LEGAL PROTECTION OF INDIVIDUALS IN THE EUROPEAN COMMUNITIES

VOLUME II

LEGAL PROTECTION OF INDIVIDUALS IN THE EUROPEAN COMMUNITIES

Volume II

REMEDIES AND PROCEDURES

A. G. TOTH, Dr. Jur., Ph.D.

Senior Lecturer in Law at the University of Strathclyde, Glasgow

Foreword by

Judge A. M. Donner

Member and Former President of the Court of Justice of the European Communities

1978

NORTH-HOLLAND PUBLISHING COMPANY
AMSTERDAM • NEW YORK • OXFORD

Library of Congress Catalog Card Number: 77 10931
North-Holland ISBN for volume II: 0 444 85045 7
North-Holland ISBN for the set: 0 444 85046 5

Publishers;
North-Holland Publishing Company
Amsterdam — New York — Oxford

Sole distributors for the U.S.A. and Canada;
Elsevier North-Holland, Inc.
52 Vanderbilt Avenue
New York, N.Y. 10017

Library of Congress Cataloging in Publication Data
Toth, A G
Legal protection of individuals in the European communities.

Bibliography: p. 295
Includes index.
CONTENTS: v. 1. The individual and community law. — v. 2. Remedies and procedures.
1. Persons (Law)—European Economic Community countries. I. Title.
Law 346'.4'012 77-10931
ISBN 0-444-85046-5

PRINTED IN THE NETHERLANDS

TO MY WIFE

The Community is governed by the rule of law. . . . . A genuine rule of law in the European context implies binding rules which apply uniformly and which protect individual rights.

Court of Justice of the European Communities, *Report on European Union*, 15 July 1974

Foreword

In saying that it is a real pleasure to introduce the book of Dr. Toth, I am expressing a sentiment that has been growing during the reading of his manuscript. It was as if somebody took one away from the daily round involved in the upkeep and cleaning of the building erected by an evolving jurisprudence and led you some distance away to take a look at the whole. The author takes you on a conducted tour of the legal Community chapel, as a good connoisseur he looks for the general principles of its construction, points out the nature of the building materials and explains how those have influenced the results. He explains how the placing of the main supporting pillars (the actions) determine the form and divisions of the building. We are made to understand why the walls and the roof must needs have received the form and place which they were given (or are being given, for the work is not yet finished) to offer an optimal space and function. Some of the beauties are pointed out. The enthusiastic guide does not find failures, at the most he sees inadequacies or gaps, which, we are told, are due to the unfinished state of the building and are certain to be remedied. And so we are left with a general impression of harmony and consistence, of a well-conceived equilibrium between the necessities which confronted the builders and the scarcity of materials they were furnished with.

The daily practitioner, used to working in the rafters or to strengthening the faulty masonry, is perhaps overconscious of deficiencies in construction and, in his scepticism, may perceive behind what is being shown as logical and ingenious, the haphazard nature of the solution and only the skilful use of plaster and paint. But it is pleasing to meet with another approach and to discover that others see the purpose and general lines of the practitioner's effort so much more clearly than he does himself and that some of them even find beauty and logic in what to him were matters of necessity. Meanwhile let the practitioner beware of too much satisfaction. There is a difference between him and the teacher. The teacher has to introduce the new apprentice or the casual visitor to the building as a whole and to try to make him familiar with it. To be able to do that he should not start with details, but take the thing as a unity. He must stress the foundation in reason of the construction and the cohesion of its various elements, if he wants his public to distinguish the essentials and so to learn to find their way in it for themselves. Once the apprentice starts working on his own, he will discover the bewildering detail and the unsatisfactory parts soon enough. But even when he has become a seasoned worker, it remains useful sometimes to stop a moment and come down (or come up) to listen to the guide and have the general design and the primary goals explained once again. Such an effort should make him thankful for the manner in which his daily work is put in a larger perspective and the sense of his efforts explained; he will return to his troublesome work feeling that, whatever the everyday deceptions, it is worthwhile and has purpose to it. You might even be beguiled into thinking your chapel to be something like a cathedral!

This describes the pleasure Dr. Toth's book gives me. It also indicates my appreciation and admiration. Not that I agree with all his observations and explanations. The mason will never completely agree with the guide; neither will the practitioner with the teacher. But it would be wrong to interrupt and try to correct or amplify his explanations. That would rob an introduction of its clarifying and illuminating force and sin against what Dr. Toth thinks is one of the fundamental principles of Community law, i.e. the principle of effectiveness (II, p. 232). Should one think that this is a somewhat double-edged compliment — in the sense of: what the author tells you may sound very well, but it is not really so — he would be completely wrong. Of course, it is gratifying when, after you have laboured for some twenty years in some secluded legal arbour, somebody writes a book about it of up to 500 pages — especially if he concludes that by and large you have done rather well. I mean that the reservation which I may have against some passages are nothing as compared to the happy surprise of meeting with an approach to the Community system of legal remedies, an approach which to me is so novel as to be little short of revolutionary. It puts the subject-matter and its problems in a perspective that I, and I think most of my generation, would never have thought of adopting, but one, which once it is offered, proves itself, systematically speaking, completely legitimate and, what is more, seems to open many interesting possibilities.

It is in two respects that I found Dr. Toth's text particularly novel.

In the first place it is characterized by its lack of historical explanations. When an elder generation tends to see the development of Community law as a process of growth and describes it according to a step-by-step method (we did this in the beginning, and of necessity then we had to do that and in consequence we were brought to such-and-such a conclusion), under the hands of Dr. Toth everything is presented as an achieved and well-proportioned system of legal protection. Where most would stress the complementary relationship of the Community system to the much more self-contained legal orders of the Member States, he presents it as a self-sufficient arrangement and stresses its inner logic. His development is entirely systematical and lacks those historical aperçus which to an elder generation are yet a matter of course. The axis of his exposition is formed not by external elements such as the objectives of the authors of the Treaty, but is formed in something that is inherent in every legal system (or should in a lawyer's view be inherent in it), to wit: the legal protection of the individual. In doing so he also succeeds in delivering himself from the partisan impression that gives so many treatments of Community law the taste of a tract for the Community idea. He takes, as it were, the Community legal system as such and asks what are its qualities and potentialities as regards the protection of the citizen.

And therein lies the second revolutionary gesture. He offers us a complete survey of the judicial remedies in Community law, the 'action against Member States' included, but he organizes it around the theme of protecting *the individual.* Those who grew up with Community law from the start have always put the accent on the constitutional aspect of the relations between the national systems of law and the Community system, between the powers of the institutions and those of the Member States and their authorities. We stressed, if I am allowed a pun, those aspects where we experienced stress. The 'grand arrêts de la Cour' were to us the Van Gend & Loos-ruling and the Costa-E.N.E.L. one and we found our main problem in the functioning of 'direct effect' and in the 'primacy' of Community law. Dr. Toth, although recognizing the importance of these rulings and problems, does away with this approach by asking what was the legal sense of this 'constitutional' scrimmage. And when he comes up with the answer, that it was the right of the individual as a citizen of the Common Market, he is able to base himself on the wording of these rulings itself. In doing so, he puts things in a very proper and adequate perspective and reminds us that the real judicial question was not: who has power to do what? but: to what end have these powers been given?, and his conviction is that this end must have been the raising of a roof over the heads of the individual people, capable of ensuring that they may in fact enjoy the advantages and rights that, in their better moments, the makers of the Treaties envisaged. I think this revolutionary in the best — but unhappily nearly forgotten — sense of the word: a turning around of things which puts them in their proper place.

The author will be the first one to observe that his approach is not so novel as I found it and there are some quite eminent predecessors who have shown him the way. In that he is right; in a certain way he might even be said to pick up a thread that more often guided the infant treatises on the role of the Court under the ECSC Treaty, but that for some time became neglected after the entry into force of the Treaties of Rome. Even then the individual was never forgotten; especially writers of a younger generation have always been more interested in the place and the protection of the individual. But Dr. Toth is, as far as I can see, the first one to place his treatment of the judicial functions in Community law in this perspective as being the most important and, in the long run, more conducive to its better understanding. I would be untrue to myself if I admitted that it is the only legitimate approach. But I welcome it as the sign that the study of Community law may be entering into a new phase, where it will be enriched by the cultivation and development of aspects that hitherto remained in the dark or were considered as being of only a secondary importance.

As an old practitioner I feel proud and honoured to have been invited to appear as a godfather at the baptism of this book. It seems a strong healthy child destined to a long life and a happy growth, that promises to become a leader among its future fellows and to be capable of not a few worthwhile contributions to life in common, viz. the Community and its law.

A. M. DONNER

Preface

Twenty-five years of European integration have brought considerable political, economic and social advantages to the Member States and their nationals. Integration, however, is not limited to those areas alone. The construction of a United Europe cannot take place except under the rule of law and within a strictly defined legal framework. Thus legal integration, both in the form of creating uniform common rules and harmonising existing national laws, necessarily accompanies and in certain respects even precedes integration in other fields.

This places individuals — natural and legal persons — in an unprecedented position. While remaining under the political authority of their own States within the bonds of nationality, they become increasingly subject to the legal (legislative, executive, judicial) authority of the Communities, to the extent to which such authority is being transferred to the latter. Formerly owing allegiance to one Sovereign only, they now find themselves confronted with two. They stand at the intersection of two legal orders, applicable concurrently, which create rights and obligations, prohibitions and restrictions for them, sometimes cumulatively, sometimes to each other's exclusion, sometimes independently of one another. The clear-cut bilateral relations between the State and the individual, or between individuals, have now been replaced, in areas within Community competence, by a complex web of tripartite relationships involving the Community institutions, the Member States and their nationals. To the traditional dichotomy between the 'private interests' of the citizen and the 'public interests' of the State a new dimension has been added by the emergence of the concept of 'common interests' represented by the Communities, which affects them both.

All this necessitates a definition of the position of the individual in relation to Community institutions, the Member States and other individuals. It also requires an exploration of the means of legal protection available to him, at both Community and national level, vis-à-vis those other subjects of Community law. The emphasis on 'legal' (i.e. judicial) protection is justified by the absence at the present time of a satisfactory 'political' protection by a directly elected parliamentary body. An inquiry of this kind may help to throw some light on the question whether the individual has not been made to sacrifice more of the traditional rights and liberties enjoyed in a democratic society than is warranted by the ultimate objectives of the integration process. Or, conversely, whether the rights and advantages created by the very same process are not liable to be made ineffective by what the European Court of Justice has called the 'inertia and resistance' of the Member States. In short, whether the 'Community citizen' enjoys adequate safeguards in respect of his rights, arising both from national and Community law, as required by the very concept of the rule of law by which the Communities are governed.

It is the object of this book to investigate these questions. Volume I sets out to define the status of the individual in the Community legal order, more particularly in the light of the nature, scope, sources and fundamental principles of Community law (Part I). Volume II deals with the various remedies and procedures that are available to individuals, both in the European Court of Justice (Part II) and in national courts (Part III), in order to enforce their substantive Community rights and to protect themselves against illegally imposed obligations, restrictions and sanctions. While, inevitably, the Community Court of Justice stands in the centre of these investigations, the book does not purport to provide an exhaustive treatment of the Court. Thus it does not deal with the Court's internal organisation, nor with those aspects of its jurisdiction which play no or only a minor part in the protection of individual rights. Nor are staff cases as such covered, although they are fully considered insofar as they lay down generally applicable rules and principles. Thus, apart from the procedure before the Court and some general aspects of its jurisdiction, Part II is limited to a discussion of the five main forms of action (actions for annulment, for failure to act, for damages, against sanctions and against Member States). References for preliminary rulings are dealt with in Part III. As regards the topics falling within the scope of the book, however, the intention has been to present a systematic, comprehensive and up-to-date exposition of the law. While an attempt has been made to place the rules and principles discussed in the wider context of the Treaties' objectives and the European Court of Justice's underlying philosophies, a practical approach is followed throughout.

This work is a lawyer's book, aimed primarily at legal practitioners, legal advisers in commercial and industrial undertakings, Government officials, European and national civil servants, who must expect to find themselves increasingly called upon to deal with cases involving questions of Community law. It is hoped that it will prove a useful tool also for law teachers and students, especially for those studying Community law at an advanced or postgraduate level. Volume I, which covers some more general topics, may be found suitable for use as a student textbook in an undergraduate course in Community law. As a whole, the book is designed to complement specialised works dealing with various areas of substantive Community law and thus fill a gap in existing legal literature.

The subject-matter of the book is regulated by relatively few provisions of the Community Treaties and acts of institutions. For the most part it is governed by the case-law of the Court of Justice. While the decisions of the Court must not be treated as generally binding 'precedents', they play an extremely important role in the structure of Community law. Over the quarter of a century of its existence, the Court of Justice has laid down, with a remarkable degree of consistency, a considerable body of rules and principles relative to the subject-matter of these volumes which fill in the many gaps left open by the Treaties or define the concepts employed by them. Most of these have now passed into the general corpus of Community law where they have acquired, as it were, an independent existence. One of the major objectives of this work has been to collect, analyse and present in a systematic way these rules and principles, thus attempting to provide a comprehensive coverage of the relevant case-law of the Court. This includes the opinions of the Advocates-General which have been considered throughout alongside the Court's decisions. The opinions are always referred to separately where they (a) elucidate a point of law which is not, or only cursorily, dealt with by the Court or (b) present an extensive analysis, or give account of the genesis, historical background, etc. of a rule or principle and (in either case) are not incompatible with the decision of the Court. By contrast, they are not as a rule mentioned separately where they (a) have been substantially adopted by the Court and incorporated in its judgment or (b) are incompatible with the latter. National decisions available in English translations are also covered. An attempt has been made throughout to follow the legal terminology used in the European Court Reports. The notes have been prepared with the intention of giving as full references as possible to the relevant decisions and opinions on all major points dealt with in the text. They thus may be used as a 'guide' to the case-law of the Court. It is thought that this may be helpful to practitioners in the preparation of a case and to academics in the carrying out of further research. Although the manuscript was completed in January 1977, it has been possible to incorporate at the proof stage the most important decisions that the European Court and some of the national courts handed down by the end of 1977.

In conclusion, I wish to thank Judge A. M. Donner for the honour he has done me in finding time amidst his many other commitments to contribute his generous Foreword. I am very grateful to Professor John W. Bridge, of the University of Exeter, for undertaking the task of reading the whole manuscript and for making so many valuable comments and suggestions. These have greatly helped in improving the text. For any remaining errors the responsibility is mine alone. I am also grateful to Mrs. Elaine Smith, of the Law School Secretariat at the University of Strathclyde, who has typed the entire manuscript — efficiently, conscientiously and always cheerfully. I would like to acknowledge the patience with which my Publishers have accepted successive delays on my part in the completion of the project, and the efficiency and care with which they have produced the book.

Finally, my thanks are due to my wife for her unfailing encouragement, support and, above all, patience during the whole time of preparation and writing. To her this book is gratefully dedicated.

Glasgow
1 January 1978 A. G. TOTH

Table of Contents

VOLUME I

PART I: The Individual and Community Law

Chapter 1: Nature and Scope of Community Law

Chapter 2: Sources of Community Law

Chapter 3: Status of the Individual in Community Law

PART II

Legal Protection by the European Court of Justice

CHAPTER 4

The European Court of Justice: Jurisdiction and Procedure

401. Jurisdiction and forms of action

The task of the Court of Justice of the European Communities is, in general, to ensure that in the interpretation and application of the Community Treaties and of the rules laid down for their implementation, the law is observed.[1] This implies that the Court has as its duty, on the one hand, to control the legality of the conduct of the institutions as well as the conformity with Community law that of the Member States and, on the other hand, to safeguard the rights and legitimate interests of all those subject to Community jurisdiction, i.e. the Communities themselves, the Member States and private individuals. In so doing the Court can only follow strictly legal, but not moral or political, considerations. It is a Court of law that must do justice according to law alone.[2] The 'law' whose observance the Court must ensure and against which it must measure the legality of the institutions' conduct is the supranational law of the Communities, i.e. the body of written and unwritten rules and principles binding on the Communities as derived from the various (primary, secondary and tertiary) sources.[3] Primarily, the task of the Court is to interpret and apply that law as the Court finds it, and not to utter opinions and criticisms as to its appropriateness, nor to suggest its revision.[4] Nevertheless, the Court may find itself faced with situations where the law is silent, obscure or inadequate. In such cases, lest it commit a denial of justice by pronouncing *non liquet*, the Court may inevitably be compelled to embark upon what may be called progressive development of the law and thus fill the gaps and adjust the law to the requirements that life presents.[5] For this purpose, the Court may draw upon the laws of the Member States,[6] the general principles of law[7] or the rules of public international law[8] and may use the various techniques of interpretation.[9]

In order to enable the Court of Justice to carry out its tasks, the Treaties have conferred upon it a precisely delimited jurisdiction. The exercise of that jurisdiction is governed by the simultaneous operation of three fundamental principles which pervade all its aspects, and basically determine the nature and scope of the various forms of action to be discussed in this book. These principles relate to the (a) separation, (b) exclusiveness and (c) express conferment of powers. They are examined below in turn.

(a) *Separation of powers*
The principle of separation of powers applies both in the relationship between the Communities and the Member States and in the relationship between the various Community institutions. In the former context the principle gives effect to the autonomous nature of the Community legal system. It implies that the jurisdiction of the Community institutions, including the Court of Justice, is strictly separated from that of the national organs, including the courts. The Court of Justice, on the one hand, and the national courts, on the other, are completely independent of one another within their respective spheres of competence. Accordingly, the European Court has no jurisdiction to interpret, apply, enforce, repeal or annul legislative or administrative acts of the Member States, nor to pronounce upon their validity under national law, even though such acts have been performed in the application of Community provisions. All this is within the competence of the Member States' organs.[10] Nor is the European Court structurally superimposed upon national courts and proceedings in the sense that decisions taken in those proceedings could be challenged in the European Court. It follows that any overlapping of the respective jurisdictions entrusted to the Community and the national authorities is in principle excluded.[11]

In the relationship between the Community institutions, separation of powers gives effect to the fundamental principle of institutional balance which governs all aspects of Community activity. According to this principle, each institution is assigned precisely defined tasks which it must carry out within the limits of its respective powers.[12] Thus it is the task of the Council and the Commission to prepare, enact and carry into effect Community legislation in consultation with the European Parliament and other consultative bodies, while it is the task of the Court of Justice to control the legality of that legislation and implementation. This task obtains increased importance at the present stage of the Communities' development which is characterised by the absence of an effective political control over the institutions' activities. But it is not the task of the Court of Justice to participate in the legislative process by substituting its judgments and judicial opinions for the decisions of the Council and the Commission, especially where the latter act in exercise of wide discretionary powers. Thus, following the classic distinction made in French administrative law between *contentieux de l'annulation* (*recours pour excès de pouvoir*) and *contentieux de pleine juridiction*,[13] in actions concerning the legality of the institutions' conduct (i.e. actions for annulment[14] and for failure to act[15]), the jurisdiction of the Court of Justice is strictly limited. It is limited to reviewing the objective legality of the act or omission in question, without considering its suitability or adequacy in the light of the underlying economic and other relevant circumstances. Clearly, that would mean replacing the legislative discretion by judicial evaluation. For the same reasons, the Court has the sole power of declaring an illegal act to be void or an illegal omission to be contrary to the Treaties, while leaving it to the relevant institution to take the measures necessary to comply with its judgment. The Court has no competence to substitute its own decision for the challenged act, nor to vary its terms, nor to award damages or any other form of redress.[16] By contrast, in actions involving subjective rights based on economic (pecuniary) considerations, such as compensation for damages caused by the institutions,[17] review of pecuniary sanctions imposed by them,[18] and certain other matters expressly specified by the Treaties,[19] the jurisdiction of the Court of Justice is necessarily unlimited or plenary. Here the Court is free to deal with all aspects of the case, factual or legal. It may not only review the strict legality of the institutions' conduct but also evaluate the underlying economic, monetary, etc. considerations and all concomitant circumstances. The Court may not merely annul but also vary the act in question by increasing or reducing the penalty imposed, and may award appropriate damages, even acting of its own motion.[20] In other words, it possesses the full powers of an ordinary civil court that are necessary to enable it to adjudicate as required by the particular type of action before it. On account of the nature of such proceedings, the exercise of these powers will not involve the Court in trespassing upon the competences of the other institutions.[21]

(b) *Exclusiveness of powers*

It follows from the principle of the separation of powers that in all those cases where the European Court has been given jurisdiction by or under the Treaties, its jurisdiction is exclusive. This excludes the possibility of submitting one and the same question, simultaneously or successively, to the decision of both the national courts and the European Court.[22] In other words, any overlapping (concurrence) of their respective jurisdictions is in principle excluded. Consequently, to the extent to which the European Court has jurisdiction in any given matter, a prior exhaustion of the domestic judicial or administrative remedies is neither necessary nor possible. Failure to do so cannot therefore prevent admissibility of an action that otherwise properly falls within the Court's jurisdiction.[23] The only exceptions to these rules seem to arise in cases involving the non-contractual liability of both the Member States and the Communities for damage caused by the national authorities in implementation of Community provisions. Here, depending on the circumstances of the case, prior exhaustion of the domestic administrative and judicial remedies may become a prerequisite for an action before the European Court, and the possibility of a concurrent jurisdiction may also arise. This follows from the fact that the principle of exclusiveness operates both ways: the fact that a matter properly falls within the competence of the national courts excludes that matter being submitted to the European Court in circumvention of the national jurisdiction.[24] Where jurisdiction is not conferred upon the Court of Justice, disputes to which any of the

Communities is a party are not on that ground excluded from the jurisdiction of the courts or tribunals of the Member States.[25] The principle of exclusiveness also applies in the relationship between the European Court of Justice and the International Court of Justice and other courts and tribunals adjudicating on the basis of public international law, insofar as the European Court has exclusive jurisdiction over disputes between the Member States concerning the interpretation or application of the Treaties and secondary legislation.[26]

(c) *Express conferment of powers*

Unlike most municipal courts and the International Court of Justice,[27] the European Court of Justice is not authorised by a general and all-embracing clause to deal with any legal dispute submitted to it within the material scope of application of Community law. The Articles specifying the Court's tasks[28] do not by themselves confer jurisdiction upon it; they amount to no more than a mere general declaration of principle which is filled with material content only by the subsequent, more detailed provisions.[29] It follows from the principle of the separation of powers that the Court, just as the other institutions of the Communities, may act only within the limits of the powers conferred upon it by the Treaties.[30] This has as a consequence that the Court has jurisdiction only where jurisdiction has been expressly conferred upon it by or under a particular provision of the three basic Treaties,[31] or by or under a subsequent agreement to which all the Member States are parties.[32] Since the jurisdictional provisions of the E.C.S.C. Treaty differ, in some cases considerably, from those of the E.E.C./Euratom Treaties (which are for the most part identical), the Court of Justice is in effect subject to three different sets of jurisdictional rules.

It follows from the foregoing that every single proceeding brought before the Court must have its legal basis in an express jurisdictional clause. The Court usually examines in the context of admissibility,[33] and *ex officio* if necessary,[34] whether its jurisdiction has been properly invoked. The requirement that every application must be 'admissible' under a particular provision means, in effect, that a remedy in the European Court exists only if expressly granted by one of the jurisdictional clauses. In other words, in the system of the Treaties, 'jurisdiction' and 'remedies' are synonymous concepts. Since the jurisdictional rules are mandatory in nature, the Court has no authority to depart from them. Consequently, it has no 'residual' or 'reserve' powers, i.e. competence to entertain cases not expressly coming under its jurisdiction in order to afford judicial protection to private individuals who might otherwise be deprived of all legal redress at both national and Community level. The system created by the Treaties differs from national law precisely in that it does not guarantee complete legal protection in a general fashion. The Court has to determine the limits of the supranational protection of individual rights strictly in accordance with the express provisions of the Treaties.[35]

The jurisdiction of the Court of Justice encompasses a variety of proceedings that do not easily admit of classification according to any material criterion. In particular, it is submitted that any attempt at their classification according to traditional jurisdictional categories, such as international, constitutional, administrative, civil, disciplinary, etc. proceedings, is futile as such categories necessarily lack any precision of meaning in a supranational context. On the other hand, most, if not all, of the various proceedings may usefully be grouped into three broad classes according to formal (procedural) criteria. These are: direct actions, references for preliminary rulings and requests for advisory opinions. Direct actions may further be divided according to the result which they seek to attain, which may be an alteration in the existing legal position (*Gestaltungsklage*, such as an action for annulment or an action against sanctions), or the performance of a specific act (*Leistungsklage*, such as an action for damages) or a mere declaration (*Feststellungsklage*, such as under the E.E.C./Euratom Treaties an action for failure to act or an action against Member States). These divisions are useful in practice in that they help delimit the respective scope and effect of the various forms of action. This is necessary because the Treaties' system of remedies is based on the principle of non-interchangeability of proceedings, that is, the rule that each form of action has a strictly defined scope and that consequently none can be used for a purpose for which it is not the proper remedy. The mutual relationship between the various types of action must always be determined in the light of this principle.[36] Detailed consideration in this book is restricted to those forms of action which are most directly relevant to the legal protection of individuals and which therefore occupy a central position in the Treaties' system, i.e. direct actions for annulment, for failure to act, for damages, against sanctions and against Member States, as well as references for preliminary rulings.

402. Admissibility of action

It follows from what has been said in the preceding Section[1] that the Court of Justice has jurisdiction to entertain any given action only insofar as the applicant has been granted by the Treaties the right to bring that particular action and the various conditions laid down for the institution thereof have been complied with. The same applies, *mutatis mutandis*, to references for preliminary rulings. Thus, before the Court may start considering the substantive issues (merits) of a case, it must first investigate whether it has jurisdiction to do so and whether the various conditions for the bringing of the case have been fulfilled. In other words, it must consider the 'admissibility' of the action or reference. This the Court may do either at the request of the parties or acting of its own motion (*ex officio*).[2] The normal (and logical) procedure is to examine the question of admissibility *in limine litis*,[3] either as a separate procedural issue (i.e. where the defendant puts forward a preliminary plea of inadmissibility)[4] or, more usually, as the first step in the proceedings. Nevertheless, since the issue of admissibility goes in essence to the jurisdiction of the Court, the parties are not prevented from raising that issue at any later stage in the proceedings.[5]

As will be seen below, the question of admissibility encompasses a variety of issues, mainly of procedure and form, which to some extent vary as between the different forms of action. Nevertheless, in the system set up by the European Treaties, issues of admissibility acquire a much wider than merely formal or procedural significance. In their entirety, they essentially determine the scope of the judicial protection open to private individuals under Community law.[6] Generally speaking, it may be said that any question is one of admissibility whose decision is necessary, not in order to settle the substantive issues of the case, but to enable the Court to proceed to such settlement. Thus, a decision as to the admissibility of an action is made primarily with reference to the person of the applicant and the nature and subject-matter of his claim (i.e. what he is asking for) and not with reference to the submissions and arguments that he puts forward in support of that claim. The question whether the grounds of the claim are pertinent or well-founded belongs to the substance of the matter. Very broadly, then, it may be said that an action is admissible if the applicant possesses a right of action and the capacity to institute proceedings,[7] the application is made in the prescribed form and within the prescribed time-limits and the Court of Justice is competent to grant what is requested.[8]

It follows from this strict separation of issues of admissibility and those of substance that a plea of inadmissibility cannot in principle be upheld where its consideration would involve an examination of the merits of the case.[9] Moreover, the admissibility or inadmissibility of a principal claim necessarily entails that of any ancillary claim based on it.[10] It also follows from the concept of admissibility as explained above that in Community law there is no place for further analogous concepts known in municipal or international law such as, for example, that of 'absolute inadmissibility', which would in itself mandatorily bar any examination (even from a formal point of view) of an application.[11] Nor is it possible to challenge the jurisdiction of the Court of Justice on the ground that the dispute in question is 'not justiciable' on account, for example, of its basically political nature.[12] It is clear that in the system of Community law there are only two possibilities: upon examination an application or a reference either satisfies the formal and procedural requirements laid down by the Treaties, in which case it is admissible and the Court has jurisdiction to entertain it, or it does not, in which case it has to be dismissed as inadmissible. A *tertium genus* does not exist.

Whilst the various issues that may conceivably be raised in the context of admissibility cannot be stated exhaustively, the following is a list of questions that the Court of Justice usually examines in that context: whether the Court has jurisdiction to entertain the application[13] or reference[14] before it (this is usually examined separately from and prior to the question of admissibility);[15] whether the applicant in a direct action has a right of action (*locus standi*)[16] and the requisite capacity to institute proceedings[17] and whether the national court in a reference proceeding for a preliminary ruling has the competence to refer;[18] whether the applicant has a legal interest in bringing the action or in making a particular submission (i.e. whether there exists a valid cause of action);[19] whether the act in question is subject to challenge by the applicant;[20] whether there is an actionable failure to act;[21] whether the action has a subject-matter or purpose[22] and whether that subject-matter has been correctly stated in the originating application;[23] whether the applicant relies on a ground which can give rise to an action[24] and whether that ground has been correctly stated in the originating application;[25] whether any other formalities regarding the originating application have been complied with;[26] whether any procedural prerequisites for bringing the action (such as e.g. compliance with any obligatory preliminary administrative procedures) have been fulfilled;[27] whether the time-limit for the bringing of the action has been observed;[28] whether the action is not premature;[29] whether a particular claim or submission is not out of time,[30] immaterial,[31] irrelevant,[32] or beyond the Court's powers;[33] whether the action has been brought in the proper forum (i.e. European Court of Justice or national courts),[34] under the proper Treaty Article,[35] against the proper defendant[36] and for a purpose for which it is the proper form of remedy;[37] whether the case is not already *res judicata*[38] or *lis pendens* (i.e. relates to the same facts, has the same subject-matter and incorporates the same conclusions as a case already pending before the Court);[39] whether the applicant's legal representative has proper authority[40] and whether the specific requirements relating to the following special forms of procedure have been complied with: intervention,[41] third party proceedings,[42] revision of judgments[43] and interpretation of judgments.[44]

403. Right of action and capacity to institute proceedings

In all forms of direct action discussed in this book, the jurisdiction of the Court of Justice may only be invoked against the Community institutions or the Member States, and only by a person or body who/which possesses both a right of action (*locus standi*) and capacity to institute proceedings. These two concepts, although usually occurring in the same context, have different meanings and do not necessarily exist together. Thus in the system of Community law, a right of action is a right granted by an express Treaty provision to bring a particular form of action before the European Court, subject to the various conditions and limitations governing that form of action. Generally speaking, such a right is granted only to the subjects of Community law, that is, to the Community institutions, the Member States and individuals. Third countries and international organisations do not (at least in the proceedings considered in this book) *ipso jure* enjoy *locus standi* in the Court of Justice,[1] although the jurisdiction of the Court may be extended to them (just as to any other person) by virtue of an arbitration clause contained in contracts concluded by or on behalf of the Communities with such countries, organisations or persons whether the contract is governed by public or private law.[2]

The right of action of Community institutions and Member States is subject to broadly similar conditions, but that of individuals is in general more restricted and the nature and scope of the restriction varies under the three basic Treaties and as between the different forms of action. Thus under the E.C.S.C. Treaty certain types of action are open only to 'undertakings' and 'associations' as defined specifically for the purposes of that Treaty.[3] In these cases entities not regarding themselves as falling within those categories have nevertheless a right of action at least for the limited purpose of challenging their (correct or erroneous) inclusion therein by the institutions.[4] Certain other types of action under the E.C.S.C. Treaty, and all proceedings under the E.E.C./Euratom Treaties are available to 'natural or legal persons' in general. In the absence of any limitation upon these concepts, it must be assumed that they encompass all such persons irrespective of nationality, residence, place of incorporation, establishment, etc. Nationals of, and legal persons (corporations) set up in, non-Member States thus have a right of action to the same extent as those belonging to the Communities. Thus, for example, a non-Community parent company and its intra-Community subsidiary equally have *locus standi* to challenge measures addressed to and concerning them both.[5] The right of action of the institutions, Member States and individuals (who will be referred to as 'private parties' in distinction from the former) will be considered in detail in subsequent Chapters in the context of the various forms of action.[6]

While the right of action ensures access to the forum of the Court of Justice, the capacity to institute proceedings (or, more precisely, the capacity to be party to proceedings) is a necessary prerequisite for the exercise of that right. The former is always a matter of express conferment by Community law; the latter is, in the case of natural persons, an inherent quality recognised by law, and in the case of legal persons, a quality attributed by law. The question, therefore, whether an entity has a right of action is always one of Community law, while the question whether that entity has the requisite capacity to bring an action is usually one of the relevant national system of law. This is, in the case of a natural person, the law that governs his personal status (usually the law of nationality or domicile) and, in the case of a legal person (corporation), the law that governs its legal status (usually the law of incorporation or establishment). It follows that where a corporation (company, association, etc.) is properly constituted according to the terms of the relevant national law and recognised by it as a 'legal person', it must be regarded as having the consequent capacity to institute proceedings also for the purposes of Community law.[7]

Nevertheless, possession of legal personality under national law is not a necessary prerequisite for a body corporate to appear as a party to proceedings before the European Court. Basing itself on a realistic theory of corporate personality, the Court of Justice has recognised the capacity of bodies not having legal personality both to institute proceedings before it in their own name and to intervene in proceedings instituted by others, provided that they display at least the characteristics which are at the foundation of such personality, in particular the ability, however circumscribed, to undertake autonomous action and to assume liability. Indeed, organisations formed for the express purpose of representing and protecting the collective interests of their members, such as trade unions and other professional associations, could hardly perform their functions if, on the basis of a formalistic approach to legal personality, they were denied the capacity to afford such representation and protection where it may be most needed, i.e. in judicial proceedings. Thus the Court of Justice has recognised that trade unions and other staff associations of European officials, which are endowed by their rules with the necessary independence to act as responsible bodies in legal matters and are sufficiently representative, have the capacity to institute proceedings even in the absence of formal legal personality.[8] It has also recognised that a national union of consumers, an association formed to represent and protect the collective interests of its members, amongst other things, in judicial proceedings, but not deemed to have legal personality under national law, has the capacity to intervene in proceedings pending before the Court.[9] On the other hand, while upholding the above principles, it has denied the capacity to intervene to a Staff Committee set up within a Community institution, as being a mere internal agency of that institution to which its statutory activities have been limited, and as lacking even a minimum of independence and responsibility.[10]

Nevertheless, the exercise of the capacity to be a party to legal proceedings thus recognised is subject to the various conditions and limitations that determine the right of action granted by the Treaties (especially the E.E.C./Euratom Treaties) to natural and legal persons and by the Staff Regulations to officials in respect of the different forms of action. The overall effect of these conditions and limitations (which will be considered in detail in their appropriate contexts) is that trade unions and other professional associations may only bring actions for the protection of their own functional-organisational rights and interests, that is, rights and interests which are connected with their intrinsic functions and involve them as separate entities in law.[11] On the other hand, they are not entitled to institute proceedings in their own name for the defence of the general (collective) interests of their members, even if they comprise all those individuals who belong to the group which they represent. Nevertheless, they may still be able to perform their functions by putting their case to the Court in the form of intervention in proceedings brought by their individual members.[12]

404. Representation

Representation before the Court of Justice is compulsory at all stages of the proceedings, whether written[1] or oral[2] and for all parties and other participants, such as, for example, the intervener.[3] The only exceptions seem to be lawyers, who may personally appear before the Court in their own case,[4] and applicants for legal aid.[5] The Member States and the institutions of the Communities are represented by an agent appointed for each case. The agent may be assisted by an adviser or by a lawyer entitled to practice before a court of a Member State. Other parties must be represented by one (or more)[6] lawyer entitled to practice before a court of a Member State. University teachers being nationals of a Member State whose law accords them a right of audience enjoy the same rights before the European Court as are accorded to such a lawyer.[7] The professional status (i.e. admission to, suspension or disbarment from, practice and the effect of the latter on the power to represent, etc.) of a lawyer is determined according to his own national law.[8] He must lodge at the Registry of the Court a certificate that he is entitled to practice before a court of a Member State.[9] Apart from this, he is not subject to any other formality; in particular, he does not have to produce a power of attorney in due form for the bringing of an action, except where his authority is disputed.[10] Legal persons governed by private law must nevertheless supply proof that authority has been properly conferred on their lawyers by someone authorised for that purpose.[11] Legal representatives must have an address for service in Luxembourg as well as a person who is authorised and willing to accept service.[12] Agents, advisers and lawyers enjoy before the Court of Justice such immunities, privileges and facilities as are necessary to the independent exercise of their duties and to the proper conduct of the proceedings; advisers and lawyers are subject to the powers of the Court in respect of their conduct.[13]

It seems that in the United Kingdom the term 'lawyer' includes both barristers (advocates) and solicitors, but by virtue of a working agreement between the Bar Council and the Law Society in England and Wales solicitors are precluded in certain circumstances from taking part in the oral presentation, and from undertaking the written presentation, of cases.[14] No similar arrangements seem to have been adopted in Scotland.

405. Languages

The language of a case before the Court of Justice is one of the six official languages of the Communities (i.e. Danish, Dutch, English, French, German, Italian) or Irish.[1] In references for preliminary rulings the language of the case is the language of the national court or tribunal which refers the matter to the Court. In other cases the language of the procedure is normally chosen by the applicant, except where the application is made against a Member State or a natural or legal person having the nationality of a Member State, in which case the language of the procedure is the official language of that State, and except where the Court authorises the use of another of the seven languages mentioned above.[2]

The language of the case must as a general rule be used at all stages of the proceedings, written and oral, in all supporting documents, in the minutes and decisions of the Court, and by all parties and other participants.[3] Nevertheless, an intervener is bound to use the language of the case only from the moment when he is allowed to intervene and so he may draw up his application in any other language.[4] Production of ducuments in one of the official languages of the Communities, even if they are not accompanied, as required,[5] by a translation into the language of the case, will nonetheless make the Court aware not only of their actual existence but also of their contents as the Court of Justice, like the other institutions, is multilingual by virtue of a presumption *juris et de jure*.[6] Witnesses and experts unable to express themselves in one of the seven languages mentioned above, may be authorised by the Court to give evidence in another language.[7] Also Judges and Advocates-General may use one of the seven procedural languages other than the language of the case.[8] In both of these situations it is the duty of the Registrar to arrange for translation into the latter. Although judgments of the Court are published in all six official languages, only the version drawn up in the language of the case is authentic.[9]

406. Written procedure

The ordinary procedure before the Court of Justice consists of two main parts: written and oral. Where necessary, preparatory inquiries may take place between the two parts. Separate provisions apply to certain special forms of procedure, which are considered later.[1] The essential rules governing the first stage of the ordinary procedure are summarised in this Section, those relating to the second and third stages are outlined in subsequent Sections.[2]

Generally speaking, the written stage, which is not open to the public,[3] is by far the most important part of the procedure before the Court of Justice. It consists of the communication by the Registrar to the parties and to the institutions whose measures are in dispute, of the various pleadings, such as applications, defences, replies, rejoinders, statements of case, observations, as well as of all papers and documents submitted in support or of certified copies thereof.[4]

A case is brought before the Court by an originating application addressed to the Registrar and accompanied by such specified documents as are relevant to the type of action in question.[5] The application must state the name and permanent residence of the applicant; the name of the party against whom the application is made; the subject-matter of the dispute and the grounds on which the application is based (*causa petendi*); the 'form of order' sought by the applicant, i.e. his claims or conclusions (*petitum*); and the nature of any evidence founded upon by him.[6] Joint application by several applicants is admissible, provided that the conclusions refer to the same measures or to measures which concern them all equally,[7] are based on the same grounds and advance the same arguments.[8] Likewise, joint presentation in one single application of various main heads of claim (e.g. for annulment, for a declaration of failure to act, for an award of damages, etc.) concerning related matters,[9] or the inclusion of subsidiary[10] or alternative[11] claims for the event that the main claim is dismissed, is also admissible. The Registrar must give notice in the Official Journal of the European Communities of the date of registration of the application originating the proceedings, the names and permanent residences of the parties, the subject-matter of the dispute and the submissions made in the application.[12]

The Court of Justice examines *ex officio* if the requirements as to the form of application have been complied with.[13] For reasons to be explained below, it is particularly important that the subject-matter of the application, the grounds on which it is based and the conclusions should be stated adequately. To what extent and in what detail these elements must be specified depends on the nature of the application in question. Generally, the Court of Justice and its Advocates-General do not insist on too rigid and formalistic requirements. They always attempt to give the terms in which an application is set out an interpretation which is both reasonable, corresponds to the applicant's true intentions and satisfies, as far as possible, the requirements of the law. In other words, they look for an interpretation that enables the Court to avoid dismissing the application as inadmissible on the purely formal ground of defective drafting.[14] The decisive consideration seems to be that an application should be held admissible on formal grounds as long as the alleged defects are not such as to prevent the defendant and any third party concerned from effectively defending its interests, or to hinder the Court in the exercise of its judicial review.[15]

As regards, more specifically, the subject-matter of the application (including the facts), this must be defined with sufficient precision to enable it to be examined properly. Any contested measures of the defendant institution, forming the subject-matter of the dispute, must be clearly indicated and enclosed.[16] As regards the grounds on which the application is based (*causa petendi*), only a brief statement thereof, and not an exhaustive treatment of all the issues, is required. Failure to designate the relevant Treaty provisions upon which the action is founded, or a mistake or inaccuracy made in that respect, cannot entail the inadmissibility of the application.[17] The Court of Justice will of its own accord apply the correct provision, and exercise its unlimited jurisdiction if so required by it, provided that it can ascertain that provision from the facts relied on and the arguments advanced.[18] In the case of an action for annulment, it is not necessary precisely to follow the terminology of the Treaties in specifying the grounds on which a claim for annulment is based. Adequacy of the presentation of these grounds is judged by reference to its substance rather than to its language. A tolerably clear presentation is quite sufficient. Nevertheless, a mere abstract statement of grounds totally unrelated to the facts as set out is not enough. Where, for example, the ground invoked is infringement by the defendant institution of Community law, the provisions allegedly infringed must be clearly indicated.[19] A general reference to the grounds, submissions and arguments put forward in another case is not admissible.[20] Advisory opinions by outside experts submitted by the applicant in support of his case, which do not reflect on all points his opinion cannot be considered as integral part of the grounds and arguments.[21] In the case of an action for damages, the grounds of the application must indicate the defendant institution's fault, i.e. the wrongful act or omission causing the injury, which is a necessary element of liability. Furthermore, the application must show at least in broad outline how the calculation of the amount of the damages is made up.[22] Nevertheless, exact figures on which that calculation is based need not necessarily be produced, especially where the collection of copious documentary evidence is impossible prior to the lodging of the application. Such figures can be presented at later stages in the proceedings (see below).[23] The question whether the grounds given are sufficient for claiming the specified amount concerns the assessment of the damage and thus relates not to the admissibility but to the substance of the case.[24]

As regards, finally, the conclusions or claims (*petitum*), they must be presented in an exact, unequivocal manner. They must specify the remedy sought, i.e. the precise result at which the applicant desires the Court to arrive on the basis of the grounds advanced. The Court of Justice is bound by the *ne ultra petita* rule, according to which it cannot generally go beyond what is requested by the applicant. In the absence of an exact statement of the claim, the Court would risk either giving judgment *ultra petita* or failing to give judgment on all heads of the conclusions. An imprecise statement of claims would moreover prejudice the rights of the defence.[25] Amendment of the conclusions is likewise subject to the strictest requirements as regards its precision and form.[26] A conclusion which has merely an abstract character cannot be justified by a sufficient degree of legal interest worthy of protection and will be dismissed as inadmissible.[27]

The application must be served by the Registrar upon the defendant.[28] Within a period of one month (which is extendable) after service, the defendant is required to lodge a defence, stating the name and permanent residence of the defendant; the points of fact and law relied on; the form of order sought, i.e. the conclusions; and the nature of any evidence founded upon by him.[29] If the defendant fails to lodge a defence in the proper form within the time prescribed, the Court may give judgment by default in accordance with the procedure laid down for that purpose.[30] The application originating the proceedings and the defence may be supplemented within the time-limits fixed by the President of the Court by a reply from the applicant and by a rejoinder from the defendant.[31] In reply or rejoinder a party may indicate further evidence, giving reasons for the delay in indicating it. However, no fresh issue may be raised in the course of proceedings unless it is based on matters of law or of fact which come to light in the course of the written procedure. If in the course of the written procedure one of the parties raises a fresh issue which is so based, the President of the Court may allow the other party additional time to answer on that issue. The decision on the admissibility of the issue is reserved for the final judgment.[32]

The foregoing provisions express an essential procedural principle and explain the vital importance of adequately stating the issues of fact and law, and in particular the grounds and conclusions, in the originating application. In practice, these provisions mean that in his reply, as in the whole course of the subsequent oral procedure, the applicant cannot generally go beyond the scope of the application and the defence. In particular, he cannot introduce new grounds, submissions and conclusions not already set out in the application;[33] he cannot amend or modify those set out therein (e.g. change from one type of action to another);[34] he cannot specify or challenge additional measures,[35] etc. New issues may be raised only as a result of a step taken by the defendant, i.e. insofar as they are based upon materials first produced in the defence.[36] A point raised at a late stage will nevertheless be considered by the Court of its own motion if it concerns its jurisdiction,[37] public interest[38] or public policy.[39] Withdrawal in the reply or during the oral procedure of a ground[40] or a conclusion[41] contained in the application is permissible.

Nevertheless, the Court of Justice and its Advocates-General do not interpret and apply the above rules in a strict and formalistic manner. By distinguishing between the introduction of new grounds or new heads of claim and the introduction of new arguments, the Court enables a ground, conclusion or argument already stated in the application with sufficient clarity to be developed, amplified or completed in the reply or during the oral proceedings.[42] The relaxation of the above rules is especially noticeable in respect of actions for damages which are subject neither to time-limits (unlike e.g. actions for annulment and for failure to act) nor to compliance with a preliminary procedure (unlike e.g. actions against Member States). It has thus been recognised that a change from a request for a declaratory judgment made in the application to one for an order for performance does not amount to an amendment of the conclusions nor to fresh issues. Consequently, where the originating application is confined to a request for a declaration establishing the Community's non-contractual liability, a subsequent request made in the reply or in the oral procedure that the Community be ordered to pay a specific amount by way of damages, is admissible.[43] Likewise, it is admissible to produce in the reply exact figures for the calculation of damages already claimed in the application as well as to rectify a calculation put forward therein.[44]

Finally, it may be noted that at any time during the proceedings the Court may order that for the purposes of the written or oral procedure or of its final judgment, a number of related cases concerning the same subject-matter shall be dealt with jointly.[45] In practice the Court orders joinder where different applicants challenge the same measure on substantially the same grounds,[46] where different applications relate to the same facts, have the same subject-matter and are supported by the same submissions,[47] or where joinder is in the interests of the proper administration of justice.[48] The aim is to avoid giving two or more separate judgments which might allow of conflicting interpretations. Joinder of intended future actions, not yet formally brought, to one already before the Court, is impossible.[49] The decision to join cases may subsequently be rescinded.[50]

The written procedure ends with the Judge Rapporteur's preliminary report as to whether a preparatory inquiry is necessary. Where the Court orders such an inquiry, the Court may undertake it itself, or may assign it to a Chamber which may then exercise the powers vested in the Court. Where the Court decides to open the oral procedure without an inquiry, the President of the Court is required to fix the opening date.[51]

407. Preparatory inquiries

The purpose of the preparatory inquiries is to determine issues of fact where the Court finds this necessary in order to enable it to give judgment. Since the procedure before the European Court is basically inquisitorial, it is for the Court to decide, acting either of its own motion or on application by a party, whether to order a particular measure of inquiry. The measures that may be adopted are as follows: the personal appearance of the parties; a request for information and production of documents; oral testimony; expert's reports and an inspection of the place or thing in question. The measures of inquiry may be conducted by the Court itself or by the Judge Rapporteur.[1] The Court may require both the parties and the Member States/institutions not being parties to the case to produce all documents and supply all information which the Court considers necessary for the proceedings.[2] Production of documents by the institutions includes the minutes relative to the adoption of the challenged measure.[3] Generally, the mere fact that a document is confidential, or is described as such, is insufficient to render it privileged from disclosure in the Court. The Court cannot in principle found a decision upon facts and documents of which the parties themselves, or one of them, are not able to have knowledge and form an opinion.[4] Application by a party for the production of documents by another party must be made during the written stage of the procedure.[5]

Witnesses are summoned by an order of the Court and heard in accordance with the provisions laid down in the Rules of Procedure.[6] Defaulting witnesses may be fined.[7] The Court may at any time entrust any individual, body, authority, committee or other organisation it chooses with the task of giving an expert opinion on specific points expressly referred to that person or body and in accordance with the provisions laid down in the Rules of Procedure.[8] The parties may object to a witness or to an expert.[9] Perjury on the part of a witness or expert is punishable under the criminal law and jurisdiction of his own State.[10] The Court may, on application by a party or of its own motion, issue letters rogatory for the examination of a witness or expert by the competent judicial authority of his place of permanent residence.[11] It is the duty of the Registrar to draw up minutes of every hearing which constitute an official record.[12] When the preparatory inquiry has been completed, the President of the Court fixes the date for the opening of the oral procedure.[13]

408. Oral procedure

The oral procedure consists of the reading of the report presented by the Judge Rapporteur,[1] the hearing by the Court of agents, advisers and lawyers and of the opinion of the Advocate-General as well as the hearing, if any, of witnesses and experts.[2] It is the task of the President of the Court to establish the cause list.[3] Subject to the power of the President to order that a case be given priority over others or be deferred, and subject to the primacy of certain types of cases,[4] the Court deals with the cases before it in the order in which the preparatory inquiries in them have been completed.[5] The proceedings are opened and directed by the President who is in general responsible for the proper conduct of the hearing. The hearing is in public, unless the Court, of its own motion or on application by the parties, decides otherwise for serious reasons. The oral proceedings in cases which are heard *in camera* are not published.[6] During the hearing the President, the Judges and the Advocate-General may put questions to the agents, advisers or lawyers of the parties.[7] The latter may address the Court only through their legal representatives.[8] The Court may also order any measure of inquiry to be taken or that a previous inquiry be repeated or expanded.[9] It may order the re-opening of the oral procedure.[10] On the whole, the hearing is usually brief as the main arguments of the parties are already set out in the written pleadings. The Advocate-General delivers his opinion orally at the end of the oral procedure. Following this, the President of the Court declares the oral procedure closed.[11] It is the duty of the Registrar to draw up minutes of every hearing. The minutes are signed by the President and by the Registrar and constitute an official record. The parties may inspect them at the Registry and obtain copies at their own expense.[12]

At any time prior to the Court's giving its decision the proceedings may be discontinued and the case removed from the register either at the written request of the applicant[13] or if the parties reach a settlement of their dispute and intimate to the Court the abandonment of their claims.[14] The latter provision does not, however, apply to certain types of proceedings.[15] In an action for annulment the consent of the defendant to the withdrawal during the oral procedure of one of the applicants is not required.[16] Where the measure whose annulment is sought is repealed by the relevant institution during the course of the proceedings, the action is rendered without subject-matter and there is then no occasion for the Court to give a judgment.[17] However, a mere withdrawal of the measure as from a certain date without its repeal with retroactive effect will not necessarily render the action without subject-matter, as the applicant may still have an interest in having the measure declared illegal retrospectively.[18]

409 Decisions of the Court of Justice

Upon the conclusion of the oral procedure, the Court proceeds to the deliberation of the case. The deliberations of the Court are and remain secret.[1] Only those Judges who were present at the oral proceedings may take part in them. Every participating Judge must give his view and the reasons for it. The opinion reached by the majority of the Judges after final discussion determines the decision of the Court.[2] A single judgment is always given and no separate or dissenting opinions are published.

Decisions may be rendered either by judgment or by order. Judgments are given to determine the substantive issues (merits) of the case; orders to deal with interim procedural and ancillary matters and with applications for interim relief. Apart from the names of the participating Judges, Advocate-General, Registrar, parties and their representatives, the judgment consists of three main parts: (a) a summary of the facts and of the conclusions, submissions and arguments of the parties; (b) the grounds for the decision (*motifs*) and (c) the operative part (*dispositif*), including the decision as to costs.[3] The judgment usually carefully distinguishes between issues of admissibility and of substance, dealing first with the former. The distinction between the grounds and operative part is important from the point of view of *res judicata*. The *res judicata* effect of a judgment results from the operative part taken together with the decisive grounds on which it is based.[4]

The judgment is delivered in open court; the parties must be given notice to attend to hear it. They are served with certified copies of it, the original being deposited at the Registry.[5] The judgment becomes binding from the date of its delivery.[6] Clerical mistakes, errors in calculation and obvious slips in it may be rectified by the Court of its own motion or on application by a party made within two weeks after the delivery of the judgment.[7] Within one month after service, any party which considers that the Court has omitted to give a decision on a particular point at issue or on costs, may apply to the Court to supplement the judgment. Upon receiving the written observations of the opposite party, the Court decides both on the admissibility and on the merits of the application.[8] This provision cannot, however, be invoked by the parties to the main action in a reference procedure for a preliminary ruling.[9] It is the duty of the Registrar to arrange for the publication of 'Reports of Cases before the Court', which as a rule contain the judgments, orders and the Advocates'-General opinions.[10]

410. Costs and legal aid

In all contentious proceedings before it, the Court of Justice must adjudicate upon costs even if the parties have made no submissions in this respect.[1] Separate rules apply to preliminary ruling procedures.[2] The Court gives a decision as to costs in its final judgment or in the order which closes the proceedings.[3] Such a decision is enforceable in the national courts.[3a] As a matter of practice, the judgment or order of the Court merely states who is to bear the costs, without quantifying them. The taxation of the costs takes place either by agreement between the parties or, in the absence thereof, by an order of the Court (see below). Generally speaking, there are three main rules as to how costs are to be disposed of between the parties. These are as follows:

First, normally the unsuccessful party is ordered to pay the costs, but only if they have been asked for in the successful party's conclusions.[4] Where the successful party has made no formal submissions on this matter, he must bear his own costs.[5] Likewise, where neither party has made any submission on costs, each must be ordered to bear his own costs.[6] Where there are several unsuccessful parties it is for the Court to decide how the costs are to be shared.[7] The unsuccessful party is to pay also the costs of the intervener who has intervened on the successful party's side.[8] A person whose application to intervene is dismissed[9] or who has intervened on the unsuccessful party's side,[10] must bear his own costs as well as those caused by his application or intervention, as the case may be. Nevertheless, in special circumstances even an unsuccessful intervener may be ordered to bear his own costs only.[11] The question whether the costs of an application for the adoption of an interim measure (e.g. suspension of operation or enforcement of the challenged act)[12] must always be dealt with in the same way as the costs in the main action, is not clear. It would seem that where such an application fails, its costs must be borne by the applicant irrespective of whether he is[13] or is not[14] successful in the main action, unless special considerations justify the application of either of the two rules to be discussed immediately below.[15]

Secondly, where each party succeeds on some and fails on other heads, or where the circumstances are exceptional, the Court may apportion the costs, i.e. order that the parties bear their own costs in whole or in part.[16] Such will be the case, for example, where the applicant is successful as to admissibility while the defendant is successful as to the merits.[17] The Court has regarded as an 'exceptional circumstance' justifying apportionment of costs (including in some cases the costs of the preparatory inquiries): the complexity of the questions as to admissibility;[18] the fact that it was the defective drafting of the challenged measure that caused the (unsuccessful) applicant to bring the action;[19] the existence of a wrongful act or omission on the part of the defendant institution giving rise to an action for damages (even if the action fails)[20] or, in the absence thereof, the fact that the applicants had at least 'sufficient reason' to consider themselves injured by that institution's conduct,[21] etc.

Thirdly, the Court may order even a successful party to pay costs which the Court considers that party to have unreasonably or vexatiously caused the opposite party to incur.[22] Such is the case, for example, where it is some blameworthy conduct on the part of the defendant institution that has induced the applicant to institute, in safeguarding his rights, what in the end turns out to be an unnecessary and unsuccessful action. Such blameworthy conduct may be e.g. the giving to a non-binding measure the appearance of a binding decision;[23] the adoption of two measures where one would have been enough and thereby causing the applicant to bring two actions instead of one,[24] etc. Conversely, the applicant may cause unreasonable or vexatious costs by failing to discontinue an action after the defendant institution has withdrawn the contested measure[25] or after the Court of Justice has rendered a judgment clarifying an important disputed issue in a similar case,[26] or by negligently failing to produce certain documents prior to the adoption of the disputed measure which could have convinced the institution not to take that measure.[27]

In addition to the above-mentioned general rules, the following provisions apply in special situations:

First, a party who discontinues or withdraws from proceedings is ordered to pay the costs, unless the discontinuance or withdrawal is justified by the conduct of the opposite party. If the opposite party has not asked for costs, the parties bear their own costs.[28]

Secondly, where a case does not proceed to judgment the costs are in the discretion of the Court.[29] Although in such cases the Court does not have to consider to what extent the application was admissible and well-founded,[30] it may, and usually does, take into account, in the applicant's favour, the fact that he was justified in believing that the bringing of the action was necessary.[31]

Thirdly, in proceedings instituted by Community officials and servants against the institutions, the institutions must always bear their own costs, except where these have been caused unreasonably or vexatiously by the opposite party.[32]

Except for avoidable costs and registry charges,[33] proceedings before the Court are free of charge.[34] Accordingly, recoverable costs are only the sums payable to witnesses and experts[35] and expenses necessarily incurred by the parties for the purpose of the proceedings, in particular the travel and subsistence expenses and the remuneration of agents, advisers or lawyers.[36] Any dispute regarding the costs to be recovered is settled by a Chamber of the Court on application by the party concerned.[37] The application is not subject to time-limit and may be made whenever one of the parties, including the intervener, disputes the costs.[38] Where the dispute concerns remuneration of lawyers, the Court will not tax the fees which are owed by the parties to their own advisers and lawyers but will only determine the extent to which the sum representing such remuneration is recoverable against the party ordered to pay the costs. Consequently, the Court cannot take account of the agreement reached between the parties and their lawyers.[39] In the absence of any provision in Community law as to scale fees, the Court has discretion to make its own assessment of the features of the case, paying regard to the subject-matter and nature of the action, its importance from the standpoint of Community law, the difficulties of the case and the volume of work involved for the lawyer. Thus the fact that an intervener relied to a large extent on the arguments of the party which it supported (e.g. Commission) may be taken into account.[40] Expenses and fees can only be recovered insofar as they relate to the actual proceedings before the Court of Justice. Costs relating to any stage prior to the application to the Court (e.g. to compulsory preliminary procedures, etc.) are not recoverable.[41] Moreover, only the remuneration of counsel representing a private party before the Court may be regarded as necessary expenses of legal assistance. Further expenses incurred as a result of employing an adviser in addition to counsel (which is quite permissible) cannot be recovered. Thus the fees of the lawyer compulsorily engaged in Luxembourg for the purpose of accepting service of documents,[42] are recoverable only insofar as they represent remuneration for that particular service, and not insofar as additional services (e.g. receiving the party, giving him legal advice and information, etc.) are also involved.[43]

Finally, costs necessarily incurred by a party in enforcing a judgment or order of the Court must be refunded by the opposite party on the scale in force in the State where the enforcement takes place.[44]

A party who is wholly or in part unable to meet the costs of the proceedings may at any time apply for legal aid. The application must be accompanied by evidence of the applicant's need of assistance, and in particular by a document from the competent authority[45] certifying his lack of means. If the application is made prior to proceedings which the applicant wishes to commence, it must briefly state the subject of such proceedings.[46] Where the Court decides that a person is entitled to receive legal aid, it orders that a lawyer be appointed to act for him. The person may choose his own lawyer, subject to acceptance by the Court.[47] Legal aid may be withdrawn[48] and the Court may order the sum advanced to be refunded in whole or in part.[49]

411. Time-limits

In the reckoning of any period of time prescribed by the basic Treaties, the Statutes of the Court or its Rules of Procedure for the taking of any procedural step, the day of the event from which the period is to run is excluded. Time continues to run during vacations. If the period would otherwise end on a Sunday or on an official holiday[1] it is extended until the end of the first following working day.[2]

The period of time allowed for commencing proceedings against a measure adopted by an institution runs from the day following the receipt by the person concerned of notification of the measure or, where the measure is published, from the 15th day after publication thereof in the Official Journal of the European Communities.[3] Where the *dies a quo* is uncertain, for example because the institution has failed to send its notification by registered or recorded delivery with an acknowledgement of receipt and it cannot produce any other evidence as to the date of posting or receipt, the benefit of doubt must be given in favour of the applicant.[4] The institution may prove the date of posting by its register of outgoing mail.[5] All procedural time-limits are extended on account of distance;[6] the extension is dependent solely on where the applicant (and not his lawyer) has his habitual place of residence at the time from which the period begins to run and during that period.[7] Because of this extension, in the reckoning of time-limits for taking procedural steps the only relevant date is that of lodgement at the Registry.[8] The date of posting is immaterial.[9] Documents must therefore be sent on such a date that they can arrive in time, bearing in mind the method of dispatch. Alternatively, documents may be lodged in person; outside the opening hours of the Registry they may be validly lodged with the janitor who will record the date and time of such lodging.[10] Expiry of time-limits cannot be remedied (or circumvented) by various procedural devices such as, for example, the qualification of a belated application as a request for intervention in similar parallel proceedings.[11] Nevertheless, rights cannot be prejudiced in consequence of the expiry of a time-limit if the party concerned can prove the existence of unforeseeable circumstances or of *force majeure*.[12] Such an unforeseeable circumstance may be, for example, the fact that documents do not reach the Court until four days after their arrival in Luxembourg. By way of exception to what has been said above, such a circumstance justifies treating the date of arrival in Luxembourg as the date of lodgement at the Registry.[13]

412. Special forms of procedure

The general procedural rules so far considered are subject to certain derogations and modifications in respect of certain special forms of procedure. These are discussed below.

(a) *Suspension of operation or enforcement (stay of execution) and other interim measures*

Generally speaking, actions brought before the Court of Justice do not have suspensory effect.[1] Nevertheless, the Court may, if it considers that circumstances so require, order that application of the contested act be suspended.[2] Moreover, the Court may in any case before it prescribe any necessary interim measures.[3] An application to suspend the operation of any measure adopted by an institution is however admissible only if the applicant is challenging that measure in proceedings before the Court. An application for the adoption of any other interim measure is admissible only if it is made by a party to a case before the Court and relates to that case.[4] The application must be made by a separate document and in accordance with the general provisions relating to the form of applications.[5] A request made in the application originating proceedings will be inadmissible.[6] Although in principle it is for the applicant to decide at what stage of the proceedings to make a request for a stay of execution, there are obvious objections to granting such a request when it is introduced very late in the proceedings, for example after the closing of both the written and the oral procedures and at a time when the Court has already started its deliberations upon the merits of the case. Clearly, when the judgment can be expected in a few weeks' time, only very rarely will there be a need for urgent interim relief.[7]

The application for a stay of execution or for other interim measures is served on the opposite party who may submit written or oral observations.[8] The President of the Court may order a preparatory inquiry and a hearing but may grant the application without such inquiry and even before the observations of the opposite party have been submitted. Nevertheless, such a decision may be varied or cancelled.[9] Where the parties are not opposed in law regarding the interim measure requested, the President may order that measure without opening the oral procedure which thus becomes unnecessary.[10] Where the President refers the application to the Court, the Court must give it absolute priority.[11]

The decision on the application takes the form of a reasoned order from which no appeal lies.[12] The enforcement of the order may be made conditional on the lodging of security by the applicant.[13] The interim measure lapses either on the date fixed by the order or, in the absence thereof, when final judgment is delivered.[14] On application by a party, the order may at any time be varied or cancelled on account of a change in circumstances.[15] Rejection of an application for an interim measure does not bar the applicant from making a further request on the basis of new facts.[16] The above rules also apply, *mutatis mutandis*, to applications to suspend the enforcement of a decision of the Court or of a measure of the other institutions.[17]

The order containing the interim measure has a strictly provisional effect and can in no way prejudice the decision of the Court on the merits of the case.[18] It follows that both the admissibility and the substance of an application for such a measure must in principle be judged without respect to the admissibility and the chances of success of the main action.[19] Nevertheless, in practice, in assessing whether the interim relief is necessary the Court cannot entirely ignore the latter factor. If the main action clearly appears well-founded, or if there is at least a strong presumption in favour of its being well-founded (*fumus boni juris*), the Court will be inclined to grant the relief sought.[20]

Suspension of the operation of an act of the institutions is an exceptional measure in that it involves the Court in exceeding its normal judicial function of controlling legality. By paralysing, even temporarily, the effects of the institutions' activities, the Court inevitably takes on executive responsibility. It follows that the Court can grant such a suspension only exceptionally, i.e. only insofar as the suspension is shown to be absolutely necessary in view of the urgency of the matter and of the irreversible (irreparable) nature of the damage which might ensue from the immediate execution of the act in question. In assessing whether these conditions are fulfilled (in respect of which *prima facie* evidence must be produced by the applicant in his request for the suspension),[21] the Court of Justice usually takes a very strict view.[22] Thus it will not grant suspension where the applicant has not proved, *prima facie*, the urgency of the situation[23] and the threat of an irreparable injury[24] which cannot be averted or mitigated by any method other than the suspension.[25] A mere assertion that the applicant has no liquid assets or capital to pay a fine imposed by the Commission,[26] or that the measure in question causes him a 'nuisance' or 'inconvenience',[27] is not sufficient. Nor will the Court grant a stay of execution where this would result in causing third parties damage at least as serious and as irreparable as that which the applicant founds upon[28] or in confronting the Court dealing with the substance of the main action with an irreversible (as opposed to provisional) situation.[29] Moreover, the fact that the applicant has taken no practical steps to avert or mitigate the possible damage, will go against him.[30] Where the applicant seeks substantially the suspension of operation of regulations, he must prove in a particularly clear fashion that he is concerned directly and individually.[31] Save in exceptional circumstances making it possible to single out the applicant from other persons subject to the law, the effect of a general provision (regulation) cannot be regarded as amounting to that of a 'measure' whose operation the Court is empowered to suspend.[32] Nevertheless, to limit the damage which the applicant might suffer from the provisional operation of a measure, in appropriate cases the Court may make that operation subject to certain conditions designed to keep the position as stable as possible in the interests of all parties pending judgment in the main action.[33]

A stay of execution is by definition only possible for a measure which can be executed. It is consequently not possible for a negative decision which rejects a request for a safeguard measure or for a grant of authorisation e.g. of a competition agreement under Article 65 (2) E.C.S.C. or under Article 85(3) E.E.C. An application for the suspension of the operation of such a negative decision will be dismissed as being without purpose (lacking relevance or pertinence), since the suspension of a refusal can never amount to the grant of the authorisation requested but refused. Such an authorisation may only be granted by the Executive (Commission) for whose decision the Court cannot in principle substitute its own order. This would be contrary to the concept of the balance of powers between the institutions.[34] For the same reasons, in such a situation the Court cannot order any other 'interim measures' either. Although such measures may go beyond the mere suspension of the operation of the contested decision, they are essentially of a conservatory nature whose purpose is to preserve the *status quo*, without giving competence to the Court to issue, even provisionally, administrative decisions for and on behalf of the Executive.[35] It will thus be outside the jurisdiction of the Court, within the context of an interim procedure, to render provisionally valid a competition agreement which the Commission has declared to be contrary to Article 85(1) E.E.C. (and which has consequently become void in pursuance of Article 85(2)), and in respect of which the Commission has refused to grant an exemption under Article 85(3) E.E.C.[36]

(b) *Procedural issues*

A preliminary objection relating, for example, to the admissibility of the action and any other procedural issue may be raised by a party by means of a separate application stating the grounds of fact and law relied on and the form of order sought.[37] The opposite party is invited to make submissions and the Court may also order a hearing.[38] The Court may decide on the application by means of a separate judgment or may join it to the substance of the case and reserve its decision for the final judgment.[39] The Court usually adopts the first solution where the preliminary issue can be settled without great difficulties or long investigations or where it involves a question of principle, a purely abstract and general problem that can easily be separated from the merits of the case. This is generally the position where the defendant institution raises a preliminary objection of inadmissibility on the grounds, for example, that the application is out of time[40] or that the applicant lacks *locus standi.*[41] In such cases only the issue of admissibility is argued in the pleadings and at the hearing and the Advocate-General also confines his opinion to that issue.[42]

By contrast, the Court will reserve its decision for the final judgment where the plea of inadmissibility seems not very well-founded or too unimportant to merit a separate judgment, or where it is interrelated with the substantive issues or can be judged more easily in the light of the more complete considerations given to the substance of the case.[43]

The Court may at any time of its own motion consider whether there exists any absolute bar to proceeding with a case and will then give its decision in accordance with the rules discussed above.[44] Such an absolute bar exists, for example, where the action constitutes a *lis pendens* because it is directed against an act which is merely a confirmation of an earlier act which is already being challenged on the same grounds in another action pending before the Court.[45]

(c) *Intervention*

The right to intervene in legal proceedings before the Court of Justice is regulated differently by the E.C.S.C. and E.E.C./Euratom Statutes. Under the E.C.S.C. Statute any natural or legal person establishing an interest in the result of any case submitted to the Court may intervene in that case.[46] No distinction is made between the Community institutions, Member States, and private parties (undertakings, associations, Member States of a Federal State having legal personality in public law, such as the *Länder* of West Germany,[47] private individuals). As a result, it is possible for private parties to intervene in cases between institutions, between Member States or between Member States and institutions, provided that they can establish a sufficient interest. It is thus possible, for example, for private parties to intervene in an action brought by a Member State against the Commission under Article 88 E.C.S.C.,[48] provided that they are directly affected by the decision whereby the Commission records a failure of that State to fulfil a Treaty obligation and lays down provisions for implementation. Nevertheless, since such an action concerns the relations between public authorities, an intervention by private parties can have as its sole object the interpretation of the Treaty provision allegedly infringed, excluding any further issues, such as the time-limit fixed by the Commission for the fulfilment of the obligation or the methods of execution of a possible coercive measure. Discussion of these questions must occur solely between the principal parties.[49] As regards intervention by a Member State, the general interest that all Member States as Contracting Parties have in the observance of the Treaty cannot justify an intervention in any and every action. The interest of an intervener State must be related to the issues raised by the particular action in which it wishes to take part and to the conclusions of one of the parties which the intervener must support or oppose.[50] Generally, an 'interest', which is a prerequisite for any intervention under the E.C.S.C. Treaty, must be established with reference to the 'result' of the case, i.e. to the operative part of the final judgment which the parties ask the Court to deliver, and with reference to the conclusions of one of the parties and not to the grounds put forward in support of them. Thus an interest in the success of abstract legal arguments is not sufficient to justify an intervention.[51] This is equally the case under the other Statutes as well.[52]

Under the E.E.C./Euratom Statutes, Member States and Community institutions enjoy a privileged position in that they have been given a right to intervene in any case before the Court of Justice without establishing an interest in the result of that case.[53] By contrast, the same right is open to other persons only if they can establish an interest in the result of a case submitted to the Court, but this right does not include intervention in cases between Member States, between Community institutions, or between Member States and institutions.[54] The right to intervene is granted to 'any person' in the widest possible sense which includes not only natural and legal persons but also bodies not having legal personality if they display at least the characteristics which are at the foundation of such personality, in particular, the ability to undertake autonomous action and to assume liability. Thus associations and unions (including trade unions) formed for the representation and protection of producers, consumers, officials, etc. and possessing the necessary independence to act as responsible bodies in legal matters, may intervene in cases in whose result they can establish an interest.[55] Since the interest of the intervener need not be distinct from that of the party whom he/it supports, associations concerned with the general and special interests of a trade or profession have a legitimate interest in defending, by way of intervention, the interests of their members.[56] In fact, in the system of the E.E.C./Euratom Treaties intervention is a procedure particularly well suited to associations which are generally not entitled to institute proceedings in their own name for the protection of the collective interests of their members.[57] Nevertheless, entities which lack even the basic aspects of legal personality, i.e. a minimum of independence and responsibility (e.g. the Staff Committees set up as purely internal agencies within the Community institutions) have no capacity to intervene.[58]

In addition to the existence of an interest in the outcome of the case, the right to intervene is under all three Statutes subject to the further condition that the intervener's submissions must be limited to supporting the conclusions of one of the parties or, at least under the E.C.S.C. Statute, to requesting the rejection of the conclusions of the opposite party.[59] These alternatives do not necessarily refer to the same situation, for example where the intervener who supports the defendant raises preliminary objections as to the admissibility of the main action, which the defendant failed to present. Under the E.C.S.C. Statute at least, this is admissible.[60] Generally, in the determination of the admissibility of the intervention only the objective and not the nature of the intervener's submissions is relevant. Thus he may put forward arguments different from, or even contrary to, those of the party which he is seeking to support and which arguments the latter expressly disavows. It would seem that he may also introduce new evidence and supporting documents.[61] The only important requirement is that his conclusions should support those of the party on whose side he intervenes. Clearly, it would deprive the intervention procedure of any meaning if the intervening party were prevented from advancing any argument of his own.[62]

It follows from the foregoing that in Community law intervention is not a very effective way of protecting individual rights. The legal limits imposed on the intervener may in certain situations have the consequence that he will be unable to prevent an injury being done to his rights. It is perhaps unfortunate, therefore, that the Statutes and the Rules of Procedure do not contain provisions for other forms of intervention, such as the compulsory joinder of third parties (i.e. compulsory intervention) or interpleader proceedings whereby a third party might pursue claims of his own against both parties to the principal action, as is known in the procedural laws of certain Member States.[63] Nevertheless, third parties are well advised to avail themselves of whatever legal protection intervention may afford in respect of proceedings to which they are strangers. Should they, due to their own fault, miss the opportunity to intervene, they will have lost an important right which can no longer be made good by any exceptional review procedure available under Community law, such as, for example, third party proceedings.[64]

An application to intervene must be made before the opening of the oral procedure[65] and in the prescribed form.[66] It must contain, amongst other things, the reasons for the intervener's interest in the result of the case and submissions supporting or opposing the conclusions of a party to the original case.[67] The grounds for those submissions must be stated only after the intervention has been allowed.[68] The parties to the principal action must be given an opportunity to submit their written and oral observations.[69] The right to intervene does not automatically arise with the submission of the application; it arises only from the order whereby the Court allows the intervention.[70] In such a case the intervener must accept the case as he finds it at the time of his intervention.[71] Intervention is possible also in proceedings for the adoption of interim measures.[72]

(d) *Third party proceedings*

Under Community law third party proceedings are the proper remedy to contest a judgment which has been rendered without the participation of the third party concerned and which is prejudicial to his rights. Their importance in the system of legal protection set up by the Treaties is underlined by the fact that, in the absence of an ordinary appeals procedure, they supply one of the only two means available for reviewing judgments given by the Court of Justice.[73] An application originating third party proceedings may be brought by Member States, Community institutions and any other natural or legal persons within two months of the publication of the original judgment in the Official Journal of the European Communities.[74] It must be directed against all the parties to the original case. The application must be made in the form prescribed for applications originating proceedings in general[75] but must, in addition, state how the judgment contested is prejudicial to the rights of the third party and indicate the reasons why the latter was unable to take part in the original case.[76] These two requirements, compliance with which constitutes an essential condition for the admissibility of the application, are further considered below.

The first of the above requirements implies that only persons whose rights have been prejudiced by the contested judgment are entitled to bring third party proceedings. The applicant must supply full and conclusive particulars of what constitutes the prejudice to his rights. Such prejudice may equally consist of a material or a non-material damage, such as damage to the reputation of an individual or to the dignity and prestige of a Member State. Moreover, the injury may arise from the legal effects (i.e. the operative part) just as from the decisive grounds of the judgment. If the legal effects flow equally from two or more grounds, each of them may be the source of the prejudice. Nevertheless, a judgment which in its grounds merely states the legal consequences of certain national measures without determining their legality with reference to Community law, cannot adversely affect the sovereignty of the State which had lawfully issued those measures, even if as a result the State must amend its legislation on the subject.[77]

The second requirement mentioned above implies that any party who could have been heard or who could have taken part in the original case will be unable to institute third party proceedings. Both the efficient administration of justice and the principle of legal certainty[78] demand that persons interested in the result of an action pending before the Court be precluded from asserting their rights once a judgment has been delivered settling the question in dispute. It is precisely to meet this requirement that the right of voluntary intervention has been made available to third parties whose interests are involved.[79] The right to open third party proceedings is therefore limited to persons who, though called upon to take part in the original case, were unable to do so for good and sufficient reasons and to persons who, due to no fault on their part, were not in a position to intervene voluntarily in the principal action. Generally, where the subject-matter of, and the conclusions submitted in, the original case were duly published in the Official Journal of the European Communities as required by the Rules of Procedure,[80] third parties cannot claim to have been unaware of that case. If they missed the opportunity to intervene owing to their own negligence, they cannot later assert an interest which was put in issue in the original case, especially if their conclusions are identical with those already put forward therein. Third party proceedings will be admissible in such a situation only if the subject-matter and the conclusions in the principal action, as published in the Official Journal, did not disclose any direct and specific interest which the third party could have established in order to intervene voluntarily in that action.[81]

The third party may apply for a stay of execution of the contested judgment in accordance with the relevant rules.[82] The Court will however order a stay of execution only if the facts and circumstances of the case are sufficient to warrant such an order.[83] The effect of a successful application for third party proceedings is that the Court will vary the contested judgment on the points on which the submissions of the third party are upheld.[84]

(e) *Revision*

Revision is one of the only two exceptional review procedures that are available against judgments of the Court of Justice.[85] An application for revision of a judgment may be made only on discovery of a fact which is of such a nature as to be a decisive factor and which, when the judgment was given, was unknown to both the Court and to the party claiming the revision.[86] Discovery of a fact unknown only to the interested party but known to the Court, does not constitute a sufficient ground for revision. Nor does discovery of a fact which did not exercise a decisive influence upon the judgment of the Court.[87] Generally, the procedure of revision cannot be used as an expedient for the re-opening of a judgment without serious reasons.[88]

An application for revision must be lodged within three months of the discovery of the new facts[89] and not later than 10 years after delivery of the judgment.[90] The application must be made against all parties to the original case, and in the form prescribed for applications originating proceedings in general.[91] It must indicate the points on which the judgment is contested together with all supporting facts and evidence.[92] The Court must first decide on the admissibility of the application by means of a separate preliminary judgment which, if the application is found admissible, will be followed by a further judgment on the merits in accordance with the Rules of Procedure.[93]

(f) *Interpretation of judgments*

If the meaning or scope of a judgment is in doubt, the Court of Justice has jurisdiction to construe it on application by any party or any institution of the Communities establishing an interest therein.[94] This provision represents one of the rare applications in modern law of the old maxim *ejus est interpretari cujus est condere* and is thus an exception to the rule according to which the Court becomes *functus officio* in delivering its judgment.

Interpretation by the Court of its own judgments is subject to the following three conditions. First, the application must be made by a person who was a party to the case in which the judgment was given, or by a Community institution. An application by third parties is inadmissible.[95] Where, however, several actions had been brought against the same measure and the measure was annulled in one of them, the applicants in the other proceedings may be considered as 'parties' to the judgment of annulment, provided that they had invoked the same grounds as those on which that judgment was based.[96] Secondly, the applicant must establish an interest in the interpretation. An interest will usually exist if the applicant has no other means of ascertaining the correct meaning of the judgment.[97] Thirdly, there must exist a doubt or difficulty as to the meaning or scope of the judgment. For the purposes of the admissibility of the application, it is sufficient that the applicant should allege the existence of an ambiguity or obscurity by showing that the parties give different meanings to the text of the judgment. Clearly, if the defendant does not deny the interpretation put forward by the applicant, then the meaning and scope of the judgment is not 'in doubt'. On the other hand, the question whether a judgment is or is not in fact ambiguous or obscure appertains to the examination of the merits of the case and will be decided by reading its operative part together with the decisive grounds and the applicant's conclusions.[98] Moreover, the doubt must concern the meaning and scope of the judgment as regards the relationship between the parties thereto and the particular issues settled thereby. Controversies relating to the possible 'external' effects of the judgment on cases other than that in which the ruling was given and on persons other than the parties thereto, cannot be settled by means of requesting the judgment's interpretation. Such disputes in reality concern the broader issue of the extent of the binding force of the Court's decisions in general, which must be ascertained not by the interpretation of a particular judgment but by the interpretation of the relevant rules of Community law determining the legal effects of the Court's decisions. A clarification of this sort can therefore more usefully be sought by way of reference proceedings which encompass also judgments of the Court of Justice.[99] Finally, the difficulty must concern a matter actually decided by the judgment. It follows, on the one hand, that the only parts of the judgment whose interpretation may be requested are those which express the decision of the Court, i.e. the operative part taken together with the decisive grounds. The Court cannot interpret incidental passages (*obiter dicta*) and those which only complete and explain the basic reasoning. On the other hand, the Court cannot rule upon problems which had not been settled by the judgment. The parties may not, by means of a request for interpretation, ask for a new decision on new disputes.[100]

An application for interpretation of a judgment is not subject to time-limit.[101] It must be made against all the parties to the case in which the judgment was given and in the form prescribed for applications originating proceedings in general.[102] It must therefore contain the conclusions of the applicant[103] and must moreover indicate the judgment in question as well as the passages whose interpretation is sought.[104] The parties must be given an opportunity to submit their observations. The Court gives its decision in the form of a judgment,[105] which will be binding not only on the applicant but also on any other party affected by the passage interpreted.[105a]

(g) *Preliminary rulings*

In preliminary ruling procedures under Article 177 E.E.C./Article 150 Euratom,[106] the decision of the national court or tribunal referring a case to the European Court must be notified to the Court by the court or tribunal concerned. The procedure is automatically set in motion as soon as such a notification is received by the Court.[107] The decision is then notified by the Registrar to the parties, to the Member States and to the Commission, and also to the Council if the act whose validity or interpretation is in dispute originates from the Council. Within two months of this notification the parties, the Member States, the Commission and, where appropriate, the Council are entitled to submit statements of case or written observations to the Court.[108] Where, owing to the special (summary) nature of the national proceedings, the reference order was made without the hearing of the prospective 'defendant', the principle that the rights of the parties must be protected may require that the opportunity to submit observations be extended also to such a 'defendant' even though he has no official standing as a party to the case.[109] In the case of references under the 1971 Protocol concerning the interpretation by the Court of the Convention on Jurisdiction 1968, which are governed by the same procedural rules as ordinary references under the Treaties,[110] also the new Member States are entitled to submit observations although they are not yet parties to the Convention.[111]

After the statements of case or written observations have been lodged (or if these documents have not been lodged within the time prescribed), the proceedings continue according to the general procedural rules as laid down by Articles 44 *et seq.* of the Rules of Procedure[112] and thus include the preliminary report by the Judge Rapporteur,[113] the preparatory inquiries where necessary[114] and the oral procedure.[115] Nevertheless, owing to the restricted standing in preliminary ruling procedures of the parties to the main action,[116] not all the provisions of the Rules of Procedure that follow Article 44 can properly be applied in a corresponding manner to reference proceedings. Thus the parties to the main action cannot make a joint application to the President to defer the case;[117] they cannot ask the Court to supplement[118] or interpret[119] its judgment (only the national court making the reference and the institutions may do so); they cannot discontinue the proceedings[120] and third parties who are not involved in the main action and who have no right to submit statements of case or written observations may not intervene.[121] Nor is the recovery of costs and the recoverability of expenses necessarily incurred by the parties for the purposes of a reference procedure (e.g. remuneration of lawyers) governed by the relevant provisions of the Rules of Procedure.[122] These provisions have been designed solely for contentious proceedings and cannot be extended to preliminary rulings which are of a quite different nature.[123] In reference proceedings the costs incurred by the institutions and the Member States which have submitted observations are not recoverable. Since such procedures are merely a step in the main action pending before the national court, it is for that court to decide, in application of national law, as to the costs incurred by the parties.[124] As regards, finally, the representation and attendance of the parties, the Court may take account of the Rules of Procedure applicable before the national court or tribunal which has made the reference.[125] In special circumstances the Court may grant, as legal aid, assistance for the purpose of facilitating the representation and attendance of a party.[126]

Cases referred for a preliminary ruling which are of an essentially technical nature or concern matters for which there is already an established body of case-law, may be assigned by the Court to the Chambers. Nevertheless, a case may not be so assigned if a Member State has exercised its right to submit a statement of case or written observations (unless it has signified that it has no objection), or if an institution expressly requests in its observations that the case be decided in plenary session.[127]

(h) *Other special forms of procedure*

In addition to the special procedures discussed in this Section, separate provisions have been laid down for the following proceedings: judgments by default and applications to set them aside;[128] staff cases;[129] appeals against decisions of the Arbitration Committee under Article 18 of the Euratom Treaty;[130] special procedures under Articles 103 to 105 of the Euratom Treaty;[131] opinions under Article 228 of the E.E.C. Treaty and under Article 95(4) of the E.C.S.C. Treaty;[132] disputes between Member States under Article 89 of the E.C.S.C. Treaty;[133] proceedings by third parties under Articles 63(2) and 66(5) of the E.C.S.C. Treaty.[134]

CHAPTER 5

Action for Annulment

501. Nature and scope of action

In the system of remedies instituted by the European Treaties, action for annulment occupies a central position. It fulfils two different functions which in some national legal systems are performed by means of separate procedures available under quite different conditions. One of these functions is to provide a judicial means of controlling the legality of the binding acts of the Community institutions (Council and Commission) which is absolutely necessary in the absence of an effective political control by an elected parliamentary body. The action thus enables the European Court of Justice to ensure observance of objective law as required by the Treaties[1]. Its second function is to afford legal protection to all those subject to the legislative and executive competence of the Communities, and in particular to individuals, whose rights and legitimate interests may be adversely affected by the institutions' illegal positive (active) conduct. Thus, action for annulment combines certain aspects of abstract judicial review of the constitutionality of legislation (*abstrakte Normenkontrolle*) with certain features of judicial review of executive action. It achieves the former by requiring the Court to check the objective conformity of secondary Community law with the Treaties as the Communities' Constitutions,[2] and the latter by empowering the Court to annul Community measures within the framework of individual, fact-related complaints brought by a defined circle of aggrieved persons. In the former context the European Court acts in the public interest as the guardian of legality; in the latter it is required to defend certain defined private interests recognised bv the legislator as worthy of protection.

The merger of these two, diverse functions within the framework of one type of remedy is explained by the fact that in Community law, in the absence of a strict separation of 'legislative' and 'administrative' functions and measures as understood in municipal law,[3] both general (normative) and individual acts, affecting respectively the public and the private spheres of interest, can in principle be issued by the same institutions (Council or Commission) under similar conditions. This justifies the creation of one single remedy in respect of both types of acts.[4] This remedy takes on the form of a contentious proceeding brought against the Council or Commission and aimed at the annulment by the European Court on specified grounds[5] and with *erga omnes* and *ex tunc* effects of an act of the defendant alleged by the applicant to be illegal, with the consequence that the defendant is required to take the necessary measures to cancel the effects caused by the annulled act.[6] By its nature, it is what is termed in German law a *Gestaltungsklage*, i.e. an action for an alteration of the legal position and not a mere *Feststellungsklage*, i.e. action for a declaration. The judgment of the Court is therefore neither declaratory of an already existing nullity,[7] nor does it have the character of an advisory opinion similar to those emanating from the International Court of Justice.[8] Since in principle all binding acts of the institutions are subject to annulment, whether of the normative or of the individual type, any authorisation of the Court to go beyond the sole task of reviewing the objective legality of the challenged measure would mean overstepping the purely judicial function by engaging the Court in what is basically the law-making process. This would contradict the principle of the institutional balance within the Communities. The Court may not, therefore, subject to certain exceptions, review the appropriateness or expediency of the measure or the underlying considerations involving questions of economic policy, in the light of which it has been taken. Nor can it vary or correct the measure itself or afford any remedy other than annulment. In other words, its jurisdiction is strictly limited.[9]

Neither intending to introduce an *actio popularis*, nor to authorise the European Court to act of its own motion, the Treaties ensure that both functions of action for annulment, mentioned above, are properly performed by delimiting in a novel and characteristic way the circle of persons entitled to engage the control machinery at the Court's disposal. This circle could in principle be defined in three different ways. First, by expressly specifying those having an unqualified right of action. Secondly, by prescribing a certain degree of legal interest as a prerequisite for bringing the action.[10] Thirdly, by determining in respect of each category of Community acts who may challenge them, by requiring a particular and close relationship between the act challenged and the person appealing against it; a relationship that amounts to a direct and specific interference by the former with the rights and legally protected interests of the latter. The Treaties make use of all three solutions although only very rarely, and by way of exception only, of the second. They specify the Member States, the Council and the Commission[11] as privileged persons who are entitled to an unqualified right of action without having to show any particular legal interest in the act in question. These are therefore enabled to seize the Court in the public interest by simply alleging that there has been a violation of objective law. By contrast, the right of action of persons other than these is defined by reference, on the one hand, to the nature of the measure challenged, and, on the other, to the way in which, and the extent to which, the measure affects them. As a result, these persons (private parties) have either no right at all to engage the control mechanism of the Court in respect of certain acts (mainly general, normative acts), or they can do so only by complying with strict requirements of admissibility centred mainly around the effects of the act upon them. While this arrangement is certainly not designed to enable individuals to use the action for annulment for the purpose of abstract control of the objective legality of Community action in general, and of any control of legislative action in particular (subject to certain variations between the E.C.S.C. and E.E.C./Euratom Treaties), it is still able to provide a reasonably high degree of legal protection if used in combination with other devices designed for that purpose, such as the defence of illegality[12] and preliminary rulings,[13] or with other types of action, such as action for damages,[14] to which these limitations do not apply and which make up, at least in part, for the limited possibilities inherent in the action for annulment insofar as individuals are concerned.[15]

While these other avenues of legal remedy may be useful in supplementing the action for annulment in certain respects, it is necessary clearly to delimit their respective fields of application. In the first place, there is a close and inherent connection between action for annulment and action for failure to act as these in fact form the two sides of the same broad remedy, i.e. control of the legality of the institutions' conduct. The former is used to review positive (active), while the latter to control negative (passive), conduct.[16] At the same time the two actions are mutually exclusive of one another. An action for annulment cannot be used parallel to, or in substitution for, an action for failure to act for a purpose for which the latter is the proper remedy. Thus, where there already exists an actionable failure to act, a subsequent measure relating to the same subject-matter (e.g. a belated express decision refusing to act) can no longer be challenged for annulment, as this would be clearly superfluous.[17] Also, where a certain activity cannot be elicited by means of an action for failure to act, the express denial of that activity can also not be the subject of an action for annulment. Otherwise the limitations on the former could be evaded by recourse to the latter.[18]

The same principles apply between action for annulment and action for damages. The former cannot be used, for example, for the purpose of having a decision annulled whereby an institution refuses to pay compensation and thus implicitly establish a right thereto. Where the real aim of an action is to obtain a finding that an institution is responsible for a wrongful act or omission, then it is not really an action for annulment but one for damages. Such finding cannot arise from proceedings based on one of the grounds of illegality but only from proceedings founded upon the special conditions of official liability.[19] Also, there is a close connection between action for annulment and action against sanctions, the latter being in fact always aimed at the annulment of the measure imposing the sanction. It is therefore subject to the rules of action for annulment, with the difference that the Court has, in actions against sanctions, unlimited jurisdiction.[20]

Finally, an action for annulment cannot be used in circumstances in which a reference for a preliminary ruling under Article 177 E.E.C./Article 150

Euratom is the proper remedy. Action for annulment can only be brought against acts taken by the Community institutions within Community jurisdiction, while a preliminary ruling may be sought in the context of acts taken by national organs within national jurisdiction in implementation of Community measures whose interpretation or validity is in question. Thus, where national organs act as agencies for and on behalf of the Communities but in accordance with the provisions of domestic law as to competence, procedure and form, for example in collecting the Communities' own resources,[21] all disputes concerning their actions, such as e.g. the assessment of individual parties with regard to duties and levies, should be solved, in accordance with Community law, by the national authorities in the forms laid down by national law. Consequently, reimbursement of duties alleged to have been illegally imposed by Community measures (and therefore illegally collected by the national agencies), cannot be achieved by means of an action for annulment brought before the European Court against those measures (quite apart from the question whether they are, on account of their nature, challengeable by individuals at all).Instead, it must be sought before the competent national courts where the question of the interpretation and validity of the Community measures forming the legal basis of the assessment may be raised and, if necessary, resolved by way of a reference for a preliminary ruling. Thus a delimitation between action for annulment and preliminary rulings is at the same time delimitation between Community and national jurisdictions.[22] Nor does the European Court have competence, within the framework of an action for annulment, to deal with alleged infringements of Community law by Member States and the consequent illegality of certain national measures. For this purpose a separate form of action, to be brought by the Commission against the Member State, is available.[23]

Owing to its central importance in the system of remedies, it is action for annulment that has in practice been resorted to most often of all types of direct action. The fact that most of the proceedings brought by private parties have been dismissed as either inadmissible or unfounded indicates the restrictive nature of the right of action granted to individuals by the Treaties. Thus, under the E.C.S.C. Treaty, of the eighty-seven decided cases[24] (of which eighty were brought by private parties and seven by Member States), only eighteen were successful (fourteen brought by private parties[25] and four by Member States[26]) and resulted in the partial or total annulment of the challenged act. Nineteen cases were dismissed as inadmissible (all brought by private parties), fourty-eight as unfounded (fourty-five brought by private parties, three by Member States) and two did not result in substantive ruling. Under the E.E.C. Treaty, of the fifty decided cases[27] (of which thirty-four were brought by private parties, thirteen by Member States and three by Community institutions), only fourteen were successful (nine brought by private parties,[28] four by Member States[29] and one by the Commission[30]) and resulted in partial or total annulment. Twenty-one cases were dismissed as inadmissible (twenty instituted by private parties, one by a Member State) and fifteen as unfounded (five instituted by private parties, eight by Member States and two by the institutions).

502. Absolute nullity and voidability

In accordance with the national laws of the Member States, Community law distinguishes between the formal (external) validity and the substantive (internal) legality of the acts of the institutions. Accordingly, when an act complies with the essential requirements of form, i.e. originates with the competent authority and is taken with due regard to the procedural and formal conditions laid down by the Treaties,[1] it must be regarded as valid and applicable, irrespective of its material legality, as long as it is not repealed by its author or annulled by the European Court of Justice. In other words, the very existence of the act creates the presumption of its validity which can only be nullified by repeal or annulment. Generally, therefore. the illegality of an act does not entail its absolute (i.e. *ab initio*) nullity or non-existence, but makes it voidable subject to the conditions of an action for annulment.[2] If such an action is not instituted within the proper time-limit, the act becomes definitive and is no longer challangeable for annulment, still less can its absolute nullity be invoked, although it may be declared inapplicable by the Court in certain circumstances.[3] These rules are dictated by the general requirement of legal certainty[4] which would be greatly jeopardised by the sometimes unpredictable consequences of a declaration of absolute nullity especially of a normative act which has been in force and relied upon in good faith for a long period of time and may have given rise to a large number of further implementing acts.

The position is somewhat different where the defect is in form. Generally, in most cases formal defects do not affect the nature or existence of the act and they, too, render the act voidable rather than null and void *ab initio*, as is shown by the fact that lack of competence and infringement of an essential procedural requirement are included amongst the grounds on which an act can be annulled by the European Court.[5] Nevertheless, absolute nullity is conceivable, within strictly defined limits, in really extreme cases involving very serious and evident defects of competence (e.g. a clear lack of power or its usurpation by the institutions), of procedure (e.g. lack of deliberation) or of form (e.g. lack of signature or publication).[6] Thus a measure taken by the institutions in a field which falls within the exclusive competence of the Member States would lack all legal foundation in Community law and would, accordingly, probably be declared by the European Court as being null and void *ab initio*.[7] Also, the giving of reasons may in exceptional circumstances amount to such an essential, indeed constitutive, element of a measure that its absence may entail the non-existence (i.e. absolute nullity) of the measure with the consequence that an action brought for its annulment may have to be dismissed as inadmissible for lack of subject-matter.[8] This solution, however, seems to represent an extreme view of the importance of reasoning as a formal requirement, and it is more usual for lack of adequate reasons to be regarded as a ground for annulment than to constitute a defect entailing absolute nullity.[9]

503. Legal interest (cause of action)

Broadly speaking, in order for an action for annulment to be admissible it is necessary that the applicant should have a legally relevant interest, recognised by the law as worthy of protection, in the institution of the action and in the annulment of the act challenged. Although the existence of a legal interest is a general requirement for the bringing of all types of action before the European Court of Justice, it has a special significance in the context of action for annulment due mainly to the nature and central position thereof in the system of legal remedies.

In connection with annulment proceedings the question of legal interest arises in two different contexts. Firstly, it is correct to say in general that the concept of interest lies at the basis of the action and belongs to its very nature. Nevertheless, the Treaties have not explicitly made the proof of an interest a general (and in itself sufficient) prerequisite for the admissibility of the action while leaving to the European Court the task of defining by case-law more closely when that interest is 'sufficient'. Instead, the Treaties themselves regulate in precise terms the question of admissibility and they do this in two different ways. Firstly, they grant certain parties (Member States and institutions) an unqualified right of action. These parties are consequently not required to show any particular legal interest when instituting any particular action. In other words, the mere fact of an objective violation of law establishes their interest in the matter since, as representatives of the public interest, they are presumed to have a general interest in the judicial control of the objective legality of any Community action.[1] Secondly, the Treaties define in strict and precise terms the conditions for admissibility in respect of each category of Community acts for other, non-privileged applicants (private parties) who in the absence of a specific relationship to the subject-matter of a Community measure are not entitled to demand objective compliance with the Treaties by the institutions. This definition is based not upon the notion of legal interest but upon the nature of the act challenged and upon the 'concern' of the applicant, i.e. the way in which, and the extent to which, it affects him. While under the E.C.S.C. Treaty this concept of 'concern' leaves some room for the Court to resort, by way of an extensive interpretation, to the wider and less precise concept of 'interest' in deciding upon the admissibility of private applications, under the much stricter terms of the E.E.C./Euratom Treaties, which refer to 'direct and individual concern', this is no longer possible. Here, the notion of interest, in this sense of the word, plays hardly any role.[2]

However, the question of legal interest also arises in a second context. It expresses the general idea that a party may seize the Court of Justice of an action or of a particular submission only if and when he is genuinely and objectively in need of the Court's protection and if the Court is in the position of affording the kind of protection sought. In other words, he must have a valid cause of action. To satisfy that requirement, it is in the first place necessary that the measure complained of should be one capable of adversely affecting the applicant.[3] This will be, in general, the case not only where the measure imposes burdens or obligations upon him, but also where it grants certain advantages to others (particularly to the applicant's competitors) which are not available to him and which correspond to certain disadvantages falling upon him. Since a possible annulment of such a measure on the grounds submitted would imply that its author would have to replace it with another one which would in all likelihood be more favourable to the applicant's position, his legal interest in bringing an action for annulment is generally recognised, and even more so where he is in competition with those in the more favoured position.[4] Similarly, an applicant will have an interest in having a general measure (i.e. a regulation) declared illegal and inapplicable to him where, in the circumstances of the case, the execution of the judgment would oblige the administration to take a more favourable new decision by taking into account the rights which the illegal provisions had failed to observe.[5] Moreover, if the contested measure contains a defect of such a nature as to render it illegal, it will adversely affect the applicant who must be able to make an application against it even though the measure was adopted at his own request. In other words, in such circumstances the maxim *volenti non fit injuria* will not apply.[6]

By contrast, a person is not adversely affected by a so-called confirmatory act, i.e. a measure which is limited to confirming (refusing to repeal or amend) a previous one which could have been, but was not, challenged by the applicant within the proper time-limit. Such an act is not actionable.[7] This does not, however, apply if there is a new factor such as to alter the essential legal or factual conditions and circumstances which governed the adoption of the original act. Such a new factor is capable of re-establishing a sufficient legal interest. Where, for example, the European Court has rendered a judgment casting doubt upon the legality of the original measure (but without pronouncing upon its validity), the subsequent refusal of the institution to repeal that measure is not a mere confirmatory act but amounts to a new decision and, as such, is subject to challenge within the prescribed time-limit.[8] This principle cannot, however, justify an evasion of the rules relating to time-limits.[9] Nevertheless a measure which re-enacts an earlier one, i.e. deals with the same subject-matter and has the same effects, is not a confirmatory act and is once again subject to appeal within the proper time-limit notwithstanding the possible continued existence of the earlier measure.[10]

To establish legal interest it is further necessary that the applicant should pursue an aim which is not only legally possible to attain but which is reasonable and 'makes sense'. This is not the case, for example, where an application (or a part of it) is directed at the joinder of a possible future action to the current one (which is impossible),[11] or at an activity which the defendant has no power to carry out,[12] or at a finding which is already the subject-matter of a separate action pending before the Court (objection of *lis pendens*)[13] or where a complaint simply fails to disclose any legal interest requiring protection[14] or discloses only an abstract ('academic') interest.[15]

A legal interest in bringing an action for annulment is generally assessed at the day on which the application is made. Later changes cannot affect the existence of the interest, although may render the action without subject-matter. Thus repeal with *ex nunc* effect by a Member State, after institution of proceedings, of a national measure whose alleged inconsistency with Community law is the subject-matter of the complaint, will not cause the applicant to lose his interest in seeking a judgment from the European Court to the effect that the measure was contrary to Community law. Such a finding may entail legal consequences for him for the time during which the measure had been in force.[16] Once the existence of a legal interest in the annulment of a measure has been established, it entitles the applicant to challenge any aspect of the measure on any of the four grounds of action[17] without having to show additional particular legal interest in respect of the criticised aspects of the measure or of the grounds relied upon.[18]

Although, as pointed out above, Member States and Community institutions are not required to show any particular legal interest in the annulment of any Community measure, they, too, must have a valid cause of action in order to seize the Court of Justice. While in the majority of cases it is assumed that such cause of action exists, the European Court is always ready to examine if that is the case where it is in doubt or expressly challenged.[19]

504. Parties

Under the E.C.S.C. Treaty, the general rules as to action for annulment are governed by Articles 33 and 34 to which the discussions in this Chapter are almost exclusively limited. Under Article 33, an action for annulment may be instituted against the Commission (formerly High Authority) only.[1a] The action may be brought by Member States, the Council, undertakings and associations of undertakings. While the right of action of the Member States and the Council is unqualified,[1] that of other parties (hereinafter: private parties) is limited in three respects. First, in order to bring an action, a private party must qualify as an undertaking or an association within the technical meaning of these terms as specifically defined for the purposes of the E.C.S.C. Treaty.[2] Persons other than undertakings or associations, such as private individuals[3] or Community officials,[4] cannot institute proceedings under Article 33. An association which has as its object to promote and to protect the general interests of its members, has standing as an applicant as soon as a measure of the Commission affects certain interests, however divergent they may be, which the association protects assuming that the other two requirements are also met.[5] Secondly, a private party must possess legal capacity to institute court proceedings in general,[6] although in most cases such capacity will naturally follow from the fact that an entity is recognised as an undertaking or association. Thirdly, a private party must satisfy the conditions for admissibility of action which Article 33 lays down in respect of undertakings and associations.[7]

Under the E.C.S.C. Treaty, action for annulment may also be brought under special provisions outside Article 33 by and against a wider or narrower circle of persons than those specified therein. These special provisions are not, however, considered in detail in this book partly because they refer back to the general rules of Article 33 (although may in certain respects derogate from those rules) and partly because they are not available to private parties (individuals) at all. Into the former category fall Articles 63(2)(2), 65(4)(2) and 66(5)(2); into the latter Articles 37 and 38 E.C.S.C. These provisions may be summarised as follows.

Article 63(2)(2) gives, by way of exception, a right of action to purchasers of Community coal and steel, although this right is without prejudice to the general rules of Article 33. Articles 65 and 66 apply to an enlarged concept of undertaking which includes, in addition to coal and steel producing undertakings, also those engaged in distribution.[8] Article 65(4)(2) provides, without any further specification, for 'the right to bring actions before the Court' against rulings of the Commission on the compatibility with Article 65 of certain prohibited agreements and decisions. It seems, however, that this right of action is subject to the general conditions for admissibility as laid down by Article 33, both as regards the parties entitled to bring such action[9] and as regards the nature of the challengeable decision and the time-limit for action.[10] Article 66(5)(2) enables 'any person directly concerned' to institute proceedings 'as provided in Article 33' against a decision by which the Commission declares a concentration unlawful and orders consequential measures under Article 66. By way of derogation from Article 33, however, the Court has unlimited jurisdiction to assess whether the transaction in question is a concentration, and the institution of proceedings has suspensory effect. As regards the persons covered by it, Article 66(5)(2) must be interpreted broadly so as to extend legal protection to any (even non-Community) undertaking whose rights and legitimate interests may be directly affected by a relevant Commission decision. As regards the cases governed by it, however, Article 66(5)(2) must be interpreted restrictively as presenting a derogation from the general provisions as to action for annulment. It cannot be applied to cases other than those expressly mentioned in it; for example it cannot grant to such an enlarged circle of persons the right of action for failure to act.[11]

Article 37 E.C.S.C. enables proceedings to be instituted in the Court for the annulment of a decision in which the Commission, acting at the request of a Member State, recognises or refuses to recognise the existence of fundamental and persistent disturbances in the economy of that State and, in the former case, orders remedial measures. That Article, however, does not specify what party or parties may institute such proceedings. Since an action under Article

37 involves an assessment of the general economic situation of the Member State concerned and of the appropriateness of the measures taken, it brings into issue the political responsibilities of the Member States and of the Commission in the matter of reconciling national and Community interests. In such circumstances undertakings and associations do not possess a standing to invoke Article 37; this right is strictly reserved to the Member States.[12] Since moreover in such proceedings the Court must, exceeding the limited jurisdiction which it possesses under Article 33, exercise exceptional powers (i.e. unlimited jurisdiction) to control the likewise exceptional powers granted by Article 37 to the Commission, these proceedings cannot be instituted by private parties even under Article 33 either considered by itself or in conjunction with Article 37.[13] Finally, under Article 38 E.C.S.C. the Court may, on grounds of lack of competence[14] or infringement of an essential procedural requirement,[15] annul acts of the European Parliament or of the Council. However, application for this purpose may be made only by a Member State or the Commission and not by private parties.[15a] In the E.C.S.C. Treaty there are no provisions for an action for annulment against the Court of Justice or other bodies such as the Consultative Committee.

Under the E.E.C. Treaty, the general rules relating to action for annulment are contained in Articles 173, 174 and 176 to which Articles 146, 147, 149 correspond verbatim in the Euratom Treaty. Discussion in this Chapter is limited to these provisions taken together with the closely connected Article 184 E.E.C./Article 156 Euratom. Under Article 173 E.E.C./Article 146 Euratom an action for annulment may be instituted against the Council and the Commission. The inclusion of the Council is explained by its increased role and legislative powers in the two later Communities as compared with its position in the Coal and Steel Community. On the other hand, action for annulment cannot be brought against the European Parliament, the Court of Justice[15b] or the Economic and Social Committee. Although in their external legal relations with the Member States and third parties, including proceedings in the national courts, the Economic and Euratom Communities are always exclusively represented by the Commission,[16] such a monopoly of legal representation does not exist before the European Court of Justice. Action for annulment can never be directed against the Communities as such (although only these, and not their institutions, possess legal personality)[17] but must be brought exclusively against the individual institution which has issued the contested measure. It is thus not possible, by naming the Community as defendant, to make the Council a party to proceedings aimed at the annulment of a measure of the Commission or *vice versa* (e.g. for the purpose of obtaining documents or other information in the exclusive possession of that institution or on the ground that the budgetary and financial powers of the Communities, insofar as they are relevant to the solution of the matter, are distributed amongst the various institutions). Consequently, an action is inadmissible to the extent to which it is directed against the wrong institution.[18] Since, however, each of the Communities is a single entity in law, a judgment of the Court which has the force of *res judicata* with regard to one institution will have the same force with regard to the particular Community as a whole.[19]

Under Article 173 E.E.C./Article 146 Euratom an action for annulment may be brought by a Member State, the Council, the Commission and by any natural or legal person. The other institutions of the Communities as well as territorial units of the Member States, such as, for example, members of a Federal State, cannot appear as applicants although the latter may institute proceedings in their capacity as 'legal persons' of public law. As under the E.C.S.C. Treaty, the Member States, the Council and the Commission occupy a privileged position in that they possess an unqualified right of action.[20] In contrast to the E.C.S.C. Treaty, however, the concept of the other parties ('natural or legal persons', hereinafter: private parties) is nowhere defined in the E.E.C./Euratom Treaties. This, as well as the reference to 'any' such person, justify the broadest possible interpretation that may include, in principle, even Community officials.[21] Thus, in order to possess a right of action, it is not necessary for a natural person to be a national of, and/or resident in, a Member State; nor for a legal person to have been formed in accordance with the law of a Member State and/or to have its registered office, central administration or principal place of business within the Community.[22] Any natural or legal person whose rights or legally protected interests have been impaired by a measure of the Council or the Commission can bring an action against the latter provided that he/it satisfies the following two requirements. First, he/it must possess legal capacity to institute court proceedings in general.[23] Secondly, he/it must meet the conditions for admissibility of action laid down by Article 173 E.E.C./Article 146 Euratom in respect of natural or legal persons.[24]

Under the E.E.C. Treaty, too, an action for annulment may be brought outside Article 173 although subject to the general conditions laid down therein. Thus under Article 180(b) any Member State, the Commission or the Board of Directors of the European Investment Bank may institute proceedings against measures adopted by the Board of Governors of that Bank. Under Article 180(c) Member States or the Commission may bring action against measures adopted by the Board of Directors of the Bank but only on certain specified grounds. In contrast to Article 37 E.C.S.C., decisions of the Commission taken under the corresponding Article 226 E.E.C. authorising Member States to take protective measures to remedy any serious difficulty arising in the national economy during the transitional period, are not subject to the Court's unlimited jurisdiction and thus may be challenged by all parties by way of the ordinary annulment procedure under Article 173. Nevertheless, the Court's power of review takes on special importance in such cases as the Commission has discretionary powers under Article 226.[25]

Finally, it may be noted that under all Treaties the bringing of an action by several parties by means of joint applications is possible provided that the applications refer to identical measures or to measures which concern all applicants equally,[26] are based upon identical grounds and advance identical arguments.[27]

505. Acts subject to challenge under the E.C.S.C. Treaty in general

Under Article 33 E.C.S.C. only decisions and recommendations of the Commission (High Authority) can be the subject of an action for annulment. Acts of the other institutions or acts of the Commission (High Authority) which do not, independently of their form, constitute decisions or recommendations within the meaning of Article 14 E.C.S.C.,[1] for example opinions, cannot in principle form the subject of such action.[2] A series of different but related acts as well as severable provisions of an individual act can be attacked by one single action as in principle (in the latter case) partial annulment is possible.[3] Member States and the Council, having an unqualified right of action, can challenge any decision or recommendation, whether general (normative) or individual, whether addressed to them or to others, and whether having any specific legal effect upon them or not. The mere fact of an objective violation of the law establishes their interest in the matter.[4] Thus a Member State can seek the annulment of a Commission decision addressed to undertakings situated in another Member State[5] or to the Government of another Member State.[6]

While the above rules are clear in themselves in that they are based upon the essential unity of Articles 14 and 33 E.C.S.C. (only the binding measures as defined in Article 14 can be the subject of an action for annulment under Article 33), difficulties may arise in practice in determining whether certain informal acts of the Commission, its internal divisions, officials or auxiliary bodies, such as letters, communications, notifications, statements, internal instructions, etc., constitute decisions or recommendations in the sense of Article 14 and are therefore subject to annulment. In principle, the legal protection of all those subject to the Community legal order requires that they should be able to identify by its very form a binding measure (decision or recommendation), which may involve serious legal consequences for them, in order to be able to institute proceedings for annulment within the prescribed time-limit. It follows that for a measure to amount to a decision (recommendation) those to whom it is addressed must be enabled to recognise clearly that they are dealing with such a measure. Consequently, if a minimum of formalities and procedural requirements prescribed by Community law[7] is not observed, then the addressees are entitled, in general, to infer that the measure in question does not entail any legal obligation for them. Nevertheless, non-compliance with some inessential formal or procedural requirement will not deprive an act of its binding nature as long as the fundamental conditions underlying the concept of a decision within the meaning of the Treaty are otherwise satisfied. In other words, it is the object and the contents, rather than the form, that determines the nature of an act. It follows that a decision (recommendation) must appear as a measure taken by the Commission, acting as a body, intended to produce legal effects and constituting the culmination of the decision-making process within the Commission, whereby the Commission gives its definitive ruling on the matter in a form from which its nature can be identified. Any measure, therefore, which, in particular, does not appear to have been debated and adopted by the Commission as a collective body and authenticated by the signature of one of its members, cannot be regarded as a decision (recommendation).[8]

These definitions imply that the following measures cannot normally be regarded as binding decisions in the sense of Article 14 E.C.S.C. and are not, therefore, subject to challenge under Article 33 E.C.S.C.: letters originating from a Director-General of the Commission and containing a 'request' (rather than imposing an obligation) to do something, in spite of the peremptory nature of the terms used;[9] acts taken, under whatever title or designation, by Departments of the Commission acting on their own authority;[10] letters signed by mere officials or Heads of Department acting in personal capacity and not in the name and on behalf of the Commission,[11] even where they contain a premature notification of an intended future formal decision[12] (unless the decision itself is adopted by the Commission by the time the action is considered by the European Court);[13] a letter addressed by the Commission to one of its own subordinate organisations, even though published subsequently in the Official Journal and qualified as a decision by an official of the Commission, where it only interprets an earlier decision and the Commission has not followed the particular procedure required for its adoption as a formal act (such a letter, being in fact a directive of an internal nature addressed by an administrative superior to the departments under his control and intended to guide the working of those departments, is capable of creating obligations only for the recipient bodies but not for outside persons);[14] the reasons and statements set out in the preamble to a decision which merely explain the aims pursued by the Commission but which expressly refrain from stating the precise rules to be drawn up in the future (these constitute merely an expression of intention not binding upon the Commission);[15] an individual provision of a decision which does not set out any rule having legal affect of any kind, either generally or with respect to specified persons, but amounts purely to an internal measure;[16] interim statements confirming only that the applicant's case is under consideration and that the necessary decision will be taken;[17] confirmatory acts after the expiry of the time-limit within which the act confirmed could have been challenged;[18] the General Report published by the Commission annually on the activities of the Communities[19] and the Audit Board's report[20] (these being intended for the European Parliament and the Committee of Presidents, respectively, it is for these bodies to judge whether they are sufficiently complete and not for the European Court to review their contents in actions brought by private parties).[21] Moreover, statements originating from officials of the Commission cannot have any influence on the interpretation of its decisions.[22]

By contrast, the following measures do amount to challengeable decisions: a letter from the Commission determining in an unequivocal manner the action which it will take in a situation where certain conditions are operative, in other words, a letter which sets out a rule capable of being applied (camouflaged decision);[23] a letter from the Commission refusing in a definitive form a request for exemption from an obligation and affirming the existence of that obligation which the applicant has denied (the letter in fact settles a point of law),[24] although that part of a letter of rejection which does not introduce any new elements into the legal relationship between the Commission and the applicant is not a decision open to challenge independently of the decision itself;[25] the application of a general decision to a concrete case constitutes a decision and not a mere interpretation of the general decision;[26] and finally a notification by an auxiliary body set up by the Commission and exercising delegated powers, which represents the final word of the administration and creates an obligation for the recipient, is a challengeable decision (although Article 33 E.C.S.C. only provides for action against the Commission's own decisions, such a notification by an auxiliary body must be regarded as equivalent to these, in order not to deprive the Community subjects from the legal protection afforded by that Article).[27]

506. Acts subject to challenge under the E.C.S.C. Treaty by private parties

Unlike Member States and the Council, undertakings and associations do not possess an unqualified right of action under Article 33 E.C.S.C. Their right is restricted in respect of the acts whose annulment they can seek before the Court of Justice. They may institute proceedings only against decisions or recommendations concerning them which are individual in character or against general decisions or recommendations which they consider to involve a misuse of powers affecting them. Thus, in order to decide whether an action brought by a private party against an act of the Commission is admissible, three questions have to be examined in the following logical order. First, whether the act in question constitutes an actionable decision or recommendation according to the criteria discussed in the previous Section.[1] Secondly, if it is such a decision (recommendation) it is then necessary to consider whether it is general or individual in character. Thirdly, if it is a general decision (recommendation) the question is whether it involves a misuse of powers affecting the applicant and if it is an individual decision (recommendation), whether it concerns the applicant. These questions will be considered below in turn.

While, for the purposes of action for annulment, the E.C.S.C. Treaty distinguishes between general and individual decisions,[2] it fails to define these respective concepts. Unlike the position under the E.E.C./Euratom Treaties which, by defining the corresponding concepts of a regulation and a decision, have given a mandatory starting point to the European Court,[3] the E.C.S.C. Treaty has left it to the Court to work out suitable definitions in its case-law. In so doing, the Court was from the beginning confronted with the possibility of resorting to similar concepts existing in the national legal systems of the Member States. Most of those systems distinguish between general administrative acts (*Rechtsverordnungen, règlements*) and individual administrative acts (*Verwaltungsakte* and *Allgemeinverfugungen, actes individuelles et collectifs*). The former are used to regulate a general and impersonal factual situation by means of normative provisions which resemble, at least from the substantive point of view, the provisions of a statute which they in most cases supplement. The latter are used to apply the general rule to specified individual cases and persons. However, not only does the definition of these concepts differ as between the various Member States, but it is in certain respects not very clear even within the same legal system. Moreover, in national law the distinction between general and individual administrative acts serves purposes which are quite different from those envisaged by the Treaty. In national law, the distinction is made to determine such matters as the conditions for the issuance of the act, the issuing authority, the type of remedy available against the act, etc. Under the Treaty, however, these aspects are of no particular importance since all acts are issued by the same institution under broadly similar conditions and are subject to the same remedy. For all these reasons, resort to analogous concepts and definitions of national law has not proved to be very helpful and could, on the contrary, have been misleading. Instead, the European Court has had to seek definitions which are suited to the peculiar requirements of Community law taking into account, on the one hand, the absence of a clear distinction between legislative and administrative competences in the usual sense[4] and, on the other hand, the fact that the line drawn between general and individual measures basically determines the extent to which individuals enjoy judicial protection as against the considerable powers of the institutions. Thus a balance has had to be struck between the private interests of the individual which require a wide definition of the concept of individual decisions and the public interest which, on the contrary, demands that certain measures having an overall importance for the Community as a whole should not be challengeable in defence of such private interests.[5]

The general or individual character of a decision must be determined in the light of the foregoing considerations. It results, in principle, directly from the contents and not from the form of the decision and must be established by objective criteria. Thus, a general decision may be defined as a quasi-legislative act originating from a public authority and having normative effect *erga omnes*.[6] Accordingly, a decision is a general decision if it lays down normative principles, specifies in the abstract the conditions for their application, and sets out the legal consequences which it entails. It regulates in an identical manner an indeterminable number of cases; its rules are applicable to any situation coming within the conditions specified for its application.[7] It is a general decision either if the identity of the individual undertakings to which it applies cannot be determined from it because it requires further implementing measures or if it is applicable to all undertakings (and all transactions) falling within its scope by reason only of the fact that they are producers of coal or steel within the Community, without any other requirement. The fact that its application is territorially delimited or that it consists of detailed and concrete rules applicable to different situations and having detailed, concrete and varied effects upon different undertakings does not detract from its general character and does not turn it into a series or collection of individual decisions. This is so even though the applicant association includes all undertakings referred to in the decision, and only those. Otherwise all undertakings in the Community could form themselves into one association and claim that the decision is individual even if it applies to them all. In other words, the individual or general character of a decision cannot depend upon whether the applicant is an undertaking or an association.[8] Finally, a decision which amends or modifies an earlier general decision will itself have the same character and will be a general decision.[9]

Once it is established that the challenged measure is a general decision, the right of undertakings and associations to request its annulment, although not totally excluded as under the E.E.C./Euratom Treaties,[10] is severely restricted in that they can proceed with the action only if they consider the decision to involve a misuse of powers affecting them.[11] This requirement does not, however, mean that the applicant has to prove, in the context of admissibility, that a misuse of powers has actually been committed. It is sufficient, to ensure admissibility of the action, that the applicant should formally allege a misuse of powers affecting it and make out a *prima facie* case, by convincingly specifying the reasons, facts and circumstances which in its opinion give rise to or indicate the probability of such misuse of powers. Strict proof will be necessary to establish that the application is well-founded, i.e. it belongs to the merits of the case. An association can allege misuse of powers with respect to one or more of the undertakings which are its members.[12] Since no other ground can be put forward, the action is admissible only to the extent that it is based on misuse of powers. But even the ground of misuse of powers is not admissible inasmuch as it is based on the same arguments as are also put forward in support of any other grounds of action simultaneously invoked.[13]

Moreover, the applicant has to show that the alleged misuse of powers 'affects' it by giving convincing reasons why the adoption of the contested decision is directly prejudicial to its interests. In other words, it must invoke a specific injury affecting its individual interests, an injury which distinguishes it from all other undertakings. The mere circumstance that the application of the decision might be discriminatory or incomplete is not enough since the remedy against such a possibility lies in contesting the individual measures implementing the general decision, for which all four grounds of action are available. If the decision affects a large number of applicants in the same degree, it will generally be impossible to maintain that it directly damages the individual interests of each of them and that it is vitiated by a misuse of powers 'affecting them'.[14] Nevertheless this notion cannot be pushed so far as virtually to require that the decision should in reality be an individual one, i.e. a disguised individual decision taken in the form of a general decision for the purpose of preventing an action by private parties (whereby the misuse of powers would consist precisely in the act of disguising). What it means is simply that the applicant must be the direct object or the victim of the misuse of powers which it alleges. In other words, under the E.C.S.C.

Treaty undertakings and associations can challenge also general decisions in the proper sense of the term.[15]

Once the action has been found admissible, a private party in pleading to the merits of the case continues to be restricted to the sole ground of misuse of powers affecting it. There are two reasons for this. One is that if it could invoke the other grounds of action as well, it, as a private party, would have virtually as extensive a right of action against general decisions as the Member States and the Council. This would clearly run counter to the intention of the Treaty which has introduced a very clear distinction between private parties and Member States/Council and between individual and general decisions. The Treaty did not intend to enable private parties to challenge the 'constitutionality' (i.e. conformity with the Treaty) of general decisions which are in fact quasi-legislative acts. That such decisions can still be challenged on the ground of misuse of powers is an exception explained by the fact that here it is still the individual element that is predominant. The second reason is that once misuse of powers has been established, annulment must necessarily follow and there will be simply no need for invoking further grounds.[16] The only situation in which a private party can plead all four grounds of action against a general decision occurs when the general decision is challenged by way of a plea of illegality, i.e. in an action directed against an individual decision alleged to be invalid because the general decision on which it is based is illegal. But here the purpose is to obtain annulment of the individual, and not of the general, decision.[17]

Where the applicant does not invoke misuse of powers, it can only contest a measure if it is an individual decision concerning it. This requirement implies that the decision has two distinct characteristics: first, it must be 'individual' and secondly, it must 'concern' the applicant. As regards the former, the concept of an 'individual' decision has been interpreted by the European Court widely, in favour of individuals, and with due regard to the notion of legal interest.[18] Accordingly, the individual nature of a decision must be determined with reference to its contents and not to its form or addressee. To be able to bring an action against a decision, it is enough for a private party to show that it is not general but possesses the characteristics of an individual act without its being necessary that it should possess these characteristics with respect to the applicant. Thus a decision is individual if it applies to undertakings which are specified by name or whose identity can be ascertained trom it, and governs specific, concrete situations connected with such undertakings. Likewise, it is individual if it relates solely to a specific activity of a public authority designated by name. The question whether it is addressed to the applicant, to somebody else or even to a Member State (whether or not the applicant's own State) is immaterial. Once satisfying these requirements, even a disguised individual decision (i.e. one having all the appearances of a general decision) remains an individual one.[19] It follows that if a decision is individual as regards certain undertakings (i.e. those to which it is addressed), it is necessarily individual as regards all. It cannot, therefore, at the same time be considered as general with regard to third parties.[20]

As to the second requirement, an individual decision always 'concerns' the applicant (in addition to the obvious case where the decision is addressed to it) as soon as it affects its position,[21] that is to say, it is capable of impairing its legally protected interests, without its being necessary that the applicant's subjective rights be also impaired and that it alone, or almost alone, be affected.[22] Thus a decision will concern the applicant if it authorises, for example, the imposition by a Member State upon it (or, if it is an association of undertakings, upon its members) of extra financial burdens[23] or, *a fortiori*, where it arises out of a request made by the applicant itself.[24] For the purpose of admissibility of the action, the fact that a decision concerns the applicant need not be proved conclusively. It is sufficient for the applicant to make out a *prima facie* case, i.e. to make an allegation of an impairment of its legally protected interests, supported by all relevant considerations. In this respect, therefore, the concept of legal interest plays a decisive part.[25] Once a decision satisfies both the above requirements, i.e. it is both individual and concerns the applicant, it is subject to challenge by private parties on all four grounds of action.[26]

An important practical consequence of this wide interpretation of the concept of individual decision is that under the E.C.S.C. Treaty it is possible for undertakings and associations in effect to challenge before the European Court measures of Member States (not necessarily their own State) thought to be violating Community provisions, which affect them adversely even though addressed to others. Thus, government measures favouring certain industries and having an impact on conditions of competition may be contested by undertakings that are injured by these measures. One legal means for this is an action for the annulment of the Commission's decision containing the authorisation on which the national measure, discriminating in favour of domestic undertakings, is based. Such a decision will be an individual decision in relation to, and will concern, not only the domestic undertakings benefiting from it, but also such undertakings of the other Member States adversely affected by it as can show a sufficient interest by establishing a special position distinct from that of the rest of the Community undertakings operating in the same field (i.e. coal or steel). This will especially be the case where the undertakings adversely affected by, and those benefiting from, the measure are in competition, i.e. carry on the same productive activity within the Common Market, sell the same products and obtain their supplies from the same sources. In such circumstances, the undertakings discriminated against are certainly 'concerned' by the Commission's individual decision.[27]

Another legal means available for the same purpose is a request addressed to the Commission to open Article 88 proceedings[28] against the Member State concerned. The decision of the Commission whereby it refuses to take the measure requested, i.e. to state that the Member State has failed to fulfil an obligation under the Treaty, will possess, with respect to the requirements of

Article 33, the characteristics which the positive decision refused would have had. If the latter would, if taken, have dealt with a particular measure passed by a Member State in violation of Community law, it would have been an individual decision. Consequently, the decision by which the Commission refused to take this individual decision will itself have an individual character and as such may be contested by undertakings which are concerned by it.[29] Alternatively, a failure of the Commission to open Article 88 proceedings as requested, can be the subject of an action for failure to act.[30]

Moreover, the decisions of the Commission authorising under Article 65(2) E.C.S.C. specialisation, joint buying or joint selling agreements including trading regulations of sales agencies and contracts of association of wholesalers are also of an individual nature. Such authorisations merely rule upon the legal validity of the actual decisions taken by particular, individual undertakings which decisions do not, by virtue of authorisation, lose their character as acts of private law. As they cannot be considered as quasi-legislative acts passed by a public authority in the exercise of its normative competence, the Commission's decision authorising them cannot be regarded as such either.[31] Similarly, decisions of the Commission ruling under Article 65(4) E.C.S.C. on the compatibility with Article 65 of certain prohibited agreements and decisions, are also of an individual nature as determining the legal validity of specific acts of particular undertakings or associations. In an action for the annulment of such decisions, the right of action of undertakings engaged in distribution (which is granted by way of exception, only for the purposes of proceedings connected with Articles 65 and 66 E.C.S.C.)[32] is not limited to cases where such undertakings themselves are parties to the agreement in question, but also extends to situations where the Commission's decision directly affects their sphere of interest.[33]

507. Acts subject to challenge under the E.E.C./Euratom Treaties by Member States/institutions

In the system of the E.E.C./Euratom Treaties, the range of actionable Community acts is essentially determined by the nature and identity of the applicant. Where the applicant is a Member State, the Council or the Commission, the Community meaures that can be the subject of an action for annulment are not specified by name, but the Court of Justice is given jurisdiction to review the legality of all 'acts' of the Council and the Commission other than recommendations or opinions.[1] In defining what particular measures this wide power encompasses, two considerations are of importance. First, since the provisions of the Treaties relating to judicial remedies[2] and those relating to the material and formal requirements of Community acts[3] form a coherent system, the term 'act', whenever it occurs in the former, must be given a meaning which covers all categories of binding measures listed in the latter (regulations, directives, decisions) or assimilable thereto, but does not extend the Court's authority so far as to take cognisance of expressions of intention which cannot, on account of their nature and effects, be regarded as, or assimilated to, those measures. Secondly, since the real nature of an act is determined by its substance, i.e. its subject-matter, contents and legal effects, rather than by its form and designation, the fact that a measure is not given a form or title corresponding to one of those explicitly mentioned in the Treaties, does not in itself exclude it from judicial review. Since the only measures expressly excluded from the ambit of an action for annulment instituted by Member States/institutions are recommendations and opinions, i.e. non-binding measures,[4] such an action must be available against all 'acts' of the Council and Commission which are designed to produce legal effects, irrespective of their nature, form or designation. The very aim of an action for annulment when brought by a Member State/institution, that of ensuring observance of the law in the interpretation and application of the Treaties, could not be achieved if the availability of this procedure would be limited merely to categories of acts expressly mentioned by the Treaties.[5]

It follows that in addition to regulations,[6] directives[7] and decisions,[8] any measure of the Council or the Commission can be challenged by Member States/institutions which is designed to lay down a course of action binding on any of the Community subjects, i.e. Member States, institutions or individuals, and produces definite legal effects in the relationships between them. The addressee of the measure,[9] its effects upon the rights or interests of the applicant, are completely irrelevant factors since the Member States/institutions, as privileged parties, enjoy an unqualified right of action which they may exercise in respect of any objective violation of the law whether or not their rights or interests are involved.[10] It is, however, doubtful whether this broad concept of an actionable Community 'act' also includes the international agreements of the Communities (in the first place of the Economic Community) with third countries and international organisations. It is true that these agreements are concluded by means of a Council decision which brings them, at least so far as the Communities are concerned, within the scope of secondary Community law.[11] The fact, however, that provision has been made in the Treaty for their submission, prior to their conclusion, to the scrutiny of the European Court in respect of their compatibility with the Treaty[12] would seem to indicate that the possibility of their being contested after they had come into force was not envisaged by the drafters. Clearly, such a possibility would create considerable difficulties and complications.[13] It is, moreover, difficult to see how the Court, as an internal organ of one of the contracting parties (i.e. of the Community) could annul an agreement which is binding on both or all parties under general international law. This would clearly amount to a breach of the agreement from the point of view of international law, even if annulment might be justified under Community law.

It may be noted finally that where the contested measure originates with the Council it is also necessary that the Council should have acted in its capacity as a Community institution and not as an organ of the collectivity of the Member States.[14] An action against an 'act' of the Council will be admissible only to the extent to which the Council acted in the former capacity, that is to say, exercised an authority which at the material time was already conferred on the Communities and dealt with a subject-matter which fell within Community competence. Only where this is the case can the measure have definite legal effects both in the relations between the Community and the Member States and in the relationships between the institutions.[15] Measures adopted by the Council in exercise of the supplementary powers conferred upon it by the Treaties[16] always constitute Community 'acts' which are subject to judicial review.[17]

508. Acts subject to challenge under the E.E.C./Euratom Treaties by private parties

Generally speaking, the right of action of private parties is limited under all three Community Treaties as compared with that of the Member States/institutions, but this limitation is different in nature and more severe in degree under the E.E.C./Euratom Treaties. In the system of these Treaties, natural and legal persons are subject to a dual restriction, a 'double barrier', which they have to overcome cumulatively in order to ensure admissibility of an action for annulment. The first restriction consists of limiting the range of challengeable acts, on account of their legal nature, to certain specified categories only. The second restriction further narrows down the circle of such acts, on account of their legal effects, by requiring a close and specific relationship between them and the applicant. As a result, natural and legal persons can challenge only such act of the Council and the Commission as falls into one of the following three categories:

(1) decision addressed to the applicant;
(2) decision addressed to another person;
(3) decision in the form of a regulation;

but if the act falls into the second or third category it is further necessary that it should be of direct and individual concern to the applicant.[1] These various requirements are considered in detail in the subsequent Sections.[2]

The system of legal protection thus created by the E.E.C./Euratom Treaties differs from that of the E.C.S.C. Treaty[3] in two important respects. First, the E.C.S.C. Treaty defines the extent of the right of action of private parties by reference to the distinction made between general and individual decisions. It does not completely exclude that right in respect of general decisions but merely restricts its exercise to the sole ground of misuse of powers affecting the applicant. By contrast, the E.E.C./Euratom Treaties make the distinction between regulations and decisions the pivot of the whole system of legal protection and clearly deny to natural and legal persons the right to challenge on any ground whatever measures which are genuinely (and not only in appearance) law-making in character, irrespective of their legal designation.[4] These include, in the majority of cases, regulations and directives. The exclusion of regulations from the reach of individual challenge may be explained on several grounds. Owing to the structure and economic scope of the E.E.C. Treaty, regulations play a fundamental part amongst the secondary sources of Community law as quasi-legislative acts designed to implement the Treaty in the most vital areas and affecting most aspects of the economic life in the Community.[5] Due further to the legislative process in that Community, regulations are very often worked out with considerable difficulty only, and by way of political compromise between the Member States both at the preparatory stages and in the framework of the Council. Their annulment with *erga omnes* and retroactive effects[6] necessarily entails extremely grave consequences and must therefore be restricted to the most serious cases of objective illegality. Since the primary function of an action for annulment when used against genuine law-making measures is precisely to provide an instrument for controlling objective legality (rather than one for protecting individual rights), it is the Member States and the institutions which are in the best position to judge when to make use of that instrument. Making it available to anyone whose interests may be prejudiced by a regulation might lead to permanent litigation and open the way to a real *actio popularis* which could jeopardise legal security and the proper functioning of the Community. When, however, a regulation does interfere with subjective rights in a direct and special way through the effects of an individual measure taken in its implementation at either Community or national level, or by causing ascertainable individual damage, it is only reasonable that its validity or legality should be contestable by those individuals whose rights or interests are prejudiced. It is thus as a necessary corollary to the restriction on the private persons' right of direct action that the Treaties provide various indirect means for the latter to challenge regulations whenever this is necessary for the protection of their subjective rights. Such indirect means are the defence of illegality,[7] preliminary rulings[8] and in certain circumstances action for damages,[9] i.e. where the Community's liability rests upon the illegality of a regulation. The essential difference between all these cases and a straightforward action for annulment, however, is that the successful indirect challenge will not entail the annulment of the regulation with *erga omnes* and retroactive effect but merely its inapplicability in the particular case concerned.[10]

The second difference between the E.C.S.C. and E.E.C./Euratom systems of legal protection is that the former is based entirely on the legal nature of the contested measure while the latter introduces an additional, second criterion which takes into account the legal effects of that measure as well. Thus, if under the E.C.S.C. Treaty a decision is individual in character objectively, that is, with respect to anyone, it is regarded as such with respect to the applicant also. It is then subject to challenge without regard to its legal effects as soon as it 'concerns' the latter, that is, affects his legally protected interests but without necessarily impairing his subjective rights. Under the E.E.C./Euratom Treaties the fact that a measure, viewed objectively, is an individual decision does not in itself open the way to an action (unless it is addressed to the applicant personally) but must also have close and specific legal effects in relation to the latter, i.e. must not only 'concern' him but must concern him 'directly and individually'. In establishing the existence of such specific legal effects or 'concern', the legitimate interests of the applicant play hardly any part.[11]

From the foregoing it becomes apparent that the E.E.C./Euratom Treaties lay down more restrictive conditions than does the E.C.S.C. Treaty for the admissibility of applications for annulment by private individuals and that in so doing they have deliberately departed from the system set up by the latter. In interpreting and applying the E.E.C./Euratom provisions it is therefore not permissible to rely upon the relevant provisions of the E.C.S.C. Treaty, nor upon the case-law developed by the European Court under it. Being presented with a considered choice and a clear wording, the European Court and its various Advocates-General, while recognising the limitations of the system, have repeatedly rejected any attempts by private parties at widening the scope of legal protection of individuals through a more generous or extensive interpretation. This they have done even though the system may create situations where private parties are virtually deprived of any legal protection at both Community and national level.[12]

509. (1) Decision addressed to the applicant

Community law requires decisions of the Council and the Commission to indicate the names of their addressees.[1] Natural and legal persons to whom/which a decision is addressed have an unqualified right to bring an action for the annulment of such a decision. Such a right is warranted by the individual character of the decision as a legal act and by its direct binding effect upon the addressee. Since the provisions of the Treaties relating to judicial protection[2] and those relating to the material and formal requirements of Community acts[3] form a coherent system, the concept of a decision for the purposes of the former is, in principle, the same as that defined by the latter.[4] In order, therefore, to establish whether an act of the Council or Commission is a decision open to challenge by private parties recourse must be had to the relevant definitions of the Treaties.[5] In practice, the majority of contested acts falling into this category are decisions issued by the Commission in competition matters holding an agreement, decision or concerted practice to constitute an infringement of Article 85(1) E.E.C.; and/or refusing an application for exemption under Article 85(3) E.E.C.; and/or requiring the infringement to be terminated, with or without the imposition of a penalty. All such decisions are subject to challenge by the addressees without any difficulty (the question of admissibility usually does not even arise); but where the applicant is a composite legal person (e.g. an association) the decision must be addressed to it as such and not to one or some of its members.[6] Difficulties may, however, arise where an individual act addressed to the applicant does not have the title of 'decision' and has the appearance of a mere non-binding measure (recommendation, opinion, communication, notification, etc.), or where such an act, although entitled 'decision', is, by its nature, a purely 'confirmatory' measure. These two situations must be considered further.

Natural and legal persons, just as Member States and institutions, cannot institute an action for annulment against an act, even if addressed to them, which is either by its title or by its true legal nature a recommendation, opinion or any other non-binding measure. It follows by implication that the express denial of such an act can also not be the subject of an action for annulment.[7] Thus, in particular, individuals cannot challenge an act of the Commission whereby the latter refuses their request to initiate an Article 169 procedure against a Member State which in their opinion has violated Community law. Quite apart from the fact that the various procedural steps provided for by Article 169 E.E.C./Article 141 Euratom take place between the Commission and the Member State concerned only, and are thus not addressed or directed to individuals, none of those steps has the character of a binding and enforceable act and therefore their refusal cannot be regarded as such either.[8]

In some cases to determine whether a certain act (communication, notification, etc.) of the Commission which constitutes a mere interim step in a procedure pending before it, should be regarded as a binding (and hence actionable) decision or a non-binding opinion, may cause real difficulties. This is the case, in particular, in procedures instituted by the Commission in competition matters under Regulation 17 which Regulation does not always use clear and consistent terminology in distinguishing between formal decisions and other informal interim measures. In such a situation the delimitation of a binding decision from a non-binding act is governed by the following two important principles. First, the silence of an instrument in a matter which affects the protection of the rights of individuals should not lead to the interpretation which is least favourable to them. Thus the fact that an enabling instrument does not specifically provide for a measure to be taken in the form of a decision, and the fact that the measure actually taken is not explicitly so designated, does not necessarily exclude its having the character of a binding decision. On the contrary, it must be regarded as a decision so as to fall under judicial control if otherwise individuals would be left without protection in respect of disadvantageous consequences (e.g. a threat of sanctions) that such a measure may indirectly entail for them. Secondly, it is not the form or title of an act but its substance, that is, its subject-matter, content and legal effects, that is decisive in defining its true legal nature.

Thus a decision proper is characterised by the following two criteria. First, it must be a definitive expression of intention although it need not necessarily mark the definitive stage of a procedure. It may have a provisional character and may, in effect, amount to no more than an interim measure (e.g. request for information, order to carry out verifications, etc.) in a procedure the final stage of which may be still far off. Secondly, it must produce legal effects in the sense of having an obligatory character although it is not necessary that it should confer rights or impose obligations; it may be of a mere declaratory nature or it may revoke rights or exempt from obligations. It follows that a definitive act of the Commission involving adverse legal effects for the addressees by bringing about a distinct alteration in their legal position and applying to them compulsorily, is not a mere opinion but a decision. Although the elevation of a mere procedural step to the rank of an actionable decision might slow down the progress of the whole procedure, this possibility cannot weaken the guarantees instituted by the Treaties to protect individual rights.[9]

While, from the point of view of substance, the criteria for the delimitation of a binding decision from a non-binding act largely coincide under the E.E.C./Euratom and E.C.S.C. Treaties,[10] the case is not entirely the same when it comes to questions of form. Unlike the position under the E.C.S.C. Treaty, under the E.E.C./Euratom Treaties the fact alone that a communication or notification was not signed by the President or a Member of the Commission but only by the acting Director-General, does not prevent it from being an actionable measure provided that the latter was acting on behalf of the Commission and that he expressed the Commission's point of view. The case-law of the Court developed on this point under the E.C.S.C. Treaty is therefore not of binding application in the context of the E.E.C./Euratom Treaties.[11] Where, however, a letter contains a Director-General's own personal opinion, it cannot commit the Commission as a whole especially if the signatory is not authorised to enter into such a commitment.[12]

Insofar as 'confirmatory' measures are concerned, i.e. measures confirming in force or, what amounts to the same, refusing to repeal or amend existing acts, these must be judged by reference to the act confirmed. Thus, generally, an individual negative decision given in response to a request only constitutes an act capable of being attacked if the positive measure requested but refused would itself have been challengeable. Where, for example, a claim by an individual is directed at the amendment of a regulation, which can only be achieved by an act which itself is in the nature of a regulation, the rejection of the claim by means of an individual decision addressed to the applicant is not subject to an action for annulment as it is not in reality an individual decision but an act confirming the regulation.[13]

510. (2) Decision addressed to another person

A Community act which qualifies as a genuine decision may be challenged not only by the addressee alone, but also by other natural or legal persons. The only (although essential) difference between the two situations is that where the applicant is the addressee of the contested decision, he must meet one requirement only, that is, he must claim an impairment of his legally protected interests.[1] Where, on the other hand, the applicant is not the addressee of the decision, he must satisfy an additional condition: he must prove that the decision concerns him directly and individually.[2] He need not, however, also demonstrate that he is in fact the true addressee of the act, that the decision is only in appearance addressed to the other person but is in reality meant to produce legal effects for him. Such a further requirement would narrow down the right of action of private parties to an excessive degree, not contemplated by the drafters of the Treaties.

This means that the action for annulment is available in respect of the so-called 'double-faced' acts, i.e. acts that create 'reflex effects' for persons other than those for whom they are primarily designed.[3] In practice, mainly (although not exclusively) the following two kinds of Community measures fall into this category. First, decisions of the Commission granting or refusing to grant an exemption from Article 85(1) E.E.C. according to the relevant rules of competition law. In either case, the decision will inevitably produce 'reflex effects' for third parties by virtue of the *erga omnes* nature of the confirmation of the validity or nullity, as the case may be, of the agreement, decision or concerted practice in question, which follows from such a decision. Persons other than the addressees may challenge these decisions provided that they can prove the existence of a direct and individual concern.[3a] Secondly, decisions of the Commission fixing prices or granting or refusing to grant to Member States tariff quotas or an authorisation to take certain protective measures, e.g. to suspend the application of the Common Customs Tariff, to exclude from Community treatment certain products originating in third countries but already in free circulation within the Community, etc. All such decisions are addressed to one or more Member State but clearly affect the position of those importers/exporters to whom the prices fixed or the protective measures authorised are applied. Again, such persons may in principle contest these decisions although the requirement to prove that they are directly and individually concerned will restrict their right of action considerably.

It follows from the foregoing that private parties may challenge not only Community decisions addressed to other natural or legal persons but also decisions addressed to Member States (not necessarily to their own State). Clearly, these two different types of decision may produce widely different legal effects. The latter may in fact have, by requiring in some cases for their implementation the taking of legislative measures at the national level, repercussions in the Member State(s) to which they are addressed which are very similar to the effects of a genuine normative act.[4] That, in spite of such effects, decisions addressed to Member States may in principle be subject to challenge by private parties, may be explained on several grounds. First, just as under the E.C.S.C. Treaty,[5] the decisive factor is the legal nature, and not the legal effect, of the act concerned. If it is an individual decision, within the definition of the Treaties, with respect to one person (i.e. the Member State to which it is addressed), because it governs an individual legal relationship and is binding on that particular person alone, it cannot be, at the same time, a general measure with respect to third parties whatever its further legal effects.[6] It should therefore be subject to review as an individual decision although its further legal effects will be taken into account in the context of the examination of 'individual concern'.[7] Secondly, the Treaties neither define nor limit the scope of the words 'another person'. The natural meaning of those words justify the broadest interpretation in accordance with the principle that provisions of the Treaties which concern legal remedies available to individuals must not be interpreted restrictively. The Treaties being silent on this point, a limitation must not therefore be presumed. Since Member States, just as constituent States in a Federal State or municipalities, are all 'persons', i.e. legal persons governed by public law, they must all fall within the scope of the provision in question.[8] Finally, complete exclusion of decisions addressed to Member States from the ambit of action for annulment by private individuals would unreasonably restrict the legal protection of the latter. While their interests may be paramount in such decisions, they have virtually no means of compelling their own State to institute proceedings against decisions unfavourable to them. Just as under the E.C.S.C. Treaty, they must, therefore, be put in the position of safeguarding their rights and interests themselves.[9]

511. (3) Decision in the form of a regulation

While an act of the Council and the Commission which qualifies as a decision is subject to challenge by private parties, one which constitutes a genuine regulation is not.[1] Thus the line drawn between decisions and regulations basically determines the extent to which natural and legal persons enjoy judicial protection under the E.E.C./Euratom Treaties. The narrower the scope of the concept of decision, the more restrictive that protection. This becomes particularly obvious in cases where the contested act does not at first sight unequivocally belong to either category, i.e. it has all the appearances of a regulation (it is so entitled and apparently contains general provisions) but is alleged, and, upon further analysis, found, to be a decision or a measure analogous to a decision. In such cases, in order to establish whether an action for annulment instituted by private parties is admissible, two questions have to be examined in the following logical order. First, whether the act designated as a regulation is a regulation in appearance only and is, according to its true legal nature, in reality a decision. Secondly, if it has been found to be a decision, whether it is by virtue of its legal effects of direct and individual concern to the applicant.[2] Since these two conditions for admissibility have to be fulfilled cumulatively, it is not enough, in principle, to prove separately either that the act is a decision or that it is of direct and individual concern to the applicant. It follows that where either of the two questions is answered in the negative, an examination of the other becomes unnecessary.[3] For this reason the European Court does not, in practice, always follow the above order but, without first examining the legal character of the act, deals immediately with its legal effects.[4] This is usually the case where the action seems likely to be dismissed as inadmissible because of a lack of direct and individual concern.

Moreoever, the Court does not always clearly distinguish between the two conditions for admissibility which, as a result, tend to merge. Thus the nature of an act, i.e. whether it is a decision or a regulation, is often determined in the light of its effects, i.e. whether it concerns the applicant directly and individually.[5] Where it so concerns him, it is accepted as an actionable decision without any further investigation into its legal nature (contrary to what has been said above) as in the European Court's opinion the aim of the Treaties is to ensure the judicial protection of individuals in all cases where they are directly and individually concerned by a Community act, which is not directed to them, in whatever form it appears.[6] Although such a merger or reduction to one of the two criteria for admissibility does not immediately seem to follow from the logic of the Treaties' system of legal protection, it becomes justified in the light of the Court's interpretation of the concepts of direct and (especially) individual concern, which are separately considered below.[7]

In examining the legal nature of the contested act, the starting point is that the E.E.C./Euratom Treaties, unlike the E.C.S.C. Treaty,[8] make a clear distinction between the concept of a decision and that of a regulation. In principle, therefore, the two concepts can never overlap but must be contrasted with one another. It follows that a binding Community act or an individual provision thereof (other than a directive which in any case can never be challenged by private parties) must in theory always be capable of being classified either as a decision or as a regulation. The same measure cannot be both a decision and a regulation at the same time, nor can it belong to a third category. Thus when the Treaties speak of a decision in the form of a regulation, they do not intend to introduce a *tertium genus* but envisage the case of a provision which is only in appearance a regulation but which, in substance, does not have the quality of a regulation but that of a decision. Whether it is the one or the other, must be decided in the light of the technical definitions given by the Treaties of decisions and regulations[9] and by taking into account its object and content, not merely its official title. The main criterion for the distinction must be sought in the individual or general application of the provision in question.[10]

According to the above considerations, a measure will be a regulation (and thus excluded from challenge by private parties) if it is essentially of a legislative (normative) nature, i.e. it applies not to a limited number of persons, defined or identifiable, but to categories of persons viewed impersonally, in a general and abstract manner, or to objectively determined situations, and involves immediate legal consequences in all Member States. It will be a regulation if it applies to the applicant solely by virtue of his belonging to a group or class of persons, or because of his participation in a business activity, to whom/which the measure applies in a general manner. The fact that the provision's scope of application is materially or territorially limited, that it has unequal legal effects upon different products or persons subjected to its operation according to the particular character of their situation or activities, that it is possible to determine with more or less precision the number or even the identity of the persons to which it applies at a given moment, does not alter the provision's character as a regulation, provided that it clearly applies by virtue of an objective factual or legal situation defined by the provision itself and that it is not possible to ascertain, at the moment of its adoption, the class of persons to which it will apply during the course of its existence.[11] Moreover, a provision which amends, repeals or revokes a measure of general application or determines its application in time, has the same general character as the measure which it qualifies.[12] Thus, except for cases involving a misuse of powers, the fact alone that individual provisions of a transitory regulation forming an integral part of a group of old and new regulations which it attempts to reconcile, have retroactive effect and thus the number and identity of the persons to which they apply are ascertainable at the time of their adoption, does not deprive them of their character as a regulation and does not make them into individual decisions.[13]

By contrast, a measure will be a decision (and thus subject to challenge by private parties) if it is essentially of an administrative (individual) nature, i.e. it governs an individual legal relationship and applies to a limited number of defined or identifiable persons. What distinguishes such a measure from a regulation in the first place is that it is of individual concern to specific persons.[14] It is precisely the individual character of a provision as it affects natural or legal persons that justifies giving those persons the right to bring action and assimilating their position to that of an addressee. It follows that where a measure entitled a regulation contains provisions which are capable of being not only of direct but also of individual concern to certain natural or legal persons, those provisions will not have the character of a regulation and may therefore be challenged by such persons without prejudice to the question whether the measure as a whole can be correctly termed a regulation.[15] Such is the case, in particular, where the number (quantity) and identity of persons, products or transactions to which a regulation (or some of its provisions) applies is, either by virtue of certain distinguishing criteria included in the regulation or by reason of the individual course of action pursued in the past by those affected, determined and known or at least ascertainable at the time when the regulation is adopted. A regulation (or an individual provision of a regulation) of this kind which applies exclusively to identifiable persons or to specific past (and therefore closed) situations is in reality not of a normative character, even if it is one of a number of related measures having a legislative function. It is, rather, an act in the nature of a decision or collective decision (*Allgemeinverfügung, acte collectif*), that is, a series or bundle of individual decisions taken in the form of a regulation. Each one of these decisions affects the legal position of each of the persons concerned and is therefore subject to challenge by him.[16]

As pointed out at the beginning of this Section, the line drawn between decisions and regulations fundamentally determines the extent to which natural and legal persons enjoy judicial protection under the E.E.C./Euratom Treaties. From the foregoing discussion it becomes apparent that in its case-law the European Court of Justice has drawn that line in such a way as to give the concept of decision the narrowest possible scope. Basically, the Court uses one criterion only to distinguish a decision from a regulation: the class of persons affected. Thus the Court classifies as individual decisions only those measures for which the number of addressees is objectively fixed at the time when the measure is adopted, and conversely, classifies as regulations or normative acts all those measures for which the number of persons affected cannot be determined at that moment because it is liable to fluctuate during the period of validity of the measure.

Such a narrow definition of a decision has been criticised mainly on two grounds. First, that it is not capable of taking sufficient account of certain intermediate or mixed forms which, since a third category does not exist, fall to be classified as regulations although they are in the nature of a general decision or a regulation for a particular case, i.e. have effects analogous to those of a decision rather than possessing a normative character. Should the criterion whether an act deals with a particular or concrete case be recognised as decisive, such intermediate forms could more properly be classed as decisions even though they may affect an indeterminate number of persons. Secondly, a too narrow interpretation of the concept of a decision does not pay heed to the basic constitutional principle of comprehensive judicial protection. This principle, too, would require a more flexible and liberal treatment of what is certainly not only one of the most important but also one of the most difficult questions concerning the legal protection of individuals in the European Communities.[17] The Court, however, has not been prepared to admit that its own interpretation of the respective concepts of decision and regulation is more restrictive of individual rights than warranted by the texts of the Treaties. It has been unwilling to widen that interpretation lest the concept of a decision be enlarged to such an extent as to endanger the system of remedies laid down by the Treaties which, in the Court's opinion, permits individual persons to apply for an annulment only of specific decisions addressed to them or of measures which affect them in an analogous manner.[18]

512. Direct concern

In defining the group of persons who are 'concerned' by a decision, it is important first of all to distinguish between those who are prejudiced by, and those who benefit from, that decision. In examining the admissibility of an action, it is necessary to limit the category of persons 'concerned' to those who are prejudiced, i.e. whose rights or legally protected interests are impaired, while excluding those who may benefit from the measure in question.[1] Under the E.C.S.C. Treaty, a decision which is individual in character can be challenged by private parties as soon as it 'concerns' them in the above sense.[2] Under the E.E.C./Euratom Treaties this is however not enough; an individual decision which is not addressed to the applicant can be challenged by him only if it concerns him both 'directly' and 'individually'. Although these two requirements have to be satisfied cumulatively, they are not mutually interdependent. Since they refer to quite different qualities of a decision, the one may well exist without the other.[3] This makes their separate examination not only possible but even desirable, in accordance with the usual practice of the European Court of Justice. Indeed, in some cases the Court has found it appropriate to examine the second condition first, holding that if the applicant is not individually concerned by a decision it becomes unnecessary to enquire whether he is directly concerned.[4] The converse proposition is, of course, also correct. The notion of direct concern is considered in this, that of individual concern in the following Section.[5]

The concept of direct concern has somewhat different meaning and significance according to whether the contested measure is a decision addressed to a Member State, or a decision addressed to another natural or legal person, or a decision taken in the form of a regulation. In all cases, however, it is clear that the criterion of 'directness' is not used simply to measure the gravity of the impairment of the applicant's rights or interests. Nor is it intended to refer merely to a causal connection (which may be both direct and indirect) between the challenged act and the rights or interests impaired. Rather, it expresses the fact that the decision produces immediate, automatic and inevitable (not merely possible) disadvantageous legal effects upon the applicant. Thus the difference between 'direct' and 'indirect' concern is characterised, on the one hand, by the absence or presence of an intermediary with an independent power of decision between the authority taking the measure and the results that follow from it, and, on the other hand, by the inevitability or mere probability with which those results follow from that measure.

Thus, generally, a decision, irrespective of its form or addressee, will concern the applicant directly if it imposes a disadvantage on, or denies an advantage to, a class of persons of which the applicant is a member (or, conversely, grants an advantage to, or terminates a disadvantage which had been imposed on, the applicant's competitors) and if these results follow automatically and necessarily from the decision.[6] Where, however, the results are merely likely to follow (but depend upon the intervention of certain persons or upon the fulfilment of certain conditions) there will be no direct concern. Thus, unlike the position under the E.C.S.C. Treaty,[7] the mere fact that a measure (for example by granting aid to certain undertakings only) is likely to influence existing conditions of competition in the relevant market is not sufficient for every market participant having a competitive relationship with the addressee of the measure to be considered as being directly (and individually) concerned by that measure. Only under special circumstances, for example, if the discriminatory measure has a direct effect on the applicant's position in some other, specific way, e.g. by prejudicing his position in the system for the allocation of any production or other quotas that may exist in the relevant sector, can he claim to be directly (and individually) concerned by it.[8]

While the foregoing considerations apply generally, the concept of direct concern requires further interpretation in the most important category of cases, namely, where the contested decision is addressed to a Member State but is intended to produce legal effects for individuals within that State. Such a situation often arises by virtue of the peculiar structure of Community law which necessitates a two-tier (i.e. Community and national) legal action in those areas where the Community institutions either do not possess the requisite powers directly to legislate for individuals within the Member States or have entrusted the latter to act as agents for the Communities in carrying out certain tasks. In such cases the Member States must co-operate with the institutions by giving effect to their measures.[9] Thus the Community decision will be followed by a national action and only the latter, not the former, will produce direct legal effects for individuals. In such circumstances the answer to the question whether an individual is directly concerned by the Community measure will in general depend upon whether or not that measure leaves any margin of discretion to the Member State to interpose its own sovereign power of decision between the Community act and its effects upon the individual. Where the Community act is not mandatory but merely enabling, i.e. contains an authorisation of which the Member State is entirely free to avail itself or not, the discretionary power of the latter will usually prevent individuals from being directly concerned by the Community decision. Such a decision does not confer any rights on possible beneficiaries of any measures which the Member State concerned might later take under the authorisation and which alone will be of direct concern to the beneficiary.[10] The position is not different where the Community decision is a negative one, i.e. contains a refusal to grant an authorisation (e.g. to suspend customs duties) or a tariff quota at a reduced rate of duty or duty free. In such cases it is entirely within the Member State's political discretion to decide whether or not to challenge the decision of refusal, that is, to pursue its original aim, just as it was entirely within its discretion to make a request for the authorisation in the first place. Moreover, even if a private individual could successfully challenge such a decision and obtain a positive measure instead, he could still not directly benefit from it: it would again be left to the discretion of the State concerned to implement the authorisation by the opening of tariff quotas or by taking any other suitable national measure. The individual would, again, be powerless to compel the State to make use of the power granted. Consequently, a decision rejecting a request for authorisation does not concern private persons in any different manner than would the positive decision granting it. In the absence of direct concern, there is no reason why individuals should be able to challenge such decisions.[11]

By contrast, a Community decision addressed to a Member State will in principle directly concern individuals where it leaves no discretion to the Member State in the matter of implementation or where the latter has, in advance or subsequently, committed itself to use its discretionary power in a certain way or renounced its exercise altogether. Thus even an authorisation to take protective measures may, although the Member State is in principle free to refrain from using it, directly concern a private party where the national authorities had in advance informed the latter that they would reject his application for an import licence as soon as the Commission had granted them the requisite authorisation to do so. The fact that the Member State had requested the authorisation with precisely the particular person in view, and that it had indicated its intention to make use of it in a particular way, will establish direct concern on the part of the person in question.[12]

Likewise, a Commission decision retroactively confirming, amending or abolishing a protective measure taken by a Member State may be of direct concern to individuals where by virtue of a mandatory provision of Community law such decision is 'immediately enforceable'. This means, in effect, that the decision is 'directly applicable' within the Member State and concerns the interested parties as directly as the national measure which it replaces. Where the decision merely confirms a protective measure already taken, it is in fact not simply an authorisation but also a validation of that measure and must have the same legal effects.[13] Moreoever, where a Member State acts merely as an agent of indirect Community administration and its role is restricted to a purely technical execution of a Community task (e.g. collecting customs duties and levies, paying out refunds, issuing import or export licences, etc. for and on behalf of the Communities) without any possibility for the intervention of its own discretionary power of decision, it is the Community measure which the Member State implements and not the national act of execution that directly governs the situation of individuals and is consequently of direct concern to them.[14]

To sum up, the concept of direct concern refers to a situation where Community power reaches beyond the Member State and 'catches' the individual directly. This is what justifies granting to the latter immediate remedy in the European Court irrespective of whom the Community measure is addressed to. It follows that there is a close connection between the concept of 'direct concern' and that of 'direct applicability'.[15] Although they are not governed by entirely identical criteria, they play a mutually complementary role in the system of the legal protection of individuals. In fact, they may be envisaged as the two sides of the same coin in that they regulate different aspects of the same problem: the position and protection of individuals in relation to Community provisions which directly penetrate into the national legal order. The concept of direct applicability is the means whereby individuals can enforce in national courts rights which they derive from such provisions. The concept of direct concern, on the other hand, enables individuals to seek protection in the European Court in respect of disadvantageous legal consequences arising for them from such provisions. Although the European Court has interpreted this latter concept narrowly (just as it has interpreted the former widely), such interpretation is, it is submitted, the only one that is in accordance with the system of remedies which the Treaties intended to create in favour of individuals.

513. Individual concern

Since in the system of the E.E.C./Euratom Treaties a decision is by definition always an act of an individual character, the question arises why the Treaties have not found it sufficient to confine the right of action of private parties simply to decisions, but, on the contrary, have found it necessary further to limit that right to decisions which are of individual concern to the applicant (unless specifically addressed to him). The imposition of this second restriction has been made necessary by the fact that there are certain measures which, according to their nature, satisfy all the criteria of a decision (i.e. they govern an individual legal relationship and are binding on a limited number of defined or identifiable persons) but produce wider legal effects which are in fact analogous to those of general (normative) provisions. Such are, in the first place, decisions addressed to Member States which may in general affect the position within those States of abstractly defined categories of persons whose identity is not ascertainable at the time of their adoption. Judged solely by their nature, such measures as decisions should in theory be challengeable by individuals, but judged by their legal effects, they must be equated with legislative measures in respect of which no right of action exists for private persons. It is precisely to resolve this possible discrepancy between legal nature and legal effect that the Treaties have introduced the criterion of individual concern.

The primary purpose of this concept is to help distinguish genuine decisions from regulations, in other words, provisions which produce true individual legal effects from those producing normative effects for persons other than those to whom they are formally addressed.[1] Such persons may only claim to be individually concerned if a provision directed to others affects them either by reason of certain attributes which are peculiar to them or by reason of special circumstances which differentiate them from all other persons, and therefore distinguishes them individually just as if they were the addressees.[2] Consequently, if a provision affects them only by reason of a commercial activity which may at any time be practiced by any person or in their capacity as members of an abstractly defined group the actual or potential membership of which is illimitable and therefore unascertainable at the time of the adoption of the provision, they will not be individually concerned. In other words, in such circumstances the provision is in fact legislative, rather than individual, in its effects whether it is a decision proper or a (real or alleged) decision taken in the form of a regulation.[3]

It follows that where a provision is intended to apply Community-wide to a commercial activity or to affect an abstractly defined group of commercial operators, the purely contingent circumstance that a person alone happens to carry out that activity or belong to that group in a given Member State at any given time subsequent to the adoption of the provision, is not such as to distinguish that person from all other potential participants and to make him individually concerned for the purposes of an action for annulment.[4] Moreover, a professional association or organisation (including trade unions), formed for the protection of the collective interests of a category of persons and acting in its capacity as the representative of its members, cannot be considered as being individually concerned by a measure affecting the general interests of that category. Any other solution would result in the grouping, under the heading of a single legal person, of the interests properly attributed to the members of a category who have been affected as individuals by genuine regulations. This would derogate from the system of the Treaties which allows applications for annulment by private individuals only of decisions which have been addressed to them or of acts which affect them in a similar manner.[5]

From such a definition of the concept of individual concern follows that in practice a decision is of individual concern only to those persons (apart from the addressee) whose number and identity is in one way or another unalterably and objectively defined and therefore ascertainable at the moment when the decision is taken so that the author of the measure is in a position to know whose interests and position its decision will exclusively affect. Only in such circumstances are these persons differentiated from all other persons and singled out just as if they were the addressees. If this condition is satisfied, the small or large number of the persons who are individually concerned or the territorial scope of application of the measure (i.e. whether it applies in one, some or all the Member States) is of no relevance. Nor is the question whether or not the author of the measure actually knows the identity of those persons. The circumstance that is capable of so individualising a person can only be a past conduct on his part (that is to say, a conduct preceding in time the adoption of the measure) corresponding to the distinguishing criteria of the measure, for example the submission of an application for import or export licence or for advance fixing of levies or refunds where the measure applies exclusively to those persons who had submitted such applications, or to products in respect of which such applications had been submitted, during a certain period prior to its adoption,[6] or the lodging of an application under Article 3(2), (6) of Regulation 17.[7]

Thus the concept of individual concern, as interpreted by the European Court of Justice, always has a retrospective aspect. Such interpretation may seem, just as that of direct concern, unduly narrow, but, it is submitted, it is perfectly in accordance with the system of legal protection of individuals as laid down by the Treaties. That system is based on the distinction between normative and individual measures and in making that distinction the Court uses exactly the same criteria as in defining the concept of individual concern. In the final analysis, therefore, the concept of an individual measure and that of a measure which is of individual concern to a person become synonymous.[8]

514. Grounds of action

Generally speaking, an act of the institutions taken in infringement of any of the written or unwritten, substantive or procedural rules that make up the body of Community law is illegal and, as such, ought in theory to be subject to annulment by the European Court. In a broader sense, therefore, any essential violation of any of the rules discussed earlier in the context of the sources of Community law[1] ought, as resulting in a materially or formally defective act, to be regarded as constituting a valid ground on which to base an application for judicial review. However, the European Court possesses such wide (virtually unlimited) powers of supervision over the legality of the institution's conduct and over the validity of their acts in reference proceedings for preliminary rulings only.[2] By contrast, in direct actions for annulment the Court has been given jurisdiction to declare acts void only where the alleged defect(s) correspond(s) to one or more of the following four specified grounds of illegality on which alone can the annulment be based:

(1) lack of competence;
(2) infringement of an essential procedural requirement;
(3) infringement of the Treaties or of any rule of law relating to their application;
(4) misuse of powers.

In addition, an individual act may also be annulled on a fifth ground, namely, that another act (usually a general, normative measure), which has served as its legal basis, is itself illegal on any of the above four grounds (defence of illegality). These four (five) grounds, which will be considered individually below,[3] are the same under the E.C.S.C. and E.E.C./Euratom Treaties and apply equally to Member States, institutions and private parties. The case-law of the European Court developed on this point under the E.C.S.C. Treaty may, therefore, generally be resorted to under the E.E.C./Euratom Treaties.

The distinction made between the four grounds of action generally corresponds to empirical classifications adopted in certain national (e.g. French, Belgian, to some extent Italian) administrative laws.[4] It has as its main purpose the identification of the possible faults in an act that the legislator recognises as being of such gravity as to entail the act's annulment. Broadly speaking, the first and second grounds enable such formal and procedural defects to be invoked as are neither negligible nor so grave as to lead to absolute nullity,[5] while the third ground provides the means for questioning the act's substantive legality. It is, therefore, the most important and most general of all grounds. By contrast, the fourth ground relates not to the act's objective (formal or material) legality but to the subjective intentions of the institution in adopting it. This ground plays a particularly important role under the E.C.S.C. Treaty where in certain circumstances it is the only one that can be relied upon.[6] No such distinction, however, exists under the

E.E.C./Euratom Treaties although here, too, misuse of powers plays a significant part in controlling the institutions' discretionary powers.[7] These later Treaties have deliberately adopted a different approach to the whole question of legal protection, an approach which clearly does not attach so much importance to the distinction made between the various grounds of action.[8] The practice of the European Court under the E.E.C. Treaty shows that almost any well substantiated infringement (other than a really minor one) of Community law in its broadest sense can be relied upon to establish the illegality of a measure and can in principle lead to its annulment. This is only a natural consequence of the fact that the various grounds are drawn up in such wide terms that they virtually encompass between themselves almost all conceivable grounds of illegality. A clear differentiation between them is made even more difficult by the fact that they overlap considerably so that in certain cases the classification of an infringement according to the clear-cut terms used by the Treaties is virtually impossible.[9]

The foregoing relationship between the various grounds of action has important practical consequences both for the parties and for the Court of Justice. As regards the parties, whilst the applicants must, in theory at least, found their action on one or more of the four grounds, they are not required in their pleadings, and in particular in the originating application (which must contain a brief statement of the grounds on which the action is based),[10] strictly to follow the legal terminology and order used by the Treaties. Whether the presentation of the grounds of action is adequate for the purpose of admissibility will be determined by reference to their substance rather than to the legal terms used. Thus, it is sufficient if it becomes reasonably clear from the application which of the grounds specified by the Treaties is being relied upon.[11] Whilst the Court will dismiss arguments which are clearly irrelevant to the challenged measure, it is nevertheless prepared to extract from the applicant's arguments the essential grounds on which the action is meant to be founded,[12] and is even willing to consider grounds not expressly mentioned in the Treaties.[13] On the other hand, a mere abstract statement of the grounds is not enough; they must relate to the facts as the latter are set out in the application. A broad reference for example to 'excess of power' (*excès de pouvoir*), which is a general term of municipal law capable of covering all grounds of action, or to a violation of Community law, without defining what constitutes such an excess of power or which particular rule of Community law has been violated, will not satisfy the requirements of admissibility.[14]

As regards the Court of Justice, the question is whether and to what extent the Court is bound by the terms of the pleadings in considering the various grounds of action. Is the Court limited to examining merely the particular ground(s) invoked or can it, acting of its own motion, *ex officio* declare an act void upon any of the four grounds even if that ground has not been pleaded or has been pleaded only belatedly? Whilst it is a general rule that the Court cannot of its own accord bring a case before itself, once a case has been properly instituted by an applicant both alternatives are in principle tenable. On the one hand, it may be argued that the Court is restricted to the grounds actually invoked as it is not its task to act on behalf of the parties and to make up for omissions committed by them. According to the *ne ultra petita* principle[15] the judicial function is exhausted by giving judgment in respect of what has been requested from the Court. On the other hand, the Court would not be fulfilling its task of ensuring that in the interpretation and application of the Treaties the law is observed if, following a kind of rigid formalism, it should refuse to annul an act which is patently illegal just because the particular ground of illegality has not been pleaded.

The European Court itself has developed a practice which gives due weight to both of these considerations. Generally speaking, it limits its enquiries to the particular ground(s) put forward by the applicant unless public interest, public policy or the need properly to fulfil its task of exercising judicial review over legality requires it to do otherwise. As maintenance of the institutional balance within the Communities is a matter which generally affects public interest and public policy, and the giving of adequate reasons for every binding measure is a necessary prerequisite for the exercise of legal control, overstepping by the institutions of their competence and their failure to consult the consultative bodies or to give adequate reasons for binding acts are matters which will usually (although not automatically) be examined by the Court of its own motion and which may lead to *ex officio* annulment.[16] In exceptionally serious cases, as seen above,[17] those defects may even entail absolute nullity. By contrast, the Court will not consider a misuse of (discretionary) powers of its own accord because that presupposes the making of subjective judgments.[18] Whether it is prepared to examine *ex officio* infringement of the Treaties or of any rule of law relating to their application, depends on the circumstances of each individual case,[19] although, clearly, any step taken by the Court in this direction of its own motion tends to limit the responsibility of the parties for the conduct of the case and for the choice of their arguments.[20] What is certain is that the Court will not examine the legality of a measure which the applicant has evidently not intended to criticise, in order not to interfere with the scope which the applicant wished to give to its action.[21]

Finally, it may be noted that annulment on any of the four grounds has exactly the same legal effect, although the particular ground on which the Court bases its judgment may play an important part in determining the nature and contents of the measure which the institution concerned has to take in order to comply with the judgment of the Court.[22] Where more than one ground is invoked, it is in the discretion of the Court to decide in what order to examine them, and the fact that any one of them is well-founded, leading in itself to annulment, will usually make an examination of the rest superfluous.[23]

515. (1) Lack of competence

Lack of competence as a ground of action gives effect to the general principle that a measure is invalid (and therefore voidable) if it originates from a body which does not possess the requisite powers for its adoption. The Community institutions will act outside their competences whenever they exercise a power which has not been conferred upon them by Community law. The institutions' powers are defined by reference to three distinct types of relationships, i.e. those between the Communities and the Member States, those between the various institutions themselves, and those between the Communities and third countries. A lack of competence may therefore arise in three different sets of circumstances. First, where an institution (Council or Commission) exercises a power not transferred to the Communities from the Member States or acts in an area not placed under Community competence.[1] Secondly, where it exercises a power conferred upon another institution or upon two institutions jointly and not, or not properly, delegated to it or exceeds the limits of delegated powers.[2] Thirdly, where it exercises a Community competence in relation to a non-Member State or its subjects (e.g. extraterritorially) in circumstances not authorised by general international law.[3] Any infringement of the rules, already discussed in earlier Chapters,[4] relating to the Communities' competences in their relationships with the Member States and third countries and to the division of powers inside the Communities between the institutions, will result in an illegal measure which may be challenged and annulled on the ground of lack of competence.

By contrast, a failure by an institution to observe only the extent of its competence in the exercise of an otherwise legitimate power, will fall under the heading of infringement of the Treaty rather than that of lack of competence, since the limits of the institutions' powers are determined by the substantive provisions of the Treaties.[5] In such a situation, however, there is a clear overlap between the two grounds of action and for reasons explained above[6] it will matter little in practice whether the action is based on the one or the other. The only consideration that could possibly make a difference is that if such a situation were to be regarded as falling under the heading of lack of competence, then, as this ground concerns public policy, the European Court could examine it *ex officio* even if that ground is not formally pleaded by the applicant.[7]

516. (2) Infringement of an essential procedural requirement

This ground of action gives effect to the general requirement that in the preparation, adoption, presentation and communication of their measures public authorities must observe certain basic rules as to form and procedure,[1] infringement of which may have as a consequence, depending upon its nature and degree of seriousness, either that no binding measure will come into existence at all[2] or that the measure will suffer from such a defect as to lead to its absolute nullity[3] or, more usually, to its annulment. Broadly speaking, the function of these formal and procedural requirements is to ensure that the measures of the institutions are taken with every guarantee of care and prudence,[4] and their observance is, particularly where they are laid down by the Treaties themselves, subject to an *ex officio* review by the European Court of Justice.[5]

In order to have an effect on the validity of a measure, the infringement must be of an 'essential' procedural requirement. What amounts to an 'essential requirement' or, perhaps more correctly, to an 'essential infringement' of a procedural requirement, depends to a large extent both on the nature and purpose of the measure and on the degree of legal protection required by its addressee.[6] Thus, more detailed and stricter requirements apply to individual measures affecting the legal position of private persons (e.g. decisions in competition matters, decisions requiring information, measures imposing obligations or enforceable pecuniary sanctions, etc.) and to the procedures relating to their adoption, such as the so-called 'administrative proceedings' which the Commission must follow in E.E.C. competition cases. These more detailed rules will be discussed separately in a subsequent Chapter.[7] Generally speaking, procedural requirements whose infringement usually constitutes a ground of action may be divided into three groups, i.e. those relating to the (a) preparation; (b) form; and (c) communication of the measure. These are examined below in turn.

As regards the preparation and adoption of Community measures, usually the following two types of infringement may be invoked as grounds of invalidity. First, the failure to consult the various consultative bodies where consultation is required by a provision of primary or secondary Community law. These bodies include, as the case may be, the E.C.S.C. Council and Consultative Committee;[8] the European Parliament; the E.E.C./Euratom Economic and Social Committee and, in E.E.C. competition matters, the Advisory Committee on Restrictive Practices and Monopolies.[9] While consultation must be proper so that an unofficial informing of the body concerned is not enough,[10] the opinion received need not be in the form of a separate act, but may be included in the minutes of the body consulted. Nor need it be set out, considered or, insofar as it contains dissenting views, refuted in the institution's measure; a simple statement to the effect that it has been obtained is quite sufficient.[11]

A second type of actionable infringement arises from a failure to give effect to the general principle of *audiatur et altera pars,*[12] i.e. failure to give parties whose interests may be perceptibly affected by a measure the opportunity to make their points of view known before the measure is finally adopted. This includes, in particular, the omission to give a Member State a hearing in certain situations,[13] e.g. before its failure to fulfil a Community obligation is recorded in a decision by the Commission according to Article 88(1) E.C.S.C.[14] It also includes, amongst other things, the failure to inform undertakings clearly and in good time of the essence of conditions to which the Commission intends to subject an exemption under Article 85(3) E.E.C. or of objections that may possibly entail imposition of sanctions. Such failure would mean to deprive them of the opportunity to submit observations to the Commission as required by Community law.[15] In such a situation the

Commission must take a new decision after hearing the undertakings' views.[16]

As regards the form of the measure, whilst insignificant (alleged) formal irregularities remain irrelevant,[17] the giving of no or insufficient reasons will always constitute an infringement of an essential procedural requirement, inadequate reasoning being treated for this purpose as equivalent to the total absence of reasoning.[18] In fact, in the structure of Community law, the requirement to give adequate reasons for every binding act fulfils more than a mere formal function. Its purposes are, first, to enable the general public to ascertain if the Community institutions properly carry the provisions of the Treaties into effect and thus to act as a kind of restraint upon their actions as well as a guarantee against arbitrariness. Secondly, to afford the parties directly affected by a measure an opportunity of defending their rights. Thirdly, to enable the European Court properly to exercise its supervisory function over the legality of the institutions' conduct.[19] It is these objectives that determine the criteria in the light of which the adequacy of reasoning must be assessed. These criteria are, on account of the identical function of reasoning, the same under the E.C.S.C. and E.E.C./Euratom Treaties[20] and, under the latter, the same in the context of a direct action for annulment as under a reference for a preliminary ruling.[21]

Broadly speaking, a statement of reasons must be deemed adequate when it sets out, in a concise but clear and relevant manner, all the essential legal and factual considerations upon which the operative part of the measure is based and thus enables both the parties concerned and the Court to discover the principal reasons which have led the institution to the adoption of the measure. General considerations which apply without distinction to other cases, or which are limited to repeating the wording of the Treaties or refer to 'information collected' without specifying it, or which are otherwise vague and inconsistent, are not enough.[22] In other words, the statement of reasons must be such as to validly substantiate the measure. It must enable the Court clearly to recognise the facts and considerations held by the institution to be decisive and to determine whether on the basis of those facts and considerations the measure is well-founded or unfounded in law. In short: it must be capable of being reviewed judicially.[23] Once this requirement is satisfied, there can be no question of an infringement of an essential procedural requirement even though the reasoning is not drawn up with that degree of precision and clarity that might perhaps be desirable or possible.[24]

Subject to the above requirements, the statement of reasons may be limited to the most important aspects of the measure as a whole. It is not necessary to support with reasons exhaustively and independently every single provision in it,[25] nor to give an overall theoretical analysis of all the objectives and criteria of the measure, especially of those not considered by the institutions (correctly or incorrectly) to be relevant. The omission of irrelevant considerations will not constitute a defect.[26] Further, the institutions may restrict themselves to stating their own interpretation of the Treaty provisions on which a measure is based. They are not required to reject or to discuss other alternative interpretations,[27] nor possible arguments and obections that may conceivably be raised by those affected by the measure.[28] Nor need an act be based solely on grounds invoked by the Member States previously consulted by the institutions; the latter must evaluate all the material facts whether or not called in aid by the Member States.[29] Although a decision which fits into a well-established line of decisions may be reasoned in a summary manner, for example, by a reference to those earlier decisions or to general rules laid down in earlier measures,[30] where the institutions considerably depart from the previous cases they must supply an additional, more detailed statement of reasons.[31] There is, of course, nothing to prevent them from basing a new decision which is identical with an earlier one on fresh grounds if the reasons for the earlier decision are no longer valid.[32]

While the foregoing rules as to reasoning apply, broadly speaking, to all types of Community measures, certain categories of acts are governed by more specific and in some respects different requirements. Subject to the common rules, it is correct to say that the extent of the duty to state reasons depends on the nature of the act in question and on the context in which it is adopted. Generally, stricter requirements apply to individual decisions affecting the legal position of private persons, especially where such decisions are taken without a previous administrative enquiry which would enable those concerned to be fully informed of the circumstances in which, and the reasons for which, the measure is taken, than to acts concerning solely the Member States or the other Community institutions (e.g. Commission). The latter, being closely involved in the Community decision-making process and therefore aware of the circumstances surrounding the adoption of the measure, already enjoy all the legal safeguards which the giving of reasons is designed to afford.[33]

Also, legislative acts of a general application (e.g. E.E.C./Euratom regulations) are subject to less strict criteria than decisions addressed to individuals. The reasoning of the former may be confined to showing the overall situation that has led to its adoption and the general objectives that it is designed to achieve. It need not list all the facts, often very numerous and complex, which have prompted its introduction, still less need it supply an evaluation of those facts whether in detail or in outline.[34] Where such a general measure forms an integral part of a complex system of similar measures, its reasoning must be considered and assessed in the context of the system as a whole. Even though it may not in itself be exhaustive, it may still satisfy the requirements if it is capable of being clarified in the light of the other (earlier) measures of which those pursuing their activities in the particular area cannot be unaware.[35]

The requirement of reasoning is likewise relaxed in respect of the price-fixing decisions of the Commission taken under agricultural regulations. These need not be reasoned individually; a reference to a previous decision containing a statement of reasons will be sufficient. Since reasoning should be proportional to the practical realities and the time and technical facilities available for the making of the decision, the Commission is entitled to confine itself to setting out in a general form the essential points which it has taken into consideration and the procedure which it has adopted. The concrete facts themselves upon which the Commission is relying in making the price-fixing decision do not have to be revealed.[36]

By contrast, decisions of the Commission which impose pecuniary obligations enforceable within the Member States[37] must be supported by precise and detailed reasoning. In particular, under the E.C.S.C. Treaty the statement of reasons must contain an accurate and detailed breakdown of the heads of the debt to which the decision is giving executory force. The same applies to decisions imposing pecuniary sanctions, e.g. a surcharge for delay in payment due from the applicant, whose amount must, too, be determined and explained by a detailed statement of account. Only such a statement will enable the Court to check the legality and accuracy of the imposition and calculation of the principal amount demanded and the rate of interest actually applied. Reference to previous decisions will not, in such circumstances, be sufficient.[38] In every other respect, decisions imposing fines under the E.C.S.C. or E.E.C. competition rules are subject to the general requirements of reasoning. They must state clearly and logically all the elements of fact on which the legal justification of the fine is based and the considerations leading to its imposition. The Commission is however not required to discuss and to refute all the arguments and objections which the parties may have raised in the course of the administrative proceedings.[39]

Finally, special considerations apply to measures taken by the institutions in the exercise of a discretionary power, such as, for example, the decisions of the Commission taken in implementation of Community competition law (e.g. decisions granting or refusing to grant an authorisation under Article 65(2) E.C.S.C. or an exemption under Article 85(3) E.E.C.). Such decisions by their nature involve an assessment of economic factors and circumstances and thus fall, to some extent, outside the usual limits of judicial review.[40] Their reasoning is, therefore, the main means through which the Court can control their legality. It follows that in the case of such measures the requirement to give reasons varies according to the degree of the discretionary nature of the power exercised. Generally, the wider the discretion, the greater the chance for its arbitrary use (i.e. misuse) and consequently the stricter the requirement for reasoning. Precisely because the Court possesses only a limited power of supervision over the merits of the decision, the statement of reasons must always be such as to enable it to ascertain at least if the institution has acted within the limits of its discretionary powers (which the Court must observe) and in accordance with the provisions of the Treaties. Even stricter requirements apply where the exercise of a discretionary power is dependent upon the pre-existence of certain conditions specified by the Treaties, as is the position, for example, in the case of authorisations and exemptions in competition matters. In such cases extensive reasoning is indispensable and it must always clearly show that those conditions have been fully satisfied. The reasoning must enable the parties and the Court to determine the facts and circumstances on the basis of which the institution has arrived at the conclusion that the necessary conditions have been met so that the Court can review whether that conclusion is well-founded in fact and in law.[41]

It is easy to see that for the above-mentioned reasons and particularly in the case of discretionary measures, the question of adequacy of reasoning is always partly linked to the substance of the case, i.e. to the legality of the measure. Since the reasoning is sufficient only insofar as it legally justifies the act, it may assume, especially in such cases, a significance that goes beyond a mere procedural requirement and bears upon the question of legality. However difficult in given cases separation of these two aspects may be, the practice of the European Court is to examine separately, wherever possible, the question of the formal sufficiency of reasons from that of their substantive correctness. Under the heading of 'infringement of an essential procedural requirement' the Court usually only deals with the former, since here the Court is only concerned with the question whether the statement of reasons is such as to enable it to exercise its judicial function properly. Whether the reasons are correct in substance and justify the measure in law is normally examined in connection with the question of legality, i.e. under the heading of 'infringement of the Treaty or of any rule of law relating to its application'. Accordingly, submissions challenging the material accuracy of reasons, their sufficiency or consistency in relation to the conclusions drawn from them, or the facts alleged by the institution and their legal evaluation, belong to the substance of the case, that is, to the sphere of review of the legality of the reasons and not to that of a mere procedural defect.[42] Finally, it may be noted that on account of the strict requirements set by the European Court in respect of the obligation to give reasons, inadequate reasoning has so far been the most successful single ground of action under both the E.C.S.C. and E.E.C. Treaties.

Thirdly, as regards the communication of the measure, whilst publication of general law-making measures is an essential condition for their formal validity,[43] irregularities in the procedure of notification of individual decisions are regarded as external to the acts themselves and thus cannot vitiate them. They do not therefore constitute infringement of essential procedural requirements but in certain circumstances may prevent the time for bringing an action for annulment from starting to run.[44] On the other hand, a failure to communicate a measure in the proper language as required by Community law[45] constitutes a legal defect which could, under given circumstances, affect the validity of the measure.[46]

517. (3) Infringement of the Treaties or of any rule of law relating to their application

Undoubtedly, infringement of the Treaties or of any rule of law relating to their application is the most general and the most important of the four grounds of action. Due perhaps to a somewhat imprecise use of language, this ground may at first sight appear to be so broad as virtually to subsume all the others as infringement of the rules relating to competence, procedure and proper use of powers, which rules are laid down in the Treaties, always constitutes at the same time infringement of the Treaties as well. In practice, however, there are important differences between this and the three other grounds although, as seen above,[1] it is not always easy or practicable to make a clear distinction between them. The main difference is that while the first, second and fourth grounds enable the Court to control the formal validity of Community measures and the subjective intentions of the institutions in taking them, the third ground provides the only legal basis for reviewing, most importantly of all, the objective and substantive legality of those measures, i.e. their material conformity with the rules and principles of Community law.

The relationship between the three other grounds and this one in reality corresponds to that between a *lex specialis* and a *lex generalis*. Accordingly, any infringement of Community law is usually brought before the Court on the third ground unless it can be shown to constitute one of the other three, more special, grounds. Thus in addition to alleged infringements of substantive Treaty provisions, which always fall under the third heading,[2] the European Court will examine under the same heading, for example, the following complaints: excessive exercise of an otherwise existing competence (as opposed to a total lack of competence);[3] material inaccuracy (as opposed to formal inadequacy)[4] of reasons;[5] erroneous findings of fact; misinterpretation and misapplication of the Treaty,[6] etc. By contrast, an injury unavoidably caused to private interests in the course of the regulation of economic activities in the public interest will not constitute an infringement of the Treaty, provided the institutions have acted with due care and have observed the principle of proportionality.[7]

The broad reference to the Treaties and to any rule of law relating to their application virtually encompasses the whole body of written and unwritten Community law. In order to ascertain what are the rules whose infringement constitutes a ground for annulment, one must therefore look into the primary, secondary and tertiary sources of Community law.[8] While there is no problem in identifying the basic Community Treaties, certain difficulties might arise in defining the concept of 'rules of law relating to their application'. Broadly speaking, this concept refers to general and abstract rules[9] which are binding upon the institutions.[10] These rules arise, in the first place, from the so-called secondary legislation.[11] This means that until and unless acts of the institutions are formally repealed or amended, they are binding upon the institutions themselves no less than they are binding upon any other subject of Community law and that the institutions must observe their provisions just as they must observe the provisions of the Treaties. Conflicts between Community measures must be resolved, according to the principle of the hierarchy of secondary sources, by giving priority to the Council's acts over those of the Commission, to 'basic' acts over 'implementing' measures and to earlier acts over later ones, unless the latter are clearly intended to repeal or amend the former.[12] Thus the validity of a measure standing lower in the hierarchy of norms is impaired by its incompatibility with one standing higher, while in the case of two measures of equal rank (e.g. two Council regulations) the validity of the one later in time may, contrary to the *lex posterior* and *lex specialis* principles, be impaired by its incompatibility with the earlier one, even though the former is not based legally on the latter and constitutes a *lex specialis* in relation to it.[13]

Rules of law relating to the application of the Treaties include, moreover, unwritten law, i.e. those general principles of law which have been recognised by the European Court of Justice as forming part of Community law.[14] Acts of institutions which are incompatible with such general principles are liable to annulment.[15] It is submitted that these rules include furthermore such provisions of general (customary) international law and such obligations arising from treaties as are binding upon the Communities.[16] It is thought that the validity of acts of the institutions taken in infringement of such provisions and obligations may be challenged not only in reference proceedings for preliminary rulings but also in direct actions for annulment, under certain circumstances.[17] By contrast, national laws of the Member States do not, as a rule, form part of the body of rules whose infringement may lead to annulment. Actions based on alleged violations of national laws are inadmissible.[18]

The fact that the third ground of action enables the European Court to exercise wide powers in reviewing the legality of the institutions' conduct raises the difficult question of how far those powers should extend. The problem is whether there should be any limits to the judicial review of executive action in the European context and, if so, where such limits should be drawn. The European Treaties deal, for the most part, with matters of economic policy and give, particularly the E.E.C. Treaty, wide discretionary powers to the institutions for the purpose of implementing those policies. The latter must therefore very often take decisions involving evaluation of economic facts, circumstances and tendencies, market conditions, etc. Such decisions do not easily admit of judicial control for at least three reasons. First, the rapid changes of economic life necessitate quick adjustments in economic policies whose flexibility cannot be hampered by subjecting them to necessarily rigid legal regulation. Secondly, the question whether an economic measure is necessary or suitable cannot usually be judged in the context of the normal judicial process by applying abstract legal rules and standards and by drawing logical conclusions. Such measures can be appraised only in the light of the realities of economic life itself, and must be subject to political, rather than legal, control. Thirdly, it would be contrary to the fundamental principle of institutional balance within the Communities to make the European Court the supreme decision-making body by enabling it to substitute, under the disguise of judicial review, its own views of economic policies to be pursued by the Communities, for those of the Council and Commission.[19]

For the above-mentioned reasons Article 33 of the E.C.S.C. Treaty places an express limitation upon the Court's powers by providing that in reviewing the legality of the Commission's conduct, the Court may not examine the evaluation of the situation, resulting from economic facts or circumstances, in the light of which the Commission took its decisions or made its recommendations, save where the Commission is alleged to have misused its powers or to have manifestly failed to observe the provisions of the Treaty or any rule of law relating to its application. In practice, this provision requires a distinction to be made between ascertainment of facts and economic circumstances upon which a measure is based and the consequences which the Commission draws from them. While findings of fact can be challenged before the Court, their evaluation lies outside its control, unless the Commission is accused of misuse of powers or of a manifest failure to observe the Treaty.[20]

In contrast with misuse of powers, which as a separate ground for annulment can be invoked on its own in all appropriate cases,[21] manifest failure to observe the Treaty does not constitute an independent ground of illegality but is a special case of the ground of infringement of the Treaty. The difference between them is that a manifest failure to observe the Treaty implies a higher degree of infringement, a serious misconstruction and misapplication of the provisions of the Treaty resulting from an obvious error in the evaluation of the economic situation in the light of which the challenged measure was taken. It can be put forward only to enable the Court to examine the evaluation of that situation. For that purpose, a prior complete proof of a manifest failure is not required (for this would straightaway lead to the annulment of the measure on the ground of infringement of the Treaty), but nor is a mere assertion of it sufficient (for this would lead to a mere formality). What is required is that the allegation should be supported by a *prima facie* evidence, i.e. the applicant must show that in the given economic situation there was *prima facie* no need for the measure taken in order to achieve a basic Treaty objective. The task of the Court then is precisely to ascertain whether the measure challenged was necessary.[22]

In the absence of an obvious error or misuse of powers, examination by the Court cannot extend to an appreciation of the necessity or desirability of the measure because such examination would exceed the limits of that control of legality which the Court may exercise under the Treaty. It would involve assessment of the complex market situation, the structural and economic factors, in view of which the measure was taken.[23] The Court must, accordingly, limit itself to considering the strict legality of the measure.[24] Since authorisation by the Commission of certain agreements under Article 65(2) E.C.S.C. usually involves an assessment of complex economic factors, it falls to some extent outside the Court's jurisdiction.[25]

The E.E.C. Treaty contains no express provision corresponding to that of the E.C.S.C. Treaty discussed above. It is nevertheless clear that similar principles must apply to the economic processes within the Economic Community also. Thus whenever the Treaty has conferred upon the Council or the Commission discretionary powers for the purpose of formulating economic policies or carrying into effect those laid down by the Treaty, for the purpose of granting exemptions, authorisations or permitting derogations from the Treaty, or whenever the Council has delegated similar powers to the Commission, the jurisdiction exercisable by the European Court over measures taken under such powers is strictly limited to the extent necessary to ensure the greatest possible freedom of action to the institutions. In particular, the Court has no power to enter the sphere of suitability or expediency, i.e. to examine whether the measure is good, appropriate or adequate, since this would mean the replacement of the legislative discretion by that of the Court. Nor can the Court substitute its own evaluation of the economic situation for that of the institutions.

It is at the same time clear that even the exercise of discretionary powers cannot be unlimited and that it cannot escape judicial review altogether. Improper exercise of discretionary powers may in principle lead to the annulment of the resulting act on the ground of infringement of the Treaty or of any rule of law relating to its application. Thus the Court will examine under this heading whether the institution has not, in exercise of its discretionary powers, violated the Treaty, secondary Community law or general principles of law;[26] whether it has not exceeded the limits of its discretion;[27] whether it has not based its evaluation of the situation on materially inexact facts;[29] and whether that evaluation, although based on materially exact facts, is still not manifestly wrong as containing a patent error or constituting a misuse of powers.[30] Where, moreover, the Treaty or the enabling act of the Council lays down certain criteria, principles or conditions for the use of the discretionary power, the institution must exercise that power within the framework of such criteria, principles and conditions. Disregard for or misinterpretation of these criteria, use of the power in the absence of the preconditions, may amount to an infringement of the Treaty or of a rule of law relating to its application and may lead to the annulment of the measure. Only the actual area of discretion to which the balancing and evaluation of the various criteria belong is not subject to judicial review, except on the grounds of obvious error or misuse of powers,[31] although in given cases it may be difficult to determine where exactly that area begins.[32]

518. (4) Misuse of powers

It follows from both the functional nature of the Communities' legal existence and the attributed nature of the institutions' competences[1] that the powers conferred upon the latter are strictly purpose-bound, i.e. can be exercised only for the general and particular purposes for which they have been granted.[2] Misuse of powers occurs if the institutions use their powers for a purpose other than the one for which those powers have been given. Although the concept of the misuse of powers as a ground of illegality is wider in some and narrower in other Member States,[3] it would seem that the European Court of Justice has accepted the narrower definition of the concept which is based entirely on the subjective intentions (motives) of the institutions in adopting their acts. Accordingly, in order to establish misuse of powers it is necessary, first, to uncover the real intentions of the institutions, that is, the object pursued by them in taking the measure challenged and, secondly, to show that this object is different from the one which they ought to have pursued under the Treaties.[4] Or, to put it differently, one must first establish the existence of a power and then the use of that power with an aim other than that for which it has been granted.[5] It is not necessary, however, that the institutions should pursue a wrong object intentionally; misuse of powers occurs already if they do so through a serious lack of foresight and circumspection amounting to a misconstruction of, and thus a disregard for, the true purpose of the law.[6] Moreover, it is not necessary that the object pursued should be illegal, i.e. prohibited or not expressly authorised by the Treaties; misuse of powers can occur if the object, though legitimate in itself, is not the one that ought to have been pursued or primarily pursued in the exercise of the power in question.[7]

Where the Treaties set out more than one objective, which is the case, for example, in the introductory Articles to each of the three basic Treaties,[8] which cannot all be pursued simultaneously in all circumstances in their entirety, the institutions are required to ensure their permanent reconciliation and, if this is not possible, must, in exercise of their discretionary powers, give some of them such priority as appears necessary in the light of the relevant facts and economic circumstances. Giving priority to certain of these objectives while disregarding or neglecting others to an extent which is not justified by the circumstances in the light of which the measure is taken may constitute misuse of powers, although giving temporary priority and thus only partially failing to achieve the required compromise may not.[9] Thus the violation in the regulation of economic affairs of the principle of the equality of consumers[10] and, more generally, that of non-discrimination,[11] which constitute objectives governing the actions of the institutions in the use of their powers, may amount to a misuse of powers with respect to the persons deliberately discriminated against.[12] Nevertheless, misuse of powers, when alleged in relation to the fundamental provisions of the Treaties laying down the basic objectives and principles of the Communities, must be proved in exactly the same way as in the case of any other Treaty provisions, i.e. by evaluating the true purpose of the measure challenged.[13]

Where, as happens frequently, the institutions are led by more than one objective, the existence of a misuse of powers must be examined in the light of the most important one. Accordingly, the presence of an unjustified subsidiary motive together with a justified one will not result in a misuse of powers provided that it is the latter that clearly predominates and that the measure does not infringe upon the essential aim which the institution was supposed to have pursued in the use of the powers.[14] Thus, for example, a measure which is otherwise in conformity with the Treaties will not be invalidated on the ground of misuse of powers just because the additional consideration of administrative convenience, that is, the aim of avoiding administrative complications, also played a certain part in its adoption,[15] or because it was used to carry out a test case.[16] By contrast, misuse of powers will occur whenever the institutions, finding themselves faced with a situation which necessitates the application of a particular provision or procedure in the Treaties, nevertheless proceed under another provision with the sole, or at least predominant, purpose of avoiding the guarantees and safeguards of the former (correct) provision or procedure.[17]

It follows from its narrow (subjective) interpretation that misuse of powers must be distinguished strictly from the other grounds of action, especially from lack of competence and infringement of the Treaties. Such a distinction is easy to make, at least in theory, if it is borne in mind that misuse of powers can exist only if the following two conditions are cumulatively fulfilled: first, the institutions must be in the possession of the requisite power to act in the given case, and secondly, that power must be discretionary. Where the requisite power is missing, the institutions cannot 'misuse' it, that is, use it for a wrong purpose; and where it is present but can only be used in a certain way strictly specified by the Treaties, leaving the institutions no choice between alternative solutions (so-called fettered competence, *compétence liée*), it cannot be 'misused' either: it can only be used illegally or nor used at all. The former situation (where the power is missing) constitutes a case of lack of competence; the latter (where the conditions laid down by the Treaties are disregarded) one of infringement of the Treaties, while the situation where the extent of existing powers is exceeded probably both; but none will amount to misuse of powers. In other words, in establishing misuse of powers neither the existence or lack of competence nor the objective legality or illegality of the resulting measure can play any part. This is in complete accordance with the system of the Treaties which have adopted a wide concept of 'infringement of the Treaties' as the main ground of action, covering all cases of objective illegality, and a narrow concept of misuse of powers as an independent ground of action not part of the former, covering, so to speak, cases of 'subjective illegality'.

The real importance of the above distinction becomes apparent in those cases where the Treaties specify misuse of powers as the only ground of action. This occurs basically in two situations. The first is under the E.C.S.C. Treaty only, where individuals (undertakings and associations) have a right of action against general decisions and recommendations on the sole ground of misuse of powers.[18] The second arises under all three Treaties in respect of measures involving the evaluation of economic facts and circumstances and the exercise of discretionary powers[19] (including, under the E.C.S.C. Treaty, a failure to take such measures)[20] which can be challenged, apart from a patent error, on the ground of misuse of powers only. It is evident that any attempt at extending the concept of misuse of powers to include cases of lack of competence or objective Treaty violation would upset the system of legal protection as laid down by the Treaties by enlarging the right of action of private parties against general measures (under the E.C.S.C. Treaty) and the Court's jurisdiction in respect of discretionary powers in a way not contemplated by the drafters of the Treaties.[21]

It is for these reasons that, for example, exercise of regulatory powers in situations where the Treaties only grant supervisory powers (i.e. the taking of a regulatory measure, such as an E.C.S.C. decision, instead of a recommendation) does not constitute a misuse of powers but only a lack of competence as it does not show in itself that the institution has pursued objectives other than those for which the powers have been conferred.[22] By contrast, the delegation by the institutions of discretionary powers to bodies not set up by the Treaties without retaining a sufficient degree of control over their exercise, will amount to a misuse of powers and not to lack of competence.[23] Nevertheless, a certain degree of overlap between these various grounds of action, and in particular between misuse of powers and infringement of the Treaties, is inevitable. The simple reason for this lies in the imprecise concept of discretionary powers which, on the one hand, may be subject to a narrower or wider interpretation depending on the circumstances of the individual case; and, on the other, cannot escape judicial supervision altogether. Thus certain situations are conceivable where an infringement may be construed either as a misuse of powers or as an infringement of the Treaties or both, e.g. the taking of discriminatory measures.[24]

It is easy to see that because of its very nature, to prove misuse of powers may present difficult problems. On the one hand, the institutions enjoy the 'presumption of innocence', i.e. they are presumed to have pursued legitimate objectives in their actions until and unless the opposite is proved.[25] On the other hand, what needs to be proved is their subjective intents and motives which are not usually recognisable from the act itself (not even from the reasoning), nor are they easily ascertainable by any other usual means, especially by private parties who may not have access to the relevant documents. The problem is made even more difficult by the fact that the objective elements of the measure, such as its effects, lawfulness, compliance with requirements of form, procedure and competence, are, for reasons discussed above, largely irrelevant.

Because of the nature of things, the European Court sets fairly high standards of proof; it accepts only objective, relevant and consistent facts as evidence of a misuse of powers.[26] Free and unsubstantiated interpretation of the institutions' intentions, mere imputation to them of concealed purposes, vague allegations of a 'departure from the legitimate objectives of the Treaty' unsupported by any explicit argument, imprecise presentation of facts, etc. are generally not acceptable.[27] Even certain errors of fact do not *ipso facto* constitute proof of misuse of powers unless it is shown that the institution, by reason of a serious lack of foresight and circumspection amounting to a misconstruction of the legal objective, has followed aims other than those for which the powers have been granted.[28] On the other hand, the Court will admit as evidence any relevant correspondence and declarations of the institution as well as *travaux préparatoires* including deliberations of the consultative bodies.[29] Nevertheless, an omission to set out or to refute in the disputed measure dissenting opinions expressed in the consultative bodies will not be considered as proof of a misuse of powers.[30] The Court can, moreover, ascertain the objects pursued by ordering production of the minutes of the institution's relevant meetings.[31] On the whole, it has been due to the difficulties in proving the presence of misuse of powers that this ground, although invoked perhaps in the largest number of cases, has so far been the least successful.

519. Defence of illegality

The validity of an act may be called in question not only by reason of formal or material defects inherent in the act itself, but also by reason of defects in the provision in pursuance of which the act has been issued. It follows from the concept of the hierarchy of secondary Community sources[1] that an illegal general measure cannot, even if its validity has not formally been challenged, give rise to a lawful and hence enforceable individual measure taken in its implementation since the defects of the former will necessarily taint the validity of the latter. Where, therefore, a general provision is executed by means of an individual decision, those whose legal position is affected by the latter can, in support of an action for its annulment, rely not only upon the four grounds of action relating to it, but may also invoke the illegality of the general provision which has served as the legal basis for the individual act. This can be done by means of the so-called defence of illegality. Not only does this device provide an additional (fifth) ground of action, but it enables the European Court to avoid the clearly undesirable position of having to give effect to an illegal law-making measure which has not been challenged within the prescribed time-limit (either because its defects have not come to light in time or because those who have realised its defects have not had the *locus standi* or the interest to challenge it) and which can, after the expiry of the time-limit, no longer be contested.

Moreover, in the context of Community law the defence of illegality has the additional importance of extending and completing the legal protection of individuals in respect of general normative acts. While, as seen above,[2] Community law does not recognise a sufficient degree of legal interest in natural and legal persons to enable them in general to challenge, in direct actions for annulment. genuine law-making measures (under the E.E.C./Euratom Treaties), or to challenge such measures on all four grounds of action (under the E.C.S.C. Treaty), such legal interest will be generated whenever normative measures are being applied, by means of individual decisions, to individual persons, cases and situations. To deny, in such circumstances, to those affected any means of contesting the validity of the underlying law-making act would not only mean depriving them of all legal protection but would also offend the fundamental principle of legality by virtually compelling the Court to enforce an illegal measure. Thus the defence of illegality makes up, at least in part, for the limitation which the Treaties have imposed on the individuals' right of action and grants the latter an important indirect means of legal protection. In that respect it fulfils a similar function in the system of legal remedies to preliminary rulings which, although subject to somewhat different rules, give effect to the same legal principle by enabling private persons to challenge, in proceedings before national courts, the validity of Community measures where these have been implemented (i.e. applied to individual cases) by national organs.[3]

The principle of the defence of illegality is formulated differently in the different Treaties. The E.C.S.C. Treaty gives effect to it in the context of actions against pecuniary sanctions and periodic penalty payments and this might give the impression that it intends to limit its application to decisions imposing such sanctions only. It provides that in support of an action against such decisions a party may, under the same conditions as generally apply to action for annulment, contest the legality of the decision or recommendation which that party is alleged not to have observed and in respect of which the sanction has been imposed.[4] By contrast, the E.E.C./Euratom Treaties contain the more general provision that notwithstanding the expiry of the period within which a Community measure can be contested[5] any party may, in proceedings in which a regulation of the Council or the Commission is in issue, plead the four grounds of action in order to invoke before the Court of Justice the inapplicability of that regulation.[6] It has, however, been held that the concept of the plea of illegality incorporates a general legal principle which would probably apply even in the absence of any express provision in the Treaties. The narrow wording of the E.C.S.C. Treaty cannot therefore prevent that principle from being applied in a general fashion to any other case not explicitly mentioned in the Treaty in more or less the same way as it applies under the E.E.C./Euratom Treaties. Any limitation of its application to pecuniary sanctions would render the exercise of the right of action granted to undertakings difficult, if not impossible, as it would require them to seek out in every general decision, within the short period of one month, those provisions which could possibly adversely affect them at some future date.[7] Generally speaking, therefore, the circumstances in which a party can raise the plea of illegality are largely the same under all Treaties and the case-law of the European Court under the earlier E.C.S.C. Treaty may be relied upon in the context of the later E.E.C./Euratom Treaties.

The defence of illegality does not constitute a *sui generis* form of action and does not in itself enable parties to introduce separate proceedings before the European Court. It merely serves to extend the existing remedies by providing an additional ground of action in certain cases; it is a means and not an end in itself. It follows that it can be raised only in the context of proceedings brought before the Court under some other provision of the Treaties and then only incidentally and with limited effect. It cannot be used parallel to or in substitution for actions for annulment or preliminary rulings for the purpose of extending the right of action of private persons in circumstances where such right does not exist under the Treaties, or for the purpose of referring questions to the European Court independently of national courts. It can be invoked only in proceedings pending before the European Court and not in connection with proceedings pending before national courts even if the latter raise questions concerning the validity of a regulation. Such a question can be referred to the European Court in the framework of the preliminary ruling procedure and by the national court only. Any other solution would, on the one hand, eliminate the restrictions imposed by the Treaties in respect of subject-matter and time-limits on private parties' right of action for annulment, and on the other hand, fundamentally alter the relations between the national courts and the European Court in the matter of preliminary rulings.[8]

Broadly speaking, therefore, the plea of illegality is only a means for enabling a party to prove, in support of an action for the annulment of an individual decision, that the latter has no foundation in law, by relying upon the irregularity (invalidity or illegality) of a general decision/regulation upon which the individual decision has been based. Since the aim of the plea is not to bring about the annulment of the general decision/regulation but only to obtain a declaration of its inapplicability for the purpose of the annulment of the individual decision, it is not subject to the usual restrictions which apply to a direct action for annulment in respect of *locus standi* and time-limits. In particular, it may be put forward by 'any party' including Member States/institutions and private parties alike, irrespective of the fact that the former could, and the latter could not, have challenged the general decision/regulation within the one or two months' time-limit.[9] That the plea is still open to Member States/institutions after the expiry of the time-limit is explained by the fact that the defects of the general measure may not clearly emerge until it is applied to individual cases and this may not take place until after the relatively short time-limit has expired.[10] Moreover, also private parties may, in challenging the general measure, rely on all four grounds of action (but only on those) without any restrictions.[11] Although the plea may be raised in respect of the general act without any time-limit, this does not permit the time-limit to be avoided within which the action for the annulment of the individual decision must be brought.[12]

From the fact that the defence of illegality incorporates a general principle of law of universal application, two important consequences follow. The first is that where the validity of the challenged individual act depends on the legality of a general provision, the European Court will examine *ex officio* whether the latter provision is lawful, even if the plea of illegality has been put forward by the applicant neither expressly nor by implication (or only by implication) whenever this is justified by the requirement of safeguarding objective legality in general, or protecting individual rights in particular.[13] The second consequence is that the possible use of the defence of illegality is not necessarily limited to situations expressly mentioned by the Treaties. In addition to actions for annulment, which represent its main field of application, it may be invoked in actions for failure to act, particularly under the E.C.S.C. Treaty where the failure of the Commission to issue the requested measure within the prescribed period is to be taken as an implied decision of refusal against which, insofar as it is an individual decision, the defence of illegality is available in the same way as against an express individual decision.[14] It may, moreover, be invoked in disputes between the Communities and their officials to challenge illegal provisions of the Staff Regulations or other general measures on the basis of which individual decisions have been issued, even though the former do not expressly confer the right to enter the plea of illegality.[15] It is submitted that the plea might also be raised in actions for damages, not, of course, to obtain annulment of an individual decision but to show that such a decision (which is the alleged cause of the damage in question) is illegal as issued under an illegal general measure.

The position is more problematic in preliminary rulings and actions against Member States. Owing to the peculiar, non-contentious nature of the preliminary ruling procedure, the defence of illegality cannot be raised by a party to the national proceedings before the European Court as this would inevitably alter the scope of the questions referred whose determination is within the exclusive competence of the national court making the reference.[16] As regards actions against Member States under Article 169 E.E.C./Article 141 Euratom (and analogous actions by Member States against the Commission under Article 88 E.C.S.C.), two different situations must be distinguished. The first arises where the Member State concerned is accused of having violated an individual decision which it has failed to challenge within the proper time-limit. In such a case the fundamental principle of legal certainty, which prevents the validity of an act being questioned indefinitely, does not allow the plea of illegality to be raised in order to re-open, out of time, discussions concerning the legality of the individual decision.[17] In the second situation it is a regulation with the non-observance of which the Member State is charged. Whether in such a case it can obtain acquittal from the charge by raising, out of time, the plea of illegality in respect of the regulation, is, in the absence of decided cases, not clear. While the wide wording of Article 184 E.E.C./Article 156 Euratom would seem to support an affirmative answer, the nature of the proceedings under Article 169 E.E.C./Article 141 Euratom would appear to require a negative solution.[18]

It follows from the preceding considerations that, generally, the defence of illegality can be raised against general decisions/regulations only. It would basically contradict the principle of legal certainty if the validity of individual decisions could be called in question, by means of the plea of illegality, long after the time-limit for their annulment has expired. Where therefore an individual decision is based on a decision which is also individual, the defence of illegality is not available.[19] It is, moreover, necessary that there should be a direct and actual juridical link between the challenged individual decision and the general decision/regulation whose illegality is pleaded. In other words, the individual decision must constitute a direct and immediate application (implementation) of the general measure; it must legally be based upon it. Where this is not entirely the case, the plea of illegality is only admissible to the extent to which it refers to those provisions of the general measure which form the legal basis of the individual act or constitute a determining factor in relation to it. In the absence of such a close relationship, a possible declaration of inapplicability of the general measure could have no repercussions on the validity of the individual act, nor would the annulment of the latter necessarily involve the inapplicability of the former. Thus the plea of illegality, whose primary aim is to challenge the very legal foundations of the contested act, would be meaningless. It cannot therefore be invoked where either there is an intermediate measure between the individual and general act or these constitute parallel measures both based on the same legal concept.[20] Where, however, two individual decisions are contested at the same time which are so closely related to one another as virtually to constitute a single whole, the plea of illegality already raised in respect of the one can be used in relation to the other as well, since both must necessarily derive their validity from the same general measure.[21] It goes without saying that the individual decision must be a genuine decision which is by its nature subject to challenge; where it is not (e.g. a letter merely refusing to declare a regulation inapplicable to the applicant), it cannot be used to challenge the legality of the underlying general measure.[22] Finally, it may be noted that, unlike private parties, Member States / institutions may invoke the defence of illegality not only in support of an action for the annulment of an individual decision, but also to support the annulment of a regulation which directly implements another ('basic') regulation since their right of action is not limited to individual acts.[23]

The effects of a successful defence of illegality are twofold. First, the general decision / regulation will be declared inapplicable and secondly, the contested individual decision, which is the subject-matter of the action, will be annulled for lack of a valid legal basis. The declaration of inapplicability of the general measure is made by way of an incidental finding in the grounds of the judgment and has a strictly limited (relative) effect. It applies exclusively in the context of the case in which it is made, with respect to the parties involved (*inter partes*) and for the future only (*ex nunc*). Moreover, it can in no way alter the legal effects of the general measure, which is no longer subject to annulment because of expiry of time-limit, except to the extent to which it has been made more specific by the individual act.[24] It follows that a judgment containing a declaration of inapplicability does not (at least as regards the past) have an effect equivalent to the objective annulment of the general measure[25] and hence it is subject to the ordinary rules of *res judicata*.[26] It cannot consequently be relied upon by third parties for the purpose of challenging, out of time, individual decisions which also had their legal basis in the same general provision which has now been declared illegal. Such a possibility would lead, in effect, to a retrospective re-opening of a situation, created by the individual decisions, which upon the expiry of the time-limits for their annulment had become final. This would unduly enlarge the scope of the plea of illegality and would be basically incompatible with the principle of legal certainty.[27] As regards the future, however, the provision declared illegal, although formally remaining in force until repealed or amended by the institution which issued it, may be regarded as virtually 'dead'. This is because either the institutions will refrain from applying and enforcing it,[28] or, if not, the Court will find it repeatedly inapplicable in subsequent actions brought within the proper time-limits. This explains why a declaration of illegality is sometimes regarded as having *erga omnes* effect.[29]

520. Time-limits for action

Action for annulment must be instituted within strict time-limits which are one month under the E.C.S.C. Treaty[1] and two months under the E.E.C./Euratom Treaties.[2] These time-limits apply to both Member States/institutions and private parties as applicants but are extended by various degrees on account of their distance from the seat of the Court of Justice.[3] They give effect to the fundamental principle of legal certainty[4] which prevents the validity of binding Community measures being brought into question indefinitely. Apart from situations falling within the scope of the defence of illegality[5] and certain exceptions expressly provided for by the Treaties, which are discussed elsewhere,[6] expiry of these time-limits in principle places an absolute prohibition upon the re-opening of the question of validity of Community acts unless there is a new factor present of a nature to change the essential legal or factual conditions and circumstances that may give rise to annulment. An application submitted outside the time-limits is, therefore, inadmissible.[7]

The periods for bringing action, once expired, cannot be revived by means of various procedural devices. Thus, for example, a judgment of the European Court anulling a measure cannot be relied on by persons other than the actual parties to the case and those directly affected by the annulled measure, as constituting in a subsequent case a new factor of the kind mentioned above, capable of causing time to start to run anew after it has expired.[8] This is so even though the annulment is based on a declaration of illegality of a common underlying general measure.[9] Moreover, purely confirmatory decisions, i.e. decisions merely confirming or refusing to repeal or amend previous acts which have become definitive by reason of their not having been contested within the proper time-limits, cannot have the effect of setting a fresh time-limit in favour of the applicant.[10] This means, in practice, that an applicant who fails to bring an action within the period of one or two months against an act constituting a formal, legally binding measure, cannot remedy his own omission by appealing to the institution concerned for a repeal or amendment of the act in question and then by instituting proceedings either for the annulment of the decision whereby his request is refused[11] or for failure to act if the institution fails to respond,[12] as the case may be. In contrast to confirmatory decisions, an act which deals with the same subject-matter as an earlier one and has the same effects, is once again subject to the period for annulment notwithstanding the existence of the earlier act.[13]

Since the periods prescribed by the Treaties for instituting proceedings are mandatory in nature, they are not subject to the discretion of the parties or of the Court. In other words, even an express or implied consent of the defendant institution to dispense with their strict observance in a given case cannot be taken into account.[14] On the contrary, since the periods are a matter of public interest, their expiry may be pleaded at any time in the proceedings even as late as the oral stage, and the Court must examine, acting, if necessary, of its own motion, whether they have been observed.[15]

The day from which the time-limits start to run (*dies a quo*) is determined by the nature of the contested measure. Broadly speaking, the act which sets time running in any given case is the final definitive measure of the institution which has binding force. Unlike the case of Community officials, whose right of action is governed by the special rules of the Staff Regulations, under the general system of the Treaties there is no means for lodging a purely administrative complaint with the institutions with the effect of suspending the operation of the time-limits for action; only a direct application to the Court is possible within those time-limits.[16] Where a series of acts are very closely (inseparably) connected with one another, a party may in the framework of an action brought within time against the last link of the chain also contest the legality of earlier steps even though an action against these would be out of time.[17]

Where the Treaties provide for the publication of the measure (i.e. E.C.S.C. general decisions/recommendations, E.E.C./Euratom regulations),[18] the time-limit runs from the fifteenth day after publication thereof in the Official Journal of the European Communities.[19] The date on which the measure is adopted or on which it is to enter into force or become operative is irrelevant. Where the Treaties provide for the notification of the measure (i.e. E.C.S.C. individual decisions/recommendations; E.E.C./Euratom directives and decisions), the time-limit runs from the day following the receipt by the applicant of the notification thereof.[20] The E.E.C./Euratom Treaties additionally provide that in the absence of notification to the applicant, the time-limit runs from the day on which the measure came to the knowledge of the latter.[21] This provision has obviously been intended for situations where a measure which is not subject to publication is challenged by a party other than the addressee, which can be both a Member State/institution and a natural or legal person provided that in the latter case the measure is of direct and individual concern to the applicant.[22]

The interpretation and application of this provision may give rise to certain difficulties in practice. First, it is not quite clear what the starting date (*dies a quo*) is where a measure which need not be, but has actually been, published in the Official Journal (e.g. a decision addressed to a Member State) is attacked by a party other than the addressee (e.g. by a natural or legal person). In one such case[23] the Advocate-General expressed the opinion that since the relevant Treaty provisions had been so drafted, in the interests of legal certainty, as not to cause any difficulty in ascertaining the commencement of the time-limits, if a measure was actually published, whether or not it had to be, the period was to run from its publication. This view seems to be supported also by the wording of the Court's own Rules of Procedure[24] which contain the phrase: 'Where the measure is published', instead of 'Where the measure is required to be published'. Nevertheless, the Court decided in the same case that the time-limit commenced 'at the latest', not with the publication of the measure in the Official Journal of the Communities, but with the publication of the national implementing provision in the Member State's own domestic Official Journal, because it was then at the very latest that the contested measure 'must have come to the knowledge of the applicants'. In other words, here the concept of taking knowledge prevailed over that of publication.

A second ambiguous situation arises where a measure which is not subject to publication (e.g. a decision) is published in the Official Journal but only summarily, in the form of a brief notice, and not in its entirety. The question then, again, is whether for interested third parties to whom the full text of the measure has not been notified, the period of limitation starts to run from the date of this partial publication or from the (later) date of their acquiring knowledge of the full measure. According to one view, the notice in the Official Journal must be taken to constitute 'publication' within the meaning of the Treaties which sets time running because it can in itself form the basis for an action for annulment.[25] According to another view, in order for a party to decide whether or not to challenge a measure before the Court, it must know the entire content of the measure. Consequently, the date of taking knowledge, and not that of publication, must be regarded as decisive, although legal certainty and the interests of the recipient of the measure require that such third parties should, if they wish to protect their rights, take the necessary steps within a reasonable period of time after publication to obtain the full text of the measure either from the institution itself or from any relevant national body. Only such action as is brought after unreasonably long and unexcused delay should be rejected as inadmissible.[26] While this second view is undoubtedly more correct as taking more account of the interests of all those involved, in the absence of a decision by the European Court on the point it is impossible to determine precisely how long that 'reasonable period' should be at the end of which interested third parties must be presumed to have acquired sufficient knowledge of the full decision. Where, however, not even a summary of the measure is published in the Official Journal, third parties cannot normally be blamed for not displaying diligence in obtaining its full text, should they acquire knowledge of its existence from any other source, e.g. through their trade associations or national authorities.[27]

Finally, certain irregularities in the procedure of notification, e.g. notification of a measure addressed to a non-Community undertaking to its intra-Community subsidiary, may have the effect of preventing the time for bringing an action from starting to run although not beyond the date when the addressee actually does acquire knowledge of it.[28]

521. Consequences of successful action

Continuity of legislative and administrative action requires that acts of the institutions which are formally in force should in principle be carried out so long as a judgment of the European Court of Justice has not held them illegal. Apart, therefore, from the very exceptional case of absolute nullity[1] and unless the Court has itself ordered suspension of the application of the contested measure, a device used by the European Court very sparingly,[2] an act challenged by an action for annulment remains fully operative until the Court has delivered its judgment. If the action is well founded, the Court of Justice shall declare the act concerned to be void[3] within the scope of the action, in accordance with the *ne ultra petita* principle.[4] Such a judgment will have the effect of completely reversing the legal position prevailing until that moment, with *erga omnes* and *ex tunc* (retroactive) effect. The annulled act must, accordingly, be regarded as if it had never existed in law and the parties to the dispute must be restored to their original legal position (*restitutio in integrum*).[5] In having effects going beyond the parties to the case, such a judgment is the only exception to the strict rule of *res judicata*.[6] It follows from the *erga omnes* effect of annulment that an act already annulled in a different case prior to the Court's giving judgment, cannot adversely affect the applicant's rights or interests. In such a situation the Court will declare that there is no occasion for it to render a further ruling.[7]

Where a particular provision is severable from the rest of the measure, partial annulment is possible even to the extent of deleting only certain words from the challenged act.[8] Partial annulment, if requested, is particularly justified where a measure, taken as a whole, is favourable to the interests of the applicant (e.g. a Commission decision granting an exemption under Article 85(3) E.E.C. subject to certain conditions) and its annulment *in toto* would mean going *ultra petita*. Total annulment in such circumstances might involve adverse consequences for the applicant as a result of his successful action.[9] Where, however, the contested provision is so intimately linked with the rest of the measure that its separate annulment would render the latter legally meaningless or ineffective, the same principle of *ne ultra petita* may compel the Court to declare the application inadmissible rather than to annul the entire measure.[10]

Although in principle annulment has retroactive effect, such an effect cannot always be achieved in practice. Where an act has been in force for some time before its annulment, it may have produced results and situations which for legal or practical reasons can no longer be undone. Moreover, if the act is of the law-making type, it may have given rise to a number of further acts implementing it generally or in individual cases which, too, would have to be regarded as non-existent as being rendered without legal foundation. This might create unpredictable results and might jeopardise legal certainty as well as contradict the principles of good faith and protection of confidence.[11] To avoid such clearly undesirable consequences, the E.E.C./Euratom Treaties authorise the Court of Justice to state, in the case of a regulation and if it considers this necessary, which of the effects of the regulation which it has declared void shall be considered as definitive.[12] This provision enables the Court not only to restrict the retroactive effect of a judgment annulling a regulation so as to protect acquired rights,[13] but also to extend the effects of the annulled regulation into the future until such time as the relevant institution has replaced it by a new one so as to avoid discontinuity of its operation during the interim period.[14] Although the Treaties grant this power to the Court in the case of regulations only, it is submitted that since it is the nature and the content not the designation and form of a measure that is decisive, the Court may exercise that power also in the case of other law-making measures irrespective of their titles, e.g. decisions having normative effect and perhaps also in the case of directives which have similar indirect effects within the Member States.

It follows from the fundamental principle of the separation of legislative and judicial powers within the European Communities and the consequent limited nature of the Court's jurisdiction in annulment proceedings[15] that the judgment of the Court in such proceedings can have only one, purely negative effect, that of annulling (declaring void) the contested measure. It can neither replace nor amend (vary) the measure (although in practice a partial annulment consisting of deleting certain words only may come very near to the concept of amendment),[16] nor can the Court award damages or deliver a mere declaratory judgment. It must refer the matter back to the institution whose act has been declared void and it is then for that institution to take the necessary measures to comply with the judgment of the Court.[17] The Court cannot in principle substitute itself for the Council and Commission and cannot therefore prescribe, not even indicate, to the latter what particular measures to take. It follows that any submission in the application requesting the Court to instruct the institutions to take specified measures is inadmissible.[18]

The institutions thus retain a certain margin of discretion, within the bounds of the judgment, in selecting the appropriate measure.[19] In so doing they must re-assess the situation in the light of the judgment, taking into account not only the operative part thereof but also the decisive grounds and any relevant observations made by the Court. The particular measure which they have to take in any given case will depend on the nature and subject-matter of the annulled act as well as on the grounds on which annulment is based. Generally speaking, the institution must re-consider the disputed question and resolve it in accordance with Community law as stated by the Court's judgment.[20] The measure taken must in principle amount to a full restitution of the original legal position (*restitutio in integrum*).[21] Thus where the act annulled is one of general application, the institutions are under an obligation to do everything in their power to eliminate all the consequences which derived from it *ab initio*[22] (unless the Court has restricted the retroactive effect of annulment), i.e. repeal or amend any general or individual measures that may have been issued under it, insofar as this is still possible with due respect being paid to the principles of legal certainty, good faith and protection of confidence. Where the act annulled is a 'negative decision', i.e. one refusing to grant an authorisation, exemption or any other request, the grant of that request may become a legal obligation on the institution, depending upon the reasons for the Court's judgment.[23] Thus where the ground for annulment is a material infringement of Community law, the institution will have to take the measure which it previously refused by the contested decision. Annulment of a 'positive decision' on the ground of material breach of Community law necessitates the adoption of a new measure. By contrast, where the ground for annulment is a mere formal or procedural defect (e.g. lack of competence or reasoning, failure to consult the consultative bodies or to hear interested parties, etc.) the institution may re-issue the same measure (in an amended form where necessary) after having rectified the defect. In re-issuing a measure which has already been the subject of a judgment of annulment, the institutions are, however, not entitled to include parts which were criticised by the operative part or the decisive grounds of the Court's judgment.

In the case of a partial annulment, the unannulled parts of the act must be regarded as confirmed by the European Court. They may therefore be reproduced unaltered in the new measure and where they grant a right or authorisation to the applicant they cannot be revoked or amended by the institution in the course of the working out of its new measure. Such parts have in fact the benefit of *res judicata* and, if reproduced, cannot be contested by a further action for annulment.[24] Annulment on whatever ground moreover implies for the author of the measure the obligation to revoke or at least not to apply a subsequent measure which simply confirms the one annulled.[25]

It goes without saying that the measures taken by the institutions are subject to renewed judicial control in the framework of a possible further action for annulment. Such an action may be brought by all those to whom the judgment of the Court annulling an act of an institution is addressed, since they are all directly concerned with the way in which the institution executes that judgment. In such an action the Court will examine whether the measures give effect to the Court's judgment of annulment and whether they correctly apply the rules of Community law as indicated therein.[26] If the institution fails to take within a reasonable time the necessary steps to comply with the judgment, the E.C.S.C. Treaty expressly provides that proceedings for damages may be instituted before the Court.[27] It is submitted that action for failure to act is also available in such a situation under all three Treaties and according to the ordinary rules relating to such action.[28]

Under the E.E.C./Euratom Treaties the obligation of the institutions to comply with the Court's judgment does not include an obligation on the part of the Communities to make good any damage that may have been caused by the annulled act. Such damage may be recovered by means of separate action under Articles 178, 215(2) E.E.C./Articles 151, 188(2) Euratom which is governed entirely by its own different rules. Although illegality of a Community act as established by a judgment of annulment may be an important factor in establishing the Communities' non-contractual liability, it ensures in itself neither the admissibility nor the success of such an action for damages.[29] By contrast, under the E.C.S.C. Treaty the Commission must, in exercise of the powers conferred upon it, take steps to ensure equitable redress including, where necessary, the payment of appropriate damages, for any harm resulting directly and specially from the measure declared void where the Court holds that measure to involve a fault of such a nature as to render the Community liable.[30] This provision can however be applied only where the principal action for annulment is successful. In itself it can serve as an independent legal basis neither for a claim for damages[31] nor for a request for the annulment of a measure taken in execution of a judgment of annulment.[32]

It may be noted that although the obligation to give effect to the Court's judgment of annulment is imposed by the Treaties only on the institution whose act has been declared void, the *erga omnes* effect of such a judgment may require also third parties to take appropriate actions. Thus the annulment of a Council regulation may entail for the Commission and/or the Member States the obligation no longer to apply the measures adopted by them in the implementation thereof and even to repeal such measures formally in the interests of legal certainty. The same obligation may arise for Member States in respect of a Community directive/decision annulled by the European Court which has been implemented by national measures. These implementing measures, having lost their legal foundations, must be regarded as illegal.

CHAPTER 6

Action for Failure to Act

601. Nature and scope of action

The system of remedies instituted by the Treaties would be incomplete if Community institutions were subject to judicial control only in respect of their positive actions while they could evade the obligations imposed upon them by simply failing to act. The Treaties are based on the principle that legal protection should be available against any illegal conduct of the institutions, whether it manifests itself in a positive or in a negative (passive) attitude. An action for annulment[1] provides adequate remedy only against the former but is not suitable to compel an institution to act. For this purpose the action for failure to act is available. These two forms of action may, in fact, be envisaged as the two sides of the same coin: they constitute, in a broader sense, the two aspects of the same general remedy, i.e. review by the European Court of the legality of the institutions' conduct.[2] In order to afford effective protection they should, in principle, form a 'watertight' system in the sense that any illegal behaviour of the institutions should be assailable by the one or by the other. Thus, an action for failure to act should in theory be always available where an action for annulment is not, i.e. in situations where an institution duly called upon to take action in fulfilment of an obligation, fails to adopt, within a prescribed period of time, a formal even if adverse or unsatisfactory act which itself is in turn subject to an action for annulment. The institution's complete silence or response by an informal act, not subject to annulment, should open the way for an action for failure to act. In practice, however, such a 'watertight' system exists only under the E.C.S.C. Treaty,[3] while under the different provisions of the E.E.C./Euratom Treaties the two remedies do not interlock without gap. This is due to the fact that here an institution may prevent an action for failure to act by adopting an informal act which is not, at the same time, subject to annulment.[4] This arrangement considerably weakens the legal protection which the action for failure to act ought, by its nature, to afford.

On the other hand, the two procedures are mutually exclusive of each other; the range of application of the one ends where that of the other begins.[5]

Thus an action for failure to act cannot be used parallel to, or in substitution for, an action for annulment for a purpose for which the latter is the proper remedy, e.g. to bring about annulment of an act which can no longer be challenged in annulment proceedings because the time-limit for the latter has expired.[6] Similarly, an action for failure to act is no longer available where the institution requested to act responds within the proper time-limit by a formal, even though adverse or unsatisfactory, measure. Against this an action for annulment is the only remedy.[7] In this sense the action for failure to act is subsidiary to the action for annulment; and under the E.C.S.C. Treaty it is, in fact, regarded as a 'variation' or 'special case' of the latter.[8]

In practice, action for failure to act has been resorted to on much fewer occasions and with much less success than action for annulment. Under the E.C.S.C. Treaty, of the sixteen decided cases[9] (of which fifteen were brought by private parties and one by a Member State) only two have been successful,[10] most of the rest being dismissed as inadmissible. Under the E.E.C. Treaty, in none of the ten cases so far decided[11] (all brought by private parties) has the applicant been able to pass the test of admissibility due mainly to the restricted standing of private parties as compared with the E.C.S.C. Treaty.[12] No action has yet been brought under the Euratom Treaty. As there are substantial differences between the E.C.S.C. and E.E.C./Euratom systems,[13] these will be considered separately below.

602. Parties (E.C.S.C)

Under the E.C.S.C. Treaty, the general rules governing the action for failure to act are laid down by Article 35 to which discussion in this Chapter is limited. Under this Article, action may be brought against the Commission (formerly High Authority) only. The other Community institutions are not subject to judicial control in respect of their illegal omissions. In defining the circle of parties entitled to institute proceedings, a distinction must be made between the two stages of the proceedings, i.e. the obligatory preliminary procedure before the Commission that must precede every action and the action before the Court of Justice itself. The preliminary procedure[1] may be initiated by the Member States, the Council, undertakings and associations of undertakings. Since any one of these bodies that can show an interest in the act which the Commission is required to take (and which will eventually be the subject-matter of the action) may set in motion the preliminary procedure, it seems that before the Commission the Member States and the Council, on the one hand, and undertakings and associations (hereinafter: private parties), on the other, have the same standing.[2] Thus, apart from the common requirement of having an interest in the matter, a private party must meet only one additional condition to be entitled to appeal to the Commission, namely, it must qualify as an undertaking or association within the technical meaning of these terms as specifically defined for the purposes of the E.C.S.C. Treaty.[3] A person that cannot so qualify, e.g. a private individual acting in his private capacity in defence of his personal interests, cannot avail himself of the procedure in Article 35.[4]

The position is different at the second stage of the proceedings, i.e. in the actual action before the Court of Justice. Since this is in reality an action for annulment, the Member States and the Council will assume their privileged position which they enjoy in such action, while private parties must satisfy the conditions for admissibility which Article 33 lays down for undertakings and associations in respect of annulment proceedings.[5] Although Article 35 does not expressly specify who may bring action before the Court, it is submitted that only the parties entitled to initiate the preliminary procedure may do so,[6] and from among these only the party which actually raised the matter with the Commission can appear as applicant.[7] This follows from the requirement, to be discussed later, that the application instituting proceedings must strictly follow the wording of the request to the Commission both as to the substantive claim and as to the legal grounds on which the claim is founded. Moreover, the application must be accompanied by documentary evidence of the date on which the matter in question was raised with the Commission.[8] In most cases only the party which made the original request will be able to comply with these requirements. If there are more than one applicant, all of them must have participated in the making of the request.[9]

Apart from Article 35, the E.C.S.C. Treaty contains a number of provisions affording specific remedies for the Commission's failure to act in specified situations (Articles 37, 58(1), 59(1), 59(5), 59(6), 61(3)). These provisions are, however, not considered in this book partly because they are only available to Member States and partly because, with the exception of Article 37, they provide for non-judicial remedies. Undertakings and associations do not have a standing before the European Court to invoke Article 37.[10]

603. Concept of failure to act (E.C.S.C.)

There are two general conditions, applicable to all parties, for the bringing of an action for failure to act. First, there must be a 'failure to act' on the part of the Commission. Secondly, the action must be preceded by a preliminary procedure. The first condition is discussed in this, the second in the following Section.[1]

The Commission's failure to act may arise in two different situations. First, where the Commission is required by the Treaty or by rules laid down for its implementation, to take a decision or make a recommendation and fails to fulfil this obligation. The Commission must, therefore, be under a clear obligation to act, and the outcome of such action must be either a decision or a recommendation.[2] The obligation to act may arise either from the Treaty itself, or from a binding act within the scope of secondary legislation. As Article 88 E.C.S.C.[3] imposes a clear obligation upon the Commission to call upon Member States to fulfil their Community obligations whenever the

Commission considers that they have failed to do so, an omission to use this power of control gives right to an action for failure to act.[4] By means of this action it is thus possible not only for other Member States but also for undertakings and associations to compel the Commission to open Article 88 proceedings against a Member State which in their opinion has violated Community law.[5] Under the E.E.C./Euratom Treaties this is not possible.[6] On the other hand, a mere failure of the Commission to repeal or revoke one of its own earlier acts which is no longer subject to an action for annulment for expiry of time-limit, does not constitute an actionable failure to act[7] except where there has occurred a new fact of a nature to alter the essential circumstances and conditions which governed the adoption of the original act.[8] This is because an applicant cannot in principle be permitted, by using the procedural device of an action for failure to act, to ask for the annulment of measures which might have been declared void if proceedings had been instituted within the proper time-limits.[9]

The Commission's failure to act may, secondly, also arise in a situation where the Commission is not obliged but merely empowered, by the Treaty or by rules laid down for its implementation, to take a decision or make a recommendation, and abstains from doing so. However, in that case an action lies only if such abstention constitutes a misuse of powers.[10] Consequently, the action must be founded on the sole ground of misuse of powers.[11] In situations where the Commission is not required but merely authorised to act and the ground of misuse of powers is not invoked, the action will be inadmissible as it fails to fulfil the requirements of the Treaty.[12]

604. Preliminary procedure (E.C.S.C.)

Before an action for failure to act may be instituted before the Court of Justice, the party wishing to bring the action must go through an obligatory preliminary procedure. This is a very strict requirement non-compliance with which entails inadmissibility of the action.[1] The procedure is the same in respect of all parties and both forms of the Commission's failure to act. As a first step, an interested party which considers that the Commission has failed to act, must 'raise the matter' with the Commission. This means, in particular, that he must, by a formal communication addressed to the Commission, specifically and unequivocally request the adoption of a particular measure. He must specify in detail the contents of the measure requested; generalities such as 'the taking of sufficient and appropriate measures' will not suffice.[2] The communication to the Commission must, moreover, possess 'peremptory' or 'threatening' character so as to reveal sufficiently clearly that it is intended to constitute the obligatory preliminary step to be followed by an action before the Court, if necessary. The Commission must be able to recognise that it is a legal act which makes time run for the bringing of the action. Anything less than a clearly worded request formally putting the Commission on notice to act (e.g. a courteous letter containing general complaints) is insufficient to make the ensuing action admissible.[3] As far as its form is concerned, the act requested can only be a formal decision or recommendation; a non-binding act, such as an opinion, cannot be obtained by means of this action. Although the Treaty lays down no time-limit for the making of the request, unreasonably long delays are not permitted as incompatible with the requirements of legal security and continuity of Community action. An unjustified long interval (e.g. eighteen months) between the time when a party obtains knowledge that the Commission will not take a certain measure and the date of the formal request initiating the preliminary procedure will render the ensuing action inadmissible.[4]

Following the request, the Commission has two months within which to act. If at the end of two months it has not taken any decision or made any recommendation, proceedings may be instituted before the Court of Justice within a further one month. It follows that the failure to act can be cured only by a formal decision or recommendation adopted within two months. A communication from the Commission which is neither in its form nor in its contents a decision or recommendation will not prevent the bringing of an action. Nor will a simple stalling reply which only reiterates and explains the prior legal position of the Commission or which states that the request is under consideration, nor any other preliminary measure relating to the preparation of a formal act. Nor can the Commission successfully argue that the two months' limit is not sufficient for it to adopt the requested measure.[5] According to general procedural rules, the time-limit of two months starts to run from the day following the receipt of the request and continues to run during vacations.[6] The Court examines of its own motion whether no decision has been taken within the period of two months, even if the Commission admits that to be the case.[7]

It is not quite clear whether the two month time-limit refers to the actual taking of the decision or to its communication to the applicant. The following variations are possible. First, a decision is taken within the time-limit but reaches the applicant after the expiration of two months, although before the institution of formal proceedings before the Court. In that case an action for failure to act will be deprived of its legal basis as no failure will exist at the time of the bringing of action. Consequently, the action for failure to act will be inadmissible, while at the same time an action for annulment becomes available.[8]

Secondly, a decision is taken after the expiry of the time-limit and reaches the applicant after the institution of formal proceedings. Its effect upon the action will then depend on whether it contains a grant or refusal of the request. If it contains the requested measure (positive decision), then the action is rendered without object and the Court will refrain from giving a ruling. But the Commission will have to bear the costs of the proceedings as its positive decision shows that the applicant's case was well founded.[9] If the decision refuses the request (negative decision), it will not deprive the action of its legal basis. The Commission's silence at the end of the time-limit has to be interpreted as an implied decision of refusal[10] which opens a right of action to the applicant unconditionally and once and for all. A subsequent express negative decision cannot affect the existence of the implied decision of refusal which alone is the basis for the action. Consequently, a second action brought for the annulment of this belated express decision will be held inadmissible as superfluous.[11]

Thirdly, a decision is not only taken but also reaches the applicant within the two months' time-limit. In the case of a negative decision refusing to take the requested measure, an action for failure to act will no longer lie as there is no longer a failure to act. An action for annulment becomes, however, available against the express decision of refusal.[12] In the case of a positive decision containing the requested measure an action becomes clearly unnecessary. A decision which may not be intended by the Commission to comply with the applicant's request and which does not in fact explicitly rule on all the points contained in the request (and therefore is not the same measure as was sought for) but which nevertheless settles, at least indirectly, the questions raised by the applicant, will prevent an action for failure to act. Such action lies only if the Commission makes no decision at all in the matter referred to in the applicant's request. Nevertheless, the partial or inadequate decision is subject to an action for annulment.[13]

From what has been said above it becomes apparent that the E.C.S.C. Treaty has instituted, in the form of the actions for annulment and failure to act, a 'closed' system of remedies. Since the failure to act means the absence of an express, formal decision,[14] it can be remedied only by an express, formal decision which is, in turn, subject to an action for annulment. An informal, non-binding act cannot prevent an action for failure to act. Thus whenever an interested party sets in motion the preliminary procedure with a view to compelling the Commission to take a certain measure, only two alternatives are possible. Either there will be a formal act (taking or refusing to take the measure) against which an action for annulment is open, or there will be no formal act at all in which case an action for failure to act is available. This also explains why the two actions are in logic mutually exclusive, that is, why they cannot both be admissible in respect of the same situation at one and the same time.[15]

From the point of view of the ensuing action, the preliminary procedure is important in three respects. First, the request addressed to the Commission will provide the starting point for the various time-limits granted to the parties concerned.[16] Secondly, by calling upon the Commission to take a particular measure within a defined period the applicant gives it an opportunity, before going to Court, to reconsider the legality or otherwise of its inaction. Unnecessary litigation can thus be avoided.[17] Thirdly, and most importantly, the request made to the Commission determines the limits within which the subsequent action can be brought before the Court and within which the Court will examine whether the Commission has in fact failed to act. The implied refusal (which is to be inferred from the inaction) can only exist with regard to an express request.[18] The applicant cannot, therefore, include in his application instituting proceedings the non-performance of an act which he has not specifically requested.[19] Nor can he change the claim and the legal grounds of his action from those expressed in the original request, in other words, the grounds upon which the application is founded[20] must not be fundamentally different from those on which the request has been based. A fundamental difference will entail inadmissibility of action.[21] Finally, the request will determine the nature of the implied negative decision which the Commission is deemed to have taken.[22]

605. Action before the Court of Justice (E.C.S.C.)

If the Commission has not adopted a formal act within the period of two months, proceedings may be instituted before the Court against the implied decision of refusal which is to be inferred from the silence of the Commission on the matter. At this point the Treaty thus adopts a fiction, i.e. that the Commission's silence constitutes an 'implied decision of refusal'. The action is to be brought, therefore, not against the Commission's silence but against its (implied) refusal to take the requested measure.[1] This has the important consequence that, technically, the action will be one for the annulment of the implied negative decision and, as such, will be governed in all respects by the rules relating to actions for annulment.[2] That is why it is often said that under the E.C.S.C. Treaty an action for failure to act is just a variation, a special case of action for annulment.[3]

Although, in theory, all the rules discussed in the Chapter dealing with actions for annulment[4] apply *mutatis mutandis*, for practical purposes the following points need emphasising. The time-limit for bringing the action is one month which starts running from the end of the two months reckoned from the date of the lodging of the original request with the Commission. The position of the various parties having *locus standi*, which was the same during the preliminary procedure, becomes different in the action before the Court. Member States and the Council, as privileged parties, may in principle invoke any of the four grounds of action[5] (although the grounds of lack of competence and infringement of an essential procedural requirement are by their very nature less likely to be invoked against an implied decision) unless they challenge a failure to act which is in connection with an authorisation and not an obligation, in which case they can rely on misuse of powers only.[6] In the case of undertakings and associations, the distinction between general and individual acts (decisions and recommendations) becomes relevant.[7] The Court, therefore, has to examine the nature of the implied negative decision from this point of view. It will be determined by the nature of the decision which the Commission has been requested, but has failed, to take. The implied decision of refusal will be a general decision if the measure which the Commission has failed to take would have been, if taken, a general act; and an individual decision if it would have been an individual act.[8] It need not, however, be individual in relation to the applicant, i.e. it is not necessary that the decision should have been addressed to him, or should have affected him alone or almost alone. It could equally have been directed to, or have affected, another undertaking or even a Member State (which need not necessarily be the applicant's own State). It is enough (and at the same time necessary) that it should concern the applicant personally.[9]

It may be noted that it is precisely because of such interpretation of the concept of 'individual decision' that under the E.C.S.C. Treaty it is possible for private parties (i.e. undertakings and associations) to challenge measures of Member States (not necessarily their own State) adversely affecting them although addressed to others. Thus government measures favouring certain industries and having an impact on conditions of competition or imposing special levies on certain industries may be contested by undertakings that are injured by these measures. Accordingly, Luxembourg steel producers could challenge (although in the event unsuccessfully) the legality under Community law of measures of their own Government subsidising the price of coal sold for household purposes by imposing a levy upon the sale of coal purchased by Luxembourg industry.[10] Likewise, French undertakings could challenge special discriminatory railway tariffs introduced by the German Government[11] and Dutch undertakings could contest the legality of Government bonuses paid to miners in the German coal-mining industry.[12] The legal means for this is either an action for the annulment of the Commission's authorisation on which the national measure is based[13] or, if it is not based on any authorisation, a request addressed to the Commission to open Article 88 proceedings against the Member State concerned.[14] A failure of the Commission to open these proceedings can be the subject of an action for failure to act. This is in fact possible because the act whereby the Commission is to call upon the Member State under Article 88 to comply with its Treaty obligations is to be regarded as an 'individual decision' which 'concerns' the applicant if the challenged national measure is such.[15] It is evident that such a construction of the combined effects of Article 88 and the action for failure to act affords considerable protection under the E.C.S.C. Treaty to private parties against national measures violating Community law. Such a protection does not exist under the E.E.C./Euratom Treaties.[16]

The consequence of the distinction between general and individual implied negative decisions is that if the implied negative decision is an individual one, the applicant private party is in principle entitled to found upon all four grounds of action (except insofar as the failure to act arises in connection with an authorisation and not an obligation). If, on the other hand, it is a general decision, it can be challenged only on the ground of misuse of powers.[17] Nevertheless, just as in the case of the Member States and the Council, the grounds of lack of competence and infringement of an essential procedural requirement will by their very nature be less likely to be invoked against an implied decision. Thus the fact alone that an implied negative decision is not based upon any declared reasons cannot constitute an infringement of an essential procedural requirement and cannot vitiate the decision, even if the decision which the Commission was required (but has failed) to take must be reasoned.[18] Furthermore, insofar as the implied negative decision is an individual decision, the defence of illegality[19] may be raised in the same way as in the case of an express decision.[20]

606. Consequences of successful action (E.C.S.C.)

The fact that an action for failure to act is, in effect, aimed at the annulment of an (implied) decision, determines the nature and consequences of the Court's judgment. The Court will not merely limit itself to an examination whether there has been, contrary to the provisions of Community law, a failure to act. It will examine the applicant's case, which must strictly be founded upon his request addressed to the Commission,[1] on merits, and annul the decision of refusal only to the extent that it finds the latter to be illegal on any of the four grounds of illegality. The legality of the implied refusal to act depends primarily on the legality of the acts which the applicant asked the Commission to take or withdraw.[2] Thus an action for failure to act is 'well founded' and successful only to the extent to which the original request was legally justified, i.e. the Commission should have taken the measure requested.[3] If the action is successful, the Court's judgment will not be purely declaratory of a failure to act, but it will annul (declare void) the Commission's implied negative decision. Such judgment means in fact to say that the Commission is not justified in not taking the requested measure, in other words, that the Commission is under an obligation to act. However, the Court cannot instruct the Commission as to what specific measures to take; this would be tantamount to the Court substituting itself for the Commission which is not permitted.[4] Just as in an action for annulment, the Court must confine itself to referring the matter back to the Commission which must then take the necessary steps to comply with the judgment according to Article 34 E.C.S.C.[5] In particular, from that moment on the Commission must act within the framework of the Court's judgment; it must re-examine the matter and take the measures that necessarily follow from the execution of the judgment of annulment.[6] Since the legal effects of the judgment flow not merely from the operative part but also from the decisive grounds on which it is based,[7] the Commission must take the judgment as a whole into account, including any relevant observations made by the Court, in establishing what measures are necessary to comply with it. As the sole object of an action for failure to act is the implied decision of refusal which appears from the silence of the Commission, the Court will entertain an action only insofar as it is directed to the annulment of the implied negative decision. Any submissions going beyond annulment, e.g. by requesting the Court to order the Commission to take specified measures, are inadmissible.[8]

607. Relationship between E.C.S.C. and E.E.C./Euratom systems

Action for failure to act under the E.E.C./Euratom Treaties is on many important points different from its counterpart under the E.C.S.C. Treaty.

These differences have their reasons in, and broadly correspond to, the differences between the actions for annulment under the two systems. This is understandable considering that the action for annulment and action for failure to act form a coherent system of remedies, each being characterised by the same features peculiar to the E.C.S.C. Treaty on the one hand, and the E.E.C./Euratom Treaties, on the other.[1] The main differences between the two systems concern the parties,[2] the conditions,[3] the consequences[4] of action and the position of private parties[5] while the similarities relate to the preliminary procedure.[6] As regards its nature, under the E.C.S.C. Treaty an action for failure to act is, as a special case of an action for annulment, what is termed in German law a *Gestaltungsklage*, i.e. an action for an alteration of the legal position, while under the E.E.C./Euratom Treaties it is a *Feststellungsklage*, i.e. an action for a declaration. But perhaps the most important difference is that the protection which this action affords to private parties under the E.E.C./Euratom Treaties is considerably smaller than that under the E.C.S.C. Treaty.[7] The relationship between the two systems is that wherever there is a clearly recognisable intention on the part of the drafters of the E.E.C./Euratom Treaties to depart from the solutions of the E.C.S.C. Treaty, the principles laid down by the European Court in its case-law under the latter, cannot be applied in the framework of the former. Any other solution would clearly be contrary to the letter and the spirit of the Treaties.[8] Where, however, there is no substantial difference between the two systems, the case-law developed by the European Court under the E.C.S.C. Treaty is freely applicable to actions brought under the E.E.C./Euratom Treaties.[9]

608. Parties (E.E.C./Euratom)

Under the E.E.C./Euratom Treaties action for failure to act is governed solely by Articles 175, 176 and Articles 148, 149, respectively. Under these provisions action may be brought against both the Council and the Commission. The inclusion of the Council is explained by its increased role and legislative powers in the two later Communities as compared with its position in the Coal and Steel Community. On the other hand, action cannot be brought against the European Parliament, the Court of Justice or the Economic and Social Committee. Just as action for annulment, action for failure to act must be directed against the particular institution whose conduct is challenged.[1] Proceedings may be instituted by the Member States, the 'other institutions of the Community' and natural or legal persons. The reference in the Treaties to the 'other institutions of the Community' instead of their designation by name, clearly a piece of bad draftsmanship, creates ambiguities in two respects. Strict interpretation of this phrase in the actual context could lead, on the one hand, to the exclusion of the Council and the Commission from, and, on the other hand, to the inclusion of the Court of Justice and the European Parliament in, the circle of possible applicants. This, clearly, could not have been the intention of the drafters. 'Other institutions' thus cannot mean 'institutions other than the Council and the Commission', but 'institutions other than the one whose inaction is being challenged'. In other words, the Council and the Commission may mutually contest each other's omissions. 'Other institutions' cannot, moreover, be taken to include the Court of Justice although it is without doubt an institution of the Communities.[2] The Court cannot bring action for annulment and it would be equally incompatible with its judicial function if it could cite before it the Council and the Commission in respect of their inaction and thus be party and judge in the same case. The inclusion of the European Parliament is less problematic although it has no *locus standi* in actions for annulment, nor under the E.C.S.C. Treaty at all.[3] The Economic and Social Committee not having the status of an institution, the 'other institutions' referred to are, accordingly, the Council, the Commission and the European Parliament. These as well as the Member States enjoy privileged position just as in an action for annulment[4] although they, too, must comply with the requirements as to the compulsory preliminary procedure.[5]

The concept of 'natural or legal persons' (hereinafter: private parties) must be given the same wide interpretation as for the purposes of action for annulment.[6] Any such person whose rights or legally protected interests have been impaired by an illegal inaction of the Council or the Commission is, accordingly, entitled to institute proceedings provided that he/it has the requisite capacity to sue[7] and satisfies the various conditions of admissibility which the Treaties have laid down for private parties.[8]

609. Concept of failure to act (E.E.C./Euratom)

Two general conditions must be fulfilled before action can be instituted. First, there must be a 'failure to act' on the part of the Council or the Commission. Secondly, the action must be preceded by a preliminary procedure. The first condition is dealt with in this, the second in the following Section.[1]

In the E.E.C./Euratom system the concept of 'failure to act' is different from that adopted in the E.C.S.C. system.[2] Under the E.E.C./Euratom Treaties, a failure of the Council or Commission to act is subject to judicial review only insofar as it constitutes an 'infringement of the Treaty.' Accordingly, failure to act means the omission of an act the adoption of which is obligatory upon the institution.[3] The institution must be under a clear legal obligation to take a certain action so that the failure to take action constitutes a breach of a duty. A failure to exercise a mere discretionary power or to take a measure dictated by mere considerations of expediency is not sufficient: this type of negative conduct is not subject to judicial control.[4] The failure to act must, in other words, be illegal.

In practice, in order for an action to succeed, it is not enough to refer in general terms to a 'violation of the Treaty'. The applicant must specify the exact provisions of Community law which in his opinion require the

Council or Commission to take the measure sought by him.[5] The provisions founded on must impose upon the institution a particular obligation to take, and at the same time create a corresponding subjective right in the applicant to demand, the requested measure. The general duty of the Commission under Article 155 E.E.C./Article 124 Euratom to ensure that Community law is observed by all those subject to it, i.e. individuals as well as Member States, is too general an obligation to serve as a basis for an action for failure to act. It does not confer upon individuals enforceable rights to demand particular measures.[6] Reliance on Article 155 E.E.C./Article 124 Euratom alone will not, therefore, ensure admissibility of action.[7] It is, moreover, doubtful whether interested parties possess an abstract right, enforceable by action for failure to act, to demand prompt and due consideration (as distinct from, or in addition to, the taking of a specified measure) whenever they make a complaint to an institution. Nevertheless, it is a duty incumbent upon any public body (*nobile officium*) to reply within a reasonable period to serious approaches made by interested parties and directed against a measure coming within its competence. Failure to do so may result in an otherwise unnecessary litigation where the institution may have to bear part of the costs.[8]

The obligation to act must, strictly speaking, arise from the Treaties (as supplemented or amended), but it is submitted that it may equally arise from a wider concept of 'Community law' including, in addition to the Treaties, secondary legislation. This is so since any obligation arising from the latter derives its binding force ultimately from the Treaties and any infringement of secondary legislation can be interpreted, in turn, as an infringement of the Treaties themselves.[9] Such a wider interpretation is also suggested by an analogy with the E.C.S.C. system which clearly stipulates that the obligation to act may arise either from the Treaty or from any 'rules laid down for the implementation thereof'.[10] 'Infringement of the Treaty' must therefore be taken to mean infringement of the Treaty or of any rule of law relating to its application, as in the case of an action for annulment.[11]

The categories of measures which are the subject-matter of the obligation to act and whose omission constitutes an actionable failure to act, differ according to whether the applicant is a Member State/institution or a private party. The European Court has stated generally that the concept of an act that can be the subject of an action is the same for the purposes of both actions for annulment and actions for failure to act, since both actions are in fact only different aspects of one and the same legal remedy.[12] It is, however, thought that this statement is correct only where the applicant is a private party.[13] In the case of Member States/institutions as applicants, while an action for annulment is not available against non-binding acts such as recommendations and opinions,[14] no such limitation exists in respect of action for failure to act. The latter is thus open in respect of any act,[15] binding[16] or non-binding,[17] which the Council or Commission has failed to take provided the inaction constitutes an infringement of Community law. Since the concept of 'act' is to be taken in its widest possible meaning so as to include any measure addressed to anyone. Member States/institutions may use this action to procure general, law-making measures to the same extent as individual measures addressed either to Member States or to institutions or to private parties. And this is possible without their having to show any particular legal interest in the act concerned on the assumption that they have a general interest in seeing that the institutions duly carry out their Community duties.[18] On the other hand, neither Member States/institutions nor private parties may, by using the procedural device of an action for failure to act, seek the annulment of an act in a situation where a direct action for annulment is no longer possible for expiry of time-limit. If they could request the Council or the Commission to repeal or revoke one of its own earlier acts and in case the institution fails to do so, bring an action for illegal failure to act, this would open a way of action that would run parallel to action for annulment, but without being subject to the conditions of the latter. This is clearly inadmissible.[19]

610. Preliminary procedure (E.E.C./Euratom)

Action for failure to act is admissible only if the requirement for an obligatory preliminary procedure has been complied with. Since the essential features of this procedure are similar in the E.C.S.C. and E.E.C./Euratom systems, the case-law developed by the European Court on the subject under the former[1] can be relied on in the context of the latter.[2] Briefly, as a first step, the institution concerned has to be called upon to act. In this respect it is necessary, just as in the E.C.S.C. system, that the prospective applicant should put the institution formally on notice to act. This is achieved only by indicating to it with unequivocal clarity the acts which it is required to take and by advising it of the applicant's intention to go to Court or at least to use 'all means of appeal', should it refrain from acting. Requests that do not amount to this will not suffice.[3] The institution then has two months within which to act. If within the two months the institution has not defined its position, the action may be brought within a further period of two months. It is seen that on this point a major difference exists between the E.C.S.C. and E.E.C./Euratom systems. In the former, the institution can only avoid an action by adopting, within the two months, a formal decision or recommendation; in the latter a 'definition of position' already brings about that effect. The meaning of this 'vague and comprehensive' expression[4] is examined in the following Section.[5]

611. Definition of position (E.E.C./Euratom)

In the E.E.C./Euratom system, an action lies only if the institution has not 'defined its position' within two months of the request addressed to it by the applicant. 'Definition of position' in this context means an express declaration of the view taken by the institution of the subject-matter of the request and the merits of the case.[1] Thus, for example, the Commission's reply to a request asking it to initiate Article 169 proceedings against a Member State,[2] that in the Commission's view the Member State has not violated Community law, amounts to a 'definition of position' and, if notified within the prescribed time-limit, is sufficient to prevent an action. That is so even if the reply itself is not a binding act and is, therefore, not subject to annulment.[3] It follows that a reply which in the final analysis constitutes a refusal to act in the way requested may amount to a declaration of position and may stop an action.[4] Nevertheless, an interim reply which merely informs the applicant that his request is being studied and which does not involve any clarification of attitude on the substantive issues of the request, does not amount to a definition of position. Even an indication to the effect that in the Commission's view there is no possibility for bringing an action on the basis of the applicant's request amounts in itself to a mere statement of an opinion and does not constitute a taking of position in response to the request. That is so even if such an indication implies a refusal to act on the part of the institution, as an implied refusal does not equal a taking of position; rather it is the typical case for which the action for failure to act is provided.[5] In contrast, a brief statement to the effect that the Commission is 'not under any obligation to adopt any measure' with respect to the request does, even if not reasoned, constitute, as an express refusal to act, a definition of position. Thus a clear distinction must be made between an express refusal to act and a failure to act (even though implying a refusal to act), between an expressed intention (even though negative) and the total lack of any expression of intention. The former does, and the latter does not, constitute a 'definition of position'.[6]

While, therefore, under the E.C.S.C. Treaty an actionable 'failure to act' means failure to take a binding act (decision or recommendation),[7] in the E.E.C./Euratom system it means failure to take a position, or adopt an attitude, whether by means of a binding or non-binding act. The adoption of an act different from the one sought or deemed necessary by the interested parties, or the adoption of a negative decision, does not fall within the concept of 'failure to act'.[8] It follows that the institution concerned may remedy its failure to act and thus prevent an action by any of the following measures taken within two months: (a) formal (i.e. binding) act granting the request;[9] (b) formal act refusing the request; (c) formal act containing a measure other than that requested; (d) informal (i.e. non-binding and non-reasoned) taking of position or declaration of an attitude expressing a willingness or unwillingness to act.[10] Since of these measures (a), (b) and (c) may, under certain circumstances, not, and (d) may never, be challenged for annulment, the situation may arise that, depending on the form in which the institution chooses to reply, a party may be left without any judicial remedy whatsoever against the institution's conduct, neither the action for failure to act, nor the action for annulment being available.[11] This is obviously a very serious gap in the system of remedies set up by the E.E.C./Euratom Treaties, a gap which affects the legal position of Member States/institutions and private parties alike and one which under the E.C.S.C. Treaty does not exist.[12]

It is submitted that this anomalous situation does not necessarily follow from the text of the Treaties, it is rather more a result of the interpretation which the European Court has given to the term 'definition of position'. It could, therefore, be corrected by simply construing that term as meaning 'definition of position by a formal (i.e. binding) act' which act would then be subject to annulment in the usual way. This would greatly increase the legal protection of private parties, would complete the E.E.C./Euratom system of remedies and would bring it more into line with that of the E.C.S.C. Treaty.

612. Consequences of successful action (E.E.C./Euratom)

The E.E.C./Euratom Treaties do not employ the fiction of an 'implied negative decision' but introduce a different concept, that of dilatoriness. An action for failure to act is, accordingly, not an action for annulment (i.e. annulment of an implied decision of refusal inferred from the silence of the institutions), but an action for a declaration. The Court is asked to establish, first, the dilatoriness of the institution in defining its position with regard to the applicant's request, and secondly, that this constitutes an infringement of Community law.[1] All that the Court can do is to examine whether the Treaties or secondary legislation impose a clear obligation to take the requested measure and whether, if so, that obligation has been fulfilled. It follows that the applicant cannot request, and the Court cannot order, specific measures to be taken by the Council or the Commission (still less can the Court's judgment itself be regarded as a substitute for such measures); in fact the indication of such measures in the statement of claim is inadmissible. Nevertheless, the applicant will attain practically the same result since in the case of a successful action the institution whose failure to act has been declared contrary to Community law is required by the Treaties to take the necessary measures to comply with the judgment of the Court of Justice. Since the legal effect of the judgment flows not merely from the operative part but also from the decisive grounds on which it is based,[2] the institution must take the judgment as a whole into account, including any relevant observations made by the Court, in establishing what measures are necessary to comply with it. Thus a mere reading of the judgment will indicate the measures by the adoption of which alone is it possible to terminate the infringement.[3] Should the institution still fail to take the required measures, another action for failure to act is the only remedy. To this all the rules discussed in this Chapter apply, including the requirement for a (second) preliminary procedure. The obligation of the Council and Commission to comply with the Court's judgment is clearly separated from the obligation of the Communities to make good any damage that may have been caused by the institutions' inaction. The latter obligation is governed entirely by the principles laid down by Article 215(2) E.E.C./Article 188(2) Euratom[4] and forms no part of the institutions' duty to execute the Court's judgment rendered in the action for failure to act.

613. Special position of private parties (E.E.C./Euratom)

Generally speaking, private parties may bring an action for failure to act under the same conditions as Member States/institutions. Most of the rules discussed above apply to them accordingly. Nevertheless, there is one major difference between the respective position as applicants of Member States/institutions and private parties. This concerns the categories of measures that it is possible to elicit by means of an action. As seen above,[1] Member States/institutions can request the adoption of any binding or non-binding act, addressed to anyone, including general (i.e. law-making) measures as well as individual decisions. By contrast, private parties can only bring an action if an institution has failed 'to address' to them 'any act' other than a recommendation or an opinion. The question, therefore, arises what exactly are the measures that private parties may seek through this action.

Generally speaking, the admissibility of an action brought by private parties depends on both the nature and the addressee of the measure which the applicant wishes to obtain, and not on one of these elements alone.[2] As regards the nature of the measure, while recommendations and opinions are expressly excluded from the ambit of the action,[3] it clearly follows from the system of judicial protection instituted by the E.E.C./Euratom Treaties in favour of private parties that measures of general application, such as regulations and directives, are not covered either.[4] In theory, therefore, the only measure which can be requested from among those mentioned in Article 189 E.E.C./Article 161 Euratom[5] is a decision.[6]

As regards the addressee of the measure, two different opinions have been put forward and it would seem that the European Court itself has not been consistent in clearly following the one or the other. The first view is based on the assumption that unlike the E.C.S.C. Treaty, the E.E.C./Euratom Treaties created two distinct legal remedies in the form of action for annulment and action for failure to act. While a private party can bring annulment proceedings against measures which, although adopted in the form of a regulation or a decision addressed to another person, affect him directly and individually,[7] he can use the action for failure to act only to obtain an act which by its very nature and wording is addressed to him. He cannot institute this action if he is not the addressee of the measure requested, even if the measure affects him directly and individually. In other words, the addressee of the measure requested can only be the person making the request.[8]

According to a second view, the action for annulment and action for failure to act form one and the same legal remedy and therefore the concept of an 'act' that can be the subject of the action is necessarily the same for the purposes of both proceedings. An action for failure to act is, therefore, available in respect of all acts which are subject to annulment, even if not addressed formally (if taken) to the person bringing the action provided they concern him directly and individually. Should this not be so, the undesirable situation might arise in certain cases that the existence or absence of a judicial remedy would depend on the (arbitrary) conduct of the institution to which a request was submitted. If the institution responds by a formal act (either granting or refusing the request), an action for annulment would be available whether or not the applicant is the addressee of that act as long as it affects him directly and individually. Should, however, the institution fail to respond at all, the applicant would be deprived of any legal remedy if he is not the addressee of the measure requested even if it affects him directly and individually. It also follows from this view that if the requested measure is an act which by its nature and destination is not subject to an action for failure to act, the express denial of that act can also not be the subject of an action for annulment.[9]

It would seem that while the first view is supported by a strict interpretation of the Treaty text, the second is more in accordance with the logic of the system of remedies open to private parties under the E.E.C./Euratom Treaties. However, because of the narrow construction by the European Court of the concepts of direct and individual concern,[10] it is doubtful whether even the second view could to any significant extent enlarge the restricted scope that an action for failure to act has for private parties.

To sum up, in order that an action for failure to act brought by a private party may be admissible, the following six requirements must cumulatively be satisfied:

(1) the institution concerned has been formally called upon to act;
(2) the institution has not defined its position within two months;
(3) the time-limit of two months for the bringing of action has been observed;
(4) the institution is under an obligation to take the measure requested;
(5) the measure is an act to be addressed to the applicant;
(6) the measure is a binding act.

It will be seen that because of the presence of the last two requirements, the rights of private parties as applicants are considerably limited as compared with those of Member States/institutions. In particular, this limitation means that unlike the latter, private parties cannot use this action to procure: (1) general (normative) acts; (2) acts addressed to others; (3) non-binding acts. These limitations are further considered below.[11]

614. (1) Limitation as to normative acts (E.E.C./Euratom)

Strictly speaking, measures of general application, such as regulations and directives, are not explicitly excluded from the scope of action for failure to act. Since, however, this action and the action for annulment form a coherent system of remedies, it is generally agreed that a measure which by its very nature is not subject to annulment proceedings by private parties, cannot be procured by them by means of an action for failure to act either. This view gains further support from the rule that the measure requested must be an act 'addressed to' the applicant which by implication excludes regulations, directives and all acts of a general regulatory character as these can never be addressed to particular private persons.[1] For the same reasons, legislative proposals to be submitted by the Commission to the Council are also excluded as these form an intrinsic part of the Community law-making process.[2] In defining whether or not an act is a 'general measure' the same considerations apply as in the case of an action for annulment.[3] Thus it is not the title and form but the substance and nature of the act that is decisive. In general, private parties cannot request a measure which would be applicable not to a limited class of addressees, specified or identifiable, but to categories envisaged abstractly and as a whole. Or, conversely, they can only request measures which are issued by reference to the particular legal position of the applicant, applying to him in a special way, and affecting him directly and individually. What is important in this respect is the final objective pursued by the applicant in bringing his action.[4]

In particular, private parties cannot use an action for failure to act to compel the Commission to call upon a Member State by means of an Article 169 procedure[5] to amend or repeal a national law believed by the applicant to be in violation of Community law. Quite apart from other considerations to be discussed below,[6] the final outcome of such a procedure would be a general, law-making measure at the national level which it is clearly not within the reach of private parties to elicit.[7] Nor can they request a measure (whatever its nature and form) the adoption of which would necessitate an examination by the Commission of the compatibility of a national Bill with Community law. Such a measure, too, is clearly outside the scope of an action for failure to act.[8] Where the measure requested would in fact have the effect of amending an earlier measure which is of general application, it would itself have the same legal scope, i.e. it would be a general measure and would therefore not be addressed to the applicant. Such a measure cannot be obtained by private parties.[9] That is the case *a fortiori* where the request is clearly directed at the amendment of a regulation which could only be achieved by a legal act which would itself be a regulation.[10]

615. (2) Limitation as to acts addressed to others (E.E.C./Euratom)

A private party can, by means of an action for failure to act, elicit only such acts as are 'addressed' to him. As seen,[1] it is not quite clear whether this provision is to be interpreted as limiting the range of acts that may be sought by private parties to such as are formally to be 'addressed' to the applicant (which in the terminology of Article 189 E.E.C./Article 161 Euratom can only be a decision sent to him),[2] or as also including such acts as are 'directed' to him in a material sense only, i.e. formally addressed to others but affecting him directly and individually (which would include, in addition to a decision sent to the applicant, a decision taken in the form of a regulation and a decision addressed to another person).[3] It is, nevertheless, certain that the act to be obtained cannot be a genuine general (normative) measure, i.e. a regulation, because such a measure is both by its nature and its wording always addressed to everybody in general and to nobody in particular. Nor can it be a directive or a decision addressed to a Member State (unless perhaps such a decision directly and individually affects the applicant) mainly because these acts, needing further implementing measures at the national level, would, in the end, lead to a general legislative or administrative enactment. Such measures, as seen,[4] cannot be elicited by private parties. So the limitation discussed in this Section and that considered in the previous Section are closely related to one another and are in fact only two different expressions of the same conception.

It is precisely because of this limitation that private parties cannot under the E.E.C./Euratom Treaties obtain a finding from the Commission that a Member State has failed in one of its obligations under Community law; nor can they compel the Commission by an action for failure to act to initiate an Article 169 procedure[5] against a Member State which they consider has violated Community law. That is so because the various procedural steps provided for by Article 169 E.E.C./Article 141 Euratom take place inherently and necessarily between the Commission and the Member State concerned. They take the form of acts which are issued to the latter and not in any way or sense 'addressed' or 'directed' to the private party who requested the Commission to act. These acts cannot, therefore, be procured by means of an action, should the Commission be reluctant to take action against the Member State. This is a clear and intentional departure from the E.C.S.C. Treaty where, due to its different construction, an action for failure to act is available to private parties for the same purpose.[6] Within the framework of the E.E.C./Euratom system, the E.C.S.C. case-law of the European Court on this point is inapplicable.[7] It is clear that this limitation of the action for failure to act presents a further serious weakness in the system of legal protection of individuals as they have virtually no remedy at the Community level against a Member State violating Community law by national measures.[8]

616. (3) Limitation as to non-binding acts (E.E.C./Euratom)

The category of measures that private parties may obtain by an action is further limited to acts other than recommendations or opinions, that is to say, to acts of a binding nature.[1] Any measure that is not a formal (i.e. binding) act within the meaning of Article 189 E.E.C./Article 161 Euratom[2] such as, for example, an advice, is clearly outside the scope of the action.[3] In determining whether a measure is or is not a 'binding' act, its content and scope and not its title or form is decisive. Thus a private party cannot evade this limitation by requesting, instead of a mere opinion, a formal decision binding upon him, if the subject-matter of the decision would not, in essence, amount to more than a mere advice. Such a measure would not be a decision but an opinion.[4]

Since both measures of general application (i.e. regulations and directives) and measures of a non-binding character (i.e. recommendations and opinions) are excluded from the scope of the action, the only acts that can in theory be requested by private parties from among those mentioned in Article 189 E.E.C./Article 161 Euratom, are decisions (possibly further limited to decisions addressed to the applicant). However, the Treaty itself does not use the word 'decisions'; it provides that 'any act' can be the subject of an action that satisfies the requirements discussed above. The question therefore arises whether the term 'act' has the same meaning as the word 'decision'. It has been suggested that behind the different expressions there lies a different meaning and that the Treaties intended to give the term 'act' a wider scope and content than that commonly attributed to a formal 'decision' under Article 189 E.E.C./Article 161 Euratom. 'Acts' should thus be understood as meaning all measures that may give rise to certain legal effects; all those whereby an institution is bound in a certain way, including what are called in German law 'real acts', i.e. purely material acts which entail legal effects quite independently of the intention of those who performed them. 'Acts' that might be requested by private parties could, accordingly, consist in certain steps or measures of a procedural character such as e.g. hearing of interested third persons in competition proceedings. The right of private parties to bring action to compel hearing and other similar procedural steps in competition matters[5] should therefore not be excluded merely because these steps may not strictly speaking have the character or title of a formal 'decision' within the meaning of Article 189 E.E.C./Article 161 Euratom.[6]

This argument gains very strong support from the wide construction which the European Court itself has given to the concept of a decision in similar situations in annulment proceedings, bringing certain procedural steps with definitive legal effects within the range of actionable decisions.[7] A corresponding extension, in suitable cases, of the scope of measures that can be elicited by means of an action for failure to act seems not only justifiable but logically necessary since the concept of an 'act' that can be the subject of an action is in principle the same for the purposes of both proceedings.

On the other hand, in the absence of any decided case on the point, it is more doubtful whether an exemption under Article 85(3) E.E.C. in conjunction with Article 6 of Regulation 17, a negative clearance under Article 2 of Regulation 17 or a decision requiring termination of an infringement under Article 3 of Regulation 17, may be procured by a private party by means of an action for failure to act. Unlike a hearing, all these measures are taken in the form of a formal 'decision'[8] so that no problem arises in that respect. However, there are other difficulties. All three provisions contain the phrase 'the Commission may . . .' instead of 'the Commission shall . . .' grant the respective measures, and this might be interpreted as meaning an authorisation for, rather than an obligation upon, the Commission. If that be correct, no action lies.[9] It has been suggested that the word 'may' expresses only the legal authority, and not the discretionary power, of the Commission to take the respective decisions. Accordingly, when the prerequisites are fulfilled the Commission no longer has a discretion to deny them. As there is then a clear obligation to act (and a corresponding subjective right in the private party to demand action), a failure to do so may give rise to an action.[10] Even if this interpretation should be endorsed by the European Court, it is still difficult to see how an interested third party can procure a decision requiring termination of an infrigement of Articles 85 or 86 E.E.C. Such a decision will be clearly addressed, not to the party making the request, but to those participating in the restrictive practice which constitutes the infringement complained of. An action for failure to act will be admissible only if the concept of the addressee of a decision is to be widened so as to include anyone showing a direct and individual concern.[11]

CHAPTER 7

Action for Damages

701. Nature and scope of action

In the course of the normal performance of their tasks, the institutions of the Communities, in the first place the Council and the Commission, may commit certain acts or omissions which may, directly or indirectly, cause material damage to those subject to their jurisdiction and even to third persons. Such a possibility is the more likely to arise in the Community context as the institutions' activities are carried out overwhelmingly in the economic sphere where, by the nature of things, even a limited measure of improper intervention (or a lack of it) may have far-reaching harmful effects. By virtue of a general and elementary principle of law prevailing in both the national and international legal order, any wrongful act or omission involving an injury entails the obligation to make reparation for it.[1] Thus, in one form or another, all the Member States recognise the responsibility of public authorities for injurious consequences arising from their official activities. The same responsibility must also attach to the Communities as a natural but necessary corollary to their exercise of sovereign powers transferred to them from the Member States. Accordingly, all three Treaties contain provisions governing the substantive conditions under which the Communities must bear liability for damages caused by their institutions or servants in the performance of their duties.[2] However, these provisions cannot be invoked, and thus the question of liability cannot be raised, within the framework of actions for annulment or for failure to act, even where the injury is connected with an illegal formal act or omission. This is partly because the jurisdiction of the European Court in such actions does not include the power fully to investigate all aspects of fact and law and to order pecuniary reparation, and partly because the duty of the institutions to eliminate the effects of the illegal conduct by restoring the *status quo ante* (*restitutio in integrum*) does not, at least under the E.E.C./Euratom Treaties, include the obligation to make good the damage caused by such conduct.[3] In other words, the Treaties have deliberately and carefully separated, both substantively and procedurally, the power of the European Court to review the legality of Community action from the power to establish liability for the consequences of such action. For the latter purpose, the Treaties have instituted a separate, third form of legal proceedings which thus complements in an important respect those discussed in the previous Chapters.[4]

For the above-mentioned reasons the action for damages must be seen as a distinct and independent form of judicial recourse which has its own special function in the system of remedies created by the Treaties and is subject to conditions designed to suit its own particular purpose. It is based on a type of jurisdiction which is entirely different from that which the Court exercises in actions concerning legality. It is distinguished from the action for annulment and failure to act by reason of its aim, grounds and effects. Its aim is not to contest the objective legality of the institutions' conduct and to bring about the annulment of an illegal act or the adoption of a particular measure, but to establish subjective rights to financial compensation for actual losses sustained. Its grounds are not the four grounds of action on which the annulment of a measure can be sought, but the existence of a wrongful act or omission, i.e. an official fault, on the part of the institutions or their servants committed in the performance of their duties. Its effects do not extend so far as to allow a direct control over the activities of the institutions through the annulment, with *erga omnes* and retroactive effect, of a measure or through the establishment of an obligation to take a measure, but are restricted to the payment of specified damages, i.e. an act affecting the applicant alone. The jurisdiction of the Court in actions concerning legality is strictly limited; in actions for damages it is plenary or unlimited.[5] In other words, by its nature an action for damages is not what is termed in German law a *Gestaltungsklage*, i.e. an action directed at the alteration of the legal position, but it is basically a *Leistungsklage*, i.e. an action aimed at the performance of a specific act (financial compensation). This, however, does not exclude the possibility of its being presented in certain special circumstances in the form of a *Feststellungsklage*, i.e. application for a declaration of Community liability based not on existing but future damage which is imminent and foreseeable with sufficient certainty.[6]

It follows from its autonomous nature that the action for damages is not in principle subsidiary to the two actions concerning legality and that, consequently, the various restrictions as to admissibility imposed by the Treaties upon private parties in the context of the latter are not applicable to it. This has the important consequence that even though an action for damages may be founded on the illegality of a formal, binding act or a failure to act (which is in fact mostly, if not necessarily always, the case) this does not in itself require, at least under the E.E.C./Euratom Treaties,[7] the antecedent establishment of such illegality by means of separate proceedings, available under much stricter conditions, such as an action for annulment or for failure to act or a reference for preliminary ruling. It would basically contradict the principle of independence of legal remedies as well as the requirements for a proper administration of justice and procedural economy and, in general, the need for an effective legal protection of individuals, if such a prior exhaustion of other remedies concerning legality were to be made a *sine qua non* condition for an action for damages. Whilst, as will be seen below,[8] the substantive law governing the Communities' non-contractual liability usually regards the illegality of an act or failure to act causing damage as a precondition for the establishment of such liability, the law relating to remedies and procedure does not consider the prior, formal annulment of that act, or a prior, formal declaration of illegality in respect of that failure to act to be a prerequisite for the admissibility of an action invoking such liability. Rather, the European Court has the necessary power to examine as an incidental matter within the framework of such an action the legality of the conduct alleged to have caused the injury, provided such examination properly falls within its own jurisdiction and not within that of the national courts.

It further follows from the above-mentioned principles and requirements that even the fact that in certain special circumstances an action for damages could bring about a financial result identical or similar to that which a successful action for annulment or failure to act could produce, and thus enable private parties to achieve an aim which they could not have achieved under the much stricter conditions of the latter, is also not of such a nature as to prevent the admissibility of the former. Even if determination of liability may in substance be coupled with a review of legality, the conditions for the admissibility of an action for damages must be established separately from those governing actions for annulment or failure to act. It is precisely these factors that underline the importance of action for damages in the overall system of remedies as a form of recourse that can, at least in part, make up for the rather limited rights that private individuals enjoy in respect of the other forms of action.[9]

The conceptual separation of claims involving liability from those founded on illegality does not, however, have the practical consequence of the former having always and necessarily to be asserted in the framework of separate proceedings. In principle, it is possible to put forward a claim for damages in an action brought primarily for annulment or for failure to act, either as a second main submission or as a subsidiary claim. The former case usually occurs where it is apparent that the measures to be taken by the defendant institution to restore the *status quo* as required in the event of a successful action, would not lead to a complete elimination of the damage. In such a situation the admissibility of each of the two claims is usually judged separately according to their own different rules.[10] This is, however, not the case where the question of liability is so closely connected with that of legality that the inadmissibility of the request for annulment must inevitably bring with it the inadmissibility of the claim for damages.[11] Where the claim for damages is submitted only as a subsidiary claim, it may be held admissible in spite of the inadmissibility of the main request for annulment or for failure to act, provided it is not founded on an alleged illegality of the defendant institution's act or omission and thus is independent of the main application.[12]

It is nevertheless clear that the principle of the independence of legal remedies cannot extend so far as to allow an action for damages to be used parallel to, or in substitution for, an action for annulment (or failure to act) for a purpose for which the latter is the proper remedy. Not only would this be contrary to general principles governing the mutual relationships between the various actions,[13] but would definitely upset the balance of the system of remedies by enabling parties circuitously to pursue an objective which may not be attainable by them at all or attainable only under entirely different conditions (*Erschleichung des Rechtsweges*). Thus an action can properly be instituted as one for damages (and can thus benefit from the less stringent conditions governing admissibility of such actions) only if it is clearly distinguishable from an action for annulment by reason of its aim, grounds and effects. Where the real aim is not to obtain compensation for a damage actually suffered but to attain a financial advantage by the cancellation of a measure denying it (which measure has become definitive through its not having been challenged within the proper time-limits); where moreover the ground of the claim is not the existence of a breach of official duty, but the illegality of the measure; and where finally the effects of the action would not go beyond what would normally follow from a successful action for annulment, it is not in reality an action for damages but one for annulment. Its admissibility will be governed by the rules relating to the latter, especially as regards time-limits. In other words, it is not possible to remove, out of time, by means of an action for damages the adverse financial consequences of a measure which could have been, but was not, challenged in time by an action for annulment. The failure of the person adversely affected to use the proper legal remedy to avoid the damage will exclude his right to demand compensation. The same principles apply, *mutatis mutandis*, to the relationship between action for damages and action for failure to act.[14]

Nor can, moreover, an action for damages be used as a vehicle for bringing before the European Court disputes arising between individuals and national authorities in connection with alleged damages caused by the latter in the course of the domestic implementation of Community provisions.[15] Where such disputes raise the question of the invalidity of the Community provisions so implemented, this question may properly be brought before the European Court only in the framework of a reference for a preliminary ruling under Article 177 E.E.C./Article 150 Euratom. Thus, where the damage consists solely of the undue payment to the national authorities of certain sums (import or export levies and charges, compensatory amounts, countervailing duties, etc.) alleged to have been improperly levied by the latter in application of a Community provision, a claim directed exclusively at the reimbursement of such sums will involve a dispute which is purely internal to the relationship between the applicant and the national authority and not one which can in principle engage the non-contractual liability of the Communities. An action for the repayment of such sums (including any interest claimed) must therefore be brought in the competent national courts (which must settle the dispute by applying Community law as to substance and national law as to competence, procedure and form) and directed exclusively against the authority which imposed them, and not, in the disguise of an action for damages, in the European Court against the Community institutions.

This is so even though the imposition of the payment is based on a specific Community provision, and without regard to the question whether the improper nature of the imposition was due to the irregularity of the underlying Community measure or only to the erroneous application by the national authority of an otherwise valid Community rule. In the former case, however, i.e. where a charge was wrongly imposed because the Community provision itself was illegal or invalid (which the national court can ascertain by means of a reference to the European Court for a preliminary ruling), the Community may have to bear subsidiary liability for any damage that cannot be recovered from the national authorities in the national proceedings. In such a case an action for damages will lie before the European Court provided that the applicant has previously exhausted all available domestic administrative and judicial remedies in order to obtain reimbursement of the payment wrongly made and provided that the other material conditions for the Communities' non-contractual liability are also met.[16] In such a case, moreover, the Community will be liable for any consequential damage that the person concerned may have suffered over and above the undue payment of the charge, such as indemnification which he had to pay in respect of cancelled transactions, unexpected financial outlays, losses on outstanding contracts, loss of profit, harm caused to him by adverse competitive conditions created by the imposition of the charge, etc.

Where, in other words, the damage suffered does not exclusively consist of irregular payment of sums to national authorities, but includes additional losses caused by other factors directly or indirectly imputable to the institutions so that the reimbursement of the sums improperly collected cannot amount to full compensation, two different courses of action must be pursued by the applicant. One is action before the competent national courts for reimbursement according to national law, the other is action before the European Court for damages according to Community law. Although the two proceedings are in principle independent of one another as having entirely different subject-matters and being founded on entirely different legal grounds, the former must always precede the latter in situations where the question of Community liability is inseparably linked to that of the legality of the national implementing measure which only the national court is competent to establish.[17] The position will not in principle be different where the basic claim is directed not at the repayment of sums incorrectly paid but, on the contrary, at the payment of sums (e.g. export refunds, carry-over payments, etc.) due to the applicant from the Member State under Community law which the Member State has refused to pay.[18]

By contrast, a direct action for damages in the European Court is always admissible where the prior exhaustion of the national remedies could not, in the individual circumstances of the case, lead to the compensation sought. This is the case where the damage complained of was caused not by a positive

Community measure but by an omission (e.g. an omission to provide for the payment of a certain kind of sum) which the national authorities, including the courts, could not cure for lack of the requisite powers. In such circumstances there will be no intervening national act between the source of the damage (the Community conduct) and the person suffering it, in respect of which the national courts could provide a remedy.[19] Also, the European Court is necessarily the proper forum in situations where the validity of the national implementing measure causing the damage becomes challengeable only in the light of the retroactive effect of a later Community provision so that the applicant could not, at the appropriate time, have brought the matter before the competent national courts.[20]

Although the foregoing distinction drawn between national remedies and action for damages may put private claimants in a disadvantageous position by depriving them in certain cases of a direct access to the European Court (and thereby of a direct indemnification from the Communities), it is made logically necessary by a number of different considerations. In the first place, positive Community law requires that the payments in question be collected by the national authorities on behalf of the Communities in accordance with the substantive provisions of Community law but subject to the procedural and formal provisions of national law.[21] Consequently, disputes arising in connection with the collection (which is thus an act of domestic law) are a matter solely for the national courts to settle under national law. Moreover, dealing with such disputes would inevitably involve the European Court in reviewing the legality of the measures actually causing the alleged damage, that is, national measures taken in implementation of Community law. Although, as seen above, the European Court is competent to review, in the framework of actions for damages, the legality and validity of the provisions causing the injury, it may do so only insofar as the provisions are those of Community law. Reviewing national measures is a matter within the sole jurisdiction of national courts making use where necessary (i.e. where it is alleged that the invalidity of the measure in question is due to the illegality of the underlying Community provisions) of the preliminary ruling procedure under Article 177 E.E.C./Article 150 Euratom. Reference of the parties to the national courts in such cases, far from being a circuitous procedure, is a necessary consequence of the separation of powers between the Communities and national authorities and is only a logical extension of the rule which excludes direct actions for annulment in the European Court against national implementing measures.[22]

It is, moreover, difficult to see how the Communities' liability could arise towards individuals in a situation where there is no direct link between the illegal (which does not in itself mean wrongful) conduct of the institutions and the person suffering the injury. Such conduct may have consequences in the legal relationship between the Communities and the Member State (e.g. the Communities may have to pay back to the Member State the amount that the State has improperly collected and paid into the Community funds) but cannot affect the relationship which the improper collection has created between the nation authority and the individual. Finally, in the light of what has been said above as to the relationship between action for annulment and action for damages, it is even arguable that a claim directed solely at the recovery of sums wrongly paid as a result of an illegal measure is, by reason of its aim, ground and effect, not in reality an action for damages but one for the annulment of the measure and must, therefore, be governed, as regards both substance and jurisdiction, by the rules relating to the latter.

In practice, action for damages has been resorted to on much fewer occasions and with much less success than action for annulment. Under the E.C.S.C. Treaty, of the twenty decided cases[23] (all brought by private parties) only one was successful (in part),[24] two were dismissed as inadmissible, the rest as unfounded. Under the E.E.C. Treaty, of the twenty-one decided cases[25] (all brought by private parties) only in three did the Court of Justice recognise, in principle, the liability of the Community, but in two of those cases no final ruling on damages has ever been given,[26] while the third case was subsequently dismissed as the applicant could not prove any loss.[27] Of the remaining eighteen cases, four were dismissed as inadmissible, twelve as unfounded and two as partly inadmissible and partly unfounded.

702. Jurisdiction

Whilst actions for annulment and failure to act always fall within the exclusive competence of the European Court of Justice, action for damages based on the Communities' non-contractual liability may pose certain jurisdictional problems. These problems arise from the fact that the Treaties confer jurisdiction in such actions upon the European Court by reference to, and within the framework of, the substantive provisions governing non-contractual liability,[1] without however exactly defining the limits of that liability. As will be seen in a subsequent Section,[2] the E.C.S.C. Treaty (which is more specific on this point) establishes the liability of the Community for any injury caused 'in carrying out this Treaty' either by a wrongful act or omission on the part of the Community acting 'in the performance of its functions' (*faute de service*) or by a personal wrong committed by a Community servant 'in the performance of his duties' (*faute personnelle*).[3] The E.E.C. and Euratom Treaties establish the Communities' liability for any damage caused by their institutions or by their servants 'in the performance of their duties'.[4] In respect of non-contractual liability thus defined, the Treaties subject the Communities to the exclusive application of the substantive rules of Community law and ensure the uniform implementation of these rules and the independence of the institutions by giving the Court of Justice exclusive jurisdiction.[5]

However, as regards non-contractual liability for damage caused by the Community institutions or servants outside the 'application of the Treaties' and outside the 'performance of their duties' the Treaties are silent, from which it follows that such liability is governed not by Community law but, in accordance with the rules of private international law, by the law of the place where the event giving rise to liability occurs (*lex loci delicti*). Consequently, any action involving non-contractual liability in this wider sense must be brought not before the European Court but before the competent national courts. It must be directed, where the wrongful act causing the injury is imputable to an institution, against the relevant Community which alone has legal personality and, where it is imputable to a Community servant, against him personally as he alone will be liable.[6] Whilst the Communities do not in such proceedings enjoy immunity in the national courts,[7] the problem of the immunity of the Community officials and servants may arise insofar as the act in question was 'performed by them in their official capacity'.[8] The question whether this is the case, as well as the quite different question whether the act was not committed 'in the performance of duties' (and, accordingly, whether the proceedings should not have been instituted before the European Court), may in doubtful cases be clarified by a reference for a preliminary ruling under Article 177 E.E.C./Article 150 Euratom. While these two concepts overlap in the majority of cases, they are not entirely identical. Thus the circumstance that an act was (or was not, as the case may be) performed by a servant in his 'official capacity', and that a decision was taken to that effect by the competent institution with regard to the waiver of his immunity, does not prejudge the answer to the question whether the same act was committed 'in the performance of duties', which is governed not by the rules on immunity but by the entirely different rules on non-contractual liability. If it was so committed, the personal liability of the servant is absorbed by that of the Community even where he was not acting in his 'official capacity'.[9]

It follows from this arrangement that Community and national jurisdictions are carefully separated as regards both the substantive law applicable and the forum in which proceedings may be instituted, with the exact dividing line between the two being determined by the scope which is to be given to the concept of 'act committed in the performance of duties'. This decisive criterion is further considered in a later Section.[10] Since it is inconceivable that an act giving rise to liability could fall, at one and the same time, both within and outside the performance of duties, the possibility of joint liability on the part of the Communities and their servants, and the concurrent jurisdiction of the European Court and national courts, is excluded in this respect.

The position is, however, different where the injury arises in the course of the national implementation of Community measures, that is, where it is connected with an activity of the organs or officials of the Member States carried out in the performance of Community tasks. As seen in other contexts,[11] in such cases the national authorities do not, strictly speaking, act as direct 'agents' for the Communities, but rather as the internal organs of the Member States designated by the latter for the purpose of performing an obligation falling upon them from their membership of the Communities. In executing substantive provisions of Community law, the national bodies usually remain subject to the domestic rules as to competence, procedure and form and thus their implementing acts must necessarily appear as manifestations of the sovereign powers of both the Communities and the Member States. In such circumstances the question of liability is determined according to whether the wrongful act or omission that is the cause of the injury is imputable (a) to the Community institutions; (b) to the national organs; or (c) to both of them jointly.

In the first case, the liability is in principle the Communities', although for reasons explained in the previous Section[12] it may have to assume a subsidiary character in relation to that of the Member States and may, depending on the circumstances in which it is invoked, be enforceable in the European Court only after the exhaustion of all available national administrative and judicial remedies.

In the second and third cases, in the absence of any relevant provisions in the Treaties the liability of the national authorities and officials cannot be assimilated to that of the Community servants and, consequently, it cannot be attributed to the Communities (even though they have performed a Community duty) except, perhaps, to the extent that they have acted under a direct and specific authorisation or under a delegation of Community powers.[13] This is the more so as the European Court, which would alone be competent to deal with the matter, has no power in actions for damages to judge the conduct of the national authorities by the criteria laid down by Community law on non-contractual liability, which would alone be applicable. It follows that where the damage arises from a wrongful act or omission that is imputable solely to the national authorities, it is for the Member State to bear full responsibility in regard to the injured party in the framework of national proceedings and according to the provisions of the national law on State liability. This is so *a fortiori* where the act giving rise to the damage is taken outside the implementation of Community provisions and constitutes a clear violation thereof.[14] It is an altogether different matter that the Communities may be held liable for an illegal failure of the Commission to exercise the supervisory powers conferred upon it by the Treaties to ensure fulfilment by the Member States of their Community obligations, if it can be proved that such a failure is the direct cause of the damage.[15]

Where, finally, the injury is caused by a conduct that is illegal and wrongful under both Community law and national law (i.e. the damage is contributed to by both the Community and national organs), it will create joint liability in the Communities and the Member State and the matter will fall within the concurrent jurisdiction of the European Court and the national courts. Since, however, the European Court can only entertain actions of this kind against the Communities and apply Community law, while the national courts can only deal with actions brought against the national authorities and apply domestic law, there is at present no forum in which, and no legal system under which, proceedings could be instituted against both debtors jointly. Separate actions may have the disadvantage either of inadequate or excessive damages being awarded by the two different courts applying different rules or of the injured party being driven from pillar to post without being able to find satisfaction in either forum.[16] Whether, in the event of full compensation being awarded by one of the forums against one of the debtors, there is a legal means for it to obtain re-imbursement from the other, is doubtful.

Finally, the position is, again, different where the injury arises from the conduct of neither the Community institutions and servants, nor the national organs and officials, but from that of a body or agency set up by the institutions in the form of a company under the private law of a Member State with delegated powers to carry out certain Community tasks (e.g. to administer the scrap equalisation scheme). The liability of such an agency for damages arising from its strictly commercial activity is governed by national law and falls within the jurisdiction of the competent national courts. When however the injury is caused by an activity performed by the agency in its capacity as a public authority and in connection with its public duties, it will directly give rise to the liability of the Communities and the matter will be subject to the jurisdiction of the European Court.[17]

703. Parties

Under all three Treaties, the Communities alone are liable, each within its own field of competence, to make good any damage caused by their institutions or by their servants in the performance of their duties.[1] Action for damages within the framework of non-contractual liability must, therefore, always be brought before the European Court of Justice and against the relevant Community. As the personal liability of Community servants towards third parties is absorbed by the liability of the Communities, it is neither necessary nor possible to institute proceedings against the servants themselves (in addition to, or in substitution for, action brought against the Communities), either in the European Court or in the national courts, for the recovery of damages caused by them in the performance of their duties.[2] The personal liability of the servants towards the Communities is governed by the Staff Regulations and the Conditions of Employment and is subject to the jurisdiction of the European Court.[3]

While the liability is the Communities' (since they alone possess legal personality and financial resources), the question arises which institution should represent them in actual proceedings before the Court of Justice. In the case of the Coal and Steel Community, this question gives rise to no problem as that Community is always represented by its institutions 'each within the limits of its powers'.[4] Since under the E.C.S.C. Treaty only the Commission has powers the exercise of which is capable of causing damage to third parties (i.e. to persons other than Community officials), in actions brought by such parties the Coal and Steel Community is always represented by the Commission alone. This is so even though the responsibility for the adoption of a particular act may be divided between the Commission and the Council, as when the Commission has acted subject to the Council's consent and conditions imposed by it.[5]

By contrast, in their 'external' relations with the Member States and third parties, including proceedings in the national courts, the Economic and Euratom Communities are always represented by the Commission only.[6] However, just as in the case of actions for annulment and failure to act,[7] such a monopoly of representation does not exist before the European Court of Justice. It is in the interests of a good administration of justice that where Community liability is involved by reason of the act or omission of one of the institutions, the Communities should be represented before the Court by the institution or institutions against which the matter giving rise to liability is alleged. Thus, where a matter has its origin both with the Commission and with the Council, the first for having made a proposal and the second for having legislated, proceedings may be instituted against the relevant Community 'as represented by the two institutions' jointly.[8] It follows that the Commission's responsibility for rules which it has not itself laid down can arise only if it has made an appropriate proposal to the Council.[9] In practice, however, applications for damages are usually directed against the relevant institution(s) and not specifically against the Community, but this cannot entail their inadmissibility as not affecting the rights of the defence.[10] Since the European Parliament and the Court of Justice do not seem to be capable of 'causing' damage to third parties (i.e. persons other than their own officials) 'in the performance of their duties', their acts or omissions cannot, in principle, engage the non-contractual liability of any of the three Communities. Those two institutions cannot therefore appear as defendants in actions for damages other than those brought by their own officials.[11]

In defining the circle of persons entitled to institute proceedings under the E.C.S.C. Treaty, a distinction must be made between actions under Article 34 and those under Article 40. Article 34 grants only an indirect right of action for damages which must always be preceded by an action for annulment or for failure to act, as the case may be.[12] The circle of parties to which such a right is granted is strictly limited to undertakings and groups of undertakings in the technical meaning of these terms as specifically defined for the purposes of the E.C.S.C. Treaty.[13] In other words, an action under Article 34 is not even available to all those who are entitled to institute an action for annulment.[14] Such a limitation does not apply to actions brought under Article 40, which may be instituted by any natural or legal person without restriction (including the Member States) who/which have suffered an injury as a result of Community activity. This includes non-Community undertakings and associations as well as private individuals. Such an extension of the right of action is justified both by the text of Article 40 itself, which simply speaks of 'the injured party' without any qualification, and by the independent nature of the action for damages to which the various restrictions relating to action for annulment do not apply. The reason for this is that while the legislative and executive powers of the Commission are, as a result of the limited scope of application of the E.C.S.C. Treaty, necessarily restricted to Community (i.e. coal and steel producing) undertakings (which justifies a corresponding restriction upon the right to bring action for annulment), the exercise of such powers may entail injurious consequences even for natural or legal persons who are not subject to the jurisdiction of the Community. In the absence of a *locus standi* before the European Court, such persons would be left entirely without legal protection as they cannot, by virtue of the European Court's exclusive jurisdiction, recover in the national courts damages caused by the Community in carrying out the Treaty.[15]

The range of persons entitled to bring action under the E.E.C. and Euratom Treaties is likewise unlimited. It includes, as in the case of actions for annulment and failure to act,[16] any natural or legal person (including the Member States) without regard to nationality, residence, place of establishment, registered office, central administration, etc. Article 215(2) E.E.C./Article 188(2) Euratom only contain provisions of substantive law, determining the conditions for a claim for damages, without laying down any procedural requirement as to the admissibility and the manner of implementation of such a claim. These must therefore be elaborated by the Court itself. The same applies to Article 178 E.E.C./Article 151 Euratom, which merely confer jurisdiction upon the Court in respect of such claims.[17] It follows that private parties are not subject to the various restrictions which limit their right of action for annulment. An action for damages is in principle always admissible provided that the following three requirements are met. First, the applicant must possess legal capacity to institute court proceedings in general.[18] Secondly, the matter must be within the jurisdiction of the European Court.[19] Thirdly, the applicant must allege an injury arising from an act or omission of the Communities capable of affecting him adversely.[20] The injury must have been sustained by the applicant himself; it is not enough to maintain that a damage has been caused to another person. Thus, for example, associations (including trade unions) cannot institute action in defence of the personal proprietary interests of their members; they may avail themselves of this remedy only to enforce a collective right to reparation or where they have themselves suffered a damage.[21] On the other hand, the question whether the injury is substantiated by sufficient grounds as regards both its existence and magnitude, relates not to the admissibility but to the merits of the case.[22]

704. General conditions for liability

The Treaties do not determine in precise terms the general conditions for, and the limits of, the Communities' non-contractual liability which forms the legal basis for an action for damages. Article 40 E.C.S.C. simply refers to a 'wrongful act or omission' on the part of the Community committed in the performance of its functions and to a 'personal wrong' committed by a servant of the Community in the performance of his duties.[1] Article 215(2)

E.E.C./Article 188(2) Euratom, on the other hand, do not contain these terms but refer, generally, to the 'non-contractual liability' of the Communities which is to be determined 'in accordance with the general principles common to the laws of the Member States'. It is, therefore, from these concepts that the conditions for, and the limits of, Community liability must be derived.

The term 'non-contractual liability', as it occurs in Article 215(2) E.E.C./Article 188(2) Euratom, means 'administrative liability', i.e. liability for breach of official duty (*Amtshaftung*) and not general (civil law) liability. It refers to the same concept as 'governmental liability' in the Member States, that is, liability of the State for damages caused by illegal and wrongful acts of its organs in the performance of their functions. It follows that, strictly speaking, the term 'non-contractual liability' is not precise: it only covers one class within the very broad concept of 'non-contractual' (i.e. tortious, delictual) liability, namely, that arising in the course of the performance of Community duties and functions. Under the Treaties the Communities are obliged to make good damages only if caused by their institutions or by their servants 'in the performance of their duties', and under the E.C.S.C. Treaty it is further necessary that the damage should have been caused 'in carrying out this Treaty'. Injury caused outside the performance of duties gives rise to the civil law liability of the Communities which falls to be determined by the national courts in accordance with the *lex loci delicti*.[2]

The dividing line between the two areas is, however, not clearly defined. Generally speaking, non-contractual liability within the meaning of the Treaties covers, as regards the conduct of the institutions, first, the damaging consequences of the legal measures whereby the Communities manifest their quasi-sovereign powers; and secondly, damages caused by a malfunctioning of the administration arising from defective departmental organisation or negligent administrative action. In either case, the wrongful act or omission is 'anonymous', that is to say, it cannot be associated with the activities of any specific person. This liability further covers those personal acts of the Community servants which, by virtue of an internal and direct relationship, are the necessary extension of the tasks entrusted to the institutions. On the other hand, non-contractual liability under the Treaties does not seem to cover damages arising in the course of the 'civil' life of the Communities, e.g. in connection with the possession and administration of Community assets (buildings, installations, dangerous materials, etc.) or damages arising from purely physical acts connected with the day-to-day running of the departments. Nor does it cover accidents caused by a servant while he is using his private car for transport during the performance of his duties, except where this has been made necessary by a case of *force majeure* or by other exceptional circumstance of such overriding importance that without the servant's using private means of transport the Community would have been unable to carry out the tasks entrusted to it.[3]

It follows from the foregoing concept of 'non-contractual liability' that the reference to the 'general principles common to the laws of the Member States', by which it must be determined, is a reference to the various national laws (including, since the date of accession, the laws of the three new Member States) concerning administrative (governmental) liability and not to those relating to general (civil law) liability. The reference is made to 'general principles' and not to detailed rules: the Court cannot therefore follow what is called the 'minimum theory' or 'the lowest common denominator', i.e. recognise a right to compensation only to the extent to which the positive law of each Member State provides for it. On the contrary, the Court is left relatively free in the doctrinal assessment of the individual problems and in the establishment of the general conditions for responsibility, provided it remains within a framework common to the laws of the Member States. While the Court cannot derive principles from the laws of only one or a few of the Member States, it may give favourable consideration to what appears in the light of 'evaluative comparative law' to be the most appropriate and most judicious of all comparable solutions, taking into account the particular objectives and nature of Community law.

It is thus clear that by referring to the broad concept of 'common general principles', the Treaties deliberately left it to the European Court to work out, by a combination of comparative and creative activity, the general conditions for the non-contractual liability of the Economic and Euratom Communities. It is equally clear that in so doing the Court is not entering wholly uncharted territory. Using more or less similar methods (without being expressly instructed to do so) it had already built up a considerable body of case-law under Article 40 E.C.S.C. defining the essential features of administrative liability as based on the concept of 'wrongful act or omission'. This earlier case-law may be drawn upon also in the context of the two later Communities since, in spite of differences in detail, the three Communities' tasks and organisation have too much in common not to have the same substantive solutions. Thus, in spite of the different formulation of the Treaty texts, a coherent body of rules is bound ultimately to emerge governing the liability of all three Communities, no matter under which Treaty a particular case or aspect was decided. It is in the light of this emerging body of case-law that the general conditions for non-contractual liability have to be examined.[4]

Broadly speaking, four conditions must be satisfied before the Communities' liability for damages may be established. These are as follows:

(1) there must exist an injury;
(2) there must exist a causal connection between the injury alleged and the conduct with which the institutions are charged;
(3) the conduct of the institutions must be illegal;
(4) the conduct of the institutions must be culpable (wrongful).[5]

It follows both from the texts of the Treaties and from the nature of things that the first and the second conditions must always exist since, clearly, in the absence of an 'injury' which has been 'caused' by the institutions, the question of Community liability and the right to compensation cannot arise.

The position is, however, far less clear regarding the third and the fourth requirements (and their mutual relationship) which represent, respectively, the objective and the subjective aspects of the concept of liability. The case-law of the Court does not seem to have yet unequivocally settled whether the joint presence of illegality and culpability must in every case be regarded as a *sine qua non* condition for the Communities' liability or whether such liability may arise, at least under exceptional circumstances, even in the absence of either or both of these requirements. Nor is it clear whether illegality *ipso facto* entails culpability or only where additional factors are present. In theory, four different variations are possible in this respect, none of which can be regarded as ruled out with final effect yet at the present stage of the development of the law on liability. These are as follows. First, both the objective condition (illegality) and the subjective condition (culpability) of liability must be established in every case independently of one another and according to different criteria. Secondly, illegality in itself may create liability without culpability. Thirdly, culpability in itself may create liability without illegality. Fourthly, the existence of a damage caused by the institutions may in itself establish liability without the proof of either illegality or culpability. Moreover, further problems present themselves in connection with both of these prerequisites. In the context of illegality, the question is whether liability can ever arise from illegal normative acts (the problem of the so-called 'legislative injustice', *normatives Unrecht*) and, if so, under what conditions. In the context of culpability the further question concerns the extent to which the injured person's conduct may exclude or limit the liability of the Communities (the problem of the so-called contributory culpability). All these problems will be examined in turn in the appropriate context.[6]

705. (1) Nature, proof and assessment of damage

Broadly speaking, in order to establish the liability of the Communities, there must exist a damage which is (a) certain and specific; (b) proved; and (c) quantifiable. These three criteria relate to the (a) nature; (b) proof; and (c) assessment of damages, respectively, and are examined in that order below.

(a) *Nature of damage*
Generally, Community law requires that there must exist an actual and certain damage which is both appreciable and definitive. Unless and until such damage can be proved by the applicant, there is no 'injury' to give rise to a compensation even though the existence of a wrongful act or omission on the part of the institutions could be or has been established.[1] In other words, the damage must have been crystallised by the time the claim for compensation is made and must be clearly specified by the applicant. An application which concerns only a potential future loss which it is not possible either to

estimate at once or to regard as certain to ensue will be dismissed as premature.[2] Where, however, the injury is imminent and definable with sufficient certainty, the Court may be asked, in accordance with general principles common to the laws of most Member States, to give a declaratory judgment on the liability of the Communities even if the damage cannot yet be precisely assessed. In certain circumstances it may prove necessary, to prevent even greater harm being done, to bring the matter before the Court as soon as the cause of damage is certain. In such circumstances the applicant may reserve the right later to specify the amount of the damage which the relevant Community would have eventually to make good and restrict himself for the time being to asking for a finding of the Community's liability.[3]

Not only must the damage be certain but it must also be specific, i.e. affecting the applicant's interests in a special and individual way. Thus the normal disadvantages inevitably following from a financial arrangement or scheme set up for the benefit of all Community undertakings operating in a particular sector or for the benefit of the public at large and affecting all commercial operators by virtue of general and objective criteria, cannot constitute an 'injury' giving a right to compensation.[4] Otherwise it would be possible for individual undertakings virtually to cancel the effects of the scheme by claiming as damages the amounts whereby they are disadvantaged by its operation.[5]

(b) *Proof of damage*

Generally, the onus to prove an injury allegedly suffered lies with the injured party. He must provide conclusive evidence as to the existence and exact amount of the damage to enable the Court to make the necessary assessment and award appropriate compensation.[6] Overall statistical figures showing disadvantageous trends in trade, the interpretation of which is doubtful, will not suffice.[7] Nor can the applicant escape the burden of proof by reducing its claim to nominal damages.[8] Since what has to be proved is the actual damage which the applicant has specifically suffered in the sense discussed above, the furnishing of adequate proof may involve considerable difficulties in certain circumstances and the failure or inability of the injured party to do so has, in fact, led to the dismissal of the application in a number of cases.[9] Although the onus is on the applicant, this does not absolve the defendant from the obligation to collaborate with him, by producing relevant documents and information which it alone possesses as a Community institution, with a view to enabling the Court to decide whether the damage is sufficiently proved.[10]

(c) *Assessment and quantum of damages*

Not only must the damage be certain and specific but it must also be quantifiable, i.e. expressed or capable of being expressed in a specified sum of money.[11] This also follows from Article 40 E.C.S.C. which limits the Court's jurisdiction to ordering 'pecuniary reparation' only. Although such an express provision does not occur in Article 215(2) E.E.C./Article 188(2) Euratom, it would seem that under those Treaties, too, the Court will not entertain a claim aimed at the payment of 'any kind of damages' or at 'compensation in other forms' than a defined sum of money, as not being sufficiently specific.[12] Generally, the applicant is expected to quantify the damage in the originating application (if this is at all possible at that stage) and to show, at the same time, at least in broad outline, how his calculation thereof is made up.[13] Although he need not necessarily produce the exact figures on which that calculation is based. That can be done at later stages in the proceedings (e.g. in the reply).[14] Alternatively, the applicant may restrict himself in his original application to requesting the Court to give a declaration on the liability of the Community only, while reserving his right to specify the amount of the damage at a later stage.[15] Also, the applicant may ask the Court to rule in an interlocutory judgment that the Community is obliged to make reparation for the loss allegedly suffered and not to rule on the exact extent of the loss and the amount of the compensation until after receiving an expert's report.[16] The Court uses this technique of an interlocutory judgment in situations where the amount of the compensation cannot be determined at the given stage of the proceedings at all (although the liability of the Community has been established) or where it could not be determined exactly without encroaching upon the legislative discretion of the defendant institution. In such cases the Court will reserve the fixing of the amount of the compensation either by agreement between the parties to be reached within a certain period of time or, in the absence thereof, by itself on the basis of detailed figures submitted by the parties or, if necessary, by experts.[17]

As to the assessment of the damage, this involves the Court in comparing the financial situation as it actually is with what it would have been if the wrongful act or omission had not been committed. This determines both the methods of assessment and the quantum of damages. As regards the methods, the Court, of course, always aims at an exact assessment of the damage based on all the available evidence which, as seen above, must be produced by the injured party. Nevertheless, as the Court is involved in reconstituting a fictitious situation, it may be faced with circumstances in which certain elements of the damage cannot be calculated with a complete guarantee of accuracy. Instead of refusing any reparation at all, the Court is prepared to accept in such cases realistic approximations, such as averages based on comparisons, reached by sampling methods habitually used in economic surveys, provided that the basic facts are sufficiently reliable.[18]

As regards the quantum of damages, the Court determines this so as to represent full compensation for the loss actually sustained, directly or indirectly, as a result of the wrongful act or omission (*damnum emergens*). This includes not only the direct loss brought about by the wrongful conduct (e.g. payment of an import levy imposed without valid legal cause or loss of an export refund or compensatory amount illegally denied) but also any additional expenses necessarily and reasonably incurred as an indirect consequence thereof (e.g. indemnification paid for the cancellation of contracts made necessary by the wrongful conduct)[19] as well as interest from the date of bringing the action.[20] The Court is also prepared in principle to grant compensation for lost profits (*lucrum cessans*), although it seems to be more cautious in quantifying this owing to the essentially speculative nature of commercial transactions. Depending on the individual circumstances of the case, the Court may award only partial reparation for lost profits especially where the applicant has entered into a transaction in spite of being aware of the possibility of its becoming frustrated.[21] There is no compensation for loss of profit where the intended transaction that could have given rise to the profit has not materialised due to the wrongful act or omission.[22] Nor where the claim is based on the principle of the protection of legitimate expectation which principle merely ensures that no loss is suffered by reason of an unexpected change in the legal position but does not under all circumstances guarantee the making of profits.[23] Where the damage is of a non-material nature ('moral injury' such as injured feelings, emotional stress, trouble and difficulties, loss of social prestige, presumably also loss of business reputation, etc.) the Court awards compensation in the form of general damages (*préjudice moral*) quantified by itself on equitable principles as opposed to special damages (*préjudice matériel*) which can only be awarded if there exists a financial loss.[24] Although the Court appears to have so far granted general damages in staff cases only, it is submitted that there is no compelling reason why such damages should not be awarded, in appropriate cases, even outside the employment relationship.

706. (2) Causal connection

The existence of an injury cannot in itself establish the liability of the Communities. It is also necessary that the injury should have been 'caused' by the conduct (act or omission) of the Community institutions or servants. Any damage resulting not from such conduct but directly from the basic Community Treaties themselves or from an instrument which forms an integral part thereof (e.g. the Act of Accession) cannot give rise to non-contractual liability on the part of the Communities.[1] The causal connection between the wrongful act or omission and the damage alleged must be direct, immediate and exclusive. It must be proved by the applicant; in the absence of such proof the action will be dismissed as unfounded.[2]

It is clear, however, that in practice it is not always easy to establish such a causal relationship especially in view of the fact that in the field of economic and commercial activity the cause of an event can be traced back to numerous factors, objective as well as subjective, operating simultaneously or successively and producing direct as well as indirect effects. Using a negative definition, it may be said that there is no causality involving liability where the same result would have occurred in the same way even without the wrongful Community act or omission in question.[3] The converse proposition, i.e. that the requisite causality exists whenever it can be shown that the damage would not have occurred without the Community action, is, however, not always correct. Although it is theoretically true that any circumstance, near or remote, without which an injurious effect would not have been produced can be considered as its cause, the fact that a Community conduct is one of several such circumstances may not in itself be sufficient to establish a causal connection entailing non-contractual liability. For that purpose, a damage will be regarded as 'direct' only if it derives from the culpable conduct of the institutions and does not depend on the intervention of other causes, whether positive or negative. Where, therefore, a contributory cause also can be shown to exist, it must always be examined whether it is not of such a nature as to break the chain of causation between the Community conduct and the damage.[4]

In the context of Community law, such a contributory cause may, in particular, consist in an act or omission of a Member State or of the person suffering the injury himself. As regards the former, generally the fact that the primary cause of the damage is an action or default of a Member State which is contrary to Community law, is sufficient to break the chain of cause and effect.[5] Where, however, such a conduct has been made possible by an illegal failure of the Commission to exercise the supervisory powers conferred upon it by the Treaties to ensure fulfilment by the Member States of their Community obligations, it is this failure that will be regarded as the direct cause of the damage. The liability will therefore be the Communities', provided the applicant can prove that his loss was caused by the illegal national measure.[6] Where the cause of the damage can be traced back equally to an illegal action on the part of the Member State and to one on the part of the Communities (e.g. to a Community act illegally authorising such a national action), the liability will be borne by the Member State and the Community jointly.[7]

As regards the conduct of the party suffering the injury, a possible negligence on his part involving a failure to recognise the possibility of the occurrence of the damage and to take action to avoid it, may operate as a contributory cause thereto and as such may break the chain of causation between the institutions' conduct and its harmful effects. Thus the fact that the damage comes about because of a mistaken belief generated in the applicant by a misleading, incomplete or imprecise information, statement, undertaking etc. made or given by the institutions, in itself capable of establishing their liability, is not necessarily such as to bring about the requisite causality. What is decisive is not whether such a conduct actually caused the wrong impression on the applicant's part but whether it could and should have caused such an error in the mind of a 'prudent and experienced trader'. Where it can be shown that it is the applicant's own lack of foresight and circumspection that is the primary cause of the damage, in other words, where his negligence has contributed to its occurrence, the chain of causality will be broken and the institutions' liability will not be established.[8]

707. (3) Illegality of institutions' conduct

As discussed above,[1] the non-contractual liability of the Communities covers damages caused by their institutions or servants 'in the performance of their duties'. The institutions perform their official duties basically in two different ways. First, by enacting legal measures in the exercise of their quasi-sovereign powers and secondly, by carrying out ordinary official (administrative) activity necessary for the putting into operation, or for the supervision of putting into operation, of those measures. It follows that damages in connection with the performance of official duties may arise basically in two different situations. First, as a direct consequence of the legal measures whereby the Communities manifest their powers and secondly, as a consequence of the malfunctioning of the administration arising from defective departmental organisation or negligent administrative action. Where proceedings are brought in respect of a damage that has arisen in the second way, the claim for compensation will be founded upon the restricted concept of official fault involving negligent or defective administration, bad organisation, lack of supervision etc.,[2] and not on the more fundamental notion of the illegality of the underlying measure in connection with whose execution the injury occurred. In such situations the question of liability can be, and usually is, disengaged from that of legality and is examined by the Court quite separately from and independently of the latter. This is so irrespective of whether the claim for compensation appears as a subsidiary claim in proceedings brought primarily for annulment or failure to act[3] or whether it is presented in the framework of a *sui generis* action for damages.[4] This situation is not considered further in this Section.

The position is more complex where the damage alleged has occurred as a direct result of a binding Community measure or of a failure to take such a measure. In such a case the question of liability is usually dependent upon, and therefore inseparably linked to, that of the legality of the measure or default. However, the mutual relationship of the two questions raises a number of complex procedural and substantive issues. From the point of view of procedure, the main problem is whether these two, quite different questions, which require quite different considerations on the part of the Court of Justice, should be dealt with in the framework of one single action or should be the subject of two distinct proceedings. Basically, three different solutions are conceivable. First, to have the illegality of the act or omission established in an action for annulment or failure to act and, once this has been achieved, to bring separate proceedings for damages. Secondly, to bring two parallel applications simultaneously, or to submit two principal claims in the same application, one for annulment (or for failure to act) and the other for damages. Thirdly, to institute one single proceeding for damages only and to raise, within the framework of that proceeding, the question of illegality together with that of liability.

The idea underlying the first of these solutions has in part been incorporated in Article 34 E.C.S.C. That Article requires the Commission, as part of its obligation to comply with a judgment of the Court declaring an act void, to pay appropriate damages in certain circumstances in respect of harm resulting directly and specially from the act annulled and, should the Commission fail to do so within a reasonable time, enables proceedings for damages to be instituted before the Court. Obviously, this provision represents a *lex specialis* in relation to Article 40 which is the *lex generalis* governing action for damages under the E.C.S.C. Treaty. It has been meant for the particular case where compliance with a judgment of annulment, even taking into account its retroactive effect (*restitutio in integrum*), is not sufficient to eliminate all the harmful consequences caused by the act annulled.[5]

The relationship between Article 34 and Article 40 is, however, not quite clear. What seems to be certain is that in the case of a successful action for annulment damages arising from the act annulled may only be recovered under Article 34.[6] On the other hand, the question whether damages arising from an allegedly illegal positive act which has not yet been annulled can be recovered only through the roundabout way of an action for annulment under Article 33 followed by compensation under Article 34, or whether such illegality can be invoked in support of a direct action for damages under Article 40, has been deliberately left open by the European Court of Justice.[7] So far the Court has only decided that an illegal inaction may be relied upon to support an action brought under Article 40 without previously having been made the subject-matter of an action for failure to act.[8] Should the Court find it impossible to extend the same solution also to cases where the damage is caused by a positive measure, then, it is submitted, in such cases only the following two alternatives remain open.

Either the complete separation of the question of legality from that of liability with the result that in actions brought under Article 40 the Court would never be able to consider claims for damages based upon the illegality of Community acts. Such claims could only be enforced through an action for annulment brought under Article 33 followed, in suitable cases, by compensation under Article 34. Not to mention the disadvantages arising from the circuitousness of such proceedings, this solution would restrict the scope of Article 40 to cases of secondary importance, i.e. to those where the claim for damages is based upon grounds other than illegality, such as the narrower concept of official fault involving defective departmental organisation, negligent administrative action and the like.[9]

As an alternative solution, Article 34 would be the only avenue open in cases where the injured party is capable of obtaining adequate redress through an action for annulment followed by compensation. However, a direct action for damages under Article 40 would be available where this is not the case, for example because the injured party cannot satisfy the conditions for admissibility as laid down by Article 33 (e.g. he/it is not a Community undertaking or association; the act causing the damage is not actionable by private parties; the damage has come to light only after the expiry of the one month time-limit, etc.) and thus cannot make use of

Article 34 at all. In such cases, the legality of a Community measure could be challenged in support of a claim for damages under Article 40. This solution seems to gain support from the fact that by its own provision the application of Article 40 is 'without prejudice to the first paragraph of Article 34' which phrase, in the interpretation of the Court, prevents any possibility of reference to Article 34, and on the contrary relates to cases where Article 34 is not applicable.[10] Since, however, Article 34 lays down stricter conditions for reparation (i.e. 'direct and special harm') than does Article 40, the above solution has the disadvantage of putting non-Community undertakings and associations in a more favourable position than that of Community subjects. As neither of the two alternatives is entirely satisfactory, it would seem that the same considerations of the independent nature of legal remedies and effective protection of individuals[11] which prompted the Court to allow under Article 40 an action for damages founded upon an inaction not previously declared illegal, also militate very strongly in favour of a similar solution in cases where the cause of the damage is a positive measure.

In the E.E.C./Euratom Treaties, there is no provision similar to Article 34 E.C.S.C. Under those Treaties, therefore, there is in principle nothing to prevent the question of the illegality of an act or omission, on which an action for damages is based, from being raised within the framework of such action or, alternatively, in an action for annulment (or for failure to act) brought simultaneously and jointly with it.[12] However, when this happened for the first time under the E.E.C. Treaty, the European Court, while finding the action for damages admissible, dismissed it on merits on the ground that the act which was the alleged cause of injury had not previously been annulled. The Court held that an administrative measure which had not been annulled could not of itself constitute a wrongful act on the part of the Communities inflicting damage upon those whom it affected. The latter could not therefore claim damages by reason of that measure. Since in the case the compensation sought by the applicant was equivalent to the customs duties and turnover tax which he had to pay in consequence of the decision in question, the granting of his request would have meant nullifying the legal effects upon him of the contested decision still in force. This the Court felt unable to achieve in the framework of an action for damages.[13]

The necessary and far-reaching implication of this decision would have been that, in spite of the absence in the E.E.C. Treaty of a provision similar to Article 34 E.C.S.C., under that Treaty, too, compensation for damages arising from an illegal measure would have been made dependent upon the successful prior completion of an action for the annulment of the measure in question. This decision of the Court has, however, been subject to strong criticisms mainly on the grounds that the rule expressed therein does not constitute a general principle common to the laws of the Member States as required by Article 215(2) E.E.C., nor does it follow from the system of the Treaty itself; that when the act causing injury is a general measure (regulation, directive) or a measure addressed to others, private parties may not at all be in a position to bring about its annulment, at most they might be able to obtain a declaration of their invalidity by means of a preliminary ruling[14] or defence of illegality[15] but even that at a considerable difficulty and after a lengthy process and this would make their right to compensation granted by the Treaty almost or entirely illusory; that the rule would shorten the period of five years within which action for damages may be brought;[16] and that it is always possible that an injury will arise or become known only after the period for an action for annulment has expired.[17] Moreover, the rule is illogical since a measure which has not been annulled creates the presumption of its formal validity only but not that of its material legality.[18] It can well be tainted with such illegality as to constitute a wrongful act leading to liability. Seemingly influenced by such criticisms, the Court has subsequently reversed its decision and has by a series of judgments firmly established the independent nature of action for damages.[19]

As a result, the antecedent annulment of the measure causing the damage, or the establishment of its illegality, by means of separate proceedings is not necessary; the issue of illegality may be pleaded by the applicant and must be examined by the Court as an incidental matter in the framework of an action for damages. This is so irrespective of any limitations to which the applicant would be subject, were he to raise the same question in the framework of an action for annulment or for failure to act. Even the fact that a successful claim for damages might bring about the virtual cancellation of the effects of the measure of default in question is of no consequence. Thus the relationship between the question of legality and that of liability, viewed from the procedural aspect, is governed by the general principles, already considered in an earlier Section,[20] which determine the relationship between actions for annulment and for failure to act, on the one hand, and action for damages, on the other.

The mutual relationship of the concepts of illegality and liability raises intricate, and not yet fully clarified, substantive issues as well. These issues may be grouped around the following three questions. First, whether illegality of the institutions' conduct must always be regarded as a condition precedent for Community liability. Secondly, what are the grounds for illegality when the question is raised in the context of liability. Thirdly, whether liability can ever arise for illegal legislative acts (the problem of the so-called 'legislative injustice', *normatives Unrecht*). These three questions are examined separately below.

(a) *Illegality as precondition for liability*

Generally speaking, the non-contractual liability of the Communities requires that the act or omission allegedly causing the injury be illegal.[21] A measure or default which has not been shown to be illegal cannot normally constitute a wrongful act or omission or cause illegal damage to individuals.[22] Consequently, a failure to establish illegality is usually taken as sufficient proof of the absence of any breach of official duty and leads to the dismissal of the action as unfounded, without the Court considering the other conditions for liability.[23] In practice, the European Court almost invariably enters into an investigation of the substantive legality or illegality of the act or omission causing the damage, just as it would do in an action for annulment or for failure to act.[24] Such an examination may nevertheless be rendered in whole or in part superfluous by an intervening decision of the Court given in another case (e.g. in the form of a preliminary ruling) and confirming the validity of the act in question, unless new grounds are raised by the applicant tending to cast doubt on that validity.[25]

While the foregoing explanation of the relationship between illegality and liability is certainly correct as a general proposition, there are signs in the case-law that the European Court might under exceptional circumstances accept (although this has not occurred so far) that Community liability may arise even in the absence of illegality, provided certain conditions are satisfied. Thus, relying upon the doctrine of 'equal apportionment of public charges' as developed by the French *Conseil d'Etat*, certain French undertakings maintained that the Community was liable to pay compensation for the 'abnormal and particular loss' which they had suffered as a result of a regulation, not otherwise illegal, fixing in a discriminatory manner the amount of certain import subsidies.[26] That doctrine, explained in French administrative law by the theory of government liability founded on risk, gives effect to the idea that if the equality of the citizens in respect of the apportionment of public charges is disturbed by the effects of some legislative or administrative measure which in the general interest imposes upon them particularly heavy financial burdens, then that equality must be restored by the granting of a compensatory indemnity even if the measure is not otherwise illegal.[27] The doctrine is, however, only applicable if the following three conditions are satisfied. First, the damage must be particular to one or several persons. Secondly, it must be of abnormal severity, exceeding the burdens placed on every member of society. Thirdly, if the source of the damage is a legislative act, it must also be shown that that act was not made in the interests of public order, particularly in economic matters. The Advocate-General, while admitting that Article 215(2) E.E.C. did not necessarily exclude the application of this doctrine in Community law, suggested that the claim be dismissed as the above-mentioned three criteria were not satisfied in the particular case.[28] The Court, likewise, did not say that Community law in general excluded liability in the absence of illegality but, after an examination of the substance of the argument, concluded that in view of the particular circumstances of the case before it (i.e. the fact that the regulation was adopted to serve the general economic interest), Community liability could not arise.[29] This judgment was in turn interpreted by the Advocate-General in a subsequent case as an implicit acceptance by the Court that the Community might be liable for a valid legislative act.[30] For such an act to involve a legal wrong creating liability on the part of the Community, he added, it was not necessarily a condition precedent that it should be invalid.[31] This interpretation seems to be corroborated by other instances of the Court entering into a material examination of claims for damages submitted in spite of the absence of illegality, instead of their forthright dismissal.[32]

(b) *Grounds for illegality*

The case-law of the European Court is almost entirely silent on the question what are the grounds on which the damaging conduct of the institutions may or must be considered illegal for the purpose of establishing the liability of the Communities. When the question of illegality is raised in the context of an action for annulment, the Treaties specify four grounds on which annulment can be based.[33] It seems, however, unlikely that the same four grounds could be applicable unaltered, in their entirety, when the question of illegality is raised only as an incidental matter for the quite different purpose of proving liability in the framework of a quite different type of action. In such circumstances the four grounds of illegality seem at once too wide and too narrow.[34] Thus an essential formal or procedural defect (e.g. lack of reasoning or consultation) may render an act illegal and subject to annulment but it is conceivable that this illegality would not suffice to establish liability. Quite apart from the special requirements applicable where the measure causing the injury is a legislative act (general decision, regulation), which are further considered below, it is generally required that illegality should involve an infringement of a substantive rule of Community law although this, in itself, may still not be enough. As a rule, every illegal act, every violation of Community law, does not necessarily give rise to Community liability. It is also required that the provision violated should have been designed to protect the rights or interests of those who were injured or at least of the group to which they belonged (i.e. that it is a so-called *Schutznorm*).[35] This principle stems from German and Italian law but is also known, in one form or another, in the other Member States[36] and thus represents a general principle of law mentioned in Article 215(2) E.E.C. It follows that infringement of rules not intended to protect the rights or interests of individuals or groups of individuals but laid down solely in the interests of the Community as a whole, or of the Member States, or in the general public interests, cannot give rise to liability.[37] Nevertheless, the principle cannot be interpreted too strictly. Thus it is not necessary that the rule infringed should have been laid down exclusively for the applicant's benefit. It is sufficient if its purpose is to protect the general interests of a category of producers or traders if these interests also encompass those of the applicant. It is therefore not required that the provision infringed should be of 'direct and individual concern' to the injured party in the strict technical sense of an action for annulment.[38]

(c) *Liability for illegal normative acts*

The question of Community liability presents special problems where it is a legislative (normative) act, such as an E.C.S.C. general decision and an E.E.C./Euratom regulation, or a failure to adopt such an act, that is alleged to be the cause of the injury (the problem of the so-called 'legislative injustice', *normatives Unrecht*).

The E.E.C./Euratom Treaties are silent on the question whether charges of official liability can be based on normative measures (although they do not expressly prevent this either) especially by individuals who are not normally entitled to challenge the legality of such measures or omissions in the framework of actions for annulment or failure to act.[39] Thus the question has to be determined in the light of the general principles common to the laws of the Member States. While in some of the original Member States (e.g. France, Belgium, Luxembourg and the Netherlands) true statutory law is not in principle subject to judicial control, most of those States recognise the principle that claims for damages can be based on 'normative acts' in the broader sense of the term which includes regulations of the Executive.[40] In some States, however, (e.g. in France) an action for damages can only be founded on legislative measures (*actes-règles*) which create a general and impersonal legal position if certain strict conditions are satisfied, i.e. if the damage is abnormal, special and direct. In other words, there must be a special loss affecting individuals only.[41] Although the laws of the three new Member States do not generally recognise the liability of the State for legislative injustice, Danish law does not expressly exclude it either, and in the United Kingdom the arguments against it seem to relate mainly to Acts of Parliament and the sovereignty of Parliament rather than to subordinate legislation enacted by the Executive. Besides, all three legal systems show signs of an enlargement of State liability thus narrowing down the gap which may at present exist between their largely negative attitude and the more progressive solutions of the old Member States.[42] Considering that what is important in ascertaining the law under Article 215(2) E.E.C./Article 188(2) Euratom is not the unanimity of the legal systems of all the Member States, nor a kind of majority finding, but rather the selection of a solution which appears to be the most judicious and 'progressive' of all comparable solutions,[43] the adoption of the principle of liability for legislative injustice as an essential part of Community law seems justified.

This is even more so if account is taken of the special structure of the Community legal system. The fact that the European Parliament plays only a relatively small part in the legislative process renders it paricularly necessary to strengthen the legal protection of individuals through the Court of Justice. Thus the recognition in principle of the liability of the Communities for normative acts may in part make up for the rather limited nature of the control available to individuals over the legality of such acts. This is also in accordance with the general principle of Community law that provisions creating judicial remedies should not be narrowly construed. Finally, it follows from Article 34 E.C.S.C. that, at least under that Treaty, damages may be payable even where general decisions (i.e. normative acts) are annulled.[44]

While the foregoing considerations amply justify the recognition of Community liability for legislative injustice, it is at the same time necessary to limit that liability one way or another especially where it is invoked by individuals. The reason for this becomes apparent from a consideration of the relationship between action for damages and actions for annulment and for failure to act. An unlimited right to challenge normative acts or omissions in the context of the former might make it possible for individuals to obtain, for all practical purposes, precisely the same relief which they are deliberately precluded from obtaining by means of the latter. This would clearly open the way to circumventing the rigid limitations which the Treaties have imposed upon individuals in respect of the control of the institutions' law-making activity.[45] Moreover, where a legislative measure incorporates a decision on economic policy, which is very often the case especially in the context of the Economic Community, the Council and the Commission possess a great degree of discretionary power in the evaluation of the underlying economic factors and conditions, which power is subject to judicial control only to a limited extent.[46] It would contradict the logic of this system, and would impede the institutions' necessary freedom of action in taking economic policy decisions, if individuals were to enjoy an unqualified right to have such decisions reviewed under the disguise of seeking compensation for losses resulting from them.

It has therefore become necessary, as a logical counterpart to the lifting of all procedural restrictions upon private individuals' right to contest the legality of legislative acts or omissions in the context of action for damages, to limit the grounds on which they may do so. Thus a distinction has become inevitable between the concept of the illegality of a normative act or inaction and its capacity to create non-contractual liability on the part of its author. As a result, not every illegality, not every flaw in a provision of general application, is capable of giving rise to liability even if it might give rise to annulment or a declaration of invalidity in a different context. Where the act or omission is of a legislative nature and involves measures in the field of economic policy, the Communities are not liable for any damage suffered by individuals as a consequence of that act or omission unless it can be shown that a sufficiently flagrant violation of a superior rule of law designed to protect individuals has occurred.[47] While this condition must be applied strictly (and it is precisely because of its strict application that almost all the claims arising from legislative measures have so far been dismissed as unfounded), it cannot be interpreted extensively. It requires no more, no less, than what it says: a particularly flagrant infringement of a protective norm of superior law. Once this has been shown to exist, the liability of the Communities will arise quite irrespective of the regulative content of the provision in question (i.e. whether it applies to a particular group of individuals only or whether it has a high degree of general applicability) and of the nature of its injurious effects upon the applicant. It is therefore not necessary that the damage caused should be direct and special in other than the usual sense, or that it should be of such gravity as to threaten the existence of the applicant, nor that a higher than normal degree of culpability should exist on the part of the institutions.[48]

So far the Court of Justice has recognised only a few rules and principles which qualify as 'superior rules of law designed to protect individuals' and whose violation by the institutions is capable of establishing the liability of the Communities. First and foremost of these is the rule prohibiting discrimination (or requiring equality of treatment) as laid down in Article 7 E.E.C. with general validity for the whole Treaty and in Article 40(3) E.E.C. for the purposes of the common agricultural policy.[49] The latter requires, in particular, that the common organisation of the agricultural markets shall exclude any discrimination between producers or consumers within the Community and that any common price policy shall be based on common criteria and uniform methods of calculation. Since, however, a 'sufficiently flagrant violation' of these principles is necessary, the applicant can succeed only insofar as he can prove the existence of an obvious, serious and material discrimination committed against him.[50] So far all the claims submitted on this ground have been dismissed in the absence of such proof.[51] A second principle constituting a 'superior rule of law for the protection of individuals' is that of proportionality which can be derived from that provision in Article 40(3) E.E.C. which stipulates that the common organisation of agricultural markets may include all measures 'required to attain the objectives' set out in Article 39 E.E.C.[52]

Finally, a third principle recognised as a superior legal norm is that of protection of legitimate expectation or confidence.[53] Generally, a violation of this principle can only give rise to liability on the part of the Communities if the objective of the legal rule whose abrupt change has caused the damage has been to protect the individual interests of business operators. This is not the case, for example, where a system of compensatory amounts has been introduced in a particular agricultural sector for the purpose of warding off difficulties which monetary instability arising from the fluctuation of exchange rates might create for the common organisations of the markets in general. Such a system does not take into account the individual situations of traders and does not aim to guarantee to them a continuous protection. Where, however, the effect of the application of the system in practice is such as to induce even a 'prudent' commercial operator to omit to cover himself against the risks in question (i.e. alteration of exchange rates), such an operator may legitimately expect that for transactions irrevocably undertaken by him no unforeseeable alteration will occur which could cause him inevitable loss by re-exposing him to the risk. The Community will, therefore, be liable if, in the absence of an overriding matter of public interest, the institutions abolish with immediate effect and without warning the application of the system of compensatory amounts without adopting transitional measures which would at least permit traders either to avoid the loss resulting from the abolition of the system or to be compensated for it.[54]

In contrast to the principles mentioned above, it may be stated generally that a legal provision will not qualify as a 'superior rule of law designed to protect individuals' if it can be shown to have been adopted by its author as a matter of common concern, i.e. in the public interest, and not in the private interests of any particular group of business operators.[55]

708. (4) Culpability of institutions' conduct

Generally, the system of Community liability created by the Treaties is based on the concept of subjective and not of objective liability. This means that in addition to the objective illegality of the injurious act or omission, the subjective criterion of culpability on the part of the institutions in committing it must also be shown to exist, i.e. the illegal act or omission must constitute an official fault, a wrongful conduct (misconduct) on the part of its author. It is precisely the factor of culpability that endows the illegal act or omission with an element of fault. Were it otherwise, the circumstances in which liability can be invoked and those in which illegality may be alleged would become indistinguishable. As a result, an action for damages could be brought on exactly the same grounds as an action for annulment or for failure to act despite their very different legal consequences and despite the very different limitations imposed on the right of private parties to institute such actions.[1]

That culpability is an essential element of Community liability follows also from the very text of Article 40 E.C.S.C. which expressly refers to a 'wrongful act or omission' (*faute de service*) on the part of the Community and to a 'personal wrong' (*faute personnelle*) on the part of a servant of the Community. In fact, all the decisions of the European Court rendered under Article 40 E.C.S.C. are centred around the concept of 'wrongful act or omission', a concept borrowed originally from national law (mainly French administrative law) but re-interpreted and re-defined by the European Court for the particular purposes of Community law.

By contrast, Article 215(2) E.E.C./Article 188(2) Euratom do not contain reference to this concept, nor to any other concept of official fault. It may be due to this fact that the decisions of the Court rendered under those provisions have so far paid much less attention to the criterion of culpability than to that of illegality.[2] This may, however, equally be explained by the fact that the Court usually begins its investigations with the requirement of illegality whose presence or absence is, owing to its objective character, generally easier to prove. In most cases the absence of this condition has made it unnecessary for the Court to examine the question of fault.[3] Although, as a result, the Court has not had opportunity so far to elaborate the various aspects of the concept of culpability in sufficient detail for the purposes of the E.E.C./Euratom Treaties, this cannot be taken as an indication of an intention on its part to apply different standards for determining Community liability under these Treaties from those applied under the E.C.S.C. Treaty. In fact, in all the cases brought under the two later Treaties where the question of culpability did arise, the Court and its various Advocates-General either expressly referred to the concept of a wrongful act or omission (*faute de service*) in the sense of Article 40 E.C.S.C., or took it as self-evident that an official fault was necessary to establish liability. This also follows from the 'general principles common to the laws of the Member States' which the Court is directed to apply. It thus appears that there is no fundamental difference on this point between the E.E.C./Euratom and

E.C.S.C. Treaties. Consequently, the case-law of the Court developed on the question of fault under the latter can, with due regard being paid to the different structure of the three Communities and to the different nature of the institutions' powers under the three Treaties, generally be relied upon also in the context of the former.[4]

While it follows from the foregoing that fault is an essential element of liability, it is less clear what degree of fault is required. The laws of the Member States on non-contractual liability distinguish two different types of culpable conduct: an illegal act or omission may be committed either intentionally or negligently. Negligence may further consist either of an ordinary degree of carelessness or of a higher, graduated degree of delinquency variously called 'gross negligence' or 'grave fault' (*grobe Fahrlässigkeit, faute lourde*). Community law generally adheres to this classification, although in the context of the institutions' activities an intentional infringement of the law, an intentional commission of a wrongful act or omission is hardly conceivable. The question therefore usually is whether, in order to establish liability, an ordinary or a higher degree of negligence must be proved.

It has been suggested that, according to the criteria of national (in the first place French) case-law as applied to the responsibility of an administrative authority the role of which is limited to supervising the activities of other bodies, whenever the Commission is performing its supervisory function over the Member States or other agencies carrying out Community tasks, its liability can be engaged only if 'gross negligence' can be ascribed to it. This would require proof that the Commission has seriously neglected the supervisory duties incumbent on it according to the normal standards of diligence; that its conduct constitutes a grave and clear infringement of legal rules and involves serious financial consequences for those concerned. This requirement of graduated fault and the corresponding diminished responsibility on the part of a supervisory organ, as opposed to the requirement of ordinary fault and the corresponding greater responsibility on the part of an administrative (executive) organ, has been explained by the autonomy of the body under supervision which, as a legal person in public or private law, carries full liability towards third parties for the consequences of its actions. On the other hand, an administrative (executive) authority itself has to assume direct and full responsibility for its own activities which excludes the concept of a gross negligence. Moreover, supervision is usually exercised over a general course of conduct but not over each individual act so that certain actions of the body under supervision can temporarily escape the attention of the supervising authority.[5]

While the European Court itself has occasionally referred to 'gross negligence' on the part of the Commission in carrying out its duties of supervision,[6] it has definitely rejected the argument as unmeritorious that supervisory authorities are liable only if there is gross fault on their part. Thus, for example, where the Commission is required under Community law to confirm, amend or reject, as the case may be, every safeguard measure taken and notified to it by a Member State, it is, regardless of whether this power is classified as 'supervisory' or 'executive', under the same obligation of care as the Member State and is independently responsible for its decision.[7]

Whilst the proof of an ordinary degree of negligence on the part of the institutions thus would seem always to be sufficient to engage the liability of the Communities, it is difficult to define in general terms what particular conduct is to be regarded as 'negligent' or 'wrongful'. This, broadly speaking, depends on the nature of the activity giving rise to the damage, i.e. whether it is of the legislative, executive or supervisory type. In other words, the question of negligence requires somewhat different considerations according to whether the damage can be related more particularly to the enactment, application and interpretation, or the supervision of the execution of Community measures.

A culpable conduct may consist, in the first place, in the enactment of an improper Community measure. An examination of the question of negligence in this context may, however, give rise to some difficulty in the case of legislative measures intended to apply for a longer period of time and in respect of a large number of affected persons. Such measures, especially those involving discretionary economic policy decisions and structural changes, require complex economic analyses and difficult forecasts. Clearly, the responsibility of the institutions for the financial consequences of such measures is more of a political than of a legal nature since they usually involve the exercise of a discretionary power.[8] Nevertheless, legal liability may also arise if it can be shown that the institutions have been negligent in their enactment, i.e. if, by taking the appropriate care, they could have recognised and avoided the harmful effects. Negligence may consist, in particular, in a grave misjudgment of market relations, inexcusable forecasting errors, etc.[9] Conversely, there is no culpable negligence where, in the light of the relevant circumstances, the institutions could not have foreseen that unusual and special factors (e.g. unexpected trends in prices and market conditions) might occur which might retrospectively militate against the adoption of what otherwise appeared to be a satisfactory measure.[10] As regards the more formal aspects of enactment, the obscurity or the bad drafting of a measure cannot suffice in itself to constitute a wrongful act or omission provided that its author does not, by its conduct, mislead those concerned as to its proper interpretation and application.[11]

The culpability of the institutions may consist, secondly, in the incorrect application of an otherwise lawful provision, i.e. its application in a situation or in a way in which this is not justified because the requisite conditions have not been fulfilled.[12] Thus, for example, an authorisation of safeguard measures whose sole purpose is to prevent 'serious disturbances' likely to jeopardise an essential Community objective, in a situation where only certain 'difficulties' exist, that is, the equation of 'difficulties' with 'serious disturbances', will constitute an official fault entailing liability. In such circumstances the fault does not lie in an incorrect evaluation of the situation but in an abusive exercise of an otherwise legitimate power owing to a misinterpretation of the conditions laid down for its application.[13] It follows that there is no fault if the use of a power, or an abstention from its use, is legally justified. In other words, what needs to be proved in such situations is a clear misuse of powers.[14] It would thus seem that misuse of powers can constitute not only a ground for illegality[15] but, in certain circumstances, also a factor in establishing culpability and may thus serve as a means of controlling the institutions' discretionary powers in the framework of an action for damages. Moreover, as a separate matter, an official fault in connection with the execution of Community provisions may consist in negligent administration, such as defective departmental organisation, careless administrative action, inexcusably long delays, failure to remind Community subjects of their duties with all possible energy, etc.[16]

On the other hand, errors or defects in the interpretation of Community law, unless they are of an exceptionally grave and inexcusable nature, do not *ipso facto* constitute an official fault involving liability. Clearly, such errors can occur as a consequence of the difficult solution of complicated legal problems. Generally, therefore, if an interpretation arrived at after careful examination seems to be juridically tenable, the fact that it is subsequently reversed cannot retroactively be considered as a fault.[17] Even the fact that the institutions themselves request those concerned to obtain information from the competent departments does not necessarily involve the institutions in an obligation to guarantee the correctness of information supplied and does not make them liable for any injury which may be caused by incorrect information. Nevertheless, failure to rectify the wrong information or a long delay in doing so may create a wrongful act (omission) rendering the Communities liable.[18]

The institutions' (in the first place, the Commission's) culpability may, finally, consist in an inadequate supervision of the execution of Community provisions by the Member States or other agencies set up for that purpose. In principle, the failure of the Commission to ensure respect by Member States for their Community obligations by using the procedure laid down for that purpose in Article 88 E.C.S.C. and Article 169 E.E.C./Article 141 Euratom,[19] may constitute a wrongful omission entailing Community liability for damages caused by the illegal national measures provided the other conditions (above all, the causal connection) are also satisfied.[20] Where, however, a specific Community task (e.g. issuing certificates of origin entailing payment of subsidies out of Community funds) is entrusted to a specific national authority (e.g. Ministry of Economic Affairs), the Commission is not normally required to verify the authenticity of every single act taken by national officials in execution of that task. This is for the national authority itself. The Commission is only obliged to proceed with due care and circumspection in the selection of the appropriate authority and procedure. Lack of detailed checking on its part will be considered as a negligent omission entailing the liability of the Communities only if suspicion of an abuse or other similar circumstance justified doubt about the validity of the national measures.[21]

On the other hand, where a Community task is carried out by an agency other than a Member State, set up specifically for that purpose and acting on behalf of the institutions, lack of sufficient supervision over the activities of that agency, as required by a normal standard of care, will constitute an official fault giving rise to liability. This is so especially where the inadequacy of control has serious financial consequences for individuals and where the Commission has been aware of previous difficulties and practices incompatible with Community policy.[22]

Establishment of an official fault on the part of the institutions does not necessarily lead to the (full) liability of the Communities even if the other conditions thereof are satisfied. Such liability may be limited or excluded altogether on account of a culpable (intentional or negligent) conduct of the injured party contributing to the damage (contributory culpability). Such conduct may consist either of a positive action or of an omission to take action to avoid or to lessen the harmful effects of the institutions' behaviour.[23] Community law has so far failed precisely to define the circumstances in which contributory culpability may be established. The case-law of the Court of Justice seems to set the requirement, perhaps on the analogy of the Roman law concept of *bonus paterfamilias*, that every commercial operator subject to Community law should go about his business with the foresight and circumspection that can be expected of a 'prudent and experienced trader'. Where an injury can be attributed to the fact that the person suffering it has shown less than this standard of care, a contributory negligence will exist on his part which will exclude Community liability either by breaking the chain of causality between the injurious conduct and the damage[24] or by preventing the operation of a protective rule or principle of Community law.[25]

Whether failure by the injured party to use all available remedies in order to avoid the damage may amount to contributory negligence, is not clear. It would seem that failure to use non-judicial (i.e. administrative, political) remedies, such as lodging formal or informal administrative complaints or objections with the institutions, making representations, asking parliamentary questions, etc. cannot. Although from the practical point of view it may be desirable that the party claiming compensation should first of all approach the institution responsible, Community law does not make this a condition for the admissibility of an action for damages.[26] On the other hand, the position may be different as regards judicial remedies. Thus, in certain very special circumstances, namely, where there is such a close connection between the claim for damages and the annulment of the measure causing it that assessment of the damage is impossible without the prior decision of the Court in the matter of annulment, a failure to bring an action for annulment in good time may exclude the right to demand compensation later.[27] It is submitted, however, that this rule has the purely procedural purpose of preventing circumvention of the inadmissibility, on account of expiry of time-limit, of an action for annulment by instituting an action for damages. It cannot therefore be taken to imply contributory negligence on the part of the injured person in every case in which he could have brought separate legal action for the annulment of the damaging measure but has failed to do so. Such a requirement would be basically incompatible with the independent nature of the action for damages in the system of legal remedies.[28]

Finally, the question arises whether culpability on the part of the institutions must in every case be regarded as a *sine qua non* condition for the liability of the Communities or whether situations may be conceivable where the illegality of their conduct alone can establish liability, without proof of fault. In some cases the applicants have put forward the latter view mainly in reliance on the German doctrine of State liability for illegal intervention equivalent to expropriation of property.[29] According to this doctrine, which developed from the principle of the protection of basic rights (*Grundrechtsschutz*), the State is responsible for any direct and illegal interference by a governmental agency, even if committed without fault on its part, which amounts to a dispossession, i.e. affects the very substance and existence of a commercial or industrial undertaking. However, an injury less than that, e.g. a loss of shares in the market, loss of profitability, simple change in the conditions of supply, etc., does not suffice to establish a claim for compensation since no undertaking has a claim to the maintenance of a particular governmental protection (e.g. protective customs tariffs). It is, however, questionable whether this principle of liability without culpability may be regarded as part of Community law. It does not seem to be generally accepted in the legal systems of the other Member States, and even those few which do recognise it show appreciable differences as to its meaning and effects. Nor does it accord with the structural peculiarities of the Common Market and with the requirement for its progressive development. For these reasons the Advocates-General have suggested its rejection in Community law[30] although the Court of Justice has so far failed to give a ruling on the matter.[31]

709. Period of limitation

Community law lays down no time-limits for the bringing of actions for damages.[1] Such actions are, however, barred after a period of five years from the occurrence of the event giving rise thereto.[2] This provision relates to the material prescription of a claim for damages and does not purport to lay down a procedural time-limit. Strictly speaking, therefore, the observance of the five-year period is not subject to an *ex officio* control by the Court of Justice; its expiry may be raised by the defendant by way of an objection. It is not quite clear what is to be regarded as the 'occurrence of the event' which gives rise to an action for damages and which thus sets the period of limitation running. This expression could be taken to refer to the wrongful act or omission of the institutions causing the damage or to the damage itself. In some cases there may exist a considerable interval between the 'occurrence' of these 'events' since a damage may not materialise or become apparent until a long time after the date of the act or omission giving rise thereto. It would seem that in the interpretation of the Court of Justice the material factor is not so much the date on which the wrongful act or omission took place as the date on which the damaging effect thereof manifested itself with sufficient clarity to enable an action for damages to be instituted, due regard being paid to the requirements as to the nature, proof and assessment of damages.[3]

The five-year period of limitation is interrupted if proceedings are instituted before the Court or if prior to such proceedings an application is made by the aggrieved party to the relevant institution.[4] Such a preliminary administrative complaint, although desirable from a purely practical point of view, is in no way a condition precedent for the institution of an action before the Court of Justice.[5] It interrupts the period of limitation only if it is followed by an action for damages before the Court within the time-limits prescribed by Articles 33 and 35 E.C.S.C. or Articles 173 and 175 E.E.C./Articles 146 and 148 Euratom,[6] as the case may be. The reference to these provisions has the sole purpose of extending the five-year period of limitation by preventing the time during which the institutions deal with the preliminary complaint from being included therein. In no case can their application have the effect of shortening the five-year period. Accordingly, a failure to institute proceedings within the time-limits so specified has as sole consequence the non-interruption of the limitation period but cannot prevent the bringing of proceedings at any later date within that period.[7]

CHAPTER 8

Action against Sanctions

801. Nature and scope of action

In order to enable the Commission to carry out its task of ensuring compliance with Community law,[1] all three Treaties have, directly or indirectly, conferred upon it the power to impose sanctions upon natural and legal persons (but not on Member States)[2] in respect of specified infringements. As these sanctions may considerably interfere with the operation and finances of the penalised undertakings, it is essential that the latter should have adequate legal protection against them. Sanctions can only be imposed by means of formal 'individual' decisions, so an obvious remedy is to bring proceedings for the annulment of the decision containing the sanction in question. If, however, such proceedings were to be subject in every respect to the general rules relating to action for annulment,[3] the remedy thus provided would be inadequate for two main reasons. First, the applicants could challenge, and the European Court could annul, the decision imposing the sanction on one (or more) of the four grounds of action[4] only. This would exclude any considerations on the part of the Court other than those relating to the strict legality of the measure, such as considerations as to the expediency, the economic, political or moral desirability, the proportionality of the sanction, the assessment of economic facts or circumstances in the light of which it has been imposed, general considerations of equity, etc. Secondly, the applicants as well as the Court would be restricted to the single remedy of annulment, without being able to request and to order any variation (reduction or increase) in the amount of the (pecuniary) sanction. The Court, not being able to substitute its own evaluation and judgment for those of the Commission, could only confirm or annul the decision in question. This would unnecessarily and unreasonably restrict both the rights of the applicants and the powers of the Court of Justice. In order to avoid these limitations, all three Treaties have, directly or indirectly, conferred upon the Court unlimited jurisdiction in actions brought against sanctions.[5] The nature and scope of this jurisdiction is further considered below.[6]

Owing to the unlimited jurisdiction of the Court of Justice, action against sanctions cannot, strictly speaking, be classified as an action for annulment even though it is usually primarily aimed at the annulment of the decision imposing the sanction. At the same time, it cannot properly be regarded as an entirely different and independent, *sui generis* type of recourse either, in the sense in which, for example, action for damages is treated as a *sui generis* type of remedy.[7] The correct position seems to be to regard it as a special case, a sub-category, of the broader concept of action for annulment. It follows that their mutual relationship is determined by considerations similar to those governing the relations between a *lex specialis* and a *lex generalis*. Accordingly, action against sanctions is governed by the general rules relating to action for annulment except to the extent to which it is subject to its own special rules, to be discussed in this Chapter, arising from the Court's unlimited jurisdiction.

The close connection between these two forms of remedy becomes apparent in cases (mainly occurring in the field of the competition law of the Economic Community) in which the challenged decision of the Commission is not confined to the imposition of a sanction but contains additional measures as well. These may consist in a refusal to grant an exemption under Article 85(3) E.E.C., or in an order requiring the applicant to terminate the infringement in respect of which the sanction has been imposed. The latter may require performance of certain acts or, more frequently, abstention from the continuation of certain actions, practices or situations which have been found to be contrary to Community law.[8] In such cases the action may be directed either against the decision as a whole, or against those parts of it only which relate to the imposition of the sanction. In the former case, the proceeding will take on a mixed form. It will be an action for annulment proper, subject to the Court's ordinary (limited) jurisdiction, as regards the additional measure (decision of refusal, order for termination); while it will be an action against sanctions, subject to the Court's unlimited jurisdiction, as regards the sanction itself.[9] In the latter case, i.e. where the applicants limit themselves to contesting the imposition of the sanction only, the action will fall in its entirety within the Court's unlimited jurisdiction.[10]

In practice, action against sanctions has so far proved to be (at least under the E.E.C. Treaty) the most successful form of direct remedy available to individuals before the Court of Justice. Under the E.C.S.C. Treaty, of the seven decided cases[11] in only one has the decision imposing the sanction been annulled,[12] while in another the fine imposed has been reduced.[13] The remaining five cases have been dismissed as unfounded. By contrast, of the seventeen cases decided under the E.E.C. Treaty,[14] eight have been partly or wholly successful. In two of these cases the decisions imposing the fines have been annulled;[15] in five cases the fines have been reduced[16] while in one case some of the fines have been annulled, some reduced.[17] The remaining nine cases have been dismissed as unfounded.

802. Concept and imposition of sanctions

The concept of sanctions provided for by Community law in respect of individuals, as well as the power of the Commission to impose them, varies under the three basic Treaties. Generally speaking, the concept of sanction implies any disadvantage or penalty, whether of a pecuniary nature or not, imposed by reason of non-compliance with a legal obligation in the past, or for the purpose of enforcing compliance therewith and thus preventing a repetition of the infringement in the future. It serves both to punish and to prevent (enforce). Since the Member States have not conferred upon the Communities criminal jurisdiction within the true meaning of the term, the sanctions at the Commission's disposal are strictly of an administrative, and not penal, character. To ensure observance of Community obligations by private individuals and undertakings and to punish their infringements by means of penal sanctions remains within the criminal jurisdiction of the Member States to be exercised in accordance with the requirements of Community law.[1]

Under the E.C.S.C. Treaty, the Court has been given unlimited jurisdiction in actions against pecuniary sanctions only. A pecuniary sanction exists when the penalty as defined above consists of the payment of a sum of money. Thus, there is no pecuniary sanction subject to the Court's unlimited jurisdiction where an undertaking which has fallen into arrears with its payments of sums of money is only obliged to pay the capital sum with legitimate interest.[2] In the system of the E.C.S.C. Treaty, the notion of pecuniary sanction comprises three (and only three) kinds of penalties, i.e. fines, periodic penalty payments and surcharges. The function of fines is usually to punish an infringement which has been committed in the past, while periodic penalty payments serve as a coercive measure to ensure future conduct. Surcharges may be used for both purposes. The Commission has been given direct authorisation by the Treaty to impose upon undertakings falling within its competence specified amounts of fines and/or periodic penalty payments in respect of infringements of provisions relating to the following matters: furnishing of information;[3] investment programmes;[4] production quotas;[5] production programmes;[6] pricing practices;[7] competition;[8] concentration;[9] wages of workers.[10] Exceptionally, it may impose fines and periodic penalty payments even on natural and legal persons including non-Community undertakings.[11] It may finally impose upon undertakings surcharges in respect of delays in the payment of production levies.[12] These sanctions may lawfully be imposed only if there is an infringement of an obligation arising either directly from a provision of the Treaty, or from a decision taken by the Commission in implementation thereof. Failure of the Commission to impose a pecuniary sanction in a situation where it should have done so, cannot in itself lead to the cancellation of the same sanction lawfully imposed in another, comparable situation.[13] In the event of dual proceedings being instituted in respect of the same infringement at national and Community level, the Commission is required, should it decide to defer its own decision until the outcome of the national proceedings, to take account of the decision of the national authorities in determining any penalty that it may itself impose. Any possible cumulation of sanctions may thereby be avoided.[14]

Under the Euratom Treaty, the Commission may directly impose upon persons or undertakings various sanctions of both a financial and non-financial nature in respect of infringements of obligations relating to safeguards.[15] In cases of infringements of other obligations, the Commission has the indirect power of calling upon the Member State having jurisdiction over the offending person or undertaking to cause sanctions to be imposed in accordance with its own national law. Should the State concerned not comply with such a request within the period laid down by the Commission, the latter may bring an action before the Court of Justice to have the infringement of which the person or undertaking is accused established.[16] All the sanctions that may be directly imposed by the Commission are subject to the European Court's unlimited jurisdiction.[17]

In contrast with the two specialist Treaties, the E.E.C. Treaty does not directly authorise the Commission to impose sanctions; nor does it directly confer upon the Court of Justice unlimited jurisdiction in respect of sanctions. Instead, it authorises the Council to lay down the provisions necessary to ensure compliance with the rules and prohibitions contained in the Treaty in the fields of transport[18] and competition,[19] including provisions for appropriate penalties, and at the same time to give the Court of Justice unlimited jurisdiction in regard to such penalties.[20] The Council has so far made use of these powers by means of three Regulations implementing the provisions of the Treaty in the fields of transport[21] and competition,[22] respectively, and applying rules of competition to transport.[23] In the field of transport, Member States are required to lay down, in consultation with the Commission, appropriate penalties in respect of specified infringements.[24] In addition, the Commission is empowered to impose upon carriers and undertakings specified penalties of a pecuniary nature for infringements of obligations relating to the supplying of information[25] and the abolition of discrimination.[26] In the field of competition, including competition in transport, the Commission is authorised to impose on undertakings or associations of undertakings, within specified limits, fines in respect of intentional or negligent infringement of the obligation to supply information and to submit to investigation, and in respect of intentional or negligent infringement of the substantive provisions of competition law or of any obligation imposed pursuant thereto.[27] The Commission may also impose on undertakings or associations of undertakings, within specified limits, periodic penalty payments in order to compel them to supply information, to submit to investigation, to put an end to an infringement of, and to refrain from any act prohibited by, the substantive rules of competition law.[28] In regard to any penalty, fine or periodic penalty payment imposed by the Commission, the Court of Justice is given unlimited jurisdiction.[29]

As under the E.C.S.C. Treaty, in the system of the E.E.C. provisions on competition fines are not in principle in the nature of sanctions for enforcement; their purpose is rather to punish unlawful conduct and to prevent its repetition. Their imposition is therefore restricted neither to cases of repeated infringements which have already been established and declared prohibited by the Commission, nor to infringements continuing into the present. First infringements as well as infringements which had been terminated and thus no longer have any harmful effects are also punishable.[30] Fines and periodic penalty payments are sanctions of a strictly administrative, and not penal, character.[31] They are not directed against individuals (natural persons) but exclusively against the assets of undertakings as bodies corporate.[32]

In fixing their amount, the Commission has, within the limits laid down by Community law, a wide power of discretion and is not obliged, in the case of cumulative infringements, to determine separately the proportion of the fine relating to each of the punishable acts.[33] On the other hand, the Commission must have regard both to the gravity and to the duration of the infringement. The gravity of the infringement is to be assessed by taking into account in particular the nature of the restrictions on competition, the number and size of the undertakings concerned, the respective share of the market controlled by them within the Community and the market situation at the time when the infringement was committed.[34] Where, furthermore, the institution of two separate proceedings in respect of the same infringement at the national and Community level would lead to a cumulation of sanctions, a general equitable requirement, such as that incorporated in the E.C.S.C. Treaty,[35] demands that in fixing the amount of the fine, the Commission should take into account any sanctions already imposed by the authorities of a Member State.[36] In the event of a sanction imposed by the authorities of a non-Member State, this requirement may arise only if the two separate proceedings relate to identical acts. This will not necessarily be the case merely because the acts attracting both sanctions arise out of the same body of agreements. What is decisive is that the offending acts should have the same purpose and the same territorial impact.[37]

The power of the Commission to impose sanctions in E.E.C. competition matters is not in principle restricted to undertakings established within the Community. Its jurisdiction extends also to companies set up and operating in a non-Member State, by reason either of the harmful intra-Community effects of their actions committed outside the Community or of the illegal activities of their intra-Community subsidiaries where these can be attributed to the parent companies themselves.[38] Originally, the power of the Commission to impose sanctions was not subject to any limitation period although, even so, the fundamental requirement of legal certainty[39] prevented the Commission from delaying the exercise of that power indefinitely.[40] Today the matter is governed by Regulation[41] which subjects the authority of the Commission to impose fines or penalties in the fields of transport and competition to a limitation period of three years in the case of infringements of provisions concerning the supplying of information and the carrying out of investigations, and to a limitation period of five years in the case of all other infringements.[42] The power of the Commission to enforce decisions imposing sanctions is subject to a limitation period of five years.[43] The Regulation also provides for the interruption and suspension of these limitation periods in certain circumstances.[44]

803. Administrative procedure

Imposition of sanctions by the Commission must be preceded by a preliminary administrative procedure the broad purpose of which is to ensure the protection of the right of defence by enabling interested parties to make their points of view known as to the charges raised against them. This procedure is governed by detailed rules in E.E.C. competition matters only. The E.C.S.C. Treaty simply provides that before imposing a pecuniary sanction under the Treaty, the Commission must give the party concerned the opportunity to submit its comments.[1] The Commission can fully satisfy this requirement by sending a registered letter to this effect to the administrative centre of that party. The letter takes effect from the time when it is duly received by the addressee.[2] The Commission is not obliged to give any reasons in the subsequent decision imposing the sanction for refusing to accept the observations submitted to it.[3] On the other hand, the penalised party is free to put forward in the course of the proceedings brought against the decision of the Commission before the European Court arguments which it had not presented at the time of the preliminary procedure.[4] The Euratom Treaty merely provides for an 'appropriate legal procedure' to ensure the protection of interests that have been prejudiced by the imposition of sanctions.[5]

In E.E.C. transport matters, the party concerned must be notified in advance of the proposed sanction.[6] Before imposing a penalty in respect of submission of information, the Commission must consult all Member States concerned.[7] Before imposing a penalty on account of prohibited discrimination, the Commission or one of its officials must hear explanations from the person affected or his authorised representative.[8] In E.E.C. competition cases, including competition in transport, before imposing a fine or a periodic penalty payment, the Commission must give the undertakings or associations of undertakings concerned the opportunity of being heard on the matters to which the Commission has taken objection. The Commission may, if it consideres this necessary, also hear other natural or legal persons showing a sufficient interest.[9] In E.E.C. competition cases the administrative procedure which must precede the imposition of sanctions and of which the hearing of the parties forms a part, consists of the following successive steps or stages.[10]

(a) *Institution of proceedings*

Although the Commission usually opens proceedings in respect of infringements of competition rules by means of a formal decision, it is not this decision but the subsequent statement of objections which determines the position of the Commission vis-à-vis the undertakings against which the proceedings have been instituted. In the case of any discrepancy between the initial decision and the statement of objections (which documents may be communicated to the parties concerned either simultaneously or consecutively), the latter will prevail. Thus it is irrelevant that the possibility of imposition of sanctions is mentioned only in the statement of objections for the first time. Moreover, that statement may take account of further infringements which have occurred since the formal opening of the proceedings and which were thus not mentioned in the original decision.[11]

(b) *Statement of objections*

The Commission must inform undertakings in writing of the objections raised against them. The communication must be addressed to each of them or to a joint agent appointed by them. Although in appropriate circumstances the Commission may also inform the parties by giving notice in the Official Journal of the European Communities, a fine or a periodic penalty payment may be imposed only if the objections were notified in the above manner.[12] Notification must take place by registered letter or by delivery by hand against receipt and in accordance with the general requirements of Community law[13] and, where the addressee is resident or has its registered office outside Community territory, of international law and practice.[14] The statement of objections may be signed by the Director-General of Competition if its contents have been approved by the member of the Commission responsible for competition matters in the exercise of the powers delegated to him by the Commission.[15] Where it concerns a large number of undertakings, it may be sent to all of them in identical wording, provided that each undertaking is put in a position to discover which objection refers specifically to it.[16]

The overall importance of the statement of objections, and indeed of the whole administrative procedure, is that it gives effect to the general principle that a person whose interests are perceptibly affected by a decision of a public authority must be given the opportunity to make his point of view known.[17] Consequently, in its final decision the Commission may only impose a sanction in respect of those of the objections raised as to which the party concerned has been afforded such an opportunity.[18] Where this is not the case, the decision is liable to be annulled on the ground of infringement of an essential procedural requirement.[19] To satisfy the above-mentioned requirement, it is sufficient if the statement of objections sets out clearly, albeit concisely, the essential facts upon which the Commission bases its case. It is not, however, necessary that the entire content of the file should be communicated to the party; the latter can consult documents of importance later on in the course of the administrative procedure. Where after the presentation of the statement of objections further investigations become necessary in the course of the proceedings, these will necessitate an amendment of the statement only if the Commission wishes to introduce additional charges founded on new facts or to base its proof of the infringements in issue on substantially different grounds.[20]

When giving notice of objections, the Commission must fix a time-limit within which the parties concerned may inform the Commission in writing of their views concerning the objections raised against them. In their observations they may present all matters relevant to their defence and may attach relevant documents in proof of the facts alleged. They may also propose that the Commission hear persons who may corroborate those facts.[21] Other natural and legal persons showing a sufficient interest must upon application also be afforded the opportunity of making known their views in writing within the time-limit fixed for that purpose.[22] In fixing these time-limits the Commission must have regard both to the time required for preparation of comments and to the urgency of the case. The time-limits must be reasonable; they cannot be less than two weeks and may be extended.[23] While in a complex case the granting of the minimum period of two weeks only may be patently unreasonable,[24] a period of two months may be adequate even where the Commission itself took more than two years to carry out its investigations.[25]

(c) *Hearing of parties*

Persons on whom the Commission proposes to impose a fine or periodic penalty payment must, upon their request submitted in their written comments, be afforded the opportunity of putting forward their arguments orally.[26] For that purpose they must be summoned to attend an oral hearing on a date to be appointed by the Commission.[27] This date may be fixed at a relatively short notice; thus for example a notice of two weeks would not be unreasonably short especially where a long time (e.g. twelve months) has elapsed between the notification of the statement of objections and the hearing, during which time the parties have been able to prepare their defence.[28] The hearing must be conducted by the persons appointed by the Commission for that purpose. Members of the Commission need not be present.[29] Persons summoned to attend the hearing can appear either in person or be represented by legal representatives or by representatives authorised by their constitution. Undertakings may moreover be represented by a duly authorised agent appointed from among their permanent staff. While undertakings may thus not be represented by a representative *ad litem*, they may seek the assistance of lawyers or university teachers who are entitled to plead before the European Court of Justice, or of other qualified persons.[30] The hearing is not public. Persons may be heard either separately or in the presence of other persons. In the latter case due regard must be paid to the legitimate interests of undertakings in the protection of their business secrets. Since the purpose of the oral hearing is usually to complete and explain the written comments, where the latter are very detailed the hearing itself can take place in a shortened form.[31] The essential content of the statements made by each person heard must be recorded in minutes which must be read and approved by him.[32] For the purpose of submitting observations on the draft minutes the grant of a period of three weeks may be sufficient.[33] The minutes must be drafted and communicated to the person concerned in the appropriate language as determined by Community law.[34] Failure to do so may constitute an irregularity capable of affecting the validity of the document, especially where it would result in the minutes' containing substantial inaccuracies or omissions with regard to that person.[35] Submission of an unapproved version of the minutes to the Advisory Committee on Restrictive Practices and Monopolies and to the Commission may likewise amount to a procedural defect capable of vitiating the final decision. However, this will be the case only if the minutes were drawn up in such a way as to misrepresent in a material respect the statements made at the hearing.[36]

(d) *Opinion of the Advisory Committee*

Following the hearing of parties but prior to the taking of a final decision on the imposition of fine or periodic penalty payment, the Commission is obliged to consult the Advisory Committee on Restrictive Practices and Monopolies.[37] Omission or improper completion of this formality may constitute an infringement of an essential procedural requirement invalidating the decision.[38] The consultation must take place at a joint meeting convened by the Commission to be held not earlier than 14 days after despatch of the notice convening it. The Commission must forward to the Committee a summary of the case to be considered together with a preliminary draft decision and must indicate the amount of the fine or penalty it proposes to impose. A report of the outcome of the consultative proceedings must be annexed to the draft decision but not made public. The opinion of the Committee is not binding on the Commission.[39]

(e) *Decision of the Commission*

Although, as seen above, the final decision of the Commission concluding the administrative procedure may deal only with those objections in respect of which the parties concerned have been afforded the opportunity of making known their views,[40] it need not necessarily be an exact reproduction of the statement of objections. The Commission must in fact take into account the factors emerging from the administrative proceedings; it may leave out objections that have proved to be unfounded or may supplement and modify its arguments, both as to fact and as to law, in support of its complaints. A certain development in the Commission's position is not only not incompatible with the rights of defence but is only to be expected: this is in fact the whole purpose of the administrative procedure. The rights of defence are perfectly safeguarded so long as the decision does not charge the parties with infringements that are different from those referred to in the notice of objections and takes into consideration only facts as to which the parties have had the opportunity of stating their views.[41] As regards its form, a decision imposing a sanction requires particularly careful reasoning so as to avoid any impression of arbitrary assessment of the sanction.[42] Decisions imposing surcharges for delay in payment must contain accurate and detailed statements of account showing how the debt and the amount of the surcharge were calculated.[43] In accordance with the general rules, the statement of reasons should indicate clearly and coherently the considerations of fact and of law on the basis of which the fine or penalty has been imposed so as to acquaint both the parties and the Court with the essential factors of the Commission's reasoning. Due precisely to the administrative, i.e. non-judicial, nature of these proceedings, the Commission is not however required to enter into and refute all the arguments put forward by the parties in the course of those proceedings or define its position thereon; nor does it have to give specific reasons for its rejection of the parties' submissions. It is only at the judicial stage, i.e. before the Court of Justice, that the Commission must discuss and, if it can, refute the applicants' arguments.[44] Finally, there is in principle nothing to prevent the Commission from adopting one single decision relating to a large number of undertakings and to a series of infringements, even if some of the undertakings are unconnected with some of the infringements, provided that the decision permits each addressee to obtain a clear idea of the complaints made against it.[45]

804. Unlimited jurisdiction of the Court of Justice

For reasons explained elsewhere,[1] all three Treaties have, directly[2] or through authorisation granted to the Council for that purpose,[3] conferred unlimited jurisdiction on the Court of Justice in actions against sanctions. These actions fall automatically within the Court's unlimited jurisdiction, without its being necessary for the applicant expressly to invoke the relevant Treaty provisions.[4] Such a jurisdiction differs, within the context of such actions,[5] from the ordinary (limited) jurisdiction that the Court possesses in straightforward actions for annulment[6] in two important respects. First, the Court is not confined to an examination of the strict legality of the measure on the four grounds of action.[7] Rather, the Court is free to deal with the case in all its aspects, factual or legal. Having the complete case before it, the Court has full power to interpret and judge the facts, not in the abstract but in their relevance to the case, and thus to form its own opinion as to the existence and character of the infringement in respect of which the sanction has been imposed. In competition cases, for example, the Court has unfettered discretion to re-assess the relevant market conditions in the light of which the Commission has imposed the fine or penalty.[8] Whether, in so doing, the Court may go so far as to depart from the grounds on which the decision is based, is not clear. It would seem that whilst a mere departure (e.g. by interpreting the facts as constituting one single concerted practice instead of a series of such practices) may be permissible,[9] a complete change of the grounds (e.g. from an intentional to a negligent infringement) may not.[10]

Since an action against a sanction is, expressly or impliedly, always based on the illegality of the measure imposing it, the Court must in the first place deal with the question of legality.[11] Whilst in raising that question the applicant is clearly entitled to avail himself of the four grounds of action,[12] neither he nor the Court is restricted to those grounds. Thus the applicant may invoke, for example, self-protection as a ground for the annulment of the sanction. An infringement of Community law may be justified on the ground of legitimate self-protection where the latter is essential in order to ward off an imminent danger immediately threatening the person concerned, provided that there is no other lawful means of avoiding it.[13] On its part, the Court may annul a sanction if it finds the latter unjustified in the actual temporal and factual circumstances in which it was imposed.[14] On the other hand, since the Court has the power to vary (to be discussed below), even the existence of a defect that would normally constitute a ground for annulment (e.g. inadequate reasoning), need not necessarily lead to the annulment of the measure and to its reference back to the Commission: the Court can itself remedy the situation by amending the penalty.[15]

The second respect in which unlimited jurisdiction differs from ordinary (limited) jurisdiction concerns the power of the Court not only to annul, but also to vary the challenged measure by reducing or increasing the fine or penalty contained in it.[16] The Court may, subject to the *ne ultra petita* principle,[17] exercise that power *ex officio*, i.e. even in the absence of any formal request to that effect by the applicant.[18] The power to vary is a necessary corollary to the power to review *in toto*: the re-assessment by the Court of the case in its entirety can be meaningful only if the Court is enabled immediately to substitute its own assessment for that of the Commission by fixing, if necessary, the amount of the fine anew. In so doing, the Court will take into account not only strictly legal but also equitable considerations and any mitigating or aggravating circumstances. In other words, it will have the powers of an ordinary civil court.[19]

805. Consequences of successful action

Owing to the unlimited jurisdiction of the Court of Justice,[1] an application brought against a decision imposing a sanction may request, and the judgment of the Court may order, any one of the following three measures:

(a) annulment of the decision *in toto*, i.e. both the clauses relating to the imposition of the sanction and those containing or ordering additional substantive measures (e.g. establishment of an infringement of Community law, order for the termination of the infringement, refusal to grant an exemption in competition cases, etc.);

(b) annulment of the decision in part, i.e. only insofar as it imposes the sanction, while leaving the rest in force;

(c) reduction (in theory, also increase) of the amount of the fine or penalty imposed, while leaving the decision as a whole in force. Usually, the request for reduction is presented only as a subsidiary submission, the main submission being directed to annulment.[2]

Annulment of the substantive provisions of the decision challenged falls within the ordinary (limited) jurisdiction of the Court of Justice and the judgment will in that respect have the consequences usually attributed to such a judgment in ordinary annulment proceedings.[3] Only insofar as it deals with the question of the fine or penalty and orders cancellation, reduction or increase thereof, will the judgment be governed by specific considerations arising from the Court's unlimited jurisdiction. These considerations are discussed below.

As a sanction can be imposed only in respect of a sufficiently documented infringement of Community law, the Court will annul (cancel) any fine or penalty imposed in respect of infringements which the Court refuses to uphold.[4] Moreover, infringements which may have been induced by an act of the Commission itself (e.g. by a misleading communication) cannot be taken into consideration for the purpose of fixing the amount of the fine.[5] Generally speaking, the question whether the fine or penalty imposed is excessive is determined by the Court in the light of the following factors: gravity, duration (or frequency) and consequences of the infringement; whether it was committed intentionally or negligently; importance of the rule violated in the system of Community law; economic capacity and financial position of the applicant; the amount of the fine or penalty in relation to the maximum laid down by the relevant provision of Community law.[6] In the special field of E.E.C. competition law, the gravity of an infringement committed jointly by several undertakings is to be assessed, and the fine imposed upon them is to be apportioned, by taking into account the nature, importance and damaging consequences of the restrictions on competition; the legislative background and economic context; the number and size of the undertakings concerned; their individual conduct and respective roles in the initiation and implementation of the prohibited agreement or practice; their respective economic strength (as regards in particular the supply of raw materials) and consequent influence over the others; the respective proportions of the market controlled by them within the Community; and the overall situation of the market when the infringement was committed.[7]

The Court will reduce the fine or penalty whenever it considers it out of proportion in the light of any of the above considerations, to the extent to which the Commission has not already taken that consideration into account when assessing the sanction. The Court will also reduce the fine or penalty to the extent to which a particular infringement has not been sufficiently established.[8] The Court is furthermore prepared to take into account both extenuating and aggravating circumstances. Extenuating circumstances are, for example, peculiar financial and economic difficulties of the applicant if sufficiently proved,[9] although not a mere difficult situation due to temporarily unfavourable economic conditions;[10] the fact that the relatively long duration of the infringement was in part due to the dilatoriness of the

Commission in instituting proceedings against it;[11] the readiness of the applicant to bring the infringement to an end immediately in accordance with the Commission's decision.[12] On the other hand, the intentional commission of the infringement is regarded as an aggravating circumstance.[13] Finally, it may be noted that instead of cancelling or reducing a periodic penalty payment, the Court may grant a mere extension of the period at the end of which the payment is to take effect.[14]

CHAPTER 9

Action against Member States

901. Nature and scope of action

Although the Commission is charged in general terms with the duty of ensuring compliance with Community law,[1] it is aided in the performance of this task with the power of imposing sanctions in respect of infringements committed by individuals only.[2] In respect of Member States, the Treaties have, in substitution for direct sanctions, devised special enforcement procedures the purpose of which is to establish with legally binding effect whether a Member State has failed to fulfil an obligation arising from Community law. In the case of an affirmative finding, the Member State is required to comply with that obligation. In principle, such a procedure may be carried out in two different ways. Either the Commission may be empowered to make the finding within its own jurisdiction but subject to challenge by the Member State concerned before the Court of Justice. Or, the same power may be reserved to the Court of Justice itself, acting on the initiative of the Commission. The E.C.S.C. Treaty follows the first, the E.E.C./Euratom Treaties the second solution.[3]

Procedurally, the two solutions differ in that they result in a reversal of the role as applicant or defendant, respectively, of the Commission and the Member State before the Court of Justice. Materially, however, both procedures have the same salient features. Their subject-matter is basically the clarification by the European Court first, of the existence, nature and exact scope of an obligation that has been imposed upon a Member State by primary or secondary Community law prior to the opening of the procedure and, secondly, whether the State has fulfilled that obligation within the time-limit fixed by the Commission for that purpose. Since their primary aim is to clarify a legal position, i.e. whether an act or omission of a Member State, most usually a law, an administrative or judicial practice, or their absence, is compatible with Community law, they are both objective procedures in which any consideration of culpability is in principle ruled out. Nor is it a condition for their introduction that the Communities, the other Member States or individuals should have suffered an injury as a result of the criticised failure. Nor, moreover, is it their function to pass a moral judgment on the defaulting State. Since, however, their second essential object is to bring about a state of affairs consistent with Community law, they are both in the nature of enforcement proceedings. By inevitably putting in issue to a certain extent the prestige of the State concerned, they constitute the *ultima ratio* which enables the Community interests to be protected against any passive attitude or resistance that may exist on the part of the Member States. Based on the compulsory jurisdiction of the Court of Justice, they provide a means of settling international (more precisely: supranational) disputes which by far exceeds any procedure so far devised and accepted in general international law in order to ensure the execution of States' obligations. As the success or failure of the Community objectives is greatly dependent on the behaviour of the Member States, these procedures play a prominent part in the structure of Community law as the only legal means available to the institutions to make that behaviour conform to the Treaties.[4]

It follows from the foregoing that under Article 88 of the E.C.S.C. Treaty, the action is brought by a Member State against a declaratory decision of the Commission whereby the latter has recorded, at the end of a preliminary procedure,[5] that the State has failed to fulfil an obligation under the Treaty. Although the aim of the action is to bring about the annulment of the Commission's decision, it is fundamentally different from an ordinary action for annulment brought under Article 33 E.C.S.C.[6] The latter is directed against a binding measure whereby the Commission lays down an obligation for the Member State(s); the former against a decision whereby the Commission merely declares that the State has failed to fulfil that obligation. In this action the State cannot simultaneously (and belatedly) contest the legality of the underlying measure with whose breach it is charged. The purpose of an action under Article 88 E.C.S.C. is first, to obtain the annulment of the declaration of infringement by showing that the applicant State has complied with the obligation in question (and not by challenging the measure itself laying down that obligation). Secondly, to obtain the annulment or amendment of the measures consequent upon the declaration of infringement. It is thus not correct to say that Article 88 gives Member States a special right of action additional to that provided by Article 33; in fact the two actions serve two quite different purposes. This is the more so as under Article 88 the Court of Justice possesses unlimited jurisdiction which it could not extend to cases properly falling within Article 33, where such jurisdiction is denied.[7] Finally, an unsuccessful action under Article 88 opens the way for the Commission to impose specified sanctions upon the State concerned.[8]

By contrast, under Article 169 E.E.C./Article 141 Euratom, the Commission is not empowered to place on record by means of a binding act any infringement of Community law by a Member State. Instead, it may, following a compulsory preliminary procedure,[9] institute proceedings before the Court of Justice against the defaulting State. As to its nature, this will be a simple action for a declaration (*Feststellungsklage*) to the effect that the State has failed to fulfil an obligation under the Treaty. As there is no previous binding measure involved as to the existence of the breach, the Court is not given unlimited jurisdiction. Nor can it order, nor the Commission take, any sanction or other specific measures, even if the infringement is established. The only consequence of the successful action is that the defendant State is required to take the necessary measures to comply with the judgment of the Court.[10]

On account of these features, action against Member States fundamentally differs, as regards not only the parties but also its purpose, subject-matter and legal consequences, from action for annulment and any other type of direct action. There is, however, a possibility of overlap between it and references for preliminary rulings in that they both may, and in fact often do, have as their subject-matter the question of the compatibility of a national law or administrative practice with Community law. While the European Court will not usually refuse to entertain a reference on account of such a subject-matter alone, it will not, and cannot, in its ruling go beyond interpreting Community law, and therefore is bound to leave it to the national court to decide on the question of compatibility within its own jurisdiction although in the light of the Court's interpretation.[11] It is only in the framework of a direct action brought against the Member State whose laws are in question, which action is designed specifically for that purpose, that the Court possesses jurisdiction to decide on the compatibility of the national law with Community law and in appropriate cases to solve any conflict between the two, with final binding effect, in favour of Community law.[12]

Although designed primarily as a means of law-enforcement at the hands of the Commission, initiation of an action against a Member State is not restricted to the Commission alone. Recognising that the other Member States have an equal interest in the due performance of Community obligations, the Treaties have made it possible for them also to bring such action, in one form or another, against the defaulting State.[13] While the value of such a possibility as a further guarantee of the observance of the law cannot be doubted, its practical effectiveness is somewhat limited by the simple fact that no Member State has ever made use of it so far.

On the other hand, the Treaties have denied any direct role in the process of law-enforcement to individuals by excluding their right to bring a defaulting Member State before the Court of Justice.[14] Consequently, individuals have at present no direct remedy at Community level in respect of violations of their Community rights through national measures or omissions taken or committed by Member States in infringement of Community law. Whatever the justification for this arrangement, it cannot be denied that it constitutes a serious defect in the system of legal protection; a defect that is only partially remedied by various indirect means that are available, in different forms, under the three Treaties. Under the E.C.S.C. Treaty, individuals have been enabled, through a generous interpretation of the concept of individual decision by the European Court, to engage the control machinery at the Commission's disposal by compelling it, by means of an action for failure to act, to open Article 88 proceedings against the defaulting State in certain circumstances.[15] Due to the different construction of both actions, such a possibility does not exist under the E.E.C./Euratom Treaties.[16] Here individuals are made entirely dependent upon the Commission (and in theory, upon the other Member States) in the matter of the protection of their rights and legitimate interests at Community level in respect of violations by adverse national measures. This underlines the importance of action against Member States as the only legal means of affording that protection, and places an additional duty upon the Commission to use that means with a diligence which reflects the fact that private persons have no immediate redress.[17]

Protection of individuals through Commission action against Member States is, however, by the nature of such action, of limited effectiveness. In the first place, the primary object of such action is the general and uniform observance of Community law rather than the defence of individual rights. Private persons have, moreover, no legal means for setting in motion the enforcement procedure which may sometimes be subject to complex, and not necessarily purely legal, considerations.[18] Due to its lengthiness, this procedure may result in the condemnation of the criticised national measure only a long time after the latter had been implemented and when it has already exerted its damaging effects upon individual rights and interests. It is precisely for these reasons that the European Court has developed the doctrine of direct applicability, thus enabling individuals directly to protect their rights against Member States by means of the national courts. Proceedings by the Commission (and by the other Member States) before the European Court and by private persons before the national courts are thus mutually complementary in the system of the legal protection of individuals, even though the latter proceedings are necessarily restricted to the protection of rights and legitimate interests arising from directly applicable Community provisions.

The two procedures have, at the same time, different purposes and legal effects and thus constitute entirely different and independent remedies between which no parallel can be drawn. They are not mutually exclusive. It follows that the fact that the Commission (or a Member State) may bring before the European Court a State for alleged non-fulfilment of its obligations under Community law, and that the European Court renders a judgment on the matter (whether or not upholding the alleged failure), cannot prevent individuals from invoking the very same obligations before national courts in defence of their corresponding rights. Conversely, the fact that individuals enjoy adequate remedy at national level against an infringement by a State of a Community obligation (e.g. failure to give effect to a directly applicable provision) cannot deprive the Commission (and the other Member States) of their right to institute proceedings against that State at Community level in respect of the same obligation.[19]

In practice, under the E.C.S.C. Treaty only four actions have so far been brought against the Commission by Member States.[20] Two of these have been successful,[21] while the other two have been dismissed as unfounded. By contrast, under the E.E.C./Euratom Treaties the Court has rendered twenty-seven judgments in actions brought by the Commission against Member States.[22] Of these actions twenty-one have been well-founded, four have been dismissed as unfounded,[23] while two have been found to be partly well-founded and partly dismissed as unfounded.[24]

902. Parties

Discussion in this Chapter is limited to actions governed by Article 88 E.C.S.C. and Article 169 E.E.C./Article 141 Euratom. Under Article 88 E.C.S.C. action may be brought by a Member State against the Commission. Under Article 169 E.E.C./Article 141 Euratom proceedings may be instituted by the Commission against a Member State. The Board of Directors of the European Investment Bank may also institute similar proceedings against a Member State in respect of non-fulfilment of obligations under the Statute of the Bank.[1] Action must always be directed against a Member State as such and not against its Government or any other internal organ.

In addition to the above-mentioned provisions, the European Court of Justice has both compulsory and optional jurisdiction to entertain actions against Member States which are brought by another Member State. Under the E.C.S.C. Treaty, the Court has compulsory jurisdiction, i.e. jurisdiction not subject to the special consent of the defendant State, over any dispute between Member States concerning the application of the Treaty which cannot be settled by another procedure provided for therein.[2] Similarly, under the E.E.C./Euratom Treaties, any Member State which considers that another Member State has failed to fulfil an obligation under the Treaties may bring the matter before the Court of Justice, subject only to the completion of a compulsory preliminary procedure before the Commission.[3] This procedure may be omitted in certain specified cases.[4] Under all three Treaties, the Court has optional jurisdiction, i.e. jurisdiction subject to a special agreement between the parties, in any dispute between Member States which relates to the subject-matter of the Treaties.[5] Whether compulsory or optional, the jurisdiction of the European Court is ultimately always exclusive over disputes between Member States falling within the field of Community law, as the States have undertaken not to submit disputes concerning the interpretation or application of the Treaties (which includes secondary legislation) to any method of settlement other than those provided for therein.[6] The question whether there might conceivably be an area of disputes between Member States falling outside the interpretation or application of the Treaties but still relating to their subject-matter and which therefore might, in the absence of a special agreement between the parties, escape the jurisdiction of the European Court, seems to be purely academic.

Finally, it may be noted that in addition to the cases so far mentioned, actions may also be brought against Member States in certain special situations. Thus under all three Treaties the Court of Justice has jurisdiction to give judgment pursuant to any arbitration clause contained in a contract concluded by or on behalf of the Communities (which contract may be concluded with a Member State), whether that contract be governed by public or private law.[7] Under the Euratom Treaty only, the Commission may bring action against a Member State in the matter of granting licences[8] and for the purpose of establishing certain infringements of the Treaty by a person or undertaking.[9] Individuals are not entitled under any of the Treaties to institute proceedings against a Member State before the European Court on any ground whatsoever. Formerly, it was held admissible for a Community official to bring his own State before the Court of Justice for an alleged violation of his privileges and immunities granted by Community law, but such a possibility no longer seems to exist.[10]

903. Failure to fulfil Community obligations

The duty of the Member States to fulfil obligations arising from or under the Treaties may be derived both from the general rule of customary international law *pacta sunt servanda,* and from specific provisions of Community law itself. The former stipulates that 'every treaty in force is binding upon the parties to it and must be performed by them in good faith'.[1] The latter require, on the positive side, that Member States shall take all appropriate measures, whether general or particular, to ensure fulfilment of the obligations arising out of the Treaties or resulting from action taken by the Community institutions and that they shall generally facilitate the achievement of the Communities' tasks. On the negative side, they must abstain from any measure which could jeopardise the attainment of the objectives of the Treaties.[2]

Although the obligation of the Member States to perform the Treaties equally arises from general international law, it is different in nature from the reciprocal obligations that that law customarily imposes upon the contracting parties to a treaty. It must rather be assessed in the context of the new supranational legal order of the Communities which is based on the balance of mutual advantages and obligations and which has created a duty of solidarity between the Member States.[3] An important consequence of this is that Member States may no longer justify their failure to perform an obligation under the Treaties by invoking, on the basis of customary international law, a similar failure on the part of another Member State or even a Community institution. Rather, they must resort to the appropriate remedy against the defaulting State or institution, while duly carrying out their own obligations. In other words, they cannot take the law into their own hands. Nor can they invoke as a ground for non-compliance with secondary Community law conditions, reservations and objections expressed by them in the course of the Community law-making process, as perhaps might be the case under general international law in the context of the treaty-making process.[4]

The actual significance of the general obligation to carry out the Treaties depends in each case on the nature and contents of the particular provisions of primary or secondary Community law that needs to be executed.[5] It thus may entail a variety of acts in the most diverse areas, such as the introduction, amendment or repeal of laws, regulations or administrative provisions; taking of individual decisions; following certain court procedures (e.g. in the context of references for preliminary rulings); adaptation of budgetary procedures, practices and the functioning of certain public services so as to be able to give effect to financial obligations within the prescribed time-limits, etc.[6] In the case of directly applicable Community provisions (e.g. E.E.C./Euratom regulations), all incompatible national provisions must be repealed or amended even though the former automatically override the latter by virtue of the supremacy of Community law.[7] Until such time as the necessary legislation is passed, the relevant national authorities are absolutely prohibited from applying the conflicting domestic provisions.[8] Where necessary, appropriate measures must be adopted to facilitate the full effectiveness of the directly applicable Community rules.[9] In the case of non-directly applicable Community provisions (e.g. E.E.C./Euratom directives), the legislative or administrative measures necessary for their correct implementation must be adopted within the prescribed time-limits.[10] Infringement of any of the above obligations, whether by means of a positive action or an abstention to act, will constitute an actionable illegal conduct on the part of the Member State.

The duty to carry out Community obligations falls upon the Member States as such, and not upon their various internal organs and agencies, since it is the Member States, each taken as a whole, that are the subjects of Community law.[11] It follows that any failure to fulfil that duty will involve the responsibility of the Member State at Community level, whatever the internal organ or agency whose action or inaction is the cause of the failure, even if it is a constitutionally independent body. Thus the failure of Parliament to enact the necessary legislation to comply with Community law, or its dilatoriness in doing so, may establish the liability of the Member State just as much as acts or omissions of the Government and the administrative services placed under its authority or the failure of the judiciary (including the highest court in the land) to give effect to Community provisions and procedures (e.g. in the matter of references for preliminary rulings). Thus a Member State cannot justify its failure by invoking the provisions, procedures and practices of the internal legal or constitutional order (e.g. the principle of the separation of powers), unforeseeable political circumstances and difficulties (e.g. Governmental crises, dissolution of Parliament, etc.), the slowness of the ordinary legislative process, etc., although the Community institutions will not usually be reluctant to take account of the latter by extending the time-limit within which a Community measure must be implemented or a breach already committed rectified.[12]

904. Preliminary procedure

Before recording the failure of a Member State to fulfil a Community obligation in a reasoned decision under Article 88 E.C.S.C. or instituting proceedings against it before the Court of Justice under Article 169 E.E.C./Article 141 Euratom, the Commission must comply with the requirements for a compulsory preliminary procedure. This pre-litigation procedure is an essential and characteristic feature of action against Member States, omission of which will entail inadmissibility of the action. Its purposes are, first, to enable the Commission to ascertain the precise nature and extent of the infringement alleged; secondly, to provide the Member State concerned with an essential guarantee in respect of its right of defence; thirdly, and perhaps most importantly, to give both parties the opportunity of clarifying in co-operation with one another sometimes complex legal situations (i.e. compatibility of national and Community provisions) and thus reaching an amicable settlement. By giving the Member State an opportunity to conform to Community law, an action before the Court may be, and on many occasions in fact has been, avoided.[1] Since there are differences in the procedures under the E.C.S.C. and E.E.C./Euratom Treaties, their separate discussion seems appropriate.

(a) *E.C.S.C. Treaty*
If the Commission considers that a Member State has failed to fulfil an obligation under the Treaty, it must first call the attention of the State to this fact and give it the opportunity to submit its comments. In so doing the Commission must clearly specify the breach alleged. Where the Member State is bound to carry out a certain obligation within a given time-limit, the preliminary procedure will not be set in motion automatically by the expiration of that time-limit but presupposes an examination of the situation by the Commission and a finding that there has been a failure. Any such finding is precluded, to the benefit of the Member State, so long as the period in question has not expired.[2] The opportunity to present observations is an essential guarantee of the right of defence and must therefore be granted in substance and not merely in form. A simple exchange of letters in which the Member State concerned expresses a mere disagreement with the Commission's point of view will not constitute definitive observations. A failure to grant such opportunity will entail annulment of the ensuing decision registering the breach, on the ground of infringement of an essential procedural requirement.[3]

Having given the State the opportunity to submit its comments, the Commission will record the failure in a reasoned decision and at the same time set a time-limit for the fulfilment of the obligation. This time-limit may be shorter than the period within which the State may bring an action against the decision (i.e. two months).[4] As regards its legal nature, the 'reasoned decision' differs fundamentally from the ordinary 'decisions' that the Commission can take under Article 14 of the Treaty in exercise of its legislative and executive competences.[5] The reasoned decision under Article 88 may have as its object only the recording of the breach of a pre-existing obligation, i.e. an obligation that had already been imposed upon the Member State, either by the Treaty or by a decision or recommendation, prior to the opening of the preliminary procedure. The decision itself cannot contain any new legislative or implementing provisions. The Commission cannot, therefore, use the enforcement procedure laid down in Article 88 in order to exercise regulatory or executive powers. Especially it cannot use the reasoned decision under Article 88 for purposes which the Treaty prevents it achieving directly by means of an ordinary decision within the meaning of Article 14.[6] It follows that if a decision does not contain a declaration of a breach of a pre-existing obligation but only requires the Member State to take certain measures, then it is not a reasoned decision within the meaning of Article 88, and an action against it under that Article will be inadmissible (although an action for its annulment under Article 33 may be available).[7] Since under Article 88 the Commission is not empowered to take decisions signifying approval of acts of Member States, a letter informing a State of the discontinuation of the preliminary procedure subject to the fulfilment of certain conditions by the latter, will not constitute a decision open to action for annulment.[8]

The reasons supporting the decision as required by Article 88 must be such as to justify the declaration of a breach. They must specify not merely the provisions of Community law which in the Commission's opinion have been infringed, but also the nature and extent of the infringement. Depending on the individual circumstances of a case, the reasoned decision may thus range from a detailed specification of the conduct whereby the Member State is to fulfil its obligations to a mere setting of a general framework within which the State itself can determine its action. Where the breach alleged is of a recommendation, it must be related to the pursuit of the aim prescribed; a breach of the means of achieving that aim, as proposed by the Commission, is not sufficient since the choice of those means must be left to the Member State.[9]

Article 88 imposes a clear duty on the Commission to call upon Member States to fulfil their Community obligations whenever the Commission considers that they have failed to do so. Accordingly, it is possible for undertakings and associations to compel the Commission, by means of an action for failure to act, to set in motion the enforcement procedure. This is in fact possible because the reasoned decision addressed to the Member State is to be regarded as an 'individual decision' which 'concerns' an undertaking (and thus subject to challenge by it) whenever the adverse national measure is such. Omission to take such a decision may therefore constitute an actionable failure to act. Thus Article 88 affords considerable indirect protection to private parties against national measures violating Community law.[10] Failure by the Commission to set in motion the enforcement procedure in

Article 88 may moreover constitute a wrongful omission giving rise to the Community's non-contractual liability.[11]

(b) *E.E.C. / Euratom Treaties*
As under the E.C.S.C. Treaty, the Commission is first required to communicate to the Member State concerned a written statement of complaints clearly specifying, on the one hand, the grounds on which the Commission considers that State to have failed to fulfil an obligation under the Treaty and, on the other, the obligation broken. At the same time the Commission must invite the State to submit its observations. The opportunity to submit observations constitutes, even if the State does not consider it necessary to make use of it, an essential guarantee of the right of defence and as such, an essential formal requirement in the procedure leading to a final declaration of breach. Respect for this guarantee has the consequence that an alleged failure in regard to which the State has not been given the opportunity to present its observations cannot be considered by the Court of Justice in the ensuing action.[12] Consequently, where the Commission changes the subject-matter of its complaint at the judicial stage (e.g. to test the compatibility with Community law of a new legislation belatedly passed by the Member State to rectify the failure), it must set in motion the preliminary procedure again.[13]

The submission of observations and, possibly, of other relevant arguments and materials is usually followed by a (sometimes prolonged) dialogue between the Commission and the Member State with a view to finding an amicable settlement to the dispute. At this stage of the proceedings the Commission is still quite free to alter its original views and arguments or to abandon the charges altogether. If no mutually acceptable solution can be found, the Commission is to deliver a reasoned opinion on the matter fixing a period of time within which the Member State is required to comply with it. This reasoned opinion has two main purposes. First, to set out the Commission's definitive position as to the legal and factual grounds on which it considers the State to have failed to fulfil one of its obligations. Secondly, to specify the measures which the Commission deems to be necessary in order to put an end to the infringement. It is thus not sufficient for the Commission to ascertain the breach; it must also lay down the means suitable to remedy it. In this second respect the Commission enjoys a wide power of discretion. It may itself determine the extent to which the obligation of the Member State may be specified. It may order concrete, individual measures by the taking of which alone will it be possible for the Member State to eliminate the infringement and its past and future consequences. These measures will of course vary in accordance with the nature of the breach and the circumstances of the case.[14]

The overall importance of the reasoned opinion is (in addition to informing the State of the definitive charges raised against it) that it determines the precise limits within which the Commission can later bring the case before the Court of Justice and within which the Court can establish the Member State's failure.[15] As regards its nature and form, however, the reasoned opinion is not a binding administrative act. It cannot therefore lay down new obligations for the Member State, i.e. obligations that had not yet existed when the preliminary procedure was commenced. It amounts merely to a prelitigation stage of a procedure which may lead to an action before the Court of Justice. The assessment of the validity of this opinion merges with that of the validity of the action itself. The opinion cannot thus be challenged separately, nor in the course of the ensuing action.[16] Although it must contain a coherent statement of reasons justifying the conclusion that the Member State has failed in one of its obligations, it cannot be attacked on the ground of inadequate reasoning. The Court of Justice might not be able to uphold the breach alleged if the opinion is insufficiently reasoned and thus might have to dismiss the case, but that will be a substantive, not a formal, defect.[17]

It follows from the non-binding nature of the acts taken during the course of the administrative procedure (i.e. the original request to the Member State to submit its observations and the reasoned opinion) that refusal or failure by the Commission to take any of them cannot be subject to an action. Since, moreover, those acts are always addressed to the Member State concerned, the right of private parties to elicit them by means of an action for failure to act is excluded. Unlike the position under the E.C.S.C. Treaty, under the E.E.C./Euratom Treaties it is thus not possible for private individuals to compel the Commission to open enforcement proceedings against a Member State considered by them to have violated one of their Community rights by adverse national measures. This is so even though the Commission is otherwise under an obligation to institute the Article 169 procedure as soon as it 'considers', rightly or wrongly, that a Member State has committed an infringement.[18] The control mechanism at the disposal of the Court of Justice in respect of such infringements can therefore be engaged by the Commission or by the other Member States only, but never by private individuals.[19]

The compulsory preliminary procedure may be derogated from by the Commission in special circumstances. In some cases the Commission may issue a binding (and therefore separately challengeable) act (decision, directive) instead of the non-binding reasoned opinion, calling upon the Member State concerned to take, within a specified period of time, measures necessary to bring an infringement to an end. If the State does not comply with this act within the prescribed time, the Commission (or any other interested State) may refer the matter to the Court of Justice direct.[20] In other cases, the Commission (or any Member State) may bring certain specified matters directly before the Court of Justice.[21]

905. Action before the Court of Justice

(a) *E.C.S.C. Treaty*

Against the reasoned decision of the Commission the State concerned may institute proceedings before the Court of Justice within two months of its notification. As the decision is merely declaratory of a breach of a pre-existing obligation, the action can have no other purposes than to obtain the annulment of the declaration by showing that the State has in fact complied with the obligation in question, as well as to obtain the annulment or modification of the measures consequent upon the declaration of breach. While the Member State is entitled to dispute, in an action under Article 88, any new conditions of implementation which the decision may have set it, it cannot challenge the validity of the original measure itself that had laid down the obligation, nor bring into issue *ex post facto*, by way of a kind of defence of illegality,[1] the material questions dealt with by it. This could have been done only in an action brought under Article 33 within the proper time-limit and subject to the Court's limited jurisdiction. After the expiration of that time-limit the obligation has become definitive and no longer assailable by means of an action which is subject to the Court's unlimited jurisdiction. It also follows from the purely declaratory nature of the Commission's reasoned decision that, since it can never be put into execution, an action brought against it can never have the effect of suspending execution. Such an effect would in fact result in the suspension not of the application of the reasoned decision of the Commission but of the binding force either of the provisions of the Treaty or of the previous acts of the Commission with the non-fulfilment of which the Member State is charged. The only effect of the action is that the sanctions specified in Article 88(3)(a) and (b) cannot be imposed as long as the action is pending.[2]

(b) *E.E.C. / Euratom Treaties*

If the Member State concerned does not comply with the reasoned opinion within the period laid down by the Commission, the latter may institute proceedings against the State before the Court of Justice. The application made by the Commission to the Court must be based on the same facts, grounds and issues on which the reasoned opinion has been based, and in respect of which the Member State has been given an opportunity to present its observations. In other words, in the interests of the right of defence, there must exist an identity of subject-matter between the administrative and the judicial stages.[3]

Since default by a State is an objective concept, the judicial proceeding is essentially an objective proceeding the sole purpose of which is to obtain a declaration to the effect that the State has failed to fulfil a certain obligation within a given period of time. It follows that in bringing the case before the Court, the Commission does not normally have to show the existence of a particular legal interest since its function is to ensure, in the general interests of the Communities, that the provisions of Community law are duly carried out by the Member States.[4] Thus the action will not be rendered inadmissible for lack of interest or subject-matter by the termination of the infringement prior to the Court's giving judgment but subsequent to the expiration of the time-limit set in the reasoned opinion, e.g. because the Member State has (belatedly) complied with its obligation.[5] Even in such circumstances there may still exist a considerable public interest in obtaining a declaration as to whether the infringement has been committed at all, as such a declaration may establish the basis for the defaulting State's liability towards other Member States, the Communities, or private individuals.[6] Only compliance with the opinion within the time-limit fixed therein can stop an action before the Court. Likewise, the fact that the infringement complained of exists on paper only (because of the continuance in force of a conflicting national law) but has been terminated in practice (by means of verbal administrative directions not to apply that law) cannot affect the admissibility of the action.[7] Nor can the fact that there is no disagreement between the parties as to the substantive aspects of the case because the Member State has admitted the existence of the default. In fact, an action under Article 169 E.E.C./Article 141 Euratom does not become without object so long as the existing legal situation is not in conformity with Community law even if measures are being taken to remedy this situation in the near future and with retroactive effect.[8]

It follows from an objective concept of default that the Court of Justice has to establish its existence without examining the question of culpability on the part of the Member State, and irrespective of any political, economic, social or legal difficulties that the latter may have had, justified or unjustified, in fulfilling its obligation.[9] Such difficulties may be raised with the Community institutions according to the appropriate procedures[10] but cannot exonerate a Member State from fulfilling its duties and, consequently, cannot prevent the Court from giving a judgment concerning the default. Not even the actual initiation of the appropriate procedure, whether before or after the expiration of the period of time fixed by the Commission, can do so.[11] Nor can the fact that the State's default may have been contributed to or caused by a possible illegal act or omission of the Community institutions. This, too, must be remedied according to the proper procedure.[12]

Since the sole object of the action is to establish a failure to fulfil an existing obligation, the Member State cannot raise in defence the plea that the measure imposing that obligation is illegal, at least insofar as the measure in question is a decision (or, possibly, a directive). The legality of that measure can only be challenged in an action for annulment brought under Article 173 E.E.C./Article 146 Euratom within the proper time-limit. Failing such action, the measure becomes definitive and, just as under Article 88 E.C.S.C., it would be incompatible with the requirement of legal certainty to allow it to be contested in the quite different proceedings brought under Article 169 E.E.C./Article 141 Euratom. The only exception to this principle is where the measure is alleged to be tainted with a defect so serious that, if substantiated, the measure would lack all legal basis in the Community legal system, i.e. would be void *ab initio*. This might be the case, for example, if it was taken in a sphere which belongs exclusively to the jurisdiction of Member States. Since in such cases the measure is deemed to be non-existent in law even without formal annulment by the Court of Justice,[13] non-compliance with it cannot establish an actionable failure on the part of the Member State. The Court will therefore investigate whether this is the case without, however, entering into a full examination of the legality of the measure in other respects.[14]

Whether the defence of illegality is also excluded where the obligation with the non-fulfilment of which the Member State is charged has been laid down in a regulation, is not quite clear. As seen above, under the E.C.S.C. Treaty it is so excluded (in respect of general decisions), but the E.E.C./Euratom systems differ on this point from the E.C.S.C. system in two respects. First, under Article 169 E.E.C./Article 141 Euratom the Court does not have unlimited jurisdiction as it does under Article 88 E.C.S.C. Secondly, Article184 E.E.C./Article 156 Euratom allow, in general terms and without time-limit, any party to invoke in any proceeding before the Court of Justice the inapplicability of a regulation which is in issue in that proceeding.[15] There is no equivalent provision in the E.C.S.C. Treaty. It is therefore doubtful if the considerations which prevent both general and individual decisions from being challenged in proceedings under Article 88 E.C.S.C. are also applicable to regulations under Article 169 E.E.C./Article 141 Euratom. Upon a strict interpretation of the wording of Article 184 E.E.C./Article 156 Euratom, this does not seem to be the case.[16] Nor has the Court of Justice been reluctant to examine, in the only case in which this question has come before it so far, the legal situation created by a regulation which the defendant State has been accused of having infringed, and even to acquit the latter 'bearing in mind the equivocal nature' of that situation.[17] In other words, here the defective nature (inadequacy) of a regulation (although, strictly speaking, not its illegality) has been successfully invoked to exonerate an otherwise clearly existing default.

The bringing of the case before the Court of Justice is not subject to any limitation period. By virtue of the nature and purpose of the default proceedings, the Commission has a wide discretionary power to select the most appropriate moment for that purpose. A number of different considerations may play a part in this, such as the desire to reach an amicable settlement (which sometimes may take a long time); the nature, relative gravity and effects of the infringement; the wish not to aggravate any existing political tensions within the Community by bringing a Member State before the Court of Justice; any proposed and impending changes in the provisions violated; etc. Even a prolonged delay in the bringing of the action (e.g. six years) cannot, therefore, affect its admissibility. Nor can the considerations that have determined the choice of the appropriate time.[18] Nor is, in principle, the expediency (advisability) of the institution of proceedings subject to judicial review.[19] In view of these considerations and of the wording of Article 169 E.E.C./Article 141 Euratom ('may' instead of 'shall'), it is doubtful whether the Commission is under a legal obligation to bring the case before the Court of Justice at all.[20] In the absence of a time-limit, the Commission could in any case never be found to be failing in the performance of such an obligation.

906. Consequences of successful action

A successful action has basically different consequences under the E.C.S.C. and E.E.C./Euratom Treaties owing to the fact that under the former the action is directed to the annulment of a binding decision, whereas under the latter it is aimed at a mere declaration. Moreover, under the former the Court of Justice has unlimited jurisdiction, whereas under the latter its jurisdiction is limited.

(a) *E.C.S.C. Treaty*
If the action is well-founded, the Court of Justice will annul the reasoned decision of the Commission recording the alleged failure. In so doing the Court may, by virtue of its unlimited jurisdiction, consider all grounds, based not only upon law but also upon any matters which justify an annulment.[1] The legal consequences of the Court's judgment may vary according to the grounds on which it is based. Thus an annulment on purely formal grounds (e.g. the Commission's failure to observe the rules as to the compulsory preliminary procedure) will clearly not amount to a finding that the State has not committed a breach of its obligations. It is submitted that in such a case the Commission may record the same default in a further decision, provided that it has rectified the formal defect (e.g. it has properly carried out the preliminary procedure). Since the Commission's decision is purely declaratory, its annulment, even on substantive grounds, cannot create rights or obligations for either party. Such annulment may mean any or all of the following: (a) the Commission has incorrectly interpreted the nature and scope of the obligation allegedly broken; (b) it has incorrectly specified the conduct of the Member State necessary to comply with the obligation; (c) the State has not committed a breach.

If, on the other hand, the action is dismissed (or if the State has neither complied with the Commission's decision nor brought an action within the time-limit set therein), the Commission may, with the assent of the Council acting by a two-thirds majority, impose the following sanctions: (a) suspend the payment of any sums which it may be liable to pay to the State in question under the Treaty; (b) take measures, or authorise the other Member States to take measures, by way of derogation from the provisions of Article 4 of the Treaty, in order to correct the effects of the infringement of the obligation. By their very nature, these sanctions cannot have retrospective effect.[2] Against a decision imposing a sanction the State may bring a further action to the Court of Justice within two months of its notification. In such a case the Court will have unlimited jurisdiction. If these measures prove ineffective, the Commission must bring the matter before the Council.[2a]

(b) *E.E.C./Euratom Treaties*
If the Court of Justice finds that a Member State has failed to fulfil an obligation under the Treaties, it does not, strictly speaking, pass a sentence but delivers a purely declaratory judgment which merely notes the fact that a

Member State is at default, that a specific legal situation exists which is not in conformity with the Treaties. The judgment has no executory force and cannot impose sanctions. It cannot repeal, amend or replace national provisions found to be contrary to Community law, nor interfere directly with the legislation or administration of the Member States in any other way, e.g. by giving specific instructions as to how to remedy the situation. It is for the defaulting State to take the necessary measures to comply with the judgment of the Court.[3]

What those measures are, or should be, depends on the specific obligations infringed and on the nature of infringement as indicated in the operative part and decisive grounds of the judgment. Generally speaking, the State must eliminate the infringement and all its past and future consequences. Where the infringement consists in the continuance in force of national legislative or administrative provisions and practices (including judicial practices) that are contrary to Community law, the State is obliged to repeal, amend or replace them to the extent to which this is necessary according to the operative part and decisive grounds of the judgment. Where the infringement consists in the absence of provisions giving effect to Community law, the State must enact them. Although the Court has no power to order the Member State to take any specific steps or measures, the Commission may specify in its application the precise acts and practices by whose adoption or omission the State has committed the breach and by whose repeal, enactment, or amendment it can bring the default to an end. In the case of a successful action, the Court will thus be able to indicate with a fair degree of precision how the State has failed in fulfilling its obligation and, consequently, how it can remedy its failure.[4]

The obligation to eliminate the consequences of the infringement with retroactive effect (i.e. with an effect going back to the commencement of the infringement) includes not only legal but also financial consequences. Thus the defaulting State is obliged to re-establish the complete *status quo ante (restitutio in integrum)* and, where necessary, to pay compensation for any injury suffered. This may involve the obligation to make payment or restitution of sums illegally withheld or collected,[5] or to collect or require repayment of sums which the State has illegally failed to collect or has illegally paid out (e.g. in the form of a State aid incompatible with the Common Market).[6] In many cases, of course, it may be difficult, if not impossible, to achieve a complete retrospective redress for all the consequences of the infringement in addition to its future termination.

Insofar as the judgment of the Court of Justice declares an existing legal situation illegal, it has necessarily an *erga omnes* effect. This follows from the fact that a situation cannot continue to be regarded as lawful with respect to some whilst it is unlawful with respect to others. Everyone, therefore, i.e. the Communities, the other Member States and private persons, may rely on that illegality and on the consequences that it necessarily entails. The judgment may thus establish the basis of the liability of the defaulting Member State towards the Communities, the other Member States and all private persons within or outside its jurisdiction.[7] Likewise, any interpretation of the meaning, scope and effect of Community provisions and any statement as to the compatibility with them of national provisions, contained in the judgment, will have an *erga omnes* effect. Such an interpretation or statement will be automatically binding on all national authorities, including the courts, and individuals. The former must immediately cease to apply national provisions held to be incompatible with Community law and, where necessary, adopt all requisite measures to facilitate the full effectiveness of the latter. Individuals may enforce Community rights denied by the incompatible national measures.[8]

Since the procedure in Article 169 E.E.C./Article 141 Euratom is the only means available to the Communities to obtain the creation of a situation which conforms to Community law, it is absolutely necessary that the Member State concerned should promptly and correctly carry out the judgment of the Court, using all means at its disposal to preserve the authority and supremacy of the Community legal order. Failure to do so may give rise to a new dispute between the Commission and the State. In the absence of any sanction-power on the part of the Communities, the only means of law-enforcement is for the Commission to start a new Article 169 E.E.C./Article 141 Euratom procedure. This will include the whole preliminary procedure and the delivery of the reasoned opinion.[9] Since the previous judgment of the Court of Justice establishing the infringement constitutes *res judicata*, the subject-matter of the first procedure cannot be reopened in the second. The sole object of the latter is to obtain a second declaratory judgment to the effect that by not complying with the earlier judgment, the Member State has failed to fulfil the obligation imposed upon it by Article 171 E.E.C./Article 143 Euratom. In giving the judgment, the Court will not consider any argument put forward by the State in defence as to why it could not give effect to the earlier judgment. The only question is whether or not it has taken the necessary measures to do so.[10]

PART III

Legal Protection by National Courts

CHAPTER 10

National Courts and Community Law

1001. Jurisdiction of national courts

It follows from the dual nature of Community law as an autonomous legal order which is partially integrated into the laws of the Member States[1] that individuals have a dual system of remedies available to them in matters falling within the scope of application of that law.[2] In all cases in which the European Court of Justice has been given jurisdiction by an express provision, the remedy lies with that Court.[3] In all other cases the national courts are the proper forum. In such cases, it is in principle within their jurisdiction to interpret (although not with final binding effect), apply and enforce Community law.[4] Their competence encompasses, broadly speaking, three different functions, i.e.:

(1) the protection of Community rights of the individual;
(2) the enforcement of Community obligations imposed upon him; and
(3) the punishment of certain Community offences.

These three broad areas of competence are separately discussed in the subsequent Sections.[5]

In the United Kingdom the competence of the courts to interpret, apply and enforce Community law as part of the law of the land is primarily derived from Sections 2 and 3 of the European Communities Act 1972.[6] In pursuance of the latter provision, for the purposes of all legal proceedings any question as to the meaning or effect of any of the Treaties, or as to the validity, meaning or effect of any Community instrument must be treated as a question of law (and not as a question of fact, as would be the position if Community law were considered as foreign law). Any such question, if not referred to the European Court for a preliminary ruling, must be determined in accordance with the rules and principles laid down by any relevant decision of the European Court (S.3(1)). The courts and tribunals must take judicial notice of the Treaties, of the Official Journal of the Communities and of any decision of, or expression of opinion by, the European Court on any of the questions mentioned above. The Official Journal is admissible as evidence of any instrument or other act thereby communicated of any of the Communities or their institutions (S.3(2)). Evidence of any Community instrument may also be given in any legal proceedings by production either of a certified true copy thereof (S.3(3)) or of a copy purporting to be printed by the Queen's Printer (S.3(4)). Evidence given in accordance with the provisions of Section 3 will be sufficient evidence also in any legal proceedings in Scotland (S.3(5)).

1002. (1) Protection of Community rights

Since Community law is put into day-to-day operation mostly by national organs (with the possible exception of competition rules which are administered directly by the Commission), it is the national courts that are in the best position to afford immediate legal protection in most cases. Of the six different types of bilateral legal relationships that are governed by Community law,[1] individuals may be involved directly only in three, i.e. in legal relations with Member States (not necessarily their own State), with Community institutions and with other individuals. Accordingly, they may wish to seek legal protection in the national courts either against Member States, Community institutions or other individuals. Each of these situations raises somewhat different problems; they must therefore be considered separately below.

(a) *Protection against Member States*
Broadly speaking, the nature and scope of the protection that national courts are required (and able) to afford to individuals vis-a-vis Member States depends on two circumstances. First, whether the Community provision from which a right or legitimate interest is or purports to be derived is directly applicable or not; secondly, what the subject-matter of that right or interest is.

As regards the former circumstance, where rights are conferred upon individuals by directly applicable Community provisions[2] (including directly applicable provisions of international agreements binding on the Communities as well as on the Member States),[3] it follows from the combined effects of the doctrines of the direct applicability and the supremacy of Community law[4] that national courts are bound to protect and enforce those rights against any adverse measure or practice of the Member States which tends to prevent their free exercise. Thus in national proceedings, whether civil or criminal, individuals are entitled to challenge for incompatibility with Community law any domestic measure or practice, whether legislative or administrative, whether general or individual, whether earlier or later in time, which has the purpose or effect of interfering with their Community rights or of imposing upon them any burdens, restrictions, obligations etc. contrary to those rights. After consulting, where necessary, the European Court of Justice in the framework of a reference for a preliminary ruling[5] as to the meaning, scope and effect of the Community provision involved and as to the compatibility with it of the national measure, the national courts are obliged to afford direct and immediate protection, irrespective of the relationship that may exist in domestic law between the rights and legitimate interests of the individual and the public interests of the State concerned.[6] Where as a result of the adverse national measure taken in infringement of Community law individuals suffer damages, the national courts are also required to award appropriate compensation according to the domestic law on State liability.[7]

Nevertheless, in the absence at the present time of any relevant Community provisions, the rights conferred by Community law upon individuals must be exercised before national courts in accordance with the system of remedies and procedures available under domestic law. Community law requires no more than that adequate protection be afforded; it leaves to each Member State the task of designating the competent courts and of laying down the rules of procedure and time-limits for that purpose. It is thus for the national court to select the most appropriate of the available redresses, e.g. to decide whether to hold an adverse domestic measure null and void *in toto* or only inapplicable to the extent to which it is incompatible with Community law, and whether to take cognisance of such invalidity or inapplicability of its own motion. The only requirements set by Community law in this respect are that the national remedies, procedures and time-limits must not be less favourable than those governing the same right of action on an internal matter and that they must not make it impossible in practice to exercise rights which the national courts have a duty to protect. Thus, for example, the fixing of a reasonable period of limitation within which an action must be brought against the incompatible national measure, is not contrary to the requirements of Community law.[8]

It follows from the foregoing that while national courts are required by Community law to afford to individuals the highest degree of legal protection that is available under domestic law, the nature and scope of that protection may, and necessarily does, vary as between the Member States owing to the existing differences in the national systems of remedies and procedures. At the present stage, this is certainly a weakness of the system of legal protection set up by Community law since it involves the risk of unequal treatment of individuals according to national criteria. While consultation of the European Court through the preliminary ruling procedure may be instrumental in working out common principles for the uniform and effective enforcement of individual rights throughout the whole Community,[9] this can, by the nature of things, only alleviate but not eliminate the problem. Should the national differences assume such proportions as to cause distortion in the conditions of competition or to affect the functioning of the Common Market, harmonisation of the relevant national laws becomes imperative.[10]

Safeguarding of individual rights by the national courts plays an essential part in the overall system of legal protection provided by Community law. It complements in a vital respect the forms of action envisaged by the Treaties at Community level which do not grant individuals direct access to the

European Court against defaulting Member States. The fact that the Commission and the other Member States do have a right of action against such States, cannot be invoked to challenge the jurisdiction of the national courts. In fact, an action against a Member State before the Court of Justice and individual proceedings against the same State before national courts, have entirely different objectives and effects and are subject to different conditions. They therefore constitute two independent (parallel) forms of remedy which cannot mutually exclude or limit one another. Any restriction of the guarantees against infringements of Community law by the Member States to the former procedure would remove all direct legal protection of the individual rights of their nationals. Thus the vigilance of the latter to safeguard their rights amounts to an effective supervision in addition to the supervision entrusted by the Treaties to the Commission and to the other Member States.[11]

The position is different where an individual right or interest purports to be derived from a Community provision (including provisions of an international agreement binding on the Communities as well as on the Member States) which is not directly applicable.[12] In principle, such a provision cannot confer on private persons rights which the national courts would be bound (or even able) to protect. Such a provision is either in the nature of a mere policy decision (e.g. resolution of the Council and the Representatives of the Governments of the Member States)[13] which is legally not enforceable at all or in the nature of an agreement between States or between States and international organisations which is governed by the principles of traditional international law. These principles place such provisions beyond the reach of individuals and, usually, of the national courts. Their proper execution and observance by the Member States is under the exclusive control of the Commission and the other Member States at Community level.[14] It follows that individuals are as a rule not only unable to derive enforceable rights from a non-directly applicable provision itself, but that they are powerless to enforce the implementation of such a provision at the national level and, once implemented, to control the conformity with it of the implementing measure by way of a court action. They can derive rights from, and challenge the legality of, the national measure only, according to the ordinary avenue of remedies open to them in respect of that particular type of (legislative or administrative) measure.[15] Since these remedies vary from Member State to Member State according to the nature of the implementing measure, and since in some States no remedy may exist at all (e.g. where implementation has taken place by means of an Act of Parliament which is not subject to judicial review), the degree of legal protection will vary throughout the Community. In this respect, too, a harmonisation of the national laws may become imperative given the impact which some non-directly applicable provisions (e.g. directives) may have on the rights and interests of private individuals.

While one is justified in seeing in this area what is probably one of the least satisfactory aspects of the system of legal protection, individuals are not entirely defenceless. Depending upon the system of remedies in force in a Member State, exceptionally it may be possible to obtain annulment of an internal administrative measure on the ground that it infringes a non-directly applicable provision (e.g. a directive) which has not yet been implemented at the national level.[16] Moreover, individuals may be able to avail themselves of the preliminary ruling procedure, to be discussed in the following Chapter,[17] to establish that the provision in question is, against all appearance to the contrary, in reality directly applicable and thus enforceable in the ordinary way.[18] Also, national courts may use the same procedure to obtain interpretation of a directive by the European Court so as to ensure, regardless of the effects of the directive, that the domestic law or administrative measure adopted for its implementation is interpreted and applied in a manner which conforms to the requirements of Community law. This may be a particularly useful procedure in cases where the implementing measure is obscure, ambiguous or departs from the directive in some respect or where the interpretation of (another) national provision directly depends on a prior interpretation of a directive or of a non-directly applicable Treaty provision.[19]

The nature and scope of the protection that individuals may seek and the national courts may afford against Member States depends, furthermore, on the subject-matter of the Community right relied on. Where the right relates to the free movement of goods, the relief usually sought and granted (normally against the national Customs and Excise authorities or other relevant bodies) consists in the annulment of restrictive measures or notices of assessment of customs and/or excise duties and taxes imposed on imported or exported goods on the basis of a national law which is alleged to be incompatible with the (directly applicable) provisions of the E.E.C. Treaty relating to the elimination of customs duties[20] and quantitative restrictions,[21] to the adjustment of State monopolies,[22] and/or to the prohibition of discriminative or protective taxation[23] in respect of goods circulating between the Member States. The claim for annulment is usually accompanied, where appropriate, by one for reimbursement of amounts already paid and for damages. The importer/exporter may moreover challenge the tariff classification of the goods in question by the Customs and Excise authorities. In deciding such disputes, the national court will usually request the interpretation of the Common Customs Tariff by the European Court by way of a preliminary ruling.[24] The provisions of the Treaty on the free movement of goods may also be invoked in criminal proceedings to obtain acquittal by showing that the domestic law which has created the offence is unenforceable as being incompatible with Community law.[25]

The provisions of the Treaty on agriculture and the relevant implementing regulations may be relied on against the national agricultural intervention agencies or Customs authorities, for example, to obtain payment of export refunds or to challenge notices of assessment of import levies,[26] and of other duties and charges[27] including monetary compensatory amounts;[28] to challenge certain aspects of the national intervention mechanism;[29] to challenge the imposition of maximum prices at the domestic level;[30] to challenge forfeiture of security deposited for the issue of an import licence;[31] to obtain payment of special bonuses, premiums, amounts etc. as provided for by Community regulations,[32] to obtain compensation for damages caused by illegal intervention on the agricultural market,[33] etc. In this context, too, an interpretation of the Common Customs Tariff may become necessary.[34] The provisions of Community law on agriculture may also be invoked in criminal proceedings to show the inapplicability of the (conflicting) national law creating the offence in question.[35]

The provisions of primary and secondary Community law may be invoked against the competent national administrative authorities and welfare institutions which control the admission, establishment, registration, residence, expulsion and the conditions of employment, pay, welfare, etc. of foreign nationals and bodies corporate, to enforce the right of free movement for workers,[36] the right of establishment,[37] the right to provide services[38] and/or any ancillary rights related to these basic freedoms[39] including the right to social security benefits,[40] against any discriminatory, restrictive or otherwise incompatible national measure or practice. The same provisions may also be invoked in criminal proceedings to show the incompatibility with Community law, and hence inapplicability, of the national law creating the offence in question.[41] Insofar as a restrictive measure is taken on grounds of public policy, public security or public health, each Member State is obliged to make available to the nationals of other Member States the same legal remedies as are open to its own nationals in respect of similar measures of the administration or, at least, must enable those persons to exercise their right of defence before a competent authority other than that which adopted the measure. Furthermore, in order to be able to prepare their defence, such persons must be notified of the precise grounds upon which the measure is based. Since this double safeguard (i.e. notification of the grounds and the right of appeal) must be available effectively, not only in appearance, a restrictive measure (e.g. expulsion) cannot be executed, save in cases of urgency, until the person concerned has been able to exhaust all the remedies mentioned.[42]

(b) *Protection against Community institutions*

National courts are able to afford private individuals legal protection against the Community institutions in two, basically different ways, i.e. directly and indirectly. The need for a direct protection arises in situations directly involving individuals in litigation with the institutions outside the European Court of Justice. Such a situation may occur because in each Member State each Community enjoys the most extensive legal capacity accorded to legal persons under domestic law and is thus capable of acquiring or disposing of movable and immovable property, and of being a party to legal proceedings. To this end, the E.C.S.C. is represented by its institutions, each acting within the limits of its powers, while the E.E.C. and Euratom are represented always by the Commission.[43] Save, therefore, where jurisdiction is conferred on the Court of Justice by or under the Treaties, disputes to which any of the Communities is a party are not in principle excluded from the jurisdiction of the courts or tribunals of the Member States.[44] In practice, such disputes may arise either from a contract concluded by or on behalf of the Communities with private persons, or from a delict (tort) imputable to the institutions. As regards the former, unless the contract contains an 'arbitration clause' conferring jurisdiction upon the European Court,[45] settlement of the dispute falls within the jurisdiction of the national courts which must decide upon the Communities' contractual liability by applying the law governing the contract in question according to the rules of private international law.[46] As regards non-contractual liability, the national courts will have jurisdiction only in those (relatively few) cases which do not fall within the European Court's exclusive jurisdiction.[47] Nevertheless, in either situation, enforcement of the decision of the national courts by measures of constraint against the Communities is subject to the authorisation of the Court of Justice.[48]

Secondly, the national courts may be required to afford individuals indirect protection against the institutions in situations where private persons are affected by the institutions' acts only indirectly, i.e. through the effects of national measures taken in implementation thereof. In such cases the immediate remedy (whether it be annulment or the award of damages) lies with the national courts and must be sought against the national authority responsible for the implementing measure, although the real source of the grievance is some defect, not in that measure but in the Community provision forming its legal basis. By using the preliminary ruling procedure,[49] the national court will be able to ascertain the invalidity of the underlying Community act and order the annulment of the implementing measure and, where appropriate, award compensation accordingly. In all such cases the jurisdiction of the national courts is exclusive, at least insofar as they are in the position of affording the remedy sought.[50] Thus action may be brought against the national Customs and Excise authorities or agricultural intervention agencies to obtain annulment of a notice of assessment of an import/export levy or duty or other charge, tax, etc.,[51] the reimbursement of amounts wrongly exacted[52] or payment of sums, e.g. monetary compensatory amounts, etc., wrongly withheld,[53] on the ground that the national organ has acted in pursuance of a Community measure which itself was invalid. Likewise, in actions brought against any other relevant national administrative authority acting in implementation of a Community measure (including social security institutions), the validity or legality of that measure may be challenged.[54]

(c) *Protection against individuals*

National courts are finally called upon to afford individuals legal protection vis-a-vis other individuals in situations where rights or prohibitions of a Community origin are founded upon or invoked in defence in domestic litigations. Since Community rights affecting legal relationships between individuals can only be enforced in the national courts, the jurisdiction of the latter in these matters cannot be restricted or excluded even by (secondary) Community law itself.[55] Thus, although Community competition law is administered and enforced generally by the Commission, national courts are frequently called upon to give a decision on the civil consequences of an infringement of that law, which may include the nullity or termination of a contract, grant of damages to injured parties, etc. Thus the provisions on competition of the E.E.C. Treaty[56] may be invoked in defence in actions brought for breach of contract and consequential damages[57] or in actions for infringement of the law on unfair competition[58] to show that the contract relied on, being incompatible with those provisions, is automatically void.[59] The same provisions may also be pleaded in defence in actions brought for infringement of patent,[60] trade mark[61] or other industrial or intellectual property rights (e.g. copyright)[62] to show that an exercise of those rights is contrary to, and therefore prohibited by, the rules on competition. Similar defence may be founded on the provisions of the E.E.C. Treaty relating to the free movement of goods.[63]

Community law may, moreover, give rise to enforceable rights in the framework of the employment (master and servant) relationship. Thus employees may invoke the provisions prohibiting discrimination on grounds of nationality or sex[64] to contest any measure of their employers which tends to have discriminatory effects.[65] In addition, Community law may be relied upon in actions before national courts in various other situations.[66] Finally, it may be mentioned that the legal protection of individuals in national litigations, even in matters not falling within Community law, has been greatly strengthened by the adoption of the Convention on Jurisdiction and the Enforcement of Judgments in Civil and Commercial Matters 1968 which, in a broader sense, also forms part of Community law.[67]

1003. (2) Enforcement of Community obligations

Enforcement of the judgments (and orders)[1] of the Court of Justice (whether or not they impose obligations of a pecuniary nature),[2] of the final decisions of the Euratom Arbitration Committee,[3] of decisions of the Commission imposing certain sanctions under the Euratom Treaty[4] or imposing pecuniary obligation under the E.C.S.C. Treaty,[5] as well as of decisions of the Council and of the Commission imposing pecuniary obligations on persons other than States under the E.E.C. Treaty[6] falls within the jurisdiction of the national courts. In spite of the difference in wording between the E.C.S.C.[7] and E.E.C./Euratom[8] provisions, the procedure of enforcement is essentially the same under all Treaties; and the more detailed provisions of the later Treaties may in principle be applied to enforcement procedures carried out under the earlier E.C.S.C. Treaty.[9]

Enforcement is governed by the rules of civil procedure in force in the State in the territory of which it is carried out.[10] This is mostly, although not necessarily exclusively, the State in which the debtor has his residence or its registered office, central administration or principal place of business. Enforcement may in principle commence immediately upon the Court's delivering a judgment or upon the Commission's taking an executory decision; in the latter case it is not necessary to wait until the expiry of the time-limit for bringing an action for the annulment of the decision. In the event of such an action, the Court may grant a suspension of the enforcement (see below).

Before enforcement can be carried out, the authenticity of the judgment or decision in question must be verified (which in practice means verification of the authenticity of the signature appearing on the document) by the national authority which the Government of each Member State has designated for this purpose and has made known to the Court of Justice and to the Commission. This is the only formality that is required for the issue of an order for enforcement (writ of execution) which the designated national authority must append to the judgment or decision. When these formalities have been completed, the party concerned may proceed to enforcement in accordance with the national law, by bringing the matter directly before the competent court. From this moment on the national rules of civil procedure apply. Thus it is the national court (and not the European Court) that has jurisdiction over any questions that enforcement may raise,[10a] such as a complaint that it is being carried out in an irregular manner, i.e. not in accordance with the domestic provisions relating to enforcement of claims in bankruptcy.[11] Nevertheless, enforcement may be suspended only by a decision of the Court of Justice given in accordance with the general rules on suspension of enforcement of Community measures.[12] The above procedure applies also to enforcement of penalties imposed and other measures ordered by the Court of Justice in respect of witnesses[13] and to the recovery of sums owed to the Court on various grounds.[14]

In the United Kingdom, the authority designated to issue an order for enforcement is the Secretary of State.[15] The Community judgment or decision to which such order has been appended must be presented by the person entitled to enforce it to the High Court (in England and Northern Ireland) or to the Court of Session (in Scotland) for registration. Persons against whom enforcement is requested must be notified of the registration. Where the judgment or decision has been partly satisfied at the date of the application for its registration, it must be registered only in respect of the balance remaining payable at that date. The registration must be varied or cancelled if at a later date it is shown that the judgment or decision in question has been partly or wholly satisfied.[16]

The effect of registration is that the Community judgment or decision is, for all purposes of execution, to be of the same force and effect as if it had been a judgment or order given or made by the High Court or Court of Session on the date of registration. Proceedings for execution may be taken accordingly.[17] An order of the European Court suspending the enforcement of a registered Community judgment or decision must likewise be registered with the High Court or Court of Session and is to have the same effect as if it had been an order made by that Court on the date of its registration staying or sisting the execution of the judgment or decision.[18] Detailed rules of court have been made for the registration and execution of Community judgments or decisions in the High Court[19] and the Court of Session.[20]

1004. (3) Punishment of Community offences

Since criminal jurisdiction as such has not been conferred upon the Communities, the institutions have no power to take and enforce penal measures for the prevention and punishment of offences committed by individuals against Community law, even in areas within exclusive Community competence. In particular, the institutions have no power to adopt penal measures for the effective protection of the Communities' funds against fraudulent practices occurring especially in the field of customs and agricultural legislation. The gap thus created in the body of Community law is only partially filled by the duty of the Member States to take all necessary measures, including criminal prosecutions and proceedings, to prevent and punish breaches of Community economic law.[1] Since the material, personal and territorial scope of each national criminal jurisdiction is necessarily limited, effective protection of Community funds and other interests can only be achieved by concerted action on the part of all the Member States. This will be made possible by the proposed Protocols to be attached to the Community Treaties that will extend the jurisdiction of national courts to prosecute and punish offences against Community law in foreign countries and will also provide for a flexible form of legal assistance between the Member States.[2] The criminal liability and protection of Community officials calls for a similar co-operation of the Member States; the proposed Protocol on this matter envisages the prosecution and punishment of officials committing certain serious offences, such as corruption or breach of professional secrecy, by the courts of their country of origin in the same way as national officials.[3]

There are nevertheless two areas in which Community law already calls for a close co-operation and assistance on the part of the national criminal authorities and courts in the matter of Community offences. First, the Member States are required to treat any perjury by a witness or expert before the European Court of Justice in the same manner as if the offence had been committed before one of their courts with jurisdiction in civil proceedings. At the instance of the Court of Justice, the Member State concerned must prosecute the offender before its competent criminal court.[4] In pursuance of these provisions, in the United Kingdom a person who commits a perjury before the European Court must, whether he is a British subject or not, be held guilty of an offence and and may be proceeded against and punished in England and Wales as for an offence against Section 1(1) of the Perjury Act 1911; or in Scotland as for an offence against Section 1 of the False Oaths (Scotland) Act 1933; or in Northern Ireland as for an offence against Section 1(1) of the Perjury Act (Northern Ireland) 1946.[5]

Secondly, each Member State is required to treat any infringement by an official, servant or employee of the Euratom Community or by any other specified person of his obligation to keep secret any classified Euratom information, as an act prejudicial to its rules on secrecy and as one falling, both as to merits and jurisdiction, within the scope of its laws relating to acts prejudicial to the security of the State or to disclosure of professional secrets. Such Member State must, at the request of any Member State concerned or of the Commission, prosecute anyone within its jurisdiction who commits such an infringement.[6] In the United Kingdom, any person falling within the above categories, whether a British subject or not, who acquires any classified information, will be guilty of a misdemeanour if he communicates it to any unauthorised person or makes any public disclosure of it, whether in the United Kingdom or elsewhere, and will be subject to the Official Secrets Act 1911 to 1939. For this purpose 'classified information' means any facts, information, knowledge, documents or objects that are subject to the security rules of a Member State or of any Euratom institution.[7]

CHAPTER 11

Preliminary Rulings

1101. Nature and scope of preliminary rulings

Preliminary rulings are given by the European Court of Justice in the framework of non-contentious proceedings in response to questions referred to it by national courts and tribunals concerning the interpretation of the Treaties and acts of the institutions (under the E.E.C./Euratom Treaties only) or the validity of acts of the institutions (under all three Treaties). They are essentially in the nature of an interim step in an action which has been started in a national court and in which the substantive issues will be settled by the same court in the light of the ruling of the European Court. The primary purpose of preliminary rulings is thus to enable national courts to reach decision in cases properly brought before them but in which the decision depends on the prior clarification of legal issues falling within the exclusive jurisdiction of the European Court. Proceedings for preliminary rulings are characterised by the absence of 'parties' in the proper sense of the word as the parties to the main action are merely invited to state their case within the legal limits laid down by the national court making the reference. They are thus fundamentally different from the various direct actions available in the European Court. As contentious proceedings the latter are characterised by the presence of parties and are closed by a 'decision' (and not a 'ruling') of the Court of Justice which settles definitively the substantive points of the dispute. In view of this essential difference, the rules laid down solely for direct actions cannot, generally, without express provision to that effect, be extended to preliminary rulings.[1]

In the system of the Community Treaties, and in particular in that of the E.E.C./Euratom Treaties, to which discussion is limited in this Chapter, preliminary rulings fulfil two different but equally important functions. The first of these functions, largely governed by considerations of public policy, is directly relevant to the attainment of the fundamental Community objectives and, ultimately, of the complete economic and social integration of the Member States. Since this process is to take place within a strictly defined legal framework, it can only be successful if accompanied (and in many respects, preceded) by a corresponding legal integration. An integrated Community legal order implies that Community law is uniformly applied and, as a logically necessary precondition for that, uniformly interpreted throughout the whole Community territory. To ensure this, the Treaties have placed the interpretation of Community law with final binding effect and the determination of the validity of the acts of institutions within the exclusive jurisdiction of the Court of Justice. At the same time, they empower and, in the case of courts and tribunals of last resort, require national courts and tribunals to invoke that jurisdiction whenever this becomes necessary in the course of the application of Community law by them.

The preliminary ruling procedure is thus essential for the preservation of the coherence and Community character of the law created by the Treaties, in the face of its simultaneous application in six (now nine) different national jurisdictions. Whilst it primarily aims to avoid divergences in the interpretation of that law, it likewise tends to ensure uniformity and effectiveness in its application by providing to the national courts a means for eliminating any obstacles that might undermine such effectiveness within the legal systems of the Member States. It is thus utlimately a device enabling the European Court to play a vital part in ensuring the uniform interpretation and application as well as the progressive development of Community law in a 'decentralised' system.[2] In fact, the Court has formulated some of the most fundamental concepts and principles of Community law in the framework of the preliminary ruling procedure, such as, for example, the doctrines of the direct applicability and supremacy of Community law.[3]

Whilst the procedure for preliminary rulings is designed to channel to the European Court any dispute concerning the interpretation and validity of Community law that may arise in the national courts, it is in no way intended to superimpose the European Court upon them, nor, conversely, to subordinate the national jurisdictional systems to that of the Communities. On the contrary, it is based on a careful separation of the two systems. It implies a spirit of collaboration between the municipal courts and the European Court with mutual regard for their respective jurisdictions. This spirit of cooperation is in fact a precondition for the success of the Treaties and is indispensable in the judicial sphere just as much as it is in the political, economic and social spheres. It requires a joint effort on the part of both courts, each keeping within the frontiers of its own competence, to ensure the uniform interpretation and effective application of Community law. It excludes any idea of subjecting the national courts to unnecessary formalism which would be incompatible with the purpose of the procedure. It follows that the respective powers of the European Court and the national courts are determined by considerations which generally apply in situations where an exclusive jurisdiction is exercised parallel with ordinary jurisdictions. Basically, the jurisdiction of the European Court is strictly limited to the interpretation of Community law and to the determination of the validity of the acts of institutions, while leaving the application of that law to the national courts. The task of the European Court is thus restricted to assisting the national courts within the framework of questions put to it, in resolving a particular dispute although that restriction has as its counterpart the authority and binding force of the solutions which the Court reaches when it 'states the law'.[4]

The second function of preliminary rulings is that of affording additional legal protection to individuals by complementing and completing the system of remedies made available to them in the form of direct actions. For this purpose they can be used both in situations where no other remedy exists at all and in situations where other remedies do exist but fail to afford adequate protection. The former is the case where redress is sought against a Member State violating the Community rights of individuals by adverse national measures or practices. The latter arises where the complaint is directed against a Community institution but the bringing of an action is excluded for one reason or another.

As regards protection vis-a-vis Member States, individuals are denied any direct redress at Community level as they cannot cite Member States before the Court of Justice.[5] On the other hand, they can institute proceedings against the injurious measure or practice in the national courts and, in the framework of such proceedings, invoke the jurisdiction of the European Court to interpret the Community provision thought to have been infringed by that measure or practice. If the European Court finds this provision to be directly applicable, the national court must give effect to it within the framework stated by the Court. By virtue of the supremacy of Community law, the national court must thus enforce individual rights arising from the Community provision even in the face of any adverse national measure or practice.[6] Should the European Court find the Community provision not to be directly applicable, the national courts may still make use of the Court's interpretation to test the conformity of national implementing measures with the provision so interpreted.[7]

As regards protection vis-a-vis Community institutions, although individuals have the right to bring direct actions for annulment before the Court of Justice, they cannot exercise that right against law-making measures nor against measures addressed to the Member States, save in the exceptional case where the measure is of direct and individual concern to them.[8] Nor can they institute proceedings against any measure after the expiry of time-limits. In these respects preliminary rulings play a role similar to that of the defence of illegality[9] or of certain national procedures laid down for testing the constitutionality of statutes (e.g. in Germany and Italy). Accordingly, individuals may challenge in the domestic courts acts of the national authorities taken in implementation of 'law-making' Community measures (or of measures addressed to Member States) and in support of their case contest the validity or legality of the measures implemented. The jurisdiction of the European Court may then be invoked to give a preliminary ruling on the validity or legality of the Community provision in question irrespective of the fact that the latter is not subject to direct action by private persons. In the absence of such a remedy, it would be left entirely to the Member States (which possess an unlimited right of action) to protect the individual rights and interests adversely affected which protection they may, for political or other reasons, not always be willing to afford.[10]

It is apparent from the foregoing that, in spite of the fundamental structural differences between preliminary rulings as non-contentious proceedings and direct actions, there may be a close connection and even overlap between them as regards their subject-matter. Thus an alleged infringement of Community law by a Member State may be the subject-matter of parallel proceedings before the Court of Justice brought, on the one hand, under Article 177 E.E.C./Article 150 Euratom and, on the other, under Article 169 E.E.C./Article 141 Euratom.[11] This is in fact possible because the two proceedings constitute, by reason of their purposes and legal effects, entirely independent remedies which are not mutually exclusive.[12] Nevertheless, in the context of preliminary rulings the European Court is strictly limited to giving an interpretation of the Community provision allegedly infringed, within the framework of the questions referred and only to the extent necessary to enable the national court to render a decision on the merits of the case. It cannot pronounce upon the incompatibility of the national measures with Community law and the consequences thereof. It can do so only in a direct action brought against the Member State concerned, specifically designed for that purpose, in which the Court can deal exhaustively with all aspects of the infringement and its legal consequences.[13] It follows that a preliminary ruling given by the Court cannot in principle prejudice the outcome of any investigation that the Commission may carry out in the same matter to establish the compatibility of the national measure with Community provisions.[14]

Likewise, the legality or validity of an act of a Community institution may in principle be the subject-matter both of a reference for preliminary ruling and, at the same time, of a direct action brought either for annulment under Article 173 E.E.C./Article 146 Euratom or for damages under Articles 178, 215(2) E.E.C./Articles 151, 188(2) Euratom. This may be the case irrespective of whether the different proceedings involve the same[15] or different[16] parties and legal issues. The grounds on which the Court may investigate the legality of the act in such circumstances, as well as the consequences of its judgment, will vary according to the characteristics of each of the different proceedings.[17]

Since, however, delimitation between references for preliminary rulings and direct actions is based upon delimitation between national and Community jurisdictions, the choice between these various forms of remedy is not left to the discretion of the parties. Rather, it is determined by strict jurisdictional rules. Thus, whenever the immediate source of the grievance is an act of the national authorities taken in implementation of Community provisions, the proper remedy lies with the national authorities, including the courts, which must solve any dispute in accordance with Community law as to substance and in accordance with domestic law as to competence, procedure and form. Should the solution of the dispute depend upon the interpretation or validity of the Community provision implemented, the national courts may (or must) refer the matter to the European Court for a preliminary ruling. The aggrieved party is however not entitled to bring the case, in circumvention of the national jurisdiction, before the Court by the expedient of a direct action (either for annulment or for damages) and thus obtain a material revision of the implementing act and, in appropriate cases, damages. Such a revision would lie beyond the Court's jurisdiction. This is so even though the Community provision is the (real or presumed) cause of the grievance. A direct action before the European Court will lie only in a case in which, and to the extent to which, the national authorities are unable to afford adequate redress.[18] Thus any possible overlap of the various proceedings on grounds of subject-matter cannot lead to an overlap of Community and national jurisdictions. In view of the fact that most Community provisions affect individual rights and interests only through implementing domestic acts, such a strict separation of preliminary rulings from direct actions on jurisdictional grounds further increases the importance of the former in the system of the legal protection set up by the Treaties.

In practice, the increasing importance of preliminary rulings is shown by the fact that, excluding staff disputes, by far the most cases come before the Court of Justice on a reference from the national courts. Thus, of the five hundred and fourty-six cases so far decided by the Court under the E.E.C. Treaty,[19] not less than three hundred and fifty-four were preliminary rulings, of which three hundred and thirty-seven related to the interpretation, and fourty to the validity, of Community provisions.[20]

1102. Jurisdiction of the Court of Justice

Under Article 41 E.C.S.C., the Court of Justice has sole jurisdiction to give preliminary rulings on the validity of acts of the Commission and of the Council where such validity is in issue in proceedings brought before a national court or tribunal. Due, probably, to the fact that acts of the institutions taken under the E.C.S.C. Treaty are very rarely in issue in domestic proceedings, this jurisdiction of the Court of Justice has not been invoked so far. It will not, therefore, be discussed any further in this Chapter.

Under Article 177 E.E.C./Article 150 Euratom, the Court of Justice has jurisdiction to give preliminary rulings concerning two distinct areas, i.e. (1) the interpretation of the Treaties and the acts of the institutions; and (2) the determination of the validity of the acts of the institutions. These provisions place a double limitation upon the jurisdiction of the Court of Justice. First, the Court is restricted to the interpretation and the determination of the validity of 'Community law'. It cannot, therefore, deal with the interpretation and validity of provisions falling exclusively within the boundaries of general international (treaty) law or domestic law. The former is a task for international adjudication; the latter is one for the national courts and tribunals. The jurisdiction of the European Court thus ends where the material scope of application of Community law ends. Secondly, the Court is restricted to an abstract 'interpretation' and 'determination of the validity' of Community law. It cannot, therefore, engage in the 'application' of the law to concrete, individual persons, cases and situations. This is a task falling within the jurisdiction of the national courts.

It is thus clear that the system of preliminary rulings is based on a strict separation of functions and competences between the European Court and the national courts. Whilst the European Court is required to enable the national courts to give a decision within the limits of their jurisdiction, it must remain within the sphere of its own. It cannot, under the guise of interpretation or appraisal of validity, substitute itself for the national courts which retain the power to apply Community law to cases properly brought before them. Otherwise a conflict of competences might arise which might seriously prejudice the system of judicial review and co-operation instituted by the Treaties. Thus the dividing line between the respective jurisdictions of the European Court and the domestic courts corresponds to that between the mental processes of law 'interpretation' and 'application'. Since the abstract interpretation of Community law always takes place in the context of concrete cases which are the subject of litigation, finding a clear-cut division between the two types of activities, and the two spheres of jurisdiction that correspond to them, is one of the most delicate problems presented by the system of preliminary rulings. How the European Court has approached and solved that problem, will be further considered in the following Sections.[1]

Subject to the foregoing distinctions and limitations, the jurisdiction of the Court of Justice is dependent solely upon the existence of a valid request for a preliminary ruling from a national court or tribunal.[2] The jurisdiction of the Court is properly invoked by the formal notification to it of such a request,[3] and continues to exist as long as the request has neither been withdrawn nor become devoid of object,[4] provided that the Court is satisfied from its wording that the question(s) raised concern(s) either the interpretation or the validity of primary or secondary Community law. The Court is neither required nor authorised to review the facts, grounds and considerations which may have led the national court to its choice of questions, nor whether the reference is relevant to, or necessary for, the rendering of a decision in the main action.[5] Nor can the Court investigate whether the national court has jurisdiction to make the reference[6] (unless that jurisdiction is challenged on grounds of Community law);[7] whether the plaintiff in the main action has sufficient legal interest in the matter;[8] whether the order for reference has acquired the force of *res judicata*;[9] or whether interest in the reference has not been lost due to the occurrence of new facts or events such as, for example, the amendment of the national law concerning the case.[10] All these questions fall exclusively within the jurisdiction of the domestic courts which are free to decide whether and, if so, at what stage of the proceedings and with respect to what legal issues a ruling on a point of Community law is necessary to the solution of the dispute before them. Consequently, whenever a valid reference is made to it, the European Court must assume that the interpretation or the appraisal of the validity of the provisions on which a ruling is sought is necessary to enable the national court to give judgment, without having jurisdiction to investigate whether the provisions referred are in fact applicable to the case at issue.[11]

Since, however, it is not the task of the Court of Justice to embark upon purely academic exercises, it will refrain from giving a ruling on a question which is manifestly unrelated to the main action or in a situation which clearly does not call for an interpretation and application of the Community provisions in issue. Such a situation may occur, for example, where the national court has committed a manifest error in specifying the provisions referred;[12] where the answer given by the Court to one of the questions submitted makes it superfluous to reply to the others;[13] where the question is, in the circumstances of the case, patently irrelevant,[14] without any purpose[15] or based clearly on a misinterpretation of documents.[16] Inevitably, in such exceptional cases, the Court of Justice will have to make an appraisal of the *prima facie* relevance to the main action of the question or provision referred. The same applies where the Court itself has substantially reformulated the question submitted so as to be able to give a reply to it.[17]

Nor is the Court empowered, on the other hand, to go beyond the scope of the reference, either of its own motion or on that of the various parties entitled to submit written observations to it.[18] Except where the scope of the reference is not clearly defined,[19] the Court cannot, in accordance with the *ne ultra petita* principle,[20] deal with any question or with the interpretation or validity of any provision of Community law which has not been formally brought before it by the national court, even if that question or provision should play a part in the principal proceedings. Not only would such a practice mean exceeding by the Court of the limits of its jurisdiction, but it would deprive the above-mentioned parties of their right to submit observations in respect of points not included in the original reference.[21]

1103. (1) Interpretation of Community law

As seen in the previous Section,[1] the jurisdiction of the Court of Justice to give interpretative preliminary rulings is subject to a double limitation. The first of these limitation restricts the competence of the Court to the area of 'Community law'. The second restricts the Court to the 'interpretation' of that law. These two limitations are considered below in turn.

(a) *Limitation to Community law*

The Court's jurisdiction to interpret by way of preliminary rulings covers (and at the same time is restricted to) the whole area of primary and secondary Community law. This includes, in the first place, the 'basic' Community Treaties, i.e. the E.E.C.,[2] Euratom,[3] Merger,[4] Budgetary[5] and Accession[6] Treaties, together with the various Annexes and Protocols attached to them which form an integral part thereof.[7] Of course, interpretation of the E.E.C. Treaty includes interpretation of Article 177 itself.[8] Although the E.C.S.C.

Treaty does not provide for a similar reference procedure in respect of interpretation, the Court has power to give preliminary rulings on questions concerning the interpretation of provisions of the E.C.S.C. Treaty or its Annexes and Protocols if the same questions also concern identical provisions in the E.E.C./Euratom Treaties or their Annexes and Protocols which provisions must then be interpreted jointly.[9]

In the second place, the power of the Court covers at least such of the further Treaties concluded between the Member States as have been brought within its jurisdiction by means of express provisions. These include the Convention on Jurisdiction and the Enforcement of Judgments in Civil and Commercial Matters of 1968 and the Convention on the Mutual Recognition of Companies and Legal Persons of 1968 whose interpretation has been entrusted to the Court of Justice by means of separate Protocols.[10] Except where these Protocols provide otherwise, the interpretation of those Conventions is governed by the general rules and procedures relating to preliminary rulings.[11]

In the third place, the competence of the Court of Justice extends to the interpretation of treaties and agreements which the Communities have concluded with third States and international organisations, with or without the participation of the Member States acting jointly as co-signatories.[12] Such a competence has been explained on the grounds that, since those treaties and agreements are concluded by the Council by means of a decision, they must be assimilated, as far as the Community is concerned, to acts of the institutions. As such, they form an integral part of Community law and fall within the Court's jurisdiction.[13] Alternatively, they create obligations for the institutions and the Member States and the definition of the scope of a Member State's Community obligation is always a matter involving interpretation of Community law.[14]

The Court's jurisdiction to interpret encompasses, in the fourth place, all acts of the Community institutions in general, regardless of whether or not they have binding force[15] and are directly applicable in the technical sense of this term.[16] It thus embraces not only regulations, directives, decisions, recommendations and opinions of the Council and Commission, but also the judgments and orders[17] as well as the Rules of Procedure of the Court of Justice[18] and joint acts (e.g. resolutions) of the Council and the Representatives of the Governments of the Member States.[19] Whether it also covers measures of the Government Representatives acting on their own, is doubtful.[20]

On the other hand, it follows from the limitation under consideration that the Court of Justice has no jurisdiction to give preliminary rulings concerning the interpretation of provisions of international (treaty) law which bind the Member States outside the framework of Community law. The Court thus cannot interpret terms occurring in agreements concluded between the Member States prior to the establishment of the Communities (or even thereafter but outside the Community framework), even though the agreement deals with a subject-matter which is within Community law (e.g.

social security) and is referred to in a Community regulation as forming an integral part thereof. If, however, the question raised is capable of being understood as concerning the interpretation of Community provisions (e.g. because the terms in issue have been replaced by the corresponding provisions of a regulation), the Court will have jurisdiction to give a ruling.[21]

Likewise, the Court of Justice has no jurisdiction to interpret provisions of national law in the framework of the preliminary ruling procedure.[22] Consequently, it can neither hear arguments put forward by, nor settle disputes arising between, the parties to the main action based on or involving the interpretation or application of domestic provisions. It is for the national courts to decide over such arguments and disputes.[23] Nor can it, for example, classify a domestic charge or tax,[24] or a social security contribution or benefit,[25] from the point of view of the relevant provisions of Community law (still less under national law), although it can interpret the Community provisions in order to enable the national court to apply them correctly to the charge, tax, contribution or benefit in question. On the other hand, the Court has jurisdiction to interpret not only the meaning of a Community rule but also the nature and scope of the legal effects which Community law attributes to it within the legal systems of the Member States. In particular, the Court can pronounce upon the direct applicability of Community provisions and upon the nature and scope of the legal protection which necessarily follows from it for individuals within the Member States. These questions involve interpretation not of national (constitutional) law but of Community law.[26]

As a counterpart to the restriction imposed upon the Court, Member States are under an obligation to refrain from any measure or procedure which might distort or conceal the Community nature of a rule and thus withdraw it from the Court's jurisdiction. Any national legislation which purports to have such effect, for example by converting a (directly applicable) rule of Community law into national law, leaves unaffected the jurisdiction of the Court to give preliminary rulings in respect of that rule.[27] Nor can the power of the Court be challenged on any other grounds of national law, such as, for example, the argument that since on the basis of national law the court making the reference is obliged to apply even a conflicting domestic provision a need for the interpretation of Community law cannot arise. Such a view would be clearly tantamount to affirming the supremacy of national law over Community law.[28]

(b) *Limitation to interpretation*

It follows from the separation of functions between the national courts and the European Court that within the framework of the preliminary ruling procedure the jurisdiction of the latter is restricted, apart from the appraisal of the validity of the acts of institutions, to the interpretation of Community law. Accordingly, the Court has, in principle, no power to take cognisance of, conduct investigations into, or settle disputes between the parties concerning the assessment of the facts involved.[29] Nor has the Court authority to find that a concrete factual situation meets the conditions laid down in a Community provision and that therefore certain legal effects follow. The only course allowed to the Court is to define the scope of the letter and spirit of Community provisions while remaining at the level of generalisation.[30] Although the Court is not, in principle, prevented from admitting evidence for certain, limited purposes (e.g. to explain and complete the facts as stated in the order for reference where the conclusions to be drawn from the evidence are common ground or, where this is not the case, to ascertain the issues between the parties),[31] or from obtaining expert opinion on certain technical questions,[32] it has so far been reluctant to do so in most cases. Its practice has been, rather, to refrain from giving a ruling as requested where, in the absence of adequate information, a reply either would not be possible without a preliminary investigation of facts[33] or would risk corresponding only imperfectly to the circumstances of the case.[34]

The Court has, moreover, no jurisdiction to apply the law to a particular person, case or situation; to rule on the merits of the main action or on any disputed issue; to act as a supreme court to reconcile conflicting decisions given by the courts of the different Member States. Nor can it decide upon the compatibility of a national law or administrative practice with Community law, nor upon how the former should be brought in conformity with the latter. In other words, it cannot settle conflicts between the two legal systems. This would amount to the application of Community law to a particular case which the Court is entitled to do only in a direct action brought against the Member State whose law is in question.[35] It is therefore always a matter for the national court in the main action to apply to the particular case before it the rules of Community law as interpreted by the European Court, and to reach a decision on the question of compatibility in the light of the criteria laid down in the Court's ruling.[36]

Thus, for example, the European Court has declined jurisdiction in favour of the national courts in the following matters, holding that they concern the application rather than the interpretation of Community law: tariff classification of goods (i.e. whether the products with which the main action is concerned meet the conditions whereby they can be classified under one or another tariff heading in the Common Customs Tariff);[37] compatibility of fixing maximum prices for sugar with Community agricultural provisions;[38] standard of care that may be expected of a prudent and diligent trader;[39] existence of circumstances amounting to *force majeure*;[40] existence of a risk of overlapping of a sickness and an invalidity insurance benefit;[41] nature, location and legal effects of a sporting activity with respect to Community law:[42] existence of an abuse by an undertaking of a dominant position within the meaning of Articles 86, 90 E.E.C.;[43] existence of an arbitrary discrimination or a disguised restriction on trade through the exercise of industrial and commercial property rights within the meaning of Article 36 E.E.C.;[44] nature of a domestic duty (i.e. whether it constitutes a charge having an effect equivalent to a customs duty within the meaning of Article 13(2) E.E.C. or an internal taxation within the meaning of Article 95 E.E.C.);[45] etc.

It is, however, clear that rigid adherence to the above principles might defeat the very purpose of preliminary rulings in certain circumstances. Uniform interpretation of Community law is not an end in itself; it is rather a means to ensure uniform application of that law throughout the whole territory of the Communities. Since the most serious threat to uniform application is presented by incompatible national laws and administrative practices, one of the most important functions of preliminary rulings is to enable national courts to ascertain whether a given law or practice is in conformity with Community law. They would be left without any guidance in that vital area, should the European Court decline to give a ruling (as has been submitted in a number of cases by one of the parties or by Member States) on the grounds that what is involved is the application, rather than the interpretation, of Community law and that the matter is thus outside the Court's jurisdiction.

In order to deal with such situations, the Court has developed certain techniques or practices which enable it, while paying due respect to the jurisdictional division and the consequent limitations, to supply the national courts with as helpful and useful an interpretation as is compatible with that division. Thus the Court always looks for the real meaning and the Community relevance of the question referred. Where a question as formulated by the national court is not limited to the pure interpretation of Community law but contains elements involving the application of that law or the interpretation, application or compatibility of national law, the Court is prepared to extract from its wording that core which alone pertains to the interpretation of Community provisions and to give a ruling on it only. In most cases such a ruling will enable the national court to decide those further aspects which fall within its own jurisdiction alone.[46] Also, rather than dismiss a request as inadmissible, the Court is willing to rephrase, whenever possible, a question drawn up in so specific a language as to refer to particular persons, products, factual or legal situations, in a general and abstract manner and give a general and abstract reply to it.[47] This is often necessary where the question relates to the interpretation of the Common Customs Tariff and in essence involves the tariff classification of certain specified goods. A straightforward placing of a particular product under a particular heading would clearly amount to the application of the Common Customs Tariff (a Community provision) to a specific case. To avoid that, the Court will reformulate the question and determine, not whether the product in issue falls within a specific category, but the general and abstract criteria which govern classification under the relevant heading.[48] Nevertheless, to avoid divergent interpretation and application of a concept at the national level, in certain cases it may become necessary to give a detailed (almost individualised) answer; in such cases the interpretation and the application of the law is almost indistinguishable.[49] Also, to provide a helpful answer to the national courts, the Court has found it necessary, in a growing number of cases (especially in criminal proceedings), to examine and give a straightforward ruling on the compatibility of national provisions and practices with Community law.[50]

The fact that the Court always aims at rendering an abstract interpretation of Community law does not mean that the Court delivers its rulings in a 'vacuum'. On the contrary, in order to give a useful and helpful reply which will enable the national court to reach its own decision, the Court expects the latter to set out the factual and legal context in which the requested interpretation is to be placed. The data supplied by the court making the reference as well as the parties entitled to make submissions to the Court will provide the general framework within which the Court will examine the question and prepare an appropriate answer to it.[51] In fact, the absence of accurate information as to the national legal context may in certain circumstances compel the Court to decline to give a ruling as requested lest its reply, not corresponding to the circumstances of the case, assume a meaning different from what the Court in fact intended.[52] In such circumstances a re-submission of the same question with an indication of its relationship to the relevant legal issues may enable the European Court to give a more specific and appropriate answer.[53]

Although the European Court is not in principle permitted to go outside the scope of the questions referred to it by the national court,[54] it is not rigidly bound by the terms of the reference. Where the questions to be answered and the provisions to be interpreted have not been drawn up or specified in precise terms, the Court has the power to extract them from the wording and reasoning of the order for reference, rather than dismiss the request as inadmissible. In so doing the Court will determine the scope of its interpretation with a view to helping the national court to settle the dispute before it.[55] But even where the reference is clearly worded, the Court is not bound by the express formulation of the questions as submitted to it by the national court. In the interests of an exhaustive and proper clarification of the matter it may depart from the order of questions, may give supplementary interpretation and may have regard to all provisions which are relevant to the issues raised, provided that it does not enter the area of the application of the law.[56] In certain situations it may even have to deal with the question of validity, i.e. where the interpretation and the determination of the validity of an act are inseparably interwoven.[57]

1104. (2) Validity of acts of institutions

Uniform application of Community law can be ensured only if Community provisions have not merely the same substantive meaning but also the same validity and efficacy in all the Member States. In fact, any divergence as to the validity and binding force of Community measures in the different national jurisdictions would be much more detrimental to the coherence and uniformity of the Community legal system than a variation in their interpretation. It is therefore of paramount importance that a central authority, the European Court of Justice, should have exclusive jurisdiction to pronounce upon the validity of the acts of institutions whenever any doubt is raised in that respect in the context of proceedings brought before national courts. This is the more necessary as the domestic courts are, by virtue of the autonomous nature of Community law, in principle prevented from deciding upon the validity of Community instruments.[1] Instead, they must resort to the preliminary ruling procedure.[2]

Although the Treaties expressly refer to the 'validity' of acts of the institutions, that concept is not limited to the formal validity of such acts. Thus the jurisdiction of the Court of Justice is not restricted to merely examining whether a valid act is formally in existence or whether such an act has not lost its validity through repeal or amendment by the relevant institution or through annulment by the Court of Justice. It is inconceivable that the authors of the Treaties should have devised an important, complex and rather cumbersome procedure for such a limited purpose only. In principle, therefore, the jurisdiction of the Court in reference procedures for preliminary rulings, just as in the context of pleas of illegality,[3] extends to reviewing also the substantive legality of Community acts. Thus, in spite of the difference in wording between Article 177 E.E.C./Article 150 Euratom (which refer to 'validity') and Article 173 E.E.C./Article 146 Euratom (which use the word 'legality'), the Court of Justice can exercise the same degree of control over the legality of the institutions' conduct in proceedings for preliminary rulings as in direct actions for annulment. This further underlines the importance of the former as an additional and complementary means of legal protection in the system created by the Treaties.[4] Although both forms of remedy can thus be used for the same basic purpose (control of objective legality), there are important differences between them which concern (a) the acts subject to challenge; (b) the grounds and (c) the consequences of invalidity. These three aspects are considered below in turn.

(a) *Acts subject to challenge*

While the validity of the Community Treaties themselves cannot be challenged in court proceedings,[5] the system of preliminary rulings enables national courts to refer to the European Court all questions regarding the validity of all acts of the Community institutions without any distinction or limitation.[6] The term 'act' must therefore be understood in the broadest possible sense, covering both binding and non-binding measures.[7] The restrictions which in a direct action for annulment are imposed upon private parties in respect of law-making acts and acts addressed to others[8] are not applicable to references for preliminary rulings. Here in the interests of an extensive legal protection, private individuals are enabled to submit to judicial review, without proof of direct and individual concern, the validity and legality of regulations, directives and decisions addressed to Member States and others, no less than that of decisions addressed to them as well as recommendations and opinions.[9] Moreover, they are enabled to do so without any limitation in respect of time.[10] The only category of acts that are excluded from the ambit of preliminary rulings are those adopted by the Representatives of the Governments of the Member States meeting in Council which are, in essence, in the nature of international agreements.[11]

(b) *Grounds of invalidity*

While a direct action for annulment must be based on one (or more) of four specified grounds,[12] the jurisdiction of the Court of Justice to give preliminary rulings is, in principle, subject to no restriction as to the reasons for which the validity of Community acts can be contested. Consequently, this jurisdiction encompasses all grounds for invalidity that can conceivably be raised against such acts.[13] These include, in particular, infringement of rules of international law provided that the latter are binding upon the Communities and capable of creating rights which private individuals may invoke in a court of law;[14] infringement of generally recognised principles of Community law such as the principles of the protection of fundamental rights,[15] of proportionality,[16] of Community preference;[17] infringement of the provisions of the basic Community Treaties;[18] infringement of the provisions of another, higher-ranking Community act such as an enabling (basic) regulation;[19] excess by the Commission of delegated powers;[20] illegal subdelegation of delegated powers from the Commission to Member States;[21] lack of competence;[22] choice of an improper legislative form (e.g. regulation);[23] insufficient statement of reasons,[24] etc. Since, however, the validity of a Community instrument can only be judged in the light of Community law, recourse to rules and principles of national law, including constitutional principles such as that of protection of fundamental rights, is not admissible to challenge that validity. Such a possibility would in fact undermine the unity and efficacy of Community law.[25]

While thus in references for preliminary rulings the possible reasons for invalidity are wider than in direct actions for annulment, those grounds which may be invoked in both procedures (i.e. the four grounds of action) are subject to identical rules and limitations.[26] Thus in both cases the Court applies the same criteria in assessing both the formal aspects (e.g. adequacy of reasoning)[27] and the substantive legality of the act challenged. Where the Council or Commission enjoys a wide discretionary power in evaluating complex economic situations, the Court, just as in a direct action, will not substitute its own evaluation for that of the institution. Instead, in reviewing the legality of the exercise of such discretion, it restricts itself to examining whether the institution's assessment contains a patent error or constitutes a misuse of powers or whether the institution did not clearly exceed the bounds of its discretion.[28] To confirm its legality, it will be sufficient if a measure does not appear at the moment of its adoption as obviously inappropriate for the realisation of the objective for which the discretionary power has been granted.[29] Moreover, since the Court deals with the sole question of legality, it cannot, just as in a direct action, attach any importance to considerations of expediency or suitability.[30]

It follows from the nature and purpose of preliminary rulings that the function of the Court of Justice in such proceedings is not to review, in a comprehensive and definitive manner, the legality of the act challenged. The Court's task is solely to declare whether the doubts and criticisms put forward in that respect by the parties in the main action and expressed or indicated by the national court in its order for reference are well-founded.[31] Consequently, it is not sufficient for the court making the reference to pose a completely general question, such as whether the act in issue is invalid 'for any reason'. Instead, the national court is expected clearly to state the arguments giving rise to doubt as to validity and specify the legal grounds on which the alleged invalidity is based. Otherwise the issue would not be precisely defined, unlike the position in an action for annulment, and the European Court would have to make exhaustive enquiries into every conceivable formal or material defect that might invalidate the act in question. This could run counter to the intentions of the parties in the main action. Moreover, the ruling of the Court might thereby have a scope which might not correspond to its knowledge of the facts and, contrary to the intention of the Treaties, might go beyond the proceedings giving rise to the reference.[32] Nevertheless, just as in reference procedures involving interpretation, the Court does not follow a policy of rigid formalism towards the national courts. Thus where a question referred to it appears at first sight to be aimed at interpretation but has the real purpose of ascertaining the validity of a measure, the Court will give its ruling on the question of validity rather than send the case back to the national court with an inadequate reply.[33] Conversely, where it is the issue of validity that is raised but cannot be decided without a prior interpretation of the act, the Court will assume that a request for interpretation is also (implicitly) submitted to it and will proceed accordingly.[34]

It follows from the foregoing that where in its reference the national court clearly defines the grounds on which the validity of the measure is challenged, the European Court is in principle restricted to an examination of those grounds. The limited status of private parties in preliminary procedures usually does not permit them to raise, before the Court of Justice, new objections over and above those which they have already put forward in the national proceedings and which have been included in the reference order.[35] Where, however, the national court fails to specify the alleged grounds of invalidity or refers to them in vague and general terms only, the European Court will not refuse to consider specific complaints made by the parties (or one of them) whether or not they were already raised before the national court.[36] In any case, the Court is always willing to examine at the parties' initiative such grounds of invalidity as may be raised by the Court of its own motion. These are basically the same as in a direct action for annulment and include, for example, lack of competence, infringement of an essential procedural requirement, lack of the necessary publication, etc. but not misuse of (discretionary) powers and only to a limited extent infringement of the Treaties and rules of Community law.[37] Exceptionally, the Court is even willing to consider other objections put forward for the first time by one of the parties in its written observations and falling clearly outside the scope of the reference.[38]

(c) *Consequences of invalidity*

The consequence of illegality, if established in the context of a direct action, is the annulment of the act concerned with *erga omnes* and retroactive effect.[39] Such far-reaching consequences are carefully counterbalanced by the restrictions on the admissibility of the action in respect of acts that can be challenged, grounds that can be invoked and time-limits. By contrast, preliminary rulings are free from all those restrictions. Their aim is basically to enable the national court to reach a decision in a given case pending before it. It is therefore sufficient, and at the same time necessary, that a declaration of invalidity should have consequences which are strictly limited to that case. Otherwise the reference procedure might be used to circumvent the restrictions on the admissibility of a direct action. It follows that a measure which is declared to be invalid in the context of a preliminary ruling will not thereby become null and void. While it can no longer be applied to the parties in the principal action, it continues to be in force as regards all other persons.[40] Nevertheless, beyond this strict *inter partes* effect, a declaration of invalidity is bound to have wider consequences in certain other respects which are considered in a subsequent Section.[41]

1105. Optional references

The procedure to obtain a preliminary ruling can be set in motion only by a court or tribunal of a Member State. The parties to an action pending before such a court or tribunal, the Member States as such, their various internal (legislative, executive, administrative) agencies, or the Community institutions have no standing to refer preliminary questions to the European Court. The power of the national courts and tribunals to make a reference is generally optional, except in the case of courts and tribunals against whose decisions there is no judicial remedy under national law, where it is compulsory. The latter is considered separately in the following Section.[1]

Generally, the provisions of Article 177 E.E.C./Article 150 Euratom empower every national court or tribunal without distinction to refer any case to the European Court for a preliminary ruling when it considers that a decision on a question of Community law is necessary to enable it to give judgment.[2] In practice when a reference is made to it the European Court, in order to ascertain if it is properly seized of the question, must first satisfy itself as to whether the body submitting the request is a 'court or tribunal' of a Member State. For the purposes of preliminary rulings these concepts are interpreted according to the criteria of Community rather than national law. Although the judicial structure of the (original) Member States is based on largely common principles, it may differ in certain respects for historical or constitutional reasons. In order to ensure the uniform interpretation and application of Community law, a body may have to be recognised as a 'court or tribunal' for the purposes of making a reference, although it may not be so considered in its own national legal system. Nevertheless, in appraising its status, the European Court will apply criteria distilled from the general principles that govern judicial organisation in the different Member States.

Thus a body will be regarded as a 'court or tribunal' if it duly represents the power of the State (i.e. is properly and permanently set up under national law), exercises a judicial function (i.e. settles disputes according to rules of law) and follows an adversary procedure similar to those used in ordinary courts of law (i.e. one which ensures its independence and impartiality as well as the proper hearing of the parties).[3] The fact that the body is set up under private rather than public law,[4] that is has strictly advisory competence,[5] that it does not form part of its own domestic judicial hierarchy,[6] is irrelevant. Thus specialised bodies on the periphery of the ordinary judicial structure (such as operate especially in the field of social security) may also be entitled to submit preliminary questions, although it is still not quite clear whether this includes arbitration generally.[7] In the United Kingdom, the reference procedure is open, in addition to the ordinary civil and criminal courts, also to administrative tribunals, e.g. the National Insurance Commissioner[8] or the Employment Appeal Tribune.[8a]

The power of the courts and tribunals to refer is comprehensive. Since the efficacy of Community law cannot vary according to the various branches of the national law in which it may take effect, the admissibility of a reference does not depend on the nature of the proceedings in which it has arisen.[9] Thus references may be made in civil, criminal, administrative, fiscal, social, labour law, etc. proceedings, including non-contentious proceedings where the courts merely perform an administrative function in judicial form (e.g. keeping of the Register of Companies)[10] and including proceedings for interlocutory injunctions[11] as well as other special summary (*ex parte*) forms of procedure, e.g. where the President of the court can make an order (e.g. for payment) on a simple application by the plaintiff and without first hearing the defendant.[12]

The power of the national courts to refer is derived directly from, and governed by, the Treaties and not national law. It follows that that power cannot be taken away, fettered or interfered with in any way by acts of the institutions or provisions of domestic law. Thus the provision in Article 9(3) of Regulation 17, according to which the authorities of the Member States, including the courts, cease to have competence to apply Articles 85 and 86 E.E.C. as soon as the Commission has initiated a procedure under Articles 2, 3 or 6 of that Regulation, cannot affect the power of a national court before which the direct effect of Articles 85 and 86 is pleaded to refer questions to the European Court for a preliminary ruling even after the Commission has opened the procedure.[13] Likewise, a rule of national law whereby a court is bound on points of law by the rulings of a superior court in the same case or in a previous case (e.g. under the doctrine of precedent) cannot deprive the inferior courts of their power to refer to the European Court questions of interpretation of Community law involving such rulings. Consequently, if the inferior court considers that the ruling on law made by the superior court would lead it to give a judgment contrary to Community law, it must be able to submit the relevant questions to the European Court, unless those questions were already referred by the superior court. Thus a lower court may request a preliminary ruling not only when a case comes before it for the first time, but also when it is reconsidering the case after its judgment has been quashed or referred back for any other reason by a higher court. Clearly, if the lower courts were bound by decisions of the appeal courts on points involving Community law, this would compromise the jurisdiction of the European Court, defeat the purpose of the preliminary ruling system and, ultimately, undermine the effectiveness of Community law in general.[14] In view of these considerations it is evident that 'guidelines' and similar directions given by higher courts for the guidance of the lower courts on how to exercise their discretionary power of reference can have no binding force and are, strictly speaking, incompatible with Community law.[15] They may in fact have undesirable consequences.[16] Nevertheless, decisions of the inferior courts to refer a case to the European Court remain subject to the ordinary remedies normally available under national law.[17]

From the foregoing it follows that, subject to what is stated below, national courts and tribunals against whose decisions there is judicial remedy enjoy unfettered discretion in referring matters to the Court of Justice. They may freely decide whether to refer or not to refer, what legal issues and at what stage of the procedure to refer to the European Court.[18] Their decision and the reasons therefore are not subject to review by that Court.[19] The only prerequisites for an exercise of that discretion are, first, that a 'question' involving interpretation or consideration of the validity of provisions of Community law should be 'raised' before them and, secondly, that they should consider a preliminary ruling on that question to be 'necessary' to enable them to give judgment. A question involving Community law may be raised by one of the parties alone, by both parties jointly, or by the court itself acting of its own motion.[20] Such a 'question' is 'raised' as soon as plausible arguments are put forward which cast *prima facie* a reasonable doubt upon the meaning, scope, effect or validity of a Community provision[21] or upon the compatibility with it of a national measure or practice. A preliminary ruling on such a question becomes, generally, 'necessary' where the court assesses, on the one hand, that the clarification of the question is essential to the determination of the issues before it and, on the other hand, that the court itself would be unable to perform that task without the help of a ruling.[22] The court must make its assessment in the light of the purposes of the preliminary ruling procedure and of the interests of the parties.[23] Thus whenever a fundamental concept of Community law (e.g. 'worker') requires interpretation, a preliminary ruling becomes generally 'necessary'.[24] Interpretation of such concepts by the national courts must be regarded, to say the least, as highly undesirable as being incompatible with the very purpose of the preliminary rulings, i.e. that of ensuring uniform interpretation and application of Community law.[25] Nevertheless, a previous ruling by the European Court on the same or substantially similar questions may render a reference 'unnecessary' although it will not prevent the national court from re-submitting the point for a further ruling.[26]

The national courts are moreover entirely free to decide at what stage of the proceedings to refer.[27] Thus reference may be made even before the process of finding the facts has been completed. An early clarification of the points of Community law may enable the national court to decide what issues of fact are relevant.[28] Nor is it necessary that the domestic court should first consider issues of national law. The possibility that a solution found thereunder might make resort to Community law superfluous cannot in itself render the reference premature.[29] Generally speaking, in most cases an early reference by the courts of first instance is desirable as this can save both considerable time and expenses later.

Although upon a strict interpretation of Article 177 E.E.C./Article 150 Euratom the lower courts of the Member States enjoy complete discretion as to whether or not to refer a case to the European Court, it is submitted that there are at least two categories of questions to which this discretionary power does not extend. These concern, on the one hand, the direct applicability of the provisions of primary or secondary Community law and, on the other, the validity of a Community act. It follows from the very concept of direct applicability and the independent nature of the Community legal order that consideration of these questions falls within the exclusive competence of the European Court. Consequently, national courts of any rank have no jurisdiction to pronounce a provision directly applicable or invalid.[30] It follows that whenever such questions are raised for the first time, and it is not possible for the court to confirm the validity of the provision in question (a decision which, it is submitted, the national court has power to take), it is bound to refer the matter to the European Court.[31]

As regards the every-day practice of the lower national courts, the following are some of the considerations that usually determine the exercise, one way or another, of the discretionary power to refer. Points in favour of making a reference: a reference at the earliest possible stage in the proceedings will save time and expense;[32] an early reference may prevent conflicting decisions being given on the same substantive issues in parallel proceedings pending before courts in the different Member States;[33] an early reference does not prevent the grant of an interlocutory injunction pending the trial to preserve the *status quo*;[34] a reference is necessary if it would be impossible for the court to give judgment without a preliminary ruling;[35] a reference is not premature if there are no substantial issues of fact or of national law to be determined beforehand.[36] Points in favour of not making a reference: the question on which preliminary ruling is sought is irrelevant and has as its sole object delaying tactics;[37] allegations as to the invalidity of a Community act or incompatibility with Community law of a national measure are unsubstantiated;[38] the court is able itself to interpret the Community provisions in issue[39] or determine their validity;[40] the court is able to decide the case before it without determining the question raised[41] or by applying national law only;[42] it is preferable to leave the reference to the court of last instance;[43] reference is incompatible with the urgency of reaching a decision in summary proceedings for an interlocutory injunction;[44] a reference would be premature at the given stage in the proceedings,[45] particularly before the facts have been found.[46]

1106. Compulsory references

If a question concerning the interpretation or the validity of Community provisions is raised in a case pending before a court or tribunal of a Member State against whose decisions there is no judicial remedy under national law, that court or tribunal is obliged to bring the matter before the Court of Justice.[1] The circumstances in which the case has come before such a court or tribunal are in principle irrelevant,[2] although in interlocutory proceedings for an interim measure the obligation to refer may not arise in certain cases.[2a]

The question which particular courts and tribunals of a Member State are subject to the obligation to refer can only be determined in the light of the object and purpose of the compulsory reference system. That object is to prevent a body of national case-law not in accord with the rules of Community law from coming into existence in any Member State[2b] and not, as has been wrongly suggested,[3] to bring before the European Court 'substantial cases of the first importance worthy of reference' which alone usually come before the highest courts of the Member States. It follows that the compulsory reference system is not limited to particular courts, such as the House of Lords,[4] or to a class of courts, which stand at the summit of the judicial hierarchy and are within their respective spheres of competence courts of last instance in general and whose decisions are therefore never subject to appeal. The obligation to refer applies to any court whether of first, second or last instance whose ruling on an issue of Community law in a particular case is not subject to ordinary appeal (exceptional remedies, such as re-opening of a case, not included) for any reason whatever, i.e. whose decision in that case is final in the sense that it does not give rise to any review of the case on the request of either of the parties as regards either the facts or the law. In such situations it is, clearly, not the importance of the case as such but the finality of the decision and its possible adverse effect upon the national case-law that makes, as a matter of principle, a reference imperative.[4a]

Thus the duty to refer may encompass the lower courts, such as, for example, the Magistrates Courts, Sheriff Courts, etc. and their equivalents in other Member States,[5] appellate courts, such as, for example, the Court of Appeal, Court of Session, and their equivalents,[6] just as the highest courts themselves. Where the right of appeal against a particular decision is in principle available but subject to a discretionary leave (as may be the case with a decision of the English Court of Appeal or of the National Insurance Commissioner) and the court considers itself, for that reason, as not constituting a court against whose decision there is no judicial remedy and does not refer the matter to the European Court,[7] it is submitted that leave to appeal to the higher court cannot be refused. Otherwise a gap would be created in the system of preliminary rulings (which is envisaged as basically a closed system) that would undermine the effectiveness of Community law.[8] Failure to grant leave to appeal in such circumstances, just as any other failure to comply with the obligation to refer, will involve the Member State concerned in a breach of Community law and may make it liable to an action by the Commission or another Member State before the Court of Justice and even to pay compensation for any damage caused.[9]

The prerequisites for a compulsory reference are not the same as those for an optional reference. As seen in the previous Section,[10] the latter imply both that a 'question' of Community law should be 'raised' before a national court and that the court should consider a preliminary ruling 'necessary' to enable it to give judgment. This second requirement does not apply in the context of compulsory references.[11] The consequence is that an obligation to refer arises as soon as there are plausible reasons, put forward by one or both of the parties or perceived by the court of its own motion, casting a *prima facie* doubt upon the meaning, scope, effect or validity of a Community provision or upon the compatibility with it of a national measure or practice. On the other hand, it is submitted that it is neither necessary nor possible for the national court to assess whether the clarification of that doubt is materially essential (as distinct from being *prima facie* relevant) to the determination of the issues before it (e.g. because the dispute could be settled on the basis of — even a conflicting — national law alone), nor whether the court would itself be capable of performing that task without the help of a ruling. By so doing the court would necessarily enter an area reserved to the European Court, for such an assessment (in itself within the national court's jurisdiction) could only be made upon a prior interpretation and appraisal of the Community provision in question. Thus the courts of last resort cannot avoid their obligation to refer by saying that a preliminary ruling is not 'necessary' to enable them to give judgment. Any extension to such courts of the discretionary power of the lower courts to evaluate whether and when a reference is 'necessary' would render their obligation purely illusory. The only margin of discretion left to the national courts is to assess whether the question raised is not *prima facie* totally irrelevant to the solution of the dispute (which is not the same thing as being materially non-essential) or whether it is not manifestly unfounded, put forward belatedly, in bad faith, in pursuit of delaying tactics, or for other clearly impermissible reasons.[12] Only in this limited sense is it possible for courts and tribunals of last resort to examine whether a ruling on the question is 'necessary' to enable them to give judgment.[13] Otherwise such courts and tribunals are unreservedly required by the Treaties to refer to the European Court every question of interpretation or validity raised before them.[14]

It follows from the foregoing that the practice of some of the national courts of last instance not to refer a question to the European Court if the meaning of the Community provision involved is 'clear' (the so-called doctrine of *acte clair*)[15] is incompatible with both the wording and the spirit of Article 177 E.E.C./Article 150 Euratom. A provision becomes 'clear' only after it has been interpreted and only upon its interpretation will there be no 'question' as to its meaning and scope. Since interpretation is within the sole province of the European Court, a national court of last instance is justified in not referring a question to that Court only if the question is materially identical with one which has already been the subject of a preliminary ruling in a similar case or if the problem can be clarified by applying rules and principles developed in the Court's previous, 'established' case-law, taken as a whole. If therefore a national court of final instance does not itself interpret a Community provision or appraise its validity but simply applies an interpretation or appraisal drawn from a previous judgment of the European Court, then, and only then, will its obligation to refer cease.[16]

Since, moreover, the duty to refer extends to any matter over which the European Court has the jurisdiction of interpretation and appraisal of validity,[17] a reference cannot be denied on the grounds that what is involved is a question of compatibility of national law with Community law rather than an interpretation of the latter.[18] While interpretation of national law falls clearly outside the jurisdiction of the European Court (and consequently cases involving such interpretation need not be referred),[19] the appraisal of the nature and scope of the effect of a Community provision within the Member States does not. Since a problem of compatibility can be solved by the national court only upon a prior interpretation of the scope and effects of the relevant Community provision, a reference is mandatory in all cases where such a question arises.

1107. Content and form of references

In drawing up a reference regard must be paid both to the general objectives of the preliminary ruling system as a whole and to the particular purpose for which a ruling is sought. Thus it must be borne in mind, first, that that system is based on a strict separation of jurisdictions between the European Court and the national courts with the result that the Court can only interpret and consider the validity of Community provisions but cannot apply them to individual cases. Secondly, that the Court can do so only in order to help the national court settle the dispute before it.[1] In part different requirements will apply according to whether the reference concerns the interpretation or the validity of a Community provision.

Where the reference relates to interpretation, the national court must clearly specify which particular provisions of primary or secondary Community law it needs to have interpreted. General questions, such as 'are the provisions (of certain national laws) incompatible with the letter and the spirit of the Treaty of Rome or with the regulations, or any other obligations provided by the competent institutions created by the Treaty?' will make the task of both the European Court and the national courts more difficult.[2] It is moreover also necessary to put a precise question to the Court regarding the interpretation sought. Thus, for example, a general 'request for a preliminary ruling on the interpretation of Article 85 E.E.C. and its implementing regulations' is not sufficient.[3] Although the European Court will not dismiss such questions as inadmissible but will endeavour to extract their sense and purpose from the order for reference, its reasons and the file of the case, its power to do so is not unlimited.[4]

Although the national court is not required to furnish reasons for its reference, nor to state its own legal interpretation of the questions submitted, it is in most cases desirable that it should do so.[5] To enable the European Court to arrive at a useful interpretation, the referring court is generally expected to define precisely the subject-matter of the proceedings (including the main arguments of the parties) indicating the factual and legal context which has given rise to the request for reference and into which the interpretation is to be placed.[6] In formulating the actual questions to be referred, the court must remain at the level of abstraction. It must not put concrete cases and situations before the European Court which might involve the latter in an application, instead of interpretation, of the law.[7] Where the purpose of the question is to ascertain the compatibility of national provisions with Community law, it must be so phrased as to refer to the interpretation of the latter and not to the interpretation or the validity of the former (e.g. 'is Article ... of Regulation ... to be interpreted in such a way as to prohibit the adoption by the Member States of measures such as . . .' followed by a general description of the contents of the national measure in question without reference to it by name).[8]

Where the reference relates to the validity of a Community provision, the national court is required clearly to define the issues submitted for examination, i.e. the measure challenged, the reasons giving rise to doubt as to its validity and the legal grounds on which the alleged invalidity is based.[9]

Formulation of the actual questions to be referred is usually the task of the court making the reference. It should be composed of the same members who will eventually decide the case upon receiving the Court's ruling. Nevertheless, in exceptional cases the European Court will accept a reference even where the questions were drafted by the President of the court.[10] It will also accept supplementary questions notified to it, upon the request of one of the parties, by the national judge-rapporteur if this is justified by the subject-matter of the case and the requirement of an economical administration of justice.[11] In the framing of the questions the parties may, and usually do, play an active role. Normally the party which makes an application for a preliminary ruling presents to the court draft questions upon which the ruling is sought. Alternatively, the parties may jointly submit an agreed wording to the court which may then be incorporated in the reference[12] or may otherwise influence the court as to what questions and in what form to refer. This is the more important as, once the reference has reached the European Court, the parties are no longer able to add further questions or to alter its terms in any other way.[13] In special (summary) proceedings, where reference is made before the hearing of the defendant, it is therefore desirable to give that party an opportunity to make his comments before the case is referred to the European Court.[14]

As regards the form of the reference, neither the Treaties nor the Statutes and Rules of Procedure of the Court of Justice lay down, expressly or by implication, any particular requirements. It is thus generally permissible for the national courts to set out their request in a simple and direct way, leaving it to the Court of Justice to render a decision on that request only insofar as it has jurisdiction to do so. Subject to what has been said above, it is quite sufficient if the reference is made in a form which enables the Court to abstract from it without difficulty the questions of interpretation or validity which it contains.[15] The formal requirements are moreover satisfied by the direct transmission of the order for reference and the file of the case by the Registrar of the national court to the Registrar of the European Court.[16] The reference will therefore be proper even if the national court refers 'the parties', instead of itself referring the matter, to the European Court.[17]

In the United Kingdom special rules have been laid down concerning the form in which and the procedure according to which references are to be made. At present such rules apply to the following courts: in England and Wales: the Court of Appeal and High Court;[18] the Court of Appeal, Criminal Division;[19] the County Court;[20] the Crown Court;[21] in Scotland: the Court of Session;[22] High Court of Justiciary and other criminal proceedings;[23] the Sheriff Court.[24] The fact that no rules have so far been made for other courts (e.g. Magistrates' Courts and tribunals) cannot affect the power of these courts to make references as that power is directly conferred by the Treaties on all courts and tribunals of the Member States.[25]

The main common features of the rules applicable to the English courts are as follows. An order referring a question to the European Court may be made by the court of its own motion or on the application of either party. An order must set out in a schedule the request for the preliminary ruling of the European Court. The court may give directions as to the manner and form in which the schedule is to be prepared. The proceedings in which an order is made will normally be stayed until the European Court has given its ruling. A copy of the order is sent to the Registrar of the European Court always through the Senior Master of the Supreme Court (Queen's Bench Division) no matter which court has made the order. It may be noted that this rule does not seem to be compatible with the requirement of Community law that the decision containing the reference should be notified to the European Court by the court or tribunal which has made it.[26] In the case of an order made by the High Court, unless the court otherwise orders, the Senior Master shall not transmit the case to the European Court until the time for appealing against the order has expired or, if an appeal is entered within that time, until the appeal has been determined or otherwise disposed of. A copy of an order made by the County Court may be sent to the Senior Master on the same conditions. An order for reference made by the High Court is deemed to be a final decision and accordingly an appeal against it will lie to the Court of Appeal without leave. The period within which a notice of appeal must be served is 14 days. By contrast, refusal to make an order for reference is subject to appeal in the ordinary way, i.e. on leave as any other interlocutory decision.[27]

The rules applicable to the Scottish courts are different in certain respects. Thus only in the case of the Sheriff Court is it expressly provided that a reference may be made by the Sheriff *ex proprio motu*. In the Court of Session a reference must be made by the court in the form of a case. The court gives directions to the parties as to the manner in which the case is to be stated, drafted and adjusted. The proceedings will normally be sisted until the European Court has given a preliminary ruling. A copy of the reference is directly sent by the clerk to the Registrar of the European Court but, unless the court otherwise directs, only after the expiration of the time (14 days) for bringing an appeal against the interlocutor making the reference. In criminal proceedings notice of intention to raise a question of Community law must be given at the first diet before the accused is called on to plead to the indictment or to the complaint. The reference is transmitted by the clerk to the Registrar of the European Court together with a certified copy of the record of proceedings and of the indictment or complaint. Against the order making the reference any aggrieved party to the proceedings may lodge an appeal within 10 days. In the Sheriff Court the Sheriff himself drafts the reference within four weeks of the decision to make it. The parties may then suggest adjustments within a further four weeks. The Sheriff finally makes and signs the reference within 14 days after the expiry of that period. The proceedings are normally sisted until the European Court has given its ruling. A copy of the reference is sent by the clerk to the Registrar of the European Court but normally only after the expiry of the period of appeal against it.

1108. Appeals against references

Community law requires a national court that has made a reference to the European Court to stay its proceedings pending the outcome of the reference.[1] This requirement does not, however, imply that all proceedings in the national legal system, including normal appellate proceedings, should automatically be suspended by the fact of the reference. In all the Member States where preliminary ruling procedure as such exists as part of national law, ordinary appeals are available against interim orders or judgments making a reference.[2] From the silence of the Treaties on this question it cannot be presumed that they have intended to alter such an important procedural principle. Nor has the European Court been able to rule that appeals against orders referring cases to it are incompatible with Community law, in spite of cogent arguments to that effect based mainly on the point that such appeals fetter the discretionary power of the lower national courts although this power is derived directly from the Treaties.[3] Clearly, this is a question of domestic procedural law which falls outside the jurisdiction of the European Court. It follows, therefore, that in the case of a court against whose decisions there is a judicial remedy under national law, Article 177 E.E.C./Article 150 Euratom does not preclude a decision of such a court referring a question to the European Court for a preliminary ruling from remaining subject to the remedies normally available under national law.[4] It is, however, submitted that if the appeal against an order for reference comes before a court of last resort, that court is bound to refer the matter to the European Court under the compulsory system insofar as the determination of the appeal is based on (or involves points of) Community law, rather than purely national law.

While an order for reference has the effect of staying the national proceedings, an appeal against such order does not have as a consequence the suspension of the reference proceedings in the European Court even though it may have suspensive effect in the national law. Once the Court is properly seized of a question falling within its jurisdiction, it must, in the interests of clarity and legal certainty, abide by the reference order and continue the procedure so long as that order has neither been withdrawn nor become devoid of object.[5] In fact it follows from the independent nature of the national and Community legal orders, and from the principle of the separation of national and Community jurisdictions that arises therefrom, that the appeal against the order for reference on the one hand, and the reference proceedings on the other, should run their own independent, parallel courses. Just as Community law cannot prevent a national appellate court from taking cognisance of the appeal, but leaves the determination of its admissibility to the national court according to national law, so it cannot require (nor authorise) the European Court to appraise the effects of the appeal in application of national law. In particular, the Court is neither required, nor authorised, to discover whether the order of the national court making the reference has acquired the force of *res judicata* under domestic law; its jurisdiction to render a preliminary ruling being dependent solely on the existence of a valid reference. It is only if the reference order is quashed and consequently retroactively annulled or if it is withdrawn for any reason (e.g. withdrawal of the plaintiff, settlement, etc.) by the same court which has made it that the European Court must abstain from giving a ruling because in that case it will no longer have a valid title to do so.[6]

Undoubtedly, the above arrangements may involve the European Court in the risk of giving a judgment that may later be rendered without legal effect by a subsequent annulment of the underlying reference decision. In order to avoid such a situation, in one case[7] the Court decided, upon being informed by the national court that an appeal had been lodged against the reference order which had the consequence of suspending the execution of that order, to stay its judgment until it was notified that judgment had been delivered on the appeal. Otherwise the Court continued the proceedings, i.e. it heard arguments and the Advocate-General delivered his opinion. Being subsequently informed that the reference order had been quashed, the Court removed the case from the Register.[8] It is, however, thought that in the light of the Court's subsequent case-law, discussed above, this course of action is not likely to be repeated in the future.[9]

1109. Position of private parties

The position of private parties in reference proceedings is basically determined by the nature and purpose of such proceedings. As seen in a previous Section,[1] Article 177 E.E.C./Article 150 Euratom establishes a direct form of co-operation between the Court of Justice and the national courts by means of a non-contentious procedure, whose purpose is not to settle a dispute but to ensure uniform interpretation and application of Community law. In this procedure the parties to the main action have in principle no right to take any initiative and are merely invited to submit their observations[2] within the legal context outlined by the court making the reference. It follows that it is exclusively for the national courts to decide whether to make a reference and what its purpose, scope and subject-matter should be. These elements of a request, as defined by the court making it, are binding on both the parties and the European Court.[3] Although in the initiation and preparation of the reference the parties may, and usually do, play an active part,[4] the final selection of the issues which relate to Community law, the assessment of their relevance to the determination of the case and the final formulation of the actual questions to be referred, are within the exclusive competence of the national court. The submission of the request to the European Court moreover interrupts the proceedings before the domestic court: for the parties these proceedings must therefore remain during the whole course of the reference procedure in the same state in which they were at the moment when the order was made.

It follows from these general considerations that the parties to the main action are not entitled, in the first place, to make a direct request to the European Court for a preliminary ruling.[5] Once the reference procedure was properly instituted, the parties cannot put forward in its course new questions or supplementary arguments representing an entirely new departure from the order making the reference and seeking to extend its subject-matter or scope.[6] This would not only mean an impermissible continuation of the national proceedings before another forum, the European Court, but would prejudice the position of the other participants, in the first place the Commission, who are also entitled to submit observations. It might moreover result in a preliminary ruling which may not be relevant to the decision of the case.[7] For the same reasons, the parties cannot change the wording,[8] content or purpose of the questions referred or have them declared without object. Thus they cannot turn a question relating to the interpretation of a Community regulation into one concerning its validity by invoking the defence of illegality.[9] They cannot, by thus establishing the illegality and consequent inapplicability of the regulation, have the reference pronounced pointless.[10] In general, they cannot raise the question of validity where the reference relates to interpretation only.[11] Even where the reference is expressly concerned with the issue of validity, the parties cannot normally invoke additional legal grounds for invalidity over and above those mentioned therein,[12] except where the reference is drawn up in general terms only without specifying any such ground[13] or where the grounds so invoked could be raised by the Court of Justice of its own motion.[14] If the parties to the main action could raise before the European Court problems of validity different from those raised by the court making the reference, even if the contested measure were the same, this would upset the balance, carefully maintained by the Court, between preliminary rulings on the one hand and direct actions relating to legality on the other.[15] What the parties are entitled and even advised to do before the Court of Justice is to amplify in their written and oral submissions the scope and the grounds of their allegations concerning the invalidity of the measure in question. Failure to do so may result in an unfavourable ruling by the Court especially where the order for reference itself does not contain adequate information as to the parties' arguments.[16] Finally, the parties to the main action (who are not 'parties' before the European Court) cannot request the Court to supplement[17] or interpret[18] judgments delivered by it in previous preliminary procedures. It is exclusively for the national court which has made the reference to decide whether it has received adequate clarification by the preliminary ruling, or whether it considers it necessary to make a further reference to the Court.[19] Likewise, third parties who are not involved in the main action have no right to intervene in the case before the European Court.[20]

1110. Legal effects of preliminary rulings

The judgments of the European Court given in reference proceedings are in principle subject to the normal operation of the *res judicata* rule.[1] Accordingly, a preliminary ruling is binding on the national court which has requested it (including all lower and higher courts that may be called upon to adjudicate in the same case)[2] but, strictly speaking, only in the particular case and in respect of the parties to that case (*inter partes*). Thus the court before which the main action is pending is required to defer to the ruling as regards the points of law on which the European Court has given its decision.

Nevertheless, it follows from the nature and the purpose of the preliminary ruling system and from the special relationship between the European Court and the national court on which it is based, that the latter remains free to draw from the Court's ruling the relevant legal conclusions necessary for a definitive settlement of the case. It remains free even to the extent of not drawing any conclusions at all, for example if it discovers afterwards that the consultation was not necessary and that it can give a decision on other grounds. Also, the national court remains free to assess whether it is sufficiently enlightened by the ruling of the Court or whether certain doubts still remain which necessitate the (re-) submission of the same or further questions. Generally, there is nothing to prevent a court, if it so desires, from making a new reference even though the issues involved have already formed the subject of a preliminary ruling in the very same proceedings or in a similar earlier case. In such situations the European Court must give a new judgment, but if the question is identical with that already settled and no new factor is presented, the Court will refer the national court to the previous judgment.[3] In such circumstances the existence of a previous ruling exempts courts of last resort from their obligation to refer.[4]

It follows from the foregoing that, formally at least, preliminary rulings have no *erga omnes* effect. An earlier ruling of the Court of Justice is, strictly speaking, not binding in later disputes raising exactly the same issues, whether in the same or in a different national court. Although the legal issue (*causa petendi*) may be the same in both cases, the subject-matter (*petitum*) and/or the parties will be different.[5] Nevertheless, the operation in practice of this strict *inter partes* effect is subject to certain qualifications. In order to assess the true practical consequences of preliminary rulings, a distinction must be drawn between rulings which deal with the interpretation, and those which relate to the validity, of Community provisions.

As regards the first group, it cannot be denied that an interpretative ruling which defines the meaning, scope and effect of a Community rule is, in practice, authoritative even beyond the individual case which has given rise to it.[6] This necessarily follows already from the fact that the Court is required, in formulating its ruling, to stay at the level of abstraction, giving its interpretation a general scope so as to avoid being involved in the application of the law to the circumstances of the particular case. Furthermore, it would defeat the very purpose of the preliminary ruling system if, in solving a dispute, a national court could disregard relevant interpretative rulings in reliance on their strict *inter partes* effect. Thus, whenever a question of Community law which has already been subject to interpretation by the European Court comes before a lower national court, that court will either apply that interpretation or submit the question to the Court for a further ruling.[7] Otherwise an interested party may bring the matter before a court of last resort which will then be obliged to use one of these two alternatives.

Through this 'watertight' system interpretative rulings cannot fail to acquire a *quasi-* (or material) *erga omnes* effect. This is because, as seen above, any further ruling given on the same question will be the same as the previous one unless new factors are presented of such a weight as to induce the Court to alter its interpretation. Even this latter possibility disappears where the preliminary ruling deals with the direct applicability of a Community provision. Since the legal character of a directly applicable rule, once established, cannot change,[8] the ruling confirming it must necessarily have a definitive effect which can no longer be challenged successfully. For all intents and purposes, such ruling will apply *erga omnes*. Indeed, interpretative preliminary rulings cannot fail to have such far-reaching consequences if the ultimate objective of the uniform interpretation and application of Community law is to be attained. In the light of these considerations it becomes clear why it is essential that the 'watertight' nature of the system should be maintained. This can be achieved only if all courts and tribunals follow the compulsory reference procedure, whatever their status in the internal judicial hierarchy, if their decision in the concrete case is not subject to appeal, without having the same type of discretionary power as is enjoyed by lower courts in the matter of appraising whether a reference is 'necessary'.[9]

As regards, secondly, preliminary rulings concerning the validity of Community measures, their legal consequences depend on whether validity is upheld or denied. As a rule, the Court does not examine and confirm the validity of an act in general, but strictly in relation to the specific arguments and complaints raised in the order for reference as amplified by the submissions of the parties.[10] The validity of an act so confirmed is therefore not definitive. While the act must be given effect by the national court in the particular case, it may be challenged subsequently, by the same or different parties, either by way of a further request for preliminary ruling or in a direct action. It seems, however, that the Court will automatically, i.e. without reconsidering the case, uphold the validity of the measure as previously established, insofar as no new legal grounds and complaints are presented capable of casting doubt upon that validity.[11] To that extent, therefore, the previous preliminary ruling seems to have a *quasi-* (i.e. material) *erga omnes* effect (the status of a 'precedent')[12] just as one dealing with interpretation. Where, however, a party relies on new grounds, arguments or evidence not presented to the Court in the previous case, or amplifies those already presented, which are capable of calling in question the validity of the measure, it would appear that the Court will not refuse to reconsider the case[13] and, if necessary, declare the act invalid. In this respect, therefore, the effect of the previous ruling is strictly *inter partes*.

The position is different where the Court of Justice declares an act invalid. In such cases the consequences of the preliminary ruling are in certain respects similar to, although not identical with, those of a declaration of inapplicability made in the context of a plea of illegality.[14] Such a ruling applies exclusively in the framework of the case in which it is given, with respect to the parties involved (*inter partes*) and for the future only (*ex nunc*). It does not have the effect of making the act in question null and void[15] and therefore does not entail the retrospective consequences of an annulment.[16] As a result, the act (and necessarily any measure taken thereunder by a Community institution) is inapplicable in the principal action but continues to be formally in force until repealed or amended by the institution which has issued it. It is assumed that in the interests of legal certainty the relevant institution is required to take such action within a reasonable time.

The question what effects precisely a declaration of invalidity has on the domestic laws of the Member States (and in particular on those of the court making the reference) is not quite clear. It would seem that Community law leaves the regulation of this question to national law. As seen in a different context,[17] in the case of a valid provision (which is directly applicable) Community law renders automatically inapplicable any incompatible national measure. On the other hand, in the case of an invalid provision Community law does not seem to require that all implementing domestic measures should be regarded as automatically invalid or at least inapplicable (although these, too, become 'incompatible' with Community law as giving effect to an invalid act), except perhaps to the extent to which a measure does no more than verbatim reproduce the Community rule.[18] In all other cases it is for the national authorities to draw the consequences in their legal systems of a declaration of invalidity made in a preliminary ruling.[19] While this means that the national authorities must take the steps which are necessary in accordance with their constitutional rules and procedures to repeal or amend the implementing measure which has now been rendered without legal foundation, it may happen that the national court making the reference will be unable to draw the full consequences from the invalidity until such steps have actually been taken. This depends on the legislative or administrative nature of the measure of implementation and on the power of the court to review it. Thus a court may have to continue to enforce an implementing Act of Parliament although the Community act which it implements has been declared invalid, unless the Act of Parliament conflicts with another, directly applicable rule. This clearly undesirable consequence could be avoided if the application of the principle of the supremacy of Community law were to be extended to this situation, which would put an immediate end to the *inter partes* operation of any domestic measure giving effect to an invalid Community act.

While a preliminary ruling which confirms the invalidity of an act of an institution has no general effects as regards the past, it necessarily has some such effect as regards the future. This is due to the inherently absolute (objective) nature of the concept of invalidity. An act which is invalid with respect to one person, must be regarded as invalid with respect to all. Thus it is inconceivable that, unless the defect has been remedied, such an act could ever be enforced, either by the Community institutions or by the national authorities, in any future situation. Should an attempt be made at its enforcement and the dispute arising therefrom come before the Court of Justice, either by way of a reference or in a direct action, it is to be expected that the Court will repeatedly uphold its invalidity.[20] To this extent, at least, a preliminary ruling declaring an act invalid cannot fail to have a *quasi-* (i.e. material) *erga omnes* effect.

1111. Principles of interpretation

Interpretation of legal texts is not merely an essential, but an inherently necessary part of the judicial function. Before a judge can perform his task of applying an abstract legal provision to a concrete factual situation, he must ascertain the meaning of that provision. Interpretation and application of the law are thus inseparably connected, being two different phases of one and the same mental process.

Judicial interpretation is made necessary, in the first place, by the fact that words do not have inherent meanings; they are only symbols of things and concepts and have such meaning as is attributed to them by the common consensus of those speaking the same language. In theory, therefore, every legal text (and every word in it) needs interpretation before it can be applied. Very often this is in part done by the text itself, i.e. at least insofar as a word may have more than one meaning or a meaning that is different from that commonly attributed to the word in everyday usage. Mostly, however, a word for word interpretation of the text takes place in the mind of the judge only and not as a separate step in the judicial process.

Secondly, interpretation of a legal text is made necessary by the general principle that a court cannot commit a denial of justice by pronouncing *non liquet* in a situation where the law is silent, obscure or inadequate.[1] Rather, it is the duty of the court to ascertain the applicable rule by interpreting the relevant texts and thus to fill any lacunae in the body of the law.

Thirdly, even assuming that careful drafting could eliminate any gaps in the law at the moment when the new legislation comes into effect (which is doubtful), no abstract legal formula can ever be devised that could cover all future contingencies that life itself can produce. It is the nature of the judicial function that application of abstract rules and principles to concrete cases always requires a certain degree of 'adjustment' in the law which is achieved by means of interpretation. It is precisely such case-to-case 'adjustments' that ultimately ensure the necessary evolution of the law that life demands.

In order to solve the various problems arising in the judicial process, legal writing and case-law has developed certain rules and methods of interpretation. As all courts of law are confronted with the same basic types of problem, these rules and methods are necessarily the same (or substantially similar) in the national, international or supranational contexts. The difference is in accentuating one or the other of them, depending on the nature of the text to be interpreted and on the legal system in which the interpretation is to take place. Thus, generally speaking, three principal methods of interpretation may be distinguished whose aim is to discover, respectively, the objective meaning of the words actually used, in the context of the instrument as a whole (grammatico-logical and systematic interpretation); the subjective intention of the legislator or, in the case of a contract/treaty, the common intention of the contracting parties (historical interpretation); the object and purpose of the particular provision as well as of the instrument as a whole (teleological interpretation). All three methods are known and used by municipal as well as international courts and tribunals;[2] they are known and used in combination with one another by the European Court of Justice. Thus the general pattern of interpretation followed by the Court in most cases, whether in direct actions or in reference proceedings, is to examine in turn the wording, general scheme and spirit of the provision in question as well as its position in the system of the particular

Treaty in which it occurs and its role in the light of that Treaty's objectives.[3] Where the provision is one of an act of secondary legislation, it is examined in the light of the spirit, system and objectives of both the act itself and the relevant Treaty provisions under which the act was adopted.[4]

According to the above pattern, the first step in the process of interpretation is to examine the wording of the provision in question.[5] Since no preparatory work (*travaux préparatoires*) has been made public in respect of the basic Community Treaties which would clearly express the intention of the Contracting Parties, the Court usually bases its interpretation upon the text in the form in which it has been drafted and gives it the significance which flows naturally from or comes as close as reasonably possible to the literal and logical meaning of the words.[6] This is also required by the general principle of legal certainty.[7] According to the strict rules of this grammatico-logical method, every difference in wording between two consecutive texts on the same subject-matter must be presumed to connote a difference in meaning and legal content, and a corresponding intention to depart from the previous text.[8] Since, however, the European Treaties were not drafted (partly for lack of time) with the same degree of precision as is expected of national statutes and codifications, slight divergences in the text of cognate provisions cannot be given the same importance as in the interpretation of national laws.[9] Moreover, unlike some national courts, the European Court does not usually accept *a contrario* arguments, i.e. that an express application by the Treaties of a rule to a certain situation excludes the application of the same rule to any other situation not expressly mentioned (*expressio unius est exclusio alterius*), unless no other interpretation is adequate and compatible with the express wording, context and object of the provision.[10]

Generally, where upon an examination of its wording the Court finds that a provision is absolutely clear and unequivocal, no further interpretation is necessary in accordance with the principle *in claris non fit interpretatio*.[11] The text may then be applied as it stands.[12] Where, however, literal interpretation fails to give a definite answer or leads to a conclusion which runs counter to common sense, to the basic principles of Community law or to its rational (logical) application,[13] it is necessary to go beyond the text and have recourse to equity,[14] to the 'spirit' of the law (*ratio legis*) and, to a lesser extent, to the real or presumed intention of the legislator (i.e. in the case of primary Community law, to the intention of the Contracting States).[15] Very often all this is done to confirm a result already arrived at by literal interpretation.

The fact that the intention of the Contracting States plays only a subsidiary role in the interpretation of the Community Treaties may be explained on several grounds. In the first place, as already pointed out above, no *travaux préparatoires* exist from which such intention could be ascertained. On the other hand, it is very doubtful whether the positions adopted by the heads of delegation to the Intergovernmental Conference preparatory to the Treaties of Rome at the beginning of 1957, as well as the unilateral explanations and declarations made in some of the Member States on the occasion of the Parliamentary ratification of the three basic Treaties, can be regarded as constituting true preparatory work. Even if they could be so considered, they could certainly not be held against the new Member States of the enlarged Communities.[16] Nor is there any guarantee that they would be instrumental in uncovering the real common intention of the contracting States as the very existence of an obscurity or gap in an international treaty text is often the result and the sign of the absence of such a common intention.[17]

Nevertheless, these considerations do not completely eliminate the historical method of interpretation in Community law. *Travaux préparatoires* are perhaps the most important, but not the only, means of discovering the intention of the legislator. Such intention may also be revealed by other relevant concomitant conduct of the author of a text. Thus an act immediately applying a rule in practice, adopted by the authors of the rule at the same time as the rule itself, is usually endowed with an interpretative significance of the first importance. Where the Member States simultaneously laid down a rule in the Treaties (e.g. definition of agricultural products in Article 38(1) E.E.C.) and fixed some facets of its application (e.g. Annex II to the E.E.C. Treaty listing agricultural products), then it is quite permissible to draw conclusions from the latter as to the way in which they intended to apply the former.[18] As regards secondary Community law, although the deliberations of the Council are secret, the legislative process preceding the final adoption of an act is generally not, and where relevant documents may throw light on the intentions of the legislator in the preparation of the act in question, they may be used as a means of interpretation.[19]

Finally, and perhaps most importantly, a provision must be interpreted according to its position in the system of the Treaty (systematic interpretation) and in the light of its own as well as the Treaty's purposes and objects (teleological interpretation). In the practice of the European Court these two methods appear as two sides of the same coin and are therefore usually employed simultaneously. They represent a dominant, and without doubt the most characteristic, feature of the Court's own particular way of interpretation. The Court's basic tenet is that each of the three Community Treaties represents a logical whole governed by its own general principles and objectives. Each Treaty is structured in such a way that each internal sub-division (i.e. Part, Title, Chapter in the E.E.C. Treaty, Title and Chapter in the E.C.S.C. and Euratom Treaties) likewise represents a logical unit governed by its own principles and objectives. The same applies, in principle, also to most individual Articles. It follows that the meaning and scope of a provision is basically determined, first, by its position within the Article in which it appears,[20] secondly, by the position of that Article within the system (i.e. Chapter, Title, Part) of the Treaty[21] and. thirdly, by the principles and objectives relevant to that particular Article,[22] Chapter, Title,[23] Part and Treaty. This method of interpretation is based on a combination of two general propositions. The first is that, in principle, the provisions of a Treaty must be read together and, insofar as possible, reconciled with one another since they mutually complement and supplement each other.[24] The second is that the introductory Articles to each Treaty[25] lay down obligatory general principles and objectives whose pursuit is indispensable for the achievement of the relevant Community's tasks. Their scope of application extends over the whole spectrum of that Treaty and consequently they are decisive for the interpretation of those more detailed provisions which give effect to them.[26]

The far-reaching consequences of this combined systematic-teleological method of interpretation may be highlighted by the following three examples. First, it has led the European Court to confirm that the Economic Community has treaty-making power in the field of transport even in the absence from the Treaty of a specific authorisation to that effect. The Court has held that in such circumstances regard must be had to the whole scheme of the Treaty no less than to its individual provisions. The placing of Article 210, which provides in general terms that 'The Community shall have legal personality', at the head of Part Six of the Treaty, devoted to 'General and Final Provisions', means, the Court has said, that in its external relations the Community enjoys the capacity to establish contractual links with non-Member States over the whole extent of the field of objectives defined in Part One, which includes transport, with which Part Six has to be read together.[27] Secondly, the Court has reached the conclusion that merger of large undertakings might amount to a prohibited abuse of a dominant position, by interpreting the relevant Article 86 E.E.C. (which Article itself is silent on this point) in the light of the general principles and objectives laid down in Articles 2 and 3(f) E.E.C.[28] Thirdly, confronted with the question whether the rules relating to the free movement of workers (Articles 48 to 51 E.E.C.) were applicable to the sphere of sea transport, the Court considered that Title IV of Part Two of the Treaty, dealing with Transport, was governed both by the general principles and objectives relating to the whole Treaty and by the specific principles and objectives relating to Part Two. It followed from the former (in particular from Article 2 E.E.C.) that the establishment of the Common Market referred to the whole of the economic activities in the Community; and it followed from the latter that the free movement of goods, persons, services and capital, which formed the foundations of the Common Market, had likewise to refer to the whole complex of economic activities. Since no express provision rendered the basic rules inapplicable to the sphere of sea transport, that particular area of economic activity had to be regarded as being included in their scope of application.[29]

The above examples (which could be multiplied) show how powerful a weapon interpretation can be at the hands of the Court of Justice. It enables the Court not only to make good lacunae in the body of Community law but also to ensure its further development. A dynamic interpretation makes it possible for the Court to keep the law abreast of the dynamics of economic and social life. While, as seen above, the Court does not fight shy of using that weapon in appropriate cases,[30] it is generally anxious not to invade the province of the legislator under the disguise of interpretation. It keeps within the limits set to its jurisdiction by the principle of separation of powers within the Communities. Practical considerations, prompted by economic and social realities, although important, can never influence its interpretation to such an extent as either to subvert the system established by the Treaties[31] or to make compromises and concessions on principle.[32]

In practice, the use made by the Court of Justice of the various methods of interpretation discussed above is subordinated to the operation of three fundamental principles of overriding importance. These principles are designed to ensure that the specific supranational nature of the Community legal system is duly taken into account, and given effect, in the interpretation of its individual provisions. These are the principles of (a) uniformity; (b) effectiveness and (c) protection of individual rights. They are considered in turn below.

(a) *The principle of uniformity*

The autonomous and supranational character of Community law[33] can only be preserved if its rules are uniformly applied and, as a precondition for that, uniformly interpreted throughout the entire Community territory. In the absence, therefore, of an express or implied reference to analogous concepts and definitions of national or international law, terms of Community law must be so interpreted as to obtain an autonomous, supranational and uniform meaning which is independent of any meaning that corresponding terms may possess under the national laws of the Member States, of third countries or in pursuance of conventions made under traditional international law. The requirement of uniformity cannot admit of criteria for interpretation that are subject to national law and that could thus be fixed and modified unilaterally by the national legislatures. Should this be possible, the meaning, scope and effect of a Community concept could vary from Member State to Member State. This would endanger not only the uniform but also the effective application of Community law and the protection of individual rights. It would therefore offend at the same time also against the other two, closely related principles that are considered below.

It follows that, unless proved otherwise, undefined terms appearing in Community texts which are also used in the national laws of the Member States (e.g. 'worker' and 'wage-earner';[34] 'offer';[35] 'public service';[36] 'official authority';[37] within certain limits: 'public policy';[38] 'civil and commercial matters';[39] etc.), of third countries (e.g. 'marketable quality'),[40] or in general international conventions (e.g. 'charge having an effect equivalent to customs duty';[41] 'public service';[42] etc.), must be presumed to have an independent Community meaning which must prevail over any different or conflicting meaning attributed to them in other legal systems. They must therefore be interpreted according to independent Community criteria, i.e. by reference, in the first place, to the scheme, object and purpose of the Community text in which they occur (i.e. the basic Treaties, acts of the institutions, ancillary Conventions) and, in the second place, to the general principles of Community law. Only such an interpretation can lead to a result which will be compatible with the principle of uniformity.[43] For the same reasons, unofficial interpretations contained in informal communiqués issued by the Council or the Commission cannot supply authentic criteria for the interpretation of Community texts. Owing to their non-binding nature, the uniform application of such communiqués in all the Member States cannot be guaranteed.[44]

The principle of uniformity further requires that Community texts of general application (e.g. regulations or directives and decisions addressed to all the Member States) should be interpreted in the light of their versions in all the official languages of the Communities.[45] All these versions being equally binding, no single one of them can be regarded as the solely authentic text. In cases of divergences between the various translations, an attempt must be made to derive a meaning common to all of them from the scheme, object and purpose of the provision. In the absence of such a meaning, preference must be given to the interpretation that is least onerous for Community subjects, provided that it suffices to achieve the purpose served by the text. This is justified on the assumption that the legislator did not intend to impose stricter obligations or confer less rights in some of the Member States than in others.[46]

(b) *The principle of effectiveness*

In accordance with the principle *ut res magis valeat quam pereat,* basic provisions of primary and secondary Community law must be so interpreted as to obtain the widest possible scope and the fullest possible effect with a view to achieving the fundamental Community objectives. Or, to put it another way, if there are various alternatives, preference must be given to an interpretation that tends to prevent the effectiveness or validity of basic Community rules being undermined.[47] This principle is of paramount importance especially in the interpretation and application of the provisions laying down the foundations of the Economic Community, i.e. the free movement of goods, persons, services and capital, and of the corresponding principle of equality of treatment or non-discrimination.[48] To ensure the effective operation of these fundamental provisions, the various exceptions and derogations allowed by the Treaty[49] must be interpreted and applied restrictively. The scope of such exceptions and derogations must be fixed uniformly by Community law. It cannot exceed the particular objective for which each of the exception clauses was inserted in the Treaty. If that objective can equally be achieved by various national measures, only those are permissible which hinder the operation of the Common Market the least. In other words, the exceptions to and derogations from the basic provisions must be interpreted in such a way as to avoid the effectiveness of the Treaty being defeated by unilateral national measures.[50] Also, since in principle integration under the E.E.C. Treaty is of a comprehensive character and is not to take place separately according to economic sectors,[51] particular provisions relating to individual sectors must be interpreted narrowly by reason of their exceptional nature.[52] Finally, the principle of effectiveness enables such implied powers to be attributed to the Community institutions as are necessary for a proper and effective implementation of the provisions of the Treaties.[53]

(c) *The principle of the protection of individual rights*

This principle applies to the interpretation of both substantive and procedural provisions of Community law. In the context of substantive law, it implies that where a provision is silent or obscure it must be given a meaning that is the least unfavourable to individuals, i.e. affords to them the widest possible freedom of action that is still compatible with Community interests in general and with the purpose of that provision in particular.[54] Provisions which confer substantive rights and economic or social advantages upon individuals cannot be interpreted strictly. On the contrary, they must be interpreted extensively so as to conform to the purpose and spirit of the Community rules on the free movement of persons, as well as to the higher principle of social justice and other principles of Community law especially designed to protect individuals (e.g. those of non-discrimination, legal certainty, proportionality, protection of confidence, of acquired rights, and of fundamental rights in general, etc.).[55] Preference must always be given to an interpretation that best serves the overall interests of European integration, not only of the economy but of the people as well.[56]

Similar principles apply in the field of remedies and procedures. Generally, the provisions of the Treaties enabling individuals to bring action in the Court of Justice in defence or enforcement of their substantive Community rights must not be interpreted restrictively to the detriment of the person concerned. Consequently, where the Treaties are silent or obscure on the point, a limitation in this respect may not be presumed,[57] Nor may the silence or obscurity of a Community text in any matter which affects the protection of the rights of individuals lead to the interpretation which is least favourable to them.[58] Nevertheless, these principles cannot result in an interpretation which would disregard the clear limitations placed by the Treaties on the system that they have created for the legal protection of individuals.[59]

Application in practice of these principles of interpretation has enabled the Court of Justice considerably to extend the scope of the remedies made available by the Treaties. Thus the Court has confirmed the right of E.C.S.C. officials to bring before it a direct action against their own States without first exhausting other Community or domestic remedies,[60] just as it has recognised in principle the right and the capacity of entities other than 'natural and legal persons' (e.g. associations, trade unions) to appear before it as parties to legal proceedings.[61] Also, the Court has extended under the E.C.S.C. Treaty the application of the plea of illegality from pecuniary sanctions to all other cases.[62] It has recognised the right of non-Community undertakings and associations as well as private individuals to bring action for damages under the E.C.S.C. Treaty.[63] By establishing the principle of independence of legal remedies, the Court has separated the action for damages from actions for annulment and failure to act thus making it possible for individuals to avail themselves of the former without having to comply with the much stricter requirements of the latter.[64] By giving a wide interpretation to the concept of 'decision' and, under the E.C.S.C. Treaty, to that of 'individual decision', the Court has extended the right of private parties to challenge the acts of the institutions.[65] As regards procedure and form, the Court interprets the relevant provisions in such a way as to pay due respect to the interests of the parties, to the requirements of procedural efficiency and, generally, to those of a proper administration of justice.[66] It never insists on a rigid and unnecessary adherence to the formalities in judging the admissibility of actions or of any further procedural steps.[67]

In conclusion, it must be pointed out that the three principles of interpretation discussed above are mutually and inseparably interrelated. Each one of them is meaningless without the others. In fact, they must be envisaged as three aspects of one and the same general idea, i.e. to use the instrument of judicial interpretation in such a way as to promote the ultimate objectives of the Communities, the economic and social integration of the Member States and of their peoples, in the most appropriate and efficient manner. A provision of Community law which lacks a uniform meaning in all the Member States is both ineffective and detrimental to individual rights. Conversely, individual rights cannot be duly protected unless the Community provisions conferring them are interpreted and implemented uniformly and effectively. This explains why the doctrine of direct applicability, which has been arrived at by the Court of Justice upon a Treaty interpretation giving effect mainly to the principle of the protection of individual rights,[68] has inevitably had to be accompanied by the doctrine of the supremacy of Community law which, in turn, is based on the principles of uniformity and effectiveness.[69] As has been pointed out in another context, the former without the latter is clearly meaningless.[70] Put in a broader perspective, the three principles of interpretation must be seen as the essential cornerstones of the whole idea of European integration,[71] being the prerequisites for the simultaneous attainment, as required by the Treaties,[72] of the economic and social progress of the Member States and of the constant improvement of the living and working conditions of their nationals. The one without the other is inconceivable.

Notes

1. Decisions of the European Court of Justice are referred to by their official case numbers only. For the names of the parties, see Table of Cases at p. 327. References are to the official English translations in the *European Court Reports*. Where official translations have not yet been published, references are to any other available English translations or, in the absence thereof, to the official French versions in the *Recueil de la Jurisprudence de la Cour de Justice*.

2. Decisions of national courts, other than British courts, are referred to by the nationality of the court followed by a serial number whereby the names of the parties and the court giving the decision can be identified in the Table of Cases at p. 327. Decisions of British courts are referred to in the usual manner by the names of the parties.

3. Except for official publications of the Community institutions, bibliographical references are not as a rule contained in the footnotes. A detailed list of works relevant to the subject-matter of the individual Chapters and, where appropriate, Sections, can be found at p. 297.

4. The first number indicates the page-number, the second the number of the note.

Section 401

3 1 Arts. 31 E.C.S.C., 164 F.E.C.. 136 Euratom.
2 Case 81/72 [1973] ECR 591 *per* A.G.; 62/76 [1977] ECR 223-224 *per* A.G.
3 See Chapter 2 above.
4 Cases 1/54, 2 Val. 33-34; 16 and 17/62 [1962] ECR 478; 40/64 [1965] ECR 227.
5 Cases 7/56 and 3 to 7/57, 2 Val. 757. See further § 219 above.
6 See § 220 above.
7 See § 221 above.
8 See § 222 above.
9 See § 1111 below.
4 10 See further §§ 102 above, 501, 701, 702, 1101 below.
11 Case 6/60, 2 Val. 826.
12 Arts 3 E.C.S.C., 4 E.E.C., 3 Euratom. See further § 206 above.
13 *Cf.* Cases 3/54, 1 Rec. 149 *per* A.G.; 1/55, 2 Rec. 38 *per* A.G.; 1/56 *ibid.*, pp. 448-449 *per* A.G.
14 See Chapter 5 below.
15 See Chapter 6 below.
5 16 See further §§ 501, 517, 521, 606, 612 below.
17 See Chapter 7 below.
18 See Chapter 8 below.
19 *Cf.* e.g. Arts. 37, 66(5)(2) E.C.S.C. (see further § 504 below), Art. 88 E.C.S.C. (see §§ 901, 906 below), Art. 95(4) E.C.S.C., Art. 12(4) Euratom in conjunction with Art. 144(a) Euratom.

20 Cases 44/59, 2 Val. 796; 23/69 [1970] ECR 559.
21 See further §§ 701, 804 below.
22 *German No. 1* [1963] CMLR 254; *German No. 28* [1969] CMLR 290-291; *Italian No. 4* [1965] CMLR 15-16; *Italian No. 5* [1966] CMLR 27; *Italian No. 6* [1965] CMLR 8-9; *Italian No. 7, ibid.*, pp. 293 *et seq.*; *Italian No. 8, ibid.*, pp. 133-134; *Italian No. 9* [1967] CMLR 170-172.
23 Arts. 40(3) E.C.S.C., 183 E.E.C., 155 Euratom. Cases 6/60, 2 Val. 826-827; 65/74 [1975] ECR 333-334 *per* A.G.
24 See further §§ 501, 701, 702, 1101 below.
6 25 Arts. 40(3) E.C.S.C, 183 E.E.C., 155 Euratom.
26 See § 902 below.
27 See Art. 36(1) of the Statute of the International Court of Justice.
28 Arts. 31 E.C.S.C., 164 E.E.C., 136 Euratom.
29 Cases 23/68 [1969] ECR 53 *per* A.G.; 66/76 [1977] ECR 310 *per Curiam*, 314 *per* A.G.
30 Arts. 3 E.C.S.C., 4 E.E.C., 3 Euratom.
31 I.e. Arts. 33-43, 47, 63(2), 65(4), 66(5) and (6), 88, 89, 92, 95(4) E.C.S.C.; Arts. 93(2)(2), 169-186, 192, 215(2), 225(2), 228(1) E.E.C.; Arts. 12(4), 18(1) and (2), 21(3) and (4) and (5), 38(3), 81(3) and (4), 82(4), 83(2), 103(3), 104(3), 105(2), 141-158, 164, 188(2) Euratom.
32 *Cf.* e.g. Arts. 10, 13, 30 of the Merger Treaty 1965; Art. 1 of the Protocol on the Privileges and Immunities of the European Communities 1965; Protocols of 3 June 1971 relating to the interpretation of the Convention on Jurisdiction 1968 and of the Convention on Mutual Recognition of Companies 1968; Art. 67 of the Association Agreement of 1961 between the E.E.C. and Greece; Art. 25 of the Association Agreement of 1963 between the E.E.C. and Turkey; Art. 7 of the Internal Agreement of 1969 on the implementation of the Yaoundé Convention of 1969; Art. 7 of the Internal Agreement of 1969 on the implementation of the Arusha Agreement of 1969; Art. 1(3) of the Treaty of Accession, etc.
33 See further § 402 below.
34 Cases 31/69 [1970] ECR 32.
35 Cases 12/63 [1963] ECR 89 *per Curiam*, 92 *per* A.G.; 66/76 [1977] ECR 310.
7 36 See further §§ 501, 601, 701, 801, 901, 1101 below.

Section 402

1 See § 401 above.
2 Cases 6/54, 2 Val. 208; 7 and 9/54, *ibid.*, p. 141; 6/60 *ibid.*, p. 824; 25/62 [1963] ECR 111-112 *per* A.G.; 26/62 *ibid.*, p. 18 *per* A.G.; 67 to 85/75 [1976] ECR 405-406 *per Curiam*, 419 *per* A.G.; 109 and 114/75 [1977] ECR 389 *per* A.G. (Order).
3 Cases 44, 46 and 49/74 [1975] ECR 398 *per* A.G.
4 See further § 412(b) below.
8 5 Cases 20/71 [1972] CMLR 948 *per* A.G.; 32/71 *ibid.*; 67 to 85/75 [1976] ECR 405-406 *per Curiam*, 419 *per* A.G.
6 Case 25/62 [1963] ECR 111-112 *per* A.G.
7 See further § 403 below.
8 Cases 9 and 11/71 [1973] CMLR 535-536 *per* A.G.; 43/72 [1973] ECR 1080-1081 *per* A.G.
9 Cases 26/68 [1969] ECR 153; 22/70 [1971] CMLR 359.
10 Case 28/65 [1966] ECR 491-492.
11 Case 3/54, 1 Rec. 147-149 *per* A.G. referring to the Italian concept of '*improponibilità*'.
12 Such a view was put forward by the A.G., but not accepted by the Court, in Case 81/72 [1973] ECR 591.
13 *Cf.* e.g. Case 31/69 [1970] ECR 32.
14 *Cf.* e.g. Case 10/69 [1969] ECR 315.
15 *Cf.* e.g. Case 6/60, 2 Val. 821-824.
16 *Cf.* e.g. Cases 9 and 12/60, 32 ILR 414 *et seq.*
17 *Cf.* e.g. Case 175/73 [1974] ECR 925-926.

9 18 *Cf.* e.g. Case 61/65 [1966] ECR 272-273.
19 *Cf.* e.g. Cases 9 and 11/71 [1973] CMLR 551; 72/74 [1975] ECR 411.
20 *Cf.* e.g. Cases 16 and 17/62 [1962] ECR 477 *et seq.*; 22/70 [1971] CMLR 356-357.
21 *Cf.* e.g. Case 48/65 [1966] ECR 27.
22 *Cf.* e.g. Case 7/61 [1962] CMLR 53.
23 *Cf.* e.g. Cases 9 and 12/60, 32 ILR 418.
24 *Cf.* e.g. Case 4/69 [1971] ECR 335-336.
25 *Cf.* e.g. Cases 19 and 21/60, 2 and 3/61 [1962] CMLR 279.
26 *Cf.* e.g. Case 74/74 [1975] ECR 544.
27 *Cf.* e.g. Cases 17/57, 2 Val. 713; 7/61 [1962] CMLR 54-55.
28 *Cf.* e.g. Case 22/70 [1971] CMLR 359.
29 *Cf.* e.g. Cases 56 to 60/74 [1976] ECR 740-741.
30 *Cf.* e.g. Case 25/62 [1963] ECR 108.
31 *Cf.* e.g. Case 48/69 [1972] CMLR 620.
32 *Cf.* e.g. Cases 12/68 [1969] ECR 114; 188/73 [1974] ECR 1107.
33 *Cf.* e.g. Case 30/59, 29 ILR 89.
34 *Cf.* e.g. Case 96/71 [1973] CMLR 383.
35 *Cf.* e.g. Cases 10 and 18/68 [1969] ECR 483.
36 *Cf.* e.g. Case 100/74 [1975] ECR 1418 (Order).
37 *Cf.* e.g. Case 59/65 [1966] ECR 550.
38 *Cf.* e.g. Case 14/64 [1965] ECR 58.
39 *Cf.* e.g. Cases 58 and 75/72 [1973] ECR 516; 109 and 114/75 [1977] ECR 389 *per* A.G. (Order).
40 *Cf.* e.g. Case 14/64 [1965] ECR 57-58.
41 *Cf.* e.g. Case 109/75 R [1975] ECR 1200 (Order). See further § 412(c) below.
42 *Cf.* e.g. Cases 9 and 12/60 [1962] ECR 180 *et seq.* (Third Party Proceedings). See further § 412(d) below.
43 *Cf.* e.g. Case 37/71 Rev. [1973] ECR 298-299. See further § 412(e) below.
44 *Cf.* e.g. Case 24/66 Bis. [1973] ECR 1602-1603. See further § 412(f) below.

Section 403

1 Cases 21 to 24/72 [1975] 2 CMLR 11 *per* A.G.
10 2 Arts. 42 E.C.S.C., 181 E.E.C., 153 Euratom. *Cf.* the two Association Agreements mentioned at note 32 in § 401 above. By virtue of an arbitration clause it is, of course, also possible to invoke the jurisdiction of the Court against a third country, international organisation or private person.
3 See § 301 above.
4 Case 67/63 [1964] ECR 160-161.
5 Case 6/72 [1973] ECR 253 *per* A.G.
6 See Chapters 5-9 below.
7 Cases 18/57, 2 Val. 255; 16 and 17/62 [1962] ECR 483 *per* A.G. *Cf.* also Art. 38(5)(a) R.P. which requires an application originating proceedings made by a legal person governed by private law to be accompanied by the instruments constituting and regulating that legal person.
11 8 Cases 175/73 [1974] ECR 925-926 *per Curiam*, 930-932 *per* A.G.; 18/74 *ibid.*, pp. 943-945 *per Curiam*, 948-951 *per* A.G.; 72/74 [1975] ECR 409-411 *per Curiam*, 413 *et seq.*, esp. at 416-418 *per* A.G.
9 Cases 41, 43 to 48, 50, 111, 113 and 114/73 [1973] ECR 1468-1469 (Order). See further § 412(c) below.
10 Case 15/63 [1964] ECR 51 *per Curiam*, 53 *et seq. per* A.G. (Order).
11 *Cf.* e.g. Case 8/72 [1973] CMLR 21 *per Curiam*, 12 *per* A.G.
12 Cases 16 and 17/62 [1962] ECR 479-480 *per Curiam*, 483, 486 *per* A.G., and see the Cases mentioned at note 8 above. See further §§ 412(c), 513, 703 below.

Section 404

1 Art. 37(1) R.P.
2 Arts. 28 E.C.S.C. Statute, 29 E.E.C. Statute, 30 Euratom Statute, Art, 58 R.P.

3 Art. 93(2) R.P.
12 4 *Cf.* e.g. Case 20/65 [1965] ECR 847.
5 Art. 76(2) R.P.
6 *Cf.* e.g. Case 4/65 [1965] ECR 1099.
7 Arts. 20 E.C.S.C. Statute, 17 E.E.C. Statute, 17 Euratom Statute.
8 Case 18/57, 2 Val. 255-256.
9 Arts. 38(3), 40(1) R.P.
10 Case 14/64 [1965] ECR 57.
11 Arts. 38(5).. 40(1) R.P.
12 Arts. 38(2), 40(1) R.P.
13 Arts. 20 E.C.S.C. Statute, 17 E.E.C. Statute, 17 Euratom Statute, Arts. 32-36 R.P. *Cf.* e.g. Case 1/60, 2 Val. 665.
14 Solicitors are prohibited (1) from taking part in the oral presentation of cases referred under Arts. 41 E.C.S.C., 177 E.E.C., 150 Euratom from the Supreme Court or the House of Lords and, in any such case in which a barrister is instructed on the reference, from undertaking the written presentation except in conjunction with the barrister; (2) in any other case in which a solicitor is acting for a party which is the U.K Government or a corporation incorporated in the U.K. or a natural person ordinarily resident in the U.K. and in which a barrister is instructed to appear, from taking part in the oral presentation or from undertaking, except in conjunction with the barrister, the written presentation. A solicitor is under no obligation to instruct a barrister in this class of case but he may not instruct an outside solicitor. If he requires another English lawyer, it must be a barrister. See Annual Statement of the General Council of the Bar, 1970-71, p.38.

Section 405

1 Art. 29(1) R.P. See also § 215 above.
2 Art. 29(2) R.P.
13 3 Art. 29(3) R.P.
4 Case 30/59, 29 ILR 86.
5 Art. 29(3) R.P.
6 Case 1/60, 2 Val. 665.
7 Art. 29(4) R.P.
8 Art. 29(5) R.P.
9 Arts. 30(2), 31 R.P.

Section 406

1 See § 412 below.
2 See §§ 407, 408 below.
3 Cases 9 and 12/60 [1962] ECR 182 (Third Party Proceedings).
4 Arts. 21 E.C.S.C. Statute, 18 E.E.C. Statute, 18 Euratom Statute. For the formalities regarding the signing, dating, copies, annexes, translations, etc. of pleadings in general, see Art. 37 R.P.
5 These documents are specified by Arts. 22(2) E.C.S.C. Statute, 19(2) E.E.C. Statute, 19(2) Euratom Statute, 37(1) and (4), 38(3) to (6) R.P.
6 Arts. 22(1) E.C.S.C. Statute, 19(1) E.E.C. Statute, 19(1) Euratom Statute, 38(1) R.P. The Statutes also mention the description of the signatory (i.e. the applicant's legal representative), but this is no longer included in Art. 38(1) R.P. as amended.
7 Cases 18 and 19/64 [1965] ECR 796.
8 Case 13/57, 2 Val. 588.
14 9 Cases 7 and 9/54, 2 Val. 138.
10 Cases 7/56 and 3 to 7/57, 2 Val. 768.
11 Case 42/71 [1973] CMLR 177.
12 Arts. 16(6) R.P., 25 I.R.
13 Cases 19 and 21/60, 2 and 3/61 [1962] CMLR 279-280. *Cf.* also Art. 38(7) R.P.
14 Cases 27 and 39/59, 2 Val. 810-811; 25 and 26/65 [1967] ECR 43; 15/70 [1970] ECR 982-983 *per* A.G.; 8/71 [1973] CMLR 907 *per* A.G.; 40/75 [1976] ECR 12 *per* A.G. (in all

three cases the Court seems to have accepted the A.G.'s Opinions by implication); 50/74 [1975] ECR 1013-1014; 95 to 98/74, 15 and 100/75 *ibid.*, pp. 1634-1635.

15 Case 74/74 [1975] ECR 544. See also the Cases mentioned in notes 16, 23 and 25 below.

16 Cases 30/68 [1970] ECR 310-311; 4/69 [1971] ECR 335-336.

17 Cases 12/68 [1969] ECR 115; 15/70 [1970] ECR 982-983 *per* A.G. See also the Case mentioned in note 18 below.

18 Cases 7/56 and 3 to 7/57, 2 Val. 768; 2 to 10/63 [1963] ECR 341. See also § 804 below.

19 Cases 19 and 21/60, 2 and 3/61 [1962] CMLR 279-280. See also § 514 below.

20 Cases 9/55, 2 Val. 126; 19 and 65/63 [1965] ECR 546.

15 21 Case 111/63 [1965] ECR 696.

22 Cases 25/62 [1963] ECR 119-120 *per* A.G.; 40/75 [1976] ECR 12 *per* A.G.

23 Cases 29, 31, 36, 39 to 47, 50 and 51/63 [1965] ECR 934-935. See also § 705 below.

24 Cases 56 to 60/74 [1976] ECR 742.

25 Cases 46 and 47/59 [1962] ECR 419.

26 Case 33/59 [1962] ECR 388 *per Curiam*, 394 *per* A.G.

27 Case 15/67 [1967] ECR 402.

28 Art. 39 R.P. For the way in which service is effected, see Art. 79 R.P.

29 Art. 40 R.P.

30 Arts. 35 E.C.S.C. Statute, 38 E.E.C. Statute, 39 Euratom Statute, Art. 94 R.P.

31 Art. 41 R.P.

32 Art. 42 R.P.

16 33 Cases 2/54, 2 Val. 41; 9/55 *ibid.*, p. 126; 18/57 *ibid.*, p. 258; 27 to 29/58 *ibid.*, p. 393; 44/59 *ibid.*, pp. 795-796; 19 and 21/60, 2 and 3/61 [1962] CMLR 280; 108/63 [1965] ECR 9.

34 Cases 17/57, 2 Val. 713; 83/63 [1965] ECR 633; 67 to 85/75 [1976] ECR 405-406.

35 Cases 1/58, 2 Val. 230-231; 30/68 [1970] ECR 310.

36 Case 11/64 [1965] ECR 298.

37 Case 31/69 [1970] ECR 32.

38 Case 2/54, 2 Val. 41.

39 Case 4/73 [1974] ECR 512 *per* A.G. See also § 514 below.

40 Case 13/60 [1962] ECR 100.

41 Cases 16 to 18/59, 2 Val. 269; 73/74 [1975] ECR 1510 *per Curiam*, 1520 *per* A.G.

42 Cases 2/54, 2 Val. 40; 2/56 *ibid.*, p. 239; 2/57 *ibid.*, p. 506; 9 and 12/60, 32 ILR 418; 18/60 [1962] ECR 203; 28/64 [1965] ECR 249.

43 Cases 25/62 [1963] ECR 108 *per Curiam*, 117-118 *per* A.G.; 19, 20, 25 and 30/69 [1970] ECR 338; 63 to 69/72 [1973] ECR 1253 *per Curiam* (by implication), 1273-1274 *per* A.G.; 56 to 60/74 [1976] ECR 740-742 *per Curiam*, 750 *et seq. per* A.G.

44 Cases 29, 31, 36, 39 to 47, 50 and 51/63 [1965] ECR 934-935.

45 Art. 43 R.P.

46 Cases 36 to 38 and 40/59, 2 Val. 276; 19 and 20/74 [1975] ECR 517.

47 Cases 112, 144 and 145/73 [1974] ECR 974; 10 to 14/75 [1975] ECR 1068.

48 Cases 27 and 39/59, 2 Val. 806.

17 49 Cases 42 and 49/59, 32 ILR 386.

50 Art. 43 R.P. *Cf.* e.g. Cases 19 and 65/63 [1965] ECR 574-576 (Order).

51 Arts. 44, 46 R.P.

Section 407

1 Art. 45 R.P.

2 Arts. 23, 24 E.C.S.C. Statute, 21 E.E.C. Statute, 22 Euratom Statute.

3 Case 2/54, 2 Val. 43.

4 Cases 42 and 49/59, 32 ILR 395; 110/75 [1976] ECR 1634-1635 *per* A.G.

5 Case 173/73 [1974] ECR 726 *per* A.G.

6 Arts. 28 E.C.S.C. Statute, 23, 25 E.E.C. Statute, 24, 26 Euratom Statute, Arts. 47, 51 R.P.

7 Arts. 28 E.C.S.C. Statute, 24 E.E.C. Statute, 25 Euratom Statute, Art. 48 R.P.

8 Arts. 25 E.C.S.C. Statute, 22 E.E.C. Statute, 23 Euratom Statute, Arts. 49, 51 R.P.

9 Art. 50 R.P.

10 Arts. 28 E.C.S.C. Statute, 27 E.E.C. Statute, 28 Euratom Statute, Art. 110 R.P.; Arts. 6, 7 S.R.P. See § 1004 below.

11 Arts. 26 E.E.C. Statute, 27 Euratom Statute, Art. 52 R.P.; Arts. 1 to 3 S.R.P. In the United Kingdom the Evidence (European Court) Order 1976, S.I. 1976 No. 428 enables evidence for proceedings before the European Court to be taken at the request of that Court. For this purpose the Order makes Sections 1-3 of the Evidence (Proceedings in other Jurisdictions) Act 1975 applicable to the European Court of Justice. Section 1(4) of the Perjury Act 1911 (c.6) and Section 1(4) of the Perjury Act (Northern Ireland) 1946 (c.13) N.I. shall have effect in relation to proceedings in the European Court as they have effect in relation to proceedings in tribunals of a foreign State.

12 Art. 53 R.P.

18 13 Art. 54 R.P.

Section 408

1 In practice the report is usually not read and the hearing accordingly opens with the speeches of the parties.

2 Arts. 21 E.C.S.C. Statute, 18 E.E.C. Statute, 18 Euratom Statute.

3 Arts. 28 E.C.S.C. Statute, 31 E.E.C. Statute, 32 Euratom Statute.

4 See Art. 85 R.P.

5 Art. 55 R.P.

6 Arts. 26 E.C.S.C. Statute, 28 E.E.C. Statute, 29 Euratom Statute, Art. 56 R.P.

7 Art. 57 R.P.

8 Art. 58 R.P.

9 Arts. 28 E.C.S.C. Statute, 29 E.E.C. Statute, 30 Euratom Statute, Art. 60 R.P.

10 Art. 61 R.P.

11 Art. 59 R.P.

12 Arts. 27 E.C.S.C. Statute, 30 E.E.C. Statute, 31 Euratom Statute, Art. 62 R.P.

13 Art. 78 R.P. *Cf.* e.g. Cases 19 and 65/63 [1965] ECR 574-576 (Order).

14 Art. 77 R.P.

15 I.e. to actions for annulment and for failure to act under Arts. 33 and 35 E.C.S.C., 173 and 175 E.E.C., 146 and 148 Euratom, see Art. 77 R.P.

16 Case 13/57, 2 Val. 589.

17 Cases 5, 7 and 8/60, 32 ILR 550.

18 Cases 16 to 18/59, 2 Val. 269.

Section 409

19 1 Arts. 29 E.C.S.C. Statute, 32 E.E.C. Statute, 33 Euratom Statute.

2 Art. 27 R.P.

3 Arts. 30 E.C.S.C. Statute, 33 E.E.C. Statute, 34 Euratom Statute, Art. 63 R.P.

4 See further § 219 above.

5 Arts. 31 E.C.S.C. Statute, 34 E.E.C. Statute, 35 Euratom Statute, Art. 64 R.P.

6 Art. 65 R.P.

7 Art. 66 R.P.

8 Art. 67 R.P.

9 Case 13/67 [1968] ECR 197 (Order).

10 Art. 68 R.P., Art. 24 I.R. For the languages in which the reports are to be published and the determination of the authentic version, see § 405 above.

Section 410

1 Arts. 32 E.C.S.C. Statute, 35 E.E.C. Statute, 36 Euratom Statute, Case 5/55, 2 Val. 64.

2 See § 412(g) below.

20 3 Art. 69(1) R.P.

3a Case 4/73 (Enforcement) [1977] ECR 3 (Order). See § 1003 below.

4 Art. 69(2) R.P.

5 Cases 1/54, 2 Val. 36-37; 16/61 [1962] ECR 307; 23, 24 and 52/63 [1963] ECR 225; 53 and 54/63 *ibid.*, pp. 248-249.

6 Cases 30/67 [1968] ECR 121; 22/70 [1971] CMLR 363.
7 Art. 69(2) R.P. *Cf.* e.g. Case 13/57, 2 Val. 589-590.
8 Cases 7 and 9/54, 2 Val. 156; 14/61 [1962] ECR 276; 19/61 *ibid.*, p. 378; 4/73 [1974] ECR 509.
9 Case 111/63 [1965] ECR 718.
10 Cases 3 to 18, 25 and 26/58, 2 Val. 345; 24 and 34/58 *ibid.*, p. 362; 30/59, 29 ILR 102.
11 Cases 40 to 48, 50, 54 to 56, 111, 113 and 114/73 [1975] ECR 2024-2025.
12 See § 412(a) below.
13 Case 67/63 [1964] ECR 166.
14 Cases 19 and 65/63 [1965] ECR 561.
15 Cases 16 to 18/59, 2 Val. 269.
16 Art. 69(3)(1) R.P. *Cf.* e.g. Cases 1/54, 2 Val. 36; 2/54 *ibid.*, p. 44; 16/61 [1962] ECR 307.
17 Cases 3/54, 2 Val. 51; 4/54 *ibid.*, p. 55; 8/57 *ibid.*, p. 532; 15/57 *ibid.*, p. 501; etc.
18 Cases 2 and 3/60, 32 ILR 405; 55 to 59 and 61 to 63/63 [1964] ECR 230.
19 Cases 14/63 [1963] ECR 374; 26/66 [1967] ECR 127.
20 Cases 5, 7 and 13 to 24/66 [1967] ECR 267; 169/73 [1975] ECR 136.
21 Cases 16 and 17/59 [1962] ECR 423; 153/73 [1974] ECR 697; 56 to 60/74 [1976] ECR 747.
22 Art. 69(3)(2) R.P.
21 23 Cases 20/58, 2 Val. 607; 16 to 18/59 *ibid.*, p. 269; 28/63 [1963] ECR 236; 23, 24 and 52/63 *ibid.*, p. 225; 53 and 54/63 *ibid.*, p. 249. Cf. also Case 88/76 [1977] ECR 727.
24 Cases 15 and 29/59, 2 Val. 563; 35/62 and 16/63 [1963] ECR 208.
25 Cases 5, 7 and 8/60, 32 ILR 550.
26 Cases 55 to 59 and 61 to 63/63 [1964] ECR 238 *per* A.G
27 Case 18/62 [1963] ECR 282.
28 Art. 69(4) R.P. *Cf.* e.g. Case 13/57, 2 Val. 589-590.
29 Art. 69(5) R.P.
30 Case 103/63 [1964] ECR 429.
31 Cases 7 and 9/54, 2 Val. 156; 75/69 [1970] ECR 543.
32 Art. 70 R.P.
33 For these, see Art. 16(5) R.P. and Arts. 17 to 22 I.R.
34 Art. 72 R.P.
35 For these, see Art. 51 R.P. *Cf.* e.g. Cases 40 to 48, 50, 54 to 56, 111, 113 and 114/73 [1975] ECR 2025.
36 Art. 73 R.P.
37 Art. 74 R.P.
38 Cases 9 and 58/65 [1968] ECR 260 (Order).
39 Cases 6/72 [1975] ECR 496 (Order); 4/73 *ibid.*, p. 987 (Order).
40 See the Cases in notes 39 above and 41 below.
22 41 Case 75/69 [1970] ECR 902-903 (Order).
42 See § 404 above.
43 Cases 20 and 21/63 [1964] ECR 622-623 (Order).
44 Art. 71 R.P. See § 1003 below.
45 In the United Kingdom the competent authority is the Secretary of State, see Annex I to the S.R.P.
46 Art. 76(1) and (2) R.P.
47 Arts. 4 and 5 S.R.P.
48 Art. 76(4) R.P.
49 Art. 76(5) R.P. *Cf.* e.g. Cases 19 and 65/63 [1965] ECR 561.

Section 411

1 A list of official holidays drawn up by the Court is contained in Annex I to R.P.
2 Art. 80 R.P.
3 Art. 81(1) R.P. See also § 520 below.
4 Cases 32 and 33/58, 2 Val. 624. In that case the Court accepted as possible (although

improbable) that a letter posted in Brussels on May 12th did not arrive in France (Savoie) before May 26th.
5 Case 42/58, 2 Val. 638. In that case the Court held it impossible that a letter posted in Luxembourg on August 1 should not arrive in middle-France (near Paris) before September 17th.
6 Art. 81(2) R.P.; Annex II to R.P. For the United Kingdom the extension is 10 days.
23 7 Case 28/65 [1966] ECR 491.
8 Art. 37(3) R.P.
9 Cases 36 to 38, 40 and 41/58, 2 Val. 596.
10 Art. 1(1) I.R.
11 See note 9 above.
12 Arts. 39 E.C.S.C. Statute, 42 E.E.C. Statute, 43 Euratom Statute.
13 Cases 25 and 26/65 [1967] ECR 42-43.

Section 412

1 See § 521 below.
2 Arts. 39(1) and (2) E.C.S.C. 185 E.E.C., 157 Euratom. For derogations from this rule, see Arts. 66(5) E.C.S.C., 83(2) Euratom.
3 Arts. 39(3) E.C.S.C., 186 E.E.C., 158 Euratom.
4 Arts. 33 E.C.S.C. Statute, 36 E.E.C. Statute, 37 Euratom Statute, Art. 83(1) R.P.
5 I.e. in accordance with Arts. 37 and 38 R.P., see Art. 83(3) R.P. See § 406 above.
6 Cases 108/63 [1965] ECR 9; 32/64 *ibid.*, p. 372.
7 Cases 3 to 18, 25 and 26/58, 2 Val. 333.
24 8 Art. 84(1) R.P.
9 Art. 84(2) R.P.
10 Case 27/76 R [1976] ECR 429 (Order).
11 Art. 85 R.P.
12 Art. 86(1) R.P.
13 Art. 86(2) R.P.
14 Art. 86(3) R.P.
15 Art. 87 R.P.
16 Art. 88 R.P.
17 Art. 89 R.P. See § 1003 below.
18 Arts. 33 E.C.S.C. Statute, 36 E.E.C. Statute, 37 Euratom Statute, Art. 86(4) R.P.
19 Cases 18/57, 2 Val. 252 (Order); 25/62 R2 [1963] ECR 128-129 (Order).
20 Case 50/69 R [1969] ECR 455, 457 *per* A.G. (Order) referring to Cases 43, 45 and 48/59, 2 Val. 782-783 (Order).
21 Art. 83(2) R.P.
22 *Cf.* e.g. Cases 19/59 R, 2 Val. 265 (Order); 25/62 R1 [1963] ECR 124-125 (Order); 27/68 R [1969] ECR 275-276 (Order); 50/69 R *ibid.*, pp. 454 *et seq.* *per* A.G. (Order); 71/74 R and RR [1974] ECR 1034 (Order).
23 *Cf.* e.g. Cases 160-161/73 R [1973] ECR 1053-1054 (Order).
24 *Cf.* e.g. Case 6/72 R [1972] CMLR 692-693 (Order). Where, however, the applicant can show such a threat, the Court will grant a stay of execution, *cf.* e.g. Cases 20/74 R [1974] ECR 339 (Order) and 45/71 R [1972] CMLR 696-697 (first half) (Order), where the Court ordered the temporary suspension of the operation of certain provisions of Commission Decisions requiring the applicants to terminate infringement under Arts. 85 and 86 E.E.C., respectively.
25 Case 44/75 R [1975] ECR 641 (Order).
26 Case 53/65 R [1966] ECR 18 (Order).
27 Case 45/71 R [1972] CMLR 697 (second half) (Order).
25 28 Case 3/75 R [1975] ECR 6 (Order).
29 Case 44/75 R [1975] ECR 641 (Order).
30 *Ibid.*
31 For the reasons for this, see §§ 508, 511 below. For the concept of 'direct and individual concern', see §§ 512, 513 below.

32 Case 44/75 R [1975] ECR 640 (Order).
33 Case 3/75 R [1975] ECR 6 (Order).
34 See § 401 above.
35 Cases 19/59 R, 2 Val. 265 (Order); 25/62 R1 [1963] ECR 124-125 (Order); 50/69 R [1969] ECR 450-451 *per Curiam*, 454 *et seq. per* A.G. (Order); 109/75 R [1975] ECR 1201-1202 (Order).
36 Case 71/74 R and RR [1974] ECR 1034 (Order).
37 Art. 91(1) R.P.
26 38 Art. 91(2) and (3) R.P.
39 Art. 91(4) R.P.
40 Cases 21 to 26/61 [1962] ECR 80 *per* A.G.
41 Cases 16 and 17/62 [1962] ECR 482 *per* A.G. *Cf.* e.g. Cases 63/69 [1970] ECR 210, 69/69 *ibid.*, p. 393, etc.
42 *Cf.* e.g. Case 8/71 [1973] CMLR 906 *per* A.G.
43 Cases 106 and 107/63 [1965] ECR 430 (Order); 16 and 17/62 [1962] ECR 482 *per* A.G.; 41 to 44/70 [1975] 2 CMLR 520 *per* A.G.
44 Art. 92 R.P. *Cf.* e.g. Cases 31 and 33/62 [1962] ECR 512 (Order).
45 Cases 58 and 75/72 [1973] ECR 516; 45 and 49/70 [1971] ECR 475; 109 and 114/75 [1977] ECR 389 *per* A.G. (Order).
46 Art. 34(1) E.C.S.C. Statute.
47 Case 13/60 [1962] ECR 143-144 (Order).
48 See § 901 below.
27 49 Case 25/59, 2 Val. 313-314.
50 Cases 9 and 12/60 [1962] ECR 182 (Third Party Proceedings).
51 Case 111/63 [1965] ECR 717-718 (Order).
52 Cases 56 and 58/64 [1966] ECR 383, 386 (Order).
53 Arts. 37(1) E.E.C. Statute, 38(1) Euratom Statute, Case 15/63 [1964] ECR 54 *per* A.G. (Order).
54 Arts. 37(2) E.E.C. Statute, 38(2) Euratom Statute.
55 Cases 16 and 17/62 [1962] ECR 488 (Order); 41, 43 to 48, 50, 111, 113 and 114/73 [1973] ECR 1468-1469 (Order); 175/73 [1974] ECR 926; 18/74 *ibid.*, p. 945; 72/74 [1975] ECR 410. See § 403 above.
56 Cases 16 and 17/62 [1962] ECR 488 (Order); 41, 43 to 48, 50, 111, 113 and 114/73 [1973] ECR 1468-1469 (Order).
57 Cases 16 and 17/62 [1962] ECR 486 *per* A.G. See §§ 403 above and 513, 703 below.
58 Case 15/63 [1964] ECR 51 *per Curiam*, 53 *et seq. per* A.G. (Order).
59 Arts. 34(2) E.C.S.C. Statute, 37(3) E.E.C. Statute, 38(3) Euratom Statute, Art. 93(2) (e) R.P.
28 60 Cases 42 and 49/59, 32 ILR 387.
61 Art. 93(2)(f) R.P.
62 Case 30/59, 29 ILR 86 (Order), 89-90.
63 Cases 9 and 12/60 [1962] ECR 187-188 *per* A.G. (Third Party Proceedings); 12/69 [1969] ECR 584.
64 See (d) below in this Section.
65 Art. 93(1) R.P. Cases 36 to 38, 40 and 41/58, 2 Val. 596.
66 Art. 93(2) R.P.
67 Art. 93(2)(d) and (e) R.P.
68 Art. 93(5) R.P.
69 Art. 93(3) R.P.
70 Case 30/59, 29 ILR 86 (Order).
71 Art. 93(5) R.P.; Case 30/59, 29 ILR 89-90.
72 Case 109/75 R [1975] ECR 1200 (Order). For such proceedings, see (a) in this Section above.
29 73 The other is revision, for which see (e) in this Section below.
74 Arts. 36 E.C.S.C. Statute, 39 E.E.C. Statute, 40 Euratom Statute, Art. 97(1) R.P.
75 *Cf.* Arts. 37 and 38 R.P., see § 406 above.

76 Art. 97(1) R.P.
77 Cases 9 and 12/60 [1962] ECR 183-184 *per Curiam*, 190-191 *per* A.G. (Third Party Proceedings).
78 See § 221 above.
79 See (c) in this Section above.
80 Art. 16(6) R.P.; Art. 25 I.R. See § 406 above.
30 81 Cases 42 and 49/59 [1962] ECR 157-159 *per Curiam*, 162 *per* A.G. (Third Party Proceedings); 9 and 12/60 [1962] ECR 181-183 *per Curiam*, 186 *et seq. per* A.G. (Third Party Proceedings).
82 Art. 97(2) R.P. See (a) in this Section above.
83 Cases 42 and 49/59 [1962] ECR 169 (Order) (Third Party Proceedings).
84 Art. 97(3) R.P.
85 The other is third party proceedings, for which see (d) in this Section above.
86 Arts. 38(1) E.C.S.C. Statute, 41(1) E.E.C. Statute, 42(1) Euratom Statute.
87 Case 1/60, 2 Val. 664-665.
88 Case 115/73 Rev. [1974] ECR 673.
89 Art. 98 R.P.
90 Arts. 38(3) E.C.S.C. Statute, 41(3) E.E.C. Statute, 42(3) Euratom Statute.
91 *Cf.* Arts. 37 and 38 R.P. See § 406 above.
92 Art. 99 R.P.
93 Arts. 38(2) E.C.S.C. Statute, 41(2) E.E.C. Statute, 42(2) Euratom Statute, Art. 100 R.P. Cases 1/60, 2 Val. 664; 37/71 Rev. [1973] ECR 298; 56/75 Rev. (not yet reported).
94 Arts. 37 E.C.S.C. Statute, 40 E.E.C. Statute, 41 Euratom Statute.
95 Case 24/66 bis. [1973] ECR 1603.
31 96 Case 5/55, 2 Val. 60-61 *per Curiam*, 1 Rec. 286 *et seq. per* A.G.
97 *Ibid.*
98 *Ibid.* pp. 61-62 *per Curiam*; 110/63 A [1966] ECR 291-292 *per Curiam*, 295 *per* A.G.
99 Cases 70/63 A [1965] ECR 279-280; 24/66 bis. [1973] ECR 1603 *per Curiam*, 1605-1606 *per* A.G. In this Case the applicant sought an interpretation of the judgment in Cases 5, 7 and 13 to 24/66 [1967] ECR 245, in particular whether that judgment was also binding upon national courts before which parallel actions had been brought, based on the same facts. See also § 1103 below.
100 Cases 5/55, 2 Val. 62-63 *per Curiam*, 1 Rec. 287 *et seq. per* A.G.; 110/63 A [1966] ECR 295 *per* A.G.
101 Case 5/55, 2 Val. 59-62.
102 *Cf.* Arts. 37 and 38 R.P., § 406 above.
103 Case 110/63 A [1966] ECR 291-292.
104 Art. 102(1) R.P.
105 Art. 102(2) R.P.
105a Cases 41, 43 and 44/73 (Interpretation) [1977] ECR 464.
32 106 See Chapter 11 below.
107 Cases 28 to 30/62 [1963] ECR 38.
108 Arts. 20 E.E.C. Statute, 21 Euratom Statute. For the procedure in cases provided for in Art. 41 E.C.S.C., see Art. 103(3) R.P.
109 Case 2/73 [1973] ECR 893 *per* A.G.
110 Art. 5(1) of the Protocol of 3 June 1971, Art. 103(2) R.P. The same rules apply also to references under the other Protocol of 3 June 1971, concerning the interpretation of the Convention on the Mutual Recognition of Companies 1968 and to references under any other future agreement.
111 Cases 12/76 [1976] ECR 1483-1484; 14/76 *ibid.*, p. 1514-1516 *per* A.G.
112 Art. 103(1) R.P.
113 See § 406 above.
114 See § 407 above. Case 51/75 [1976] ECR 854 *per* A.G.
115 See § 408 above.
116 See § 1109 below.
117 Under Art. 55(2) R.P.
118 Under Art. 67 R.P., Case 13/67 [1968] ECR 197 (Order).

119 Under Art. 102 R.P., Case 13/67 [1968] ECR 197 (Order).
120 Under Art. 77 R.P.
121 Under Art. 93 R.P., Cases 6/64 [1964] ECR 614-615 (Order); 19/68 [1968] ECR 479. See in general Case 62/72 [1973] ECR 279 *per* A.G.
122 I.e. Arts. 69 to 75 R.P.; in particular Arts. 73 and 74 R.P.
123 Case 62/72 [1973] ECR 275-276 *per Curiam*, 279 *et seq. per* A.G.
33 124 *Ibid. Cf.* e.g. Case 13/61 [1962] ECR 54 where the Court for the first time settled the question of costs in preliminary ruling procedures. For alternative solutions suggested by the A.G., see *ibid.*, p. 71.
125 Art. 104 R.P.
126 Ibid. In *R.* v *Marlborough St. Stipendiary Magistrate, Exp. Bouchereau* [1977] 1 CMLR 274 the High Court (Queen's Bench Division) has declared that a legal aid certificate granted under section 28(2) of the Legal Aid Act 1974 by a Magistrate's Court extends to and covers reference proceedings under Art. 177 E.E.C. arising from the proceedings for which the certificate was originally granted. No such provision for legal aid however is available when the party in question is a company, see *Maxims Ltd.* v *Dye* [1977] 2 CMLR 418 *per* Graham J.
127 Art. 95(1) R.P.
128 Art. 94 R.P.
129 Arts. 95(2) and (3), 96 R.P.
130 Art. 20 Euratom Statute, Art. 101 R.P.
131 Arts. 105, 106 R.P.
132 Arts. 107 to 109 R.P.
133 Arts. 41 and 42 E.C.S.C. Statute.
134 Art. 43 E.C.S.C. Statute.

Section 501

34 1 Arts. 31 E.C.S.C., 164 E.E.C., 136 Euratom. Case 22/70 [1971] CMLR 357.
2 *Ibid.*, pp. 341-342 *per* A.G.
3 See § 206 above.
35 4 Cases 7 and 9/54, 2 Rec. 124-125 *per* A.G.; 8/55 *ibid.*, pp.247-248 *per* A.G.
5 See §§ 514 to 518 below.
6 See § 521 below. Case 50/69 R [1969] ECR 455 *per* A.G. (Order).
7 See § 502 below.
8 Case 22/70 [1971] CMLR 341-342 *per* A.G.
9 Cases 3/54, 1 Rec. 149 *per* A.G.; 1/55, 2 Rec. 38 *per* A.G.; 1/56 *ibid.*, pp. 448-449 *per* A.G.
10 On the question of legal interest, see further § 503 below.
11 Only the Council under the E.C.S.C. Treaty. See further § 504 below.
36 12 See § 519 below.
13 See § 1101 below.
14 See § 701 below.
15 See in general Cases 3/54, 1 Rec. 173-174 *per* A.G.; 7 and 9/54, 2 Rec. 123-124 *per* A.G.; 8/55, 2 Val. 101 *per Curiam*, 2 Rec. 246 *et seq. per* A.G.; 24 and 34/58, 6 Rec. 621 *et seq. per* A.G.; 16 and 17/62 [1962] ECR 482, 485-486 *per* A.G.; 9 and 11/71 [1973] CMLR 533 *per* A.G.; 43/72 [1973] ECR 1078-1079 *per* A.G.; 153/73 [1974] ECR 699 *per* A.G.
16 See § 601 below.
17 Cases 7 and 9/54, 2 Val. 143-144; 32 and 33/58 *ibid.*, pp. 626-627; 109 and 114/75 [1977] ECR 387 *per* A.G. (Order). The converse proposition is also correct, see § 601 below.
18 Case 15/70 [1970] ECR 980 *per Curiam*, 984 *per* A.G. See further § 601 below.
19 Cases 42 and 49/59, 32 ILR 386. See further § 701 below.
20 See §§ 801, 804 below.
37 21 Art. 6 of Council Decision 70/243 and Arts. 4 and 8 of Council Regulation 729/70, of 21 April 1970 and Arts. 1, 2 and 13 of Council Regulation 2/71 of 2 January 1971.
22 See in general Cases 96/71 [1973] CMLR 383; 43/72 [1973] ECR 1082 *per* A.G.; 99/74 [1975] ECR 1540 *per Curiam*, 1542-1543 *per* A.G.; 46/75 [1976] ECR 79-80; 26/74 *ibid.*, p. 686. See further §§ 701, 1101 below.

23 See Chapter 9 below. *Cf.* also Cases 40 to 48, 50, 54 to 56, 111, 113 and 114/73 [1975] ECR 2074 *per* A.G.

24 As of 31 December 1976. Staff Cases and actions brought solely for the cancellation or reduction of pecuniary sanctions are not included. For the latter, see § 801 below. Joined Cases have been counted as one Case.

25 Cases 9/56, 2 Val. 457; 10/56 *ibid.*, p. 481; 18/57, *ibid.*, p. 245; 4 to 13/59 *ibid.*, p. 640; 24 and 34/58 *ibid.*, p. 345; 36 to 38 and 40/59 *ibid.*, p. 270; 30/59, 29 ILR 85; 18/62 [1963] ECR 259; 67/63 [1964] ECR 151; 8/65 [1966] ECR 1; 49/65 *ibid.*, p. 73; 2/65 *ibid.*, p. 219; 9 and 58/65 [1967] ECR 1; 25 and 26/65 *ibid.*, p. 33.

26 Cases 1/54, 2 Val. 18; 2/54 *ibid.*, p. 37; 66/63 [1964] ECR 533 (here the action was dismissed as unfounded, except that the Court annulled one word only in the challenged decision); 28/66 [1968] ECR 1.

27 See note 24 above.

28 Cases 106 and 107/63 [1965] ECR 405; 56 and 58/64 [1966] ECR 299; 8 to 11/66 [1967] ECR 75; 62/70 [1972] CMLR 160; 6/72 [1973] ECR 215; 17/74 [1974] ECR 1063; 19 and 20/74 [1975] ECR 499; 40 to 48, 50, 54 to 56, 111, 113 and 114/73 *ibid.*, p. 1663; 29/75 [1976] ECR 431.

29 Cases 24/62 [1963] ECR 63; 13/72 [1973] ECR 27; 151/73 [1974] ECR 285; 47/75 [1976] ECR 569.

30 Case 81/72 [1973] ECR 575.

Section 502

38 1 See §§ 206, 215 above.

2 Cases 7/56 and 3 to 7/57, 2 Val. 763; 15 to 33, 52, 53, 57 to 109, 116, 117, 123, 132 and 135 to 137/73 [1974] ECR 191 *per Curiam*, 197 *per* A.G.; 6 and 11/69 [1969] ECR 539 *per Curiam*, 550 *per* A.G.; 50/69 R *ibid.*, pp. 454-455 *per* A.G. (Order); 102/63 [1964] ECR 713 *per* A.G.

3 I.e. in the context of a defence of illegality or of a reference for preliminary ruling. See §§ 519, 1104, 1110 below.

4 See § 221 above.

5 See §§ 515, 516 below.

6 Cases 15 to 33, etc. /73 [1974] ECR 197 *per* A.G.; 19 and 21/60, 2 and 3/61 [1962] CMLR 265-266 *per* A.G.; 102/63 [1964] ECR 713 *per* A.G.; 6 and 11/69 [1969] ECR 550 *per* A.G.

7 Cases 6 and 11/69 [1969] ECR 539.

8 Cases 1 and 14/57, 2 Val. 692-693 where the Court held an opinion issued by the High Authority under Art. 54(4) E.C.S.C. without giving reasons, to be non-existent in law.

39 9 *Cf.* e.g. Cases 18/57, 2 Val. 259; 8 to 11/66 [1967] ECR 93-94. See further § 516 below.

Section 503

1 Cases 2 and 3/60, 32 ILR 402-405; 43/72 [1973] ECR 1078 *per* A.G.

2 Cases 3/54, 1 Rec. 173-174 *per* A.G.; 7 and 9/54, 2 Rec. 123-125 *per* A.G.; 8/55 *ibid.*, pp. 246-247 *per* A.G.; 24 and 34/58, 6 Rec. 621-624 *per* A.G.; 16 and 17/62 [1962] ECR 485-486 *per* A.G.; 10 and 18/68 [1969] ECR 491 *per* A.G. For the definition of the concept of 'direct and individual concern', see further §§ 512 and 513 below.

40 3 This condition is expressly laid down by Art. 91 of the Staff Regulations and thus applies to Community officials in the first place, *cf.* e.g. Cases 17/68 [1969] ECR 69; 26/68 *ibid.*, p. 153; 39/69 [1970] ECR 272; 46/69 *ibid.*, p. 281; 66/75 [1976] ECR 601-602. It is, however, submitted that it forms in a broader sense a general prerequisite for the admissibility of actions for annulment brought by private parties also, *cf.* Cases 16 to 18/59, 2 Val. 269; 109 and 114/75 [1977] ECR 389 *per* A.G. (Order).

4 Cases 24 and 34/58, 2 Val. 351-352 *per Curiam*, 6 Rec. 621-623 *per* A.G.; 4/73 [1974] ECR 504.

5 Case 20/68 [1969] ECR 243. See also § 519 below.

6 *Ibid.*, p. 242 *per Curiam*, 248-249 *per* A.G.

7 Case 1/76 [1976] ECR 1024.

8 Cases 42 and 49/59, 32 ILR 388, 391; 24/69 [1970] ECR 151.

9 Cases 43/64 [1965] ECR 397; 34/65 [1966] ECR 531. See further § 520 below.
10 Case 2/57, 2 Val. 507.
41 11 Cases 42 and 49/59, 32 ILR 386.
12 Case 18/69 [1970] ECR 255.
13 Cases 9 and 11/71 [1973] CMLR 551; 45 and 49/70 [1971] ECR 475; 58 and 75/72 [1973] ECR 516; 109 and 114/75 [1977] ECR 389 *per* A.G. (Order). *Cf.* however Cases 59 and 71/69 [1970] ECR 629 where in the circumstances of the case the Court found that the applicant had a legal interest in bringing two actions for annulment.
14 Cases 56 and 58/64 [1966] ECR 338-339; 88/76 [1977] ECR 726.
15 Case 15/67 [1967] ECR 402.
16 Cases 7 and 9/54, 2 Rec. 132-134 *per* A.G.; 14/63 [1963] ECR 371.
17 See §§ 514 to 518 below.
18 Cases 24 and 34/58, 6 Rec. 623-624 *per* A.G.
19 Cases 2 and 3/60, 32 ILR 402; 22/70 [1971] CMLR 358-359.

Section 504

1 See §§ 503 above and 505 below.
1a Case 66/76 [1977] ECR 310.
2 See § 301 above.
3 Case 12/63 [1963] ECR 89.
4 Case 10/55, 2 Val. 731.
5 Cases 7 and 9/54, 2 Val. 142; 8/57 *ibid.*, p. 517; 9/57 *ibid.*, p. 535; 13/57 *ibid.*, p. 586.
42 6 See § 403 above.
7 See § 506 below.
8 Art. 80 E.C.S.C. See further § 301 above.
9 Case 12/63 [1963] ECR 89.
10 Cases 18/57, 2 Val. 252-253; 1/58 *ibid.*, p. 221.
11 Case 12/63 [1963] ECR 89 *per Curiam*, 93 *per* A.G.
43 12 Cases 2 and 3/60, 32 ILR 402-405.
13 *Ibid. Cf.* also Cases 13/63 [1963] ECR 175-177 *per Curiam*, 181-183 *per* A.G.; 73 and 74/63 [1964] ECR 20-21 *per* A.G.
14 See § 515 below.
15 See § 516 below.
15a Case 66/76 [1977] ECR 310.
15b Case 91/76 [1977] ECR 229.
16 Arts. 211 E.E.C., 185 Euratom. See § 101 above.
17 See § 101 above.
18 Cases 25/60 [1962] ECR 35 *per* A.G.; 15/63 [1964] ECR 53-55 *per* A.G. (Order); 18/63 *ibid.*, p. 96; 27/63 *ibid.*, p. 136 *per Curiam*, p. 142 *per* A.G.; 79 and 82/63 *ibid.*, pp. 265-266 *per Curiam*, 271-272 *per* A.G.; 28/64 [1965] ECR 247; 43/64 *ibid.*, p. 395; 100/74 [1975] ECR 1418 (Order). Under the E.C.S.C. Treaty such a problem does not arise, partly because under Art. 6 that Community is represented by its institutions 'each within the limits of its powers', and partly because under Art. 33 only the Commission can be named as defendant.
44 19 Cases 79 and 82/63 [1964] ECR 266. As to *res judicata*, see § 219 above.
20 See §§ 503 above and 507 below.
21 Cases 43, 45 and 48/59, 2 Val. 782, 784. In disputes between officials and the Communities the Court of Justice's jurisdiction is founded upon Arts. 179 E.E.C., 152 Euratom and upon the special and therefore exclusive provisions of Arts. 90 and 91 of the Staff Regulations issued under those Articles, see e.g. Cases 175/73 [1974] ECR 925-926; 18/74 *ibid.*, pp. 943-945 *per Curiam*, 948 *per* A.G. In the above Cases, however, the Court confirmed that in the absence of the Staff Regulations, Arts. 173 E.E.C., 146 Euratom applied to officials.
22 See further §§ 110 and 301 above.
23 See § 403 above.
24 See §§ 508 to 513 below.

25 Cases 13/63 [1963] ECR 175-177 *per Curiam*, 181-183 *per* A.G.; 73 and 74/63 [1964] ECR 12-13 *per Curiam*, 20-21 *per* A.G.; 37/70 [1971] CMLR 252-253 *per Curiam*, 245 *per* A.G.; 72/72 [1973] ECR 385 *et seq*. Although Art. 226 E.E.C. applied only during the transitional period, the almost identical Art. 135 of the Act of Accession applies, until the end of 1977, in relation to the new Member States and as between the original and new Member States.
26 Cases 18 and 19/64 [1965] ECR 796.
27 Case 13/57, 2 Val. 588. See § 406 above.

Section 505

45 1 See §§ 207, 208 above.
2 With the exception of opinions provided for by Art. 54(5) E.C.S.C. Cases 1 and 14/57, 2 Val. 694-695.
3 Cases 1/54, 2 Val. 22; 2/54 *ibid.*, p. 40; 3/54 *ibid.*, p. 49; 4/54 *ibid.*, p. 54; 2/56 *ibid.*, p. 236. See further § 521 below.
4 See §§ 503, 504 above.
5 Case 66/63 [1964] ECR 533.
6 Case 28/66 [1968] ECR 1.
7 See § 215 above.
46 8 Cases 23, 24 and 52/63 [1963] ECR 223-224; 28/63 *ibid.*, pp. 235-236; 53 and 54/63 *ibid.*, p. 247-248 *per Curiam*, 252 *per* A.G.; 54/65 [1966] ECR 195. For the rules relating to signature and delegation of powers in the single Commission of the three Communities, see §§ 206 and 215 above. For the question whether the requirements discussed in the text are still applicable, see Cases 109 and 114/75 [1977] ECR 387-388 *per* A.G. (Order).
9 See the Cases mentioned in the previous footnote.
10 Cases 53 and 54/63 [1963] ECR 252 *per* A.G.; 66/63 [1964] ECR 546.
11 Cases 42 and 49/59, 32 ILR 385.
12 Cases 35/62 and 16/63 [1963] ECR 204. However, the fact that the terms of the letter might reasonably have led the applicant to believe that the decision in question had already been taken, will influence the Court's ruling on costs, see § 410 above.
13 Cases 15 and 29/59, 2 Val. 560.
14 Cases 20/58, 2 Val. 605-607; 32 and 33/58 *ibid.*, p. 633. In such a case, too, the fact that the Commission has encouraged the applicant to bring an action by wrongly describing the letter as a decision, has an effect on costs, see § 410 above.
15 Cases 16 to 18/59, 2 Val. 268-269.
16 *Ibid.*
17 Cases 42 and 49/59, 32 ILR 385.
18 *Ibid.*, pp. 388-391. See further § 503 above.
19 Art. 18 of the Merger Treaty.
20 Art. 78d E.C.S.C.
21 Case 18/62 [1963] ECR 281-282.
22 Cases 53 and 54/63 [1963] ECR 247.
23 Cases 8/55, 2 Val. 99; 1 and 14/57 *ibid.*, p. 695.
47 24 Case 14/59, 2 Val. 543.
25 Cases 41 and 50/59, 2 Val. 679.
26 Cases 42 and 49/59, 32 ILR 388.
27 Cases 32 and 33/58, 2 Val. 625.

Section 506

1 See § 505 above.
2 For the purposes of this Section, the word 'decision' includes also 'recommendation' as these two types of act are subject to the same rules.
3 See § 511 below.
48 4 See § 206 above.
5 Cases 3/54, 1 Rec. 171-175 *per* A.G.; 7 and 9/54, 2 Rec. 123-126 *per* A.G.; 8/55 *ibid.*, pp. 246-249 *per* A.G. See also §§ 206, 501, 503 above and 508 below.

6 Cases 8/55, 2 Val. 101; 18/57 *ibid.*, p. 256; 3 and 4/64 [1965] ECR 459 *per* A.G.

7 Cases 10/57, 2 Val. 568; 13/57 *ibid.*, p. 587; 36 to 38, 40 and 41/58 *ibid.*, p. 597; 3 and 4/64 [1965] ECR 454.

49 8 *Ibid.*; Cases 8/55, 2 Val. 98-99; 7 and 9/54, 2 Rec. 126 *per* A.G.; 55 to 59 and 61 to 63/63 [1964] ECR 227-228 *per Curiam*, 234 *per* A.G.

9 Cases 36 to 38, 40 and 41/58, 2 Val. 597.

10 See §§ 508, 511 below.

11 For the concept of misuse of powers, see further § 518 below.

12 Cases 3/54, 2 Val. 49, 51; 4/54 *ibid.*, p. 54; 8/55 *ibid.*, p. 100; 2/57 *ibid.*, p. 506; 8/57 *ibid.*, p. 517; 13/57 *ibid.*, pp. 587-589; 10/57 *ibid.*, p. 568; 36 to 38, 40 and 41/58 *ibid.*, p. 597; 55 to 59 and 61 to 63/63 [1964] ECR 227-228; 3 and 4/64 [1965] ECR 454.

13 See §§ 515 to 518 below.

14 Cases 55 to 59 and 61 to 63/63 [1964] ECR 227-228; 3 and 4/64 [1965] ECR 455 *per Curiam*, 462 *per* A.G.

50 15 Case 8/55, 2 Val. 100 *per Curiam*, 2 Rec. 253 *per* A.G.

16 Cases 8/55, 2 Val. 100-101; 36 to 38, 40 and 41/58, 5 Rec. 369 *per* A.G.; 3 and 4/64 [1965] ECR 461-462 *per* A.G. For a contrary view, see Cases 3/54, 1 Rec. 148 *per* A.G.; 8/55, 2 Rec. 259 *per* A.G.

17 Cases 25 and 26/65 [1967] ECR 43-44. See further § 519 below.

18 See § 503 above.

19 Cases 7 and 9/54, 2 Val. 141-142 *per Curiam*, 2 Rec. 121-122, 126 *per* A.G.; 8/55, 2 Val. 100 *per Curiam*, 2 Rec. 246 *per* A.G.; 18/57, 2 Val. 257.

51 20 Case 18/57, 2 Val. 256.

21 *Ibid.*, p. 257.

22 Case 30/59, 29 ILR 88.

23 Cases 7 and 9/54, 2 Val. 142.

24 Case 13/60 [1962] ECR 99.

25 Case 30/59, 29 ILR 88. *Cf.* also Cases 10 and 18/68 [1969] ECR 490-491 *per* A.G., comparing this system with that of the E.E.C. Treaty, for which see § 512 below.

26 Cases 8/55, 2 Val. 99-101; 18/57 *ibid.*, p. 257; 24 and 34/58 *ibid.*, p. 352.

27 Cases 24 and 34/58, 2 Val. 351-352 *per Curiam*, 6 Rec. 621-624 *per* A.G., where the Court annulled in part, at the request of some French undertakings, a High Authority decision authorising the German Government to maintain in force special discriminatory domestic railway tariffs.

28 See Chapter 9 below.

52 29 Case 30/59, 29 ILR 88 where the Court annulled at the request of a Dutch coal mining undertaking a High Authority decision refusing to declare that, by financing from public funds tax free bonuses granted to miners in the German coal mining industry, the German Government acted contrary to the prohibition laid down in Art. 4(c) E.C.S.C. (prohibition of State subsidies).

30 See Chapter 6 below.

31 Case 18/57, 2 Val. 256-257.

32 See §§ 301, 504 above.

33 Cases 18/57, 2 Val. 252-253; 1/58 *ibid.*, pp. 220-221.

Section 507

1 Arts. 173(1) E.E.C., 146(1) Euratom.

2 In particular, Arts. 173 to 177 E.E.C., 146 to 150 Euratom.

3 Arts. 189 to 191 E.E.C., 161 to 163 Euratom.

53 4 See § 213 above.

5 Case 22/70 [1971] CMLR 356-358 *per Curiam*, 341 *per* A.G. In that case the Court held that a Council discussion regarding the negotiation and conclusion by the Member States of the European Road Transport Agreement was an actionable Community act as it was designed to lay down a course of action binding on both the institutions and the Member States. *Cf.* also Cases 16 and 17/62 [1962] ECR 478; 8 to 11/66 [1967] ECR 99 *per* A.G.

6 See § 210 above.

7 See § 211 above.
8 See § 212 above.
9 *Cf.* e.g. Case 13/63 [1963] ECR 165.
10 See §§ 503, 504 above.
11 See further § 205 above.
12 Art. 228(1) E.E.C. There is no corresponding procedure under the Euratom Treaty.
13 Opinion 1/75 [1975] ECR 1360-1361.
14 See further § 217 above.
54 15 Case 22/70 [1971] CMLR 353, 358 *per Curiam*, 342-343, 350-351 *per* A.G.
16 See § 214 above.
17 Case 38/69 [1970] ECR 56 *per Curiam*, 62-63 *per* A.G.

Section 508

1 Arts. 173(2) E.E.C., 146(2) Euratom.
2 See §§ 509 to 513 below.
3 See § 506 above.
4 See further § 511 below.
55 5 See further § 210 above.
6 See § 521 below.
7 See § 519 below.
8 See § 1101 below.
9 See §§ 701, 707 below.
10 Cases 16 and 17/62 [1962] ECR 478-479 *per Curiam*, 482-483, 486-487 *per* A.G.; 25/62 [1963] ECR 107 *per Curiam*, 112-114 *per* A.G.; 9 and 11/71 [1973] CMLR 533 *per* A.G.; 43/72 [1973] ECR 1078-1079 *per* A.G.
56 11 Cases 16 and 17/62 [1962] ECR 485-486 *per* A.G.; 25/62 [1963] ECR 115-116 *per* A.G.; 106 and 107/63 [1965] ECR 434 *per* A.G.; 10 and 18/68 [1969] ECR 490-491 *per* A.G. See further §§ 503 above and 512, 513 below.
12 Cases 16 and 17/62 [1962] ECR 478 *per Curiam*, 482, 487 *per* A.G.; 38/64 [1965] ECR 213 *per* A.G.; 40/64 *ibid.*, pp. 227-228 *per Curiam*, 235 *per* A.G.; 10 and 18/68 [1969] ECR 490-491 *per* A.G.; 134/73 [1974] ECR 16 *per* A.G.; *German No. 25, Brinkhorst-Schermers* pp. 152 *et seq.*

Section 509

1 See § 215 above.
2 In particular Arts. 173 E.E.C., 146 Euratom.
3 Arts. 189 to 191 E.E.C., 161 to 163 Euratom.
4 Cases 16 and 17/62 [1962] ECR 478 *per Curiam*, 484-485 *per* A.G.; 8 to 11/66 [1967] ECR 99 *per* A.G. *Cf.* also Case 22/70 [1971] CMLR 341 *per* A.G.
5 See further §§ 212 above and 511 below.
6 *Cf.* e.g. Cases 8/72 [1973] CMLR 12 *per* A.G.; 19 and 20/74 [1975] ECR 499; 71/74 *ibid.*, p. 563.
57 7 Case 15/70 [1970] ECR 979-980 *per Curiam*, 984 *per* A.G.
8 Case 48/65 [1966] ECR 27. See further § 615 below.
58 9 Cases 8 to 11/66 [1967] ECR 90-93 *per Curiam*, 99-106 *per* A.G. In that case the Court decided that a 'communication' by the Commission under Art. 15(6) of Regulation 17 was not a mere opinion but an actionable decision within the meaning of Art. 189 E.E.C.
10 *Ibid.*, p. 101 *per* A.G. For the E.C.S.C. Treaty, see § 505 above.
11 Case 42/71 [1973] CMLR 183-184 *per* A.G., referring to Case 48/65 [1966] ECR 19. See also *ibid.*, p. 31 *per* A.G. See further §§ 206 and 215 above.
12 Case 71/74 [1975] ECR 582.
13 Cases 42/71 [1973] CMLR 187 *per Curiam*, 184 *per* A.G.; 96/71 *ibid.*, p. 383 *per Curiam*, 368-369 *per* A.G. On the question of legal interest in challenging confirmatory measures in general, see § 503 above.

Section 510

1 See § 503 above.

59 2 For this, see further §§ 512, 513 below.

3 Cases 25/62 [1963] ECR 113 per A.G.; 10 and 18/68 [1969] ECR 490-491 *per* A.G.

3a Case 26/76 (not yet reported), where the Court confirmed the existence of a direct and individual concern.

4 See § 212 above.

5 See § 506 above.

60 6 Cases 25/62 [1963] ECR 106-107 *per Curiam*, 113-114 *per* A.G.; 16 and 17/62 [1962] ECR 484 *per* A.G. See also § 212 above.

7 See § 513 below.

8 Case 25/62 [1963] ECR 106-107 *per Curiam*, 112-113 *per* A.G.

9 *Ibid.*, pp. 112-113 *per* A.G. In that case the European Court held, contrary to the views of the Commission, that individuals were in principle entitled to challenge decisions addressed to Member States, subject to the proof of direct and individual concern. The case involved an action brought by a German importer against a Commission decision addressed to Germany, refusing to authorise the latter to suspend in part the application of the C.C.T. in respect of fresh clementines. The action was, however, dismissed as inadmissible as the applicant could not prove that the decision concerned him directly and individually. The European Court gave similar rulings concerning the possibility of actions by private parties against decisions addressed to Member States in Case 1/64 [1964] ECR 416-417, where a Belgian company challenged a Commission decision addressed to France; in Case 69/69 [1970] ECR 392 *et seq.* where three Belgian companies contested a Commission decision addressed to Belgium and Luxembourg; and in Cases 38/64 [1965] ECR 207-208; 106-107/63 *ibid.*, pp. 410-411; 62/70 [1972] CMLR 170; 29/75 [1976] ECR 441 *et seq.* in which Cases various German companies challenged decisions of the Commission addressed to Germany.

Section 511

1 See §§ 508, 509, 510 above.

2 Cases 30/67 [1968] ECR 120; 6/68 *ibid.*, p. 414 *per Curiam*, 417 *per* A.G.; 63/69 [1970] ECR 210-211 *per Curiam*, 215-216 *per* A.G.; 41 to 44/70 [1975] 2 CMLR 521 *per* A.G.; 42/71 [1973] CMLR 187 *per Curiam*, 184-185 *per* A.G.; 72/74 [1975] ECR 414-415 *per* A.G.; 100/74 *ibid.*, p. 1401 *per Curiam*, p. 1411 *per* A.G.; 101/76 [1977] ECR 806.

3 Cases 16 and 17/62 [1962] ECR 485 *per* A.G.; 63/69 [1970] ECR 215-217 *per* A.G.; 42/71 [1973] CMLR 185 *per* A.G.; 72/74 [1975] ECR 415 *per* A.G.; 101/76 [1977] ECR 813 *per* A.G.

4 Cases 40/64 [1965] ECR 226; 72/74 [1975] ECR 409; 41 to 44/70 [1975] 2 CMLR 534-535.

61 5 Cases 16 and 17/62 [1962] ECR 478-480; 63/69 [1970] ECR 210-212; 41 to 44/70 [1975] 2 CMLR 534-535; 100/74 [1975] ECR 1401-1403 *per Curiam*, 1411 *per* A.G.

6 Case 69/69 [1970] ECR 393.

7 See §§ 512 and 513 below.

8 See § 506 above.

9 See §§ 210, 212 above.

10 Cases 16 and 17/62 [1962] ECR 478-479 *per Curiam*, 484-485 *per* A.G. An almost identical decision was given in Cases 19 to 22/62 [1962] ECR 497 *et seq.* Case 101/76 [1977] ECR 806, 808.

62 11 *Ibid.*, Cases 30/67 [1968] ECR 120-121; 6/68 *ibid.*, pp. 414-415. In the latter Case the Court refused to characterise Art. 9(3) of Council Regulation 1009/67 on the common organisation of the market in sugar as a decision because this provision applied to the applicant only by virtue of his capacity as a seller of raw beet sugar, without any further specification. Neither the fact that the number or even the identity of producers and sellers affected by the provision could be ascertained, nor the fact that it regulated the price system differently in respect of the different sugar products, altered its nature as a regulation. The A.G., however, concluded that the provision was by its nature a regulation for a particular case rather than a normative act, i.e. a decision in the form of a regulation and that since it concerned the applicant directly and individually, the action was admissible, *ibid.*, pp. 417 *et seq.* Case 63/69 [1970] ECR 210-212 where the

Court refused to treat Commission Regulation 1670/69, designed to adapt the operation of the intervention mechanisms of the common organisation of the agricultural markets to the devaluation of the French Franc on 8 August 1969, as an individual measure just because the assessment of the compensatory charge and subsidy provided for therein could affect commercial operators in an unequal fashion on account of their different geographical situation. The Court considered as decisive the fact that the object of the measure was not to compensate individual entrepreneurs but to even out the consequences of devaluation for the agricultural price mechanism. See also Cases 64/69 [1970] ECR 225-227; 65/69 *ibid.*, pp. 233-234.

12 Case 6/68 [1968] ECR 415.

13 Cases 63/69 [1970] ECR 211-212 *per Curiam*, 217-218 *per* A.G., 64/69 *ibid.*, pp. 226-227; 41 to 44/70 [1975] 2 CMLR 522-524 *per* A.G. interpreting the previous decisions; 100/74 [1975] ECR 1413-1414 *per* A.G. also interpreting the above decisions.

14 See further § 513 below.

15 Cases 16 and 17/62 [1962] ECR 478-479 *per Curiam*, 484-485 *per* A.G.; 30/67 [1968] ECR 121; 100/74 [1975] ECR 1411 *per* A.G.

16 Cases 41 to 44/70 [1975] 2 CMLR 534-535 *per Curiam*, 521-523 *per* A.G., where the European Court held that Commission Regulation 983/70 was in fact not a regulation for the purposes of Art. 173(2) E.E.C. but a group of individual decisions, since by it the Commission in effect denied the applicants (and other importers) licences to import table apples at a time when the number of applications for licences that would be affected by this 'regulation', and the quantities applied for, were determined. Case 100/74 [1975] ECR 1401-1403, where the Court held an application for the annulment of Commission Regulation 2546/74 admissible, by saying that the Regulation was in fact in the nature of an individual measure since it applied to a fixed and known number of cereal exporters, i.e. to those who, having had advance fixing prior to the abolition of the export refunds, still had current export licences on the date when the Regulation took effect.

63 17 Case 6/68 [1968] ECR 417 *et seq. per* A.G. In that Case the A.G. concluded that the contested act was an actionable decision in the form of a regulation, while the Court held that it was in fact a regulation and dismissed the action as inadmissible. Contrast this with Case 100/74 [1975] ECR 1401-1403 *per Curiam*, 1413-1414 *per* A.G., where, conversely, the A.G. concluded that the challenged measure was a regulation and that accordingly the action should be held inadmissible, while the Court recognised that it was a decision and held the application admissible.

18 Cases 16 and 17/62 [1962] ECR 478-480; 40/64 [1965] ECR 227; 6/68 [1968] ECR 415; 101/76 [1977] ECR 808.

Section 512

1 Cases 10 and 18/68 [1969] ECR 492 *per* A.G.; 41 to 44/70 [1975] 2 CMLR 523-524 *per* A.G.

64 2 See § 506 above.

3 Cases 38/64 [1965] ECR 211-213 *per* A.G.; 69/69 [1970] ECR 397-400 *per* A.G. In the former Case the A.G. found that the challenged decision concerned the applicant directly but not individually; in the latter Case, conversely, that the decision concerned the applicant individually but not directly.

4 Cases 25/62 [1963] ECR 107; 1/64 [1964] ECR 417; 38/64 [1965] ECR 208; 40/64 *ibid.*, pp. 226-227.

5 See § 513 below.

6 Case 100/74 [1975] ECR 1402-1403; 26/76 (not yet reported), especially *per* A.G.

7 See § 506 above.

65 8 Cases 10 and 18/68 [1969] ECR 480-482. In that Case Italian sugar refineries brought action for the annulment of three decisions whereby the Commission granted aid from the FEOGA to certain other sugar refineries in Italy. The decisions were addressed to the Italian Government and to the respective recipients of the aid. The applicants claimed to be directly and individually concerned as the aids granted were capable of altering the conditions of competition on the Italian sugar market by advantaging

their competitors. However, the Court found that the aids had no direct effect on the allocation of quotas as laid down by Regulations 1009/67 and 1027/67 and so the applicants were not directly and individually concerned.

9 See § 101 above.

10 Cases 25/62 [1963] ECR 114-115, 120 *per* A.G.; 1/64 [1964] ECR 420-421 *per* A.G.; 106 and 107/63 [1965] ECR 434-435 *per* A.G.; 100/74 [1975] ECR 1410-1411 *per* A.G.; 69/69 [1970] ECR 393-394 *per Curiam*, 397-399 *per* A.G. In the last mentioned Case, the Court held that the applicants, three Belgian firms which imported and refined aluminium, were not directly (and individually) concerned by a decision of the Commission which refused to allow Belgium and Luxembourg to open for 1968 a tariff quota for unwrought aluminium.

11 See the Cases mentioned in the previous footnote.

66 12 Case 62/70 [1972] CMLR 170-171. In that Case the Court held that the applicant, a German import company, was both directly and individually concerned by a decision of the Commission authorising the Federal Republic of Germany under Art. 115 E.E.C. to exclude from Community treatment certain products originating in a third country and already in free circulation within the other Member States of the Community. See also § 513 below. Similar situation arose in Case 29/75 [1976] ECR 441 *et seq*.

13 Cases 106 and 107/63 [1965] ECR 411. In those Cases the Court held that a Commission decision retroactively authorising certain safeguard measures regarding import of maize taken by the Federal Republic of Germany under Art. 22 of Regulation 19 was of direct (and individual) concern to certain importers of cereals. See also § 513 below.

14 Cases 38/64 [1965] ECR 211-212 *per* A.G.; 41 to 44/70 [1975] 2 CMLR 534-535 *per Curiam*, 524 *per* A.G. In the latter Cases the Court held that a decision of the Commission laying down the conditions for the issuance of import licences for table apples, taken in the form of a regulation, was of direct concern to the applicants since the national authorities were required to issue or to deny import licences by mechanically applying those conditions, without having any independent power of evaluation or decision. See further § 513 below.

15 Cases 25/62 [1963] ECR 114-115 *per* A.G.; 38/64 [1965] ECR 211 *per* A.G.; 69/69 [1970] ECR 397 *per* A.G.; 9/70 *ibid.*, p. 846 *per* A.G.

Section 513

67 1 See § 511 above.

2 Cases 25/62 [1963] ECR 107 *per Curiam*, 115-116, 121 *per* A.G.; 1/64 [1964] ECR 417 *per Curiam*, 422 *per* A.G.; 38/64 [1965] ECR 208 *per Curiam*, 213 *per* A.G.; 40/64 *ibid.*, p. 226; 42/71 [1973] CMLR 187; 96/71 *ibid.*, pp. 368-369 *per* A.G.; 72/74 [1975] ECR 410; 100/74 *ibid.*, p. 1403. See also the Cases mentioned at notes 10 and 11 in § 511 above.

3 Case 25/62 [1963] ECR 107. In that Case the Court held that the applicant, a German importer of southern fruits, was not individually concerned by a Commission decision refusing to authorise Germany to suspend in part the C.C.T. for fresh clementines, since the disputed measure affected him only by reason of a commercial activity which could be practised by anyone at any time. See also the Cases mentioned in the previous footnote.

68 4 Case 1/64 [1964] ECR 417. In that Case the Court held that the applicant, a Belgian firm producing glucose, was not individually concerned by a decision of the Commission authorising the French Government to levy countervailing charges, as a protective measure, on imports of glucose from all Member States except Italy, although the applicant was the only Belgian undertaking with an economic interest in the matter. Case 38/64 [1965] ECR 208, where the Court held that the purely accidental circumstance that the applicant, a German importer of cereals, was the only firm to apply for an import licence was not sufficient to establish individual concern on its part with respect to a Commission decision, addressed to Germany, fixing the c.i.f. prices for a particular produce imported into the Community. In Case 40/64 [1965]

ECR 226 the Court held that a regulation fixing reference prices for certain fruits affected the import trade in general and did not therefore individually concern the applicants.

5 Cases 16 and 17/62 [1962] ECR 479-480; 72/74 [1975] ECR 409-410 *per Curiam*, 416-417 *per* A.G.

6 Cases 106 and 107/63 [1965] ECR 411-412 *per Curiam*, 417-418 *per* A.G. In that Case German importers of cereals challenged a Commission decision retroactively authorising certain safeguard measures taken by the German Government regarding import of maize. The Court held that since the only persons concerned by these measures were those importers who had requested an import licence during the course of a certain day, their number and identity was sufficiently specified and ascertainable to be individually concerned by that decision. In Case 62/70 [1972] CMLR 170-171 the Court held that the applicant, a German import company, was individually concerned by a Commission decision authorising the German Government under Art. 115 E.E.C. to exclude from Community treatment certain products because when the Commission adopted the decision it was aware that the authorisation was to extend to all applications for import licences which were already pending before the German authorities on the day when the German Government had requested the authorisation. Similar situation arose in Case 29/75 [1976] ECR 441 *et seq*. In Cases 41 to 44/70 [1975] 2 CMLR 534-535 the Court held a Commission Regulation to be of individual concern to the applicants since when the Regulation was issued both the market situation and the quantities of products for which individual applications for import licences had been lodged were taken into account and since no new applications could be added. In Case 100/74 [1975] ECR 1403, too, the Court held a Commission Regulation to be of individual concern to the applicants since it affected, by virtue of certain distinguishing criteria, a fixed number of traders identified by the fact that they had applied for advance fixing during a particular period prior to the adoption of the Regulation. It may be noted that these are the only five Cases in which the Court has so far recognised the existence of both direct and individual concern.

7 Case 26/76 (not yet reported) *per Curiam* and *per* A.G. This is now the sixth case confirming direct and individual concern.

8 See § 511 above; cf. also Case 101/76 [1977] ECR 813 *per* A.G.

Section 514

69 1 See Chapter 2 above.

2 See § 1104 below.

3 See §§ 515 to 519 below.

4 Case 3/54, 1 Rec. 149 *et seq. per* A.G.

5 See § 502 above.

70 6 See § 518 below.

7 *Ibid.*

8 Case 34/62 [1963] ECR 151 *per* A.G.

9 *Cf.* e.g. Cases 2/54, 2 Val. 40; 3/54 *ibid.*, p. 45; 4/54 *ibid.*, p. 52; 9/56 *ibid.*, pp. 467, 471; 66/63 [1964] ECR 553 *per* A.G.; 28/66 [1968] ECR 17 *per* A.G.

10 See § 406 above.

11 Cases 19 and 21/60, 2 and 3/61 [1962] CMLR 279-280.

12 Case 4/73 [1974] ECR 504-505.

13 *Cf.* e.g. Case 108/63 [1965] ECR 10 where the Court held that the principle of estoppel should not be dismissed out of hand as a ground of action just because written Community law does not mention it as such.

14 Cases 19 and 21/60, 2 and 3/61 [1962] CMLR 279-280.

71 15 See § 406 above.

16 Cases 1/54, 2 Val. 35; 2/54 *ibid.*, pp. 40-41; 6/54 *ibid.*, p. 210; 18/57 *ibid.*, p. 258; 19/58, *ibid.*, p. 368; 14/59 *ibid.*, p. 549; 66/63 [1964] ECR 553 *per* A.G.; 4/73 [1974] ECR 512 *per* A.G. *Cf.* also Case 5/67 [1968] ECR 109 *per* A.G.

17 See § 502 above.

18 Cases 7 and 9/54, 2 Val. 152; 5/67 [1968] ECR 109 *per* A.G.

19 *Cf.* e.g. Case 14/59, 2 Val. 549.

20 Case 5/67 [1968] ECR 109 *per* A.G.
21 Case 14/59, 2 Val. 550.
22 See § 521 below.
23 Cases 9/56, 2 Val. 467 *et seq.*; 18/57 *ibid.*, p. 257; 42 and 49/59, 32 ILR 399; 67/63 [1964] ECR 166.

Section 515

72 1 See further §§ 101, 108 above.
2 See further § 206 above.
3 See further §§ 109 and 110 above.
4 See Chapters 1 and 2.
5 Case 66/63 [1964] ECR 553 *per* A.G.
6 See § 514 above.
7 Cases 19/58, 2 Val. 368; 3 to 18, 25 and 26/58, *ibid.*, p. 334; 14/59 *ibid.*, p. 549; 66/63 [1964] ECR 553 *per* A.G.

Section 516

1 For these rules, see further § 215 above.
2 See further § 505 above.
3 See § 502 above.
73 4 Case 6/54, 2 Val. 210.
5 *Ibid.*; Cases 1/54, 2 Val. 35; 2/54 *ibid.*, pp. 40-41; 18/57 *ibid.*, p. 258.
6 Cases 1 and 14/57, 3 Rec. 228-229 *per* A.G.; 9 and 10/56, 4 Rec. 106 *per* A.G.; 31/59, 6 Rec. 205-206 *per* A.G.; 36 to 38 and 40/59 *ibid.*, p. 912 *per* A.G.; 18/62 [1963] ECR 280; 5/67 [1968] ECR 95; 13/72 [1973] ECR 39 *per Curiam*, 48 *per* A.G.; 80/72 *ibid.*, p. 651.
7 See § 803 below.
8 E.g. under Art. 60(1) E.C.S.C., see Cases 1/54, 2 Val. 35; 2/54 *ibid.*, pp. 38-41; 6/54 *ibid.*, p. 210.
9 As required by Art. 10 of Regulation 17, see Case 41/69 [1970] ECR 710 *per* A.G. See further § 803 below.
10 Case 1/54, 2 Val. 35.
11 Cases 2/54, 2 Val. 38-41 *per Curiam*, 1 Rec. 118 *per* A.G.; 4/54, 2 Val. 54; 6/54 *ibid.*, p. 209.
12 See § 221 above.
13 *Cf.* e.g. Case 13/63 [1963] ECR 173-174.
14 Case 20/59, 2 Val. 308.
15 Art. 19 of Regulation 17. See further § 803 below.
74 16 Case 17/74 [1974] ECR 1079-1081.
17 Cases 56 and 58/64 [1966] ECR 338-339.
18 Cases 2/54, 2 Val. 40-41; 18/57 *ibid.*, p. 259; 13/60 [1962] ECR 100, and see the Cases mentioned in the following footnotes.
19 Cases 2/56, 2 Val. 237; 8/57 *ibid.*, pp. 258-259; 36 to 38 and 40/59, 6 Rec. 911 *et seq.* *per* A.G.; 24/62 [1963] ECR 69 *per Curiam*, 73 *per* A.G.; 3/67 [1968] ECR 31.
20 Cases 24/62 [1963] ECR 73, 79 *per* A.G.; 34/62 *ibid.*, p. 152 *per* A.G.; 8 to 11/66 [1967] ECR 108 *per* A.G.
21 Case 78/74 [1975] ECR 438 *per* A.G. See in this respect further § 1104 below.
22 Cases 6/54, 2 Val. 209; 2/56 *ibid.*, p. 237; 18/57 *ibid.*, pp. 258-259; 14/61 [1962] ECR 275; 24/62 [1963] ECR 69-70; 1/63 *ibid.*, p. 312; 3/67 [1968] ECR 31.
23 Cases 34/62 [1963] ECR 147 *per Curiam*, 152 *per* A.G.; 13/63 *ibid.*, p. 175.
24 Cases 14/61 [1962] ECR 275; 40 to 48, 50, 54 to 56, 111, 113 and 114/73 [1975] ECR 1931.
25 Cases 2/56, 2 Val. 237; 8/65 [1966] ECR 7; 29/67 [1968] ECR 279-280.
26 Cases 34/62 [1963] ECR 142; 41/69 [1970] ECR 690.
75 27 Cases 3 to 18, 25 and 26/58, 2 Val. 344.
28 Cases 2/56, 2 Val. 237; 24/62 [1963] ECR 73 *per* A.G.; 29/67 [1968] ECR 279-280; 48/69 [1972] CMLR 629-630.
29 Case 34/62 [1963] ECR 147.

30 Cases 1 and 14/57, 2 Val. 693.
31 Case 73/74 [1975] ECR 1514.
32 Case 34/62 [1963] ECR 147.
33 Cases 22/70 [1971] CMLR 362; 13/72 [1973] ECR 39 *per Curiam*, 48 *per* A.G. *Cf.*, however, Case 29/75 [1976] ECR 452-453 *per* A.G.
34 Cases 18/62 [1963] ECR 280; 5/67 [1968] ECR 95; 80/72 [1973] ECR 651.
35 Case 78/74 [1975] ECR 431 *per Curiam*, 438 per A.G. This Case came before the Court under Art. 177 E.E.C. and not under Art. 173 E.E.C., but the principles are the same.
76 36 Cases 16/65 [1965] ECR 887-889; 41 to 44/70 [1975] 2 CMLR 532 *per* A.G.
37 Arts. 92 E.C.S.C., 192 E.E.C. See further § 1003 below.
38 Cases 9/56, 2 Val. 467; 1/63 [1963] ECR 313.
39 Cases 29/67 [1968] ECR 279-280; 41/69 [1970] ECR 689-690; 55/69 [1972] CMLR 645-646; 56/69 *ibid.* See further § 803 below.
40 See § 517 below.
77 41 Cases 18/57, 2 Val. 258-259; 36 to 38 and 40/59, 2 Val. 277 *per Curiam*, 6 Rec. 911 *et seq. per* A.G.; 13/63 [1963] ECR 174-175: 66/63 [1964] ECR 543-545 *per Curiam*, 553-554 *per* A.G.; 8 to 11/66 [1967] ECR 93-94; 6/72 [1973] ECR 246-249; 19 and 20/74 [1975] ECR 519-520.
42 Cases 2/56, 2 Val. 237; 14/61 [1962] ECR 275-276 *per Curiam*, 284 *per* A.G.; 13/63 [1963] ECR 174-175 and 176 *et seq. per Curiam*, 183-184 *per* A.G.; 66/63 [1964] ECR 543 *et seq. per Curiam*, 553-554 *per* A.G.; 40 to 48, 50, 54 to 56, 111, 113 and 114/73 [1975] ECR 1931.
43 See § 216 above.
44 Cases 48/69 [1972] CMLR 620; 52/69 *ibid.*, p. 639; 53/69 *ibid.*
45 See § 215 above.
46 Case 41/69 [1970] ECR 686. See further § 803 below.

Section 517

78 1 See §§ 514, 515, 516 above.
2 *Cf.* e.g. Cases 1/54, 2 Val. 22 *et seq.*; 9/56 *ibid.*, p. 469.
3 See § 515 above.
4 Case 6/54, 2 Val. 211-212.
5 See § 516 above.
6 Case 13/60 [1962] ECR 100.
7 Case 15/57, 2 Val. 494. See further § 206 above.
8 See § 201 above.
9 Cases 19 and 21/60, 2 and 3/61 [1962] CMLR 280.
10 Case 32/64 [1965] ECR 374.
11 See §§ 206-213 above.
12 See further § 206 above.
79 13 This would seem to follow from the Court's judgment in Case 9/73 [1973] ECR 1158-1159 where the Court examined the compatibility of Council Regulation 974/71, introducing the compensatory amounts, with earlier Council Regulation 950/68 containing the Common Customs Tariff. *Cf.* however the A.G.'s opinion, *ibid.*, pp.1168-1169, who, relying on the *lex posterior* and *lex specialis* principles, expressed the view that the validity of the later regulation could not be judged by the rules of the earlier one on which it was not based and in relation to which it was a *lex specialis*.
14 See § 221 above.
15 Cases 4 to 13/59, 2 Val. 651-652; 81/72 [1973] ECR 586; 4/73 [1974] ECR 507; 70/74 [1975] ECR 807.
16 See § 222 above.
17 For a contrary view, see the A.G.'s opinion in Cases 41 to 44/70 [1975] 2 CMLR 525.
18 Case 108/63 [1965] ECR 9-10. See further § 220 above.
19 See in general Case 6/54, 1 Rec. 245 *et seq. per* A.G.
80 20 Case 6/54, 2 Val. 212-214 *per Curiam*, 1 Rec. 233 *per* A.G.
21 See § 518 below.

22 Case 6/54, 2 Val. 213-214 *per Curiam*, 1 Rec. 238 *per* A.G.
23 *Ibid.*; Cases 15 and 29/59, 2 Val. 563.
24 *Ibid.*; Cases 7 and 9/54, 2 Val. 152.
25 Cases 36 to 38 and 40/59, 2 Val. 277; 66/63 [1964] ECR 548.
81 26 Cases 10 and 18/68 [1969] ECR 495 *per* A.G.; 73/69 [1970] ECR 480 *per* A.G.; 31/70 *ibid.*, p. 1070 *per* A.G.; 95/75 [1976] ECR 368 *per Curiam*, 373 *per* A.G.; 114/76 [1977] ECR 1226 *per* A.G.
27 Cases 37/70 [1971] CMLR 253; 62/70 [1972] CMLR 171-172; 40/72 [1973] ECR 143; 154/73 [1974] ECR 30 *per* A.G.; 70/74 [1975] ECR 807; 37/75 *ibid.*, p. 1347 *per Curiam*, 1350 *per* A.G. 29/75 [1976] ECR 443.
28 Cases 5/67 [1968] ECR 96; 43/72 [1973] ECR 1073.
29 Cases 34/62 [1963] ECR 152 *per* A.G.; 37/70 [1971] CMLR 245 *per* A.G.
30 *Ibid.*; Cases 10 and 18/68 [1969] ECR 502-503 *per* A.G.; 41 to 44/70 [1975] 2 CMLR 531 *per* A.G.; 57/72 [1973] ECR 340; 43/72 *ibid.*, pp. 1073-1074 *per Curiam*. 1085-1087 *per* A.G.; 37/75 [1975] ECR 1350 *per* A.G.
31 Cases 24/62 [1963] ECR 67-68; 34/62 *ibid.*, pp. 151-152 *per* A.G.
32 Cases 73/69 [1970] ECR 480 *per* A.G.; 154/73 [1974] ECR 32 *per* A.G.

Section 518

1 See further § 101 above.
2 See further § 206 above.
3 See in general Case 3/54, 1 Rec. 149 *et seq. per* A.G.
82 4 Cases 8/55, 2 Rec. 254-255 *per* A.G.; 8/57, 2 Val. 519.
5 Cases 6/54, 2 Val. 215; 2/57 *ibid.*, pp. 507-508; 15/57 *ibid.*, p. 499.
6 Cases 8/55, 2 Val. 114; 8/57 *ibid.*, p. 524; 3 and 4/64 [1965] ECR 454 *per Curiam*, 459 *per* A.G.
7 Cases 3/54, 1 Rec. 149 *et seq. per* A.G.; 8/55, 2 Rec. 255 *et seq. per* A.G.
8 Arts. 1-5 E.C.S.C., 1-8 E.E.C., 1-3 Euratom.
9 Cases 9/56, 2 Val. 477; 8/57 *ibid.*, pp. 524-527; 17/67 [1967] ECR 464-465 *per* A.G.; 28/66 [1968] ECR 13. See also § 203 above.
10 Art. 3(b) E.C.S.C.
11 Art. 7 E.E.C. See further § 304 above.
12 Case 8/57, 2 Val. 523.
13 *Ibid.*, p. 519.
14 Cases 1/54, 2 Val. 22, 36; 8/55 *ibid.*, p. 112.
15 Cases 2/57, 2 Val. 507-511; 15/57 *ibid.*, p. 499-500.
83 16 Cases 52 and 55/65 [1966] ECR 172 *per Curiam*, 182-183 *per* A.G.
17 See the Cases mentioned at note 15 above and Cases 6/54, 2 Val. 215; 8/57 *ibid.*, p. 521. *Cf.* also Case 48/69 [1972] CMLR 633 *per Curiam*, 593 *per* A.G.
18 See § 506 above.
19 See § 517 above.
20 See § 603 below.
21 Cases 3/54, 1 Rec. 169-170 *per* A.G.; 8/55, 2 Rec. 254-255 *per* A.G.
84 22 Cases 3 and 4/64 [1965] ECR 455.
23 Case 9/56, 2 Val. 470-480. See also § 206 above.
24 See also § 517 above.
25 Cases 3/54, 1 Rec. 152 *per* A.G.; 8/55, 2 Rec. 254-255 *per* A.G.
26 Cases 18 and 35/65 [1966] ECR 117.
27 Cases 3 to 18, 25 and 26/58, 2 Val. 345; 19/58, *ibid.*, p. 369; 48/69 [1972] CMLR 633 *per Curiam*, 593 *per* A.G.
28 Case 8/55, 2 Val. 114.
29 Case 6/54, 2 Val. 215.
30 Case 4/54, 2 Val. 54-55.
85 31 Cases 2/54, 2 Val. 43; 3/54 *ibid.*, p. 51.

Section 519

1 See § 206 above.
2 See §§ 506, 508, 511 above.
86 3 Cases 9/56, 2 Val. 463-465 *per Curiam*, 4 Rec. 101-102 *per* A.G.; 15/57, 4 Rec. 202-206 *per* A.G.; 36 to 38, 40 and 41/58, 5 Rec. 370 *per* A.G.; 9 and 11/71 [1973] CMLR 533 *per* A.G.; 43/72 [1973] ECR 1078-1079 *per* A.G.
4 Art. 36(3) E.C.S.C.
5 See § 520 below.
6 Arts. 184 E.E.C., 156 Euratom.
7 Cases 9/56, 2 Val. 463-465; 32 and 33/58 *ibid.*, p. 627-628.
87 8 Cases 31 and 33/62 [1962] ECR 506-507 *per Curiam*, 509-510 *per* A.G.; 44/65 [1965] ECR 970-971 *per Curiam*, 974-977 *per* A.G. See § 1109 below.
9 Cases 31 and 33/62 [1962] ECR 510 *per* A.G.
10 Case 32/65 [1966] ECR 414 *per* A.G.
11 Case 9/56, 2 Val. 463-465 *per Curiam*, 4 Rec. 101-102 *per* A.G.
12 Cases 31 and 33/62 [1962] ECR 507 *per Curiam*, 510 per A.G.
13 Cases 14/59, 2 Val. 548-549; 29/67 [1968] ECR 275-276; 44, 46 and 49/74 [1975] ECR 394.
88 14 Cases 32 and 33/58, 2 Val. 627; 42/58 *ibid.*, p. 639. See further § 605 below.
15 Cases 20/71 [1972] CMLR 958 *per Curiam*, 948-949 *per* A.G.; 32/71 *ibid.*; 44, 46 and 49/74 [1975] ECR 394.
16 Case 44/65 [1965] ECR 970-971 *per Curiam*, 974-977 *per* A.G. See § 1109 below.
17 Cases 3/59, 2 Val. 376-377; 6 and 11/69 [1969] ECR 550 *per* A.G.
18 See further § 905 below.
19 Cases 1/63 [1963] ECR 319-322 *per* A.G.; 67/63 [1964] ECR 171 *per* A.G.; 21/64 [1965] ECR 187-188; 36/64 *ibid.*, pp. 336-337.
89 20 Cases 1/58, 2 Val. 230; 41 and 50/59 *ibid.*, p. 680; 31 and 33/62 [1962] ECR 506-507; 18/62 [1963] ECR 279; 1/63 *ibid.*, pp. 319-322 *per* A.G.; 21/64 [1965] ECR 187-188; 32/65 [1966] ECR 409-410 *per Curiam*, 414-415 *per* A.G.
21 Cases 25 and 26/65 [1967] ECR 44.
22 Case 96/71 [1973] CMLR 370 *per* A.G.
23 *Cf.* e.g. Case 32/65 [1966] ECR 409-410 *per Curiam*, 414-415 *per* A.G., although here the plea was unsuccessful in the absence of a direct link between the two regulations.
24 Cases 9/56, 2 Val. 464-465; 31 and 33/62 [1962] ECR 507; 43/72 [1973] ECR 1079 *per* A.G.
25 See further § 521 below.
26 See § 219 above.
27 Cases 15 to 33, 52, 53, 57 to 109, 116, 117, 123, 132 and 135 to 137/73 [1974] ECR 191-192 *per Curiam*, 196 *per* A.G.
90 28 This happened in the Cases mentioned in the previous footnote.
29 *Cf.* Cases 28 to 30/62 [1963] ECR 41 *per* A.G.

Section 520

1 Art. 33(3) E.C.S.C.
2 Arts. 173(3) E.E.C., 146(3) Euratom.
3 See § 411 above.
4 See § 221 above.
5 See § 519 above.
6 See § 411 above.
7 Cases 1/58, 2 Val. 231; 3/59 *ibid.*, pp. 376-377; 21/64 [1965] ECR 187; 34/65 [1966] ECR 531; 2/71 [1972] CMLR 437 *per* A.G.
8 Cases 43/64 [1965] ECR 397; 34/65 [1966] ECR 531.
9 Cases 15 to 33, 52, 53, 57 to 109, 116, 117, 123, 132 and 135 to 137/73 [1974] ECR 191 *per Curiam.*, 196 *per* A.G. See also § 519 above.
10 Cases 24/69 [1970] ECR 151; 53/70 [1971] ECR 608; 33/72 [1973] ECR 480 *per Curiam*, 485 *per* A.G. See further § 503 above.

11 Case 2/71 [1972] CMLR 444 *per Curiam*, 436-438 *per* A.G.
12 Case 102/63 [1964] ECR 712 *per* A.G.
13 Case 2/57, 2 Val. 507.
91 14 Cases 4/67 [1967] ECR 372; 24/69 [1970] ECR 150-151 *per Curiam*, 154-155 *per* A.G.
15 See the Cases mentioned in the previous footnote and Cases 79/70 [1971] ECR 696; 33/72 [1973] ECR 480 *per Curiam*, 484 *per* A.G.
16 See note 11 above.
17 Cases 12 and 29/64 [1965] ECR 118; 18 and 19/64 *ibid.*, p. 797.
18 See further § 216 above.
19 Arts. 33(3) E.C.S.C., 173(3) E.E.C., 146(3) Euratom in conjunction with Art. 81(1) R.P.
20 *Ibid.*
21 In the light of Art. 81(1) R.P. this must probably be taken as meaning the day following the one on which the measure came to the knowledge of the applicant.
22 See further § 510 above.
23 Cases 31 and 33/62 [1962] ECR 508 *per Curiam*, 510-511 *per* A.G.
24 Art. 81(1) R.P.
92 25 This view was put forward by the Commission in Cases 10 and 18/68 [1969] ECR 488 *per* A.G.
26 This view was expressed by the A.G. in the same Cases, *ibid.*
27 Case 69/69 [1970] ECR 396-397 *per* A.G.
28 Cases 48/69 [1972] CMLR 620; 52/69 *ibid.*, p.639; 53/69 *ibid.*

Section 521

93 1 See § 502 above.
2 See § 412(a) above.
3 Arts. 34 E.C.S.C., 174 E.E.C., 147 Euratom.
4 See § 406 above.
5 Cases 50/69 R [1969] ECR 454-455 *per* A.G. (Order); 22/70 [1971] CMLR 358; 9 and 11/71 [1973] CMLR 533 *per* A.G.; 43/72 [1973] ECR 1078 *per* A.G.
6 See § 219 above.
7 Cases 3/54, 2 Val. 50; 4/54 *ibid.*, p.54; 28 to 30/62 [1963] ECR 41 *per* A.G.
8 Cases 18/62 [1963] ECR 283; 66/63 [1964] ECR 546; 56 and 58/64 [1966] ECR 351.
9 Case 17/74 [1974] ECR 1081 *per Curiam*, 1090-1091 *per* A.G.
10 Case 37/71 [1972] ECR 489-490.
11 See § 221 above.
12 Arts. 174(2) E.E.C., 147(2) Euratom.
13 Cases 9 and 11/71 [1973] CMLR 533 *per* A.G.; 91/75 [1976] ECR 238 *per* A.G.
94 14 Case 81/72 [1973] ECR 586.
15 See § 401 above.
16 See e.g. Case 66/63 [1964] ECR 546. See also the argument of the High Authority in Case 2/56, 2 Val. 236.
17 Arts. 34(1) E.C.S.C., 176(1) E.E.C., 149(1) Euratom.
18 Cases 30/59, 29 ILR 89 *per Curiam*, 7 Rec. 71-73 *per* A.G.; 42/71 [1973] CMLR 185-186 *per* A.G.; 5/71 [1971] ECR 992 *per* A.G.
19 Cases 7 and 9/54, 2 Rec. 133 *per* A.G.; 2/56, 2 Val. 236; 42 and 49/59, 32 ILR 398; 14/61 [1962] ECR 268.
20 Case 22/70 [1971] CMLR 358.
21 See the Cases mentioned at note 5 above, and Case 4/69 [1971] ECR 343 *per* A.G.
22 Cases 15 to 33, 52, 53, 57 to 109, 116, 117, 123, 132 and 135 to 137/73 [1974] ECR 197 *per* A.G.
23 Case 50/69 R [1969] ECR 457 *per* A.G. (Order).
95 24 Cases 14/64 [1965] ECR 58 *per Curiam*, 64 *per* A.G.; 17/74 [1974] ECR 1081 *per Curiam*, 1091 *per* A.G. See also § 219 above.
25 Cases 45 and 49/70 [1971] ECR 475.
26 Cases 14/61 [1962] ECR 268; 30/76 [1976] ECR 1725 *et seq.*
27 Art. 34(2) E.C.S.C.

28 See Chapter 6 below.
29 Arts. 176(2) E.E.C., 149(2) Euratom. Case 4/69 [1971] ECR 343. *per* A.G. See further § 701 below.
30 Art. 34(1) E.C.S.C. See further § 707 below.
96 31 Cases 41 and 50/59, 2 Val. 680.
32 Cases 36 to 38, 40 and 41/58, 5 Rec. 372 *per* A.G.

Section 601

97 1 See Chapter 5 above.
2 Cases 15/70 [1970] ECR 979; 9 and 11/71 [1973] CMLR 538 *per* A.G.; 42/71 *ibid.*, p.186 *per* A.G.
3 See § 604 below.
4 See § 611 below.
5 See § 604 below.
98 6 See §§ 603, 609 below. The converse proposition is also correct, see § 501 above.
7 See § 604 below.
8 See § 605 below.
9 As of 31 December 1976. Staff Cases are not included. Joined Cases have been counted as one Case.
10 Cases 30/59, 29 ILR 85 (this Case started as an action for failure to act but was later transformed into an action for annulment); 42 and 49/59, 32 ILR 382.
11 See note 9 above. One Case ended without judgment.
12 See § 613 below.
13 See § 607 below.

Section 602

1 See § 604 below.
2 Cases 7 and 9/54, 2 Val. 138. It seems that the Court adopted this view contrary to the A.G.'s opinion who suggested that since an action for failure to act is only a specific case of action for annulment, the conditions for admissibility which the Treaty lays down in respect of the latter for private parties must already apply to the preliminary procedure. Accordingly, the distinction made between Member States/Council and private parties in respect of challengeable acts should apply already before the Commission in respect of its failure to act, see 2 Rec. 114 *et seq. per* A.G.
3 See § 301 above.
99 4 Cases 9 and 12/60, 32 ILR 414; 12/63 [1963] ECR 89 *per Curiam*, 92-93 *per* A.G.
5 See § 605 below and see also § 504 above.
6 Cases 7 and 9/54, 2 Rec. 114 *et seq. per* A.G.; 12/63 [1963] ECR 92 *per* A.G.
7 Thus it does not seem possible that for example the original request is made by a Member State and the action is brought by an undertaking.
8 Art. 22(2) E.C.S.C. Statute, Art. 38(4) R.P. See further § 406 above.
9 Cases 24 and 34/58, 6 Rec. 625 *per* A.G.
10 Cases 2 and 3/60, 32 ILR 403. See also § 504 above.

Section 603

1 See § 604 below.
2 See §§ 207 and 208 above.
3 See in general Chapter 9 below.
100 4 Cases 7 and 9/54, 2 Val. 139; 30/59, 29 ILR 87-88.
5 *Cf.* also Case 48/65 [1966] ECR 29-30 *per* A.G. See also § 605 below.
6 See § 615 below.
7 Cases 34/59, 2 Val. 776; 21 to 26/61 [1962] ECR 78.
8 Cases 42 and 49/59, 32 ILR 388. See also § 503 above.
9 Cases 21 to 26/61 [1962] ECR 78 *per Curiam*, 80 *per* A.G.
10 See § 518 above.
11 Cases 42 and 49/59, 32 ILR 390.
12 Cases 19 and 21/60, 2 and 3/61 [1962] CMLR 279.

Section 604

1 Cases 17/57, 2 Val. 713 *per Curiam*, 5 Rec. 39 *per* A.G.; 24 and 34/58, 2 Val. 360.
2 Case 75/69 [1970] ECR 542-543.
101 3 Cases 17/57, 2 Val. 713 *per Curiam*, 5 Rec. 40 *per* A.G.; 22 and 23/60, 32 ILR 546.
4 Case 59/70 [1971] ECR 652-654. For a criticism of this judgment, see Case 7/71 [1972] CMLR 459 *per* A.G.
5 Cases 42/58, 2 Val. 639; 42 and 49/59, 32 ILR 386-387; 21 to 26/61 [1962] ECR 76; 109 and 114/75 [1977] ECR 384 *per* A.G. (Order).
6 Art. 80(1) R.P.; Cases 32 and 33/58, 2 Val. 626. See further § 411.
7 Cases 32 and 33/58, 2 Val. 626; 42/58 *ibid.*, p.638; 21 to 26/61 [1962] ECR 76.
8 Cases 5 to 11 and 13 to 15/62 [1962] ECR 459-460.
9 Cases 7 and 9/54, 2 Val. 143, 156; 75/69 [1970] ECR 542-543.
102 10 See § 605 below.
11 Cases 7 and 9/54, 2 Val. 143-144; 32 and 33/58, *ibid.*, p.626; 17/57, 5 Rec. 38 *et seq. per* A.G.; 109 and 114/75 [1977] ECR 386 *et seq. per* A.G.(Order).
12 Case 30/59, 29 ILR 87.
13 Cases 5 to 11 and 13 to 15/62 [1962] ECR 459-460.
14 Cases 42 and 49/59, 32 ILR 387.
15 Case 109 and 114/75 [1977] ECR 387 *et seq. per* A.G. (Order).
16 Cases 17/57, 2 Val. 713; 22 and 23/60, 32 ILR 546. See also Art. 22(2) E.C.S.C. Statute.
17 *Ibid.*
18 Case 75/69 [1970] ECR 546 *per* A.G.
103 19 *Ibid.*, pp.542-543 *per Curiam*; Cases 24 and 34/58, 2 Val. 359-360; 21 to 26/61 [1962] ECR 78 *per Curiam*, 81 *per* A.G.
20 As required by Art. 38(1)(c) R.P. See further § 406 above.
21 Cases 41 and 50/59, 2 Val. 681.
22 See § 605 below.

Section 605

1 Cases 7 and 9/54, 2 Val. 143.
2 *Ibid.*, p.140.
3 Cases 7 and 9/54, 2 Rec. 116 *et seq. per* A.G.; 12/63 [1963] ECR 89 *per Curiam*, 92 *per* A.G.
4 See Chapter 5 above.
5 See §§ 514-518 above.
6 See § 603 above.
7 See § 506 above.
8 Cases 7 and 9/54, 2 Val. 141-142; 42 and 49/59, 32 ILR 389; 109 and 114/75 [1977] ECR 390 *per* A.G. (Order).
104 9 See the Cases mentioned in the previous footnote and Case 30/59, 29 ILR 88.
10 Cases 7 and 9/54, 2 Val. 152.
11 Cases 24 and 34/58, 2 Val. 345.
12 Case 30/59, 29 ILR 85.
13 See the Cases mentioned at note 11 above.
14 See the Cases mentioned at notes 8, 9 and 12 above. For Article 88 proceedings see further Chapter 9 below.
15 Cases 7 and 9/54, 2 Val. 141-142; 30/59, 29 ILR 88; 48/65 [1966] ECR 29-30 *per* A.G. See also § 603 above.
16 See § 615 below.
17 Cases 7 and 9/54, 2 Val. 141-142; 42 and 49/59, 32 ILR 389.
18 Cases 7 and 9/54, 2 Val. 155; 109 and 114/75 [1977] ECR 390 *per* A.G. (Order).
105 19 See § 519 above.
20 Cases 32 and 33/58, 2 Val. 627; 42/58, *ibid.*, p.639.

Section 606

1 See § 604 above.
2 Cases 42 and 49/59, 32 ILR 390.

3 Cases 32 and 33/58, 2 Val. 632-633; 42/58 *ibid.*, pp. 639-643. *Cf.* also Case 30/59, 29 ILR 85.
4 See § 521 above.
5 See § 521 above.
6 Cases 7 and 9/54, 2 Rec. 114-115, 120, 133 *per* A.G.; 42 and 49/59, 32 ILR 398.
7 See § 219 above.
8 Cases 30/59, 29 ILR 89; 75/69 [1970] ECR 542.

Section 607

106 1 See § 601 above and the Cases quoted at note 2 in that Section.
2 See § 608 below.
3 See §§ 609, 611 below.
4 See § 612 below.
5 See § 613 below.
6 See § 610 below.
7 Case 48/65 [1966] ECR 29 *per* A.G.
8 *Ibid.*, p.30; Cases 9 and 11/71 [1973] CMLR 537 *per* A.G.
9 *Cf.* e.g. Case 8/71 [1973] CMLR 908 *per* A.G.

Section 608

1 See § 504 above.
107 2 Arts. 4 E.E.C., 3 Euratom.
3 In March 1969 the European Parliament itself considered making use of its powers under Art. 175 E.E.C. by instituting proceedings against the Council for its failure to implement a 1960 proposal, adopted by Parliament under Art. 138 E.E.C., calling for direct elections by universal suffrage. See, *3rd Gen. Rep. EC (1969)* pp.415, 418-419.
4 See §§ 503, 504 above, 609 below.
5 See §§ 610, 611 below.
6 See §§ 301 and 504 above.
7 See § 403 above.
8 See § 613 below.

Section 609

1 See § 610 below. Arts. 175(1) and (2) E.E.C., 148(1) and (2) Euratom.
2 See § 603 above.
3 Case 6/70 [1970] ECR 822 *per* A.G. *Cf.* also Case 48/65 [1966] ECR 32 *per* A.G.
4 Cases 10 and 18/68 [1969] ECR 494 *per* A.G.
108 5 *Ibid.*, p.483 *per Curiam.*
6 Case 6/70 [1970] ECR 822 *per* A.G.
7 For instances where Art. 155 E.E.C. was invoked, without success, see, in addition to the Case mentioned at the previous footnote, Cases 15/70 [1970] ECR 978 *et seq.*; 15/71 [1972] CMLR 58.
8 Cases 103/63 [1964] ECR 429 *per Curiam*, 432-433 *per* A.G.; 109 and 114/75 [1977] ECR 390-391 *per* A.G. (Order).
9 *Cf.* Cases 10 and 18/68 [1969] ECR 483 where the European Court referred in this context to the provisions of 'Community law' rather than to provisions of the 'Treaty'.
10 See § 603 above.
11 See § 517 above.
12 Case 15/70 [1970] ECR 979.
13 See § 613 below.
14 See § 507 above.
15 For the concept of 'act', see § 507 above.
16 I.e. regulations, directives, decisions. See §§ 210-212 above.
17 I.e. recommendations, opinions and also proposals to be submitted by the Commission to the Council under various Treaty provisions. See § 213 above.

109 18 See §§ 503, 608 above.
19 Cases 10 and 18/68 [1969] ECR 483. See also § 603 above.

Section 610

1 See § 604 above.
2 *Cf.* e.g. Case 8/71 [1973] CMLR 908-909 *per* A.G.
3 *Ibid.*
4 Case 48/65 [1966] ECR 29 *per* A.G.
5 See § 611 below. Art. 175(2) E.E.C., 148(2) Euratom.

Section 611

110 1 Case 6/70 [1970] ECR 822 *per* A.G.
2 For Article 169 proceedings, see in general Chapter 9 below.
3 Case 48/65 [1966] ECR 27.
4 *Ibid.*, p.32 *per* A.G.
5 Case 6/70 [1970] ECR 821 *per* A.G.
6 Case 15/70 [1970] ECR 983 *per* A.G.
7 See § 604 above.
8 Case 8/71 [1973] CMLR 912. In that Case the act requested by the applicant was a 'formal hearing' by the Commission under Art. 19(2) of Regulation 17 in conjunction with Art. 5 of Regulation 99/63. While refusing to adopt a position on the question whether the applicant had a 'sufficient interest' to be heard formally within the meaning of the above provisions, the Commission agreed to receive written observations from, and also to have an informal 'discussion' with the applicant. The Court held this to be an 'act' or 'attitude' sufficient to make an action for failure to act inadmissible.
9 Where the request is granted only after the bringing of the action, the Court may, without considering the admissibility and substance of the application, apportion the costs, see Case 103/63 [1964] ECR 429.
10 Cases 48/65 [1966] ECR 27 *per Curiam*, 32 *per* A.G.; 15/70 [1970] ECR 983 *per* A.G.; 8/71 [1973] CMLR 912; 42/71 *ibid.*, p.187.
11 Such a situation has arisen in two notable Cases. In Case 48/65 [1966] ECR 26 *et seq.*, the applicant brought two actions against the Commission's 'declaration of its position' in effect refusing to institute Art. 169 proceedings against the Federal Republic of Germany: one for annulment and another for failure to act. The Court held both to be inadmissible, the former because the 'declaration of position' was not a binding act and thus not subject to annulment, the latter because it being duly notified within the two months, there was no failure to act. In Case 42/71 [1973] CMLR 187 *et seq.*, the applicant again brought two actions against a formal notification by the Commission rejecting a request to amend a previous regulation. The action for failure to act was held inadmissible because the notification did constitute an 'adoption of a position', while the action for annulment was inadmissible because the 'position adopted', although a formal act, was not subject to challenge by private parties as it related to the amendment of a regulation which can be requested by Member States/institutions only. In this respect see also § 614 below.

111 12 See § 604 above.

Section 612

1 Cases 9 and 11/71 [1973] CMLR 537-538 *per* A.G.
2 See § 219 above.
3 Case 8/71 [1973] CMLR 906-907 *per* A.G.
4 See in general Chapter 7 below.

Section 613

112 1 See § 609 above.
2 Cases 103/63 [1964] ECR 433 *per* A.G.; 48/65 [1966] ECR 30 *per* A.G.; 15/71 [1972]

CMLR 56 *per* A.G. The Court usually refers to the 'form and legal nature' of the act, *ibid.*, p.59; Case 134/73 [1974] ECR 11.

3 Arts. 175(3) E.E.C., 148(3) Euratom. See § 616 below.

4 Cases 8/71 [1973] CMLR 908 *per* A.G.; 42/71 *ibid.*, p.186 *per* A.G.; 134/73 [1974] ECR 11. See also § 614 below.

5 See §§ 206, 210-213 above.

6 See the Cases mentioned at note 4 above and Case 48/65 [1966] ECR 30 *per* A.G. But see § 616 below.

7 See § 508 above.

8 Cases 103/63 [1964] ECR 433 *per* A.G.; 48/65 [1966] ECR 30 *per* A.G. This view was also advocated by the Commission and seems to have been adopted by the Court in Case 15/71 [1972] CMLR 55-56, 59.

113 9 Cases 15/70 [1970] ECR 980; 15/71 [1972] CMLR 55-56 *per* A.G.; 42/71 [1973] CMLR 186 *per* A.G.; 134/73 [1974] ECR 11 *per Curiam*, 14 *per* A.G. In this last-mentioned Case the Court dismissed an action on the ground that the applicant wished to procure a provision of a general regulatory character and 'not an act concerning it directly and individually'.

10 See §§ 512 and 513 above.

11 See §§ 614-616 below.

Section 614

114 1 Case 134/73 [1974] ECR 11. In that Case the applicant, a German oil mill operator, requested the inactment of a regulation for an additional subsidy for oil mills far from the production areas. The Court dismissed the action as inadmissible as the applicant's object was to procure a provision of a general regulatory character which could not be described as an act addressed to him as required by Art. 175(3) E.E.C.

2 *Ibid.*

3 See § 511 above.

4 Cases 103/63 [1964] ECR 433 *per* A.G.; 6/70 [1970] ECR 822 *per* A.G.; 15/71 [1972] CMLR 56-57 *per* A.G.; 42/71 [1973] CMLR 186 *per* A.G.; 134/73 [1974] ECR 15 *per* A.G.

5 See in general Chapter 9 below.

6 See § 615 below.

7 Case 103/63 [1964] ECR 433 *per* A.G. In that Case the applicants, German transport companies, requested the Commission to take action against the Federal Republic under Art. 169 E.E.C. with a view to obtaining amendment of a German statute fixing, in their opinion in violation of Regulation 19, too low intervention prices for cereals. The Court, however, was not required to give judgment on the substantive issues as the Commission did, during the course of the proceedings, institute Art. 169 proceedings against Germany. In his opinion, the A.G. expressed the view that the action was inadmissible.

8 Cases 6/70 [1970] ECR 818-819; 15/70 *ibid.*, pp. 979-980. In both Cases the applicants, Italian landowners, sought a decision from the Commission fixing the terms and procedures to be followed by them in concluding the leases of their agricultural property at a time when a Bill on the fixing of agricultural rents, allegedly violating Community law, becomes law in Italy. Both actions were held inadmissible.

9 Case 15/71 [1972] CMLR 59. In that Case the applicant, a German import-export company, sought a Commission decision enabling and compelling the Member States to grant the benefit of the Community system to imports of goods of Algerian origin from Algeria effected during 1963, at a time when that country had already ceased to be a part of the Common Market. The Court held the action inadmissible on the ground that the act requested would in effect amend an earlier decision of general application and as such could not be described as a measure to be addressed to the applicant.

10 Case 42/71 [1973] CMLR 186 *per* A.G.

Section 615

1 See § 613 above.

2 For A.G.'s opinions supporting this view, see the Cases mentioned at note 8 in Section 613 above. In Cases 15/71 [1972] CMLR 59 the European Court held the action to be inadmissible not because the measure sought by the applicant was a general provision, but because it could not, as such, 'either from its form or its legal nature, be described as a measure that would have to be notified to the applicant firm within the meaning of Art. 175(3)'.

115 3 This follows from Arts. 173(2) E.E.C., 146(2) Euratom, see § 508 above. For A.G.'s opinions supporting this view, see the Cases mentioned at note 9 in § 613 above. Such an interpretation would seem to follow also from the view expressed by the European Court in Case 15/70 [1970] ECR 979 that 'the concept of a measure capable of giving rise to an action is identical in Arts. 173 and 175, as both provisions merely prescribe one and the same method of recourse'.

4 See § 614 above.

5 See in general Chapter 9 below.

6 See §§ 603, 605 above.

7 Case 48/65 [1966] ECR 29 *et seq. per* A.G. In that Case the applicants, German import companies, requested the Commission to initiate Art. 169 proceedings against the Federal Republic with a view to abrogating a certain tax which they thought was imposed in violation of Art. 95 E.E.C. The A.G. submitted, amongst other things, that the action was inadmissible as the measures requested concerned the Federal Republic only and would not be meant for or addressed to the applicants. The Court found the action inadmissible on the grounds that the Commission had defined its position within the prescribed time-limit. See also Cases 103/63 [1964] ECR 433 *per* A.G. (the Court was not required to give judgment) and 6/70 [1970] ECR 820-821 *per* A.G.

8 For remedies against the Member States at the national level, see § 1002 below.

Section 616

1 Cases 48/65 [1966] ECR 32 *per* A.G.; 15/71 [1972] CMLR 58 *per* A.G.

2 See §§ 206, 210-213 above.

3 Case 6/70 [1970] ECR 818-819 where the measure requested was an 'advice' on the behaviour to be followed by the applicants when faced with a possible conflict between their national law and Community law. The action was held inadmissible.

116 4 Case 15/70 [1970] ECR 978-980.

5 See Art. 19(2) of Regulation 17 and Art. 5 of Regulation 99/63.

6 Case 8/71 [1973] CMLR 907-908 *per* A.G. The Court seems to have implicitly endorsed such an interpretation as it has not found the action inadmissible purely on the grounds that the act requested has been a 'hearing' and not a formal decision, *ibid.*, p.912. See also note 8 in § 611 above. It may be noted that even if the right to be heard could not be enforced by means of an action for failure to act, any interested third party who has not been heard contrary to Art. 19(2) of Regulation 17, can contest the Commission's final decision taken in his absence in an action for annulment on the ground of infringement of an essential procedural requirement, provided that the decision concerns him directly and individually. See in this respect § 516 above.

7 See § 509 above.

8 This follows indirectly from Arts. 19(1) and 21(1) of Regulation 17.

117 9 See § 609 above.

10 C. W. Oberdorfer, A. Gleiss, M. Hirsch, *Common Market Cartel Law*, 2nd ed. (1971), §§ 113, 316, 324, pp. 94, 142, 164; A. Deringer, *The Competition Law of the European Economic Community* (1968), §§ 405-406, 2024, 2033, pp.127, 268-269, 270.

11 See §§ 613, 615 above. The possibility for an action seems now to follow implicitly from the decision of the Court in Case 26/76 (not yet reported).

Section 701

118 1 In the *Chorzow Factory (Indemnity) Case*, the Permanent Court of International Justice stated that 'it is a principle of international law, and even a general conception

of law, that any breach of an engagement involves an obligation to make reparation.' P.C.I.J. (1928) Ser, A. No.17, p.29.

2 Arts 34, 40 E.C.S.C.; 215(2) E.E.C.; 188(2) Euratom. See further § 704 below.

3 See § 521 above. For the position under the E.C.S.C. Treaty, see § 707 below.

119 4 See Chapters 5 and 6 above.

5 Cases 3/54, 1 Rec. 149 *per* A.G.; 1/55, 2 Rec. 38 *per* A.G.; 1/56 *ibid.*, pp.448-449 *per* A.G. See further § 401 above.

6 Cases 9 and 12/60, 32 ILR 415-417 *per Curiam*, 7 Rec. 445 *et seq. per* A.G., dealing with the relationship between actions for damages and actions for failure to act under the E.C.S.C. Treaty; Cases 4/69 [1971] ECR 336 *per Curiam*, 342-343 *per* A.G., and 153/73 [1974] ECR 692 *per Curiam*, 699 *per* A.G., dealing with the same question under the E.E.C Treaty; Cases 5/71 [1971] ECR 983 *per Curiam*, 990 *et seq. per* A.G. 9 and 11/71 [1973] CMLR 551 *per Curiam*, 532 *et seq. per* A. G.; 59/72 [1973] ECR 806-807 *per* A.G.; 43/72 *ibid.*, p.1069 *per Curiam*, 1078-1083 *per* A.G.; 99/74 [1975] ECR 1539; 56 to 60/74 [1976] ECR 741 *per Curiam*, 751-752 *per* A.G., all these Cases and opinions deal with the relationship between actions for damages and actions for annulment under the E.E.C. Treaty. *Cf.* also Case 44/76 [1977] ECR 407.

7 For the position under the E.C.S.C. Treaty, see § 707 below.

120 8 See § 707 below.

9 See the Cases mentioned at note 6 above.

10 Case 25/62 [1963] ECR 119 *per* A.G. In that Case the Court, while rejecting the application for annulment as being inadmissible, did enter into an examination of the merits of the claim for damages.

11 Cases 4/67 [1967] ECR 373; 96/71 [1973] CMLR 383; 72/74 [1975] ECR 410-411.

12 Cases 19 and 21/60, 2 and 3/61 [1962] CMLR 281.

121 13 See §§ 501 and 601 above.

14 Cases 59/65 [1966] ECR 550-551 *per Curiam*, 555 *per* A.G.; 4/67 [1967] ECR 373; 53/70 [1971] ECR 608-609. In all these Cases Community officials' actions for annulment of decisions refusing promotion to a higher grade or appointment to a post with a higher salary were held inadmissible for expiry of time-limits. Consequently, it was also inadmissible for them to claim as damages the differences between their actual salaries and those that would have been due to the grade or post sought. See in this respect also Cases 9/75 [1975] ECR 1182-1183 and 58/75 [1976] ECR 1159 *per* A.G. See further Cases 5/71 [1971] ECR 992 *per* A.G.; 9 and 11/71 [1973] CMLR 533 *per* A.G.; 15 to 33, 52, 53, 57 to 109, 116, 117, 123, 132 and 135 to 137/73 [1974] ECR 188 *per Curiam*, 194 *per* A.G.; 72/74 [1975] ECR 410-411.

15 On the division of jurisdiction in actions for damages between national courts and the European Court, see further § 702 below.

122 16 See § 704 below.

17 Cases 5, 7, 13 to 24/66 [1967] ECR 263-264; 30/66 *ibid.*, p.298; 96/71 [1973] CMLR 383; 46/75 [1976] ECR 79-80 *per Curiam*, 86-87 *per* A.G.; 26/74 *ibid.*, pp.686-687 *per Curiam*, 690-692 *per* A.G.

18 Case 99/74 [1975] ECR 1538-1540.

123 19 Cases 43/72 [1973] ECR 1069 *per Curiam*, 1076-1084 *per* A.G.; 126/76 (not yet reported).

20 Cases 74/74 [1975] ECR 543 *et seq.*; 67 to 85/75 [1976] ECR 406.

21 Art. 6 of Council Decision 70/243 and Arts. 4 and 8 of Council Regulation 729/70, of 21 April 1970 and Arts. 1, 2 and 13 of Council Regulation 2/71 of 2 January 1971.

22 See § 501 above.

124 23 As of 31 December 1976. Staff Cases are not included. Joined Cases have been counted as one Case. All actions have been brought under Art. 40 E.C.S.C.

24 Cases 29, 31, 36, 39 to 47, 50 and 51/63 [1965] ECR 911 and [1966] ECR 139. Here five applicants were successful while nine applications were dismissed as unfounded.

25 As of 31 December 1976. Staff Cases are not included. Joined cases have been counted as one case.

26 Cases 5, 7 and 13 to 24/66 [1967] ECR 245 (where the Court dismissed some of the applications as unfounded) and Case 30/66 [1967] ECR 285. See note 16 in § 702 below.

27 Case 74/74 [1975] ECR 533 (Interlocutory Judgment) and [1976] ECR 797 (Final Judgment).

Section 702

1 Arts. 40(1) and (2) E.C.S.C., 178 E.E.C., 151 Euratom.
2 See § 704 below.
3 Art.40(1) and (2) E.C.S.C.
4 Arts. 215(2) E.E.C., 188(2) Euratom.
5 Cases 9 and 12/60. 32 ILR 418; 5, 7 and 13 to 24/66 [1967] ECR 270 *per* A.G.; 9/69 [1969] ECR 335-336 *per Curiam*, 339, 345-346 *per* A.G.; 9 and 11/71 [1973] CMLR 536 *per* A.G.; 42/72 [1973] ECR 1080, 1082 *per* A.G.
125 6 See the Cases mentioned in the previous footnote.
7 Arts. 40(3) E.C.S.C., 183 E.E.C., 155 Euratom.
8 Art. 12(a) of the Protocol on the Privileges and Immunities of the European Communities of 8 April 1965.
9 Cases 5/68 [1968] ECR 402 *per Curiam*, 408 *per* A.G.; 9/69 [1969] ECR 335-336 *per Curiam*, 343-346 *per* A.G.
10 See § 704 below.
11 See §§ 101, 109 above.
126 12 See § 701 above.
13 Case 23/59, 2 Val. 658-659 *per Curiam*, 5 Rec. 528 *per* A.G.
14 Case 60/75 [1976] ECR 55-56.
15 See § 706 below.
127 16 This happened in fact in Cases 5, 7 and 13 to 24/66 [1967] ECR 266-267 and 30/66 *ibid.*, pp.300-301 where the European Court, while establishing the liability of the Community in principle, postponed giving a final judgment on the actual amount of damages until the competent national courts have decided upon the question of the concurrent liability of Germany. For an unsuccessful request by one of the parties for the interpretation of the European Court's judgment, see Case 24/66 bis. [1973] ECR 1599. See also *German No. 31* [1969] CMLR 244 *et seq.*
17 Cases 18/60 [1962] ECR 204-205 *per Curiam*, 208 *per* A.G.; 14, 16, 17, 20, 24, 26 and 27/60 and 1/61, 32 ILR 411.

Section 703

1 Arts. 40(1) and (2) E.C.S.C., 215(2) E.E.C., 188(2) Euratom. The original text of Art. 40 E.C.S.C. distinguished between *faute de service* (wrongful act or omission of an institution) and *faute personnelle* (personal wrong of a Community servant) and in respect of the latter, made the servant alone liable towards third parties. Only when the injured party was unable to obtain satisfaction from the servant, had the Court power to order the Community to pay compensation. Mainly to bring it more into line with the E.E.C./Euratom Treaties, Art. 26 of the Merger Treaty of 1965 amended this arrangement.
2 Case 9/69 [1969] ECR 335-336 *per Curiam*, 343-344, 346 *per* A.G. See further § 702 above. For a definition when a damage is caused 'in the performance of duties', see § 704 below.
3 Arts. 40(2) E.C.S.C., 215(3) E.E.C., 188(3) Euratom.
4 Art. 6 E.C.S.C. See § 101 above.
128 5 Cases 33/59 [1962] ECR 397 *per* A.G.; 9 and 25/64 [1965] ECR 324 *per* A.G.
6 Arts. 211 E.E.C., 185 Euratom. See § 101 above.
7 See §§ 504, 608 above.
8 Cases 63 to 69/72 [1973] ECR 1247-1248; 44/76 [1977] ECR 405.
9 Cases 56 to 60/74 [1976] ECR 756 *per* A.G.
10 See the Cases mentioned at note 8 above. In Cases 79 and 82/63 [1964] ECR 272 the A.G. has expressed the opinion that an action for damages cannot lie against the Community as such but must be brought against the institution which is alleged to have caused the damage.

11 The Parliament seems to be excluded simply because its acts have no legally binding effect and therefore cannot 'cause' injury. The position of the Court of Justice appears to be more doubtful. One could argue that a judgment of the Court can be legally 'faulty' (nothing that is human is absolutely perfect) and can, therefore, give rise to a claim for damages. On the other hand, it would be a contradiction in terms, a legal impossibility, to suggest that a judgment can also be 'illegal' (a second essential requirement) as a judgment is always supposed to state the 'law'. Moreover, because of the one-tier system, the Court would have to review its own judgment which would contradict the *nemo judex in re sua* principle.

12 See §§ 521 above and 707 below.

13 See § 301 above.

14 See § 504 above.

129 15 Cases 9 and 12/60, 32 ILR 417—418 *per Curiam*, 7 Rec. 445 *et seq. per* A.G. See also § 701 above.

16 See §§ 504, 608 above. However, Community Officials must bring their Actions under Art. 179 E.E.C. and Arts. 90 and 91 of the Staff Regulations, not under Arts. 178, 215(2), see Cases 9/75 [1975] ECR 1181; 48/76 [1977] ECR 298.

17 Cases 72/74 [1975] ECR 417—418 *per* A.G.; 56 to 60/74 [1976] ECR 751—752 *per* A.G.

18 See § 403 above.

19 See §§ 701 and 702 above.

20 Case 99/74 [1975] ECR 1539. See further § 705 below.

21 Case 72/74 [1975] ECR 411 *per Curiam*, 418 *per* A.G.

22 Cases 56 to 60/74 [1976] ECR 742; 5/71 [1971] ECR 993 *per* A.G.

Section 704

1 Since the Community is now alone liable for both its institutions and servants, the distinction made by Art. 40 between 'wrongful act or omission' and 'personal wrong' has lost much of its earlier significance. See note 1 in § 703 above.

130 2 See further § 702 above.

3 Cases 9/69 [1969] ECR 335-336 *per Curiam*, 340-343, 346 *per* A.G.; 14, 16, 17, 20, 24, 26 and 27/60 and 1/61, 32 ILR 408-412; 9 and 12/60, 7 Rec. 450 *per* A.G.

131 4 Cases 9 and 12/60, 7 Rec. 469 *per* A.G.; 25/62 [1963] ECR 116-117 *per* A.G.; 9 and 25/64 [1965] ECR 326 *per* A.G.; 5, 7 and 13 to 24/66 [1967] ECR 269-273 *per* A.G ; 9/69 [1969] ECR 339-340 *per* A.G.; 5/71 [1971] ECR 989-990 *per* A.G.; 63 to 69/72 [1973] ECR 1259-1260, 1274 *per* A.G. On the concept of general principles of law as a source of Community law, see further § 221 above.

5 Cases 25/62 [1963] ECR 120 *per* A.G.; 5, 7 and 13 to 24/66 [1967] ECR 273-274 *per* A.G.; 4/69 [1971] ECR 337 (in that Case the Court did not mention the fourth requirement); 5/71 [1971] ECR 994, 998-999 *per* A.G.; 63 to 69/72 [1973] ECR 1260-1272 *per* A.G.; 153/73 [1974] ECR 693; 26/74 [1976] ECR 693-694 *per* A.G.

132 6 See §§ 705-708 below.

Section 705

1 Cases 23/59, 2 Val. 657-658; 14, 16, 17, 20, 24, 26 and 27/60 and 1/61, 32 ILR 408, 412; 19 and 21/60, 2 and 3/61 [1962] CMLR 283; 18/60 [1962] ECR 206; 4/65 [1965] ECR 1112; 49/65 [1966] ECR 82; 51/65 *ibid.*, p. 97; 54/65 *ibid.*, pp. 197-198; 26/68 [1969] ECR 156; 67 to 85/75 [1976] ECR 408; 74/74 *ibid.*, pp. 804-806. In the last-mentioned Case the Court dismissed an application for damages although in a previous interlocutory judgment ([1975] ECR 550-551) it had in principle established the liability of the Community for any loss that may have been caused to the applicant by the unforeseeable withdrawal of the compensatory amounts. The reason for dismissing the action was that the loss envisaged at the time of the interlocutory judgment did not materialise and that therefore there was no 'damage' to be compensated for.

133 2 Cases 55 to 59 and 61 to 63/63 [1964] ECR 229; 9 and 25/64 [1965] ECR 320-321. In the latter Case the Court dismissed the claim as premature because the consequences of the High Authority's alleged fault were not at the time of the judgment capable of being calculated.

3 Cases 56 to 60/74 [1976] ECR 741-742 *per Curiam*, 752-754 *per* A.G. In those Cases Court held admissible an application brought in July 1974 for a declaration that the Community was bound to make good the damage which the applicants were going to suffer during the 1974/75 cereal marketing year by reason of the alleged discriminatory rules on prices and aids contained in various Council Regulations. *Cf.* also Case 44/76 [1977] ECR 407.

4 Cases 14, 16, 17, 20, 24, 26 and 27/60 and 1/61, 32 ILR 407; 9 and 58/65 [1967] ECR 12. 'Special' damage is expressly required by Art. 34 E.C.S.C. only. In the first of the above-mentioned cases the Court, whilst making the statement discussed in the text, left open the question whether Art. 40 E.C.S.C. also required that the damage must be peculiar to the applicant. The statement however seems to imply an affirmative answer.

5 Case 153/73 [1974] ECR 706 *per* A.G.

6 Cases 55 to 59 and 61 to 63/63 [1964] ECR 229; 13/69 [1970] ECR 14.

7 Case 26/74 [1976] ECR 687-688 *per Curiam*, 694-695 *per* A.G.

8 *Ibid.*

9 See the Cases mentioned at notes 1, 6 and 7 above.

10 Cases 29, 31, 36, 39 to 47, 50 and 51/63 [1965] ECR 943-944 *per* A.G.

11 Case 1/55, 2 Val. 725; 10/55 *ibid.*, p.737.

134 12 Case 5/71 [1971] ECR 908.

13 Case 68/63 [1965] ECR 605.

14 Cases 25/62 [1963] ECR 119-120 *per* A.G.; 29, 31, 36, 39 to 47, 50 and 51/63 [1965] ECR 934-935; 40/75 [1976] ECR 12 *per* A.G. See further § 406 above.

15 Cases 25/62 [1963] ECR 108 *per Curiam*, 117-118 *per* A.G.; 56 to 60/74 [1976] ECR 741-742. See also § 406 above.

16 Case 74/74 [1975] ECR 544.

17 *Ibid.*, pp. 550-551. For the final judgment of the Court in that Case, see [1976] ECR 797. See also Cases 29, 31, 36, 39 to 47, 50 and 51/63 [1965] ECR 941; 5/71 [1971] ECR 993 *per* A.G.; 63 to 69/72 [1973] ECR 1271-1273 *per* A.G.

18 Cases 29, 31, 36, 39 to 47, 50 and 51/63 [1965] ECR 938-939 *per Curiam*, 943-944 *per* A.G.

135 19 Cases 5, 7 and 13 to 24/66 [1967] ECR 265-266; 30/66 *ibid.*, pp. 299-300.

20 Case 58/75 [1976] ECR 1155, where the Court awarded legal interest at 8% from the date of the administrative complaint lodged by the applicant in a Staff dispute. The A.G. submitted that interest should be paid from the time when the damage occurred. *ibid.*, p. 1164.

21 See the Cases mentioned at note 19 above.

22 *Ibid.*

23 Case 74/74 [1975] ECR 550. See further § 707 below.

24 Cases 7/56 and 3 to 7/57, 2 Val. 769-770; 68/63 [1965] ECR 604-605; 110/63 *ibid.*, p. 667; 12/66 [1967] ECR 167; 10 and 47/72 [1973] ECR 772; 61/76 [1977] ECR 1436.

Section 706

1 Case 169/73 [1975] ECR 134.

2 Cases 18/60 [1962] ECR 206; 36/62 [1963] ECR 296-298; 29, 31, 36, 39 to 47, 50 and 51/63 [1965] ECR 944 *per* A.G.; 5, 7 and 13 to 24/66 [1967] ECR 278 *per* A.G.; 26/68 [1969] ECR 156; 4/69 [1971] ECR 346 *per* A.G., 153/73 [974] ECR 693; 169/73 [1975] ECR 135-136 *per Curiam*, 148 *et seq. per* A.G.; 40/75 [1976] ECR 8-9 *per Curiam*, 13-15 *per* A.G.; 26/74 *ibid.*, p.688 *per Curiam*, 694-695 *per* A.G.; 56 to 60/74 *ibid.*, pp.759-760 *per* A.G.; 74/74 *ibid.*, pp.809-810 *per* A.G.

3 Cases 29, 31, 36, 39 to 47, 50 and 51/63 [1965] ECR 954 *per* A.G.; 5, 7 and 13 to 24/66 [1967] ECR 278 *per* A.G.

136 4 Case 169/73 [1975] ECR 148 *et seq.*, esp. at 151 *per* A.G.

5 Case 99/74 [1975] ECR 1544 *per* A.G. In that Case the Court did not consider the question of causation as it dismissed the action as inadmissible.

6 Cases 9 and 12/60, 32 ILR 420 *per Curiam*, 7 Rec. 475 *per* A.G. In those Cases the applicants based their claim for damages on the failure by the High Authority to use the procedure in Art. 88 E.C.S.C. to enforce respect by France for the rule of free

circulation of goods as laid down in Art. 4(a) E.C.S.C. In Case 4/69 [1971] ECR 336 the applicant based its application on the failure of the Commission to use its powers under Arts. 97(2), 155 and 169 E.E.C. to obtain the abolition or reduction of a German Tax alleged to be contrary to Arts. 95 and 97(1) E.E.C. In Case 40/75 [1976] ECR 7-9 the applicant claimed compensation for damages suffered by reason of a failure by the Commission to initiate the procedure in Art. 93(2) E.E.C., and to use the powers conferred upon it by Arts. 93(2), 155 and 169 E.E.C., to ensure that the Italian Government abolished the aid granted by it in contravention of Art. 92 E.E.C. to Italian manufacturers of certain pasta products who were in competition with the applicant. However, the Court dismissed the action as unfounded since the applicant could not prove that his loss was caused by the disputed Italian measures.

7 Cases 5, 7 and 13 to 24/66 [1967] ECR 263 *et seq. per Curiam*, 279 *per* A.G. In those Cases the causes of the damage were both the safeguard measure taken by Germany and the decision of the Commission authorising that measure.

8 Cases 36/62 [1963] ECR 296-297; 169/73 [1975] ECR 134-136 *per Curiam*, 148 *et seq. per* A.G.

Section 707

137 1 See § 704 above.

2 See further § 708 below.

3 Cases 19 and 21/60, 2 and 3/61 [1962] CMLR 281.

4 Cases 14, 16, 17, 20, 24, 26 and 27/60 and 1/61, 32 ILR 407, 409, 411. In those Cases the Court expressly refused to consider, in the framework of an action for damages brought under Art. 40 E.C.S.C., the legality or illegality of the measure in the course of whose implementation the malfunctioning of the administration causing the damage occurred.

138 5 Cases 14, 16, 17, 20, 24, 26 and 27/60 and 1/61, 7 Rec. 351 *per* A.G. See also § 521 above.

6 Cases 9 and 12/60, 7 Rec. 446 *per* A.G.

7 Cases 9 and 12/60, 32 ILR 416-417.

8 *Ibid.*, p. 417.

9 This solution was adopted by the European Court in the cases mentioned at note 4 above. The respective scopes of Arts. 34 and 40 have been interpreted by the A.G. in Cases 36/62 [1963] ECR 300 and 5/71 [1971] ECR 990-991.

139 10 Cases 9 and 12/60, 32 ILR 417; this solution seems to emerge also from the A.G.'s opinion in those Cases. See 7 Rec. 445 *et seq.*

11 See § 701 above.

12 As e.g. in Case 25/62 [1963] ECR 108.

13 *Ibid.*

140 14 See § 1104 below.

15 See § 519 above.

16 See § 709 below.

17 Cases 38/64 [1965] ECR 213 *per* A.G.; 106 and 107/63 *ibid.*, p.440 *per* A.G.; 5/71 [1971] ECR 990-992 *per* A.G.; 9 and 11/71 [1973] CMLR 532-535 *per* A.G.

18 See § 502 above.

19 See the Cases mentioned at note 6 in § 701 above.

20 See further § 701 above.

21 Cases 5/71 [1971] ECR 984 *per Curiam*, 9994 *per* A. G.; 9 and 11/71 [1973] CMLR 554-555 *per Curiam*, 549 *per* A.G.; 96/71 *ibid.*, p.383; 59/72 [1973] ECR 807 *per* A.G.

22 Cases 35/62 and 16/63 [1963] ECR 207; 84/63 [1964] ECR 334; 87/63 *ibid.*, p.484; 93/63 *ibid.*, p.511; 19 and 65/63 [1965] ECR 557.

23 Cases 4/69 [1971] ECR 337-338; 9 and 11/71 [1973] CMLR 555; 59/72 [1973] ECR 804 *per Curiam*, 812 *per* A.G.; 43/72 *ibid.*, p. 1074; 63 to 69/72 *ibid.*, p. 1253; 56 to 60/74 [1976] ECR 747.

141 24 See, in addition to the Cases mentioned in the previous footnotes, also Cases 153/73 [1974] ECR 691 *et seq.*; 74/74 [1975] ECR 543 *et seq.*; 95 to 98/74, 15 and 100/75 *ibid.*, pp.1636 *et seq.*; 67 to 85/75 [1976] ECR 408-409.

25 *Cf.* e.g. Case 59/72 [1973] ECR 803 *per Curiam*, 807-808 *per* A.G. where during the

course of the written proceedings the Court had, by a judgment rendered in a different case under Art. 177 (Case 40/72 [1973] ECR 125), affirmed the validity of the regulation which allegedly caused the damage and whose legality was challenged by the applicant.

26 Cases 9 and 11/71 [1973] CMLR 555.

27 *Ibid.*, pp.548-550 *per* A.G.

28 *Ibid.*

29 *Ibid.*, p. 555 *per Curiam. Cf.* also Cases 54 to 60/76 [1977] ECR 657, 659-660.

30 Case 169/73 [1975] ECR 141.

31 *Ibid.*

32 Cases 19 and 65/63 [1965] ECR 558.

142 33 See §§ 514-518 above.

34 It is submitted, however, that subject to the limitations on liability in respect of normative acts, discussed in the text under (c), the defence of illegality may be raised in actions for damages to show that an individual decision which is the alleged cause of the damage is illegal as issued under an illegal general measure, see § 519 above.

35 Cases 25/62 [1963] ECR 121-122 *per* A.G.; 5, 7 and 13 to 24/66 [1967] ECR 262-263 *per Curiam*, 274 *per* A.G.; 30/66 *ibid.*, p.297; 4/69 [1971] ECR 345 *per* A.G.

36 Under Art. 34 of the German Constitution, the Government is liable only where the official causing the injury violated a concrete obligation towards third parties in performing his duties and not merely an abstract rule designed to protect the public in general. In Italian law, infringement of rules created exclusively or mainly in the public interest gives rise to an action for annulment only, but does not confer a subjective right on the basis of which an action for damages could be brought. In French and Luxembourg law a claim for damages requires the infringement of a right vested in the individual.

37 Cases 9 and 12/60, 32 ILR 419-421.

38 Cases 5, 7 and 13 to 24/66 [1967] ECR 262-263 *per Curiam*, 274-275 *per* A.G.; 30/66 *ibid.*, p.297. In those Cases the Court decided that Regulation 19 and in particular Art. 22 thereof, which was the provision violated by the Commission decision causing the damage, was designed to protect the general interests of producers of and traders in the relevant agricultural products, which also encompassed the interests of the applicants who in their capacity as grain importers participated in intra-Community trade.

143 39 See §§ 511, 614 above.

40 Case 5/71 [1971] ECR 989 *per* A.G.

41 Case 25/62 [1963] ECR 121 *per* A.G.

42 Cases 63 to 69/72 [1973] ECR 1258-1260 *per* A.G.

43 *Ibid.*, Case 5/71 [1971] ECR 989-990 *per* A.G. See further § 704 above.

44 *Ibid.*

144 45 In fact it happened in some cases that private parties sought, quite legitimately, to achieve through an action for damages the same result which previously they or others had been unable to attain by an action for annulment or for failure to act. See e.g. Cases 9 and 11/71 [1973] CMLR 550 *et seq.* where the success of the action would have meant the virtual annulment of the effects of certain regulations — a result which the applicants had been unable to achieve previously in Case 65/69 [1970] ECR 233-234, which was dismissed as inadmissible. In Case 43/72 [1973] ECR 1068 *et seq.* the applicants were able to request by way of damages the payment of certain compensatory amounts for which the relevant Commission regulation failed to provide, in spite of the fact that another company had previously been unsuccessful in obtaining amendment of the same regulation, see Case 42/71 [1973] CMLR 187. In Case 153/73 [1974] ECR 691 *et seq.* the applicants were able to request as damages certain subsidies not provided for by the relevant Council regulation although previously they were unable to achieve the same result by a simple amendment of that regulation through an action for failure to act, see Case 134/73 [1974] ECR 9-11

46 See § 517 above.

47 Cases 5/71 [1971] ECR 984; 9 and 11/71 [1973] CMLR 552 *per Curiam*, 554 *per* A.G.; 59/72 [1973] ECR 803 *per Curiam*, 806-807 *per* A.G.; 43/72 *ibid.*, p.1070 *per*

Curiam, 1083 *per* A.G.; 63 to 69/72 *ibid.*, p. 1248; 153/73 [1974] ECR 693; 74/74 [1975] ECR 546 *per Curiam*, 561 *per* A.G.; 56 to 60/74 [1976] ECR 743, 54 to 60/76 [1977] ECR 658: 97/76 *ibid.*, p. 1080.

48 Cases 63 to 69/72 [1973] ECR 1260-1261 *per* A.G.; 153/73 [1974] ECR 700 *per* A.G.

145 49 See further § 304 above.

50 Case 153/73 [1974] ECR 704 *per* A.G.

51 See Cases 5/71 [1971] ECR 984-985; 63 to 69/72 [1973] ECR 1245 *et seq.*; 153/73 [1974] ECR 691 *et seq.*; 56 to 60/74 [1976] ECR 740 *et seq.*; 54 to 60/76 [1977] ECR 659.

52 Cases 63 to 69/72 [1973] ECR 1245 *et seq. per Curiam*, 1261 *per* A.G. See further § 221 above.

53 See in general § 221 above.

54 Case 74/74 [1975] ECR 549-550 where the Court held that the Commission had violated a superior rule of law, thus rendering the Community liable, by failing to include transitional measures for the protection of the confidence of traders, in the regulation withdrawing the monetary compensatory amounts. Since, however, the applicant had not been able to prove that it had actually suffered a loss, the application was dismissed by a final judgment, see [1976] ECR 804 *et seq.*; Cases 95 to 98/74, 15 and 100/75 [1975] ECR 1643 *per* A.G.; 67 to 85/75 [1976] ECR 411, 54 to 60/76 [1977] ECR 659; 97/76 *ibid.*, pp. 1077 *et seq.*

55 Cases 9 and 11/71 [1973] CMLR 554; 43/72 [1973] ECR 1086 *per* A.G.

Section 708

146 1 Cases 23/59, 2 Val. 658; 9 and 12/60, 7 Rec. 469 *per* A.G.; 33/59 [1962] ECR 395 *per* A.G.; 25/62 [1963] ECR 120 *per* A.G.; 5, 7 and 13 to 24/66 [1967] ECR 260-263 *per Curiam*, 274-278 *per* A.G.; 5/71 [1971] ECR 994, 998-999 *per* A.G.; 59/72 [1973] ECR 807 *per* A.G.; 63 to 69/72 *ibid.*, p.1270 *per* A.G.; 26/74 [1976] ECR 693 *per* A.G.

2 It is interesting to note that, for example, in Case 4/69 [1971] ECR 337, in defining the general conditions for Community liability, the Court did not mention culpability. See note 5 in § 704 above.

3 See § 707(a) and note 23 in that Section.

147 4 See § 704 above.

5 Cases 9 and 12/60, 7 Rec. 469 *per* A.G.; 33/59 [1962] ECR 396, 405 *per* A.G.; 29, 31, 36, 39 to 47, 50 and 51/63 [1965] ECR 953 *per* A.G.; 9 and 25/64 *ibid.*, pp.325-326 *per* A.G.; 5, 7 and 13 to 24/66 [1967] ECR 276-278 *per* A.G. In the last two Cases it was the Commission that invoked the requirement of 'gross negligence' in connection with its supervisory functions. The A.G., whilst not dismissing the argument as such, was of the opinion in both cases that in the given circumstances an ordinary degree of fault was sufficient to establish the liability of the Community.

6 Cases 19 and 21/60, 2 and 3/61 [1962] CMLR 281-282.

148 7 Cases 5, 7 and 13 to 24/66 [1967] ECR 262; 30/66 *ibid.*, pp.296-297.

8 Case 33/59 [1962] ECR 397-398, 406 *per* A.G.

9 Cases 63 to 69/72 [1973] ECR 1270-1271 *per* A.G.

10 *Ibid.*, p.1253 *per Curiam*; 56 to 60/74 [1976] ECR 744-745 *per Curiam*, 760 *per* A.G.

11 Cases 36/62 [1963] ECR 296 *per Curiam*, 300 *per* A.G.; 169/73 [1975] ECR 140 *per* A.G.

12 Case 26/74 [1976] ECR 688.

149 13 Cases 5, 7 and 13 to 24/66 [1967] ECR 262; 30/66 *ibid.*, p.296. In those Cases the Court held that in authorising the German Government to maintain certain safeguard measures the Commission applied the power granted to it by Art. 22 of Regulation 19 in a situation that did not justify safeguard measures and this constituted an official fault.

14 Cases 67 to 85/75 [1976] ECR 409-410.

15 See § 518 above.

16 Cases 14, 16, 17, 20, 24, 26 and 27/60 and 1/61, 32 ILR 408-412.

17 *Ibid.*, p.412; Cases 7/56 and 3 to 7/57, 2 Val. 769; 5, 7 and 13 to 24/66 [1967] ECR 276 *per* A.G.

18 Cases 19, 20, 25 and 30/69 [1970] ECR 339-340; 26/74 [1976] ECR 693 *per* A.G.

19 See in general Chapter 9 below.

20 Cases 9 and 12/60, 32 ILR 420 *per Curiam*, 7 Rec. 475 *per* A.G.; 4/69 [1971] ECR 336; 40/75 [1976] ECR 7-9. See note 6 in § 706 above.

21 Case 23/59, 2 Val. 659.

150 22 Cases 19 and 21/60, 2 and 3/61 [1962] CMLR 281-282; 33/59 [1962] ECR 405 *per* A.G.

23 Case 58/75 [1976] ECR 1154 *per Curiam*, 1162 *per* A.G.

24 See § 706 above.

25 See § 221 above.

26 Cases 5, 7 and 13 to 24/66 [1967] ECR 271 *per* A.G.; 9 and 11/71 [1973] CMLR 537 *per* A.G.; 63 to 69/72 [1973] ECR 1272 *per* A.G. See however the Case mentioned at note 23 above.

27 See the Cases mentioned at note 14 in § 701 above.

151 28 See § 701 above.

29 Cases 63 to 69/72 [1973] ECR 1273-1275 *per* A.G.; 56 to 60/74 [1976] ECR 765 *per* A.G.

30 *Ibid.*

31 Cases 63 to 69/72 [1973] ECR 1253; 56 to 60/74 [1976] ECR 747. It may be noted that in Case 59/72 [1973] ECR 812 the A.G. concluded that the question whether the Community could incur liability independently of any fault did not arise merely because the applicants did not in that particular case claim to have suffered any 'exceptional and special detriment'. It would seem to follow from this view that an exceptional and special injury could establish liability even in the absence of culpability.

Section 709

1 Cases 56 to 60/74 [1976] ECR 755 *per* A.G.

2 Arts. 40 E.C.S.C. Statute, 43 E.E.C. Statute, 44 Euratom Statute.

152 3 See § 705 above. Cases 46 and 47/59 [1962] ECR 420, 423; 5, 7 and 13 to 24/66 [1967] ECR 260.

4 See note 2 above.

5 Cases 5, 7 and 13 to 24/66 [1967] ECR 271 *per* A.G., 9 and 11/71 [1973] CMLR 537 *per* A.G.

6 See §§ 520, 604, 610 above.

7 Cases 5, 7 and 13 to 24/66 [1967] ECR 260 *per Curiam*, 271-273 *per* A.G.; 9 and 11/71 [1973] CMLR 537 *per* A.G.; 11/72 [1973] ECR 425.

Section 801

153 1 Arts, 8 E.C.S.C., 155 E.E.C., 124 Euratom.

2 Except under Art. 88 E.C.S.C. For this and, in general, for the procedure for ensuring compliance with Community law by the Member States, see Chapter 9 below.

3 See in general Chapter 5 above.

4 See §§ 514-518 above.

5 Arts. 36 E.C.S.C., 172 E.E.C., 144 Euratom.

6 See § 804 below.

154 7 See § 701 above.

8 *Cf.* e.g. Cases 6 and 7/73 [1974] ECR 255; 40 to 48, 50, 54 to 56, 111, 113 and 114/73 [1975] ECR 1913; 73/74 *ibid.*, p.1510.

9 See the first two Cases mentioned in the previous footnote.

10 Case 73/74 [1975] ECR 1510 *per Curiam*, 1520 *per* A.G.

11 As of 31 December 1976. Joined Cases have been counted as one Case.

12 Case 1/63 [1963] ECR 303.

13 Case 16/61 [1962] ECR 289.

14 See note 11 above.

15 Cases 26/75 [1975] ECR 1367; 73/74 *ibid.*, p.1491.

16 Cases 41/69 [1970] ECR 661; 44/69 *ibid.*, p.733; 45/69 *ibid.*, p.769; 57/69 [1972] CMLR 557; 6 and 7/73 [1974] ECR 223. See further § 805 below.

17 Cases 40 to 48, 50, 54 to 56, 111, 113 and 114/73 [1975] ECR 1663, where the Court annulled the fines in seven cases, and reduced them in nine cases. In respect of the latter, see further § 805 below.

Section 802

155 1 See §§ 101 above and 1004 below.
2 Cases 1/63 [1963] ECR 319-320 *per* A.G.; 21/64 [1965] ECR 187-188.
3 Art. 47(3) E.C.S.C.; *cf*. Cases 2 to 10/63 [1963] ECR 327; 29/67 [1968] ECR 263.
4 Art. 54(6) E.C.S.C.
5 Art. 58(4) E.C.S.C.
6 Art. 59(7) E.C.S.C.
7 Art. 64 E.C.S.C.; *cf*. Cases 8/56, 2 Val. 70; 1/59 *ibid*., p.74; 16/61 [1962] ECR 289; 29/67 [1968] ECR 263.
8 Art. 65(5) E.C.S.C.
9 Art. 66(5) E.C.S.C.
10 Art. 68(6) E.C.S.C.
11 Art. 66(5) and (6) E.C.S.C. For the distinction between Community and non-Community undertakings, see § 301 above. The latter's right of action is based on Arts. 36, 66(6) E.C.S.C. and Art. 43(2) E.C.S.C. Statute.
12 Art. 50(3) E.C.S.C., *cf*. e.g. Cases 1/63 [1963] ECR 319-320 *per* A.G.; 21/64 [1965] ECR 187-188.
13 Cases 2 to 10/63 [1963] ECR 340, 344.
156 14 Art. 90(2) E.C.S.C.
15 Art. 83 Euratom.
16 Art. 145 Euratom.
17 Art. 144(b) Euratom.
18 Art. 79(3) E.E.C.
19 Art. 87(2) E.E.C.
20 Art. 172 E.E.C.
21 Regulation 11 of 27.6.60. O.J. 1960, 52/1121.
22 Regulation 17 of 6,2.62. O.J. 1962, 13/204.
23 Regulation 1017/68 of 19.7.68. O.J. 1968, L 175/1.
24 Art. 16 of Regulation 11.
25 Art. 17 of Regulation 11.
26 Art. 18 of Regulation 11.
27 Art. 15 of Regulation 17; Art. 22 of Regulation 1017/68. Although these provisions specify the limits of fines in u.a., the Commission and the Court are entitled to fix the amount of the fine in a national currency in which it then becomes payable, see Cases 41, 43 and 44/73 (Interpretation) [1977] ECR 462-463.
28 Art. 16 of Regulation 17; Art. 23 of Regulation 1017/68.
29 Art. 25(2) of Regulation 11; Art. 17 of Regulation 17; Art. 24 of Regulation 1017/68.
157 30 Cases 41/69 [1970] ECR 701; 44/69 *ibid*., pp.760-761; 45/69 *ibid*., pp.805-806; 49/69 [1972] CMLR 633.
31 Art. 19 of Regulation 11; Art. 15(4) of Regulation 17; Art. 22(4) of Regulation 1017/68; Cases 41/69 [1970] ECR 722 *per* A.G.; 48/69 [1972] CMLR 570 *per* A.G.; 7/72 [1973] CMLR 869, 880 *per* A.G.; 40 to 48, 50, 54 to 56, 111, 113 and 114/73 [1975] ECR 2119-2120 *per* A.G.; *German No. 57* [1974] 1 CMLR 264.
32 Cases 14/68 [1969] ECR 24 *per* A.G.; 7/72 [1973] CMLR 880 *per* A.G.
33 Cases 40 to 48, 50, 54 to 56, 111, 113 and 114/73 [1975] ECR 2120-2121 *per* A.G.
34 Art. 15(2) of Regulation 17; Art. 22(2) of Regulation 1017/68; Cases 41/69 [1970] ECR 701; 44/69 *ibid*., p.761; 45/69 *ibid*., p.806.
35 See the text at note 14 above.
36 Case 14/68 [1969] ECR 15 *per Curiam*, 24-26 *per* A.G. See also § 221 above.
37 Cases 44/69 [1970] ECR 761; 45/69 *ibid*., p.807; 7/72 [1973] CMLR 887-888 *per Curiam*, 870 *et seq*. *per* A.G.
38 Cases 48/69 [1972] CMLR 628-629 *per Curiam*, 605-607 *per* A.G.; 52/69 *ibid*., p.640; 53/69 *ibid*.; 6/72 [1973] ECR 242; 6 and 7/73 [1974] ECR 253-255 *per Curiam*, 262-265 *per* A.G. See further § 110 above.
39 See § 221 above.
40 Cases 41/69 [1970] ECR 683; 44/69 *ibid*., pp.750-751; 45/69 *ibid*., p.795; 48/69 [1972] CMLR 621; 49/69 *ibid*., p.632; 51/69 *ibid*., p.635; 52/69 *ibid*., p.639; 53/69 *ibid*.; 54/69 *ibid*., p. 643; 55/69 *ibid*., p. 646; 56/69 *ibid*.; 57/69 *ibid*., p. 648.

41 Regulation 2988/74 of 26.11.74. O.J. 1974 L 319/1, it came into force on 1 January 1975.
158 42 *Ibid.*, Art. 1.
43 *Ibid.*, Art. 4.
44 *Ibid.*, Arts. 2, 3, 5 and 6.

Section 803

1 Art. 36 E.C.S.C.
2 Case 8/56, 2 Val. 69-70.
3 Case 21/64 [1965] ECR 188.
4 Case 16/61 [1962] ECR 302.
5 Art. 83(2) Euratom.
6 Art. 20 of Regulation 11.
7 Art. 18(3) of Regulation 11.
8 Art. 25(1) of Regulation 11.
9 Art. 19(1) and (2) of Regulation 17; Art. 26(1) and (2) of Regulation 1017/68.
10 See in general Regulation 99/63 of 25.7.63, O.J. 1963 2268; Cases 41/69 [1970] ECR 706-713 *per* A.G.; 48/69 [1972] CMLR 608-611 *per* A.G. The same administrative procedure applies also when proceedings are instituted by the Commission merely to terminate infringement of Arts. 85 or 86 E.E.C., without imposing sanctions, *cf.* Cases 56 and 58/64 [1966] ECR 338 *per Curiam*, 355 *per* A.G.; 8/72 [1973] CMLR 11-12 *per* A.G.; 6/72 [1973] ECR 240; 17/74 [1974] ECR 1077-1081.
159 11 Cases 48/69 [1972] CMLR 618-619; 49/69 *ibid.*, p. 630; 51/69 *ibid.*, p. 634; 52/69 *ibid.*, p. 637; 53/69 *ibid.*; 54/69 *ibid.*, p. 641; 55/69 *ibid.*, p. 644; 56/69 *ibid.*; 57/69 *ibid.*, p. 647.
12 Art. 2 of Regulation 99/63.
13 Art. 10 of Regulation 99/63. See § 216 above.
14 Cases 52/69 [1972] CMLR 637-638; 53/69 *ibid.* See § 222 above.
15 Cases 48/69 [1972] CMLR 618; 52/69 *ibid.*, p.637; 53/69 *ibid.*; 55/69 *ibid.*, p.644; 56/69 *ibid.*; 8/72 [1973] CMLR 21-22. See also §§ 206 and 215 above.
16 Cases 40 to 48, 50, 54 to 56, 111, 113 and 114/73 [1975] ECR 1989-1990 *per Curiam*, 2066 *per* A.G.
17 Case 17/74 [1974] ECR 1079-1081. See also § 221 above.
18 Art. 4 of Regulation 99/63.
19 See § 516 above. See also the Case mentioned at 17 above which, however, concerned not the imposition of a sanction but the granting of an exemption under Art. 85(3) E.E.C. subject to certain conditions.
160 20 Cases 56 and 58/64 [1966] ECR 338; 41/69 [1970] ECR 683-686; 44/69 *ibid.*, pp.751-752; 45/69 *ibid.*, pp.795-797; 48/69 [1972] CMLR 619; 49/69 *ibid.*, p.631; 51/69 *ibid.*, pp.634-635; 52/69 *ibid.*, p.638; 53/69 *ibid.*; 54/69 *ibid.*, pp.641-642; 55/69 *ibid.*, pp.644-645; 56/69 *ibid.*; 57/69 *ibid.*, pp.647-648; 6/72 [1973] ECR 240; 40 to 48, 50, 54 to 56, 111, 113 and 114/73 [1975] ECR 1929, 1990-1991.
21 Arts. 2(4) and 3 of Regulation 99/63.
22 *Ibid.*, Art. 5.
23 *Ibid.*, Art. 11.
24 Cases 6 and 7/73 [1974] ECR 274-275 *per* A.G.
25 Cases 40 to 48, 50, 54 to 56, 111, 113 and 114/73 [1975] ECR 1927-1928 *per Curiam*, 2066 *per* A.G.
26 Art. 7 of Regulation 99/63.
27 *Ibid.*, Art. 8.
28 Cases 51/69 [1972] CMLR 635; 55/69 *ibid.*, pp.644-645; 56/69 *ibid.*
29 Art. 9(1) of Regulation 99/63; Cases 41/69 [1970] ECR 689; 44/69 *ibid.*, pp.753-754; 45/69 *ibid.*, p.798.
30 Art. 9(2) of Regulation 99/63; Case 49/69 [1972] CMLR 631.
31 Art. 9(3) of Regulation 99/63; Case 6/72 [1973] ECR 264 *per* A.G.
32 Art. 9(4) of Regulation 99/63.
161 33 Case 41/69 [1970] ECR 686.
34 See § 215 above.

35 Case 41/69 [1970] ECR 686-687. See also § 516 above.
36 Cases 44/69 [1970] ECR 753; 45/69 *ibid.*, p.797; 48/69 [1972] CMLR 619-620 *per Curiam*, 612 *per* A.G.; 51/69 *ibid.*, p.635. See also § 516 above.
37 Arts. 10, 15(3) and 16(3) of Regulation 17; Art. 1 of Regulation 99/63.
38 Case 41/69 [1970] ECR 710 *per* A.G. See also § 516 above.
39 Art. 10 of Regulation 17; Case 45/69 [1970] ECR 798. See also § 516 above.
40 Art. 4 of Regulation 99/63.
41 Cases 41/69 [1970] ECR 691; 48/69 [1972] CMLR 619; 51/69 *ibid.*, p.635; 52/69 *ibid.*, pp. 638-639; 53/69 *ibid.*, 54/69 *ibid.*, p. 641; 55/69 *ibid.*, pp. 644-645; 56/69 *ibid.*, 57/69 *ibid.*, pp. 647-648; 40 to 48, 50, 54 to 56, 111, 113 and 114/73 [1975] ECR 1929 *per Curiam*, 2067 *per* A.G.
42 Case 16/61 [1962] ECR 322 *per* A.G. See also § 516 above.
162 43 Case 1/63 [1963] ECR 313.
44 Cases 56 and 58/64 [1966] ECR 338 *per Curiam*, 355 *per* A.G.; 29/67 [1968] ECR 279-280; 41/69 [1970] ECR 689-690; 55/69 [1972] CMLR 645-646; 56/69 *ibid.*; 6/72 [1973] ECR 240; 8/72 [1973] CMLR 20 *per* A.G.; 40 to 48, 50, 54 to 56, 111, 113 and 114/73 [1975] ECR 2067 *per* A.G. See further § 516 above.
45 Cases 40 to 48, 50, 54 to 56, 111, 113 and 114/73 [1975] ECR 1930.

Section 804

1 See § 801 above.
2 Arts. 36 E.C.S.C. 144 Euratom.
3 Art. 172 E.E.C.
4 Cases 2 to 10/63 [1963] ECR 341-342.
5 For the broad concept of 'unlimited jurisdiction' see further § 401 above.
6 See § 521 above.
7 See §§ 514-518 above.
8 Cases 41/69 [1970] ECR 704 *per* A.G.; 48/69 [1972] CMLR 574 *per* A.G.; 7/72 [1973] CMLR 867 *per* A.G.; 40 to 48, 50, 54 to 56, 111, 113 and 114/73 [1975] ECR 2112 *per* A.G.
9 Case 48/69 [1972] CMLR 591 *per* A.G.
10 Case 26/75 [1975] ECR 1390 *per* A.G.
11 *Ibid.*
163 12 Cases 2 to 10/63 [1963] ECR 342.
13 Case 16/61 [1962] ECR 303.
14 Case 26/75 [1975] ECR 1380.
15 Case 16/61 [1962] ECR 322 *per* A.G.
16 Art. 17 of Regulation 17; Art. 24 of Regulation 1017/68.
17 See § 406 above.
18 Case 8/56, 2 Val. 71.
19 *Ibid.*; Cases 1/59, 2 Val. 75-77; 16/61 [1962] ECR 307 *per Curiam*, 322 *per* A.G.; 7/72 [1973] CMLR 867, 884 *per* A.G.; 26/75 [1975] ECR 1390 *per* A.G. See further § 805 below.

Section 805

1 See § 804 above.
164 2 Cases 7/72 [1973] CMLR 867 *per* A.G.; 73/74 [1975] ECR 1510 *per Curiam*, 1520, 1528 *per* A.G.
3 See further § 521 above.
4 Cases 2 to 10/63 [1963] ECR 340; 1/63 *ibid.*, p. 313 where the Court annulled a decision imposing surcharges of 7 million lire (lack of reasoning); 26/75 [1975] ECR 1380 where the Court annulled a decision imposing a fine of 100,000 u.a.; 73/74 [1975] ECR 1515 where the Court cancelled fines ranging from BF 800,000 to BF 6,750,000 (lack of reasoning); 40 to 48, 50, 54 to 56, 111, 113 and 114/73 [1975] ECR 2021 where the Court cancelled fines ranging from 100,000 to 1 million u.a.
5 *Ibid.*, p. 2009-2010.
6 Cases 8/56, 2Val. 71; 1/59 *ibid.*, pp. 75-77; 2 to 10/63 [1963] ECR 345; 21/64 [1965] ECR 191; 45/69 [1970] ECR 805-807; 48/69 [1972] CMLR 630; 49/69 *ibid.*, p. 633;

51/69 *ibid.*, p. 636; 52/69 *ibid.*, p. 640; 53/69 *ibid.*, 54/69 *ibid.*, p. 643; 55/69 *ibid.*, p. 646; 56/69 *ibid.*; 6 and 7/73 [1974] ECR 257; 26/75 [1975] ECR 1390 *per* A.G.

7 Cases 41/69 [1970] ECR 701-702; 44/69 *ibid.*, pp. 761-762; 45/69 *ibid.*, pp. 806-807; 57/69 [1972] CMLR 650; 48/69 *ibid.*, p. 614 *per* A.G.; 40 to 48, 50, 54 to 56, 111, 113 and 114/73 [1975] ECR 2022-2023 *per Curiam*, 2120-2122 *per* A.G.

8 Cases 16/61 [1962] ECR 307 (fine of 8 million lire reduced to 4 million lire); 41/69 [1970] ECR 703 (fine of 210,000 u.a. reduced to 200,000 u.a.); 44/69 *ibid.*, p. 762 (fine of 65,000 u.a. reduced to 55,000 u.a.); 45/69 *ibid.*, p. 807 (fine of 190,000 u.a. reduced to 180,000 u.a.); 57/69 [1972] CMLR 650 (fine of 40,000 u.a. reduced to 30,000 u.a.); 40 to 48, 50, 54 to 56, 111, 113 and 114/73 [1975] ECR 2023, 2026 (fines reduced as follows: 800,000 u.a. to 200,000 u.a.; 400,000 u.a. to 80,000 u.a.; 600,000 u.a. to 150,000 u.a.; 500,000 u.a. to 80,000 u.a.; 700,000 u.a. to 100,000 u.a.; 1,500,000 u.a. to 600,000 u.a.; 1 million u.a. to 100,000 u.a.; 200,000 u.a. to 40,000 u.a.; 800,000 u.a. to 240,000 u.a.).

9 Case 21/64 [1965] ECR 191.

10 Case 16/61 [1962] ECR 307.

165 11 Cases 6 and 7/73 [1974] ECR 257 (fine of 200,000 u.a. reduced to 100,000 u.a.).

12 *Ibid.*

13 See the Cases mentioned at note 7 above.

14 Cases 2 to 10/63 [1963] ECR 345. In that Case the Court granted an extension of 7 months.

Section 901

166 1 Arts. 8 E.C.S.C., 155 E.E.C., 124 Euratom.

2 See §§ 801 and 802 above. Under the E.C.S.C. Treaty the Commission may impose sanctions on the Member States also, see § 906 below.

3 Arts. 88 E.C.S.C., 169 E.E.C., 141 Euratom.

167 4 Cases 20/59, 2 Val. 305 *per Curiam*, 6 Rec. 707-708 *per* A.G.; 7/61 [1962] CMLR 42-43 *per* A.G.; 2 and 3/62 [1962] ECR 430 *per Curiam*, 439 *per* A.G.; 8/70 [1970] ECR 970-971 *per* A.G.; 4/69 [1971] ECR 345-346 *per* A.G.; 7/71 [1972] CMLR 477 *per Curiam*, 458 *per* A.G.; 48/71 *ibid.*, p. 707 *per* A.G.

5 See further § 904 below.

6 See further Chapter 5 above.

7 Case 3/59, 2 Val. 374-377. For a contrary view expressed by the A.G., see Case 9/61 [1962] ECR 243. See further §§ 904, 905 below.

8 See § 906 below.

9 See § 904 below.

168 10 Cases 7/61 [1962] CMLR 48 *per* A.G.; 48/65 [1966] ECR 27 *per Curiam*, 30 *per* A.G.; *Belgian No. 7* [1972] CMLR 337-340 *per Procureur Général*. See further § 906 below.

11 See § 1103 below.

12 Cases 63/74 [1975] ECR 293-294 *per* A.G.; 104/75 [1976] ECR 643, 649 *per* A.G. See also §§ 106 above and 1101 below.

13 See § 902 below.

14 *Ibid.*

169 15 See §§ 603, 605 above and 904 below.

16 See §§ 615 above and 904 below.

17 Cases 29/68 [1969] ECR 181; 2/73 [1973] ECR 879 *per Curiam*, 887-888 *per* A.G.

18 See § 904 below.

19 Cases 26/62 [1963] ECR 13; 6/64 [1964] ECR 602 *per* A.G.; 57/65 [1966] ECR 216 *per* A.G.; 28/67 [1968] ECR 153 *per Curiam*, 160-161 *per* A.G.; 31/69 [1970] ECR 32, 34 *per Curiam*, 38-39 *per* A.G.; 9/70 *ibid.*, p. 846 *per* A.G. See also § 104 above and in general Chapter 10 below.

20 As of 31 December 1976. Joined Cases have been counted as one Case.

170 21 Cases 20/59, 2 Val. 294; 25/59 *ibid.*, p. 309.

22 See note 20 above.

23 Cases 31/69 [1970] ECR 25; 7/69 *ibid.*, p. 111; 26/69 *ibid.*, p. 565; 70/72 [1973] ECR 813 (brought under Art. 93(2) E.E.C.).

24 Cases 28/69 [1970] ECR 187; 7/71 [1972] CMLR 453.

Section 902

1 Art. 180(a) E.E.C.
2 Art. 89(1) E.C.S.C.
3 Arts. 170 E.E.C., 142 Euratom.
4 Arts. 93(2), 225(2) E.E.C.; 38(3), 82(4) Euratom.
5 Arts. 89(2) E.C.S.C., 182 E.E.C., 154 Euratom.
6 Arts. 87 E.C.S.C., 219 E.E.C., 193 Euratom.
171 7 Arts. 42 E.C.S.C., 181 E.E.C., 153 Euratom.
8 Art. 21(3) Euratom.
9 Art. 145(2) Euratom.
10 Case 6/60, 2 Val. 824-827. The action was held admissible under Art. 16 of the original E.C.S.C. Protocol on Privileges and Immunities in conjunction with Art. 43 E.C.S.C. This Protocol was repealed by Art. 28(2) of the Merger Treaty. The Protocol on the Privileges and Immunities of the European Communities of the same date, which replaced it, is subject to the ordinary jurisdictional rules of the basic Treaties in pursuance of Art. 30 of the Merger Treaty.

Section 903

1 As formulated in Art. 26 of the Vienna Convention on the Law of Treaties of 1969.
2 Arts. 86 E.C.S.C., 5 E.E.C., 192 Euratom.
3 See §§ 101, 102 above.
4 Cases 90 and 91/63 [1964] ECR 631; 52 and 55/65 [1966] ECR 172; 6 and 11/69 [1969] ECR 539-540; 38/69 [1970] ECR 56-57; 7/71 [1972] CMLR 477; 39/72 [1973] ECR 113-116; 52/75 [1976] ECR 284; 78/76 [1977] ECR 612.
172 5 Cases 78/70 [1971] CMLR 656; 2/73 [1973] ECR 878.
6 Cases 31/69 [1970] ECR 32; 77/69 *ibid.*, p. 246 *per* A.G.; 30/72 [1973] ECR 172; 79/72 *ibid.*, p. 671.
7 Cases 31/69 [1970] ECR 32; 167/73 [1974] ECR 371-373 *per Curiam*, 377 *per* A.G. See further § 106 above.
8 Case 48/71 [1972] CMLR 707-708.
9 *Ibid.*; 30/72 [1973] ECR 172; 39/72 *ibid.*, p. 116 *per Curiam*, 119-120 *per* A.G. See further § 210 above.
10 Cases 52/75 [1976] ECR 284; 10/76 *ibid.*, p. 1365.
11 See § 109 above.
12 Cases 77/69 [1970] ECR 243 *per Curiam*, 246 *per* A.G.; 8/70 *ibid.*, p. 966 *per Curiam*, 971 *per* A.G.; 51 to 54/71 [1971] ECR 1115-1116 *per Curiam*, 1122 *per* A.G.; 30/72 [1973] ECR 171-172 *per Curiam*, 179-180 *per* A.G.; 79/72 *ibid.*, p. 671; 52/75 [1976] ECR 283-285.

Section 904

173 1 Case 20/59, 6 Rec. 707-709 *per* A.G.
2 Case 9/61 [1962] ECR 237-238.
3 Case 20/59, 2 Val. 307-308.
4 Case 3/59, 2 Val. 377.
174 5 See § 207 above.
6 Cases 20/59, 2 Val. 304-306; 6 and 11/69 [1969] ECR 543. See also § 207 above.
7 Case 19/58, 2 Val. 367.
8 Case 17/57, 2 Val. 712.
9 Case 20/59, 2 Val. 304, 308 *per Curiam*, 6 Rec. 708 *per* A.G.
10 Cases 7 and 9/54, 2 Val. 139; 30/59, 29 ILR 87-88; 48/65 [1966] ECR 30 *per* A.G. See further §§ 603, 605 above.
175 11 Cases 9 and 12/60, 32 ILR 419-420. See further § 708 above.
12 Case 31/69 [1970] ECR 32-33.
13 Case 7/69 [1970] ECR 116-117.
14 Cases 7/61 [1962] CMLR 48 *per* A.G.; 45/64 [1965] ECR 864-865 *per Curiam*, 870-871 *per* A.G.; 30/72 [1973] ECR 169; 70/72 *ibid.*, p. 829.

176 15 See the Cases mentioned in the previous footnote. See further §§ 905 and 906 below.
16 Cases 48/65 [1966] ECR 27; 6 and 11/69 [1969] ECR 542.
17 Case 7/61 [1962] CMLR 54 *per Curiam*, 50 *per* A.G.
18 *Ibid.*, pp. 54-55.
19 Case 48/65 [1966] ECR 27 *per Curiam*, 30-33 *per* A.G. See further § 615 above.
20 Art. 93(2) E.E.C.; Cases 70/72 [1973] ECR 828-832 *per Curiam*, 834-836 *per* A.G.; 120/73 *ibid.*, p. 1481; 121/73 *ibid.*, p. 1505; 122/73 *ibid.*, p. 1521; 141/73 *ibid.*, p. 1538; 173/73 [1974] ECR 717; Art. 82(4) Euratom.
21 Arts. 225(2) E.E.C., 38(3) Euratom.

Section 905

177 1 See § 519 above.
2 Cases 3/59, 2 Val. 374-377; 20/59, *ibid.*, pp. 299, 305; 6 and 11/69 [1969] ECR 543-544.
3 Cases 45/64 [1965] ECR 864-865; 30/72 [1973] ECR 169.
4 Case 167/73 [1974] ECR 368-369. However, in Case 26/69 [1970] ECR 575 the Court deemed it necessary to examine if the Commission still had a sufficient legal interest in bringing the action in the particular circumstances of the case.
178 5 Cases 7/61 [1962] CMLR 53-54 *per Curiam*, 49 *per* A.G.; 7/69 [1970] ECR 119-120 *per* A.G.; 26/69 *ibid.*, pp. 575-576 *per Curiam*, 581 *per* A.G.; 30//72 [1973] ECR 172.
6 Case 39/72 [1973] ECR 112.
7 Case 167/73 [1974] ECR 368-373.
8 Case 8/70 [1970] ECR 971 *per* A.G. For a somewhat different opinion of the same A.G., see Cases 2 and 3/62 [1962] ECR 439.
9 Cases 38/69 [1970] ECR 57; 8/70 *ibid.*, p. 966. See also the Cases mentioned at note 12 in § 903 above.
10 E.g. application to the Commission for authorisation to take protective measures during the transitional period under Art. 226 E.E.C., or even thereafter with respect to deflection of trade under Art. 115 E.E.C.
11 Cases 7/61 [1962] CMLR 55; 2 and 3/62 [1962] ECR 430.
12 *Ibid.*, Case 7/71 [1972] CMLR 474.
13 See § 502 above.
179 14 Cases 6 and 11/69]1969] ECR 539-541 *per Curiam*, 550 *per* A.G.; 70/72 [1973] ECR 835 *per* A.G.
15 See further § 519 above.
16 This seems to follow also from the A.G.'s opinions in the Cases mentioned at note 14 above.
17 Case 26/69 [1970] ECR 578 (the A.G. arrived at the opposite conclusion, *ibid.*, pp. 587-588).
18 Cases 7/68 [1968] ECR 428; 7/71 [1972] CMLR 473 *per Curiam*, 458 *per* A.G.
19 Cases 26/69 [1970] ECR 575; 8/70 *ibid.*, p. 971 *per* A.G.
20 A negative answer seems to follow from the A.G.'s opinion in Case 7/71 [1972] CMLR 458.

Section 906

180 1 Case 20/59, 2 Val. 304-305.
2 *Ibid.*, p. 300.
2a Art. 88(3), (4) and (5) E.C.S.C.
181 3 Arts. 171 E.E.C., 143 Euratom. Cases 6/60, 2 Val. 823-824; 7/69 [1970] ECR 117. See in general the submissions of the *Procureur Général* in *Belgian No. 7* [1972] CMLR 366 *et seq*. Regarding the filling of this gap in the Treaties, see the suggestions of the Court of Justice in 'Reports on European Union', *Supplement 9/75 — Bull. EC*, p. 17.
4 Case 70/72 [1973] ECR 828-829.
5 Case 6/60, 2 Val. 823-824.
6 Case 70/72 [1973] ECR 828-829.
182 7 Case 39/72 [1973] ECR 112.

8 Cases 77/69 [1970] ECR 247 *per* A.G.; 48/71 [1972] CMLR 707-708. See further §§ 104, 106 above.
9 See § 904 above.
10 Cases 7/61 [1962] CMLR 49 *per* A.G.; 48/71 [1972] CMLR 707-708 *per Curiam*, 702 *et seq.*, 707 *per* A.G.

Section 1001

185 1 See § 104 above.
2 Cases 1/64 [1964] ECR 420 *per* A.G.; 28/67 [1968] ECR 153-154 *per Curiam*, 160 *per* A.G. See § 302 above.
3 See § 401 above.
4 *German No. 1* [1963] CMLR 254.
5 See §§ 1002, 1003, 1004 below.
6 For a discussion of Section 2, see §§ 105 and 107 above.

Section 1002

186 1 See § 109 above.
2 For the directly applicable provisions of the E.E.C. Treaty, see Annex I to this book.
3 Case 87/75 [1976] ECR 142 *per Curiam*, 146 *et seq. per* A.G.
4 See §§ 104 and 106 above.
5 See in general Chapter 11 below.
187 6 Cases 6/64 [1964] ECR 593; 20/64 [1965] ECR 35-36; 13/68 [1968] ECR 462-463 *per Curiam*, 470 *per* A.G.; 93/71 [1973] CMLR 352-354; 167/73 [1974] ECR 371; 2/74 *ibid.*, p. 659 *per* A.G.; 36/75 [1975] ECR 1229 *et seq. per Curiam*, 1241 *per* A.G.; 43/75 [1976] ECR 476; 48/75 *ibid.*, pp. 515-517; 8/77 [1977] ECR 1506.
7 Cases 39/72 [1973] ECR 112; 60/75 [1976] ECR 57 *per Curiam*, 62 *per* A.G.
8 Cases 28/67 [1968] ECR 154; 34/67 *ibid.*, p. 251; 13/68 *ibid.*, pp. 462-463 *per Curiam*, 470 *per* A.G.; 84/71 [1972] CMLR 912-913 *per* A.G.; 120/73 [1973] ECR 1483; 121/73 *ibid.*, p. 1507; 122/73 *ibid.*, p. 1523; 141/73 *ibid.*, p. 1540; 33/76 [1976] ECR 1997-1998 *per Curiam*, 2002 *et seq. per* A.G.; 45/76 *ibid.*, p. 2053.
9 Case 60/75 [1976] ECR 62.
10 In accordance with Arts. 100 to 102 and 235 E.E.C. See Cases 33/76 [1976] ECR 1998. 45/76 *ibid.*, p. 2053.
188 11 See further § 901 above and in particular the Cases cited at note 19 in that Section. See also § 1101 below. *Cf. German No. 18* [1967] CMLR 324; *Italian No. 10* [1968] CMLR 276-277; for a contrary view, see *German No. 22* [1967] CMLR 336 *et seq.*
12 For non-directly applicable provisions of the E.E.C. Treaty, see Annexe II to this book.
13 See § 217 above.
14 Cases 9/73[1973] ECR 1160-1161; 10/73 *ibid.*, p. 1194; 74/76 [1977] ECR 574-575; 78/76 *ibid.*, p. 609. See further § 901 above and the Cases mentioned at note 17 in that Section.
15 This seems to be the position also in the United Kingdom, see *Processed Vegetable Growers Association* v. *Commissioners of Customs and Excise* [1974] 1 CMLR 127-128; and also in French law, see *French No. 15* [1972] CMLR 903.
189 16 *Belgian No. 2* quoted in [1972] CMLR 360-361.
17 See Chapter 11 below.
18 *Cf.* e.g. Cases 9/70 [1970] ECR 825; 20/70 *ibid.*, p. 861; 23/70 *ibid.*, p. 881; 33/70 *ibid.*, p. 1213; 41/74 [1974] ECR 1337; 51/76 [1977] ECR 126-127; 38/77 (not yet reported), where it was possible to challenge the compatibility of national laws and administrative practices with directives which are *ex hypothesi* not directly applicable. In a series of Cases beginning with Case 2/74 [1974] ECR 631 it was possible to establish that certain provisions of the E.E.C. Treaty, *prima facie* non-directly applicable, created enforceable rights in individuals. See § 211 above.
19 Cases 32/74 [1974] ECR 1206; 67/74 [1975] ECR 305-306; 111/75 [1976] ECR 665 *per Curiam*, 670 *per* A.G.; 51/76 [1977] ECR 126-127; 78/76 *ibid.*, p. 610; *German No. 55* [1974] 1 CMLR 108-109; *German No. 61* [1975] 1 CMLR 127.
20 Art. 12 E.E.C., *cf.* e.g. Cases 26/62 [1963] ECR 1; 28 to 30/62 *ibid.*, p. 31; 27/74 [1974] ECR 1037; *Belgian No. 5* [1970] CMLR 219; *Belgian No. 7* [1972] CMLR 330. Art.

13(2) E.E.C., *cf.* e.g. Cases 33/70 [1970] ECR 1213; 94/74 [1975] ECR 699; 33/76 [1976] ECR 1989; *Italian No. 19* [1973] CMLR 152. Art. 16 E.E.C., *cf.* e.g. Cases 18/71 [1972] CMLR 4; 45/76 [1976] ECR 2043.

21 Arts. 30 *et seq.* E.E.C., *cf.* e.g. Cases 13/68 [1968] ECR 453; 4/75 [1975] ECR 843; *Italian No. 1* [1963] CMLR 136, 139; *Italian No. 13* [1970] CMLR 314.

22 Art. 37 E.E.C., *cf.* e.g. Cases 6/64 [1964] ECR 585; 13/70 [1970] ECR 1089; 45/75 [1976] ECR 181; 91/75 *ibid.*, p. 217; *German No. 43* [1971] CMLR 687.

23 Art. 95 E.E.C., *cf.* e.g. Cases 57/65 [1966] ECR 205; 28/67 [1968] ECR 143; 45/75 [1976] ECR 181; 127/75 *ibid.*, p. 1079; *German No. 29* [1969] CMLR 300; *German No. 30*, *ibid.*, p. 261; *German No. 32*, *ibid.*, p. 221.

24 *Cf.* e.g. Cases 28/75 [1975] ECR 989; 35/75 *ibid.*, p. 1205; 37/75 *ibid.*, p. 1339, etc.

25 *Cf.* e.g. Cases 82/71 [1972] CMLR 723 and 59/75 [1976] ECR 91, both invoking Art. 37 E.E.C.; Cases 8/74 [1974] ECR 837, 104/75 [1976] ECR 613 and 3, 4 and 6/76 *ibid.*, p. 1279, all invoking Arts. 30 *et seq.* E.E.C.; Case 155/73 [1974] ECR 409, invoking Arts. 2, 3(f), 5, 37, 86 and 90 E.E.C.; Cases 131/73 [1973] ECR 1555, invoking certain regulations, etc.; *Dutch No. 12* [1977] 1 CMLR 330.

26 *Cf.* e.g. Cases 5/72 [1973] CMLR 322; 11/73 [1973] ECR 919; 12/73 *ibid.*, p. 963 etc.

27 *Cf.* e.g. Cases 2/73 [1973] ECR 865; 51/74 [1975] ECR 79.

28 *Cf.* e.g. Cases 34/74 [1974] ECR 1217; 93/74 [1975] ECR 661 etc.

29 *Cf.* e.g. Case 34/70 [1970] ECR 1233.

30 *Cf.* e.g. Cases 88 to 90/75 [1976] ECR 323.

190 31 *Cf.* e.g. Cases 4/68 [1968] ECR 377; 64/74 [1975] ECR 261 etc.

32 *Cf.* e.g. Cases 32/72 [1973] CMLR 268; 93/71 *ibid.*, p, 343; 27/72 *ibid.*, p. 612 etc.

33 *Cf.* e.g. Case 60/75 [1976] ECR 45.

34 *Cf.* e.g. Cases 40/69 [1970] ECR 69; 72/69 *ibid.*, p. 427; 28/70 *ibid.*, p. 1021 etc.

35 *Cf.* e.g. Cases 190/73 [1974] ECR 1123; 31/74 [1975] ECR 47; 10 to 14/75 *ibid.*, p. 1053; 65/75 [1976] ECR 291, etc.

36 Arts. 48 *et seq.* E.E.C., *cf.* e.g. Cases 9/74 [1974] ECR 773; 41/74 *ibid.*, p. 1337; 68/74 [1975] ECR 109; 67/74 *ibid.*, p. 297; 36/75 *ibid.*, p. 1219.

37 Arts. 52 *et seq.* E.E.C., *cf.* e.g. Case 2/74 [1974] ECR 631.

38 Arts. 59 *et seq.* E.E.C., *cf.* e.g. Cases 33/74 [1974] ECR 1299; 39/75 [1975] ECR 1547.

39 *Cf.* e.g. Case 32/75 [1975] ECR 1085.

40 *Cf.* especially Case 1/72 [1973] CMLR 408. *Cf.* also Cases 75/63 [1964] ECR 177; 61/65 [1966] ECR 261; 20/75 [1975] ECR 891; 17/76 [1976] ECR 1429, etc.

41 *Cf.* e.g. Cases 48/75 [1976] ECR 497; 118/75 *ibid.*, p. 1185; 8/77 [1977] ECR 1506, etc.

42 Arts. 6, 8 and 9 of Directive 64/221, O. J. English Special Edition, 1963-1964 p. 117; Cases 36/75 [1975] ECR 1232-1233; 48/75 [1976] ECR 515-517.

43 Arts. 6 E.C.S.C., 211 E.E.C., 185 Euratom.

191 44 Arts. 40(3) E.C.S.C., 183 E.E.C., 155 Euratom.

45 Arts. 42 E.C.S.C., 181 E.E.C., 153 Euratom.

46 Arts. 215(1) E.E.C., 188(1) Euratom; Cases 9/69 [1969] ECR 339 *per* A.G.; 23/76 [1976] ECR 1818, 1821 *per Curiam*, 1825 *per* A.G.

47 On this, see § 702 above.

48 Art. 1 of the Protocol on the Privileges and Immunities of the European Communities, Case 4/62 [1962] ECR 42-43 (Order).

49 See § 1104 below.

50 See further §§ 501, 701, 702 above and 1101 below. Cases 15/71 [1972] CMLR 59; 96/71 [1973] CMLR 383; 43/72 [1973] ECR 1069 *per Curiam*, 1082-1083 *per* A.G.; 46/75 [1976] ECR 79-80; 26/74 *ibid.*, pp. 686-687.

51 *Cf.* e.g. Cases 16/65 [1965] ECR 877; 17/67 [1967] ECR 441; 73/69 [1970] ECR 467; 23/75 [1975] ECR 1279 etc.

52 *Cf.* e.g. Cases 181/73 [1974] ECR 449; 95/75 [1976] ECR 361.

53 *Cf.* e.g. Cases 78/74 [1975] ECR 421; 7/76 [1976] ECR 1213 etc.

54 *Cf.* e.g. Cases 29/69 [1969] ECR 419; 40/72 [1973] ECR 125; 11/74 [1974] ECR 877; 24/75 [1975] ECR 1149; 19/76 [1976] ECR 1243.

192 55 Case 127/73 [1974] ECR 62-63.

56 Arts. 85, 86 E.E.C.

57 *Cf.* e.g. Cases 56/65 [1966] ECR 235; 23/67 [1967] ECR 407; 48/72 [1973] ECR 77; 25/75 [1975] ECR 1103; 63/75 [1976] ECR 111, etc.
58 *Cf.* e.g. Cases 1/70 [1970] ECR 515; 22/71 [1972] CMLR 81; 8/74 [1974] ECR 837, etc.
59 Under Art. 85(2) E.E.C.
60 *Cf.* e.g. Cases 24/67 [1968] ECR 55; 15/74 [1974] ECR 1147; 16/74 *ibid.*, p. 1183 etc.
61 *Cf.* e.g. Cases 40/70 [1971] CMLR 260; 192/73 [1974] ECR 731; 51/75 [1976] ECR 811; 86/75 *ibid.*, p. 871; 96/75 *ibid.*, p. 913, etc.
62 *Cf.* e.g. Cases 78/70 [1971] CMLR 631; 127/73 [1974] ECR 51 and 313, etc.
63 Especially Arts. 30 *et seq.* E.E.C., *cf.* e.g. Cases 15/74 [1974] ECR 1147; 16/74 *ibid.*, p. 1183; 51/75 [1976] ECR 811; 86/75 *ibid.*, p. 871; 96/75 *ibid.*, p. 913; 119/75 *ibid.*, p. 1039, etc.
64 Arts. 7, 119 E.E.C. See further § 304 above.
65 *Cf.* e.g. Cases 44/72 [1973] CMLR 501; 152/73 [1974] ECR 153; 36/74 *ibid.*, p. 1405; 43/75 [1976] ECR 455; 13/76 *ibid.* p. 1333, etc.
66 *Cf.* e.g. Cases 20/64 [1965] ECR 29; 54/72 [1973] ECR 193; 77/72 *ibid.*, p. 611, etc.
67 Case 12/76 [1976] ECR 1484. See § 204 above.

Section 1003

1 *Italian No. 12* [1970] CMLR 11 *et seq.*
2 Arts. 44 E.C.S.C., 187 E.E.C., 159 Euratom.
3 Arts. 18(3), 164 Euratom.
4 Arts. 83(2), 164 Euratom.
5 Art. 92 E.C.S.C.
6 Art. 192 E.E.C.
7 Art. 92 E.C.S.C.
8 Arts. 192 E.E.C., 164 Euratom.
9 Case 108/63 [1965] ECR 10.
10 Art. 92 E.C.S.C. does not specifically mention civil procedure but refers to 'the legal procedure in force in each State' generally.
193 10a Case 4/73 (Enforcement) [1977] ECR 3-4 (Order).
11 Case 108/63 [1965] ECR 10; *Italian No. 2* [1964] CMLR 186 *et seq.*
12 Art. 89 R.P.; *Italian No. 4* [1965] CMLR 16; *Italian No. 5* [1966] CMLR 25, 27; *Italian No. 6* [1965] CMLR 5, 9; *Italian No. 7, ibid.*, p. 296; *Italian No. 9* [1967] CMLR 172.
13 Art. 48(4) R.P.
14 Art. 22(2) I.R.
15 European Communities (Enforcement of Community Judgments) Order 1972, S.I. 1972 No. 1590, Art. 3.
16 *Ibid.*
17 Ibid., Art. 4.
194 18 *Ibid.*, Art. 5.
19 Rules of the Supreme Court (Amendment No. 3) 1972, S.I. 1972 No. 1898, Rule 8.
20 Act of Sederunt (Rules of Court Amendment No. 6) 1972, S.I. 1972 No. 1982.

Section 1004

1 Cases 12/70 [1970] ECR 911 *et seq.*; 39/70 [1971] CMLR 293 *per Curiam*, 284-286 *per* A.G.; 178 to 180/73 [1974] ECR 400; 10 to 14/75 [1975] ECR 1081-1082 *per* A.G.; 50/76 [1977] ECR 150; *French No. 16* [1974] 1 CMLR 76 *et seq.*; *German No. 57 ibid.*, pp. 264 *et seq.*
2 O.J. Vol. 19 C 222, 22.9.76.
3 *Ibid.*
4 Arts. 28 E.C.S.C. Statute, 27 E.E.C. Statute, 28 Euratom Statute, Arts. 6-7 S.R.P.
5 Section 11(1) of the European Communities Act 1972.
195 6 Art. 194(1) Euratom.
7 Section 11(2) of the European Communities Act 1972.

Section 1101

196 1 Cases 13/61 [1962] ECR 61, 71 *per* A.G.; 28 to 30/62 [1963] ECR 38 *per Curiam*, 43 *per* A.G.; 44/65 [1965] ECR 971; 62/72 [1973] ECR 275.

197 2 Cases 26/62 [1963] ECR 12; 6/64 [1964] ECR 614 (Order); 61/65 [1966] ECR 281 *per* A.G.; 28/67 [1968] ECR 154; 21 to 24/72 [1975] 2 CMLR 6 *per* A.G.; 166/73 [1974] ECR 38; 107/76 [1977] ECR 973; *German No. 23* [1968] CMLR 3.

3 See §§ 104, 106 above.

198 4 Cases 13/61 [1962] ECR 50-51 *per Curiam*, 56, 69 *per* A.G.; 28 to 30/62 [1963] ECR 41-43 *per* A.G.; 20/64 [1965] ECR 48 *per* A.G.; 16/65 *ibid.*, p. 886; 127/73 [1974] ECR 69-70 *per* A.G. See further § 1102 below.

5 See §§ 901, 902 above.

6 See further §§ 106, 1002 above and 1103 below. *Cf.* also Case 107/76 [1977] ECR 980 *per* A.G.

7 See further § 1002 above.

8 See § 508 above.

9 See § 519 above.

199 10 Cases 73 and 74/63 [1964] ECR 20, 22 *per* A.G.; 38/64 [1965] ECR 213 *per* A.G. See further § 1104 below.

11 *Cf.* e.g. the following pairs of Cases, each pair involving the same infringement by a Member State: Cases 33/70 [1970] ECR 1213 (under Art. 177) and 8/70 *ibid.*, p. 961 (under Art. 169); Cases 18/71 [1972] CMLR 4 (under Art. 177) and 7/68 [1968] ECR 423 (under Art. 169); Cases 93/71 [1973] CMLR 343 (under Art. 177) and 39/72 [1973] ECR 101 (under Art. 169).

12 See further § 901 above.

13 Cases 2/73 [1973] ECR 882 *et seq. per* A.G., esp. at 887-888; 63/74 [1975] ECR 293-294 *per* A.G.; 104/75 [1976] ECR 643, 649 *per* A.G.; 111/75 *ibid.*, p. 670 *per* A.G. See further §§ 901 above and 1103 below.

14 Case 51/74 [1975] ECR 95-96.

15 *Cf.* e.g. Cases 34/74 [1974] ECR 1217 (under Art. 177 E.E.C.) and 26/74 [1976] ECR 677 (under Arts. 178, 215(2) E.E.C.).

16 *Cf.* e.g. Cases 40/72 [1973] ECR 125 (under Art. 177 E.E.C.) and 59/72 *ibid.*, p. 791 (under Arts. 178, 215(2) E.E.C.); 114/76, 116/76, 119 and 120/76 [1977] ECR 1211, 1247, 1269 (under Art. 177 E.E.C.) and 83 and 94/76, 4 and 15/77 (not yet reported) (under Arts. 178, 215(2) E.E.C.).

17 See further §§ 514, 521, 707 above and 1104, 1110 below.

200 18 Cases 96/71 [1973] CMLR 393; 46/75 [1976] ECR 79-80. See further §§ 501 and 701 above and the Cases mentioned at note 22 in § 501 and at notes 17-20 in § 701.

19 As of 31 December 1976. Staff cases are not included.

20 *10th Gen. Rep. EC (1976)* p. 337.

Section 1102

201 1 See §§ 1103 and 1104 below. *Cf.* also Case 6/64 [1964] ECR 601 *per* A.G.

2 Case 13/61 [1962] ECR 50. For the concept of 'court or tribunal', see § 1105 below.

3 Arts. 20 E.E.C. Statute, 21 Euratom Statute. See further § 412(g) above.

4 Cases 127/73 [1974] ECR 61-62; 146/73 *ibid.*, p. 147. See further § 1108 below.

5 Cases 26/62 [1963] ECR 11 *per Curiam*, 19 *per* A.G.; 28 to 30/62 *ibid.*, p. 41 *per* A.G.; 6/64 [1964] ECR 593 *per Curiam*, 602 *per* A.G.; 20/64 [1965] ECR 34; 56/65 [1966] ECR 247-248; 28/68 [1969] ECR 134; 78/70 [1971] CMLR 652 *per* A.G.; 155/73 [1974] ECR 426; 111/75 [1976] ECR 665; 78/76 [1977] ECR 610; 52/76 *ibid.*, p. 180.

6 Case 19/68 [1968] ECR 478-479.

7 Case 127/73 [1974] ECR 61-63. In that Case the jurisdiction of the national court to refer was challenged on the basis of Art. 9(3) of Regulation 17 under which the national court should have stayed the proceedings from the moment the Commission had opened a procedure under Art. 3 of the same Regulation.

8 Cases 19/68 [1968] ECR 478-479; 23/75 [1975] ECR 1313 *per* A.G.

9 Case 13/61 [1962] ECR 50. See further § 1108 below.

10 Case 43/71 [1973] CMLR 69 *per Curiam*, 65 *per* A.G.

202 11 Cases 13/68 [1968] ECR 459-460; 10/69 [1969] ECR 315.

12 *Ibid.*; Cases 26/62 [1963] ECR 19 *per* A.G.; 6/64 [1964] ECR 602 *per* A.G.; 20/64 [1965] ECR 39 *per* A.G.

13 Cases 54/72 [1973] ECR 205 *per Curiam*. 211-212 *per* A.G.; 127/73 [1974] ECR 318; 23/75 [1975] ECR 1306; 17/76 [1976] ECR 1453; 52/76 [1977] ECR 182; 62/76 *ibid.*, p. 218.
14 Case 181/73 [1974] ECR 464.
15 Case 31/74 [1975] ECR 65.
16 Case 51/74 [1975] ECR 96.
17 Case 130/73 [1973] ECR 1337-1338 *per* A.G.
18 Arts. 20 E.E.C. Statute, 21 Euratom Statute. See further § 412(g) above.
19 Cases 101/63 [1964] ECR 200; 1/71 [1971] CMLR 429 *per Curiam*, 425 *per* A.G., 10/71 [1971] ECR 729 *per Curiam*, 734, 737 *per* A.G.
20 See § 406 above.
21 Cases 73 and 74/63 [1964] ECR 18-19 *per* A.G.; 23/68 [1969] ECR 51 *per Curiam*, 57-58 *per* A.G.; 51/75 [1976] ECR 854 *per* A.G.; 119/75 *ibid.*, p. 1060. See further § 1109 below.

Section 1103

1 See § 1102 above.
2 Art. 177 E.E.C.
3 Art. 150 Euratom.
4 Art. 30 Merger Treaty.
5 Since the Budgetary Treaty merely amends the basic Treaties, without containing any new or 'independent' provisions. See § 204 above.
6 Art. 1(3) of the Treaty of Accession.
7 See § 203 above. Case 5/68 [1968] ECR 404-405 *per* A.G.
8 Thus in Cases 21 to 24/72 [1975] 2 CMLR 20 the interpretation of Art. 177(1)(b) was requested under Art. 177(1)(a). In Cases 166/73 [1974] ECR 33 and 146/73 *ibid.*, p. 139 Art. 177(2) was interpreted. *Cf.* also Case 61/65 [1966] ECR 280 *per* A.G.
203 9 Case 101/63 [1964] ECR 199-200. That Case concerned the interpretation of an identical Article (Art. 9) in the three separate Protocols on the Privileges and Immunities of the E.C.S.C., E.E.C. and Euratom prior to their replacement by a single Protocol.
10 Protocols of 3 June 1971. See further § 204 above.
11 Arts. 3 and 5, respectively, of the Protocols; Cases 12/76 [1976] ECR 1483-1484; 14/76 *ibid.*, p. 1515 *per* A.G.; 29/76 *ibid.*, p. 1550. See also notes 2 and 14 in § 1105 and notes 1 and 11 in § 1106 below.
12 Cases 40/72 [1973] ECR 125; 181/73 [1974] ECR 459-460, in both Cases the Court interpreted the Association Agreement of 1961 between the E.E.C. and Greece; Case 87/75 [1976] ECR 136 *et seq.* where the Court interpreted the two Yaoundé Association Conventions of 1963 and 1969. See also § 205 above.
13 Case 181/73 [1974] ECR 459-460. Contrary view was expressed by the A.G., *ibid.*, p. 473, who thought that the Court could only interpret such an agreement where its interpretation is relevant to the interpretation or the assessment of the validity of an act of the institutions. The Court confirmed its own view in Opinion 1/76 [1977] ECR 760.
14 Case 87/75 [1976] ECR 147 *per* A.G.
15 Case 113/75 [1976] ECR 992-993 *per Curiam*, 996-997 *per* A.G.
16 Cases 32/74 [1974] ECR 1205 *et seq. per Curiam*, 1213 *per* A.G.; 111/75 [1976] ECR 665 *per Curiam*, 670 *per* A.G.; 78/76 [1977] ECR 610 (where the Court accepted a reference for the interpretation of a non-directly applicable Treaty provision).
17 Case 24/66 bis. [1973] ECR 1606 *per* A.G. See further § 412(f) above.
18 Case 62/72 [1973] ECR 274. See further § 412(g) above.
19 Case 9/73 [1973] ECR 1161.
20 See further § 217 above.
204 21 Cases 28/68 [1969] ECR 134; 130/73 [1973] ECR 1333-1334. See also § 704 above.
22 Cases 75/63 [1964] ECR 186; 24/64 *ibid.*, p. 652; 33/65 [1965] ECR 904; 78/70 [1971] CMLR 656 *per Curiam*, 645 *per* A.G.; 9/74 [1974] ECR 778 *per Curiam*, 782 *per* A.G.; 52/76 [1977] ECR 182.

23 Cases 26/62 [1963] ECR 14-15 *per Curiam*, 19 *per* A.G.; 33/70 [1970] ECR 1226 *per* A.G.; 54/72 [1973] ECR 205; 65/75 [1976] ECR 304; 88 to 90/75 *ibid.*, p. 335; 111/75 *ibid.*, p. 669 *per* A.G.; 32/76 *ibid.*, p. 1530.

24 Cases 9/70 [1970] ECR 840; 20/70 *ibid.*, p. 876; 23/70 *ibid.*, p. 895; 29/72 [1973] CMLR 488 *per* A.G.; 77/72 [1973] ECR 622; 27/74 [1974] ECR 1046.

25 Cases 19/68 [1968] ECR 478; 23/68 [1969] ECR 50; 1/72 [1973] CMLR 407; 76/72 [1973] ECR 463; 24/74 [1974] ECR 1006-1007; 7/75 [1975] ECR 688-689; 32/75 *ibid.*, pp. 1093-1094; 93/75 *ibid.*, p. 2151.

26 Cases 26/62 [1963] ECR 11 *per Curiam*, 19 *per* A.G.; 13/68 [1968] ECR 462 *per Curiam*, 469-470 *per* A.G.

27 Cases 34/73 [1973] ECR 991; 13/76 [1976] ECR 1346 *per* A.G.

28 Cases 6/64 [1964] ECR 593-594 *per Curiam*, 601 *et seq. per* A.G.; 111/75 [1976] ECR 665 *per Curiam*, 669 *per* A.G.

29 Cases 51/74 [1975] ECR 92; 10 to 14/75 *ibid.*, p. 1082 *per* A.G.; 51/75 [1976] ECR 854 *per* A.G. See also the Cases mentioned at note 36 below.

205 30 Case 56/65 [1966] ECR 254.

31 Case 51/75 [1976] ECR 854-855 *per* A.G.; 52/76 [1977] ECR 180

32 Cases 98 and 99/75 [1976] ECR 256 *per* A.G.

33 Case 13/61 [1962] ECR 53.

34 Case 77/72 [1973] ECR 622; 52/76 [1977] ECR 182.

35 See §§ 901 and 1101 above.

36 Cases 13/61 [1962] ECR 50 *per Curiam*, 63 *per* A.G.; 26/62 [1963] ECR 14-15; 28 to 30/62 *ibid.*, p. 38; 100/63 [1964] ECR 572; 6/64 *ibid.*, pp. 592-593, 598; 20/64 [1965] ECR 34; 56/65 [1966] ECR 247-248; 61/65 *ibid.*, p. 274; 28/67 [1968] ECR 157; 28/68 [1969] ECR 134; 29/68 *ibid.*, p. 180; 5/69 *ibid.*, pp. 301-302; 28/70 [1970] ECR 1025 *per Curiam*, 1029 *per* A.G.; 30/70 *ibid.*, p. 1205; 10/71 [1971] ECR 729 *per Curiam*, 733-734 *per* A.G.; 82/71 [1972] CMLR 740 *per Curiam*, 726 *per* A.G.; 11/73 [1973] ECR 925; 45/75 [1976] ECR 194; 119/75 *ibid.*, p. 1073 *per* A.G.; *French No. 2* [1963] CMLR 246; *Italian No. 16* [1975] 1 CMLR 422; *EMI Records Ltd.* v. *CBS United Kingdom Ltd. ibid.*, p. 296. See also the Cases mentioned at notes 22, 24 and 25 above.

37 Cases 36/71 [1972] CMLR 801 *per Curiam*, 791 *per* A.G.; 183/73 [1974] ECR 485-486. But see the Cases mentioned at note 49 below.

38 Cases 65/75 [1976] ECR 307-308; 88 to 90/75 *ibid.*, pp. 338-339. But see the Cases mentioned at note 50 below.

39 Case 158/73 [1974] ECR 111.

40 Case 3/74 [1974] ECR 599.

41 Case 184/73 [1974] ECR 524.

42 Cases 36/74 [1976] ECR 1418, 1420; 13/76 [1976] ECR 1340.

43 Cases 127/73 [1974] ECR 317-318; 155/73 *ibid.*, p. 430.

44 Case 119/75 [1976] ECR 1060.

45 Case 94/74 [1975] ECR 711.

206 46 See the Cases mentioned at notes 22, 24, 25 and 36 above.

47 Cases 56/65 [1966] ECR 254 *per* A.G.; 29/72 [1973] CMLR 488-489 *per* A.G.

48 Cases 28/70 [1970] ECR 1025 *per Curiam*, 1029 *per* A.G.; 12/71 [1971] ECR 750 *per Curiam*, 757 *per* A.G.; 13/71 *ibid.*, p. 774; 14/71 *ibid.*, p. 786; 38/72 [1972] ECR 1341 *per* A.G.; 49/73 [1973] ECR 1208 *per* A.G.

49 Cases 72/69 [1970] ECR 433 *et seq. per Curiam*, 445-446 *per* A.G.; 74/69 *ibid.*, pp. 458 *et seq.*

50 Cases 51/74 [1975] ECR 94; 104/75 [1976] ECR 633 *et seq. per Curiam*, 643 *per* A.G.; 118/75 *ibid.*, pp. 1195 *et seq.*, esp. 1199; 3, 4 and 6/76 *ibid.*, pp. 1311-1313; 13/76 *ibid.*, p. 1341.

207 51 Cases 6/64 [1964] ECR 593; 33/65 [1965] ECR 904; 56/65 [1966] ECR 248; 127/73 [1974] ECR 321-322 *per* A.G.

52 Case 77/72 [1973] ECR 622.

53 Case 94/74 [1975] ECR 708 *et seq. per Curiam*, 715-716 *per* A.G., where the same questions were again submitted as in the Case mentioned in the preceding footnote.

54 See § 1102 above, notes 19 and 21.
55 Cases 101/63 [1964] ECR 200; 1/71 [1971] CMLR 429 *per Curiam*, 425 *per* A.G.; 10/71 [1971] ECR 729 *per Curiam*, 734, 737 *per* A.G.; 51/75 [1976] ECR 854 *per* A.G.
56 Cases 78/70 [1971] CMLR 652-653 *per* A.G.; 27/74 [1974] ECR 1052 *per* A.G.
57 Case 34/74 [1974] ECR 1238 *per* A.G.; 62/76 [1977] ECR 217.

Section 1104

208 1 See §§ 102, 104 above and 1105 below (p. 214). This is expressly so provided under the E.C.S.C. Treaty only, see Art. 41. *Cf.* also the Suggestions of the Court of Justice on European Union, in 'Reports on European Union', *Supplement 9/75 - Bull EC*, p. 21.
2 Case 16/65 [1965] ECR 886-887.
3 See § 519 above.
4 Cases 73 and 74/63 [1964] ECR 11 *et seq. per Curiam* (by implication), 19-20 *per* A.G.; 16/65 [1965] ECR 886-887 *per Curiam*, 893 *per* A.G. *Cf.* also Case 40/72 [1973] ECR 142.
5 See §§ 101, 103 above. As to Community Treaties with third States, see § 507 above.
6 Cases 9/70 [1970] ECR 837; 20/70 *ibid.*, p. 873; 23/70 *ibid.*, p. 892; 41/74 [1974] ECR 1348.
7 Cases 113/75 [1976] ECR 996-997 *per* A.G.
8 See § 508 above.
9 Cases 73 and 74/63 [1964] ECR 11 *et seq. per Curiam* (by implication), 20-22 *per* A.G.; 16/65 [1965] ECR 886-887; 181/73 [1974] ECR 459 *et seq.* where the plaintiff in the main action was able in effect to contest the legality of a regulation which it could not previously challenge in a direct action for annulment, see Case 96/71 [1973] CMLR 383. *Cf.* also Case 7/76 [1976] ECR 1223 *et seq. per Curiam*, 1230 *per* A.G., where the validity of a regulation was challenged which previously could not be contested in an action for damages, see Case 46/75 [1976] ECR 79-80. *Cf.* e.g. also Case 19/76 [1976] ECR 1249 *et seq.*
10 Case 16/65 [1965] ECR 899 *per* A.G.
11 See § 217 above.
209 12 See § 514 above.
13 Cases 21 to 24/72 [1975] 2 CMLR 20.
14 *Ibid.*, pp. 20-21; Case 9/73 [1973] ECR 1157. See further § 222 above.
15 Cases 29/69 [1969] ECR 424-425 *per Curiam*, 428 *per* A.G.; 11/70 [1970] ECR 1134; 25/70 *ibid.*, p. 1174. See further § 303 above.
16 Cases 73/69 [1970] ECR 473-475; 11/70 *ibid.*, p. 1134; 25/70 *ibid.*, p. 1174; 5/73 [1973] ECR 1104 *et seq.*; 99 and 100/76 [1977] ECR 872; 114/76 *ibid.*, pp. 1220-1221 *per Curiam*, 1230 *et seq. per* A.G.; 116/76 *ibid.*, pp. 1264-1266; 119 and 120/76 *ibid.*, pp. 1286-1287. See further § 221 above.
17 Case 73/69 [1970] ECR 473-475. See further § 221 above.
18 Case 5/73 [1973] ECR 1104 *et seq. Cf.* e.g. also Cases 19/76 [1976] ECR 1249 *et seq.*; 24/75 [1975] ECR 1160-1161; 62/76 [1977] ECR 218; 114/76, 116/76 *ibid.*, pp. 1220-1221 *per Curiam*, 1230 *et seq. per* A.G.; 116/76 *ibid.*, pp. 1264-1266; 119 and 120/76 *ibid.*, pp. 1286-1287.
19 Cases 5/73 [1973] ECR 1104 *et seq.*; 78/74 [1975] ECR 429-432; 5/75 *ibid.*, pp. 768-770; 95/75 [1976] ECR 366-368 *per Curiam*, 373 *per* A.G. *Cf.* also Cases 7/76 [1976] ECR 1223 *et seq.* (first question).
20 Case 37/75 [1975] ECR 1345-1347 *per Curiam*, 1349 *per* A.G.
21 Case 23/75 [1975] ECR 1299 *et seq.*
22 Case 5/73 [1973] ECR 1104 *et seq.*
23 *Ibid.*
24 Cases 78/74 [1975] ECR 429-432; 5/75 *ibid.*, pp. 768-770.
25 Cases 29/69 [1969] ECR 428 *per* A.G.; 11/70 [1970] ECR 1134. See further § 102 above.
26 See §§ 515-518 above.
27 Case 78/74 [1975] ECR 438 *per* A.G.
28 Cases 57/72 [1973] ECR 340-341; 78/74 [1975] ECR 432; 5/75 *ibid.*, p. 769; 23/75 *ibid.*, pp. 1310-1311 *per* A.G.; 55/75 [1976] ECR 30; 114/76 [1977] ECR 1226 *per* A.G.

29 Case 40/72 [1973] ECR 142.
30 Case 11/74 [1974] ECR 888 *per* A.G.
210 31 *Ibid.*
32 Cases 73 and 74/63 [1964] ECR 26 *per* A.G.; 5/67 [1968] ECR 108 *per* A.G.; 55/75 [1976] ECR 41 *per* A.G.
33 Case 16/65 [1965] ECR 886.
34 Case 29/69 [1969] ECR 428 *per* A.G.
35 Cases 5/67 [1968] ECR 108 *per* A.G.; 42/72 [1973] ECR 74 *per* A.G. See further § 1109 below.
36 Cases 5/67 [1968] ECR 95-96.
37 Cases 73 and 74/63 [1964] ECR 14; 5/67 [1968] ECR 108-109 *per* A.G. See further § 514 above.
38 *Cf.* e.g. Case 125/75 [1976] ECR 784 *per Curiam*, 792-793 *per* A.G.
211 39 See § 521 above.
40 Case 16/65 [1965] ECR 886 *per Curiam*, 899 *per* A.G.
41 See § 1110 below.

Section 1105

1 See § 1106 below. Arts. 177(2) and (3) E.E.C., 150(2) and (3) Euratom.
2 Case 166/73 [1974] ECR 38. The same applies under Art. 2 of the Protocol of 3 June 1971 concerning the interpretation of the Convention on the Mutual Recognition of Companies 1968. However, under Arts. 2 and 3 of the Protocol of the same date concerning the interpretation of the Convention on Jurisdiction 1968, the optional reference procedure applies only to courts and tribunals when they are hearing appeals and to courts and tribunals mentioned in Art. 37 of the Convention.
212 3 Case 61/65 [1966] ECR 272-273 *per Curiam*, 280-282 *per* A.G., where the European Court held that a Dutch Arbitration Tribunal (*Scheidsgerecht*), set up under private law, but subject to State supervision, to settle disputes between a Miners' Insurance Fund and its members, was entitled to submit references under Art. 177 E.E.C., although it was not a court or tribunal under Dutch law.
4 See the Case mentioned at the previous footnote.
5 Case 36/73 [1973] ECR 1308 *et seq. per Curiam* (by implication), 1317-1320 *per* A.G., where the Court accepted a reference from the Litigation Section of the Netherlands Council of State (*Raad van State*).
6 See the Case mentioned at note 3 above.
7 *Ibid.*, p. 281 *per* A.G.
8 *Re an Illness in France* [1976] 1 CMLR 248; Case 17/76 [1976] ECR 1456 *per* A.G. See further § 1107 below.
8a *Amies* v *Inner London Education Authority* [1977] 1 CMLR 342.
9 Case 82/71 [1972] CMLR 740 *per Curiam*, 727 *per* A.G.
10 Case 32/74 [1974] ECR 1205 *et seq. per Curiam*, 1213 *per* A.G.
11 Cases 29/69 [1969] ECR 424-425 *per Curiam* (by implication), 428 *per* A.G.; 78/70 [1971] CMLR 645 *per* A.G.; 107/76 [1977] ECR 973.
12 Cases 33/70 [1970] ECR 1226 *per* A.G.; 43/71 [1973] CMLR 69 *per Curiam*, 64 *per* A.G.; 2/73 [1973] ECR 875 *et seq. per Curiam* (by implication), 893 *per* A.G.; 162/73 [1974] ECR 211. *Cf.* also *Italian No. 21* [1975] 2 CMLR 271-272. All these references arose from a special summary procedure laid down by Art. 633 of the Italian Code of Civil Procedure.
13 Case 127/73 [1974] ECR 61-63. For a different opinion by the A.G., see *ibid.*, p. 79.
213 14 Cases 166/73 [1974] ECR 37-39; 146/73 *ibid.*, p. 147. For a background of these Cases at the national level, see also *German No. 54* [1974] 1 CMLR 523, esp. p. 566. The same rules and principles also apply to the reference procedure for the interpretation of the Convention on Jurisdiction 1968 under the Protocol of 3 June 1971, see Case 29/76 [1976] ECR 1556 *per* A.G.
15 See especially the 'guidelines' laid down by Lord Denning MR in *Bulmer* v. *Bollinger* [1974] 2 CMLR 115 *et seq.*
16 See note 25 below.
17 See § 1108 below.

18 Cases 26/62 [1963] ECR 19 *per* A.G.; 166/73 [1974] ECR 38.
19 See § 1102 above, and the Cases mentioned at note 5 in that Section.
20 Cases 2/73 [1973] ECR 893 *per* A.G.; 34/73 *ibid*., p. 995 *per* A.G.; 166/73 [1974] ECR 38.
21 Case 31/67 [1968] ECR 164 *per* A.G.
22 Cases 21 to 24/72 [1975] 2 CMLR 12 *per* A.G.; *German No. 14* [1966] CMLR 416; *Van Duyn* v. *Home Office* [1974] 1 CMLR 357-358, referred to by Lord Denning MR in *Bulmer* v. *Bollinger* [1974] 2 CMLR 115; *EMI Records Ltd.* v. *CBS United Kingdom Ltd.* [1975] 1 CMLR 296-297; *Re an Illness in France* [1976] 1 CMLR 248.
23 *German No. 17* [1968] CMLR 117.
24 *Re an Illness in France* [1976] 1 CMLR 248.
25 *Cf.* e.g. *R.* v. *Secchi* [1975] 1 CMLR 391 *et seq*., where, following the 'guidance' of Lord Denning MR in *Bulmer* v. *Bollinger* [1974] 2 CMLR 115 *et seq*., a Magistrate's Court itself interpreted the concept of 'worker' as used in the E.E.C. Treaty, instead of referring the question to the European Court which, it is submitted, would have been the correct procedure.
26 Cases 28 to 30/62 [1963] ECR 38-39. See further § 1110 below.
214 27 See the Cases mentioned at notes 11 and 12 above.
28 Case 158/73 [1974] ECR 116 *per* A.G. For contrary views, see *Van Duyn* v. *Home Office* [1974] 1 CMLR 358 *per* Pennycuick V.-C. and *Bulmer* v. *Bollinger* [1974] 2 CMLR 116, 120-121 *per* Lord Denning MR.
29 Case 155/73 [1974] ECR 434 *per* A.G. For contrary views, see the English Cases at the preceding footnote and also *Bulmer* v. *Bollinger* [1975] 2 CMLR 489 *per* Whitford J.
30 See further §§ 102, 104 and 1104 above, especially note 1 in § 1104.
31 Cases 16/65 [1965] ECR 886-887; 21 to 24/72 [1975] 2 CMLR 12 *per* A.G. Although here the A.G. dealt with an international agreement concluded by the Community, his conclusions apply, *a fortiori*, to the basic Treaties themselves. *Cf.* however *Schorsch Meier* v. *Hennin* [1975] 1 CMLR 26 where the Court of Appeal declared Art. 106 E.E.C. directly applicable, refusing to refer its interpretation to the European Court. In a subsequent case the House of Lords expressed the strongest reservations concerning this decision saying that such issues should be referred to the European Court for clarification, see *Miliangos* v. *Frank* [1975] 2 CMLR 596 *per* Lord Wilberforce. See in this respect also note 13 in § 104 and note 25 in § 105 above. *Cf.* also *German No. 26* [1969] CMLR 88, 96-97 where the Administrative Court of Frankfurt, relying upon its discretionary power under Art. 177(2) E.E.C., declared a Commission regulation invalid.
32 *German No. 19* [1967] CMLR 159; *EMI Records Ltd.* v. *CBS United Kingdom Ltd.* [1975] 1 CMLR 297.
33 *EMI Records Ltd.* v. *CBS United Kingdom Ltd.* [1975] 1 CMLR 297.
34 *Ibid.*
35 *Van Duyn* v. *Home Office* [1974] 1 CMLR 357-358; *Re an Illness in France* [1976] 1 CMLR 248.
36 *Van Duyn* v. *Home Office* [1974] 1 CMLR 357-358.
37 *Dutch No. 10* [1973] CMLR 518-519.
38 *German No. 5* [1964] CMLR 182; *Belgian No. 6* [1971] CMLR 78.
39 *German No. 11* [1971] CMLR 557; *German No. 17* [1968] CMLR 117; *Löwenbräu München* v. *Grunhalle Lager International Ltd.* [1974] 1 CMLR 9, 12; *Schorsch Meier* v. *Hennin* [1975] 1 CMLR 26; *Re a Holiday in Italy* [1975] 1 CMLR 188; *R.* v. *Secchi* [1975] 1 CMLR 391 *et seq*.
40 *German No. 26* [1969] CMLR 96-97.
41 *Sirdar Ltd.* v. *Les Fils de Louis Mulliez* [1975] 1 CMLR 380.
42 *Bulmer* v. *Bollinger* [1974] 2 CMLR 120-121, applied in the same Case by Whitford J. [1975] 2 CMLR 489.
43 *German No. 4* [1964] CMLR 106; *German No. 5, ibid*., pp. 182-183.
44 *Dutch No. 1* [1962] CMLR 217; *Dutch No. 4* [1967] CMLR 11; *Dutch No. 8* [1969] CMLR 201; *German Nos. 21 and 24* [1969] CMLR 178 and [1974] 1 CMLR 515.

215 45 *DDSA Pharmaceuticals Ltd.* v. *Farbwerke Hoechst AG* [1975] 2 CMLR 50-52.
46 *Bulmer* v. *Bollinger* [1974] 2 CMLR 120.

Section 1106

1 The same applies under Art. 2 of the Protocol of 3 June 1971 concerning the interpretation of the Convention on the Mutual Recognition of Companies 1968. However, under Art. 3 of the Protocol of the same date concerning the interpretation of the Convention on Jurisdiction 1968 the compulsory reference procedure applies only to the courts and tribunals indicated by name in Art. 2 point 1.

2 Case 32/74 [1974] ECR 1213 *per* A.G.

2a Case 107/76 [1977] ECR 973, where the Court has held that a court or tribunal is not required to refer a question under Art. 177(3) E.E.C. when the question is raised in interlocutory proceedings for an interim order, even where no judicial remedy is available against the decision to be taken in the context of those proceedings, provided that each of the parties is entitled to institute proceedings on the substance of the case and that during such proceedings the question provisionally decided in the summary proceedings may be re-examined and may be the subject of a reference to the Court under Art. 177. *Cf.* also *German No. 45* [1972] CMLR 998.

2b Case 107/76 [1977] ECR 973.

3 See *Bulmer* v. *Bollinger* [1974] 2 CMLR 114 *per* Lord Denning MR.

4 *Ibid.*, p. 125 *per* Stephenson L. J.; for a contrary view, see *ibid.*, pp. 113-114 *per* Lord Denning MR.

4a Case 107/76 [1977] ECR 972-973 *per Curiam* (by implication), 979-981 *per* A.G.; *German No. 65* [1977] 1 CMLR 511.

5 Case 6/64 [1964] ECR 592 where the *Giudice Conciliatore* of Milan was held to be under the obligation to refer as his decision in the concrete case was not subject to appeal on account of the small amount involved (1925 lire).

6 *German No. 40* [1971] CMLR 641; *German No. 62* [1976] 1 CMLR 279. For contrary views, see *German No. 6* [1964] CMLR 94; *German No. 11* [1971] CMLR 557; *German No. 16 ibid.*, p. 545. But see now the Case mentioned at note 2a above.

7 *Cf.* e.g. *Re a Holiday in Italy* [1975] 1 CMLR 188 where the National Insurance Commissioner held that he was not bound to refer a question to the European Court as his decision could be set aside by an order of *certiorari* made by the High Court even though an application for such an order cannot be made without the leave of the High Court. In Case 17/76 [1976] ECR 1456 the A.G. left the question open whether the National Insurance Commissioner constituted a court of appeal or a court of last resort.

216 8 Case 166/73 [1974] ECR 38.

9 See §§ 903 and 906 above. *Cf.* also the Suggestions of the Court of Justice on European Union in 'Reports on European Union', *Supplement 9/75 — Bull. EC*, p. 18, where the Court suggests various remedies for infringement of Art. 177 E.E.C. by the national courts, such as the right of the party adversely affected directly to apply to the Court of Justice or to bring an action for damages against the State, or obligatory default proceedings by the Commission.

10 See § 1105 above.

11 The phrase in Art. 177(2) 'if it considers that a decision on the question is necessary to enable it to give judgment' does not occur in Art. 177(3). Likewise the same phrase does not appear in Art. 2(2) of the Protocol of 3 June 1971 concerning the interpretation of the Convention on the Mutual Recognition of Companies 1968, dealing with compulsory references. These omissions clearly indicate the intention of the drafters not to grant courts of last resort the discretionary power to assess whether and when a reference is 'necessary'. This interpretation is only confirmed by the fact that, by contrast, the same phrase has been included in Art. 3(1) of the Protocol of the same date on the interpretation of the Convention on Jurisdiction 1968, dealing also with compulsory references. This may perhaps be explained by the fact that this latter Protocol has generally created a more restrictive right to refer (and, correspondingly, a

more restricted obligation) as compared with Art. 177 E.E.C. or the other Protocol in that it has confined that right (and obligation) to certain specified national courts and tribunals only, see note 2 in § 1105 above and note 1 in this Section. See also note 13.

12 Case 6/64 [1964] ECR 607 *per* A.G.; *Dutch No. 6* [1971] CMLR 465; *Dutch No. 7* [1967] CMLR 54; *Dutch No. 11* [1973] CMLR 168-169; *German No. 32* [1969] CMLR 243.

13 It is submitted that the opinion expressed by the A.G. in Case 29/76 [1976] ECR 1556 that the second prerequisite in Art. 177(2), i.e. 'if that court or tribunal considers that a decision on the question is necessary to enable it to give judgment', also applies to Art. 177(3) even without an express mention, is acceptable only if the word 'necessary' is given the meaning discussed in the text. The same reservations apply also to the dicta by Lords Denning and Stephenson in *Bulmer* v. *Bollinger* [1974] 2 CMLR 114 and 125. *Cf.* also Case 107/76 [1977] ECR 985 *per* A.G.

14 Cases 28 to 30/62 [1963] ECR 38; 67/74 [1975] ECR 314 *per* A.G.; *Miliangos* v. *Frank* [1975] 2 CMLR 595-596 *per* Lord Wilberforce.

15 *Cf.* e.g. *French No. 5* [1964] CMLR 481-483; *French No. 7* [1967] CMLR 359-360; *French No. 8, ibid.*, p. 368; *German No. 34* [1971] CMLR 534; *German No. 64* [1977] 1 CMLR 664. *Italian No. 22* [1975] 2 CMLR 201.

217 16 -Cases 28 to 30/62 [1963] ECR 38 *per Curiam*, 44-45 *per* A.G.; 73 and 74/63 [1964] ECR 11; *French No. 7* [1967] CMLR 360-361; *French No. 17* [1974] 1 CMLR 476; *German No. 32* [1969] CMLR 225-226; *German No. 33, ibid.*, pp. 132, 135-136; *German No. 62* [1976] 1 CMLR 279.

17 See §§ 1103 and 1104 above.

18 Reference was denied on that ground (at least in part) in *Belgian No. 4* [1973] CMLR 196-197; *French No. 3* [1965] CMLR 31; *German No. 63* [1976] 2 CMLR 422.

19 *German No. 27* [1971] CMLR 601; *German No. 33* [1969] CMLR 137-138; *German No. 57* [1974] 1 CMLR 266.

Section 1107

1 Case 10/71 [1971] ECR 734 *per* A.G.

2 *Ibid.*, p. 729 *per Curiam*, 734, 737 *per* A.G.

218 3 Case 1/71 [1971] CMLR 429 *per Curiam*, 425 *per* A.G.

4 See notes 2 and 3 above and note 55 in § 1103 above.

5 Case 17/67 [1967] ECR 460 *per* A.G.

6 Cases 12/71 [1971] ECR 750 13/71 *ibid.*, p. 774; 14/71 *ibid.*, p. 786. See also the Cases mentioned at note 51 in § 1103 and the relevant text above.

7 Cases 56/65 [1966] ECR 254-255 *per* A.G.; 82/71 [1972] CMLR 726 *per* A.G. See further § 1103 and the Cases mentioned at notes 47 in 48 in that Section above. *Cf.* also *Van Duyn* v. *Home Office* [1974] 1 CMLR 360; *Bulmer* v. *Bollinger* [1974] 2 CMLR 117 per Lord Denning MR.

8 *Cf.* e.g. Case 9/74 [1974] ECR 778 *per Curiam*, 782 *per* A.G. See further § 1103 and the Cases mentioned at note 36 in that Section above.

9 See further § 1104 and the Cases mentioned at note 32 in that Section above.

10 Case 75/63 [1964] ECR 183 *per Curiam*, 188-189 *per* A.G.

11 Case 17/72 [1974] 1 CMLR 195 *per Curiam*, 193 *per* A.G.

12 *Cf.* e.g. Case 192/73 [1974] ECR 748 *per* A.G.

13 See § 1109 below.

219 14 Case 77/72 [1973] ECR 627 *per* A.G.

15 Case 13/61 [1962] ECR 50.

16 Art. 20 E.E.C. Statute, Art. 21 Euratom Statute. See further § 412(g) above.

17 Case 101/63 [1964] ECR 199.

18 Rules of the Supreme Court (Amendment No. 3) 1972, S.I. 1972 No. 1898. Rule 11 adds a new Order 114: 'References to the European Court'.

19 The Criminal Appeal (References to the European Court) Rules 1972, S.I. 1972 No. 1786.

20 County Court (Amendment No. 2) Rules 1973, S.I. 1973 No. 847.

21 The Crown Court (References to the European Court) Rules 1972, S.I. 1972 No. 1787.

22 Act of Sederunt (Rules of Court Amendment No. 5) 1972, S.I. 1972 No. 1981.

23 Act of Adjournal (References to the European Court) 1973, S.I. 1973 No. 450.
24 Act of Sederunt (Sheriff Court Procedure Amendment No. 2) 1973, S.I. 1973 No. 543 amending the Rules in the Schedule to the Sheriff Courts (Scotland) Act 1907.
25 See § 1105 above.
26 Art. 20 E.E.C. Statute, Art. 21 Euratom Statute. See further § 412(g) above.
220 27 Judicature Act 1925, Section 31. See *Bulmer* v. *Bollinger* [1974] 2 CMLR 114 *per* Lord Denning MR, 125 *per* Stephenson L.J.

Section 1108

1 Art. 20 E.E.C. Statute, Art. 21 Euratom Statute. See further § 412(g) above.
2 Cases 13/61 [1962] ECR 58-61 *per* A.G.; 127/73 [1974] ECR 70 *per* A.G.
3 Cases 146/73 and 166/73 [1974] ECR 43-47 *per* A.G. The A.G. here suggested that the rules of English law giving an unlimited right of appeal against an order for reference made by the High Court are void.
221 4 Case 146/73 [1974] ECR 147. See also note 2 above.
5 Cases 127/73 [1974] ECR 61-62 *per Curiam*, 68-71 *per* A.G.; 146/73 *ibid*., p. 147.
6 Case 13/61 [1962] ECR 49-50 *per Curiam*, 61 *per* A.G.
7 Case 31/68 [1970] ECR 404 *per Curiam*, 408-409 *per* A.G. (Order).
8 *Ibid*., pp. 405-406.
222 9 *Cf*. Cases 120/73 [1973] ECR 1488 *per* A.G. and in particular 24/74 [1974] ECR 1012 *per* A.G.

Section 1109

1 See § 1101 above.
2 Art. 20 E.E.C. Statute, Art. 21 Euratom Statute. See further § 412(g) above.
3 See § 1102 above.
4 See § 1107 above.
5 Cases 31 and 33/62 [1962] ECR 507; *French No. 6* [1966] CMLR 484; *Bulmer* v. *Bollinger* [1974] 2 CMLR 113-114, 118 *per* Lord Denning MR.
6 Cases 94/74 [1975] ECR 712; 119/75 [1976] ECR 1060.
7 Cases 73 and 74/63 [1964] ECR 27-28 *per* A.G.
8 Case 5/72 [1973] CMLR 335.
9 See § 519 above.
10 Case 44/65 [1965] ECR 970-971 *per Curiam*, 975-976 *per* A.G.
223 11 Case 51/70 [1971] CMLR 772 *et seq*. *per Curiam* (by implication), 765-766 *per* A.G.
12 Case 17/67 [1967] ECR 451 *et seq*. where the Court refused to consider certain additional complaints made by the parties although the A.G. gave a favourable opinion in this respect, see *ibid*., p. 460. *Cf*. also Cases 42/72 [1973] ECR 74 *per* A.G.; 55/75 [1976] ECR 36 *per* A.G. See also note 15 below.
13 Case 5/67 [1968] ECR 95-96.
14 Cases 73 and 74/63 [1964] ECR 14; 5/67 [1968] ECR 108-109 *per* A.G. See further § 1104 above.
15 Case 6/71 [1972] CMLR 416-418 *per* A.G.
16 Case 11/74 [1974] ECR 888 *per* A.G.
17 Under Art. 67 R.P. See § 412(g) above.
18 Under Art. 40 E.E.C. Statute, Art. 41 Euratom Statute. See further § 412(g) above.
19 Cases 13/67 [1968] ECR 196-197 (Order); 29/68 [1969] ECR 180 *per Curiam*, 186 *per* A.G.
20 Under Art. 37 E.E.C. Statute, Art. 38 Euratom Statute. Case 6/64 [1964] ECR 614-615 (Order). See further § 412(g) above.

Section 1110

1 See § 219 above.
2 Cases 29/68 [1969] ECR 180; 21 to 24/72 [1975] 2 CMLR 12 *per* A.G.; 2/73 [1973] ECR 893 *per* A.G.; 52/76 [1977] ECR 183; *German No. 28* [1969] CMLR 289; *German No. 46*, *Brinkhorst-Schermers, Supplement* p. 71; *German No. 50* [1972] CMLR 827-828; *German No. 54* [1974] 1 CMLR 552, 565; *Italian No. 13* [1970] CMLR 320; *Italian*

No. 16 [1975] 1 CMLR 422; *Italian No. 17* [1973] CMLR 324; *French No. 11* [1969] CMLR 25; *Bulmer v. Bollinger* [1974] 2 CMLR 113 *per* Lord Denning MR. Such binding force was denied by *German No. 48* [1972] CMLR 186.

224 3 Cases 28 to 30/62 [1963] ECR 38-39 *per Curiam*, 40 *et seq. per* A.G. where the Court referred to Case 26/62 [1963] ECR 1; Case 28/67 [1968] ECR 152 *et seq. per Curiam*, 160 *per* A.G. and *German No. 22* [1967] CMLR 335-336 where the German *Bundesfinanzhof* (Federal Finance Court) requested the European Court to reconsider the interpretation it had given in Case 57/65 [1966] ECR 205; Case 29/68 [1969] ECR 179-180 where some of the questions had already been submitted by the same court in the same proceedings in Case 25/67 [1968] ECR 207.

4 See § 1106 above and the Cases mentioned at note 16 in that Section.

5 Cases 28 to 30/62 [1963] ECR 40 *et seq. per* A.G.; *Italian No. 19* [1973] CMLR 155-156; *Bulmer* v. *Bollinger* [1974] 2 CMLR 113, 115-116 *per* Lord Denning MR.

6 This has been recognised by a number of municipal courts, *cf.* e.g. *Dutch No. 3* [1964] CMLR 376; *Dutch No. 4* [1967] CMLR 10; *French No. 9* [1969] CMLR 84; *French No. 17* [1974] 1 CMLR 476; *German No. 37* [1975] 1 CMLR 615; *German No. 39* [1971] CMLR 719-720; *German No. 60* [1974] 2 CMLR 551-552.

7 *Cf.* e.g. *Dutch No. 2* [1963] CMLR 144.

8 See § 104 above.

225 9 See § 1106 above.

10 See § 1104 above. In its rulings the Court uses the formula: 'Examination of the questions referred has revealed nothing capable of affecting the validity . . .' of the act in question, *cf.* e.g. Case 55/75 [1976] ECR 34.

11 Cases 154/73 [1974] ECR 24-25 and 55/75 [1976] ECR 33 *per Curiam*, 36 *per* A.G. In both Cases the validity of the regulation challenged had already been examined and confirmed in previous preliminary rulings in Cases 5/73 [1973] ECR 1091; 9/73 *ibid.*, p. 1135 and 10/73 *ibid.*, p. 1175.

12 Case 59/72 [1973] ECR 808 *per* A.G.

13 This follows by implication from Case 59/72 [1973] ECR 803 *per Curiam*, 807-808 *per* A.G. where in a direct action for damages the applicant relied upon the illegality of a regulation whose validity was upheld by the Court in a previous preliminary ruling in Case 40/72 [1973] ECR 125.

14 See § 519 above.

15 Case 16/65 [1965] ECR 886 *per Curiam*, 899 *per* A.G. See also § 1104 above.

16 See § 521 above.

226 17 See § 106 above.

18 Case 11/74 [1974] ECR 888 *per* A.G.

19 Case 23/75 [1975] ECR 1306 *per Curiam*, 1318 *per* A.G. For an example see Case 62/76 [1977] ECR 223 *per* A.G.

20 This is what happened e.g. in Case 62/76 [1977] ECR 217-218.

Section 1111

227 1 *Cf.* Art. 4 of Code Napoleon (*Code Civil*).

2 *Cf.* Art. 31(1) of the Vienna Convention on the Law of Treaties 1969 which lays down the following main rule of interpretation: 'A treaty shall be interpreted in good faith in accordance with the ordinary meaning to be given to the terms of the treaty in their context and in the light of its object and purpose.'

228 3 Case 6/72 [1973] ECR 243, interpreting the concept of an 'abuse' within the meaning of Art. 86 E.E.C.; Case 22/70 [1971] CMLR 354-355, interpreting the E.E.C.'s treaty-making power; Case 43/75 [1976] ECR 471 *et seq.*, interpreting the direct effect of Art. 119 E.E.C. (principle of equal pay).

4 Cases 22/67 [1967] ECR 326-327; 28/68 [1969] ECR 135; 27/72 [1973] CMLR 615 *per* A.G.; 190/73 [1974] ECR 1133; 50/75 [1975] ECR 1481; 17/76 [1976] ECR 1451.

5 Cases 13/61 [1962] ECR 49; 13/60 *ibid.*, p. 128 *per* A.G.; 111/75 [1976] ECR 672-673 *per* A.G.

6 Case 15/60, 32, ILR 357.

7 Cases 1/64 [1964] ECR 420 *per* A.G.; 120/75 [1976] ECR 1013 *per* A.G., interpreting the Common Customs Tariff.

8 Cases 15/60, 32 ILR 357; 13/60 [1962] ECR 127 *per* A.G.; 24/62 [1963] ECR 79 *per* A.G.

9 Cases 13/60 [1962] ECR 126 *per* A.G.; 73 and 74/63 [1964] ECR 19 *per* A.G.; 8 to 11/66 [1967] ECR 99-100 *per* A.G.

10 Cases 8/55, 2 Val. 111; 9/56, 2 Val. 464; 15/63 [1964] ECR 54 *per* A.G.

11 Case 8/55, 2 Rec. 263-264 *per* A.G.

12 Case 38/69 [1970] ECR 63 *per* A.G.

13 Cases 14/59, 2 Val. 547; 30/59, 29 ILR 96.

14 Cases 37/72 [1973] ECR 368; 64/74 [1975] ECR 268-269; 31/75 *ibid.*, p. 1570; 94/75 [1976] ECR 159-160 *per Curiam*, 164-165 *per* A.G.; 102/75 *ibid.*, p. 1799 *et seq. per* A.G.

15 Cases 6/60, 2 Val. 830; 13/61 [1962] ECR 51 *per Curiam*, 70 *per* A.G.; 36/71 [1972] CMLR 794 *per* A.G.; 152/73 [1974] ECR 170 *per* A.G.; 34/74 *ibid.*, p. 1229 *per Curiam*, 1236 *per* A.G.; 45/75 [1976] ECR 205-206 *per* A.G.; 91/75 *ibid.*, pp. 236-237 *per* A.G.; 111/75 *ibid.*, pp. 672-673 *per* A.G.; 125/75 *ibid.*, pp. 788-789 *per* A.G.

229 16 Case 2/74 [1974] ECR 666 *per* A.G.

17 Case 8/55, 2 Rec. 263-264 *per* A.G.

18 Case 185/73 [1974] ECR 626 *per* A.G.

19 Cases 29/69 [1969] ECR 425; 72/69 [1970] ECR 435-436; 74/69 *ibid.*, pp. 462-463.

20 *Cf.* e.g. Case 59/75 [1976] ECR 100 interpreting the nature and scope of the adjustment prescribed by Art. 37 E.E.C.

21 *Cf.* e.g. Case 87/75 [1976] ECR 138, deducing the 'crucial role in the construction of the Common Market' of Arts. 9 and 13(2) E.E.C. from their position at the beginning of that Part of the Treaty reserved for the 'Foundations of the Community'. *Cf.* also Case 43/75 [1976] ECR 471 *et seq.*, interpreting Art. 119 from its position in Chapter 1, Title III of Part Three of the E.E.C. Treaty. *Cf.* also Case 24/62 [1963] ECR 67-68 *per Curiam*, 79-80 *per* A.G., interpreting Arts. 25 and 29 E.E.C. from their position in relation to Arts. 2, 3, 9 E.E.C. in the context of the Treaty as a whole.

22 *Cf.* e.g. Case 166/73 [1974] ECR 38, interpreting Art. 177 E.E.C., amongst other things, in the light of its own aims. *Cf.* also Cases 11/63 [1964] ECR 67; 61/72 [1973] ECR 310.

23 *Cf.* e.g. Case 185/73 [1974] ECR 618, interpreting the definition of agricultural products in Art. 38(1) E.E.C. in the light of the aims of the common agricultural policy laid down in Title II of Part II of the Treaty.

24 Cases 9/61 [1962] ECR 235-236; 6/72 [1973] ECR 245, speaking in particular of Arts. 85 and 86 E.E.C. See also § 203 and the Cases mentioned at notes 17-22 in that Section above.

25 Arts. 1 to 5 E.C.S.C., 1 to 8 E.E.C., 1 to 3 Euratom.

230 26 Cases 6/72 [1973] ECR 244-245; 6 and 7/73 [1974] ECR 252. See also § 203 and the Cases mentioned at notes 15 and 16 in that Section above.

27 Case 22/70 [1971] CMLR 354.

28 Case 6/72 [1973] ECR 243-245.

29 Case 167/73 [1974] ECR 369-371.

30 *Cf.* in addition to the Cases mentioned at notes 27, 28 and 29 above, Cases 13/60 [1962] ECR 112 *per Curiam*, 124-125, 141 *per* A.G.; 26/74 [1976] ECR 690 *per* A.G. referring to Case 34/74 [1974] ECR 1227 *et seq.*

231 31 Cases 92/71 [1973] CMLR 576; 91/75 [1976] ECR 238-239 *per* A.G.

32 Case 43/75 [1976] ECR 480.

33 See § 102 above.

34 Case 75/63 [1964] ECR 184-185 interpreting the terms 'worker' and 'wage-earner' as they appear in Arts. 48 to 51 E.E.C. and Regulation 3.

35 Cases 49/71 [1973] CMLR 50 *per Curiam*, 39, 42 *per* A.G.; 50/71 *ibid.*, interpreting the term 'offer' appearing in certain agricultural regulations.

36 Case 152/73 [1974] ECR 163 *per Curiam*, 168-170 *per* A.G., interpreting the term 'employment in the public service' as it appears in Art. 48(4) E.E.C. and Regulation

1612/68 as well as in Art. 13 of the European Convention on Establishment of 13 December 1955.

37 Case 2/74 [1974] ECR 654-655 interpreting the concept of 'official authority' appearing in Art. 55(1) E.E.C.

38 Cases 41/74 [1974] ECR 1350; 36/75 [1975] ECR 1231, interpreting the concept of 'public policy' as it appears in Arts. 48(3), 56(1), 66 E.E.C. and in the relevant implementing legislation.

39 Case 29/76 [1976] ECR 1551, interpreting the concept of 'civil and commercial matters' as it appears in Art. 1 of the Convention on Jurisdiction of 1968. For principles governing the interpretation of the same Convention, see also Cases 12/76 [1976] ECR 1484; 14/76 *ibid.*, p. 1508.

40 Case 12/73 [1973] ECR 974 interpreting the term 'marketable quality' appearing in Art. 6 of Regulation 1041/67.

41 Case 181/73 [1974] ECR 462-463 *per Curiam*, 469 *per* A.G. interpreting the terms 'levy' and 'charge having equivalent effect to customs duties' under the Association Agreement between the E.E.C. and Greece of 1961 and with respect to GATT.

42 See note 36 above.

43 See the Cases mentioned at notes 34 to 41 above and also Cases 15/63 [1964] ECR 54 *per* A.G.; 9/72 [1972] CMLR 935 *per* A.G.; 5/73 [1973] ECR 1122 *per* A.G.; 51/76 [1977] ECR 124-125. See further §§ 205, 220, 221 and 222 above.

232 44 Case 74/69 [1970] ECR 459.

45 For the official languages of the Communities, see § 215 above.

46 Cases 13/61 [1962] ECR 70 *per* A.G.; 19/67 [1967] ECR 354; 29/69 [1969] ECR 424-425; 51/70 [1971] CMLR 768 *per* A.G.; 6/74 [1974] ECR 1293; 91/75 [1976] ECR 235-236 *per* A.G.; 80/76 [1977] ECR 434-436; 82/76 *ibid.*, p. 349; 30/77 [1977] 2 CMLR 821.

47 Cases 48/69 [1972] CMLR 571 *per* A.G.; 166/73 [1974] ECR 38, interpreting Art. 177 E.E.C.; 5/75 [1975] ECR 775 *et seq. per* A.G.; 74/74 *ibid.*, p.557 *per* A.G. referring to Case 78/74 *ibid.*, p.433.

48 For this principle, see further § 304 above.

49 E.G. in Arts. 36, 48(3) and (4), 55(1), 56(1), 66, 115 E.E.C.

50 Cases 2 and 3/62 [1962] ECR 432, 434; 9/72 [1972] CMLR 935 *per* A.G.; 29/72 [1973] CMLR 497 and 8/74 [1974] ECR 861 *per* A.G., both interpreting the scope of the exceptions in Art. 36 E.E.C.; 152/73 [1974] ECR 162-164 *per Curiam*, 169 *per* A.G., interpreting the extent of the exception in Art. 48(4) E.E.C., i.e. 'employment in the public service'; 2/74 *ibid.*, pp.654-655, interpreting the scope of the exception in Art. 55(1), i.e. 'exercise of official authority'; 41/74 *ibid.*, p.1350 and 36/75 [1975] ECR 1231, both interpreting the extent of the limitation in Art. 48(3) E.E.C. on grounds of 'public policy; 67/74 [1975] ECR 307; 91/75 [1976] ECR 235-237 *per* A.G., interpreting Art. 37 E.E.C.; 29/75 *ibid.*, p. 443. and 41/76 *ibid.*, p. 1937, both interpreting the scope of the derogations allowed under Art. 115 E.E.C.; 12/76 *ibid.*, p. 1485, interpreting the Convention on Jurisdiction of 1968; 30/77 [1977] 2 CMLR 824, interpreting the concept of public policy.

51 See § 108 above.

52 Case 167/73 [1974] ECR 378 *per* A.G.

53 See § 206 above and the Cases mentioned at note 31 in that Section.

233 54 Cases 29/69 [1969] ECR 424-425; 38/70 [1972] CMLR 231 *per* A.G.; 58/70 *ibid.*; 104/76 [1977] ECR 842.

55 For these principles, see further §§ 221, 303, 304 above.

56 Cases 140/73 [1973] ECR 1456; 66/74 [1975] ECR 161-162; 74/74 *ibid.*, p.557 *per* A.G. referring to Case 78/74 *ibid.*, p.433; 7/75 *ibid.*, pp.695 *et seq. per* A.G.; 5/75 *ibid.*, pp.775 *et seq. per* A.G.; 32/75 *ibid.*, pp.1094-1095, 63/76 [1976] ECR 2066 *et seq.*

57 Cases 7 and 9/54, 2 Val. 141; 6/60 *ibid.*, p. 826; 25/62 [1963] ECR 106-107; 1/64 [1964] ECR 420 *per* A.G.; 41 to 44/70 [1975] 2 CMLR 524 *per* A.G.; 5/71 [1971] ECR 989 *per* A.G.; 153/73 [1974] ECR 699.

58 Cases 8 to 11/66 [1967] ECR 92-93. *Cf.* also Cases 14/61 [1962] ECR 279 *per* A.G. and 63 to 69/72 [1973] ECR 1260 *per* A.G.

59 Cases 6/68 [1968] ECR 415; 134/73 [1974] ECR 16 *per* A.G.; 66/76 [1977] ECR 310.
60 See § 902 above, and especially note 10 in that Section.
61 See § 403 above.
62 See § 519 above.
63 See § 703 above.
64 See § 701 above.
234 65 See §§ 506, 509 above.
66 Cases 59/72 [1973] ECR 807 *per* A.G.; 43/72 *ibid.*, p.1069.
67 See further §§ 406, 411 above.
68 Cases 9/70 [1970] ECR 846 *per* A.G.; 107/76 [1977] ECR 980 *per* A.G. See further § 104 above.
69 See § 106 above.
70 *Ibid.*
71 *Cf.* the Suggestions of the Court of Justice on European Union in 'Reports on European Union', *Supplement 9/75 — Bull. EC*, pp.17-18.
72 *Cf.* the Preambles to the E.C.S.C., E.E.C. and Euratom Treaties, especially to the E.E.C. Treaty.

Bibliography

The following bibliographical references are arranged according to the subject-matter of the individual Chapters and, where appropriate, Sections.

General

(Works relevant to both Volumes I and II or to more than one Chapter)

Bebr, G., Judicial Control of the European Communities. London, 1962.
Brown, L. N. and Jacobs, F. G., The Court of Justice of the European Communities. London, 1977.
Campbell, A., Common Market Law. Vols. 1-3 and Supplements. London, 1969-1975.
Colin, J.-P., Le gouvernement des juges dans les Communautés européennes. Paris, 1966.
Collins, L., European Community Law in the United Kingdom. London, 1975.
Delvaux, L., La Cour de Justice de la Communauté Européenne du Charbon et de l'Acier. Paris, 1956.
Ehle, D., Klage- und Prozeßrecht des EWG-Vertrages. Herne/Berlin, 1966.
Ehle, D., The Legal Protection of Enterprises of the Common Market within the Jurisdiction of the European Court of Justice and of National Courts. (1968-69) 6 C.M.L. Rev. 193.
Fromont, M., Rechtsschutz gegenüber der Verwaltung in Deutschland, Frankreich und den Europäischen Gemeinschaften. Köln, 1967.
Ganshof van der Meersch, W. J., Droit des Communautés européennes. Les Novelles. Bruxelles, 1969.
van Gerven, W., The Legal Protection of Private Parties in the Law of the European Economic Community, in: F. G. Jacobs (ed), *European Law and the Individual.* Amsterdam, 1976, p. 1.
Green, A. W., Political Integration by Jurisprudence. Leyden, 1969.
von der Groeben, H., von Boeckh, H. and Thiesing, J., Kommentar zum EWG-Vertrag. Vols. 1-2. 2nd ed., Baden-Baden, 1974.
Ipsen, H. P., Europäisches Gemeinschaftsrecht. Tübingen, 1972.
Laubadère, A. de, Traits généraux du contentieux administratif des Communautés européennes. (1964) 111 *Recueil des Cours* 527.
Mann, C. J., The Function of Judicial Decision in European Economic Integration. The Hague, 1972.
Neri, S., La protection juridictionnelle des particuliers dans les Communautés européennes. Heule, 1965.
Reintzsch, G., Wohlfahrt, J. and Burmester, U., Die Einzelpersonen und das Europäische Recht. Berichte über den VII. Europarechts-Kongreß der FIDE in Brüssel. (1976) 11 EuR 262.
Riese, O., Über den Rechtsschutz innerhalb der Europaischen Gemeinschaften. (1966) 1 EuR 24. (*Cf.* also, *ibid.* p. 69).
Riese, O., Über den Rechtsschutz von Privatpersonen und Unternehmen in der Europäischen

Wirtschaftsgemeinschaft, in: *Probleme des Europäischen Rechts. Festschrift für Walter Hallstein*. Frankfurt am Main, 1966, p. 414.
Schermers, H. G., Judicial Protection in the European Communities. Deventer, 1977.
Stein, E. and Hay, P., Legal Remedies of Enterprises in the European Economic Community. (1960) 9 A.J.C.L. 375.
Stein, E. and Vining, G. J., Citizen Access to Judicial Review of Administrative Action in a Transnational and Federal Context, in: F. G. Jacobs (ed.), *European Law and the Individual*. Amsterdam, 1976, p. 113.
Steindorff, E., Rechtsschutz und Verfahren im Recht der Europäischen Gemeinschaften. Baden-Baden, 1964.
Torrelli, M., L'individu et le droit de la Communauté économique européenne. Montréal, 1970.
Toth, A. G., The Individual and European Law. (1975) 24 I.C.L.Q. 659.
Ule, C. H., Empfiehlt es sich, die Bestimmungen des europäischen Gemeinschaftsrechts über den Rechtsschutz zu ändern und zu ergänzen? Gutachten für den 46. Deutschen Juristentag. Munchen/Berlin, 1966. (*Cf.* also (1966) 1 EuR 367 and (1967) 3 C.D.E. 101.)
Ule, C. H., Der gerichtliche Rechtsschutz des Einzelnen gegenüber der vollziehenden Gewalt in den Europäischen Gemeinschaften, in: *Gerichtsschutz gegen die Executive. Judicial Protection against the Executive*. Koln, 1970, Vol. 2. p. 1179.
Valentine, D. G., The Court of Justice of the European Communities. Vols. 1-2. London, 1965.
Vandersanden, G. and Barav, A., Contentieux Communautaire. Bruxelles, 1977.
Wall, E. H., The Court of Justice of the European Communities. London, 1966.
Wohlfarth, E., Everling, U., Glaesner, H.-J. and Sprung, R., Die Europäische Wirtschaftsgemeinschaft. Kommentar zum Vertrag. Berlin/Frankfurt am Main, 1960.
De individuele Rechtsbescherming in de Europese Gemeenschappen. Louvain, 1967: Deventer, 1964.
Zehn Jahre Rechtsprechung des Gerichtshofs der Europäischen Gemeinschaften. Dix ans de jurisprudence de la Cour de Justice des Communautés européennes. Kölner Schriften zum Europarecht, Vol. 1. Köln, 1965.

Chapter 1

General

Donner, A. M., The Role of the Lawyer in the European Communities. Edinburgh, 1968.
Pescatore, P., Le droit de l'intégration. Leyden, 1972.
La jurisprudence européenne après vingt ans d'expérience communautaire. Die europäische Rechtsprechung nach zwanzig Jahren Gemeinschaftsleben. VIe Congrès international de droit européen organisé par la FIDE. Ier thème: Jurisprudence sur les problèmes généraux de l'intégration. 1. Thema: Rechtsprechung zu den allgemeinen Problemen der Integration. Köln, 1976, p. 39.

Section 101

Leopold, P. M., External Relations Power of the EEC in Theory and Practice. (1977) 26 I.C.L.Q. 54. (*Cf.* also *ibid.*, p. 208).
Lesguillons, H., L'application d'un traité-fondation: le traité instituant la CEE. Paris, 1968.
Martens, J., Die rechtsstaatliche Struktur der Europäischen Wirtschaftsgemeinschaft. (1970) 5 EuR 209.
Monaco, R., The Limits of the European Community Order. (1976) 1 E.L.Rev. 269.
Neri, S., De la nature juridique des Communautés européennes. Heule, 1965.
Pescatore, P., Les relations extèrieures des Communautés européennes. (1961) 103 *Recueil des Cours* 1.
Rengeling, H.-W., Nationaler Verwaltungsvollzug von Gemeinschaftsrecht: Die Gemeinschaftskompetenzen. (1974) 9 EuR 216.
Sasse, C., Zur auswärtigen Gewalt der Europäischen Wirtschaftsgemeinschaft. (1971) 6 EuR 208.
Scheuner, U., Perspektiven einer Europäischen Union. (1976) 11 EuR 193.
La fusion des Communautés européennes. The Hague, 1965.
La Communauté et ses États membres. The Hague, 1973.

Section 102

Constantinesco, L., La spécificité du droit communautaire. (1966) 2 R.T.D.E. 1.

Constantinides-Mégret, C. Le droit de la Communauté économique européenne et l'ordre juridique des Etats membres. Paris, 1967.

Erades, L., International Law, European Community Law and Municipal Law of Member States. (1966) 15 I.C.L.Q. 117.

Iglesias Buigues, J. L. La nature juridique du droit communautaire. (1968) 4 C.D.E. 501.

Mackenzie Stuart, Lord, The European Communities and the Rule of Law. London, 1977.

Tallon, D., Le droit communautaire. (1966) 2 C.D.E. 571.

Section 103

Brinkhorst, L. J. and Kuiper, M. J., The Integration of the New Member States in the Community Legal Order. (1972) 9 C.M.L.Rev. 364.

Forman, J., The European Communities Act 1972. (1973) 10 C.M.L.Rev. 39.

Hunnings, N. M., Constitutional Implications of Joining the Common Market. (1968-69) 6 C.M.L.Rev. 50.

Ipsen, H. P., The Relationship between the Law of the European Communities and National Law. (1964-65) 2 C.M.L.Rev. 379.

Martin, A., The Accession of the United Kingdom to the European Communities: Jurisdictional Problems. (1968-69) 6 C.M.L.Rev. 7.

Mitchell, J. D. B., 'What Do You Want to Be Inscrutable for, Marcia?' (1967-68) 5 C.M.L.Rev. 112.

Mitchell, J. D. B., Kuipers, S. A. and Gall, B., Constitutional Aspects of the Treaty and Legislation Relating to British Membership. (1972) 9 C.M.L.Rev. 134.

Neri, S., Le droit communautaire et l'ordre constitutionnel italien. (1966) 2 C.D.E. 363.

Pescatore, P., Conclusion et effets des traités internationaux, selon le droit constitutionnel, les usages et la jurisprudence du Grand-Duché de Luxembourg. Luxembourg, 1964.

Pescatore, P., Das Zusammenwirken der Gemeinschaftsrechtsordnung mit den nationalen Rechtsordnungen. (1970) 5 EuR 307. *Cf.* also (1971) 6 EuR 69.

Saint-Esteben, R., Droit communautaire et droits nationaux. Paris, 1967.

Suy, E., Les rapports entre le droit communautaire et le droit interne des Etats membres. Heule, 1964.

Waelbroeck, M., Traités internationaux et juridictions internes dans les pays du Marché commun. Bruxelles, 1969.

Wohlfarth, E., Europäische und deutsche Rechtsordnung. Göttingen, 1965.

Zuleeg, M., Das Recht der Europaischen Gemeinschaften im innerstaatlichen Bereich. Köln, 1969.

Droit communautaire et droit national. Semaine de Bruges 1965. Bruges, 1965.

Gemeinschaftsrecht und nationale Rechte. V. Internationaler Kongreß für Europarecht vom 23.-26. September 1970 in Berlin, veranstaltet von der FIDE. Köln, 1971.

Section 104

Bebr, G., Directly Applicable Provisions of Community Law: The Development of a Community Concept. (1970) 19 I.C.L.Q. 257. French text in (1970) 6 C.D.E. 3.

Daig, H.-W., Die Rechtsprechung des Gerichtshofes der Europäischen Gemeinschaften zur unmittelbaren Wirkung von EWG-Bestimmungen auf die Rechtsbeziehungen zwischen Mitgliedstaaten und Gemeinschaftsbürgern. (1970) 5 EuR 1.

Dumon, F., La notion de 'disposition directement applicable' en droit européen. (1968) 4 C.D.E. 369.

Prasch, G., Die unmittelbare Wirkung des EWG-Vertrages auf die Wirtschaftsunternehmen. Baden-Baden, 1967.

Winter, J. A., Direct Applicability and Direct Effect—Two Distinct and Different Concepts in Community Law. (1972) 9 C.M.L.Rev. 425.

Section 105

Dreyfus, F., Le droit communautaire et le droit britannique interne: les solutions du European Communities Act du 17 octobre 1972. (1973) 9 R.T.D.E. 242.

Everling, U., Europaisches Gemeinschaftsrecht und nationales Recht in der praktischen Rechtsanwendung. (1967) 20 N.J.W. 465.
Pescatore, P., L'application directe des traités europeens par les juridictions nationales: la jurisprudence nationale. (1969) 5 R.T.D.E. 697.
Pescatore, P., L'attitude des juridictions nationales à l'égard du problème des effets directs du droit communautaire. (1970) 6 R.T.D.E. 296.

Section 106
Gaudet, M., Conflits du droit communautaire avec les droits nationaux. Nancy, 1967.
Gavron, R., Réflexions sur la primauté du droit communautaire. (1969) 5 R.T.D.E. 28.
Grabitz, E., Gemeinschaftsrecht bricht nationales Recht. Hamburg, 1966.

Section 107
Bebr, G., How Supreme Is Community Law in the National Courts? (1974) 11 C.M.L.Rev. 3.
Dehousse, F., La primauté du droit communautaire sur le droit des Etats membres. Rapport fait au nom de la Commission juridique au Parlement européen. (1965) 1 R.T.D.E. 212.
Gangsted-Rasmussen, N., Primauté du droit communautaire en cas de conflit avec le droit danois. (1975) 11 R.T.D.E. 700.
Hallstein, W., La primauté du droit communautaire sur le droit des Etats membres. Intervention dans le débat juridique sur le rapport de Dehousse. (1965) 1 R.T.D.E. 247.
Hay, P., Supremacy of Community Law in National Courts. (1968) 16 A.J.C.L. 524.
Lagrange, M., Du conflit entre loi et traité en droit communautaire et en droit interne. (1975) 11 R.T.D.E. 44.

Section 108
Ubertazzi, G. M., Le domaine matériel du droit communautaire. (1976) 12 R.T.D.E. 635.

Section 110
Meessen, K. M., Der räumliche Anwendungsbereich des EWG-Kartellrechts und das allgemeine Völkerrecht. (1973) 8 EuR 18.

Chapter 2

General
Lauwaars, R. H., Lawfulness and Legal Force of Community Decisions. Leyden, 1973.
Morand, C.-A., La législation dans les Communautés européennes. Paris, 1968.
Pescatore, P., L'ordre juridique des Communautés européennes. Etude des sources du droit communautaire. 2nd ed. Liège, 1973.

Section 204
Hauschild, W. M., L'importance des Conventions communautaires pour la création d'un droit communautaire. (1975) 11 R.T.D.E. 4.

Section 205
Bleckmann, A., Der gemischte Vertrag im Europarecht. (1976) 11 EuR 301.
Pietri, J.-P., La valeur juridique des accords liant la Communauté économique européenne. (1976) 12 R.T.D.E. 51 and 194.

Section 206
Brinkhorst, L. J., Implementation of (Non-Self-Executing) Legislation of the European Economic Community, including Directives, in: *Legal Problems of an Enlarged European Community*. London, 1972, p. 69.
van der Esch, B., Legal Policy in an Enlarged European Community. (1973) 10 C.M.L.Rev. 56.
Lagrange, M., Le pouvoir de décision dans les Communautés européennes: théorie et réalité. (1967) 3 R.T.D.E. 1.

Mitchell, J. D. B., Community Legislation, in: *Legal Problems of an Enlarged European Community*. London, 1972, p. 87.
Nicolaysen, G., Zur Theorie von den implied powers in den Europäischen Gemeinschaften. (1966) 1 EuR 129.
Schindler, P., Delegation von Zuständigkeiten in der Europäischen Gemeinschaft. Baden-Baden, 1972.
Teitgen, P.-H., La décision dans la Communauté économique européenne. (1971) 134 *Recueil des Cours* 589.
La décision dans les Communautés européennes. Bruxelles, 1969.

Section 207
Börner, B., Die Entscheidungen der Hohen Behörde. Tübingen, 1965.

Section 210
Louis, J.-V., Les règlements de la Communauté économique européenne. Bruxelles, 1969.
Louis, J.-V., Compétences des Etats dans la mise en oeuvre du règlement. (1971) 7 C.D.E. 627.
Ophüls, C. F., Les règlements et les directives dans les Traités de Rome. (1966) 2 C.D.E. 3.
Rabe, H.-J., Das Verordnungsrecht der Europäischen Wirtschaftsgemeinschaft. Hamburg, 1963.

Section 211
André, A., Artikel 189 Abs. 3 EWG-Vertrag als politische Norm. (1969) 4 EuR 191.
Fuiano, N., L'exécution des directives de la CEE en Italie. (1971) 7 C.D.E. 662.
Kellermann, A. E., Les directives de la CEE dans l'ordre juridique néerlandais. (1969) 5 C.D.E. 247.
Kovar, R., Lagarde, P. and Tallon, D., L'exécution des directives de la CEE en France. (1970) 6 C.D.E. 274.
Mischo, J., L'exécution des directives de la CEE au Luxembourg. (1974) 10 C.D.E. 39.
Oldekop, D., Die Richtlinien der E.W.G. Göttingen, 1968.
Rambow, G., L'exécution des directives de la Communauté économique européenne en République fédérale d'Allemagne. (1970) 6 C.D.E. 379.
Riegel, R., Überlegungen zum Problem EG-Richtlinien und nationale Rahmenkompetenz. (1976) 11 EuR 79.
de Ripainsel-Landy, D., L'exécution des directives de la CEE en Belgique. (1973) 9 C.D.E. 184.
Simmonds, K. R., Van Duyn v The Home Office: The Direct Effectiveness of Directives. (1975) 24 I.C.L.Q. 419.
Weber, N., Die Richtlinie im EWG-Vertrag. Hamburg, 1974.

Section 212
Grabitz, E., Entscheidungen und Richtlinien als unmittelbar wirksames Gemeinschaftsrecht. (1971) 6 EuR 1.

Section 213
Morand, C.-A., Les recommandations, les résolutions et les avis du droit communautaire. (1970) 6 C.D.E. 623.

Section 214
Everling, U., Schwartz, I. E., and Tomuschat, C., Die Rechtsetzungsbefugnisse der EWG in Generalermächtigungen, insbesondere in Artikel 235 EWGV. (1976) EuR Sonderheft.
Gericke, H.-P., Allgemeine Rechtsetzungsbefugnisse nach Artikel 235 EWG-Vertrag. Hamburg, 1970.

Section 215
Scheffler, H.-H., Die Pflicht zur Begründung von Maßnahmen nach den Europäischen Gemeinschaftsverträgen. Berlin, 1974.
Le Tallec, G. and Ehlermann, C.-D., Die Begründungspflicht für Rechtsakte der Europäischen Gemeinschaften. (1966) 12 A.W.D. 149. See also *Section 516* below.

Section 217

Bebr, G., Acts of Representatives of the Governments of the Member States taken within the Council of Ministers of the European Communities. (1966) 14 S.E.W. 529.

Kaiser, J. H., Die im Rat vereinigten Vertreter der Regierungen der Mitgliedstaaten, in: *Zur Integration Europas*. Karlsruhe, 1965.

Pescatore, P., Remarques sur la nature juridique des décisions des représentants des Etats membres réunis au sein du conseil. (1966) 14 S.E.W. 579.

Section 218

Blumann, C., Le Conseil européen. (1976) 12 R.T.D.E. 1.

Lauwaars, R. H., The European Council. (1977) 14 C.M.L.Rev. 25.

Section 219

Gutsche, M., Die Bindungswirkung der Urteile des Europäischen Gerichtshofes. Göttingen, 1967.

Hay, P., European Economic Community: Res Judicata and Precedent in the Court of Justice of the Common Market. (1963) 12 A.J.C.L. 404.

Matthies, H., Die Bindungswirkung von Urteilen des Gerichtshofes der Europäischen Gemeinschaften, in: *Probleme des Europaischen Rechts. Festschrift für Walter Hallstein*. Frankfurt am Main, 1966, p. 304.

Plouvier, L., Les décisions de la Cour de Justice des Communautés européennes et leurs effets juridiques. Bruxelles, 1975.

Section 220

Donner, A. M., National Law and the Case Law of the Court of Justice of the European Communities. (1963-64) 1 C.M.L.Rev. 8.

Usher, J. A., The Influence of National Concepts on Decisions of the European Court. (1976) 1 E.L.Rev. 359.

Section 221

Lecheler, H., Der Europäische Gerichtshof und die allgemeinen Rechtsgrundsätze. Berlin, 1971.

Lorenz, W., General Principles of Law: Their Elaboration in the Court of Justice of the European Communities. (1964) 13 A.J.C.L. 1.

Püttner, G., Der Schutz wohlerworbener Rechte im Gemeinschaftsrecht. (1975) 10 EuR 218.

Rüber, H.-J., Der Gerichtshof der Europäischen Gemeinschaften und die Konkretisierung allgemeiner Rechtsgrundsätze. Köln, 1970.

Section 222

Kuyper, P. J., Sanctions Against Rhodesia: the EEC and the Implementation of General International Legal Rules. (1975) 12 C.M.L.Rev. 231.

Meessen, K. M., The Application of Rules of Public International Law within Community Law. (1976) 13 C.M.L.Rev. 485.

van Panhuys, H. F., Conflicts between the Law of the European Communities and Other Rules of International Law. (1965-66) 3 C.M.L.Rev. 420.

Pescatore, P., International Law and Community Law — A Comparative Analysis. (1970) 7 C.M.L.Rev. 167.

Pescatore, P., L'apport du droit communautaire au droit international public. (1970) 6 C.D.E. 501.

Schermers, H. G., Community Law and International Law. (1975) 12 C.M.L.Rev. 77.

Chapter 3

Section 302

Constantinesco, L.-J., Die unmittelbare Anwendbarkeit von Gemeinschaftsnormen und der Rechtsschutz von Einzelpersonen im Recht der EWG. Baden-Baden, 1969. Also published in French as: L'applicabilité directe dans le droit de la CEE. Paris, 1970.

Section 303

Bridge, J. W., Fundamental Rights in the European Economic Community, in: J. W. Bridge *et al.* (eds.), *Fundamental Rights*. London, 1973, p. 291.

Edeson, W. R. and Wooldridge, F., European Community Law and Fundamental Human Rights: Some Recent Decisions of the European Court and of National Courts. (1976) 1 L.I.E.I. 1.

Fuss, E. W., Der Grundrechtsschutz in den Europäischen Gemeinschaften. 1975.

von der Groeben, H., Über das Problem der Grundrechte in der Europäischen Gemeinschaft, in: *Probleme des Europäischen Rechts. Festschrift für Walter Hallstein*. Frankfurt am Main, 1966, p. 226.

Hilf, M., The Protection of Fundamental Rights in the Community, in: F. G. Jacobs (ed.), *European Law and the Individual*, Amsterdam, 1976, p. 145.

Kropholler, J., Die Europäischen Gemeinschaften und der Grundrechtsschutz. (1969) 4 EuR 128.

Pescatore, P., Les droits de l'homme et l'intégration européenne. (1968) 4 C.D.E. 629.

Pescatore, P., Fundamental Rights and Freedoms in the System of the European Communities. (1970) 18 A.J.C.L. 343.

Pescatore, P., The Protection of Human Rights in the European Communities. (1972) 9 C.M.L.Rev. 73.

Pescatore, P., La protection des droits fondamentaux par le pouvoir judiciaire. Rapport communautaire. VIIe Congres International de Droit Européen. Bruxelles, 2-4 octobre 1975. (not yet published).

Rinck, G., Civil Liberties and the Common Market: A Study in Comparative Economic Law. (1976) *Juridical Review* 249.

Scheuner, U., Fundamental Rights in European Community Law and in National Constitutional Law. (1975) 12 C.M.L.Rev. 171.

Zuleeg, M., Fundamental Rights and the Law of the European Communities. (1971) 8 C.M.L.Rev. 446.

Section 304

Bleckmann, A., Considérations sur l'interprétation de l'article 7 du Traité CEE. (1976) 12 R.T.D.E. 469.

Schmitthoff, C. M., The Doctrines of Proportionality and Non-Discrimination. (1977) 2 E. L. Rev. 329.

Sundberg-Weitman, B., Addressees of the Ban on Discrimination Enshrined in Article 7 of the EEC Treaty. (1973) 10 C.M.L.Rev. 71.

Sundberg-Weitman, B., Discrimination on Grounds of Nationality. Amsterdam, 1977.

Chapter 4

General

Brinkhorst, L. J. and Wittenberg, G. W., The Rules of Procedure of the Court of Justice of the European Communities. Leyden, 1962.

Donner, A. M., The Court of Justice of the European Communities. (1961) I.C.L.Q. Supplementary Publication No. 1. p. 66.

Feld, W., The Court of the European Communities: New Dimensions in International Adjudication. The Hague, 1964.

Goose, P.-E., Neuere Entwicklungen im Verfahrensrecht des Gerichtshofs. (1975) 10 EuR 230.

Hammes, C. L., Gedanken zu Funktion und Verfahren des Gerichtshofs der Europäischen Gemeinschaften. (1968) 3 EuR 1.

Knaub, G., La procédure devant la Cour de Justice des Communautés européennes. (1967) 3 R.T.D.E. 269.

van Reepinghen, C. and Orianne, P., La procédure devant la Cour de Justice des Communautés européennes. Paris, 1961.

Usher, J. A., Presenting a Case before the European Court. (1976) 1 E.L.Rev. 109.

Section 401

Donner, A. M., The Constitutional Powers of the Court of Justice of the European Communities (1974) 11 C.M.L.Rev. 127.

Grementieri, V. and Golden, C. J., The United Kingdom and the European Court of Justice: An Encounter Between Common and Civil Law Traditions. (1973) 21 A.J.C.L. 664.
Hay, P., Federal Jurisdiction of the Common Market Court. (1963) 12 A.J.C.L. 21.
Lagrange, M., The Court of Justice as a Factor in European Integration. (1966-67) 15 A.J.C.L. 709.
Mertens de Wilmars, J., La jurisprudence de la Cour de Justice comme instrument de l'intégration communautaire. (1976) 12 C.D.E. 135.
Nicolaysen, G., Der Gerichtshof — Funktion und Bewährung der Judikative. (1972) 7 EuR 375.
Schermers, H. G., The European Court of Justice: Promoter of European Integration. (1974) 22 A.J.C.L. 444.

Section 406

Günther, W., Die Präklusion neuer Angriffs-,Verteidigungs- und Beweismittel im Verfahren vor dem Gerichtshof der Europäischen Gemeinschaften. Köln, 1970.

Section 407

André, A., Beweisführung und Beweislast im Verfahren vor dem Europäischen Gerichtshof. Köln, 1966.
Andre, A., Evidence before the European Court of Justice, with Special Reference to the Grundig/Consten Decision. (1967-68) 5 C.M.L.Rev. 35.

Section 410

Wolf, K., Kostenrecht und Kostenpraxis des Gerichtshofs der Europäischen Gemeinschaften. (1976) 11 EuR 7.

Section 412

Berri, M., The Special Procedures before the Court of Justice of the European Communities. (1971) 8 C.M.L.Rev. 5.
Degenhardt, F.-J., Die Auslegung und Berichtigung von Urteilen des Gerichtshofes der Europäischen Gemeinschaften. Stuttgart, 1969.
Plouvier, L., Le recours en révision devant la Cour de Justice des Communautés européennes. (1971) 7 C.D.E. 428.
Vandersanden, G., Le recours en intervention devant la Cour de Justice des Communautés européennes. (1969) 5 R.T.D.E. 1.
Vandersanden, G., Le recours en tierce opposition devant la Cour de Justice des Communautés européennes. (1969) 5 C.D.E. 666.

Chapter 5

General

Schermers, H. G., The Law As It Stands on the Appeal for Annulment. (1975) 2 L.I.E.I. 95.
Valentine, D. G., The Jurisdiction of the Court of Justice of the European Communities to Annul Executive Action. (1960) 36 B.Y.I.L. 174.

Section 501

Fromont, M., L'influence du droit français et du droit allemand sur les conditions de recevabilité du recours en annulation devant la Cour de Justice des Communautés europeennes. (1966) 2 R.T.D.E. 47.
Petersen, E., L'influence possible du droit anglais sur le recours en annulation auprès de la Cour de Justice des Communautés européennes. (1966) 2 R.T.D.E. 256.

Section 502

van Empel, M., L'acte public inexistant et le droit communautaire. (1971) 7 C.D.E. 251.

Section 505

Waelbroeck, M., La notion d'acte susceptible de recours dans la jurisprudence de la Cour de Justice des Communautés européennes. (1965) 1 C.D.E. 225.

Section 506

Buergenthal, T., Appeals for Annulment by Enterprises in the European Coal and Steel Community. (1961) 10 A.J.C.L. 227.

Section 507

Bandilla, R., Das Klagerecht der Mitgliedstaaten der Europäischen Gemeinschaften gegen Durchgriffsakte. Hamburg, 1965.

Section 508

Daig. H. W., Zum Klagerecht von Privatpersonen nach Art. 173 Abs. 2 EWG-, 146 Abs. 2 EAG-Vertrag, in: *Festschrift für Otto Riese*, Karlsruhe, 1964, p. 187.

Ehle, D., Nichtigkeitsklage privater Personen nach dem EWG-Vertrag. (1963) 16 N.J.W. 2193.

Knöpfle, R., Das Klagerecht Privater vor dem Gerichtshof der Europäischen Gemeinschaften. (1959) 12 N.J.W. 553.

Rasquin, G. and Chevallier, R.-M., L'article 173, alinéa 2 du Traité CEE. (1966) 2 R.T.D.E. 31.

Section 509

Catalano, N., Les voies de recours ouvertes aux personnes physiques ou morales contre les actes non réglementaires de la Commission CEE. (1965) 13 S.E.W. 526.

Section 510

Danner, W., Die Klagemöglichkeit privater Personen gegen Maßnahmen der Kommission, die an Mitgliedstaaten gerichtet sind, nach Art. 173 Abs. 2 EWG-Vertrag. Tübingen, 1965.

Harding, C. S. P., Decisions Addressed to Member States and Article 173 of the Treaty of Rome. (1976) 25 I.C.L.Q. 15.

Weinhardt, D., Die Klagebefugnis des Konkurrenten. Göttingen, 1973.

Werbke, A., Das Recht des Einzelnen zur Berufung auf Staatengerichtete Entscheidungen. (1970) 23 N.J.W. 2137.

Sections 512 and 513

Barav, A., Direct and Individual Concern: An Almost Insurmountable Barrier to the Admissibility of Individual Appeal to the EEC Court. (1974) 11 C.M.L.Rev. 191.

Section 516

Fikentscher, W. and Hoffman, G., Einfluß der Form eines Rechtsaktes der Europäischen Gemeinschaftsorgane auf den Rechtsschutz vor dem Gerichtshof der Europäischen Gemeinschaften. (1964) 12 S.E.W. 289. See also *Section 215* above.

Section 517

Asso, B., Le contrôle de l'opportunité de la décision économique devant la Cour européenne de justice. (1976) 12 R.T.D.E. 21 and 177.

van der Esch, B., Pouvoirs discrétionnaires de l'exécutif européen et contrôle juridictionnel. Deventer and Paris, 1968.

van der Esch, B., Discretionary Powers of the European Executive and Judicial Control. (1968-69) 6 C.M.L.Rev. 209.

Soell, H., Zur Ermessensbindung der Kommission der Europäischen Gemeinschaften am Beispiel des EGKS-Vertrages. (1970) 16 A.W.D. 297.

Section 518

Clever, F., Ermessensmißbrauch und détournement de pouvoir nach dem Recht der Europäischen Gemeinschaften im Licht der Rechtsprechung ihres Gerichtshofes. Berlin, 1967.

Fawcett, J. E. S., Détournement de pouvoir by international organisations. (1957) 33 B.Y.I.L. 311.
Meister, B. W., Ermessensmißbrauch oder détournement de pouvoir als Fehlerbestand der Nichtigkeitsklage des Montanvertrages. Bielefeld, 1971.
Weber, Y., La preuve du détournement de pouvoir devant la Cour de Justice des Communautés européennes. (1967) 3 R.T.D.E. 507.

Section 519
Barav, A., The Exception of Illegality in Community Law: A Critical Analysis. (1974) 11 C.M.L.Rev. 366.
Bebr, G., Judicial Remedy of Private Parties against Normative Acts of the European Communities: The Role of Exception of Illegality. (1966-67) 4 C.M.L.Rev. 7.

Section 521
André, A., Zur Rechtskraft und Gestaltungswirkung der Urteile des Europäischen Gerichtshofs im Anfechtungsprozess. (1967) 2 EuR 97.

Chapter 6

Barav, A., Considérations sur la spécificité du recours en carence en droit communautaire. (1975) 11 R.T.D.E. 53.
Buergenthal, T., The Private Appeal Against Illegal State Activities in the European Coal and Steel Community. (1962) 11 A.J.C.L. 325.
Catalano, N., La protection juridictionnelle indirecte dans le système des traités de Rome. (1966) 2 R.T.D.E. 371.
Czasche, H., Die Untätigkeitsklage vor dem Europäischen Gerichtshof. Göttingen, 1969.
Kundoch, H. G., Le recours en carence comme moyen juridique de promouvoir l'élection directe du Parlement européen. (1975) 11 C.D.E. 425.
Reuter, E., Le recours en carence de l'article 175 du traité de la CEE dans la jurisprudence de la Cour de justice des Communautés européennes. (1972) 8 C.D.E. 159.
Roemer, K., Die Untätigkeitsklage im Recht der Europäischen Gemeinschaften. (1966) 14 S.E.W. 1.
Soldatos, P., L'introuvable recours en carence devant la Cour de Justice des Communautés européennes. (1969) 5 C.D.E. 313.
Toth, A. G., The Law As It Stands on the Appeal for Failure to Act. (1975) 2 L.I.E.I. 65.
Wolf, K., Le recours en carence dans le droit des Communautés européennes. (1966) 9 *Revue du Marché Commun* 111.

Chapter 7

Dumon, F., La responsabilité extracontractuelle des Communautés européennes et de leurs agents. (1969) 5 C.D.E. 3.
Durand, A., Restitution or Damages: National Court or European Court. (1976) 1 E.L.Rev. 431.
Elster, T., Non-Contractual Liability under Two Legal Orders. (1975) 12 C.M.L.Rev. 91 and 254.
Fuss, E.-W., Grundfragen der Gemeinschaftshaftung. (1968) 3 EuR 353.
Gilsdorf, P., Die Haftung der Gemeinschaft aus normativem Handeln auf dem Hintergrund der Rechtsprechung des Europäischen Gerichtshofs. (1975) 10 EuR 73.
Goffin, L., Annotation to Case 25/62 *Plaumann* v *Commission*. (1963-64) 1 C.M.L.Rev. 354.
Hartley, T. C., Concurrent Liability in EEC Law: A Critical Review of the Cases. (1977) 2 E. L. Rev. 249.
Heldrich, A., Die allgemeinen Rechtsgrundsätze der außervertraglichen Schadenshaftung im Bereich der EWG. 1961.
Heldrich, A., Annotation to Joined Cases 5, 7 and 13 to 24/66 *Kampffmeyer* v *Commission*. (1967) 2 EuR 344.
Jaenicke, G., Die Staatshaftung in rechtsvergleichender Sicht, in: *Haftung des Staates für*

rechtswidriges Verhalten seiner Organe. Liability of the State for Illegal Conduct of Its Organs. Köln, 1967, p. 859.
Knöpfle, R., Das Verhältnis der Amtshaftungsklage zur Nichtigkeitsklage im Montanvertrag. (1961) 14 N.J.W. 2287.
Krüger, H., Die Abhängigkeit der Amtshaftungsklage von der erfolgreichen Durchführung der Nichtigkeits-bzw. Untätigkeitsklage im Recht der EWG. Berlin, 1976.
Lagrange, M., The Non-Contractual Liability of the Community in the E.C.S.C. and in the E.E.C. (1965-66) 3 C.M.L.Rev. 10.
Mackenzie Stuart, Lord, The 'Non-Contractual' Liability of the European Economic Community. (1975) 12 C.M.L.Rev. 493.
Much, W., Die Haftung der Europäischen Gemeinschaften für das rechtswidrige Verhalten ihrer Organe, in: *Haftung des Staates für rechtswidriges Verhalten seiner Organe. Liability of the State for Illegal Conduct of Its Organs*. Köln, 1967, p. 723.
Schermers, H. G., The Law As It Stands on the Appeal for Damages. (1975) 1 L.I.E.I. 113.
Schröder. Ersatzleistungen für rechtmäßige und rechtswidrige hoheitliche Maßnahmen der Europäischen Wirtschaftsgemeinschaft. Freiburg, 1970.

Chapter 8

Lang, J. T., The Procedure of the Commission in Competition Cases. (1977) 14 C. M. L. Rev. 155.
Mok, M. R., The Procedure of the E.E.C. Commission in Antitrust Cases. (1963-64) 1 C.M.L.Rev. 327.
Nebolsine, G., The 'Right of Defence' in the Control of Restrictive Practices Under the European Community Treaties. (1959) 8 A.J.C.L. 433.
Sedemund, J., Das Verfahren der EWG in Wettbewerbssachen. (1973) 8 EuR 306.

Chapter 9

Barav, A., Failure of Member States to Fulfil Their Obligations under Community Law. (1975) 12 C.M.L.Rev. 369.
Cahier, P., Le recours en constatation de manquements des Etats membres devant la Cour des Communautés européennes. (1967) 3 C.D.E. 123.
Cahier, P., Les articles 169 et 171 du traité instituant la Communauté économique européenne à travers la pratique de la Commission et la jurisprudence de la Cour. (1974) 10 C.D.E. 3.
Ferriere, G., Le controle de la légalité des actes étatiques par la Cour de Justice des Communautés européennes. Paris, 1968.
Mertens de Wilmars, J. and Verougstraete, I. M., Proceedings against Member States for Failure to Fulfil Their Obligations. (1970) 7 C.M.L.Rev. 385.
Schermers, H. G., The Law As It Stands Against Treaty Violations by States. (1974) 2 L.I.E.I. 111.

Chapter 10

Allen, C. G., Criminal Offences Against the Law of the European Economic Community. (1974) 11 C.M.L.Rev. 183.
Bail, C. and Lichtenberg, H., The Application of Community Law in Germany. (1972) 9 C.M.L.Rev. 234; (1975) 12 C.M.L.Rev. 275.
Bebr, G., Community Regulations and National Law (Critical Comments on Recent Decisions of National Courts). (1973) 10 C.M.L.Rev. 87.
Bebr, G., A Critical Review of Recent Case Law of National Courts. (1974) 11 C.M.L.Rev. 408.
Bigay, J., Droit communautaire et droit pénal. (1972) 8 R.T.D.E. 725.
Bridge, J. W., Community Law and English Courts and Tribunals: General Principles and Preliminary Rulings. (1975) 1 E.L.Rev. 13.

Collins, L., Remedies in the United Kingdom: Some Practical Problems of Direct Applicability, in: F. G. Jacobs (ed.), *European Law and the Individual*. Amsterdam, 1976, p. 161.
van Dijk, P., The Implementation and Application of the Law of the European Communities within the Legal Order of the Netherlands. (1968-69) 6 C.M.L.Rev. 283.
Donner, A. M., Les rapports entre la compétence de la Cour de Justice des Communautés européennes et les tribunaux internes. (1965) 115 *Recueil des Cours* 1.
Donner, A. M. *et al.* Le Juge national et le Droit communautaire. Leyden/Bruxelles, 1966.
Forman, J. and Stevens, T., The Attitude of British Courts to Community Law — the First Three Years. (1976) 13 C.M.L.Rev. 388.
Fuss, E.-W., Rechtsschutz gegen deutsche Hoheitsakte zur Ausführung des Europäischen Gemeinschaftsrechts. (1966) 19 N.J.W. 1782.
Hopt, K., The Application of Community Law in Germany. (1966-67) 4 C.M.L.Rev. 93 and 450; (1968-69) 6 C.M.L.Rev. 226; (1970) 7 C.M.L.Rev. 87; (1971) 8 C.M.L.Rev. 97 and 103.
Johannes, H., Das Strafrecht im Bereich der Europäischen Gemeinschaften. (1968) 3 EuR 63.
Johannes, H., Le droit pénal et son harmonisation dans les Communautés européennes. (1971) 7 R.T.D.E. 315.
Maestripieri, C., The Application of Community Law in Italy. (1973) 10 C.M.L.Rev. 340; (1975) 12 C.M.L.Rev. 431; (1976) 13 C.M.L.Rev. 524 and 530.
Pescatore, P., Die unmittelbare Anwendung der europäischen Verträge durch die staatlichen Gerichte. (1970) 5 EuR 56.
Suetens, L. P., The Application of Community Law in Belgium. (1964-65) 2 C.M.L.Rev. 433.
Tallon, D. and Kovar, R., The Application of Community Law in France. (1966-67) 4 C.M.L.Rev. 64 and 446; (1967-68) 5 C.M.L.Rev. 488 and 501; (1968-69) 6 C.M.L.Rev. 419 and 491; (1970) 7 C.M.L.Rev. 359; (1971) 8 C.M.L.Rev. 402; (1972) 9 C.M.L.Rev. 329; (1973) 10 C.M.L.Rev. 451; (1974) 11 C.M.L.Rev. 432.
Ubertazzi, G. M., L'impact du droit communautaire dans le procès pénal interne. (1975) 11 R.T.D.E. 196.
Usher, J., Le droit communautaire devant les tribunaux britanniques. (1975) 11 C.D.E. 560.

Chapter 11

General

Alexander, W., Questions et réponses préjudicielles dans la procédure de la Cour de Justice des Communautés européennes. Bruxelles, 1965.
Barav, A., Some Aspects of the Preliminary Rulings Procedure in EEC Law. (1977) 2 E.L.Rev. 3.
Daig, H.-W., Aktuelle Fragen der Vorabentscheidungen nach Artikel 177 EWG-Vertrag, unter besonderer Berücksichtigung von Rechtsprechung und Praxis des Gerichtshofes der Europäischen Gemeinschaften. (1968) 3 EuR 259 and 371.
Jacobs, F. G. and Durand, A., References to the European Court: Practice and Procedure. London, 1975.
Mitchell, J. D. B., Sed Quis Custodiet Ipsos Custodes? (1974) 11 C.M.L.Rev. 351.
Pepy, A., Les questions préjudicielles dans les traités de Paris et de Rome et la jurisprudence de la Cour des Communautés européennes. (1965) 1 C.D.E. 194.
de Richemont, J., L'intégration du droit communautaire dans l'ordre juridique interne. Article 177 du Traité de Rome. Paris, 1975.
Schermers, H. G., The Law As It Stands on Preliminary Rulings. (1974) 1 L.I.E.I. 93.
Tomuschat, W., Die gerichtliche Vorabentscheidung nach den Verträgen über die Europäischen Gemeinschaften. Köln/Berlin, 1964.

Section 1101

Juillard, P., Procédure des questions préjudicielles et renforcement du lien communautaire. (1968) 4 R.T.D.E. 293.
Lagrange, M., L'action préjudicielle dans le droit interne des Etats membres et en droit communautaire. (1974) 10 R.T.D.E. 268.
Mashaw, J. L., Ensuring the Observance of Law in the Interpretation and Application of the EEC Treaty: The Role and Functioning of the Renvoi d'Interpretation under Article 177. (1970) 7 C.M.L.Rev. 258 and 423.

Section 1102

Mok, M. R., Should the 'First Paragraph' of Article 177 of the E.E.C. Treaty Be Read As A Separate Clause? (1967-68) 5 C.M.L.Rev. 458.

Pepy, A., Le rôle de la Cour de Justice des Communautés européennes dans l'application de l'article 177 du Traité de Rome. (1966) 2 C.D.E. 459.

Section 1103

Mok, M. R., The Interpretation by the European Court of Justice of Special Conventions Concluded between the Member States. (1971) 8 C.M.L.Rev. 485.

Section 1104

Bebr, G., Examen en validité au titre de l'article 177 du traité CEE et cohésion juridique de la Communauté. (1975) 11 C.D.E. 379.

Couzinet, J.-F., Le renvoi en appréciation de validité devant la Cour de justice des Communautés européennes. (1976) 12 R.T.D.E. 648.

Sections 1105 and 1106

Bebr, G., Article 177 of the EEC Treaty in the Practice of National Courts. (1977) 26 I.C.L.Q. 241.

Chevallier, Commentaire de l'article 177 du Traité CEE à l'usage des juges et des justiciables français. 1964.

Cohn, E. J., Zur Vorlagepflicht von Schiedsgerichten an den Europäischen Gerichtshof. (1966) 12 A.W.D. 431.

Collins, L., Article 177 of the E.E.C. Treaty and English Interlocutory Proceedings. (1974) 23 I.C.L.Q. 840.

Constantinesco, L., Zur Vorlage nationaler Instanzgerichte an den Europäischen Gerichtshof. (Art. 177 Abs. 2 EWGV). (1967) 13 A.W.D. 125.

Hay, P., Une approche politique de l'application de l'article 177 du Traité CEE par les juridictions nationales. (1971) 7 C.D.E. 503.

Lagrange, M., The European Court of Justice and National Courts. The Theory of the Acte Clair. (1971) 8 C.M.L.Rev. 313.

Lesguillons, H., Les juges français et l'article 177. (1968) 4 C.D.E. 253.

Mok, M. R. and Hartmut, J., Schiedsgerichtsbarkeit und EWG-Vertrag. (1966) 12 A.W.D. 125.

Pepy, A., Le rôle des juridictions nationales dans l'application de l'article 177 et la jurisprudence de la Cour de Justice. (1966) 2 C.D.E. 21.

Pescatore, P., Interpretation of Community Law and the Doctrine of 'Acte Clair', in: *Legal Problems of an Enlarged European Community*. London, 1972, p. 27.

Zehetner, F., Zum Vorlagerecht nationaler Gerichte an den Gerichtshof der Europäischen Gemeinschaften. (1975) 10 EuR 113.

Section 1110

Trabucchi, A., L'effet 'erga omnes' des décisions préjudicielles rendues par la Cour de justice des Communautés européennes. (1974) 10 R.T.D.E. 56.

Section 1111

Chevallier, R.-M., Methods and Reasoning of the European Court in its Interpretation of Community Law. (1964-65) 2 C.M.L.Rev. 21.

Degan, V. D., Procédés d'interprétation tirés de la jurisprudence de la Cour de Justice des Communautés européennes. (1966) 2 R.T.D.E. 189.

Marsh, N. S., Interpretation in a National and International Context. Brussels, 1974.

McMahon, J. F., The Court of the European Communities: Judicial Interpretation and International Organisation. (1961) 37 B.Y.I.L. 320.

Ormand, R., L'utilisation particulière de la méthode d'interprétation des traités selon leur 'effet utile' par la Cour de justice des Communautés européennes. (1976) 12 R.T.D.E. 624.

Questiaux, N., Interpretation of Community Law, in: *Legal Problems of an Enlarged European Community*. London, 1972, p. 47.

Reports presented to a Judicial and Academic Conference, Court of Justice, Luxembourg, 1976.

Zuleeg, M., Die Auslegung des europaischen Gemeinschaftsrechts. (1969) 4 EuR 97.

Abbreviations

Accession Treaty	Treaty concerning the Accession of Denmark, Ireland and the United Kingdom to the E.E.C. and Euratom, 1972
Act of Accession	Act annexed to the Accession Treaty
A.G.	Advocate-General
A.J.C.L.	*The American Journal of Comparative Law*, Baltimore
A.W.D.	*Aussenwirtschaftsdienst des Betriebs-Beraters*, Heidelberg
Brinkhorst-Schermers	L. J. Brinkhorst and H. G. Schermers, *Judicial Remedies in the European Communities*, Deventer-London, 1969 + *Supplement*, 1972
Budgetary Treaty	Treaty amending certain Budgetary Provisions of the E.C.S.C., E.E.C., Euratom and Merger Treaties, 1970
Bull.EC	*Bulletin of the European Communities*, Brussels
B.Y.I.L.	*British Yearbook of International Law*, London
C.D.E.	*Cahiers de Droit Européen*, Brussels
C.M.L.R.	*Common Market Law Reports*, London
C.M.L.Rev.	*Common Market Law Review*, Leyden
Cmnd.	Command Paper
E.C.S.C.	European Coal and Steel Community; the Treaty establishing that Community, 1951
E.C.S.C. Statute	Statute of the Court of Justice of the E.C.S.C.
E.C.R.	*European Court Reports* (Reports of Cases before the Court of Justice of the European Communities), Luxembourg

E.E.C.	European Economic Community; the Treaty establishing that Community, 1957
E.E.C. Statute	Statute of the Court of Justice of the E.E.C.
E.L. Rev.	*European Law Review*, London-Andover
EuR	*Europarecht*, München and Berlin
Euratom	European Atomic Energy Community; the Treaty establishing that Community, 1957
Euratom Statute	Statute of the Court of Justice of the Euratom
Gen.Rep.EC	*General Report on the Activities of the European Communities*, Brussels and Luxembourg
I.C.J.	International Court of Justice
I.C.L.Q.	*International and Comparative Law Quarterly*, London
I.L.R.	*International Law Reports*, London
I.R.	Instructions to the Registrar of the European Court of Justice
L.I.E.I.	*Legal Issues of European Integration*, Deventer
Merger Treaty	Treaty establishing a Single Council and a Single Commission of the European Communities, 1965
N.J.W.	*Neue Juristische Wochenschrift*, München
O.J.	*Official Journal of the European Communities*, Luxembourg
P.C.I.J.	Permanent Court of International Justice
Rec., Recueil	*Recueil de la Jurisprudence de la Cour de Justice des Communautés Européennes*, Luxembourg
Recueil des Cours	*Collected Courses of the Hague Academy of International Law*, Leyden
R.P.	Rules of Procedure of the European Court of Justice
R.T.D.E.	*Revue Trimestrielle de Droit Européen*, Paris
S.E.W.	*Sociaal-economische Wetgeving*, Zwolle
S.I.	Statutory Instrument
S.R.P.	Supplementary Rules of Procedure of the European Court of Justice
Val., Valentine	D. G. Valentine, *The Court of Justice of the European Communities*, 2 volumes; London, 1965

Table of Treaties

References are to Volume, page and, where appropriate, to note. The numbers in brackets following page numbers indicate the notes at which an instrument or provision is mentioned.

1. Basic Community Treaties

2. Treaties between Member States

3. Treaties between the Communities and Third States

4. Other Treaties

Table of Community Acts

References are to Volume, page and, where appropriate, to note. The numbers in brackets following page numbers indicate the notes at which an instrument or provision is mentioned.

1. Acts of Institutions

2. Other Acts

3. Rules of Procedure

Table of National Constitutions and Laws

References are to Volume, page and, where appropriate, to note. The numbers in brackets following page numbers indicate the notes at which an instrument or provision is mentioned.

Table of Cases

References are to Volume, page and note. The numbers in brackets following page numbers indicate the notes at which a case is mentioned. Principal references are in bold type. Unless otherwise stated, decisions of the European Court of Justice are in the form of judgment.

A. Cases before the Permanent Court of International Justice and the International Court of Justice

No. 1, *Jurisdiction of the Courts of Danzig*. Advisory Opinion of 3 March 1928 P.C.I.J. (1928) Series B, No. 15. **Vol. II** 11(3).
No. 2, *Chorzow Factory (Indemnity) Case*. Judgment of 13 September 1928 P.C.I.J. (1928) Series A, No. 17. **Vol. II** 118(1).
No. 3, *Minority Schools in Albania*. Advisory Opinion of 6 April 1935. P.C.I.J. (1935) Series A/B, No. 64. **Vol. I** 111(1).
No. 4, *Reparation for Injuries Suffered in the Service of the United Nations*. Advisory Opinion of 11 April 1949. I.C.J. Reports, 1949, p. 174. **Vol. I** 6(41, 43).

B. Cases before the Court of Justice of the European Communities

1954

1/54 *France v High Authority* 2 Valentine 18; [1954-55] 1 Recueil 7. **Vol. I** 40(20), **Vol. II** 3(4), 20(5, 16), 37(26), 45(3), 71(16), 73(5, 8, 10), 78(2), 82(14).
2/54 *Italy* v *High Authority* 2 Valentine 37; [1954-55] 1 Recueil 73. **Vol. II** 16(33, 38, 42), 17(3), 20(16), 37(26), 45(3), 70(9), 71(16), 73(5, 8, 11), 74(18), 85(31).
3/54 *ASSIDER* v *High Authority* 2 Valentine 45; [1954-55] 1 Recueil 123. **Vol. I** 84(14, 19), **Vol. II** 4(13), 8(11), 20(17), 35(9), 36(15), 39(2), 45(3), 48(5), 49(12), 50(16), 69(4), 70(9), 81(3), 82(7), 83(21), 84(25), 85(31), 93(7), 119(5).
4/54 *ISA* v *High Authority* 2 Valentine 52; [1954-55] 1 Recueil 177. **Vol. II** 20(17), 45(3), 49(12), 70(9), 73(11), 84(30), 93(7).
6/54 *Netherlands* v *High Authority* 2 Valentine 203; [1954-55] 1 Recueil 201. **Vol. I** 46(19), **Vol. II** 7(2), 71(16), 73(4, 5, 8, 11), 74(22), 78(4), 79(19), 80(20, 22, 23), 82(5), 83(17), 84(29).
7 and 9/54 *Groupement des Industries Sidérurgiques Luxembourgeoises* v *High Authority* 2 Valentine 131; [1955-56] 2 Recueil 53. **Vol. I** 13(20), 38(4), 40(20), 51(62), 81(27), 85(46), 100(13), 102(27), **Vol. II** 7(2), 14(9), 20(8), 21(31), 35(4), 36(15, 17), 39(2), 41(16, 5), 48(5), 49(8), 50(19), 51(23), 71(18), 80(24), 94(19), 98(2), 99(6), 100(4), 101(9), 102(11), 103(1, 2, 3, 8), 104(9, 10, 15, 17, 18), 105(6), 174(10), 233(57).
8 and 10/54 *Association des Utilisateurs de Charbon du Grand-Duché de Luxembourg* v *High Authority* 2 Valentine 158; [1955-56] 2 Recueil 157. **Vol. I** 102(27, 28).

1955

1956

1957

1958

1964

1965

10/69 *Portelange* v *Marchant* [1969] ECR 309; [1974]1 CMLR 397. **Vol. I** 88(30), **Vol. II** 8(14), 202(11, 12).
12/69 *Wonnerth* v *Commission* [1969] ECR 577. **Vol. II** 28(63).
13/69 *Van Eick* v *Commission* [1970] ECR 3. **Vol. II** 133(6).
15/69 *Südmilch* v *Ugliola* [1969] ECR 363; [1970] CMLR 194. **Vol. I** 112(14).
18/69 *Fournier* v *Commission* [1970] ECR 249. **Vol. II** 41(12).
19, 20, 25 and 30/69 *Richez-Parise* v *Commission* [1970] ECR 325. **Vol. II** 16(43), 149(18).
23/69 *Fiehn* v *Commission* [1970] ECR 547. **Vol. II** 5(20).
24/69 *Nebe* v *Commission* [1970] ECR 145. **Vol. I** 88(32), **Vol. II** 40(8), 90(10), 91(14, 15).
26/69 *Commission* v *France* [1970] ECR 565; [1970] CMLR 444. **Vol. II** 170(23), 177(4), 178(5), 179(17, 19).
28/69 *Commission* v *Italy* [1970] ECR 187; [1971] CMLR 448. **Vol. II** 170(24).
29/69 *Stauder* v *Ulm* [1969] ECR 419; [1970] CMLR 112. **Vol. I** 85(5), 86(8,10), 108(11), **Vol. II** 191(54), 209(15, 25), 210(34), 212(11), 229(19), 232(46), 233(54).
31/69 *Commission* v *Italy* [1970] ECR 25; [1970] CMLR 175. **Vol. II** 6(34), 8(13), 16(37), 169(19), 170(23), 172(6, 7), 175(12).
38/69 *Commission* v *Italy* [1970] ECR 47; [1970] CMLR 77. **Vol. I** 71(21, 23), 76(1), 77(7), **Vol. II** 54(17), 171(4), 178(9), 228(12).
39/69 *Fournier* v *Commission* [1970] ECR 267. **Vol. II** 40(3).
40/69 *Hauptzollamt Hamburg* v *Bollmann* [1970] ECR 69; [1970] CMLR 141. **Vol. I** 5(28), 58(28, 29), 60(53), **Vol. II** 190(34).
41/69 *ACF Chemiefarma* v *Commission* [1970] ECR 661. **Vol. I** 52(68), 74(14), 85(46, 49), 87(17, 19), **Vol. II** 73(9), 76(39), 77(46), 154(16), 157(30, 31, 34, 40), 158(10), 160(20, 29), 161(33, 35, 38, 41), 162(44, 8), 164(7, 8).
44/69 *Buchler* v *Commission* [1970] ECR 733. **Vol. I** 87(19), **Vol. II** 154(16), 157(30, 34, 37, 40), 160(20, 29), 161(36), 164(7, 8).
45/69 *Boehringer Mannheim* v *Commission* [1970] ECR 769. **Vol. I** 87(19), **Vol. II** 154(16), 157(30, 34, 37, 40), 160(20, 29), 161(36, 39), 164(6, 7, 8).
46/69 *Reinarz* v *Commission* [1970] ECR 275. **Vol. II** 40(3).
48/69 *ICI* v *Commission* [1972] ECR 619; [1972] CMLR 557. **Vol. I** 6(43), 7(54), 34(21, 24), 35(25, 26, 27, 30), 52(76), 72(7), 74(17, 19, 20, 21), 81(28), 84(33, 34), 85(51), 87(19), 88(31), 94(2), 95(3), 104(48), **Vol. II** 9(31), 75(28), 77(44), 83(17), 84(27), 92(28), 157(31, 38, 40), 158(10), 159(11, 15), 160(20), 161(36, 41), 162(8, 9), 164(6, 7), 232(47).
49/69 *BASF* v *Commission* [1972] ECR 713; [1972] CMLR 557. **Vol. I** 87(19), 88(31), **Vol. II** 157(30, 40), 159(11), 160(20, 30), 164(6).
50/69 R *Germany* v *Commission* (Order) [1969] ECR 449; [1971] CMLR 724. **Vol. II** 24(20, 22), 25(35), 35(6), 38(2), 93(5), 94(23).
51/69 *Bayer* v *Commission* [1972] ECR 745; [1972] CMLR 557. **Vol. I** 87(19), 88(31), **Vol. II** 157(40), 159(11), 160(20, 28), 161(36, 41), 164(6).
52/69 *Geigy* v *Commission* [1972] ECR 787; [1972] CMLR 557. **Vol. I** 34(21, 23), 35(28), 52(76), 72(7), 74(17, 19, 20, 21), 87(19), 88(31), 95(3), 103(47), 104(48), **Vol. II** 77(44), 92(28), 157(38, 40), 159(11, 14, 15), 160(20), 161(41), 164(6).
53/69 *Sandoz* v *Commission* [1972] ECR 845; [1972] CMLR 557. **Vol. I** 34(21,23), 35(28), 52(76), 72(7), 74(17, 19, 20, 21), 87(19), 88(31), 95(3), 103(47), 104(48), **Vol. II** 77(44), 92(28), 157(38, 40), 159(11, 14, 15), 160(20), 161(41), 164(6).
54/69 *Francolor* v *Commission* [1972] ECR 851; [1972] CMLR 557. **Vol. I** 74(14), 87(19), 88(31), **Vol. II** 157(40), 159(11), 160(20), 161(41), 164(6).
55/69 *Cassella* v *Commission* [1972] ECR 887; [1972] CMLR 557. **Vol. I** 52(76), 72(7), 87(19), 88(31), **Vol. II** 76(39), 157(40), 159(11, 15), 160(20, 28) 161(41), 162(44), 164(6).
56/69 *Hoechst* v *Commission* [1972] ECR 927; [1972] CMLR 557. **Vol. I** 52(76), 72(7), 87(19), 88(31), **Vol. II** 76(39), 157(40), 159(11, 15), 160(20, 28), 161(41), 162(44), 164(6).
57/69 *ACNA* v *Commission* [1972] ECR 933; [1972] CMLR 557. **Vol. I** 87(19), 88(31), **Vol. II** 154(16), 157(40), 159(11), 160(20), 161(41), 164(7, 8).
59 and 71/69 *Brembati* v *Commission* [1970] ECR 623. **Vol. II** 41(13).
63/69 *Compagnie Francaise Commerciale* v *Commission* [1970] ECR 205; [1970] CMLR 369 **Vol. II** 26(41), 60(2, 3), 61(5), 62(11, 13).
64/69 *Compagnie Française Commerciale* v *Commission* [1970] ECR 221; [1970] CMLR 369. **Vol. II** 62(11, 13).

1970

1971

1972

21 to 24/72 *International Fruit Company* v *Produktschap voor Groenten en Fruit* [1972] ECR 1219; [1975] 2 CMLR 1. **Vol. I** 7(54), 78(16), 87(26), 94(2), 95(8, 11, 14), 96(18), 97(22), **Vol. II** 9(1), 197(2), 202(8), 209(13, 14), 213(22), 214(31), 223(2).
27/72 *Aimer* v *Einfuhr- und Vorratsstelle Getreide* [1972] ECR 1091; [1973] CMLR 612. **Vol. II** 190(32), 228(4).
29/72 *Marimex* v *Italian Finance Administration* [1972] ECR 1309; [1973] CMLR 486. **Vol. II** 204(24), 206(47), 232(50).
30/72 *Commission* v *Italy* [1973] ECR 161. **Vol. I** 58(32), 59(42), 60(51), **Vol. II** 172(6, 9, 12), 175(14), 177(3), 178(5).
32/72 *Wasaknäcke* v *Einfuhr- und Vorratsstelle Getreide* [1972] ECR 1181; [1973] CMLR 268. **Vol. I** 57(25), 58(33), 59(35, 36), 60(49), 61(57), 91(55), 111(2), **Vol. II** 190(32).
33/72 *Gunnella* v *Commission* [1973] ECR 475. **Vol. II** 90(10), 91(15).
36/72 *Meganck* v *Commission* [1973] ECR 527. **Vol. I** 92(62).
37/72 *Marcato* v *Commission* [1973] ECR 361. **Vol. II** 228(14).
38/72 *Van de Poll* v *Hauptzollamt Trier* [1972] ECR 1329. **Vol. II** 206(48).
39/72 *Commission* v *Italy* [1973] ECR 101; [1973] CMLR 439. **Vol. I** 4(22), 5(31), 56(16), 57(20, 22, 23, 25), 58(32), 60(49), 92(62), **Vol. II** 171(4), 172(9), 178(6), 182(7), 187(7), 199(11).
40/72 *Schroeder* v *Germany* [1973] ECR 125; [1973] CMLR 824. **Vol. I** 43(5), 95(8), **Vol. II** 81(27), 141(25), 191(54), 199(16), 203(12), 208(4), 209(29), 225(13).
42/72 *Lütticke* v *Hauptzollamt Passau* [1973] ECR 57; [1973] CMLR 309. **Vol. II** 124(5), 210(35), 223(12).
43/72 *Merkur* v *Commission* [1973] ECR 1055. **Vol. I** 113(21), **Vol. II** 8(8), 36(15), 37(22), 39(1), 55(10), 81(28, 30), 86(3), 89(24), 93(5), 119(6), 123(19), 140(23), 144(45, 47), 145(55), 191(50), 234(66).
44/72 *Marsman* v *Rosskamp* [1972] ECR 1243; [1973] CMLR 501. **Vol. I** 14(37), 112(7), **Vol. II** 192(65).
48/72 *Brasserie de Haecht* v *Wilkin-Janssen* [1973] ECR 77; [1973] CMLR 287. **Vol. I** 15(47), 88(30), **Vol. II** 192(57).
54/72 *FOR* v *VKS* [1973] ECR 193. **Vol. I** 113(22), **Vol. II** 192(66), 202(13), 204(23).
57/72 *Westzucker* v *Einfuhr- und Vorratsstelle Zucker* [1973] ECR 321. **Vol. I** 52(72), 59(36), 73(6), **Vol. II** 81(30), 209(28).
58 and 75/72 *Perinciolo* v *Council* [1973] ECR 511. **Vol. II** 9(39), 26(45), 41(13).
59/72 *Wünsche* v *Commission* [1973] ECR 791; [1974] 1 CMLR 61. **Vol. II** 119(6), 140(21, 23), 141(25), 144(47), 146(1), 151(31), 199(16), 225(12, 13), 234(66).
61/72 *Mij PPW Internationaal N.V.* v *Hoofdproduktschap voor Akkerbouwprodukten* [1973] ECR 301. **Vol. II** 229(22).
62/72 *Bollmann* v *Hauptzollamt Hamburg-Waltershof* [1973] ECR 269. **Vol. II** 32(121, 123), 33(124), 196(1), 203(18).
63 to 69/72 *Werhahn* v *Council* [1973] ECR 1229. **Vol. I** 83(12), 84(16), 86(13, 14, 15), 87(17), 113(21), **Vol. II** 16(43), 128(8), 131(4, 5), 134(17), 140(23), 143(42, 43, 44), 144(47, 48), 145(51, 52), 146(1), 148(9, 10), 150(26), 151(29, 30, 31), 233(58).
70/72 *Commission* v *Germany* [1973] ECR 813; [1973] CMLR 741. **Vol. I** 53(86), 75(26), 89(35), **Vol. II** 170(23), 175(14), 176(20), 179(14), 181(4, 6).
72/72 *Einfuhr- und Vorratsstelle Getreide* v *Baer-Getreide* [1973] ECR 377. **Vol. II** 44(25).
76/72 *Michel S.* v *Fonds National de Reclassement Social des Handicapés* [1973] ECR 457. **Vol. I** 97(27), **Vol. II** 204(25).
77/72 *Capolongo* v *Maya* [1973] ECR 611; [1974] 1 CMLR 230. **Vol. I** 14(33), 15(39), **Vol. II** 192(66), 204(24), 205(34), 207(52), 219(14).
79/72 *Commission* v *Italy* [1973] ECR 667; [1973] CMLR 773. **Vol. I** 62(26), **Vol. II** 172(6, 12).
80/72 *Koninklijke Lassiefabrieken* v *Hoofdproduktschap voor Akkerbouwprodukten* [1973] ECR 635. **Vol. I** 57(18), **Vol. II** 73(6), 75(34).
81/72 *Commission* v *Council* [1973] ECR 575; [1973] CMLR 639. **Vol. I** 50(53), 53(86), 65(2, 3), 84(42), 86(13, 14), 89(35), **Vol.II** 3(2), 8(12), 37(30), 79(15), 94(14).

1973

1/73 *Westzucker* v *Einfuhr- und Vorratsstelle Zucker* [1973] ECR 723. **Vol. I** 75(30), 89(35).
2/73 *Geddo* v *Ente Nazionale Risi* [1973] ECR 865; [1974] 1 CMLR 13. **Vol. I** 15(39, 45, 46),

1974

1975

102/75 *Petersen* v *Commission* [1976] ECR 1777. **Vol. I** 84(45), **Vol. II** 228(14).
104/75 *De Peijper* [1976] ECR 613. **Vol. I** 21(10), **Vol. II** 168(12), 189(25), 199(13), 206(50).
109/75 R *National Carbonising Company* v *Commission* (Order) [1975] ECR 1193; [1975] 2 CMLR 457. **Vol. II** 9(41), 25(35), 28(72).
109 and 114/75 *National Carbonising Company* v *Commission* (Order) [1977] ECR 381. **Vol. I** 72(6), 81(28), **Vol. II** 7(2), 9(39), 26(45), 36(17), 40(3), 41(13), 46(8), 101(5), 102(11, 15), 103(8), 104(9, 18), 108(8).
110/75 *Mills* v *Investment Bank* (Interlocutory Judgment) [1976] ECR 955. **Vol. I** 85(1), 87(17), 93(77).
110/75 *Mills* v *Investment Bank* [1976] ECR 1613. **Vol. II** 17(4).
111/75 *Mazzalai* v *Ferrovia del Renon* [1976] ECR 657; [1977] 1 CMLR 105. **Vol. II** 189(19), 199(13), 201(5), 203(16), 204(23, 28), 228(5, 15).
113/75 *Frecassetti* v *Amministrazione delle Finanze dello Stato* [1976] ECR 983. **Vol. II** 203(15), 208(7).
118/75 *Watson and Belmann* [1976] ECR 1185; [1976] 2 CMLR 552. **Vol. I** 14(35), 15(46), 90(46), 91(51, 53), 110(21), 111(28), 112(12-16), **Vol. II** 190(41), 206(50).
119/75 *Terrapin* v *Terranova* [1976] ECR 1039; [1976] 2 CMLR 482. **Vol. II** 192(63), 202(21), 205(36, 44), 222(6).
120/75 *Riemer* v *Hauptzollamt Lübeck-West* [1976] ECR 1003. **Vol. II** 228(7).
125/75 *Eier-Kontor* v *Hauptzollamt Hamburg-Jonas* [1976] ECR 771. **Vol. II** 210(38), 228(15).
127/75 *Bobie* v *Hauptzollamt Aachen-Nord* [1976] ECR 1079. **Vol. II** 189(23).
130/75 *Prais* v *Council* [1976] ECR 1589; [1976] 2 CMLR 708. **Vol. I** 111(31).

1976

1/76 (Opinion) *Opinion given pursuant to Article 228(1) of the E.E.C. Treaty* [1977] ECR 741; [1977] 2 CMLR 279. **Vol. I** 6(50, 51, 53), 43(5), **Vol. II** 203(13).
1/76 *Wack* v *Commission* [1976] ECR 1017. **Vol. II** 40(7).
3/4 and 6/76 *Kramer* [1976] ECR 1279; [1976] 2 CMLR 440. **Vol. I** 6(50), 7(53), **Vol. II** 189(25), 206(50).
7/76 *IRCA* v *Amministrazione delle Finanze dello Stato* [1976] ECR 1213. **Vol. I** 75(28), **Vol. II** 191(53), 208(9), 209(19).
10/76 *Commission* v *Italy* [1976] ECR 1359; [1976] 2 CMLR 699. **Vol. I** 62(26), **Vol. II** 172(10).
12/76 *Tessili* v *Dunlop* [1976] ECR 1473; [1977] 1 CMLR 26. **Vol. II** 32(111), 192(67), 203(11), 231(39), 232(50).
13/76 *Donà* v *Mantero* [1976] ECR 1333; [1976] 2 CMLR 578. **Vol. I** 14(35), 15(47), 31(53), 112(14, 16), 113(17, 18), **Vol. II** 192(65), 204(27), 205(42), 206(50).
14/76 *De Bloos* v *Bouyer* [1976] ECR 1497; [1977] 1 CMLR 60. **Vol. I** 85(50), **Vol. II** 32(111), 203(11), 231(39).
17/76 *Brack* v *Insurance Officer* [1976] ECR 1429; [1976] 2 CMLR 592. **Vol. II** 190(40), 202(13), 212(8), 215(7), 228(4).
19/76 *Triches* v *Caisse Liégeoise pour Allocations Familiales* [1976] ECR 1243; [1977] 1 CMLR 213. **Vol. II** 191(54), 208(9), 209(18).
23/76 *Pellegrini* v *Commission* [1976] ECR 1807; [1977] 2 CMLR 77. **Vol. II** 191(46).
26/76 *Metro* v *Commission*, 25 October 1977 (not yet reported). **Vol. II** 59(3a), 64(6), 68(7), 117(11).
27/76 R *United Brands* v *Commission* (Order) [1976] ECR 425; [1976] 2 CMLR 147. **Vol. II** 24(10).
29/76 *LTU* v *Eurocontrol* [1976] ECR 1541; [1977] 1 CMLR 88. **Vol. II** 203(11), 213(14), 216(13), 231(39).
30/76 *Küster* v *Parliament* [1976] ECR 1719. **Vol. II** 95(26).
32/76 *Saieva* v *Caisse Allocations Familiales* [1976] ECR 1523; [1977] 2 CMLR 26. **Vol. II** 204(23).
33/76 *Rewe* v *Landwirtschaftskammer Saarland* [1976] ECR 1989; [1977] 1 CMLR 533. **Vol. I** 14(33), **Vol. II** 187(8, 10), 189(20).
41/76 *Donckerwolcke* v *Procureur de la République* [1976] ECR 1921; [1977] 2 CMLR 535 **Vol. I** 5(31), 91(50, 52-a), **Vol. II** 232(50).
44/76 *Eier-Kontor* v *Council and Commission* [1977] ECR 393. **Vol. II** 119(6), 128(8), 133(3).

1977

11/77 *Patrick* v *Ministre des Affaires Culturelles* [1977] ECR 1199; [1977] 2 CMLR 523. **Vol. I** 14(35), 16(56).
15/77 *Schwab* v *Council and Commission* (not yet reported). **Vol. II** 199(16).
30/77 *Regina* v *Bouchereau* [1977] 2 CMLR 800. **Vol. II** 232(46, 50).
31/77 R and 53/77 R *Commission* v *United Kingdom* (Order) [1977] ECR 921; [1977] 2 CMLR 359. **Vol. I** 9(18).
38/77 *Enka* v *Inspecteur der Invoerrechten en Accijnzen*, 23 November 1977 (not yet reported). **Vol. I** 63(29), 64(36, 40), **Vol. II** 189(18).
52/77 *Cayrol* v *Rivoira*, 30 November 1977 (not yet reported). **Vol. I** 91(50, 52a).

C. Cases before National Courts

1. Cases before Belgian Courts

No. 1, *Essimex* v *Jans*, 24 November 1967, Arrondissementsrechtbank, Tongeren. [1972] CMLR 48. **Vol. I** 26(12), 61(57).
No. 2, *Corveleyn* v *Belgium*, 7 October 1968, Conseil d'Etat. [1972] CMLR 360-361 (referred to); [1970] 7 CMLR ev. 237. **Vol. I** 64(39), **Vol. II** 189(16).
No. 3, *Sociaal Fonds voor de Diamantarbeiders* v *Chougol*, 24 December 1968, Vrederechter, Antwerpen. [1969] CMLR 315. **Vol. I** 17(4), 27(17).
No. 4, *Peeters* v *Minister of Finance*, 29 April 1969, Cour de Cassation. [1973] CMLR 190. **Vol. II** 217(18).
No. 5, *Fromagerie Franco-Suisse 'Le Ski'* v *Minister for Economic Affairs*, 4 March 1970, Cour d'Appel, Bruxelles. [1970] CMLR 219. **Vol. I** 17(4), 27(17), **Vol. II** 189(20).
No. 6, *Willems, Raes & Co.* v *Dopff & Irion*, 26 May 1970, Tribunal de Commerce, Bruxelles. [1971] CMLR 75. **Vol. II** 214(38).
No. 7, *Minister for Economic Affairs* v *Fromagerie Franco-Suisse 'Le Ski'*, 21 May 1971, Cour de Cassation. [1972] CMLR 330. **Vol. I** 4(19), 17(4), 20(4), 25(8), 27(17, 18), **Vol. II** 168(10), 181(3), 189(20).

2. Cases before Dutch Courts

No. 1, *Grundig* v *Nibeja*, 12 January 1962, Hoge Raad. [1962] CMLR 205. **Vol. II** 214(44).
No. 2, *FIVA* v *Mertens*, 28 June 1962, Kantongerecht, Amsterdam. [1963] CMLR 141. **Vol. II** 224(7).
No. 3, *Grundig Nederland* v *Ammerlaan*, 20 February 1963, Gerechtshof, 's-Gravenhage. [1964] CMLR 373. **Vol. II** 224(6).
No. 4, *Gerrit Hofma* v *Grundig Nederland*, 30 September 1964, Gerechtshof, Leeuwarden. [1967] CMLR 1. **Vol. II** 214(44), 224(6).
No. 5, *Re Import Duties on Processed Beef*, 21 December 1965, Tariefcommissie. [1966] CMLR 346. **Vol. I** 26(14), 61(57).
No. 6, *Re Tax Assessment of Social Security Benefits*, 22 December 1965, Hoge Raad. [1971] CMLR 462. **Vol. II** 216(12).
No. 7, *Schetselaar* v *Geigy*, 11 February 1966, Hoge Raad. [1967] CMLR 47. **Vol. II** 216(12).
No. 8, *Vyvyx* v *Boehringer Sohn*, 14 October 1966, Gerechtshof, 's-Gravenhage. [1969] CMLR 198. **Vol. II** 214(44).
No. 9, *Van Gend & Loos* v *Inspecteur der Invoerrechten en Accijnzen, Venlo*, 26 August 1969, Tariefcommissie. [1970] CMLR 1. **Vol. I** 78(13).
No. 10, *Diederichs and Plaschke* v *The State*, 6 January 1970, Arrondissementsrechtbank, 's-Gravenhage. [1973] CMLR 509. **Vol. II** 214(37).
No. 11, *Reinvoorde* v *The State*, 7 April 1970, Hoge Raad. [1973] CMLR 163. **Vol. II** 216(12).
No. 12, *Officier van Justitie* v *de Peijper*, 6 September 1976, Kantongerecht, Rotterdam. [1977] 1 CMLR 321. **Vol. II** 189(25).

3. Cases before English Courts

Aero Zipp Fasteners Ltd. v *YKK Fasteners (UK) Ltd.*, 7 November 1973, High Court (Chancery Division). [1973] CMLR 819. **Vol. I** 19(22), 29(29).
Amies v *Inner London Education Authority*, 2 December 1976, Employment Appeal Tribunal, [1977] 1 CMLR 336. **Vol. I** 19(19), **Vol. II** 212(8-a).

Application des Gaz SA v *Falks Veritas Ltd.*, 22 May 1974, Court of Appeal [1974] 2 CMLR 75. **Vol. I** 19(23).
Attorney-General for Canada v *Attorney-General for Ontario*, 28 January 1937, Judicial Committee of the Privy Council [1937] A.C. 326. **Vol. I** 10(4).
Blackburn v *Attorney-General*, 27 February 1971, Court of Appeal [1971] CMLR 784. **Vol. I** 10(4).
Bulmer Ltd. v *Bollinger SA*, 22 May 1974, Court of Appeal [1974] 2 CMLR 91. **Vol. I** 10(7), 19(21), 20(24), **Vol. II** 213(15, 22, 25), 214(28, 42), 215(46, 3, 4), 216(13), 218(7), 220(27), 222(5), 223(2), 224(5).
Bulmer Ltd. v *Bollinger SA*, 13 May 1975, High Court (Chancery Division) [1975] 2 CMLR 479. **Vol. II** 214(29, 42).
DDSA Pharmaceuticals Ltd. v *Farbwerke Hoechst AG*, 24 June 1975, High Court (Chancery Division) [1975] 2 CMLR 50. **Vol. II** 215(45).
EMI Records Ltd. v *CBS United Kingdom Ltd.*, 13 March 1975, High Court (Chancery Division) [1975] 1 CMLR 285. **Vol. II** 205(36), 213(22), 214(32-34).
Esso Petroleum Co. Ltd. v *Kingswood Motors (Addlestone) Ltd.*, 19 April 1973, High Court (Queen's Bench Division) [1973] CMLR 665. **Vol. I** 19(22), 29(29).
Felixstowe Dock & Railway Co. v *British Transport Docks Board*, 29 July 1976, Court of Appeal [1976] 2 CMLR 655. **Vol. I** 29(29).
Haug v *Registrar of Patent Agents*, 21 February 1975, Comptroller of the Patent Office [1976] 1 CMLR 491. **Vol. I** 29(29).
Re a Holiday in Italy, 4 July 1974, National Insurance Commissioner [1975] 1 CMLR 184. **Vol. I** 19(20), 57(19), **Vol. II** 214(39), 215(7).
Re an Illness in France, 12 February 1976, National Insurance Commissioner [1976] 1 CMLR 243. **Vol. II** 212(8), 213(22, 24), 214(35).
Löwenbräu München v *Grunhalle Lager International Ltd.*, 27 November 1973, High Court (Chancery Division) [1974] 1 CMLR 1. **Vol. II** 214(39).
Maxims Ltd. v *Dye*, 1 June 1977, High Court (Chancery Division) [1977] 2 CMLR 410. **Vol. II** 33(126).
McWhirter v *Attorney-General*, 30 June 1972, Court of Appeal [1972] CMLR 882. **Vol. I** 10(4).
Miliangos v *George Frank (Textiles) Ltd.*, 4 December 1974, High Court (Queen's Bench Division) [1975] 1 CMLR 121. **Vol. I** 29(30).
Miliangos v *George Frank (Textiles) Ltd.*, 5 November 1975, House of Lords [1975] 2 CMLR 585. **Vol. I** 20(25), **Vol. II** 214(31), 216(14).
Processed Vegetable Growers Association Ltd. v *Commissioners of Customs and Excise*, 7 September 1973, Leeds VAT Tribunal [1974] 1 CMLR 113. **Vol. I** 19(19), 29(31), 62(28), **Vol. II** 188(15).
R. v *Marlborough Street Stipendiary Magistrate, Ex parte Bouchereau*, 17 January 1977, High Court (Queen's Bench Division) [1977] 1 CMLR 269. **Vol. II** 33(126).
R. v *Secchi*, 25 March 1975, Metropolitan Magistrate, Marylebone [1975] 1 CMLR 383. **Vol. I** 64(39), **Vol. II** 213(25), 214(39).
Rio Tinto Zinc Corporation v *Westinghouse Electric Corporation*, 26 May 1977, Court of Appeal [1977] 2 CMLR 420. **Vol. I** 19(22).
Salomon v *Commissioners of Customs and Excise*, 26 October 1966, Court of Appeal [1967] 2 Q.B. 116. **Vol. I** 10(4), 29(27, 28).
Schorsch Meier GmbH v *Hennin*, 26 November 1974, Court of Appeal [1975] 1 CMLR 20. **Vol. I** 10(7), 12(13), 20(24, 25), 29(30), **Vol. II** 214(31, 39).
Sirdar Ltd. v *Les Fils de Louis Mulliez*, 19 March 1975, High Court (Chancery Division) [1975] 1 CMLR 378. **Vol. II** 214(41).
Van Duyn v *Home Office*, 14 February 1974, High Court (Chancery Division) [1974] 1 CMLR 347. **Vol. I** 19(17), **Vol. II** 213(22), 214(28, 35, 36), 218(7).

4. Cases before French Courts

No. 1, *Consten* v *UNEF*, 26 January 1963, Cour d'Appel, Paris. [1963] CMLR 176. **Vol. I** 26(14).
No. 2, *Etat Français* v *Nicolas and Société Brandt*, 9 May 1963, Cour d'Appel, Amiens. [1963] CMLR 239. **Vol. II** 205(36).
No. 3, *Re Riff*, 19 February 1964, Cour de Cassation. [1965] CMLR 29. **Vol. II** 217(18).

No. 4, *Nani* v *Caisse d'Assurance Vieillesse*, 4 March 1964, Cour d'Appel, Paris. [1964] CMLR 334. **Vol. I** 41(2), 61(57).
No. 5, *Re Shell-Berre*, 19 June 1964, Conseil d'Etat. [1964] CMLR 462. **Vol. II** 216(15).
No. 6, *Torrekens* v *Caisse Régionale Vieillesse de Lille*, 1 December 1965, Cour de Cassation. [1966] CMLR 482. **Vol. II** 222(5).
No. 7, *State* v *Cornet*, 29 June 1966, Cour de Cassation. [1967] CMLR 351. **Vol. II** 216(15), 217(16).
No. 8, *Lapeyre* v *Administration des Douanes*, 5 January 1967, Cour de Cassation. [1967] CMLR 362. **Vol. II** 216(15).
No. 9, *Saarknappschaft* v *Freund*, 15 November 1967, Cour d'Appel, Colmar. [1969] CMLR 82. **Vol. I** 26(14), **Vol. II** 224(6).
No. 10, *Syndicat Général de Fabricants de Semoules de France*, 1 March 1968, Conseil d'Etat. [1970] CMLR 395. **Vol. I** 26(13).
No. 11, *Caisse Régionale de Sécurité Sociale du Nord-Est* v *Goffart*, 21 March 1968, Cour de Cassation. [1969] CMLR 24. **Vol. II** 223(2).
No. 12, *Administration des Contributions Indirectes* v *Ramel*, 22 October 1970, Cour de Cassation. [1971] CMLR 315. **Vol. I** 26(14).
No 13, *Weigel & Cie.* v *Directeur Général des Douanes*, 8 January 1971, Tribunal d'Instance, 1er Arrondissement, Paris. [1976] 1 CMLR 43. **Vol. I** 26(14).
No. 14, *Re Guerrini*, 7 January 1972, Cour de Cassation. *6th Gen. Rep. EC [1972]* p. 405 and [1976] 2 CMLR 163. note 9 (referred to). **Vol I** 26(14).
No. 15, *Aim* v *Administration des Douanes*, 12 April 1972, Cour d'Appel, Paris. [1972] CMLR 901. **Vol. I** 62(27), **Vol. II** 188(15).
No. 16, *République* v *Dumortier*, 8 January 1973, Tribunal de Grande Instance, Lille, [1974] 1 CMLR 76. **Vol. I** 6(40), **Vol. II** 194(1).
No. 17, *Garoche* v *Striker Boats (Nederland)*, 8 May 1973, Cour de Cassation. [1974] 1 CMLR 469. **Vol. II** 217(16), 224(6).
No. 18, *Administration des Douanes* v *Soc. Cafés Jacques Vabre*, 7 July 1973, Cour d'Appel, Paris. [1975] 2 CMLR 336. **Vol. I** 26(14).
No. 19, *Administration des Douanes* v *Soc. Cafés Jacques Vabre*, 24 May 1975, Cour de Cassation. [1975] 2 CMLR 336. **Vol. I** 17(5), 25(9), 26(14), 27(20).
No. 20, *Von Kempis* v *Geldof*, 15 December 1975, Cour de Cassation. [1976] 2 CMLR 152. **Vol. I** 17(4), 27(18).

5. *Cases before German Courts*

No. 1, *Saarbergwerke AG* v *Halberger Hütte GmbH*, 14 April 1959, Bundesgerichtshof. [1963] CMLR 251. **Vol. II** 5(22), 185(4).
No. 2, *Re Iron Casings*, 27 March 1963, Finanzgericht Rheinland-Pfalz. [1966] CMLR 332. **Vol. I** 67(53).
No. 3, *Re Import of Siamese Tapioca Meal*, 9 April 1963, Finanzgericht Bremen. [1964] CMLR 304. **Vol. I** 26(12), 61(57).
No. 4, *Re Potato Flour Tax*, 9 October 1963, Finanzgericht Nürnberg. [1964] CMLR 96. **Vol. II** 214(43).
No. 5, *Re Import Duties on Poultry Meat*, 23 April 1963, Finanzgericht Nürnberg. [1964] CMLR 178. **Vol. II** 214(38, 43).
No. 6, *Re Agfa-Optima'*, 30 May 1963, Oberlandesgericht München. [1964] CMLR 87. **Vol. II** 215(6).
No. 7, *Re Customs Duties on Polyethylene*, 3 September 1963, Finanzgericht Bremen. [1964] CMLR 295. **Vol. I** 65(10).
No. 8, *Re Tax on Malt Barley*, 14 November 1963, Finanzgericht Rheinland-Pfalz. [1964] CMLR 130. **Vol. I** 10(12), 45(9), 51(61).
No. 9, *Re Import of American Barley*, 17 December 1963, Verwaltungsgericht Frankfurt-am-Main. [1964] CMLR 285. **Vol. I** 3(8), 10(12), 45(10), 51(61).
No. 10, *Re Import of Siamese Tapioca Meal*, 23 March 1964, Finanzgericht Nürnberg. [1964] CMLR 310. **Vol. I** 51(61), 59(41).

No. 38, *Re Imported Thai Sand Flour,* 15 May 1970, Finanzgericht Bremen. [1971] CMLR 521. **Vol. I** 5(28), 58(28), 60(53).

No. 39, *Re Import of Tapioca Flour,* 2 October 1970, Finanzgericht Hamburg. [1971] CMLR 718. **Vol. II** 224(6).

No. 40, *Deutsche Grammophon GmbH* v *Metro-SB-Grossmärkte GmbH & Co. KG,* 8 October 1970, Hanseatisches Oberlandesgericht. [1971] CMLR 631. **Vol. II** 215(6).

No. 41, *Re Import of Dutch Barley,* 14 October 1970, Finanzgericht Rheinland-Pfalz. [1971] CMLR 733. **Vol. I** 67(54).

No. 42, *Re Levy Assessment in Berlin,* 14 January 1971, Finanzgericht Berlin. [1971] CMLR 713. **Vol. I** 33(8).

No. 43, *Re German Spirits Monopoly,* 18 January 1971, Finanzgericht Düsseldorf. [1971] CMLR 687. **Vol. I** 18(11), **Vol. II** 189(22).

No. 44, *Einfuhr- und Vorratsstelle für Getreide und Futtermittel* v *Wasaknäcke Knäckebrotfabrik GmbH,* 1 March 1971, Hessischer Verwaltungsgerichtshof. [1972] CMLR 841. **Vol. I** 8(15), 26(11).

No. 45, *Re Export Subsidies for Powdered Milk,* 30 March 1971, Bundesfinanzhof. [1972] CMLR 992. **Vol. II** 215(2a).

No. 46, *Re Lütticke GmbH,* 9 June 1971, Bundesverfassungsgericht. *Brinkhorst-Schermers, Supplement,* p. 70. **Vol. I** 8(8), 17(3, 5, 8), 26(15), **Vol. II** 223(2).

No. 47, *Baer Getreide GmbH* v *Einfuhr- und Vorratsstelle für Getreide und Futtermittel,* 16 July 1971, Hessischer Verwaltungsgerichtshof. [1972] CMLR 539. **Vol. I** 68(56).

No. 48, *Internationale Handelsgesellschaft mbH* v *Einfuhr- und Vorratsstelle für Getreide und Futtermittel,* 24 November 1971, Verwaltungsgericht Frankfurt-am-Main. [1972] CMLR 177. **Vol. I** 8(15), 26(11), 90(43), **Vol. II** 223(2).

No. 49, *Re Tax for Plant Health Check,* 26 November 1971, Verwaltungsgericht des Saarlandes. *6th Gen. Rep. EC [1972]* p. 404-405 (referred to). **Vol. I** 27(18).

No. 50, *Scheer* v *Einfuhr- und Vorratsstelle für Getreide und Futtermittel,* 29 November 1971, Hessischer Verwaltungsgerichtshof. [1972] CMLR 824. **Vol. I** 58(31), **Vol. II** 223(2).

No. 51, *Re Investment Aid,* 22 February 1972, Verwaltungsgericht Köln. *6th Gen. Rep. EC [1972]* p. 404-405 (referred to). **Vol. I** 27(18).

No. 52, *Re Levy Assessment on Frozen Beef,* 17 March 1972, Finanzgericht Berlin. [1972] CMLR 387. **Vol. I** 33(8).

No. 53, *Re Free Movement of Persons,* 29 September 1972, Verwaltungsgerichtshof Kassel, *7th Gen. Rep. EC [1973]* p. 460 (referred to). **Vol. I** 64(39).

No. 54, *Rheinmühlen Düsseldorf* v *Einfuhr- und Vorratsstelle für Getreide und Futtermittel,* 8 November 1972 and 14 August 1973, Bundesfinanzhof. [1974] 1 CMLR 523. **Vol. II** 213(14), 223(2).

No. 55, *Re Deportation of a Belgian National,* 20 December 1972, Oberverwaltungsgericht Münster. [1974] 1 CMLR 107. **Vol. I** 63(30), **Vol. II** 189(19).

No. 56, *Re Mineral Oil Tax and Inward Processing,* 15 February 1973, Hessisches Finanzgericht. *7th Gen. Rep. EC [1973],* p. 459 (referred to). **Vol. I** 63(33).

No. 57, *Re Frauds on Agricultural Levies,* 6 June 1973, Bundesgerichtshof. [1974] 1 CMLR 251. **Vol. I** 6(40), 8(8), 67(54), **Vol. II** 157(31), 194(1), 217(19).

No. 58, *Re Fees for Examination of Imported Oranges,* 8 March 1974, Bundesverwaltungsgericht. [1975] 2 CMLR 415. **Vol. I** 27(18).

No. 59, *Re Foreign Value Added Tax,* 21 May 1974, Finanzgericht Baden-Württemberg. [1975] 2 CMLR 326. **Vol. I** 64(39).

No. 60, *Internationale Handelsgesellschaft mbH* v *Einfuhr- und Vorratsstelle für Getreide und Futtermittel,* 29 May 1974, Bundesverfassungsgericht. [1974] 2 CMLR 540. **Vol. I** 7(60), 8(8, 9, 15), 17(9), 26(11), 27(18), **Vol. II** 224(6).

No. 61, *Haaga GmbH,* 5 December 1974, Bundesgerichtshof. [1975] 1 CMLR 124. **Vol. I** 63(30), **Vol. II** 189(19).

No. 62, *Re Cointreau Bottles,* 28 August 1975, Hanseatisches Oberlandesgericht. [1976] 1 CMLR 268. **Vol. II** 215(6), 217(16).

No. 63, *Re Canal Freightage of Coke,* 1 April 1976, Bundesgerichtshof. [1976] 2 CMLR 418. **Vol. II** 217(18).

No. 64, *Re Taxation of Foreign Workers,* 9 July 1976, Bundesfinanzhof. [1977] 1 CMLR 659. **Vol. I** 17(5), 26(15), **Vol. II** 216(15).

No. 65, *Hoffmann-La Roche* v *Centrafarm*, 7 October 1976, Oberlandesgericht Karlsruhe. [1977] 1 CMLR 506. **Vol II** 215(4a).

6. *Cases before Italian Courts*

No. 1, *Soc. B.P. Colussi di Milano* v *Ministero del Commercio con l'Estero*, 7 November 1962, Consiglio di Stato. [1963] CMLR 133. **Vol. I** 17(6), **Vol. II** 189(21).
No. 2, *High Authority* v *Merlini*, 29 March 1963, Tribunale, Torino. [1964] CMLR 184. **Vol. II** 193(11).
No. 3, *Costa* v *ENEL*, 24 February 1964, Corte Costituzionale. [1964] CMLR 425. **Vol. I** 25(10), 27(18).
No. 4, *Simet* v *High Authority*, 28 February 1964, Tribunale, Napoli. [1965] CMLR 10. **Vol. I** 8(15), 10(13), **Vol. II** 5(22), 193(12).
No. 5, *Feram* v *High Authority*, 23 May 1964, Tribunale Civile, Roma. [1966] CMLR 20. **Vol. I** 8(15), 10(13), **Vol. II** 5(22), 193(12).
No. 6, *Meroni* v *High Authority*, 24 June 1964, Tribunale, Milano. [1965] CMLR 1. **Vol. I** 8(15), 10(13), **Vol. II** 5(22), 193(12).
No. 7, *Alma* v *High Authority*, 30 June 1964, Tribunale, Mondovi. [1965] CMLR 290. **Vol. I** 8(15), 10(13), **Vol. II** 5(22), 193(12).
No. 8, *Acciaierie San Michele* v *High Authority*, 30 October 1964, Tribunale, Torino. [1965] CMLR 130. **Vol. I** 10(13, 16), **Vol. II** 5(22).
No. 9, *Acciaierie San Michele* v *High Authority*, 16/27 December 1965, Corte Costituzionale. [1967] CMLR 160. **Vol. I** 8(8, 15), 10(13, 16), 11(19), **Vol. II** 5(22), 193(12).
No. 10, *Costa* v *ENEL*, 1/4 May 1966, Giudice Conciliatore, Milano. [1968] CMLR 267. **Vol. I** 12(13), 17(3, 6), 18(14), 27(18), **Vol. II** 188(11).
No. 11, *Costa* v *ENEL*, 2 January 1967, Giudice Conciliatore, Milano. *Brinkhorst-Schermers, Supplement*, p. 85. **Vol. I** 27(18).
No. 12, *Barge* v *High Authority*, 24 November/18 December 1967, Tribunale, Torino. [1970] CMLR 9. **Vol. II** 192(1).
No. 13, *Salgoil* v *Ministry for Foreign Trade*, 24 September 1969, Corte di Appello, Roma. [1970] CMLR 314. **Vol. I** 17(3), **Vol. II** 189(21), 223(2).
No. 14, *Isolabella* v *Amministrazione delle Finanze dello Stato*, 16 December 1969, Corte di Appello, Milano. [1971] CMLR 479. **Vol. I** 18(10).
No. 15, *ICIC* v *Ministry of External Trade*, 18 May 1971, Tribunale Civile, Roma. *6th Gen. Rep. EC [1972]*, p. 405 (referred to). **Vol. I** 25(10).
No. 16, *Sirena* v *Eda*, 14 October 1971, Tribunale, Milano. [1975] 1 CMLR 409. **Vol. II** 205(36), 223(2).
No. 17, *Fratelli Grassi* v *Amministrazione delle Finanze*, 24 November 1971, Corte di Appello, Brescia. [1973] CMLR 322. **Vol. I** 17(4), **Vol. II** 223(2).
No. 18, *Frontini* v *Ministero delle Finanze*, 21 April 1972, Tribunale, Torino. [1974] 2 CMLR 372. **Vol. I** 8(15), 10(14, 17), 57(19), 58(27), 59(41).
No. 19, *SAFA* v *Amministrazione delle Finanze dello Stato*, 12 May 1972, Corte di Appello, Milano. [1973] CMLR 152. **Vol. I** 17(4), 27(18), 57(19), 59(41), 63(33), **Vol. II** 189(20), 224(5).
No. 20, *Ministero delle Finanze* v *Isolabella*, 8 June 1972, Corte Suprema di Cassazione. *6th Gen. Rep. EC [1972]*, p. 404 (referred to). **Vol. I** 26(12).
No. 21, *Amministrazione delle Finanze dello Stato* v *SACE*, 22 June 1972, Tribunale, Brescia. [1975] 2 CMLR 267. **Vol. I** 8(2), 9(17), 17(3), 26(15), 63(33), **Vol. II** 212(12).
No. 22, *Schiavello* v *Nesci*, 6 October 1972, Corte di Cassazione. [1975] 2 CMLR 198. **Vol. I** 8(15), 27(18), **Vol. II** 216(15).
No. 23, *Amministrazione delle Finanze dello Stato* v *UNIL-IT*, 23 March 1973, Corte di Appello, Milano. 7th Gen. Rep. EC [1973], p. 460 (referred to). **Vol. I** 67(54).
No. 24, *Frontini* v *Ministero delle Finanze*, 27 December 1973, Corte Costituzionale. [1974] 2 CMLR 372. **Vol. I** 4(19), 8(8, 9, 15), 10(14, 17), 11(19), 17(8), 26(15), 39(5), 45(10), 46(12), 57(19, 22, 23), 59(41), 60(49).
No. 25, *Ministry of Finance* v *Rocco*, 18 March 1974, Corte di Appello, Napoli. [1975] 1 CMLR 539. **Vol. I** 17(8), 27(18), 58(28), 59(41), 61(57).

No. 26, Judgement of 22 October 1975, Corte Costituzionale. *9th Gen. Rep. EC* [1975], p. 283 (referred to). **Vol. I** 26(16).

7. *Cases before Luxembourg Courts*

No. 1, *Chambre des Métiers* v *Pagani*, 14 July 1954, Cour Supérieure de Justice. [1972] CMLR 348-349 (cited); [1969] CMLR 322 and [1975] 2 CMLR 365 (referred to). **Vol. I** 27(17).

8. *Cases before Scottish Courts*

Gibson v *Lord Advocate*, 7 March 1975, Court of Session. [1975] 1 CMLR 563. **Vol. I** 11(22), 60(44, 46).

MacCormich v *Lord Advocate*, 30 July 1953, Court of Session. [1953] S.C. 396. **Vol. I** 11(22).

Annex I

Directly applicable provisions of the E.E.C. Treaty

Provision	*Directly applicable from*	*Held in*
Art. 7 (not in itself; only in conjunction with Arts. 48, 52, 59(1) or 60(3))	—	Cases 2/74 [1974] ECR 650-652 36/74 [1974] ECR 1420-1421 118/75 [1976] ECR 1196 *et seq.* 13/76 [1976] ECR 1341
Art. 12 (in conjunction with Art. 9)	1 January 1958	Cases 26/62 [1963] ECR 12-13 28 to 30/62 [1963] ECR 39 2 and 3/69 [1969] ECR 223
Art. 13(2) (in conjunction with Art. 9)	1 January 1970	Cases 33/70 [1970] ECR 1222 77/72 [1973] ECR 623 94/74 [1975] ECR 711 87/75 [1976] ECR 139 33/76 [1976] ECR 1997
Art. 16 (in conjunction with Art. 9)	1 January 1962	Cases 18/71 [1971] ECR 816 63/74 [1975] ECR 291 45/76 [1976] ECR 2052

Art. 30	1 January 1970	Case 74/76 [1977] ECR 575
Art. 31	From the time set in Art. 31(2)	Case 13/68 [1968] ECR 460-461
Art. 32(1)	1 January 1958	Case 13/68 [1968] ECR 461
Art. 37(1)	1 January 1970	Cases 59/75 [1976] ECR 101 45/75 [1976] ECR 198
Art. 37(2)	1 January 1958	Case 6/64 [1964] ECR 597-598
Art. 48	1 January 1970	Cases 167/73 [1974] ECR 371 41/74 [1974] ECR 1347 48/75 [1976] ECR 511 118/75 [1976] ECR 1197 13/76 [1976] ECR 1341
Art. 52	1 January 1970 (1 January 1973 as regards new Member States)	Cases 2/74 [1974] ECR 652 48/75 [1976] ECR 511 118/75 [1976] ECR 1197 11/77 [1977] ECR 1205
Art. 53	1 January 1958	Case 6/64 [1964] ECR 596-597
Art. 59(1)	1 January 1970	Cases 33/74 [1974] ECR 1312 36/74 [1974] ECR 1420-1421 48/75 [1976] ECR 511 118/75 [1976] ECR 1197 13/76 [1976] ECR 1341
Art. 60(3)	1 January 1970	Cases 33/74 [1974] ECR 1312 13/76 [1976] ECR 1341
Art. 85(1)	1 January 1958	Case 127/73 [1974] ECR 62

Art. 85(2)	1 January 1958	Case 48/72 [1973] ECR 86
Art. 86 (even within the framework of Art. 90)	1 January 1958	Cases 127/73 [1974] ECR 62 155/73 [1974] ECR 430
Art. 92(1) (only where implemented under Art. 94 or Art. 93(2))	—	Cases 77/72 [1973] ECR 621-622 78/76 [1977] ECR 609
Art. 93(3) (last sentence)	1 January 1958	Cases 6/64 [1964] ECR 596 120/73 [1973] ECR 1483 121/73 [1973] ECR 1507 122/73 [1973] ECR 1523 141/73 [1973] ECR 1540
Art. 95(1) (in conjunction with Art. 95(3))	1 January 1962	Cases 57/65 [1966] ECR 210-211 28/67 [1968] ECR 152-153 45/75 [1976] ECR 193 74/76 [1977] ECR 578
Art. 95(2)	1 January 1962	Case 27/67 [1968] ECR 232
Art. 119 (within certain areas only)	1 January 1962 (1 January 1973 as regards new Member States) (generally only enforceable as from date of judgment)	Case 43/75 [1976] ECR 479-481

Annex II

Non-directly applicable provisions of the E.E.C. Treaty

Provision	*Held in*
Arts. 2, 3(f) and 5	Cases 155/73 [1974] ECR 435 *per* A.G.
Arts. 5, 40(3) and 98 (except in conjunction with implementing regulations)	Case 2/73 [1973] ECR 878-879 (by implication)
Arts. 5 and 107	Cases 9/73 [1973] ECR 1161 10/73 [1973] ECR 1194
Art. 32(2) (last sentence)	Case 13/68 [1968] ECR 461
Art. 33(1) and (2)(1)	Case 13/68 [1968] ECR 461
Art. 90(2)	Case 10/71 [1971] ECR 730
Art. 92(1) (unless implemented under Art. 94 or Art. 93(2))	Cases 77/72 [1973] ECR 621-622 74/76 [1977] ECR 575 78/76 [1977] ECR 609
Art. 93 (except last sentence of Art. 93(3))	Case 6/64 [1964] ECR 596
Art. 97(1)	Cases 28/67 [1968] ECR 156 13/67 [1968] ECR 194 25/67 [1968] ECR 217 34/67 [1968] ECR 250-25
Art. 102	Case 6/64 [1964] ECR 595
Art. 107 (see above)	

Index